7,768
Michael
Morley £14.45

Fifth Edition

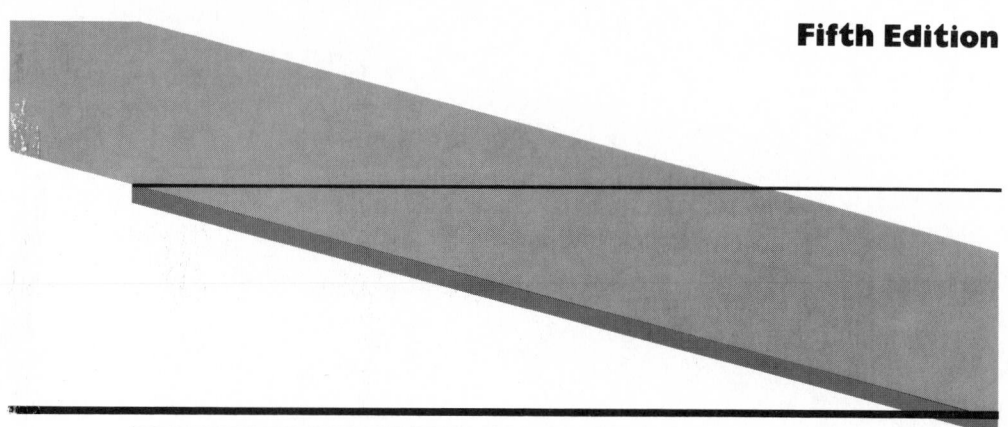

Research Methods in Social Relations

Louise H. Kidder

Department of Psychology
Temple University

Charles M. Judd

Department of Psychology
University of Colorado

with
Eliot R. Smith

Department of Psychological Sciences
Purdue University

Published for the Society for the Psychological Study of
Social Issues (SPSSI)

Holt, Rinehart and Winston
New York   Chicago   San Francisco   Philadelphia
Montreal   Toronto   London   Sydney
Tokyo   Mexico City   Rio de Janeiro   Madrid

To Bob and Liz, our best social supporters
And to our children, Graham and Charin and Jean and Emily,
   our best social relations

ACKNOWLEDGMENTS: Excerpts on pages 174–175 from Richard McCleary, *Dangerous Men: The Sociology of Parole* (Beverly Hills, CA: Sage, 1979), pp. 39, 41. Copyright © 1978 by Sage Publications, Inc. Reprinted by permission of Sage Publications, Inc. Excerpts on pages 179–181 from Donald R. Cressey, *Other People's Money: A Study in the Social Psychology of Embezzelment* (New York: Macmillan, 1953), pp. 27, 28, 29, 30, 31. Reprinted by permission of the author.

Library of Congress Cataloging-in-Publication Data

Kidder, Louise H.
  Research methods in social relations.

  "Published for the Society for the Psychological
Study of Social Issues."
  Bibliography: p.
  Includes indexes.
  1. Social sciences—Research.   2. Social sciences—
Methodology.   I. Judd, Charles M.   II. Smith, Eliot R.
III. Society for the Psychological Study of Social
Issues.   IV. Title.
H62.K473   1986   300'.72   85-27274

ISBN 0-03-002473-0

CBS COLLEGE PUBLISHING
Holt, Rinehart and Winston
The Dryden Press
Saunders College Publishing

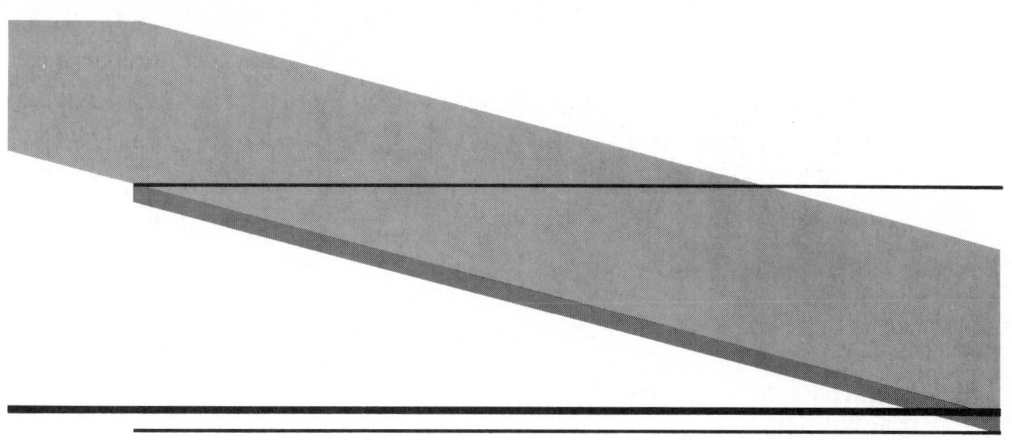

Foreword

Since its founding in 1936, the Society for the Psychological Study of Social Issues (SPSSI) has had as its primary goal the encouragement of research on significant social problems. Hence, the purposes of the Society and the development of social science research methods have been closely linked throughout SPSSI's history. The publication of the first edition of *Research Methods in Social Relations* in 1951 marked SPSSI's commitment to the role of good research methodology in our attempt to understand human behavior and its societal consequences. The book's successive editions have maintained and strengthened that commitment, representing the refinement and extension of research techniques relevant to the study and solution of social problems.

SPSSI's research philosophy is based on the premise that the study of complex social issues must be approached from multiple perspectives with a variety of research techniques. An effective program of research must be based on the recognition that different research methods complement rather than compete with each other. The authors of this edition, Louise Kidder and Chick Judd, subscribe fully to this multimethodological philosophy and have sought to introduce the reader to a broad range of methodological approaches representative of the various social science disciplines. Their goal is to provide the student of social science with an appreciation of the strengths (and weaknesses) unique to each methodology and to offset any rigid adherence to a single methodological doctrine. Both sophistication and flexibility are essential if research is to be made relevant to the social issues of the day.

A second premise on which this text is built is the conviction that a good understanding of research methods is important not only for social science researchers themselves but for an informed public as well. To a greater extent than ever before, the definition of social problems and the development of social policies are being determined by results of social research and interpretations of the meaning of those results. Thus, an understanding of the factors that affect the validity of research findings may prove critical to social and political decision makers, whether or not they ever conduct research themselves. With this need in mind, the authors have focused attention on major issues of interpretation and validity that have broad applicability to many decision-making contexts.

A unique aspect of SPSSI's publication program is that the authors of SPSSI-sponsored books contribute their efforts to the Society. Thus, SPSSI owes a great debt of thanks to all of those who have participated in the development and revision of this research methods text across the years, and, in particular, to Louise and Chick who are responsible for this excellent fifth edition.

MARILYNN B. BREWER
President, SPSSI, 1985

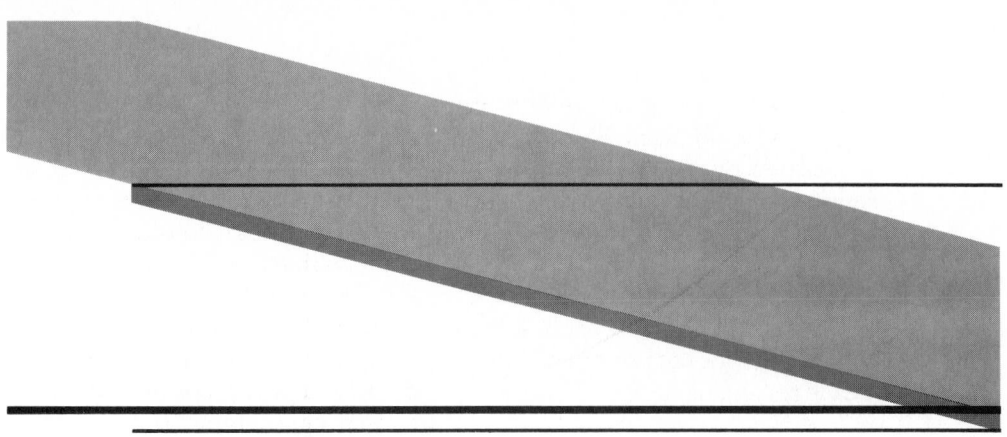

Preface

The Present and Past Editions

Research Methods in Social Relations has lived a long time and seen more generations of students than any of its authors or readers. It symbolizes tradition and change; it applies timeless issues of research design and measurement to changing methodologies and social concerns. It breaks some traditions and teaches readers to try new methods without losing sight of the old.

We begin this edition with two new chapters on the nature of knowledge and the logic of social inquiry. These chapters compare ordinary knowing with scientific methods. They also raise questions about the place of values in social research. We have added chapters which introduce new methods of data collection and analysis. New chapters on questionnaires and interviews provide an overview of these methods and step-by-step lessons in asking questions effectively. New chapters on data analysis integrate statistical analyses with the logic of research design. These chapters show how the original research design and the subsequent data analysis determine which relationships can be examined and which variables can be controlled. We have retained our discussion of experimental and quasi-experimental designs from the fourth edition. The search for plausible rival hypotheses and the necessity to rule out threats to validity remain important themes. We also have retained our discussion of participant observation, field work, and other qualitative methods.

Our goal remains true to the earlier editions — to provide multiple research strategies, multiple methods of measurement, and multiple techniques of data analysis — to allow the fullest exploration of social relations. We also maintain a commitment expressed by the earliest authors and by the sponsoring Society for the Psychological Study of Social Issues — a commitment to examine the place of values in social research. We do this both by the examples chosen to illustrate methodological issues and by the treatment of ethical issues in a chapter by Stuart Cook, one of the authors of the first edition.

Hybrid Vigor

Teachers and students who liked the earlier versions of *Research Methods in Social Relations* should find this edition even more to their liking. It has the hybrid vigor that comes from years of experimentation. It retains the eclectic quality of its predecessors, making it a book for social scientists at large. The methods we examine are applicable not just in social psychology and sociology or political science, health science or education, but span all these fields. The substantive social issues addressed by the methods are also cross-disciplinary. We have tried to make the book useful for teachers and students in many programs and departments, to provide a compendium of research methods and issues for social scientists from multiple disciplines. To paraphrase one of the techniques we discuss, ours is a "multitrait-multimethod" book.

Resourceful Skeptics

Beneath the emphasis on multiple eclectic methods are two currents that run consistently through the book. One concerns causal inferences. We state that social scientists often wish to but cannot make causal inferences, and we examine the elements of research design that make causal inference possible. The other current describes problems in measurement. We take the position that our measurements will always include a little more than intended and less than desired. We instruct the student in multiple methods of measuring and observing — being a participant observer, constructing scales and questionnaires, conducting interviews, and using archival data. Our concern with causal inference and measurement as omnipresent research problems is met by our prescription of multiple methods. We want students to approach research problems with a skeptic's eye, but we do not want them to despair of ever conducting useful research. Therefore, we supply them with a large and varied store of methods so that they become optimistic and resourceful skeptics.

Instructor's Manual

A new Instructor's Manual written by Mary Amanda Dew accompanies this edition. In it both new and seasoned instructors will find creative ideas for lectures and class exercises. The manual begins with the premise that it is impossible to learn to do research without having hands-on experience, so it provides *exercises* that can be done in class. To aid instructors with their lecture preparation, the manual provides a concise *summary* of each chapter and highlights the major points raised in the text. For each chapter the manual contains several *lecture topic suggestions*, some conceptual and some statistical. At the end of each chapter are *test questions*, short-answer as well as multiple-choice, including complete answers for both. The exercises and lecture suggestions add new ideas to enrich the course. The summaries and test questions emphasize the major ideas from the text.

Acknowledgments

Writing feels like solitary work, but the final printed product is always the work of many hands and minds. This edition of *Research Methods in Social Relations* has been made new and improved through the work of many people. Chapters 9–12 on data collection by Eliot Smith give a step-by-step guide for constructing scales and questionnaires and conducting interviews—tools that users of previous editions have described as the "nuts and bolts" of the book.

The Advisory Committee and reviewers who read some or all of the chapters sharpened our logic and updated our thinking. Those people are Richard Archer, Jeff Berman, Keith Billingsley, Susan Brandon, Richard Hofstetter, Kevin Jordan, Dave Kenny, Bernie Lieberman, Lawrence Rosen, Bob Rosenthal, Rick Scheidt, Kelly Shaver, Steve West, Larry Wrightsman, and Bob Wyer. We remain indebted to them for what they enabled us to do, even though we were not able to do everything.

The Publications Committee of the Society for the Psychological Study of Social Issues has sometimes worried about and worked on this book as much as the authors have. The members of the publications committee whose terms overlapped with the gestation and birth of this edition are Reuben Baron, Marilynn Brewer, Jeff Fisher, Dan Perlman, and Jeff Rubin. We thank them for being readers, advisors, and friends.

We also owe personal thanks to people who helped us in various ways. Eliot Smith thanks Pamela Smith and Jim Kluegel; Chick Judd thanks Dave Kenny, Jon Krosnick, Gary McClelland, Mike Milburn, and Rae Sullivan; and Louise Kidder thanks Donald Campbell, Michelle Fine, Dave Kipnis, and Ralph Rosnow.

The final printed product would not exist were it not for the people at Holt, Rinehart and Winston who saw this book through the production process: Rosalyn Sackoff, senior editor, Herman Makler, project editor, and Barbara Conner, copy editor. We thank them for their skill, expertise, and good humor.

L.H.K./C.M.J.

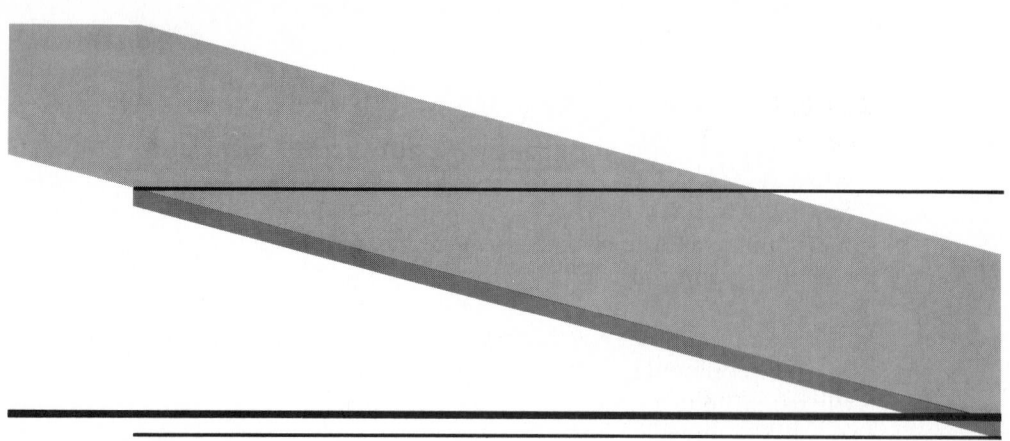

Contents

PART I

Introduction

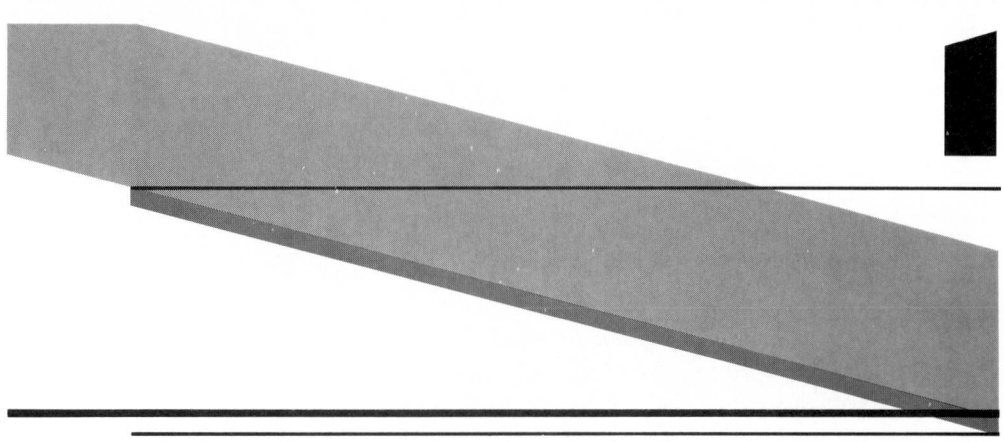

Acquiring Social Knowledge: Scientific and Ordinary Knowing

Gazing down at people from a tall building or window of a low-flying airplane gives you a different view of humanity from the one you normally have. A crowded park or congested freeway feels different when you remove yourself from the congestion and look at the crowds from afar. Somehow the distance gives you a sense of objectivity: You can observe without feeling the congestion yourself. At the same time, much would be missed if we always observed from afar. We would miss the feelings, the excitement, and the crush and enthusiasm of the crowd if we never entered into it ourselves.

Social scientists observe people from various distances, because different vantage points give different information about people, how they feel, act, and interact. Confining ourselves as social scientists to a single method or procedure limits what we can know. Some research methods allow the observer to be a participant in the group that is being observed. Other methods enable the observer to remain hidden or anonymous and to see from a distance. We will introduce you to these different methods in detail in subsequent chapters. To understand the methods of social scientific research, you must appreciate that there are multiple methods that give useful information primarily when used in combination. No one procedure or method can provide a complete description.

First, we will describe how social science is similar to and different from two other activities that you are already familiar with: physical science and ordinary knowing. Social science is similar to physical science in the logic of inquiry but different in the degree to which the objects (or subjects) under observation play an active role in the inquiry and raise questions about social values. Social science is similar to ordinary knowing in the quest to understand how people behave and relate to each other, but it is different in its systematic methods of inquiry.

We will elaborate on the following points in this chapter:

1. Social science can borrow the logic of physical science but must create different methods because the "things" we study are not inert objects but sentient beings and their interpersonal or social relations. When we study social relations among individuals or groups of people, we encounter their reactions to us as observers and we raise value-laden questions. The physical sciences also are not value-free, as Einstein pointed out when he discovered the formula for nuclear energy, but the place of values is more immediately apparent in the social sciences. Also the reactions of the observed to the observer must be taken into account.

2. Examining social relations scientifically sometimes appears to be "common sense" because most people observe and try to understand social relations daily in the process of ordinary knowing. We will show how social science differs from ordinary knowing in its deliberate search for sources of bias or invalidity.

The Place of Values in Social Research

This might seem to be an odd topic to introduce at the outset because research, any research, should be objective, and that means "not biased by someone's point of view." Values, however, represent a point of view, a judgment that "this is good and that is bad," which someone else might disagree with. Arguments about values cannot be settled by scientific evidence, much as both parties would like to believe that the evidence is on their side. Where does this leave social science?

The inextricable connection between social values and social relations requires social scientists to be aware of the implications their research can have for human welfare. They cannot extricate themselves from value questions, but they can be aware of what the implications are for various parties' welfare.

In some social research the values are so uncomplicated or noncontroversial that they almost cease to exist. For instance, in observing the use of interpersonal space in the library, it has been found that when the library is very crowded (e.g., the week before final exams), students are less bothered by a stranger sitting down right next to them than when it is uncrowded. The research seems quite uncontestable and noncontroversial: People tolerate invasions of their personal space and do not feel threatened when the invasion is unavoidable. There may be some values or political perspectives associated with this observation, but there is no apparent debate (e.g., Sommer, 1969). However, research on nonverbal gestures between men and women or between teachers and students has produced observations that raise more debate. The research shows that behaviors in such pairs are not symmetrical (Henley, 1977). In nonintimate conversations, men touch women more frequently than women touch men, and people in positions of power or authority generally do more nonreciprocal touching. What makes this research more controversial than the observations of crowding in the library is the interpretation of the data. The observations are quite straightforward; the interpretation introduces social and political beliefs and values. For instance, one interpretation of the asymmetrical touching behavior of men and women is that it is "affectionate" and is a "friendly gesture." A different interpretation, however, is that it illustrates a power differential that enables one party to invade the space of the other. The same can be said of the teacher-student observations. The "facts" must be interpreted, and this introduces different perspectives, values, and beliefs.

The act of framing a question about social relations also brings in values, beliefs, and differing perspectives. For instance, there are many studies that ask, "what are the effects of maternal employment on child development," but almost none concerning the effects of paternal employment. Is this asymmetry neutral or does it reflect cultural beliefs and values? Take another example: In the past there were many studies designed to investigate "the causes of homosexuality." There were none investigating "the causes of heterosexuality." The act of asking a question and framing it, with both an implied answer and an implicit set of values about social relations, is rarely neutral.

Contestability in Social and Physical Sciences

If you have taken a laboratory course in the natural or physical sciences, you probably remember white lab coats and physical equipment that convey this message: "This is serious; this is science." The dissection tools, microscopes, titration jars, and other uncommon instruments make it clear that this is no ordinary way of apprehending the world. This is science, and it promises to reveal information available only to science. Ordinary knowing cannot compete.

Compare this with your first introduction to social science. There were probably no lab coats or uncommon instruments involved in whatever you saw or heard. For example, perhaps you heard or read that day-care centers in the United States or communal child care in Israel created self-reliant and sociable children. If you were not opposed to the idea that mothers of young children can work and their children can prosper, you might have believed the results were true. However, if you (or someone you know) believed that mothers of young children should stay home, it would be easy to find fault with the research and conclude that the results were wrong. The results of social science appear to be more contestable than the results of the physical or natural sciences.

We do not want to suggest that there is no ambiguity in the natural sciences. Electron microscopes and other sophisticated methods of observation have a significant share of ambiguity and error. We intend merely to say that "in most people's eyes" the results of social science often appear to be more contestable than the results of natural or physical sciences.

What makes social science seem more contestable? Few people would say, "Amoebas do not reproduce by dividing in half! They reproduce just like dogs and cats; I don't care what you say with your fancy microscopes!" In contrast, a fair number of people might say, "Children of working mothers do not develop as well as children whose mothers stay home! I don't care what you say with your fancy surveys!"

We do not oppose argumentation and debate; they are essential for a science to grow and test itself. Instead we are impressed by the difference between the public acceptance of observations made by physical or natural scientists on the one hand and social scientists on the other.

Two features make social observations particularly open to debate. One is the seemingly ordinary quality of most social science methods of observation. Instead of using dissection kits or electron microscopes, social scientists often use their unadorned eyes and ears to make observations. They ask people questions, listen to their answers, and observe their behaviors. In the following chapters we will show you that the methods of social science differ in significant ways from ordinary knowing; the requirements imposed on measuring techniques are stringent and far from ordinary. For now, however, we wish to point out that to the public, social science methods sometimes look ordinary, and therefore the conclusions seem contestable.

The second feature that makes social science conclusions seem more contestable is the fact they often address issues about which there are serious, deeply felt, politically identifiable debates. It is, therefore, difficult to persuade someone that you have observed "the facts" when those facts contradict the person's beliefs, values, or political interpretations. For instance, someone who believes mothers should stay home with young children might not be dissuaded by social science data. The prior belief is deeply rooted in the person's beliefs about men and women, about family, about power, and perhaps about religion.

Social science research can never (or hardly ever) be value-free because it is an investigation of relations between people instead of between objects. We qualify this statement to say "hardly ever" and allow the possibility that some social research *might* be value-free. We leave you to find examples and to argue with classmates about whether a particular example is value-free. In reaching your own conclusion you will probably create some very convincing cases that also show how much values come into play in social research.

We do not want to leave the impression that physical and natural sciences are really scientific and social science is not. Rather, we want to give you an appreciation for the features of social science that make it particularly challenging. Research in social relations has many similarities with other forms of research. Most of this book will use language that is technical and will teach methods that are not simple. If sheer difficulty and complexity were qualifications for being considered "scientific," then social science is high on the scientific ladder. However, it sometimes looks like ordinary knowing, and it is usually embedded in a set of social and political values.

Ordinary Knowing

The study of social relations is the study of how people behave with and toward others. Defined broadly in this way, we are all students in the field of social relations. To see this, imagine yourself at a party on a weekend evening. You have expectations about how people at the party are likely to behave. Likewise you can easily think of behaviors that you are unlikely to see at the party. Reading *War and Peace*, for instance, is not a typical party activity. Not only do you have expectations about people's behavior at the party, but also you are likely to have explanations for at least some of this behavior. Suppose you saw someone at the party spill a drink on someone else. At least implicitly, you would look around to figure out why the drink was spilled and what the consequences were. Was the accident not an accident at all, but rather intended? Did it occur because the drinker already had one too many drinks? Was the party too crowded, with the inevitable jostling when too many people are jammed into a small room?

Consider another example: You are walking across campus on your first day back at school after summer vacation. Just like at the party, you have expectations about how people typically behave on returning to school. Consistent with your expectations, you see a lot of other returning students hurrying to get their course schedules approved, housing arrangements set, parking stickers purchased, and so forth. Suddenly you notice something not in keeping with your expectations. Surrounding the Dean's office is a picket line, with twenty or thirty students carrying signs. Because you did not expect this behavior the day before classes start, more or less automatically you try to figure out what's going on. That is, you try to find explanations for the behavior you are observing. Are these protestors concerned about a new and important issue on campus that you ought to be concerned about as well? Or are they malcontents, protesting because they have nothing better to do, and hence do not deserve your attention? You try to answer these questions about why the students are picketing the Dean's office by reading the signs they carry and watching them carefully for a few minutes.

As both these examples illustrate, we are all naive observers or students of social relations, regardless of what our actual profession is. All of us are engaged daily in the ordinary pursuit of understanding social relations because we all have expectations, hunches, and hypotheses about *how* people are likely to behave in given situations and *why* they behave the way they do. For instance, we expect certain behaviors at a party and not others. When someone spills a drink, we try to figure out what caused that behavior. Similarly, we expect returning students to be concerned about the same things we are. When we encounter a group of protestors, we attempt to construct some explanation for their behavior. The expectations, hunches, or hypotheses of ordinary knowledge are ultimately utilitarian. If we have ideas about how others are likely to behave with and toward us in different situations and in response to our own behavior, ultimately we can act in ways that elicit desired behaviors from others. Ordinary knowledge of social relations is useful for planning our own behaviors to reach our goals, objectives, or desired outcomes.

This does not imply that our ordinary hunches and hypotheses about others' behaviors are necessarily right. We certainly have expectations about behavior that are violated routinely. For instance, we may think it inappropriate to have too much to drink at a party. Nevertheless, someone may do just that. Likewise, when driving a car we expect others to look for oncoming cars before making a left turn. Nevertheless, people sometimes turn left in front of approaching traffic.

Not only our expectations about how others are likely to behave but also our explanations for why they behave the way they do may be wrong. For instance, after seeing the partygoer spill a drink, we may surmise that the accident was caused by mere clumsiness. This explanation might well be in error; perhaps the spill was intentional in retaliation against someone who had been insulting. Without seeing that prior insult, our explanation for the behavior would certainly be wrong. Likewise, when we first see the group of students picketing the Dean's office, we might conclude they are malcontents who do not deserve our attention. As a result, we might not listen to what they are saying and might never appreciate the fact that their grievance was legitimate.

Because our ordinary hunches, hypotheses, and explanations are ultimately constructed to help us achieve our own goals, and because we must inevitably realize that our hunches are not always correct, part of ordinary knowing involves trying to figure out when our hunches, hypotheses, and explanations are right and when they are wrong. Therefore two characteristics distinguish our ordinary knowledge of social relations. First, we have hunches and hypotheses about others' behavior. Second, we continue to examine, at least somewhat critically, those hunches and hypotheses. We are motivated both to explain others' behaviors and to figure out whether our explanations are correct. We do both routinely and spontaneously, hardly ever bothering to reflect on the fact that we are in fact studying social relations.

These two tasks also characterize scientific studies of social relations, regardless of whether the studies are conducted by psychologists, sociologists, economists, political scientists, educators, or others. They all share the goals of constructing theories of human social behavior and critically examining those theories to increase their accuracy.

The goal of this book is to examine scientific methods of studying social relations. What are the methods used to construct scientific theories of social relations? To answer this question, we will first examine how we operate routinely as ordinary observers of social relations—methods we routinely use in constructing and critically examining our hunches and hypotheses about human social behavior. Then we will compare and contrast these methods with those that characterize a scientific approach to the same phenomena.

First, what form do our ordinary hunches, hypotheses, and theories about human social behavior take? That is, what constitutes a "naive" social relations hypothesis or theory?[1] Second, what methods are ordinarily used in critically examining those hypotheses? What are the sources of support routinely used to figure out if a hypothesis is right or wrong, firmly grounded or not?

Naive Hypotheses and Theories of Social Relations

Most aphorisms or clichés about human behavior are naive hypotheses of social relations.

Birds of a feather flock together.
Absence makes the heart grow fonder.
The early bird gets the worm.

Each of these naive hypotheses has a characteristic form that is seen most clearly if we reduce it to its basic meaning.

Similarity results in increased contact.
Absence results in increased affection.
Acting on opportunities early results in success.

Each of these naive hypotheses argues that one phenomenon or behavior—the subject—causes or is associated with another phenomenon or behavior—the object. These phenomena, both subject and object, are called **constructs.** A social relations hypothesis, naive or not, concerns relationships between constructs that have to do with human social behavior. These hypothesized relationships may be causal or not. They may state that one construct **causes** another, or they may simply state that one construct tends to be found with another. In this definition, there are two notions that require elaboration. The first is the notion of constructs. The second is the notion of what is a causal relationship.

As we said, constructs are the phenomena of which a hypothesis speaks. When a hypothesis concerns causal relationships, some constructs are identified as causes and others as effects. If we believe the three naive

---

[1]By *naive* we mean a theory or a hypothesis of ordinary observers, as opposed to a theory or hypothesis of a scientist.

hypotheses presented are causal ones, the causal constructs are "similarity," "absence," and "early action." The three affected constructs are "contact," "affection," and "success." Notice that all these constructs, whether involved in a hypothesized causal relationship or not, concern general phenomena having to do with social behavior, and they all require further definition or elaboration. What, for instance, is "similarity" or "success"? Two different people may define these in different ways. Success for one person might mean having good friends, whereas for someone else it means having money or status. Thus constructs need further definitions to be tied to actual observable behavior. We do not directly see "success," for success can mean different things to different people. Rather we observe various ways of defining or measuring success (e.g., someone's stated quality of friendships or someone's average yearly income).

Our ordinary hypotheses frequently concern *causal* relationships between constructs because most of us believe that behaviors have causes. We believe, for instance, that success is not entirely the result of luck or good fortune or random events. Rather we accept the notion that it is partly affected by activities or constructs like "early action." Likewise, in arguing that similarity results in contact between people, we implicitly acknowledge that our choice of friends is not random; rather, some phenomena or constructs cause us to like or dislike others. Ordinary hypotheses by their very nature imply that human behavior is partially determined or caused. The "partially" qualification in the preceding sentence is an important one, however. For although we implicitly believe that human behavior is to some extent caused or determined, we also believe that human behavior happens as a result of random events, luck, and simply individual whims. Most people believe that human behavior has certain reliable causes, but believing in reliable causes does not necessarily make us determinists. To believe that behavior is caused does not mean that we can always perfectly predict and explain human behavior. There is still plenty of room left for luck and free will.

Social relations hypotheses vary not only in whether or not they describe a causal relationship but also in the complexity of the relationship they describe. Some hypotheses may be linked with other hypotheses to make up a social relations **theory.** For instance, the following set of hypotheses forms a small theory. Like many such sets, it takes the form of a syllogism:

Being unemployed frequently leads to personal depression.
Depression is often a cause of divorce.
Therefore, increased unemployment in society often is associated with
    higher divorce rates.

This syllogism consists of three hypotheses, the third being logically inferred from the other two. Some theories of social relations can be as simple as this, linking a few hypotheses. Others are exceedingly complex, linking many more hypotheses. For instance, some of the founding documents of this country, such as the Declaration of Independence, set forth relatively complex theories about the conditions under which people will be happy and prosper.

Hypotheses vary in complexity not only by being linked with others in theories but also by bringing in qualifying conditions or constructs that must be met for the hypotheses to be applicable. For instance, someone may hypothesize that "absence makes the heart grow fonder" but only when the absence is without other members of the opposite sex. This qualifying condition makes the hypothesis more complex than the original one. Now, instead of maintaining simply that the one construct leads to another, the hypothesis states that construct A results in construct B only under condition C. We say that A and C **interact** to produce B.

There is one very common form of qualifying condition that we often add to hypotheses: We frequently specify a group or kind of person for which a hypothesized causal effect should hold. For instance, we may say that "among males over 50, unemployment increases the probability of personal depression." We have then added a qualifying condition that specifies the group or population for whom the hypothesis is expected to be true. Adding such a condition suggests by implication that the hypothesis may not hold for other groups or populations. Because people having different backgrounds and experiences do in fact behave differently, it is generally a good idea to increase the complexity of a social relations hypothesis by adding a condition that specifies the population where the hypothesis should hold.

Social relations hypotheses thus vary both in whether or not they describe a causal relationship and in their complexity. In addition, there are differences in the confidence with which they are held or maintained. We may, for instance, firmly believe that being unemployed can cause one to be depressed. We may feel less strongly, however, about whether personal depression is a cause of divorce. Because theories are made up of sets of hypotheses, often in syllogistic form, and because these hypotheses differ in the confidence with which they are held, the syllogistic conclusion of the theory as a whole ought to be held with no more confidence than the least confident premise. Whether or not this is in fact how we operate in our ordinary understanding of social relations, however, is open to question.

So far we have discussed the nature of hypotheses, that is, what form they take and how they may vary. Once we realize that they may vary in the confidence with which they are held, we must raise the second question that was posed earlier about our ordinary knowledge of social relations. *Why* are some hypotheses held with more confidence than others? To answer this question we must know how people ordinarily gather evidence to test hypotheses.

Sources of Support for Naive Hypotheses

There are at least five sources of support routinely used to develop and modify naive hypotheses and theories: (1) speculation and logical analysis, (2) authority, (3) consensus, (4) observation, and (5) past experience.

I. Speculation and logical analysis   We often derive hypotheses and decide whether they are accurate by examining whether they are logically consistent with other hypotheses that we hold. An example of such derivation is contained in the syllogism presented previously. If we take it to be true that unemployment frequently leads to personal depression, and if we take it to be true that personal depression can often lead to marital discord and divorce, it necessarily follows that unemployment increases the chance of divorce. This final hypothesis is deduced or logically inferred from the combination of the two earlier ones. Schematically we can represent the syllogism this way:

Being Unemployed ⟶ Depression ⟶ Deviance

As this illustration makes clear, the influence of unemployment on the probability of divorce follows from the mediating or intermediary role played by personal depression in the process.

Syllogistic reasoning is frequently used to derive and modify hypotheses based on their consistency with other hypotheses. Generating support for hypotheses by such reasoning, however, is not without its pitfalls. Abelson and Rosenberg (1958) argued that logic and "psycho-logic," that is, the processes of reasoning toward consistency that we ordinarily engage in, are not necessarily the same thing. The following example illustrates the difference. Feather (1964) selected subjects who were either quite religious or not at all religious. To each group, he gave a set of syllogisms. Half of these syllogisms contained concluding hypotheses that were proreligion; half contained concluding hypotheses that were antireligion. In addition, regardless of the type of concluding hypothesis, some of the syllogisms were logically valid and others were not. An example of a logically invalid syllogism that reaches a proreligion conclusion is

Tolerance toward humankind creates love and harmony.
Christianity creates love and harmony.
Therefore, Christianity gives rise to tolerance toward humankind.

The subjects were asked to indicate whether each syllogism was logically sound or logically unsound. Results of this study showed that proreligious subjects overestimated the logical validity of invalid proreligious syllogisms and underestimated the validity of valid antireligious syllogisms.

Therefore what we ordinarily regard as a logical conclusion may be influenced not only by pure logic but also by our wishes or desires. We may invent seemingly logical justifications for hypotheses that we hold simply because we wish these hypotheses to be true. Although we strive for logical consistency in many of our beliefs, we also have a remarkable ability to ignore inconsistencies in other beliefs. For instance, it was not unusual twenty years ago to encounter white Americans who believed both that "anyone in this country can achieve whatever he or she wants" and that "blacks should not be allowed to attend the same schools as whites." When we want to ignore contradictions in our thinking, we have a remarkable capacity to do so.

2. Authority   We are likely to turn to various authorities or experts to determine what hypotheses make sense in our ordinary understanding of social relations. To figure out how to cope with a difficult child, a parent might consult the clergy, a counselor, or a teacher. To decide how to behave in a foreign country we have not visited before, we might consult someone who knows the country well. To understand why riots occur sometimes in some large cities in the summer, we might consult a sociologist or a specialist in race relations. As long as we have faith in the expert we consult, we may regard the expert's opinion as sufficient justification for a hypothesis.

Using experts to decide which are good hypotheses and which are bad is efficient as long as they are indeed expert in the area under consideration. All too often, however, we presume someone to be an expert when he or she only has the trappings of expertise without the actual knowledge to back it up. We rely on the symbols of authority without making sure that the authority knows what he or she is talking about. Consider a well-known study of obedience by Milgram (1974), in which someone with the trappings of scientific authority induced compliance from subjects who never questioned the expertise underlying it. Milgram ordered the subjects to use strong electric shocks on another person, and they were willing to follow his orders simply because he claimed to be an expert. Other studies have also shown that we frequently overestimate the expertise of so-called experts (Ross, Amabile, & Steinmetz, 1977).

In addition, we may let our beliefs and values define who we identify as an expert. This happens when we seek so-called experts merely to provide a confirmation for our hypotheses rather than a critical assessment. For instance, some might regard an astrologer as an expert on how to choose a spouse. Someone who defines the astrologer as an expert in this area is already convinced of the wisdom of astrological advice on such matters.

A final problem with reliance on authorities is that authorities may have their own interests at heart. Since authorities presumably like their status, they may provide advice that perpetuates or justifies the status quo rather than suggest novel social arrangements. If we wanted to under-stand why urban riots occur and we sought the advice of a corporate pres-ident in a community where the riot occurred, it is unlikely that he or she would identify the cause of the riots as the current economic system. A person who possesses wealth and power may be unlikely to recommend a redistribution of wealth and power in society.

In sum, in our ordinary knowledge of social relations, we seek the wisdom of authorities to help us evaluate our hypotheses and theories. Just as relying on logical analysis is not without pitfalls, so too, relying on the wisdom of authorities may lead to biased conclusions.

3. Consensus Instead of appealing to the wisdom of authorities, we may also appeal to the wisdom of our peers. We decide what are good or bad beliefs or hypotheses by finding out whether our friends agree with us. How might a mother decide when to wean a child? She might appeal to a physician as an authority. Equally likely, however, she might ask her friends when they weaned their infants. If a client in a business setting makes an unreasonable request, we might ask our co-workers why the client acted that way and how we should respond. If we want to evaluate our opinions on why high schools don't seem to be doing as good a job as they used to, we might discuss it with our neighbors. All these examples illustrate the validation of one's hypotheses or theories by social compar-ison or peer consensus.

This source of support for hypotheses is not a great deal different from the use of authorities. In both cases, others are the referent to decide what one should and should not believe. As a result, the use of consensus and social comparison is subject to the same kinds of biases and distor-tions as the use of authorities. With which of our peers will we discuss our ideas on schools? Most probably the discussion will be with people like us who are quite likely to agree on such things.

In addition, groups of people can be notoriously poor as independent judges. Groups frequently are pushed toward unanimity so that dissenting voices may not be heard (Janis, 1972). Also, the group may give the listener what he or she wants to hear, especially if the listener is highly regarded. As a result, group consensus or social comparison is often inadequate for validating hypotheses. In our ordinary understanding of social relations, however, we sometimes rely on it heavily.

4. Observation In order to determine whether our naive social relations hypotheses are correct, we routinely compare them to the observed behav-iors of ourselves and others. When they are not consistent with what we observe, we may modify or abandon them. Suppose you believed that women were able to "read" nonverbal messages more clearly than men (Hall, 1978). That is, you thought that women were more sensitive in understanding nonverbal signals that were sent to them, intentionally or not. To determine whether this hypothesis was accurate, you might watch members of both sexes in a number of different settings. If you were serious enough about examining your hypothesis, you might even do a little experiment on your own. You might, for instance, try to communicate nonverbally with some female and some male acquaintances and then see who figured out your signals more clearly.

Let's take another example. Suppose you believed that prejudice toward other ethnic groups is caused by a lack of personal acquaintance with members of those groups. To learn whether this hypothesis is accurate, you might conduct some informal interviews with various acquaintances, asking about their friendships with members of various ethnic groups. You might then see if your estimates of each person's degree of prejudice toward each group seem to be related to the number of friendships he or she had.

Such observational procedures are as full of pitfalls as the other procedures we use to support our naive hypotheses. There are four major problems in using observation to validate social relations hypotheses. We can use the example in the preceding paragraph to illustrate. First, as we argued in defining hypotheses and theories, the constructs mentioned in a hypothesis (e.g., prejudice or personal acquaintance) can mean different things to different people. One person's impression of someone's prejudice may not be the same as someone else's because different observers may look for different things. Likewise what one person means by personal friendships with members of different ethnic groups may be different from what another person means. Hence, in deciding what behaviors to observe, we might observe behaviors that do not represent or capture the construct with which our hypothesis is concerned. For instance, instead of measuring people's actual friendships, we might, when we interview them, measure how much they want to pretend to have such friendships.

Second, inferring that one construct *causes* another can be very difficult. Suppose in our example we indeed found that people who seemed more prejudiced reported fewer friendships. Such a finding does not necessarily mean that differences in contact with members of various ethnic groups *causes* differences in prejudice. It is at least as plausible that the causal effects are the other way around: that prejudice causes differences in friendship patterns. Using observation to support hypotheses can be misleading because causality can be very hard to establish.

Third, we might make our observations on a very select group of people, a group of people, perhaps, for which the hypothesis might be especially true but one that is not representative of the world at large. For instance, although it might be true that prejudice and contact with members of ethnic groups are related in our select sample of friends, they may not be related in general or in other samples. Thus, we might engage in biased sampling in such a way that we have more or less confidence in our hypothesis than we should.

Fourth, we probably are biased in deciding which observations are relevant. Snyder and Swann (1978), for instance, have shown that when testing hypotheses about individuals, people look for instances that confirm those hypotheses and tend to ignore instances not consistent with them. Thus, the very process of collecting observational data can be biased. Just as we might choose authorities who will tend to confirm our hypotheses, so too, we might judge observations as relevant or not depending in part on whether they support our hypotheses.

5. Past experience Probably we most frequently generate support for our hypotheses as students or naive observers of social relations by reflecting on or remembering past observations. We think back to instances or events that confirm the hypothesis and then we attempt to make modifications to take into account disconfirming instances.

Although the use of past experience or recollected observations is, we suspect, very frequent, it is susceptible to all the dangers inherent in the use of concurrent observation, plus others. Memory is inherently reconstructive. We do not passively store information about past observations; rather we store and organize events selectively. Theories and hypotheses are tools that we use in organizing our memories. It has been repeatedly shown that information or observations that are consistent with a theory or expectation are more easily remembered than information that is irrelevant (Johnson & Judd, 1983; Rothbart, Evans, & Fulero, 1979). Hence, it is perhaps unlikely that hypotheses will be disconfirmed by recollected observations.

Toward a Science of Social Relations

Try as we may to obtain an accurate understanding of social relations, we encounter innumerable difficulties in constructing and validating hypotheses and theories in everyday life. Acquiring knowledge about how people behave and why people behave as they do is not easy. Yet we all naively persist at it. So too does the scientist of social relations, be he or she a psychologist, sociologist, political scientist, or educator. Although the scientist's path toward acquiring knowledge about social relations is in many ways just as hazardous and difficult as the path of the ordinary knower, there are differences in how they proceed. The purpose of the concluding part of this chapter is to identify some of those differences, most of which are differences of degree rather than of kind. That is, scientists differ from the ordinary observer not so much in what they do but in how it is done. The science of social relations and the naive study of social relations are not qualitatively different from each other; the differences are subtle and, at times, hard to identify. They are nonetheless present.

The most important difference concerns the extent to which scientific studies are on the alert for biased conclusions. Scientists ideally operate as if their hypotheses and conclusions about human behavior might be in error. Social scientists look for biases and pitfalls in the processes used to support and validate hypotheses. Scientists are aware of a literature on such biases and submit their conclusions to the scrutiny of other scientists who attempt to find biases that were overlooked. The casual observer or ordinary knower often gathers evidence in support of hypotheses without being aware of or worried about the biases inherent in the process. This difference is one of degree, however. Although scientists are on the lookout for biases, they are not aware of them all. Likewise, casual observers certainly strive to be as accurate as possible in reaching their conclusions. The difference is this: *The scientist systematically studies how to avoid biases in examining hypotheses.*

Unlike the casual observer scientists always rely on observation to evaluate a hypothesis critically. They engage in empirical research to try to determine whether hypotheses are accurate and how they need to be modified to make them more accurate. Empirical research is observation that is systematic in attempting to avoid the biases. Although scientists may also use logical analysis, authorities, consensus, and past experience in evaluating hypotheses, unlike the casual observer, they ultimately engage in systematic observation or empirical research. Scientists ultimately put confidence in a hypothesis or a theory if it has been able to withstand empirical or observational attempts to falsify it.

Because of this reliance on observation, social scientists tend to be more concerned about the problem of linking up theoretical constructs with observables than are casual observers. A good scientific hypothesis contains not only statements about relationships between constructs of interest but also statements about what observable indicators or variables go with each construct. In other words, scientists who rely on empirical research are necessarily concerned with how to measure theoretical constructs. An ordinary observer using observation to support hypotheses is perhaps unlikely to spend much time thinking about what observable variables indicate constructs of interest. Scientists should be very concerned with that question.

To rely ultimately on empirical research or systematic observation to validate hypotheses means that social scientists assume that all constructs of interest can indeed be measured or observed. This is the **assumption of operationalism.** For each construct of interest in the study of social relations there must be observable features we can measure that represent the construct. This is not to say, of course, that scientists assume anything can be perfectly measured. In fact, they assume quite the contrary—that all constructs are measured with error. Nevertheless, the scientific assumption of operationalism means that all constructs of interest *can* be measured, albeit imperfectly.

Earlier we argued that one of the characteristics of a scientific inquiry is that the scientist is constantly wary of biases in attempting to validate hypotheses. Ultimately this means that scientists can never actually accept a hypothesis as correct or accurate, for the observations that support it may have been biased or in error in unknown ways. Strange as it may seem, science never can actually *prove* a hypothesis based on empirical research since that research could conceivably have been biased. The best one can do is gather a lot of empirical evidence, all of which supports or is consistent with the hypothesis, although in sum the hypothesis remains unproven in a formal sense. Although scientists of social relations, like ordinary observers, are invested in their hypotheses and ultimately wish to support them, to function scientifically means that one can never accept hypotheses as absolutely true. At best, hypotheses can withstand attempts to show that they are incorrect. There may always be other explanations for the observed data that seem to support a hypothesis, so a truly scientific stance is always a skeptical one.

What makes a scientific hypothesis a good one, then? A hypothesis gains gradual acceptance if it is repeatedly supported, survives numerous attempts to falsify it, and seems to account for observations conducted by different scientists in different settings. Because any particular observation in support of a hypothesis may be biased or in error, science requires **replication.** That is, empirical research must repeatedly reveal the same conclusions when conducted independently by different researchers. Only in this way can the biases of any one investigator or procedure be overcome. Likewise, as we have already said, scientists submit their interpretations of their research to the critical review of fellow scientists. In that way, they encourage others to find the errors or biases of interpretation that they themselves have missed.

All this sounds very laudable, and in theory it is. Yet in fact, scientists are rarely as noble as this idealized picture paints them. Scientists, like everyone else, are personally invested in what they do. They want to be right. They may even on occasion be a little more vain than most. Science does, however, provide a structure that necessitates the critical review of hypotheses and research. Although individual scientists may invest a great deal in trying to "prove" a hypothesis or in trying to demonstrate that all competitors are in error, the scientific community, by requiring that research be critically reviewed before being published, sees to it that hypotheses are usually critically evaluated, and they are only cautiously accepted by the scientific community as a whole.

A science of social relations consists of the interchange between theories and empirical research. One does research in an attempt to examine the validity of one's theories. Hence, systematic observation always starts with a question or hypothesis that motivates it. Research in turn leads to modification of hypotheses and theories. Ideally the path of science, circling between theory and observation, is always guided by a skeptical and self-critical stance.

2

Examining Social Relations Research

There are two purposes to this chapter. First, we want to explore the nature and rationale for scientific research in social relations. What is empirical research and why is it done? Second, we want to discuss ways in which any particular piece of social relations research may be sound or unsound, valid or invalid, useful or useless. In other words we will introduce criteria that can be used to judge the quality of scientific research. These criteria are the building blocks for sound social relations research.

The Purposes of Social Relations Research

We said in the first chapter that scientists of social relations conduct empirical research, or systematic observation, to support and modify theories and hypotheses about social behavior. To be more precise about the purposes of research, we need to review the nature of theories and hypotheses in social relations.

A theory about social relations has three features. First, it contains constructs that are of theoretical interest and that it attempts to explicate or account for in some way. Second, a theory describes relations among these constructs. These relations are frequently causal, specifying which constructs exert effects on which others under varying conditions. These hypothesized relations are the heart of a theory. Finally, a theory incorporates hypothesized relations or links between the theoretical constructs and observable variables that can be used to measure the constructs. These links specify the behaviors or other indicators that can be used to conduct empirical research. Nonscientific or naive theories of social relations also consist of constructs and causal relations among them, but because the scientific study of social relations relies on systematic observation to support and modify theories, a scientific theory also specifies the observable indicators that measure the constructs of theoretical interest.

A few examples will clarify what constitutes a theory. In political science there are theories about the factors that determine voters' preferences among political candidates (e.g., Campbell et al., 1960). These theories refer to political constructs such as candidate preference, party affiliation, strength of party affiliation, knowledge of political issues, and so forth. Further, the theory specifies relationships among these constructs. For instance, a theory may hold that candidate preference is determined by party affiliation, particularly among those who are relatively unknowledgeable about political issues. Notice that this example consists of a hypothesized causal relationship between two constructs under certain conditions. Finally, a good theory of candidate preference also specifies how the constructs of interest may be measured or observed. For instance, the theory may state that voter preference is best indicated by reports of voting behavior.

In sociology, there are several theories about alienation, deviance, and related constructs (e.g., Lefton, Skipper, & McCaghy, 1968). These theories talk about constructs such as alienation, education, social and peer support, poverty, and so forth. The theories also posit causal relations among constructs. For instance, they might posit that deviance develops in an environment lacking in sufficient social and peer supports, particularly when accompanied by poverty. The theory also is likely to specify the observable indicators of deviance, for example, a set or pattern of particular behaviors.

Finally, in psychology there is a developing theory concerning the adverse psychological effects of failure (e.g., Abramson, Seligman, & Teasdale, 1978; Seligman, 1975). This theory talks about constructs like failure, sense of personal control, attributions or explanations about failure, withdrawal, and so forth. The heart of the theory is contained in the hypothesized relations among constructs. For instance, failure is likely to result in withdrawal and helplessness when it is accompanied by a loss of a sense of personal control. The theory also specifies how the constructs are to be observed. For instance, failure is usually defined as receiving information that one's peers did better than oneself.

Relations among constructs (e.g., failure leads to withdrawal when accompanied by a loss of personal control) and relations between constructs and observable indicators (e.g., failure is indicated by information that one performed less well than one's peers) are the hypotheses of a theory. Thus, any theory is made up of hypotheses, which are of two sorts: (1) hypothesized relations among constructs and (2) hypothesized relations between constructs and observable indicators. Both sorts of hypotheses have characteristic forms. The first, concerning relations among constructs, typically takes the form

Construct A causes construct B for population X in condition Y.

Each of the examples of theories we discussed earlier contains hypotheses that conform to this model, although the word *cause* may be replaced with *leads to, produces,* or *is associated with.* Note, however, that in any given hypothesis, much may remain implicit. For instance, the populations or conditions for which the relationship between construct A and construct B holds may not be explicitly mentioned. A few further examples illustrate hypotheses about relations among constructs:

Contact with members of other ethnic groups decreases prejudice when in equal status settings.

Crowded classrooms in inner-city schools adversely affect educational achievement.

The social class of one's parents has a strong effect on one's aspirations in our society.

Deinstitutionalization of the mentally retarded enhances community acceptance.

The second type of hypothesis concerns relations between constructs and observable indicators. They usually are of the form

Behavior X or response Y is a valid indicator of construct A.

Examples include the following:

Delinquency may be defined as being arrested more than once prior to age 18.

The F scale is the appropriate measure of the authoritarian personality.

Ideologues are those who explicitly refer to underlying ideologies in discussing political issues.

In general, the purpose of conducting empirical research or systematic observation is to examine hypotheses. Research can be used to examine both kinds of hypotheses. Typically scientists conduct research to examine hypotheses of the first sort, making assumptions about hypotheses of the second sort. For instance, they might conduct research designed to demonstrate that "interracial contact decreases prejudice," and in the process they make assumptions about how both constructs, interracial contact and prejudice, are to be measured.

Although research that examines hypotheses of the first sort, causal relations among constructs, is perhaps more typical, research on hypotheses of the second sort is also a major occupation of scientists. Research designed to examine whether a given variable accurately or validly measures a given construct is called *psychometric* or *measurement research*. Measurement research is usually conducted by examining whether two or more ways of measuring the same construct give the same results. As we will see in later portions of this chapter, such research is vitally important to the success of research examining hypothesized causal relations among constructs. Only if we can successfully observe or measure the constructs of interest can we empirically examine hypotheses about the causal relations among constructs.

We have said that the purpose of conducting empirical research is to examine hypotheses. At this point we need to be more specific about what it means to *examine* hypotheses. There are four different functions or purposes of research that, in total, constitute the process of examining social relations hypotheses: (1) discovery, (2) demonstration, (3) refutation, and (4) replication.

Discovery

Researchers frequently gather data to attempt to discover what might be responsible for some phenomenon or behavior. For instance, in studying depressed patients we might interview and observe the patients' families to see if there are any patterns of interaction that might be responsible for the depression. In doing such systematic observation we do not as yet have a well-defined hypothesis about the causes of depression. Rather we are attempting to discover what might be plausible causes of constructs. Thus research as discovery is used primarily to develop or generate hypotheses.

When conducting research for this purpose, the researcher is operating in what is called an **inductive** manner, attempting to move from observation to the development of hypotheses, rather than the other way around.[1] Of course, research never serves solely a discovery function. In other words, the researcher never exclusively operates inductively. There is always some ill-defined or implicit theoretical orientation that guides the research, even when the researchers have no explicit hypotheses that they are examining. For instance, in the depression example, a researcher who interviews family members is implicitly assuming that causes of the depression may lie in the family and their interactions with the patient. A researcher who believed that depression was a result of a genetic or neurochemical malfunction would never look for causes in patterns of family interaction. In other words, without some kind of underlying or implicit theory, a researcher would not know where to begin looking for the causes of a given phenomenon or behavior. It is simply not possible to conduct research as pure discovery or to proceed purely inductively. Even when research is used primarily to generate hypotheses, the researcher inevitably makes theoretical assumptions in deciding what to observe or where a potential cause may lie.

Demonstration

If researchers have a hypothesis about the relations among constructs of interest, they are quite likely to gather data in an attempt to demonstrate or support the hypothesis. Suppose, for instance, that researchers believe that living in integrated neighborhoods reduces prejudice. They may then try to generate data or take observations to demonstrate the validity of this hypothesis. For instance, they might interview residents of both integrated and segregated neighborhoods about their attitudes toward various ethnic groups. If the interviews showed that those who lived in integrated neigh-

---

[1]The other way around, moving from prior hypotheses to observation or empirical research, is known as working *deductively*. When scientists use research for other purposes than discovery, they typically are operating deductively, although the distinction is not always crystal clear. We discuss deduction more in the following section on research as demonstration.

borhoods had more favorable attitudes, the research would be consistent with the hypothesis.

It is important to realize that at best research can only be consistent with or demonstrate a hypothesis. It can never *prove* the hypothesis. This point was made in the first chapter but bears reiterating here. Just because residents of integrated neighborhoods express less hostility toward other ethnic groups than residents of segregated neighborhoods, this does not mean that the hypothesis, which states that integration causes a reduction in prejudice, is correct. There are always alternative explanations equally consistent with the research results. For instance, residents of integrated neighborhoods might express less hostility because they were initially less prejudiced before they ever moved into that neighborhood. Hence, although the research is consistent with the hypothesis or demonstrates that it might be correct, there always remain alternatives that are equally consistent with the research results.

Research designed to demonstrate a hypothesis is **deductive** rather than inductive. Whereas in discovery the research is used to generate a hypothesis, here the hypothesis generates the research. Scientists, when acting deductively, start with the hypothesis, which they then seek to support or demonstrate with the data generated by research.

Once again, however, the researcher's activity is never pure deduction or pure demonstration. Although it may turn out that the research results are nearly perfectly consistent with the hypothesis that motivates the research, there are inevitably some inconsistencies or results that cannot be entirely explained by the hypothesis. The researcher then proceeds inductively, examining the data and hypothesis to determine how the hypothesis might be modified to account more perfectly for the research results. In this way, research never exclusively serves a discovery or a demonstration function, just as the researcher never reasons exclusively deductively or inductively.

Refutation

Although researchers can never conclusively prove a hypothesis, it is possible, if one proceeds with care, to refute competing hypotheses. For instance, suppose we conducted research on the integration-reduces-prejudice link that we have been discussing. Suppose we found that residents of integrated neighborhoods expressed less hostility than residents of segregated neighborhoods. We might then want to refute the competing or alternative hypothesis that residents of the two neighborhoods differed in prejudice initially, before they moved into the segregated or integrated neighborhoods. To do this we would have to conduct further research, interviewing people when they first move into integrated neighborhoods and then following them over time. If we found that initially they expressed hostility equal to that of segregated residents but that over time they developed more positive attitudes, we would have generated evidence to refute the competing hypothesis.

The process of supporting a hypothesis, and ultimately a theory that is made up of numerous hypotheses, is one of demonstration and repeated refutation of alternative hypotheses. Although in a formal sense there are always alternatives as yet unrefuted, gradually one develops confidence in a hypothesis through repeated demonstration and repeated refutations of alternatives to it. This brings us to the fourth purpose of research.

Replication

In the first chapter we argued that the researcher's biases inevitably affect how observations are gathered and interpreted. The only way to avoid these biases is to replicate the research. Replication means that other researchers in other settings with different samples attempt to reproduce the research as closely as possible. If the results of the replication are consistent with the original research, we have increased confidence in the hypothesis that the original study supported.

These then are the ways research is used to develop, examine, support, and modify hypotheses. The functions or purposes of research in examining hypotheses are not mutually exclusive. Any given study is likely to serve a number of functions simultaneously. Research to demonstrate a hypothesis usually ends up as discovery as well. Likewise, replication inevitably involves discovery and refutation, as the conditions of replications change and hypotheses must be modified to account for those changes.

The purpose of research is to inform hypotheses, to enable us to build better and more accurate hypotheses about how human beings behave. Of course, not all research is equally informative or useful in constructing and modifying hypotheses. It is to this issue that we now turn: What makes research useful or not in helping us to discover, demonstrate, revise, and ultimately support hypotheses?

Criteria for Evaluating Social Relations Research

To discuss these criteria we will use one of the examples presented earlier:

Crowded classrooms in inner-city schools adversely affect educational achievement.

Construct Validity

To conduct research that will help determine whether this is a good or bad hypothesis and whether it should be modified in some way, we first need to measure successfully the theoretical constructs of interest.

Clearly, if the researcher never examined a variable that was intended to represent "educational achievement," the research would not be very useful in figuring out whether the hypothesis needs modification. In this hypothesis two constructs are involved: Degree of crowdedness in classrooms is the first, and it is the causal one. Educational achievement is the second, and it is hypothesized to be affected. Both of these must be measured successfully, or *operationalized*, in order for the research to be useful in informing the hypothesis that motivates it. The variable used to measure the causal construct, crowdedness of classrooms, is called the **independent variable.** The variable used to assess the affected construct, educational achievement, is the **dependent variable.** These labels refer to the fact that the affected variable is presumed by the hypothesis to be "dependent" on the causal variable. The degree to which both the independent and dependent variables accurately reflect or measure the constructs of interest is known as the **construct validity** of the research. If a study has high construct validity, all the constructs in the hypothesis that motivates the research have been successfully measured or captured by the specific variables on which the researcher has gathered data.

Internal Validity

Assume we had met this first criterion for useful research, and we had good measures of both the degree of crowdedness in classrooms and students' achievement. Suppose we then gathered data on a number of classrooms and found, indeed, that in more crowded classrooms students in fact did less well. Certainly this result is consistent with the hypothesis. What we do not know, however, is whether our research supports the notion that crowdedness *causes* a decrease in achievement. When a hypothesis concerns a causal relation between constructs, as it frequently does, research is clearly more informative if it can be used to examine causality. The second criterion for useful or informative research, known as **internal validity,** concerns the extent to which conclusions can be drawn about the causal effects of one variable on another. In research with high internal validity, we are relatively more able to argue that relationships are causal ones, whereas in studies with low internal validity, causality cannot be inferred as well.

External Validity

A final criterion concerns the extent to which one can generalize the results of the research to the populations and settings of interest in the hypothesis. This is known as the research study's **external validity.** In the example we are considering, suppose the constructs were well measured (high construct validity). Suppose further that we found a relationship between crowdedness and achievement and could reasonably claim that relationship to be a causal one (high internal validity). We then would want to know further whether that causal relationship held in only the relatively few classrooms we observed in our research or whether we could generalize the causal relationships to other classrooms that we did not observe. The hypothesis states that the effect appears in all inner-city classrooms. Clearly it would not be efficient to observe them all. But we might select a few to observe so that we would have confidence in generalizing the results of our research to other classrooms. Such a study has relatively high external validity. A study from which generalization is difficult has relatively low external validity.

These three validities are the main criteria for judging the informativeness of any particular research study. (See Table 2.1.) These definitions are consistent with those of many others who have discussed research validity (Campbell & Stanley, 1963; Cook & Campbell, 1979; Cronbach & Meehl, 1955; Judd & Kenny, 1981). The reader is referred to these sources for further elaboration.

Although all three of these validities are important in evaluating research, their relative importance depends on the purposes the research is designed to serve. For instance, in research that focuses primarily on *discovering* a cause of some particular behavior, it might be sufficient initially to measure other constructs that are related to the behavior of interest, without for the time being worrying too much about whether the relationship is a causal one. In other words, in discovery research, measuring constructs well (i.e., construct validity) may be relatively more important than internal validity. Or consider research whose primary purpose is *replication*. It might be argued that such research is especially concerned with external validity, since in replication we are concerned with whether a previously obtained result continues to be found in a new setting at a different time. Because the conditions of the original research and the replication are never exactly identical, one is always examining issues of generalizability in conducting replication research.

The remaining pages of this chapter concern the factors that determine whether a study has high or low construct, internal, and external validity. Our discussion here will serve only as an introduction, however,

TABLE 2.1   Definitions of Research Validities

Construct validity	To what extent are the constructs of theoretical interest successfully operationalized in the research?
Internal validity	To what extent does the research design permit us to reach causal conclusions about the effect of the independent variable on the dependent variable?
External validity	To what extent can we generalize from the research sample and setting to the populations and settings specified in the research hypothesis?

to the question of how valid and informative research is designed and conducted. The major portion of this book is devoted to this topic as well. Hence, the remaining pages in this chapter serve as an introduction to many of the later chapters, where the same issues are considered in greater detail.

Maximizing Construct Validity

Chapter 3 extensively examines the issue of construct validity—how we measure what we want to measure. Our discussion here will give you a preliminary idea about how we decide whether given variables measure the constructs of interest.

Suppose we wanted to measure the school achievement of children in different classrooms to examine our hypothesis about the deleterious effects of crowded classrooms. There are a number of ways to measure achievement. We could give the students achievement tests; we could look at students' grades; we could ask teachers to evaluate their students verbally; and so forth. Each of these measures of achievement is called a **variable**.[2] Variables are simply rules or ways of classifying people into different categories so that those who are in the same category are more similar in some way of interest than those who are in different categories. For instance, scores on an achievement test constitute a variable that is thought to measure achievement. If we line students up according to their scores on the achievement test, we believe that students close together in that rank order are more similar on achievement than students further apart.

Actually, however, variables never measure only the construct of interest. They measure other irrelevant characteristics as well. Think about an achievement test. To some extent it does measure that which we call achievement; however, it also probably measures test-taking anxiety, motivation to do well on the day the test was administered, ability to read English, and so forth. Thus, variables measure not only the construct of interest but also what we might call constructs of disinterest—things we would rather not measure. Finally, any variable is likely to contain within it random errors of measurement. We might for instance suspect that the scores of some students on the achievement tests are affected by coding or grading errors or errors on the students' part in recording what they knew to be the correct answer.

---

[2]Variables are actually rules for classifying people or any other sorts of units into different categories. In most social relations research, we measure characteristics of people, and hence variables are ways of classifying people. However, we might use a variable to measure characteristics of houses, classrooms, cities, and many other units as well.

As is shown in Figure 2.1, any variable is most likely made up of three different components: (1) the construct of interest, (2) other things that we do not want to measure—constructs of disinterest, and (3) random errors. Therefore, if we lined students up in order of their scores on the test, that order would not be identical to the ordering that would result if somehow we could line them up according to their pure or "true" achievement. Motivation, test-taking anxiety, and random errors are also responsible in part for the ordering of students based on their achievement test performance.

A variable that has a great deal of construct validity is one that mostly measures the construct of interest, with minimal contributions from constructs of disinterest and random error. Given this, how do we know the degree to which any given variable has construct validity? Since we cannot measure "true" achievement directly, we cannot know whether the rank ordering of students on the test is similar to the rank ordering of students on "true" achievement. The only solution is to measure other variables that we think are also measures of achievement. For instance, we could look at school grades. School grades probably measure achievement, that is, the construct of interest, and they probably measure other things as well, like teachers' biases and preferences, students' extroversion, and so forth. We therefore compare the ordering of students on what we think are our two measures of achievement, test scores and grades. If the two orderings are similar, and if we believe that the only thing these two variables measure in common is achievement, the similarity of their orderings is evidence for their construct validity.

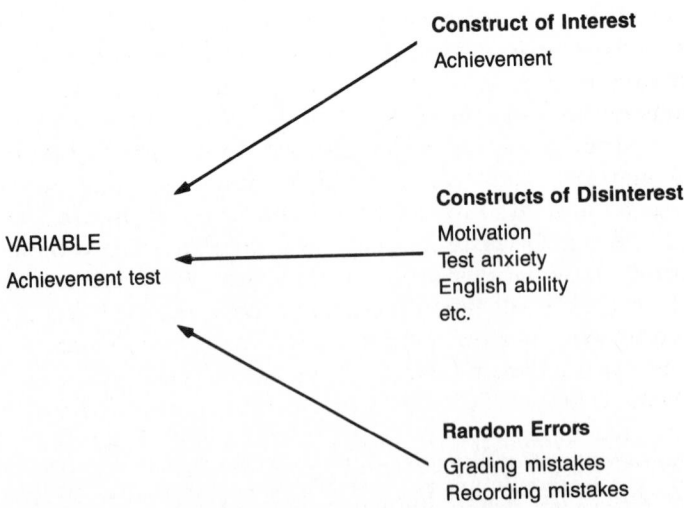

FIGURE 2.1 **Three components of a variable**

Let us review the general point. Since all variables measure not only the construct of interest but other things as well, and since we cannot know the order of people for sure on the "true" construct, the best we can do is measure another variable that we think also assesses the construct of interest and then compare orders on the two variables. If two variables that we think measure the same construct give us similar orderings of people, we have increased confidence that, in fact, each of them is measuring that construct that we think they have in common. Most fundamentally, to assure ourselves that our research has construct validity, we need to measure each construct in more than one way. Only if the different ways of measuring constructs give similar results can we have confidence that our variables in fact capture the constructs of interest. Construct validity is best examined by employing *multiple operationalizations*, or multiple ways of measuring.

The need for multiple operationalizations and how, more specifically, one examines the quality of one's variables are discussed in much greater detail in the next chapter. Here we wish to stress the importance of construct validity to research. If research is to be useful or informative in examining hypotheses, it must measure the constructs that the hypotheses talk about. If the observed variables do not have construct validity, there is no way the research can inform our theory.

Maximizing Internal Validity

In Chapters 4, 5, and 6 we discuss different research designs. Differences among designs affect the research's internal validity—the extent to which we can infer causal connections from a relationship between two variables. Our discussion of internal validity here should give you an intuitive understanding for how to maximize our ability to argue for causal connections in the research we do.

In our crowded classrooms example, suppose we went into 100 classrooms and measured their degree of crowdedness and the average student's achievement. Suppose further that our research had perfect construct validity: Our measures of both crowdedness and achievement measured those constructs and nothing else. Finally, suppose we found that the average student's achievement was ten points lower in classrooms that were classified as crowded than in classrooms that were not crowded. In other words, we found that the two variables, crowdedness and achievement, were related in the predicted direction. Could we argue from this relationship that we have evidence for a causal effect of crowdedness on lowered achievement? Of course, we could not.

A simple relationship between two variables is not enough to infer that one causes the other. In order to have causality, there must be a relationship, but by itself a relationship between two variables is not sufficient. Consider a few classic examples where relationships certainly do not imply causality. Among elementary schoolchildren it is certainly the case that those children having larger feet are better readers. Does that mean that size of feet affects reading ability? Certainly not. Age affects both, and that is why foot size and reading ability are related. Older children tend both to have larger feet and to be better readers. Another example: In England in the last century it was noticed that more babies were born where more storks were roosting. Does that mean that the presence of storks assures many births? No. What accounts for the relationship is population density. Where there are lots of people, there are lots of chimneys, where storks are fond of roosting. Likewise, where there are lots of people there are lots of babies. Hence, storks and babies are found together.

Returning to our example, assuming we have found that those classrooms classified as crowded have lower average achievement than those classified as uncrowded, why can't we argue for causality here? It is possible that students in the crowded classrooms were less able initially than students in the less-crowded classrooms. In other words, the differences in achievement may predate the students' experiences in one classroom or another. Students might be selectively placed in crowded or uncrowded classrooms according to their initial ability. Such selective placement may be intentional or not, but in either case it is clearly a reason for refraining from inferring causality. Selective placement is known, therefore, as the *selection threat* to internal validity.

How might we get around this selection threat? One way might be for us as researchers to place students in either crowded or uncrowded classrooms in such a way that we knew there were no initial differences in achievement. If we could do so, we might have confidence that any differences in achievement later on were not due to initial achievement differences. To do this we might find a group of children and measure their achievement initially. Suppose we then match boys and girls on their achievement scores, putting all the matched boys in the crowded classrooms and all the girls in the uncrowded ones. For every boy who initially had a score of 10 on the achievement test, we would find a girl with an identical score. We would then place the matched children in the crowded and uncrowded classrooms, boys in the former and girls in the latter. Such matching would mean that initially the two groups of students would not differ in achievement.

If after such matching to equate the groups initially we later found differences between classrooms, with those in crowded classrooms doing less well, we might be tempted to argue for a causal effect of crowdedness. However, we might still be in error. Although the boys in the crowded classrooms might initially have the same achievement scores as the girls in the uncrowded classrooms, they might be changing on their own at a different rate. That is, even if crowdedness of classroom made absolutely no difference to achievement, we might still observe differences between boys and girls at the end of a few months, even though they were initially the same, simply because they were changing or learning on their own at different rates. The problem is not that the boys and girls differ initially; that problem has been eliminated by matching. The problem is that the two groups may be growing or changing at different speeds. Hence, if we find a difference in achievement at a later time, we can not infer confidently that the difference is caused by the difference in classroom crowdedness. This problem is known as the *selection by maturation threat* to internal validity.

What we need is some way to equate the children in the two types of classrooms not only now but also in the future. We need to assign them to classrooms in such a way that if crowdedness had no effect on achievement, we would find no achievement difference between the two groups of children at a later time. Unfortunately there is no such characteristic of the children that we can use. Any characteristic might be related to achievement later, even if it is not now, and hence we would find differences between the two types of classrooms later even if crowdedness had no effect on achievement.

There really is only one type of variable that we could use to assign children to type of classroom to accomplish our goal. Suppose for each child we flipped a coin. Is there any reason to expect that heads or tails is related to a child's achievement now or in the future? Certainly not, just as we would not expect the result of the coin toss to be related to hair color or height. By definition, a variable whose values are randomly determined, like the flip of a coin or the throw of a die, is unrelated on average to all other variables now and in the future. Hence, if we decided who was to be in the crowded classroom and who in the uncrowded by a flip of a coin, we would expect no differences in achievement later if crowdedness made no difference.

Instead of achievement, think about hair color for a minute. Suppose we put people in crowded or uncrowded classrooms according to whether they got heads or tails on a coin toss. We certainly would not expect that as a result of our coin toss, all the brunettes would wind up in one type of class and all the blondes in the other. Rather we would expect both types of classes to have a mixture of brunettes and blondes. Since presumably type of class has no effect on hair color, we would expect the same mixture of brunettes and blondes in each type of class both now and in the future. Similarly, if achievement were unaffected by crowdedness, and if we randomly decided who was in which type of classroom, we would expect to find no difference between classrooms in achievement at a later time. If we *did find* a difference, we would believe that it must have been caused by crowdedness.

The moral of this example is that one can confidently infer causality from the relationship between two variables only if people have been randomly assigned to the levels of one of the variables. Degree of crowdedness in our example has two levels: crowded and uncrowded. If it is related to achievement later and if children were assigned to its levels (or type of classroom) on a random basis, we can argue that it, as the independent variable, had a causal effect on achievement, the dependent variable. Causal inference is possible only when students or other subjects have been randomly assigned to levels of the independent variable. (Remember—the independent variable is that which represents the causal construct in the hypothesis.) Research studies carried out in this manner, with random assignment to the independent variable, are called **randomized experiments.** They are discussed in much greater detail in Chapter 4.

Although randomized experiments are the best choice if causal conclusions are all important in research, they require the researcher to have a great deal of power or control. He or she must be able to determine who is in which sort of classroom, for example. Frequently such control over the independent variable is impossible. It would be quite unusual if a school system and parents allowed a researcher to decide who was in which type of classroom. When such control is not possible, some type of quasi-experimental or correlational research design is used instead of a randomized experimental design. These research designs are discussed in Chapters 5 and 6. Although they do not permit causal inferences with the same degree of confidence as randomized experiments do, they are essential tools for the social relations researcher. In this field, there are frequently practical and ethical considerations that force the researcher to use some design other than a randomized experimental one. Although some internal validity is sacrificed, nevertheless quasi experiments and correlational designs can yield exceedingly rich and useful information. Randomized experiments are nice, but they are not the only tools in the researcher's bag.

Maximizing External Validity

In Chapters 7 and 8 we look at procedures designed to increase the external validity of research—procedures to increase our ability to generalize the research results to the populations and settings of theoretical interest. As we did with the other validities, our purpose in the following paragraphs is to introduce the material found in those later chapters.

Returning to our example once again, suppose we had measured both constructs well and done what we could to assure internal validity; how would we insure that our research results were generalizable to the extent we desired? First, it is necessary to specify before the research is conducted the limits of desired generalization. Rather than remaining implicit in the hypothesis, the population and setting to which generalization is sought should be made explicit. We need to define precisely the group of people and the settings for which we think our hypothesis holds. For instance, we might say that crowded classrooms adversely affect achievement in fourth through sixth grades in schools located in cities having more than 500,000 residents. In this example we wish to generalize to a population of classrooms in schools. The more precise we can be about which classrooms we are concerned with, the easier generalization becomes.

Ideally, if cost and time did not matter, we might gather data from all classrooms in the population of classrooms. That is, we might see if crowdedness and student achievement are related across *all* fourth-through sixth-grade classrooms in all large cities in the country. If we gather data from the entire population and find support for our hypothesis, generalization to the desired population is no longer a problem.

Unfortunately, however, it is seldom efficient to measure every classroom or every person in the population and settings of interest. Rather, we can only afford to gather data from a *sample* taken from that *population.* To enhance generalization, we want to select that sample so that it is as similar as possible to the population as a whole. What we want is a sample that is representative of the population. How do we obtain it? Suppose we selected only fourth-grade classrooms. Are they representative of all fourth- through sixth-grade classrooms? Probably not. Suppose we selected for our sample all fourth- through sixth-grade classrooms in one particular city. Would they be representative? Probably not. The only way we can be confident about generalizing from a sample to a population of interest is to draw a random or *probability sample.* That means that instead of using any characteristic of the classroom (e.g., fourth grade only or one city only) to decide which ones are in the sample, we use a variable whose values are randomly determined. We do something like flipping a coin to determine the classrooms from which we gather data.

It is important to be clear that flipping a coin to select a sample from a population is not the same thing as flipping a coin to decide which children are assigned to which type of classroom. Using a random process to select a sample from a population is done to enhance our ability to generalize, that is, external validity. Using a random process to decide who is in which type of classroom is done to increase internal validity, that is, our ability to reach causal conclusions about the effects of classroom crowdedness.

Frequently in social relations research it is not practical to draw a probability sample. We may like to generalize to classrooms across the country, but we simply cannot afford to travel across the country to measure crowdedness and achievement in our randomly drawn sample. Generalization must then be done on a theoretical basis. We must speculate about how classrooms that we have not observed might differ from those we have; and then we must decide if those differences should influence whether crowdedness affects achievement. Such speculation ultimately requires further research to increase our confidence in its conclusion. Hence, research as replication in other settings and with other samples is an important part of maximizing external validity.

Summary

There are two major foci of this chapter. In the first, the purposes of empirical research for the scientific study of social relations were examined. We argued that research is used fundamentally to examine hypotheses. As such, research can be used for discovery, demonstration, refutation, and replication.

Discovery is the inductive process of gathering data to formulate hypotheses. Demonstration is predominately a deductive process, gathering data that one hopes are consistent with a hypothesis. Although such demonstrations can be used to support a hypothesis, the hypothesis can never in fact be proven since there always remain alternative ways to account for the same research results. Research as refutation involves the attempt to refute competing hypotheses, that is, to show that alternative explanations for previous results are not in fact valid. Finally, research as replication involves repeating research with different samples or in different settings in order to gain increased confidence in a previous demonstration. In all four cases, discovery, demonstration, refutation, and replication, the ultimate reason for gathering empirical data is to support, evaluate, and refine our hypotheses so that they do a better job of describing social relations.

In the second half of the chapter we defined three criteria that determine the extent to which research is useful in examining hypotheses: construct validity, internal validity, and external validity. Research has high construct validity if the variables that are in fact measured correspond closely to the constructs that the hypotheses discuss. Research that is internally valid permits one to reach causal conclusions about the relationship between the independent and dependent variables. Finally, in research that is high in external validity, one can generalize the results from the sample studied to the population of interest. In addition to defining these validities, we also discussed on an intuitive level the necessary conditions for achieving each one. This discussion serves to introduce the more-complete presentations in the next six chapters.

PART II

Research
Validities

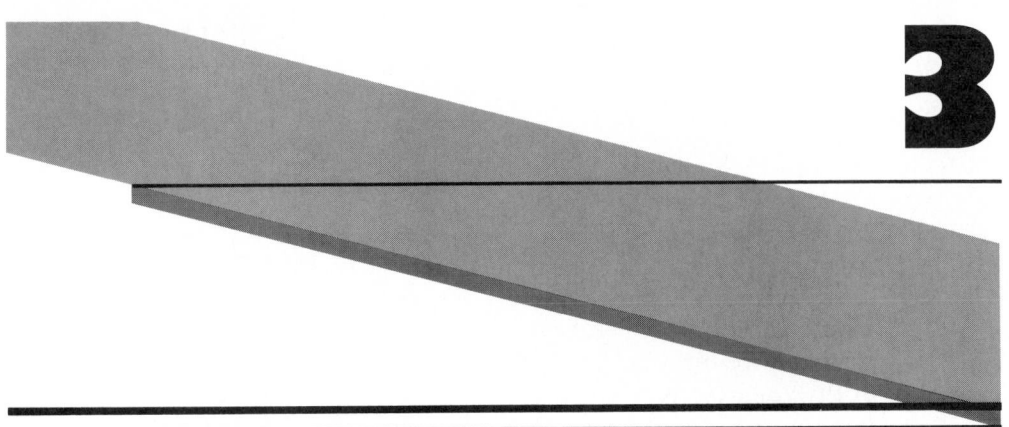

3

Measurement: From Abstract Concepts to Concrete Representations

To do any research we must be able to measure the concepts we wish to study. For instance, if we want to study social power, we need a measuring instrument. It is often difficult to develop yardsticks or scales for such abstract ideas because the fabric of social life is not flat, firm, one-dimensional, or tangible. Therefore, we can never be sure we are really measuring what we mean when we say this is a study of "social power" or any of the hundreds of abstract terms that refer to social relations. The problem a social scientist has trying to capture the shape or size of abstract concepts is like the problem a seamstress would have trying to measure an invisible, intangible piece of cloth.

Gossamer Concepts and Concrete Definitions

Social scientists do not spend much time groping in thin air hoping to find the shape of "social status." Instead they devise concrete representations which they can measure more directly. The abstract concepts are called **constructs,** the concrete representations are called **variables,** and the procedures for measuring variables are called **operational definitions.**

Constructs

Constructs are the abstractions that social and behavioral scientists discuss in their theories. They are the rich theoretical concepts that make the science interesting, terms like *social status, power, intelligence,* and *gender roles.* Because you cannot literally put your finger on any of these to measure them, you must find some concrete representations that approximate what you mean when you speak of such concepts.

Any one construct can be measured in many different ways because there are a variety of concrete representations of any abstract idea. Each of these will give us an approximate representation of the construct. For instance, power could be represented by the amount of influence a person has at work, at home, in the neighborhood, or in the mass media. Each of these gives some indication of a person's power; no one alone contains the whole truth. Each of these representations is a different *variable,* but they are all related to the *construct.* Taken together they are what we mean when we speak of power.

Variables

Variables are representations of constructs. They cannot be synonymous with a construct because any single construct has many different variables. Therefore, variables are partial representations of constructs, and we work with them because they are measurable. They suggest ways that we can decide whether someone has more or less of the construct. For instance, if we select "influence at work" as the variable to represent power, we can begin to devise ways to determine whether someone has more or less influence at work than someone else. Being more concrete than the construct, the variable suggests some steps we can take to measure it. These steps are called **operational definitions.**

Operational Definitions

An *operational definition* specifies how to measure a variable so that you can assign someone a score such as "high," "medium," or "low" social power. Operational definitions are the means by which we obtain the numbers or categories for the variables. That is, an operational definition is the sequence of steps or procedures a researcher follows to obtain a measurement. The variable may have only two possible scores such as "present" and "absent" or "high" and "low," or it may have 100 or more possible scores, as with IQ tests. Provided there are at least two possible scores or levels, it is a variable and the operational definition is at least minimally useful.

Why Operational Definitions Are Always Necessary and Often Inadequate

At the beginning of a research project a student's greatest concern is generally "what is my topic?" and the second greatest concern is "how will I measure it?" The second question can be answered only by finding or creating an operational definition, and the student rarely feels satisfied after this has been accomplished. The dissatisfaction is realistic because operational definitions are never completely adequate. They are necessary but rarely seem sufficient to capture the rich and complex ideas contained in a theoretical construct. The beauty of an operational definition is that it specifies precisely how to obtain a measurement of a variable in such a concrete and specific manner that anyone else could repeat the steps and obtain the same measurements. Its very specificity and concreteness, however, limit the breadth and depth of what we are able to measure. The following discussion illustrates the dilemma.

Suppose someone claimed to have found a way to measure people's health by "sensing the auras" that surround them. The practitioner claimed the technique worked but was so mystical and complex that no one else could use it and obtain the same readings; this would be an unacceptable operational definition. A thermometer reading of someone's temperature, in contrast, is an acceptable operational definition because it is a straightforward procedure that can be easily repeated. But what is a thermometer reading actually an operational definition of? Is it a measure of health?

Technically, a thermometer reading is a measure of how high the mercury has risen in a tube, which in turn is a measure of how warm the mercury is, which is a measure of how warm the inside of the person's mouth is. Is that a measure of health? We usually accept it as a measure of whether or not a person has a fever, but even that is debatable. We all have different thermometer readings at different times of day; at what point do we call a temperature a "fever"? At 99°F? Or 100°F? The connection between temperature and "fever" is not entirely clear. The thermometer reading, therefore, is an imperfect measure of whether or not someone has a fever. It is a less-than-adequate measure of health because the connection between temperature and health is more tenuous than the connection between temperature and fever. A person may have a normal temperature but suffer from high blood pressure or diabetes or arthritis and, therefore, not be in perfect health.

Health is a very complex abstract construct with many components: Blood pressure, blood sugar levels, white blood cell count, red blood cell count, degree of obesity, cholesterol level, history of cancer, and many other details constitute a person's state of health. A temperature reading, therefore, measures only one component of health. To obtain an adequate assessment of someone's state of health, we must take many readings and ask many questions, as a physician does during a general medical checkup. Any single measurement, such as a red blood cell count, is an operational definition of a component of health, such as degree of anemia. And each such operational definition is more acceptable as a scientific measurement of health than is an "aura" reading because "auras" are not publicly accessible. Almost anyone can learn to measure blood pressure or count red blood cells, and two people can agree in their measurements. Not so with reading auras. Scientific measurement is accomplished with operational definitions that can be used and repeated by any number of people. This is what makes operational definitions objective.

The emphasis on objectivity should not be misconstrued. It does not mean that all measurement or all observations must be quantified. Good observations and measurement can also consist of words rather than numbers. Moreover, it does not mean that a number like 100 on a thermometer or achievement test *is* that person's temperature or level of achievement. If the same person were retested with another instrument or at another moment, the number might change. Each measurement gives an approximation to the true score—and each also contains some error. The emphasis on objectivity does not guarantee truth or accuracy, but it does permit scientists to communicate with one another and with the public. It also permits anyone to challenge and check a piece of research because the operational definitions are instructions for replicating an observation.

Operational definitions are like the procedures we use to teach children about objects and concepts. We point at objects and name them. Because we cannot point with our fingers at abstract concepts, we devise a number of steps, like taking thermometer readings or achievement tests, and point to the final answer as a measure of fever or achievement level.

Early logical positivists were overzealous in their application of operational definitions. They made circular claims, such as "intelligence is what the intelligence tests measure," which left no room for debate. Such tautologies help us to understand neither the concept of intelligence nor the test used to measure it. D. T. Campbell criticizes the tautological approach, which he calls "definitional operationism" (1969c). He says that every observation is affected by a variety of factors that bear no relation to the construct we wish to measure. For instance, answers to census questions about family income or number of adults living in a home are only partly determined by the respondent's true income or family size. They are also determined by "the social interaction of the interview . . . the interviewer's appearance . . . the respondent's fear of similar strangers, such as bill collectors, welfare investigators and the law . . . " (p. 15). Paper-and-pencil measures are as vulnerable to irrelevant influences as are face-to-face interviews or observations:

> A manifest anxiety questionnaire response may in part be a function of anxiety, but it is also a function of vocabulary comprehension, of individual and social class differences in the use of euphoric and dysphoric adjectives, of idiosyncratic definitions of the key terms frequently repeated, of respondent expectations as to the personal consequences of describing himself sick or well, etc. The questionnaire situation is so obviously complex, and the instruments so poorly compensated even for such obvious sources of bias as respondent differences in vocabulary level . . . that it seems now incredible that anyone would have regarded it as definitional of a single theoretical parameter, yet such was the power of the positivist ideology that it once was [p. 15].

Any single operational definition cannot provide the one and only true measure, therefore, because it also taps irrelevant features. In the absence of other operational definitions of the same construct, we do not know how much of the measurement reflects these irrelevant features and how much reflects what we intended to measure.

A second reason for not accepting single operations as definitive measures of concepts is that doing so would logically preclude our efforts to improve measurement in science. An early critic of "definitional operationism" called it "an obstacle to scientific advance because of its exclusion of criticism" (Adler, 1947, p. 441). Campbell elaborates on this:

> One of the great weaknesses in definitional operationism . . . was that it allowed no formal way of expressing the scientist's prepotent awareness of the imperfection of his measuring instruments and his prototypic activity of improving them. Thus, while Boring was defining intelligence in terms of the Stanford-Binet, 1916 edition, Terman was already working on a revision which

would make it a less biased instrument. Missed by definitional operationism is the fact that many of the meter readings in any actual scientific activity are discarded because the scientist judges them to be in error, the meter operating imperfectly for some reason or other. Criticism of method and improvements of method are activities rendered nonsensical in a consistent logical positivism [1969c, p. 15].

A third reason to be suspicious of any claim that intelligence (or any other quality) is what any single test measures is that without a second independent test to measure the same quality, there is no guarantee that the test is related to anything other than itself. Adler (1947) devised a test to measure something he called "C_N" as follows:

The C_N Test

1. How many hours did you sleep last night? _____
2. Estimate the length of your nose in inches and multiply by 2. _____
3. Do you like fried liver? (Mark $+1$ for Yes and -1 for No.) _____
4. How many feet are there in a yard? _____
5. Estimate the number of glasses of ginger ale the inventor of this test drank while inventing it. _____

Sum = Crude C_N Score

His instructions say, "This test is to be taken daily at the same hour of the day for as long as you can take it. Then you may proceed to calculate your refined C_N rate . . . " (p. 439), and he provides an elaborate formula for the calculation of the refined rate from the crude score. If you should wonder what your C_N score represents, he says that "the test measures C_N and C_N is what the test measures" (p. 439).

Adler created this test to show the futility of trying to hide behind definitional operationism. He adds,

We are confronted here by a seemingly closed system. All criticism is excluded. C_N *is* what it was defined as, and the test is what defines it. Still C_N does not make sense; we are unable to form a concept of it [p. 439].

Unless there at at least two operational definitions of a concept, we have no way of knowing whether a particular definition is appropriate. In the case of the C_N Test, we must have some idea what C_N is to construct a second operational definition, and it is not sufficient to say that "C_N is what the C_N Test measures." That begs the question.

Campbell and Adler have identified the following errors committed by researchers who rely on *definitional operationism:* (1) They do not acknowledge the irrelevant factors and errors that contribute to a score, (2) they do not allow room for improvement, and (3) they do not tell us anything about the concept other than that it is what the test measures. In spite of these problems, however, we do not advocate abandoning operational definitions. Instead, we advocate the use of *multiple* operational definitions. If we agree that each measure is an imperfect indicator of a complex abstract concept like intelligence or social status, we can use multiple measures without violating any claims that one operational definition is supreme. In addition, by acknowledging the imperfection of all our current measures, we leave room for improvement, without which there would be little hope for scientific advance. "We are continuously confronted by the necessity of developing new concepts and new ways of measurement. There is hardly any measurement in sociology [or any social science] that is generally recognized as fully satisfactory" (Adler, 1947, p. 441).

In discussing operational definitions, we have emphasized the imperfections, errors, and fallibility of measurement because, in teaching research methods courses, we have seen students paralyzed by the fear that they have not found the *best* measure for their research. We want to inoculate students against this fear by saying *no* measure is perfect. Students should not conclude that research is impossible, but they should realize that any single operational definition is imperfect and that it is therefore wiser to choose two. Two imperfect measures are better than one. Each provides a check on the other, and each has a different set of errors or biases.

Reliability

Classical measurement theory begins with the assumption that all measurement contains some error (Guilford, 1954). Any observed score has two components:

Observed Score = True Score + Error

A reliable measure is one that has a small error component and, therefore, does not fluctuate randomly from one moment to the next. To understand reliability in measurement, consider what it means in a person. If you call someone reliable, you probably mean the person is consistent—if she tells you one thing today, she will say the same thing tomorrow. If a reliable person says she will meet you at noon tomorrow, when you appear at the assigned time and place, that person will be there. A reliable person is also one who, if she begins to tell you a story of something that happened, maintains a consistent account and does not give different versions from one hour to the next. These various definitions of a reliable person imply the person will not say one thing and do another or give different versions of the "truth" at different times.

A reliable instrument also tells the same story from one measurement instance to the next. By contrast, consider an unreliable instrument, an *elastic* ruler. If you tried to measure your height by standing on one end of the elastic ruler and holding the other to the top of your head, you would get a slightly different reading each time you measured because you would pull a little more or less on the ruler each time and it would stretch or shrink accordingly. An elastic ruler has a large error component, and that makes the observed scores unreliable. The larger the error component in relation to the true score, the less reliable the instrument.

To be reliable an instrument must also be confined to measuring a single construct and only one dimension. If an instrument simultaneously measured length and width it would not be reliable as a measure of length. Why not? To continue with the analogy of an elastic ruler, you now have to picture an elastic suit that a person could wear—something like a diver's wet suit but with greater elasticity. If the suit came in four sizes, small, medium, large, and extra large, we might try to measure people's height by seeing which suit they could fit into. However, two people of rather different heights could both fit into the large suit. One person might be 6 feet, 6 inches tall and rather thin; the other might be 5 feet, 5 inches tall and rather wide. So the size of the suit they both fit into is not a reliable measure of height because it simultaneously measures three dimensions, height, breadth, and width. If we wanted to remeasure their heights a year later, we would not necessarily obtain the same measurements even if their heights remained constant. If the 6-foot, 6-inch person gained weight, he would now wear the extra-large suit. And if the 5-foot, 5-inch person lost weight, he would fit into the medium suit. If we thought our instrument was measuring height, it would appear as though their heights had changed. The suit does not measure height alone; it also measures volume, so suit size is an unreliable measure of height. A reliable instrument must meet two conditions: It must have a small random error component and measure a single dimension.

The latter requirement applies not only to elastic rulers that contain a lot of random error but also to firm measuring devices that contain little random error. For instance, if we constructed a wooden rather than elastic device to measure height, but it again measured more than one dimension, it would not be a reliable measure of height. At the risk of sounding macabre, we will continue with the previous example; but instead of elastic suits we will use wooden boxes to measure people's height. The boxes also come in four sizes, but they are all unfortunately Procrustean and none is longer than 5 feet. (No one promised us perfect instruments.) We ask people to fit themselves into a box. The smallest box a person can fit into becomes that person's modified-height score; we might decide to add 12 inches to each score as a correction for having begun with truncated measures. Our boxes, like the elastic suits, are inadequate primarily because they do not measure only a single dimension. They also measure people's breadth and width. And because people must bend to fit in, the boxes measure a fourth construct, too—a person's agility or ability to bend. If any of these other dimensions changed—if some people became more limber or gained weight—subsequent box measures of their "height" would make it appear that they had grown taller or shorter. The measures would be unreliable. To provide reliable measurements of a construct, an instrument must measure that construct alone—and only one dimension.

There are several ways to assess the reliability of an instrument. An instrument that contains random errors or one that measures more than one dimension would fare poorly on each. The following four measures of reliability are based on correlation coefficients. A **correlation coefficient** is an index of relationship. In the case of reliability correlation coefficients, we see how much relationship there is between two attempts to measure the same construct. The two attempts may use the same measuring instrument on two separate occasions, or they may use different portions of a measuring instrument on a single occasion. A more technical definition of correlation is provided in Chapter 14. For our purposes in this chapter, it is sufficient for you to think of it simply as a measure of the strength of a relationship, or a "co-relation."

Test-Retest Correlation

By using an instrument twice on the same persons or groups, we can compute the correlation between their two scores. This correlation is a measure of the reliability of the instrument. If the instrument is reliable, people should maintain the same relative positions on the instrument. If there have been no major changes in those groups' or persons' lives, the persons who scored high on the first testing should still score high on the second. No one expects to find a perfect correlation for most measures in the social sciences because they all contain an element of error that makes the observed scores fluctuate from one testing session to the next. Even a wooden ruler might not yield identical measures of height from one time to the next because there is some slippage in placing the ruler, because people's posture changes and influences their height, because they may wear different shoes from one time to the next, and so on. Repeated readings with a wooden ruler would be more consistent from one time to the next than with an elastic ruler, however. The smaller the error component, the more consistent the readings from one measurement time to the next, and the higher the test-retest reliability of the instrument.

Split-Half Correlation

By correlating the results obtained from two halves of the same instrument, we can calculate the split-half reliability. If our elastic ruler were 200 inches long, we could measure people's height by using the first half of the ruler once, from 0 to 100 inches, and then the second half, from 100 to 200 inches. We should get approximately the same number of inches for a single person from both ends of the ruler, but they will not be identical because the elasticity creates errors. The same would happen if we had a 200-item attitude scale. We could give each person two attitude scores, based on the first hundred and second hundred items. The scores would be similar, but not identical, because the items differ and both halves of the scale include some error in their measurement. The split-half reliability of either the ruler or the attitude scale is the correlation between the scores obtained from the two halves. The more similar the scores from the two halves, the higher the correlation and the more reliable the instrument is.

There are other ways to compute split-half reliability. Rather than correlate totals from the first and second halves of an instrument, we can correlate totals made up of alternate items—odd versus even items. Either calculation gives information about the reliability or consistency of a measure. The correlation coefficients will not be identical because each set of subtotals will produce a different result. Some calculations will produce maximally dissimilar halves, as for instance, summing all items worded in a positive direction for one total and summing all items worded in a negative direction for the other total. Other calculations will produce maximally similar halves, such as summing alternate items provided they do not differ systematically in the direction of wording, tone, or content.

Because different ways of halving an instrument produce different split-half reliability coefficients, there is no single answer to the question "What is the reliability of a test?" Each instrument will have a range of reliability coefficients.

Average Item-Total Correlation

By correlating each item with the total score and averaging those correlation coefficients, we obtain another measure of the internal consistency of a test. The total score should be corrected each time so as not to include the score from the item it is correlated with. This gives a measure of how much the answer to each item agrees with the sum of answers to the other items. This reliability coefficient and the following one show whether the instrument taps the same variable with each additional item.

Average Interitem Correlation

Correlating each item with every other item and averaging those coefficients produces another internal consistency measure.

All four measures of reliability—the test-retest, split-half, average item-total, and average interitem correlation—show whether the instrument is measuring a single quality and how precisely it measures it. Using these criteria, we can evaluate Adler's C_N Test and determine how reliable it is. The test–retest reliability of his scale could be reasonably high. People's answers to one of his five questions may be stable over time—"Do you like fried liver?'' would probably elicit the same answers if asked today and a week from now. Answers to the question "How many hours did you sleep last night?'' may change from week to week, but individuals may retain a fairly constant rank ordering, such that those who sleep long hours will give answers ranging between eight and ten hours and those who sleep very little will answer between four and five hours each time they are asked. The test-retest correlation will not be a perfect $r = 1.00$, but it should be substantially greater than zero because most people have regular sleep patterns. The answers to the questions "Estimate the length of your nose in inches and multiply by two'' and "Estimate the number of glasses of ginger ale the inventor of this test drank while inventing it'' will probably produce wild guesses because few people know the length of their noses—most would probably not even know where to begin measuring if they tried—and no one would know how many glasses of ginger ale Adler had drunk. But they could remember how they guessed the first time, so answers to these two items may also have a high test-retest correlation. The item that asks how many feet are in a yard would elicit the same answer from everyone—3 feet—and a test–retest correlation would be zero because there are no consistently high and consistently low scores. With no variation in scores, there is no correlation.

Four of the five items on Adler's C_N Test could yield high test-retest correlations, therefore, and the fifth would have a zero correlation because there would be no variability of scores. The test-retest reliability of the C_N Test as a whole depends on the correlation of the total scores, however, and not on the individual items. For a test that is internally consistent, whose items all measure the same construct, the test-retest correlation of the total score is higher than the test-retest correlation of individual items. For the C_N Test, however, this is not likely to be true because the total scores represent a nonsensical sum with no apparent internal consistency.

The other three measures of reliability are all measures of internal consistency. On each of them, Adler's C_N Test would earn a low reliability rating. Consider the following fictional people and their answers to the C_N Test (Table 3.1).

TABLE 3.1 Answers to the C_N Test

Items	Jane	Jim
1. Hours slept	10	5
2. Length of nose × 2	1	3
3. Fried liver	+1	−1
4. Feet in a yard	3	3
5. Ginger ale guess	5	10
Totals	20	20

If the test were internally consistent, a person who scores high on item 1 should also score high on items 2 through 5. This is not true in our example. Jane scored higher than Jim on item 1 but lower on item 2, higher on 3, and lower on 5. There is no consistency from one item to the next because the items do not measure the same construct. Adler's C_N Test is nonsensical, and we can tell simply by looking at the items that they do not measure anything in common. With more serious instruments, the items may appear on the surface to measure one construct, such as social status, but in fact measure several related but nonidentical constructs, such as education, familiarity with classical music, and knowledge about expensive wines. These may all look like measures of social status, but in an empirical test they may not cohere. One person could have little education but know a great deal about classical music and expensive wines; another could have many educational degrees and be uninterested in music and wine. The three measures of internal consistency—split-half reliability, item-total correlations, and interitem correlations—test the extent to which an instrument measures one or several constructs. If an instrument measures one construct and with little error, it is reliable. If it measures several independent (uncorrelated) constructs, even if it does so with little error, it is not a reliable instrument but rather a collection of several reliable subscales or subinstruments.

Adler's C_N Test measures more than one construct, and because the constructs are independent of each other they will not cohere over time. For instance, if a person changes his opinion about fried liver from -1 to $+1$, we would not expect to find a corresponding change in the number of hours he sleeps each night. The questions are not measuring the same construct, and the answers would not be consistent with one another. Therefore, the total C_N score is not a reliable measure. To be reliable an instrument must satisfy two conditions: It must (1) measure a single construct and (2) measure it with minimal random error.

When we assess the reliability of an instrument we are not concerned about *which* construct it measures. We care only that it measures *some* construct in such a way that we could measure repeatedly and obtain the same results. The concern with *which* construct an instrument measures is the concern about its *validity*.

Validity

A valid measure is one that taps the construct we intend to tap. An instrument may be very reliable and tap a construct with great precision but be invalid for our purposes because it measures the wrong construct. For instance, if we wished to measure intelligence and we gave a standard IQ test in English to a group of French high school students, we may find a high test-retest reliability but have an invalid measure of those students' intelligence. Instead, we would have a measure of their knowledge of English. For French students, an English IQ test is a measure of English language proficiency rather than a measure of intelligence. That test would be an inappropriate and, therefore, *invalid* test of intelligence for that group.

Using an English language IQ test to measure the intelligence of French students is an obvious case of measuring a construct other than the one intended. Most measures in social science do not contain such gross errors, but all measures share this problem to some extent. Operational definitions inevitably include components that are not supposed to be included and exclude portions of the underlying construct that should be measured. As the underlying construct cannot be tapped directly, but only indirectly through operational definitions, we can never be sure what portion of the construct the operational definition taps and what portions are unmeasured. We know, however, that any single measure includes irrelevant components and excludes relevant parts of the underlying construct by virtue of the fact that another measure will yield slightly different results. Figure 3.1 illustrates this.

Suppose the underlying variable we wish to measure is the intelligence of a sample of French high school students. We could use an English language intelligence test as operational definition 1, a French translation of the same test as operational definition 2, and a face-to-face interview conducted by a panel of French educators as operational definition 3. Table 3.2 shows a hypothetical rank ordering of students' intelligence scores obtained from three measures.

By counting the number of agreements in the rank ordering between any two tests, we get a rough estimate of the correlation. The greater the number of agreements, the higher the correlation. The amount of agreement between operational definitions 1 and 2 is the same as the amount

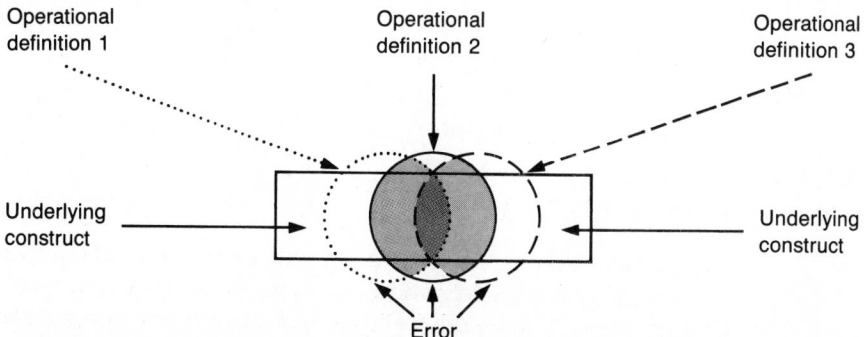

FIGURE 3.1 **Operational definitions include irrelevant components and fail to include all relevant portions of the underlying construct.**

**TABLE 3.2 Rank Ordering of Nine French High School Students'
Intelligence Scores Obtained with Three Hypothetical Measures**

Operational Definition 1 English IQ Test	Operational Definition 2 French Translation of English Test	Operational Definition 3 French Interviews
Marie	Pierre	Pierre
Pierre	Marie	Marie
Jeanne	Jeanne	Jeanne
Jacques	Jacques	Jacques
Lisa	Lisa	Lisa
Charles	Charles	Charles
Carole	Carole	Carole
Robert	Robert	Marianne
Marianne	Marianne	Robert

of agreement between operational definitions 2 and 3. In each case, two
students reverse positions, and seven remain the same. The amount of
agreement between operational definitions 1 and 3 is less—four students
change their rank orders from one test to the next, and only five remain
the same. The amount of agreement between any two measures tells us
the extent to which they are measuring the same thing. This is called the
amount of *shared* or *common variance*, and it is represented by the
darker overlapping portions of the circles in Figure 3.1. To calculate the
amount of shared variance, compute the correlation coefficient and square
that: r^2 = proportion of shared variance (see Chapters 14 and 15).

The nonoverlapping portions of the circles in Figure 3.1 consist of
two components: error and aspects of the construct that are measured by
only one operational definition. The disagreements between the measures
of intelligence obtained with the English version of the test, the French
version, and the interviews with educators arise from both the error and
unique components of the underlying variable contained in each operational definition. The error component includes both random and systematic qualities. The systematic qualities include knowledge of English for
the English version of the intelligence test and conversational skills and
poise for the interview with educators. These are not part of what we
mean by intelligence because a French student may be very intelligent but
be unable to answer a single item of the English version because that students has never studied English. Another student may receive high scores
on both written tests but become stage-struck during an interview with
French educators. Facility with English and stage presence are irrelevant
variables that are included in these two measures of intelligence. If we use
only one operational definition, we do not know how much of the observed
score represents the construct we intend to measure—intelligence—and
how much represents irrelevant qualities like knowledge of English or

conversational skills. When we use two or more operational definitions, we can correlate them, calculate the amount of common variance, and know to what extent the measures tap what we intend and to what extent they contain error. The more dissimilar the operational definitions are—like a written test and an interview—the more heterogeneous the irrelevant components. If you use maximally dissimilar operational definitions, the irrelevant components are also dissimilar, and the shared variance reflects the variable intended. The more dissimilar two methods of measurement are, the more meaningful a correlation between them is because the common variance then reflects the underlying variable rather than shared error or irrelevant components.

Reliability–Validity Continuum

Reliability and validity are two different characteristics of measurement that shade into one another. They are two ends of a continuum, and at points in the middle it is difficult to distinguish between them. For instance, in our discussion of Adler's C_N Test, we showed that it is an unreliable measure because it has no internal consistency. There is no relationship between liking fried liver and sleeping long or short hours, yet the answers to those two items are summed to produce a total score. This internal inconsistency makes the instrument unreliable and also makes it invalid. If it measures two unrelated constructs, it cannot be called a valid measure of either one because their sum is meaningless. It is like adding apples and old shoes—what would you call the sum?

Another illustration of how reliability and validity overlap appears in our earlier discussion of using elastic versus firm measures of height. We said that elastic tape measures are less reliable than firm yardsticks because they introduce more random errors. But even wooden measures are unreliable if they introduce more than one dimension or construct. The Procrustean wooden boxes that simultaneously measured a person's height, weight, and flexibility would be unreliable measures of height because "box size" (small, medium, large, or extra large) is really a measure of a combination of qualities. It is multidimensional rather than unidimensional. This makes it unreliable as a measure of height because if a person's weight changed and he could subsequently fit into a smaller box, we would mistakenly interpret it as a change in "height." The box is also an invalid measure for the same reason. If we call it a measure of "height," we are calling it by the wrong name. It is not measuring height but rather "height plus weight plus flexibility plus willingness to squeeze into tight spaces."

A third illustration shows how reliability and validity overlap: In our methods of assessing them we examine the relationship between two measurements. In the case of reliability, the two measurements come from the same instrument. In the case of validity, the two measurements come from different instruments. This seems like a clear-cut distinction, which should make it obvious that reliability is different from validity. However, they shade into one another if we recognize that the "different" instruments used to assess validity can have varying degrees of "difference." And the "same" instrument used to measure reliability can also vary in its degree of "sameness." Therefore, reliability and validity estimates lie on a continuum, as illustrated in Figure 3.2.

At one end of the continuum are correlations between identical methods of measurement. Test-retest correlations are based on the same test administered twice. At the other end of the continuum are correlations between very different methods of measuring the same variable. A paper-and-pencil test of intelligence and an interview can be distinctly different measures. Reliability estimates are correlations between identical or similar methods; validity estimates are correlations between dissimilar methods.

Both ends of the scale have some practical limits beyond which the correlations are meaningless. If the measures are so similar that they are guaranteed to produce 100 percent agreement, they would not be considered a fair test of the reliability of an instrument. For instance, if a retest were administered immediately after its initial administration and each person simply copied the answers from the first test, the perfect correlation between the test and retest measures would tell nothing about the reliability of the instrument. It would only show that people can copy their answers accurately. At the other end of the continuum, if two measures of intelligence were so different that they did not both bear some resemblance to what most people call "intelligence," their low correlation would be a foregone conclusion. For instance, a test of how well people can sight-read music would probably not correlate highly with an adult intelligence test. Sight-reading music requires intelligence, but it also requires prior training and interest in music, both of which are different from intelligence, so the correlation may be near zero. Finding maximally different methods to measure the same variable is difficult—because the more the methods differ, the less likely they are to tap the same variable.

There are several ways to evaluate the validity of an instrument, each based on finding agreement between two different assessments of the same variable.

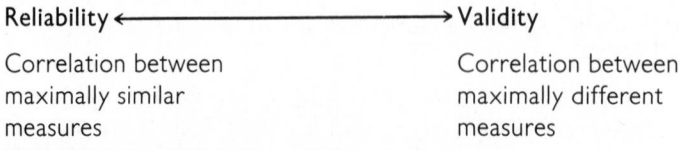

Reliability ⟵——————————⟶ Validity

Correlation between   Correlation between
maximally similar   maximally different
measures   measures

FIGURE 3.2   Reliability-validity continuum

Face Validity

Face validity is evaluated by a group of judges, sometimes experts, who read or look at a measuring technique and decide whether in their opinion it measures what its name suggests. For instance, professional speech therapists could look at a test designed to measure degrees of speech impairment and decide whether the test measures what the testers claim. Evaluating face validity is a subjective process, but we could calculate a validity figure by computing the amount of agreement among judges. The higher the percent who say it measures what it claims to measure, the higher the face validity. Every instrument must pass the face validity test either formally or informally. Every researcher who chooses an instrument is a judge who has decided that the test measures the construct he or she wishes to study. Without such minimal face validity, an instrument would not be used.

Concurrent Validity

Concurrent validity is the ability of a test to distinguish between individuals who are known to differ. For instance, if you were developing a test to measure people's political conservatism, the test should distinguish between people who belong to groups we assume differ, such as supporters and opponents of the Equal Rights Amendment. If members of these groups scored the same, the test would be a measure not of political conservatism but of something those groups shared, such as a fear of nuclear war.

Predictive Validity

Predictive validity is the ability of a test to identify future differences. For instance, the predictive validity of college entrance examinations is the ability of those tests to identify who will graduate from college and who will drop out or to predict who will receive high grades and who will receive low grades or to predict who will go on to graduate school and who will not. Depending on which of these criteria we choose, the test may have high, moderate, or low predictive validity. Predictive validity is an evaluation of a test's practical worth in foreseeing the future. It is a pragmatic approach to validity.

Convergent and Discriminant Validity: The Multitrait-Multimethod Matrix

Face validity, concurrent validity, and predictive validity are each based on an assessment of how much one method of measuring a construct agrees with other methods of measuring the same construct. They are all forms of *convergent* validation, which requires *agreement* between scores obtained with two or more instruments. This is only one aspect of construct validation. Another aspect requires a demonstration that the construct can be *differentiated* from other constructs, and to demonstrate this a researcher must show *disagreement* between two scores that presumably measure different constructs. Such disagreement is evidence of *discriminant* validity.

For instance, if there is a meaningful construct called "attitudes toward women," and if we design an instrument to measure it, we would want to demonstrate that many different methods of measuring attitudes toward women yield scores that are similar. We would also need to show, however, that attitudes toward women are distinct from other attitudes—that this is a construct apart from attitudes toward people in general or attitudes toward minority groups. To demonstrate that our instrument measured attitudes toward women and not general political liberalism or attitudes toward people in general, we would have to measure those other attitudes too and find lower correlations among measures of political liberalism, attitudes toward men, and attitudes toward women than we find when we use multiple measures of attitudes toward women. *Low* correlations with tests measuring *different* constructs demonstrate the *discriminant* validity of an instrument. The **multitrait-multimethod matrix** is a table of correlations that enables us to examine both the convergent and discriminant validity of a construct (Campbell & Fiske, 1959).

To construct this matrix you must have at least two constructs that you measure with at least two methods. The matrix of correlations looks complicated (see Figure 3.3), but the logic is simple.

The matrix is based on the principle that the more features two measurements have in common, the higher their correlation will be. Measurements can share two types of features: traits and methods. *Traits* are the underlying construct the measurement is supposed to tap; they are the *content. Methods* are the *form* of the measurement—paper-and-pencil questionnaires, face-to-face interviews, unobtrusive observations, census records, and so on. Ideally, scores should reflect only the intended trait

	Paper-and-Pencil Questionnaire		Observations of Behavior	
	Attitudes toward Women (ATW)	**Attitudes toward Men (ATM)**	**Attitudes toward Women (ATW)**	**Attitudes toward Men (ATM)**
Questionnaire { ATW	(.90)*	.30		
{ ATM	.30	(.90)		
Behavior { ATW	.70	.10	(.90)	.30
{ ATM	.10	.70	.30	(.90)

*The correlations in parentheses are reliability correlations.

FIGURE 3.3 **Multitrait-multimethod matrix of correlations between attitudes toward women and attitudes toward men**

and not be influenced by the method. In reality, the form or method of measurement also affects the score, and some of the variation in observed scores is a product of the method used to obtain the scores. A face-to-face interview about attitudes toward women, for instance, would measure not only attitudes toward women but also people's desire to appear liberal or current in their views. An English language test of intelligence would measure not only students' intelligence but also their English proficiency. A set of police department statistics on murder rates in major American cities would measure not only murder rates but also the efforts of police commissioners and mayors in those cities to be reappointed or reelected. Each attempt to measure a construct, therefore, is contaminated by aspects of the method that are irrelevant to the construct but inevitable in the measurement.

Some irrelevant aspects of methods are known and can be taken into account. For instance, if the statistics from one police department are inflated and those of another depressed for political purposes, the investigator can adjust the figures to reduce the contamination. Interviewers can try to establish rapport with their respondents to elicit honest rather than guarded or socially desirable answers (see Chapter 11). Researchers can also correct for known biases in questionnaires. For instance, people often develop preferences for circling Yes's or No's. Researchers can control these biases by wording items so that half contain positive statements and half negative statements about the topic. A person who believes in the virtue of electoral politics, for instance, would have to agree with the statement "It is important to vote because every vote counts" and disagree with the statement "Voting is wasted effort." If someone answered the questionnaire unthinkingly and chose to disagree with most items regardless of their content, that person's score would not be biased either for or against electoral politics if half the items were positive and half negative. By controlling the direction of wording, researchers can eliminate such response biases from the observed score.

In addition to these known biases and sources of contamination, however, measuring techniques include other features that an investigator cannot control, and scores, therefore, inevitably contain both a trait and a methods component. The multitrait-multimethod matrix lets a researcher assess the extent to which scores reflect the trait and the method contained in every measurement.

Because every score is made up of two elements—a trait and a method—the correlation between two sets of scores depends on how much they share both the trait and the method. Reliability coefficients are correlations between scores that reflect the same trait and the same method. Convergent validity coefficients are correlations between scores that reflect the same trait measured by different methods. The reliability coefficients of an instrument should, therefore, logically be higher than its validity coefficients because the former are based on more shared elements. The multitrait-multimethod matrix introduces two additional correlation coefficients to assess the validity of an instrument. These are both correlations between *different traits*. One is a discriminant validity correlation between different traits measured by the same method, and the other is a nonsense correlation between different traits measured by different methods. Table 3.3 depicts these correlations and their elements.

The first two correlations should be high; the last two should be low. If the third and fourth correlations are as high as the convergent validity correlations, it means the two traits are not different but are the same or highly similar. For instance, if an investigator devised two separate tests, one called Attitudes Toward Women and the other Attitudes Toward Men, the two should not be too highly correlated if they are truly separate attitudes. If the intercorrelations between these tests were like those shown in Figure 3.3, we would be satisfied that they measured two distinct traits or attitudes.

The same-trait-different-method correlation coefficients (.70) are higher than the different-trait-same-method correlations (.30) and the different-trait-different-method correlations (.10). This is justification for saying the tests measure two different traits. If, however, the matrix looked like Figure 3.4, the tests would be invalidated, not because the correlations were too low but because some of the correlations were too high.

The correlations in Figure 3.4 show that the two attitudes are very similar because they are highly correlated with one another. The correlation between two different traits measured by the same method (.80) is higher than the correlation between the same trait measured by different methods (.40). These two attitudes have no discriminant validity because they are so highly intercorrelated. If they are truly different attitudes, the correlation between them should not be higher than the convergent validity correlations of the same trait measured by different methods (.40).

Particularly if a researcher is trying to develop a test to measure a newly conceptualized trait, it is important to assess its discriminant validity to demonstrate that it is new and different. Campbell and Fiske (1959) point out that tests have been invalidated not only because of low correlations but also "because of too high correlations with other tests pur-

TABLE 3.3 Correlation Coefficients in a Multitrait-Multimethod Matrix

Coefficients	Elements Contained in the Scores That Are Correlated	
	Traits	Methods
1. Reliability correlation	Same	Same
2. Convergent validity correlation	Same	Different
3. Discriminant validity correlation	Different	Same
4. Nonsense correlation	Different	Different

	Paper-and-Pencil Questionnaire		Observations of Behavior	
	Attitudes toward Women (ATW)	Attitudes toward Men (ATM)	Attitudes toward Women (ATW)	Attitudes toward Men (ATM)
Questionnaire	⎰ATW (.90)* ⎱ATM .80	.80 (.90)		
Behavior	⎰ATW .40 ⎱ATM .30	.30 .40	(.90) .80	.80 (.90)

*The correlations in parentheses are reliability correlations.

FIGURE 3.4 Multitrait-multimethod matrix of correlations between attitudes toward women and attitudes toward men

porting to measure different things" (p. 84). If we obtained the correlations shown in Figure 3.4, we would conclude the two tests measure roughly the same attitude; and rather than talk of "Attitudes toward Women" and "Attitudes toward Men," we would rename the scales and call them both "Attitudes about Gender Roles."

Scales

A scale in social science is a set of categories to differentiate among people on any one variable. There may be as few as two categories in a scale or as many as 100 or more.

Nominal Scales

Nominal scales contain qualitatively different categories to which we attach names rather than numerical meaning. The simplest are dichotomies, with only two values, such as "male" and "female" or "homeowners" and "renters." The categories are qualitatively rather than quantitatively different. If for the sake of coding and keypunching data, we use numbers like 1 and 2 to stand for "male" and "female," respectively, the numbers have no arithmetic value. The number 2 does not mean that cases placed in that category have more of the quality than cases placed in the category numbered 1. Other examples of nominal scales are the following:

Types of urban stressors:

1 = traffic noises
2 = air pollutants
3 = crowds
4 = bureaucratic harrassment
5 = other

Living arrangements for the elderly:

1 = own home or apartment
2 = relative's home
3 = retirement home
4 = other

The list of alternatives need not exhaust all possible categories, but it should include those categories relevant to the theory and the population tested and should enable the coder to classify every case. For instance, there are many more living arrangements for elderly people than the three just listed. If, however, we designed a study to test the effects of living in one's own home, in someone else's, or in an institution, the three categories plus the unspecified "other" category would be sufficient for the purposes of that study. The inclusion of "other" enables us to classify every case.

Ordinal Scales

An ordinal scale contains categories that can be ordered by rank on a continuum. The categories have a rudimentary arithmetic meaning such as "more" or "less" of the quantity being measured. For instance, we could order occupations in terms of how much autonomy the workers have in their jobs.

1 = little autonomy (e.g., assembly line workers, keypunch operators, and check-out clerks in a large discount department store)
2 = moderate autonomy (e.g., construction workers, nurses, and taxi drivers)
3 = much autonomy (e.g., independent artists, jewelers, doctors, lawyers)

The scale states that 1 means an occupation permits less autonomy than 3 and that 2 is located in between. An ordinal scale gives only this information and does not provide any information about the distances between the values. The interval between 1 and 2 may be larger or smaller than the interval between 2 and 3. An ordinal scale does not imply anything about the arithmetic values other than that they are in order.

Interval Scales

When numbers attached to a variable imply not only that 3 is more than 2 and 2 is more than 1 but also that the size of the interval between 3 and 2 is the same as the interval between 2 and 1, they form an interval scale. Just because a scale contains values from 1 to 100, it does not automatically follow that the difference between 60 and 70 is the same as the difference between 90 and 100. For instance, if we made up a 100-item vocabulary test on which most people defined between 60 and 70 words correctly, and only two people defined 90 and one person defined 100 correctly, the gap between 90 and 100 probably represents a greater difference in vocabulary level than the gap between 60 and 70.

If the intervals represent *equal* quantities of the variable measured, they constitute an interval scale. For every unit increase on the scale, there is a unit increase in the variable. The Fahrenheit scale measures temperature in equal intervals. The temperature difference between 33 and 34 degrees is the same as the temperature difference between 36 and 37 degrees. If this seems obvious, it is because we have grown accustomed to the Fahrenheit scale and take for granted that it represents equal intervals of physical heat and cold. We cannot take for granted that social science scales represent equal intervals.

Most social science constructs are measured by ordinal rather than interval scales. For instance, if we used families' annual income as a variable to measure the underlying construct "social status," we could not assume that the dollar scale represented equal intervals of social status. The status difference in the interval between $20,000 and $40,000 in annual income is much larger than the status difference in the interval between $120,000 and $140,000. As we go up the income scale, the $20,000 difference makes less and less difference in social status. Two families with incomes of $120,000 and $140,000 are more likely to live next door to each other than are two families with incomes of $20,000 and $40,000 because the $20,000 interval represents a bigger difference in social status at the bottom end of the scale than at the top. Annual income, therefore, is not an interval scale measure of social status.

The numbers on an interval scale can be added or subtracted because the properties of the scale are such that 20 − 10 = 40 − 30. But numbers on an interval scale cannot be multiplied or divided because the scale does not have a true zero. It has an arbitrary zero. We can multiply and divide the values only if we have a ratio scale.

Ratio Scales

Ratio scales do have a true zero, and as a result the scale values represent multipliable quantities. Physical scales measuring length and weight are ratio scales: a 4-foot length of board is twice as long as a 2-foot piece; 10 pounds of feathers weight twice as much as 5 pounds. For these physical scales, zero is real and not arbitrary. Although we cannot point to anything that has 0 inches or 0 pounds, we know what those mean on our rulers or scales, and we do not arbitrarily locate 0 at any point on the scale.

Some variables used to measure social constructs look superficially like ratio measures because they have zero as the lowest score. Money as a measure of social status, for instance, gives the appearance of being a ratio scale because the variable has an absolute true zero. A person can be penniless and possess no money. This does not mean, however, that the penniless person has zero social status. A monk who takes a vow of poverty, for instance, has no money but has social status among people who respect religious orders. The most we can assume about social status measured in dollars is that more money represents more status, all other assets being equal.

If we measured happiness by how often a person smiled, we might be tempted to say that someone who smiles ten times is twice as happy as someone who smiles five times. True, ten smiles are twice as many as five smiles. Our scale, however, is to be a measure not of "smiling" but of the construct "happiness." "Number of smiles" is the variable we have chosen to measure the abstract construct "happiness," and happiness may not double as smiles do.

Even standardized and copyrighted measures such as IQ scales do not have true zeros. No psychologist would try to argue that someone with an IQ score of 150 is twice as intelligent as someone with an IQ of 75. Although the numbers can be added or multiplied and though a scale may begin with zero, it does not mean that the underlying construct has those properties. It is difficult to imagine any social construct such as happiness, social status, or power for which there is a true zero because it is always possible to imagine a case with a little less of the construct. For instance, if we devised a 10-item scale of happiness for which every answer that represented unhappiness received a zero, someone who answered all 10 items with zeros would receive a total happiness score of 0. Does that person truly have no happiness? Is it not possible to imagine someone else who might have even less happiness than that person? Social science constructs have this quality of an infinite regress at the bottom end of the scale. It is always possible to imagine a case of a little less status, a little less power, a little less happiness; and the scale, therefore, does not have a true zero. Without a true zero, a scale does not have ratios—it is not possible to say that a score of 10 represents twice as much of the construct as 5.

Measurement Presupposes Theory

The preceding discussion implies that we know what the relationship is between the variable we measure and the underlying construct that it represents. How do we know what the relationship is? The relationship between a variable like dollar income and a construct like social status is called the *epistemic correlation* (L. F. Carter, 1971). This is not a correlation that we can actually compute—because we have no direct access to the construct "social status." We can measure it only with variables like dollars or years of schooling. Hence the dilemma: How do we determine the epistemic correlation between a variable and a construct if we can only measure the construct with variables? The solution is twofold.

First, we use what we already know about both income and social status to determine what the relationship is between the two. We have an intuitive theory about the relationship of dollars to status. This is not a theory based on social science research—it is based on common sense and personal observations. For instance, most of us know by the time we are 18 that the social status difference between two families with annual incomes of $140,000 and $120,000 is *not* the same as the social status difference between two families with incomes of $40,000 and $20,000. The first difference is negligible; the second is sizable, even though in both instances the difference is $20,000. Recognizing this commonly accepted fact is one step in deciding what the relationship is between income and status. It is not a direct linear relationship like that shown in Figure 3.5. Intuition and common sense inform us that equivalent increases in dollar income do not produce equivalent increases in social status. This is one way we decide that income is not an interval scale measure of status.

The second step in determining the relationship between a variable like dollars and the construct it represents is to locate another variable that measures the same construct. Education, or years of schooling, is another measure of social status. *If* there were a direct linear relationship between income and status and if there were a direct linear relationship between schooling and status, there should be a direct linear relationship between income and schooling. If $A = B$ and $A = C$, B should equal C. But $B \neq C$ in this case. For each additional year of schooling, people do not always receive additional income. There are people with many years of schooling who have lower incomes than people with fewer years of schooling. Therefore, either income or schooling or both have a nonlinear relationship to the construct social status.

What should we assume about the relationship between status and our numerical indicators? The answer comes again from our prior knowledge about what the numbers mean. In the case of income, it is probably reasonable to assume that dollars and status are related in a curvilinear rather than linear fashion. Figure 3.6 illustrates a curvilinear relationship. This relationship means that "small differences in income make less and less difference as one becomes richer and richer" (Carter, 1971, p. 16). We cannot prove that social status has such a curvilinear relationship with

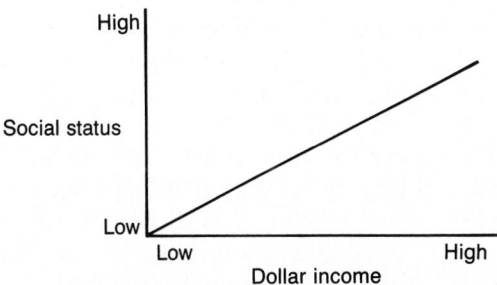

FIGURE 3.5 Direct linear relationship between income and status that is contradicted by intuition and common sense

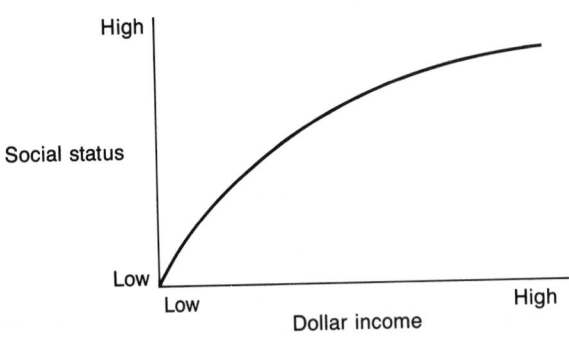

FIGURE 3.6 Curvilinear relationship between income and social status (from Carter, 1971)

income because we have no direct measure of social status. We will probably make fewer errors, however, and reach more insightful conclusions if we assume a relationship like that in Figure 3.6 instead of Figure 3.5.

The relationship between social status and education is probably neither linear like Figure 3.5 nor curvilinear like Figure 3.6, given what we know about the meaning of education. Whereas a visitor from Mars might assume the difference between 14 and 15 years of schooling is the same as the difference between 15 and 16 years, we know that completing 16 years of school means being a college graduate, and that makes a bigger difference than any of the preceding years of schooling. Employers act as though the difference between 15 and 16 years of schooling is bigger than the difference between 14 and 15 years. Education as a measure of social status has plateaus, and college graduation is one of them. Therefore, we should not assume a linear relationship between education and status, nor should we assume a curvilinear relationship like that in Figure 3.6. Instead, we can best approximate the relationship between education and status by using plateaus and assigning status increments to each plateau rather than each year of schooling. Each graduation signals an increase in status: elementary school graduate, high school graduate, and college graduate. Figure 3.7 illustrates this relationship between number of years of education and social status.

Fitting quantitative variables to abstract constructs is a bit like using a luminous ruler to measure an elephant on a moonless night. We can obtain clear numbers, but we know that the numbers do not perfectly capture the dimensions of the beast. The ruler does not bend where the elephant bends; it slips when the elephant stamps its feet; and as we grope in the dark, it is hard to tell what portions of the elephant we have measured and which parts remain untouched. When we transfer our numbers onto paper and try to sketch the elephant from the measured inches, part of our sketch is derived from what we already know about elephants— our intuition and commonsense knowledge about the shape and size of an elephant.

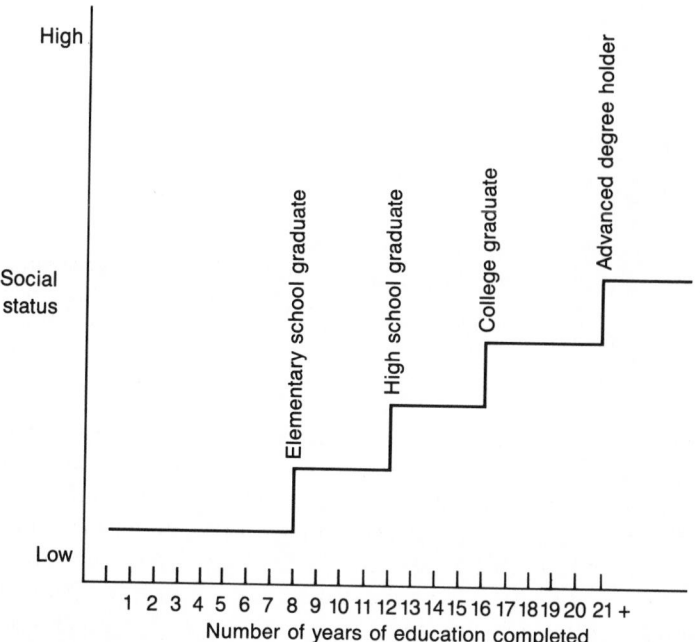

FIGURE 3.7 Relationship between number of years of education and social status

Construct Validity of Manipulated Variables

The preceding discussion refers to variables obtained by using *measurements*. The same problems of assessing validity pertain to variables that we *create* by experimental *manipulations*. For instance, instead of measuring anxiety, a researcher may manipulate people's anxiety levels, creating high anxiety in some persons and low anxiety in others. Or rather than measure people's existing levels of motivation, an experimenter may manipulate motivation by giving some subjects instructions that motivate them to do well on a task and giving others instructions that cause them to care little about their performance.

When researchers create rather than measure levels of an independent variable, we call it a **manipulated variable.** When independent variables are obtained by measurements rather than manipulations, a researcher uses the same techniques for assessing reliability and validity that are used for dependent variables. With manipulated independent variables, however, the researcher must test the manipulation by subsequently measuring its effects to determine its construct validity. For instance, if a researcher tries to create high levels of motivation by telling some subjects that their performance on a task is an indicator of their intelligence and create low motivation by telling others that the task is a measure of willingness to practice dull tasks, the researcher needs to know whether these instructions really created different levels of motivation. Perhaps they created no differences at all—because the subjects did not believe the instructions, for example. Perhaps they created no differences because all the subjects wanted to do well regardless of the nature of the task. Perhaps they created differences—but in anxiety instead of motivation. To demonstrate the validity of the manipulation, the researcher must also *measure* the subjects' levels of motivation after the instructions. If those who received the "intelligence test" message say the task is important and they intend to do well, this is partial evidence that the researcher has created a high level of motivation. However, the instructions may also have created different levels of anxiety along with levels of motivation. We would like to see evidence that only motivation, and not anxiety, was manipulated by the instructions. To do this, a researcher would have to demonstrate both the discriminant and convergent validity of the manipulation.

When researchers demonstrate the validity of their manipulated variables, they generally obtain a measure of the independent variable after they have manipulated it. This is called a *manipulation check*, and it gives evidence of the convergent validity of the manipulation. Researchers rarely take the further step of demonstrating the discriminant validity by showing that their manipulation has *not* created different levels of some other variables. Occasionally, however, when research includes this additional step, it becomes all the more persuasive.

Research critics frequently allege that an experimental treatment or manipulation in someone else's research was invalid. For instance, when Horner (1972) reported that women have more "fear of success" than men do, critics said she had not adequately manipulated the independent variable—success achieved by a woman versus success achieved by a man. What she had done was ask students to read stories about a successful medical student. Women read stories about "Anne" who was at the top of her class in medical school, and men read stories about "John," also at the top of his class in medical school. By having women read about "Anne" and men read about "John," Horner intended to have the students identify with the protagonist and thereby experience "success." She then asked the students to write stories about Anne's or John's future, and she coded their stories for the amount of fear they portrayed. Many women wrote stories about Anne's subsequent failure, saying such things as "Anne will deliberately lower her academic standing the next term . . . and Anne drops out of med school" (p. 60). Horner interpreted this as an "underlying fear of success" among the women who wrote such stories.

Other researchers, however, have pointed out that the independent variable that Horner created by giving men and women these stories was not simply "success achieved by a woman" versus "success achieved by a man." Instead, the stories portrayed Anne as successful in a nontraditional career for a women and John as successful in a traditional career for a man. Therefore, the female students were responding not only to Anne's success but also to her stepping out of her traditional gender role. Male students, on the other hand, responded to John succeeding in a career dominated by other men. If the men had read stories about "John at the top of his class in home economics," they too may have shown an underlying fear of success. The criticism, therefore, pertains to the validity of the independent variable. Subsequent researchers have said that this study illustrated fear of stepping out of traditional gender roles rather than fear of success among women (Monahan, Kuhn, & Shaver, 1974).

Summary

We began this chapter by saying that operational definitions are always essential. Without them there would be no scientific measurement. They provide a public process for reproducing and replicating measurements and manipulations so that we can assess their reliability and validity.

Operational definitions are necessary but also inevitably inadequate. They contain errors by including irrelevant components and omitting other relevant portions of the underlying construct that we want to tap. For this reason, no single operational definition completely defines the construct. Each is only an approximation. Because no single measure is 100 percent reliable or 100 percent valid, we advocate using multiple operational definitions of any construct.

With multiple measures of multiple constructs, a researcher can construct a matrix of reliability and validity correlations known as the *multitrait-multimethod matrix*. This provides a very thorough assessment of construct validity by allowing the researcher to examine both the convergent and discriminant validity of the methods and the traits being measured.

Measuring abstract constructs with concrete operational definitions involves us in a curious transaction between having an image of something and not being sure how to trace it. When we set out to measure a construct like social power, we think we know what we mean by the words. Yet when we try to devise specific procedures to tap social power, we discover that our procedures do not adequately capture what we think social power is. The concrete operational definition falls short of capturing the richness of our abstract construct. It seems as though we know what we mean by "social power" and yet we cannot devise a way to trace or measure it perfectly. All we can do is use our intuitive or theoretical understanding of the construct to guide us in selecting a measurement or manipulation that seems most appropriate. We then assess the reliability and validity of our operational definition to see how well or how poorly it measures the construct in comparison with other methods of measuring the same. As we do this, we give temporary credence to those other measures as we test the goodness of our own. D. T. Campbell describes the predicament as follows: "We are like sailors who must repair a rotting ship at sea. We trust the great bulk of the timbers while we replace a particularly weak plank. Each of the timbers we now trust we may in its turn replace. The proportion of the planks we are replacing to those we treat as sound must always be small" (1974, p. 6).

As social researchers we live with the knowledge that each of our measures is imperfect. Provided there is some agreement among the imperfect measures, we give up the search for certainty and accept consensus instead.

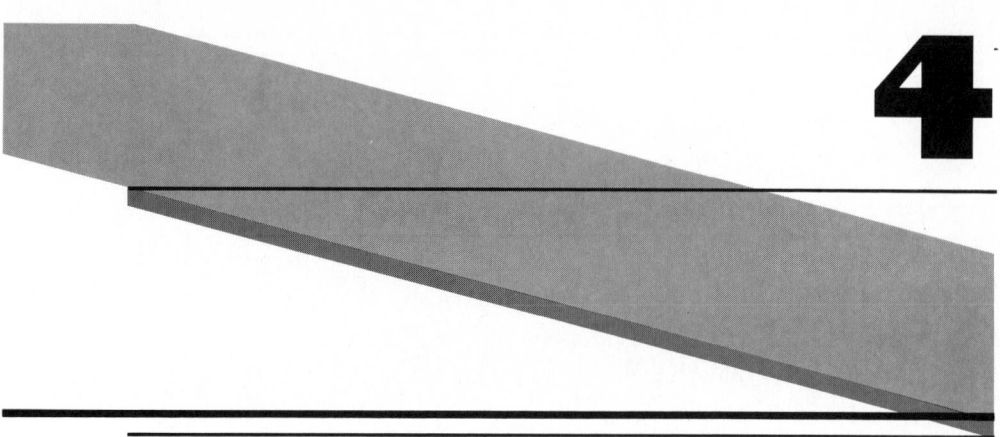

4

Randomized Experiments

Randomized experiments are highly specialized tools, and like any tool they are excellent for some jobs and poor for others. They are ideally suited for the task of causal analysis. No other method of scientific inquiry permits the researcher to say with the confidence of an experimenter, "This caused that to happen." In reading scientific reports, you find many guarded, qualified, and indirect causal statements such as "*X* seems to be a factor in determining *Y*" or "it would appear that there is a relationship between *X* and *Y*." The conclusions sound indirect and the words carefully chosen because the writers cannot make definitive causal assertions. They cannot make bold causal statements if they have not conducted randomized experiments.

We do not intend this chapter to stand as a tribute to randomized experiments, for they have their weaknesses. We point out their strengths and their weaknesses and show how they differ from other research approaches. The chief strength of randomized experiments is their internal validity. The greater the control an experimenter has, the greater the internal validity of the experiment. The same feature that promotes internal validity can jeopardize external validity. The more control an experimenter has over the subjects and the many variables that could influence the results, the more unnatural the study. Maximum control approximates an isolated laboratory with research conducted in a vacuum. The more the experimental conditions differ from real-life situations, the more difficult it is to generalize the results to naturally occurring social processes and the lower the external validity of the research. Let us examine what it means to have control in an experiment.

Controlling and Manipulating Variables

All research requires the manipulation or measurement of **variables.** Variables are qualities the researcher wants to study and draw conclusions about. For instance, if you want to study people's political behavior and understand why they vote as they do, their votes are a variable you must measure. *Variables*, as the name suggests, must vary and have at least two values. Therefore, to understand people's party preference, you must study people who vote for at least two different candidates or parties. If everyone in your study said he or she would vote for Geraldine Ferraro for vice-president, you would no longer have a variable. For most research, you have not just one but two variables, and you look at the relationship between the two. For instance, in a study of voting behavior, you could include people's religion as a second variable and examine the relationship between religion and voting preference. Political scientists and polling organizations already know a lot about the relationships between religious preference and political party preference and can often predict which candidate will win in which districts because they know the religious makeup of different parts of a city or state. Clearly there are many other variables besides religion that influence how a person will vote. A person's education, parents' party preference, income, and attitudes about specific issues such as abortion or gun control also determine how that person will vote. If you wanted to be able to *predict* people's votes, you would try to include as many of these variables as possible in your research. If, on the other hand, you wanted to understand the influence of a single variable, to see whether it affects voting, you would try to *control* all the other variables. The former is the strategy of survey researchers; the latter is the strategy of experimenters.

Experimenters ask questions like "what is the effect of televised appearances on people's votes for candidates?" Notice that the question refers to a variable the experimenter can possibly control—televised appearances. Experimenters study variables that either they or someone else can *manipulate*—like the timing or content or amount of televised political advertisements. These are called *experimental variables.* The variables we discussed earlier, such as religion, income, education, and parents' party preference, are all variables that people bring with them to a study. These are called *subject variables* or *organismic variables.* They are properties that people already possess. By contrast, experimental variables are properties that an experimenter can manipulate or expose people to. This is a major difference between experimenting and conducting nonexperimental or quasi-experimental research. Experimenters can control the variables they wish to study the effects of, or they can control who is exposed to those variables.

Experimenters may also control the influence of variables that are extraneous to the purpose of the study. For instance, if you wanted to study the influence of television advertising on voting behavior and were not interested in the effects of education, religion, and parents' party preferences, you could control for the effects of those variables in your experiment in one of two ways.

1. *Hold the other variables constant.* You can turn the variables of religion, gender, education, and attitudes into constants by choosing only Catholic men with a college education and antiabortion attitudes as participants for your experiments. This approach to controlling other variables is like the approach frequently used in natural science. If you try to study the effects of some varieties of plant food on the growth of plants, you might select a field of white pine seedlings in a particular field in Maine and feed four varieties of plant food to trees in the four quadrants

of the field. You have held constant the soil type (we assume the field has the same soil type in its four quadrants), the climate, the plant variety, and the season. You know that all these variables affect how fast plants grow, and you have controlled them in your study by limiting the experiment to one soil type, climate, plant, and season. This is an effective way to study the growing powers of your four varieties of plant food because you know the only difference between plants in the four quadrants is the type of food they received. This experiment has high internal validity—you can say quite confidently that the plant food caused differences in growth. By confining your experiment to such a narrow range of conditions, however, you have sacrificed its external validity. You do not know whether the best plant food for white pines would also be best for red oaks or for trees in warmer climates. The more you hold such other conditions constant, the lower the generalizability of your results. This technique of controlling other variables maximizes internal validity at the expense of external validity, and you may, therefore, choose not to hold all other variables constant. In the case of voting behavior, you could study the effects of television advertising on white, Catholic, college-educated men who opposed abortions if you believed that this group of people would respond to televised political advertisements in the same way as any other group. If, however, you thought they would be influenced in ways different from the larger population to which you wish to generalize, you should not try to control for the influence of religion, education, and the other variables by holding them constant. You should choose the second method instead.

2. *Randomly assign subjects to experimental conditions.* You can conduct an experiment with a heterogeneous assortment of people (or plants or voting districts) and still control for the influences of the many extraneous variables those people possess by randomly assigning people to the experimental conditions. We shall refer to the units in experimental studies as "subjects," whether they are people, plants, or collectivities like voting districts. If you include in your study people who differ in education, religion, parents' preferences, and attitudes toward abortion, you can eliminate the influence of those variables by randomly assigning people to your experimental conditions. To compare the effects of different television campaigns—one that interviews the candidate and another that interviews supporters—you can draw the subjects' names out of a hat and assign the first to watch the candidate, the second to watch the supporters, the third to watch the candidate, and so on. Provided you have the names all written on similar slips of paper and have shuffled the slips sufficiently, you have a random assignment procedure as good as any. Random assignment controls for the influence of all the extraneous subject variables that you do not want to study but also do not want to hold constant because holding them constant limits the generalizability of your study. It is the defining feature of a true experiment.

Random Assignment

Random assignment is the best way to equate two or more groups before an experimental treatment begins. This is essential for making causal inferences about the effects of an experimental treatment because the experimenter must be reasonably confident that the differences that appear at the end of the experiment between two treatment groups are the result of the treatments and not the result of some preexisting differences between the groups.

Random assignment (also called *randomization*) is not the same as random sampling (also called *random selection*). **Random assignment** is a procedure you use after you have a sample of subjects and before you expose them to a treatment. It is a way of assigning subjects to treatments so that the groups do not differ before the treatment begins. It is a "fair" procedure, whereby all subjects have an equal chance of being assigned to condition A or condition B. Drawing names out of a hat is the prototype and works as well as more sophisticated techniques, such as using a table of random numbers (e.g., Myers, 1966) or using a computer-generated list of random numbers. *Random sampling* is the procedure you use to *select* the subjects you will study. Random sampling serves not to equate two or more experimental groups but to make whatever subject group you study representative of a larger population. It is also a "fair" procedure whereby all subjects in a given population (e.g., the population of people over 21 living in North America) have an equal chance of being included in the study. Random sampling allows you to say that what you have found in this sample is true of people in the larger population. It maximizes the external validity of research. Random assignment, on the other hand, enables you to say, "X caused Y" with some degree of certainty. It maximizes the internal validity of research. We will not discuss random sampling further in this chapter; it will appear again in Chapter 7. We introduced it here to inform you that it is different from random assignment, and it is the latter that defines true experiments.

To appreciate what random assignment accomplishes and what its limitations are, consider the following experiment. You are hired by a publishing company to determine whether students learn more about research methods from attending lectures or reading a research methods book (the one the publisher is about to put on the market). The publishing company draws a random sample of undergraduate students from across the country, brings them together in your city, and pays them to take part in your study. You, therefore, do not have to worry about the representativeness or cooperation of the students. Your only concern is to determine whether students learn more from a textbook or from lectures. The simplest way to design this experiment is to assign students randomly to one of two conditions: group T, which will read the textbook and not attend lectures, and group L, which will attend lectures but not read the textbook. You measure how much they have learned by giving them all the same examination at the end of the semester. Assume for the sake of this example that the examination is an accurate and fair measure of how much people know about research methods.

By randomly assigning students to groups, you assume you have created equivalent groups. This is an assumption rather than a fact or a guarantee because there is a possibility that the groups you created were actually different, just by chance. When you toss a coin 10 times, you expect to get 5 heads and 5 tails if the coin is unbiased. You know that it is possible, however, to get 9 heads and 1 tail even from an unbiased coin. The chances of this occurring are small, but they exist. The same is true for random assignment to groups. For instance, suppose you were to evaluate the effects of listening to lectures versus reading textbooks and you had only 10 people with whom to experiment. By randomly assigning 5 people to the lecture group and 5 to the textbook group you would stand a good chance of creating groups that are roughly equivalent in current grade point average, motivation to perform well, and prior knowledge of research methods. However, there is no *guarantee* that the groups would be equivalent. There is always a chance that you accidentally assigned the most studious people to the textbook group and the most carefree people to the lecture group. Random assignment, like the flip of a coin, is a method that is fair and equal in the long run, but there is always a possibility that it will produce an unusual and unbalanced grouping, just as an unbiased coin can produce a run of 9 heads and 1 tail. The smaller the number of subjects you have available for random assignment, the less confident you can be that you have created equivalent groups. It takes only a few "accidental" assignments of subjects to create nonequivalent groups when each group has only 5 people. If each group had 50 people, the fact that the 2 people with the highest grade point averages, motivation, and prior knowledge both ended up in the same group would not have much impact on the equivalence of the two groups. Large numbers aid in achieving pretreatment equivalence of groups.

Random assignment is the "fairest" method of assignment for assessing the effects of one or more treatments. It allows you to examine differences between groups that appear after a treatment has been administered and to trust that the differences you observe were not there before the treatment. Random assignment enables an experimenter to rule out one threat to internal validity in particular—the threat of *selection*.

Five Threats to Internal Validity

To illustrate the problems of making causal inferences and maximizing internal validity, we use a hypothetical problem in which you may take the role of the researcher to experience the problems of identifying the real cause of an event. Making causal inferences is what doctors do when they try to diagnose the cause of a patient's pain or what detectives do when they identify the cause of a death. The researcher, doctor, and detective must each rule out a list of rival explanations to arrive at the most probable cause. The rival explanations are **threats to the internal validity** of the research proposition.

If you introduce a treatment that you hope will make a difference in people's lives, you would like to conclude your research with a clear statement of the form "*X* causes *Y*." You might wish to say, "Lectures make people learn" or "Lectures make people learn more than books do." Or you might wish to conclude, "Tutoring helps people who are tutored" or "Tutoring helps people who do the tutoring." These conclusions are simply stated and are much more straightforward than the actual conclusions you find at the end of research papers. Such statements have the basic form that experimenters want to assert, even if the findings are not always so simple as "*X* causes *Y*."

One reason researchers cannot always state their conclusions so simply is that there may be *other* causes of *Y* in their research. These other causes are rival explanations called *threats to validity* (see Chapter 2). Five threats to internal validity follow. Other threats exist—we discuss others in the next chapter and you can find discussion of others in an excellent book by Cook and Campbell (1975).

1. **Maturation:** any naturally occurring process within persons you study that could cause a change in their performance. Fatigue, boredom, growth, or intellectual maturation may account for changes.
2. **History:** any event that coincides with the treatment and could have a similar effect. These could be major historical events that occur in the political, economic, or cultural life of the people you are studying, or they could be minor events that occur during the course of an experiment—such as an experimenter becoming ill and having to be replaced, a disruption in the procedures because of equipment failure, or an interruption from any unwanted source.
3. **Instrumentation:** any change in your measurement procedures. If you purposefully change your measuring procedures because you have discovered a "better" way to collect data, or if your observers gradually become more experienced or careless, these changes could have effects that may be confused with those of the treatment.
4. **Mortality:** any dropout of subjects from a study. If some subjects do not return for a posttest or if subjects in a control group are more dif-

ficult to recruit than subjects in a treatment group, these differential recruitment and dropout rates could create differences that are confused with treatment effects.

5. **Selection:** any procedure of assigning or selecting subjects for treatment and comparison groups that is not random. If subjects are assigned to treatment and comparison groups on the basis of their own choice or anyone else's choice, the groups are likely to differ in ways that we cannot fully identify. Such differences may masquerade as treatment effects. Random assignment greatly reduces the chances of having a selection bias.

To see how each of these can be a rival explanation and a threat to the validity of a researcher's conclusion, imagine you have been asked to evaluate the effects of going to college on people's political attitudes. The trustees of an educational foundation would like to know whether receiving a liberal arts education actually makes people more liberal. You have the seemingly simple assignment to answer the question "Does going to college make people more liberal?" (or the question "Does it keep them from becoming conservative?"). You decide to answer this by comparing the people you now know in college with the people from your high school who did not go to college. A high school reunion gives you the opportunity to make some observations.

You find that your high school friends who have not gone to college seem more conservative than the people in your current classes. What is the cause of the difference? To conclude that going to college makes a difference, you must be able to rule out potential rival explanations.

Maturation   One rival explanation is that your high school friends who have not gone to college seem conservative not because they missed college but because they are getting older. If you think maturation is the cause of conservatism (and conversely, youth the cause of liberalism) you would expect to find your college friends showing the same signs of weariness and conservatism, for they are the same age. So you can rule out maturation as a threat to the internal validity of your study.

History   Someone might point out to you that the reason your high school friends seem conservative is not that they have missed college but that they are caught in an economic and political climate that makes everyone want to protect what they have rather than share the little wealth they still possess. This is not a very convincing argument if your college friends are caught in the same economic and political climate, so history cannot explain the difference.

Instrumentation   Is it possible that your high school friends are no more conservative than they (and you) were during high school but that your own standards of what constitutes conservatism and liberalism have changed? If you have changed your own standards, your high school friends would seem more conservative because of a change in you, not them. Such a change in measuring instrument (in this case, you) can be a threat to internal validity. However, you are now applying the same measuring instrument to both your high school and college friends, so even if your standards have changed, this is not a rival explanation for the current differences you observe. You can rule out instrumentation as a threat to internal validity.

Mortality Perhaps the people at your high school reunion are a special subset, representing the most conservative of the class. This could happen if the more liberal graduates decided not to return for reunions. Anytime you suspect that *not everyone* showed up who should have been there, you must ask yourself whether the dropouts might represent a different group if you had been able to interview or observe them. Unless you can get information on the people who do not show up, mortality is a threat to the internal validity of your study.

Selection This is the most serious of the threats to the internal validity of the study you have been asked to conduct. You need to consider the possibility that your high school friends who did not go to college and your current college friends were different types of people to begin with, with different political attitudes even before their educational paths diverged. Because they were not randomly assigned to the college and no-college groups but rather *selected* their own paths or had their paths selected for them by admissions committees, school counselors, and other advisers, there is no guarantee that they were similar to begin with. Such *selection* effects are serious threats to the internal validity of studies in which there is no random assignment. Whenever people select their own treatments or are selected by others for treatments or end up in different treatment groups by some unknown process instead of by random assignment, we have no assurance that the people in different groups were equivalent to begin with. Chances are they were not because the very fact that they selected or were selected for different treatments indicates that they were different types of people, with different preferences, different abilities, or some other characteristics that made them seem more suitable for one treatment rather than another.

Selection differences appear wherever we study naturally occurring groups. Students in small rural colleges probably differ in important ways from students in big urban universities even before they set foot on their campuses. Any comparison of graduates from small colleges and those from big universities must take this into account—the differences between those graduates may have little to do with the college experience itself and much to do with the preexisting differences between the groups.

By using experimental designs and random assignment of people to conditions, an experimenter can rule out many of these threats to internal validity. Random assignment is particularly effective in ruling out the threat of preexisting *selection* differences. It is not a cure-all, however, and we shall see that even laboratory experiments do not yield airtight causal inferences.

Examples of Randomized Experiments

To be a randomized experiment, a study need not be conducted in a laboratory. Experiments can also take place in real-life settings. The two examples we discuss in this section test the same theoretical proposition, one in the laboratory and the other in the field. The theoretical proposition is that people benefit from having a feeling of control over what happens to them. The settings range from a laboratory, in which almost everything is controlled and the experiment is conducted in a social vacuum, to retirement homes, where many events in addition to the experimental treatment affect the subjects.

A Laboratory Experiment

Glass and Singer conducted over two dozen laboratory experiments that they have published under the title *Urban Stress: Experiments on Noise and Social Stressors* (1972). They state in the preface that they were not interested in the effects of noise per se: "It is clear that most of our two dozen or so studies center around noise; yet we never considered this a 'noise' book. The use of noise stimuli in our research was simply a convenient device for studying antecedents and consequences of analogues of urban stressors" (p. xii). Noise in the laboratory was a substitute for urban social stressors such as "bureaucratic harassment and arbitrary discrimination" (p. xii). They did not study these factors directly because the experimenters would have lost the experimental control that they had in their laboratories. They wanted to maximize the internal validity of their research, possibly at the expense of external validity. How reasonable is it to generalize from the effects of noise in a laboratory to the other physical and social stressors of urban life? Each reader may have a different judgment about the generalizability or external validity of this research. The researchers themselves were "confident that the model and procedures used in our research apply equally well to all of these domains of study" (p. xii).

They examined the effects of two variations in the noise produced by an electronic noise generator. The first variation was predictability; they exposed subjects to either predictable intermittent or unpredictable intermittent noise. The experimenters measured the listeners' physiological reaction and their ability to solve graphic puzzles after being exposed to the noise. The second variation was perceived control: Listeners who perceived they had control could press a button to turn off the noise, though they were encouraged not to use it unless it was absolutely necessary. Another group of listeners had no way to turn off the noise.

These variations represent two different types of control. Being able to predict when the noise will come gives some modicum of control in the sense that you are not taken by surprise. Being able to press a button to turn off the noise gives more control, though in this case the experimenters succeeded in persuading the listeners not to use the buttons. People who had the buttons were actually exposed to as much noise as those without buttons, but the former knew that they could terminate it if they wished. The experimenters called this *perceived* rather than actual control.

The subjects were randomly assigned to treatments—they were not permitted to choose one form of noise presentation over another. The experimenters measured the listeners' physiological reactions and cognitive performance after they were subjected to one of the noise conditions. The physiological measures included palmar sweating, a sign of arousal or anxiety. The cognitive measures included solving graphic puzzles and persistence in working on puzzles that the subjects believed could be solved but that, in fact, were insoluble; persistence was taken as a measure of frustration tolerance. The experimenters also gathered other data, including the listeners' ratings of how irritating, distracting, and unpleasant the noise was.

The unpredictable intermittent noise lowered the listeners' frustration tolerance; they worked for a shorter time at the insoluble puzzles after being exposed to random noise than to predictable noise. There were no effects of the predictable versus unpredictable noise on physiological reactions. Perceived control had an effect, however. Having access to a button to turn off the noise made a difference in both the listeners' physiological reactions and their frustration tolerance. Subjects who had such control sweated less (i.e., were less anxious or aroused) and persisted longer on the graphic puzzles. Those subjects also rated the noise as less irritating, distracting, and unpleasant. Glass and Singer (1972) concluded from over two dozen experiments like these that the disruptive and disturbing effects of stress can be reduced if subjects can either predict when the stress will strike or believe they can control it by turning it off if they so choose.

Glass and Singer prefaced their book by saying it is not a book about noise but a book about urban stress. They relied on analogies, however, to study urban stress. Is the laboratory noise a good analog for the physical and social stressors in cities? And are the physiological measures of palmar sweating and the cognitive performance measures of persistence at insoluble puzzles good analogs of the effects of urban stress? These laboratory procedures are all **operational definitions** of abstract concepts such as "urban stress," "anxiety," and "frustration tolerance." An operational definition is a procedure used by the researcher to manipulate or measure the variables of the study. All research contains operational definitions of abstract concepts; they are not unique to laboratory experiments. If we were to study urban stress by going to people's neighborhoods and measuring the noise levels and asking them to rate on a scale from 1 to 100 how anxious the noise makes them and how much it affects their frustration tolerance, those measures would also be operational definitions of the more abstract concepts of "stress," "anxiety," and "frustration tolerance." Constructing good operational definitions requires appropriate and accurate procedures to measure and manipulate variables. The art of finding suitable procedures cannot be taught with a set of rules but is acquired by experience. Glass and Singer's use of noises produced in a laboratory to represent physical and social stressors produced in cities is persuasive. Their conclusions seem to be generalizable to the world outside the laboratory. The real test of external validity, however, rests on the confirmation of those findings in other settings.

Glass and Singer's experiments have high internal validity. The effects are clearly attributable to their manipulations—to the predictable versus unpredictable noises and the controllable versus uncontrollable noises. Because Glass and Singer assigned subjects to experimental conditions, it is not likely that the effects were produced by *selection* differences (the likelihood is 5 in 100). Maturation is not a plausible rival explanation because there is no reason to believe that people aged or tired differentially in the different experimental conditions. Nor is *instrumentation* a plausible explanation—the groups did not differ in how or when they were tested. *History* was constant for all the groups because they were kept in the same laboratory conditions.

Normally, we would not even bother to go through this entire list of rival explanations to assess the internal validity of a true experiment. Random assignment and careful control of experimental conditions safeguard against most of these threats to validity.

It is the *external validity* of laboratory experiments that is questionable. The best test of external validity is a replication of a study—a demonstration that the results can be repeated with different subjects, different procedures, and different experimenters.

A Field Experiment

Schulz (1976) conducted a study of the effects of control and predictability on the physical and psychological well-being of people in a retirement home. He did not set out to replicate the Glass and Singer research, and he does not talk about noise or urban stress, but he repeated some of the same ideas. We can, therefore, test the generalizability of Glass and Singer's laboratory research by seeing whether their ideas apply in another setting, an institution for elderly people.

Schulz began his experiment with the premise that "from the very young to the very old and dying, persons strive to control their environments.... Typically, however, retirement and old age precipitate an abrupt decline in control. Retirement means the loss of one of the most meaningful sources of instrumental control in life, the work role.... In addition ... many aged individuals experience further declines in their ability to manipulate and control the environment as a result of institutionalization" (p. 563). He asked residents in a retirement home if they would serve in a study of the "daily activities of aged individuals" (p. 566). Forty people agreed, and he randomly assigned them to one of four conditions. He tried to include people in the study who were not in daily contact with one another to prevent them from comparing notes and thereby arousing suspicion or contaminating the results of the study. Three of the four groups were visited by undergraduate students. The students explained that they were interested in getting to know some elderly people because they were taking a course on aging and thought they should get some first-hand experience. They also added that the experimenter thought the residents "might enjoy having someone to talk to." The experimental manipulation was the degree of control the residents had over the timing and duration of the visits. There were three variations and a fourth comparison group:

1. Controlled visits   These residents controlled both the frequency and duration of the undergraduates' visits. They called the visitors when they wanted them to come and determined how long they stayed. In the initial visit, during which the undergraduates introduced themselves, they ended by saying, "Let me write down my name and phone number for you. If you ever just feel like talking, give me a call and I'll be over."

2. Predictable visits   These residents knew when their visitors would appear, but they could not control either the occurrence or the duration of the visits. Instead, the visitors told them at the beginning of each visit approximately how long they would stay and informed them by phone when they would visit again. To make these visits comparable to the control-visit group, each visitor in this group was paired with a visitor in the control-visit group and kept a similar visiting schedule. Thus, if a resident who could *control* the visitor's appearances requested daily visits of two hours each, Schulz selected a visitor from the *predictable* group to make similar appointments every day for two hours. If another resident in the controlling group requested visits only once a week for one-half hour each, a visitor in the predictable group followed the same schedule. This ensured equivalent amounts of visiting in the two groups, and the only difference was whether the residents controlled the timing of visits or were simply able to predict when they would occur.

3. Random visits   Residents in this condition could neither control nor predict the timing of their visits. They were visited as frequently and for the same length of time as the other residents because each visitor in this condition was also paired with a visitor in the control-visit group and kept the same schedule but did not inform the resident of the time or duration of any visit. The visits were unpredictable from the resident's point of view, with the visitor stopping in unannounced and saying, "I decided to drop by and pay you a visit today."

4. No visits   These residents had no undergraduate visitors, but they were interviewed at the beginning and end of the study. The interviews measured the residents' health, psychological well-being, and activity level.

The results of Schulz's experiment confirm the idea that having control over one's environment produces physical and psychological well-being. The residents who could control or predict visits scored consistently higher on the measure of physical and psychological well-being than did the residents who received random visits or no visits. The residents who could control visits did not show any greater benefits than the residents who could predict, however, contrary to the idea that more control causes more well-being. Schulz says this "suggests that the relatively positive outcome of the predict and control groups is attributable to predictability alone."

It is difficult to interpret Schulz's finding of no difference between control and predictability. One of the cardinal rules of experimental research is that negative findings are often uninterpretable because they could be the result of many things—imprecise measurement, weak manipulations of the independent variable, careless procedures. Many negative findings are unreported because it is not clear why there were no differences. When differences between groups do emerge, however, and when there are no plausible rival explanations, the experimenter can conclude that the differences were caused by the independent variables. Random assignment and experimental designs enable the experimenter to rule out most rival explanations, and positive findings in true experiments permit the experimenter to say, "This caused that." Schulz's field experiment partially replicates Glass and Singer's earlier laboratory experiments demonstrating that people benefit when they can predict and control events in their environment. This confirmation in another setting adds to the external validity of the laboratory studies.

Independent and Dependent Variables

In true experiments we study the relationship between two types of variables—**independent** and **dependent variables.** Independent variables are the *causes* and dependent variables the *effects.* In Schulz's experiment, the visiting manipulation is the independent variable or cause. It is one variable with four values: controlled visits, predictable visits, random visits, and no visits. If the independent variable had only one value and did not vary, it would be impossible to know if it caused anything. For instance, if Schulz had introduced only controllable visits and measured the residents' health and psychological well-being after such visits, he would not have been able to conclude anything about the effects of the visits because he would have had nothing with which to compare those residents' reactions. For this reason, an experimental manipulation requires at least one experimental group and one comparison group—thereby creating an independent *variable* because there are two values, treatment and no treatment.

Schulz used several *dependent* variables or measures of *effects.* He had several measures of health status: number of types of medication used per day, quantity of medication used per day, number of trips to the infirmary per week, and a subjective assessment by the director of the home. He also used several measures of psychological well-being: the residents' reports of how much of the time they felt lonely; how much of the time they felt bored; how happy, hopeful, and useful they felt; and the activities director's rating of each person's "zest for life." Each of these measures is a dependent variable that could be influenced by the independent variable.

Experimental Versus Correlational Studies

Experimental research is not the only research in which the investigator tries to study cause-effect relationships. There are many researchers who find it impossible or unethical to assign people to conditions by a flip of a coin and yet would like to study the causes and effects in those situations. For instance, you might believe that the schools people attend determine how much they learn. It is impossible, however, to assign students to school by a flip of a coin except in some very rare instances. The quality of schools and students' academic achievement are related in complex ways, and it is difficult to make a simple cause-effect statement about the two. Most research on the relationship between schools and academic achievement is, therefore, correlational rather than experimental research. The researchers do not manipulate one variable and look at the subsequent effects on another variable. Instead they *measure* both variables and look at the relationship between the two.

The difficulty in making causal assertions with correlational research is that the relationship between the two variables could result from three possibilities:

1. Perhaps the quality of schools determines the students' academic achievement:

Quality of Schools ———→ Students' Achievement

2. Perhaps the students' academic achievements (which they get from their parents' training, their reading at home, and other nonschool activities) determine the quality of schools:

Students' Achievement ———→ Quality of Schools

3. Perhaps both the quality of schools and the students' academic achievements are determined by other causes, called *third variables*, such as parents' income and social status:

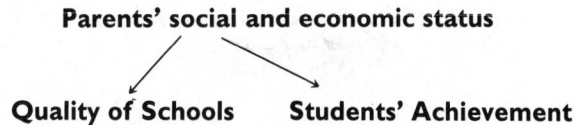

Parents' social and economic status

Quality of Schools   Students' Achievement

Deciding which of these possibilities explains the relationship between school quality and academic achievement requires a theoretical model and complex statistical analysis. We will discuss these further in our chapters on quasi-experimental designs and survey research. For now, it suffices to say that when social scientists do nonexperimental research and find a relationship between two variables, they must contend with numerous rival explanations before making their causal statements.

Experimental Designs

We use the following notation to describe different research designs:

X = a treatment, an independent variable, a cause.
O = an observation, a dependent variable, an effect.
R = subjects have been randomly assigned to the treatment conditions.

Design I. Randomized Two-Group Design

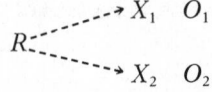

Subjects are randomly assigned to the experimental treatment group (X_1) or to a comparison group (X_2). There is a slight chance that randomization failed and that they would differ on the dependent variable $(O_1$ and $O_2)$ even if no treatment intervened. This is a small and remote possibility that is taken into consideration in the statistical analysis.

This design contains all the bare essentials for an experiment: random assignment, treatment and no-treatment groups, and observations after the treatment. We must have at least two groups to know whether the treatment had an effect, and we must have some assurance that the groups were equivalent before treatment so that we can attribute any posttreatment differences to the experimental treatment. We can rule out several rival explanations or threats to internal validity by using this design. We know the posttreatment differences are not the result of a subject *selection* bias because subjects were randomly assigned rather than personally selected into the two groups. We know the posttreatment differences are not a product of *maturation* because the two groups should have matured (aged, fatigued) at the same rate if they were tested at the same intervals after random assignment.

We can rule out other rival explanations not just by referring to the random assignment but by looking carefully at the experimental procedures to see whether it is plausible that the treatment group might have been exposed to some other events (historical events in the outside world or events within the experimental session) that the no-treatment group did not experience. If not, we can eliminate *history* as a rival explanation. If the two groups were tested or observed under similar circumstances, we can eliminate *instrumentation* differences as an explanation. Once we have eliminated these rival explanations, we can feel reasonably confident that the experimental treatment caused the subsequent difference between the two groups $(O_1$ and $O_2)$.

Many experimenters use this design or some variation of it, with two or more treatment groups. Glass and Singer's (1972) laboratory studies of the effects of noise had this design—but instead of a no-treatment comparison group, they used two alternative treatments: predictable versus unpredictable noise in one set of studies and controllable versus uncontrollable noise in another set. Design 1 is the simplest of the true experimental designs.

Design 2. Before-After Two-Group Design

$$R \begin{cases} O_1 & X_1 & O_2 \\ O_3 & X_2 & O_4 \end{cases}$$

This design has an additional set of tests or observations of the dependent variable, called *pretests*, before the experimental treatment. Pretests have several advantages. They provide a check on the randomization and let the experimenter see whether the groups were equivalent before the treatment. If the groups are not equivalent on the pretests, the experimenter can adjust the posttest measures to provide a fairer test of the treatment. Pretests also provide a more sensitive test of the effects of the treatment by letting each subject serve as his or her own comparison. Instead of comparing only O_2 and O_4, the experimenter can compare each subject's pretest and posttest scores (O_1 with O_2 and O_3 with O_4). As subjects' pretest scores all differ from one another and their posttest scores reflect some of these preexisting individual differences, the experimenter gains precision by making these intraindividual comparisons.

To understand the benefits of this pretest design, suppose you and a friend were randomly assigned to different groups in an experiment on weight loss; you were assigned to the no-treatment comparison group and your friend to the weight-loss treatment group. If you weigh 130 pounds on the pretest and 130 pounds on the posttest, it is clear that being in the comparison group did not affect your weight. If your friend weighed 160 pounds on the pretest and 150 pounds on the posttest, it is plausible that the treatment caused your friend to lose 10 pounds (assuming we can rule out maturation, history, instrumentation, and all other threats to internal validity). However, if the experimenter did not take pretest measures and looked only at the posttest weights, your friend's 150 pounds compared to your 130 would make the treatment look bad. Therefore, having pretest information in this before-and-after, two-group design gives an experimenter a more precise measure of treatment effects.

The pretest also has some disadvantages, however. It may sensitize subjects to the purpose of the experiment and bias their posttest scores. If this happens for the experimental and control groups alike, their posttest scores should be equally elevated or depressed, and pretesting alone would not be a rival explanation for a difference between O_2 and O_4. If however, the pretest affects the treatment group differently from the no-treatment group, this would appear as a difference on the posttest scores and would be indistinguishable from a difference produced by the treatment alone.

Design 2 provides no solution for this problem. Experimenters must, therefore, decide whether this is a plausible occurrence for any particular study, and if it is, they should avoid this design in favor of the simpler Design 1. Schulz (1976) used a variation of this before-after design in his study of the effects of control among retirement home residents. Instead of two groups, he had four, and all had pretests as well as posttests.

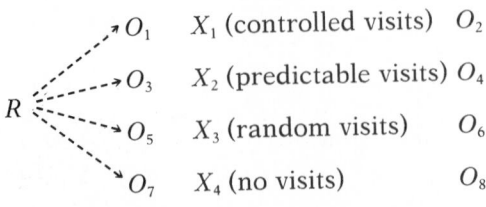

The pretests (odd-numbered O's in the preceding diagram) and posttests (even-numbered O's) contained several dependent variable measures: health status, psychological well-being, and activities. The treatments, on the other hand, were all variations of *one* independent variable. Any single independent variable may have multiple values or levels—therefore, the four X's in the preceding diagram represent not four different independent variables but four values of one independent variable called "degree of control over visitors."

Schulz did not find differences between all four groups after the treatment. Instead, he found that the first two were similar, and together they had better health than the last two, which were also similar to each other. He concluded that the important beneficial ingredient in degree of control was predictability, for that was what the first two groups had in common. In interpreting his results, Schulz was not bothered by the potential effects of pretesting alone or by the effects of pretesting in combination with the treatments because the pattern of results does not lend itself to either of those interpretations. Ruling out rival explanations depends on three things: (1) the design of the study, (2) the experimenter's knowledge of what different events (such as intrasession history) the subjects may have experienced, and (3) the pattern of results and whether that particular pattern could plausibly be explained by some events other than the experimental treatments.

The third design combines Designs 1 and 2. With this design an experimenter can test decisively whether the posttest differences were caused by the treatment, the pretest, or the combination of treatment plus pretest.

Design 3. Solomon Four-Group Design

$$
R
\begin{cases}
O_1 & X_1 & O_2 \\
O_3 & X_2 & O_4 \\
 & X_1 & O_5 \\
 & X_2 & O_6
\end{cases}
\quad
\begin{array}{c}
\text{(Design 2)} \\[1em]
+ \\[1em]
\text{(Design 1)}
\end{array}
$$

Design 3 is an expensive design because it requires four groups of subjects to test the effects of only two levels of a treatment. The four groups are needed because in addition to the treatment and no-treatment groups there are pretested and nonpretested groups.

This design offers the separate advantages of Design 1 (no interference from pretesting effects) and Design 2 (greater precision from the pretest scores as base lines against which to measure the effects of the treatment). In addition, it enables the experimenter to see whether the *combination* of pretesting plus treatment produces an effect that is different from what we would expect if we simply added the separate effects of pretesting and treatment. Such combinations, if they are different from the sum of the two individual effects, are called *interaction* effects. They are like what happens when two natural elements combine and interact to produce a new effect—hydrogen and oxygen together produce a new compound, water. The whole is different from or greater than the simple sum of the parts. In many social science problems, interactions are important. We need more than two-group designs to study these and we need more than one independent variable because an interaction results from a combination of two or more causes or independent variables. Designs with two or more independent variables are called *factorial designs.*

Design 4. Factorial Design

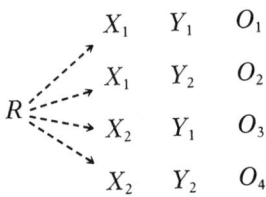

$$
\begin{array}{ccc}
X_1 & Y_1 & O_1 \\
X_1 & Y_2 & O_2 \\
X_2 & Y_1 & O_3 \\
X_2 & Y_2 & O_4 \\
\end{array}
$$

The X is one independent variable; the Y is another. In a factorial design, two or more independent variables are always presented in combination. The entire design contains every possible combination of the independent variables (also known as *factors*, hence the name, *factorial design*). If there are more than two independent variables or factors and if each has more than two values, the design rapidly mushrooms because each additional variable or value greatly increases the number of conditions. We can illustrate this with the following tables, which are the form most commonly used to diagram factorial designs.

Table 4.1 illustrates the combination of two factors or independent variables. In the language of experimental design, we call this a *two-by-two factorial design*, which means there are two factors and each has two values or levels. If we added a third factor, we would double the number of conditions if the additional factor also had two values, triple it if the

TABLE 4.1   A 2 × 2 Factorial Design

Factor Y	Factor X	
Actor's Behavior	Actor's Gender	
	Male	Female
Assertive	Assertive Male	Assertive Female
Submissive	Submissive Male	Submissive Female

TABLE 4.2   A 2 × 2 × 3 Factional Design

Factor Y	Factor Z	Factor X	
Actor's Behavior	Actor's Age	Actor's Gender	
		Male	Female
Assertive	Child		
	Adolescent		
	Adult		
Submissive	Child		
	Adolescent		
	Adult		

new factor had three values, and so on. For instance, if we added the actor's age as another factor and used three age categories—child, adolescent, adult—we would have a 2 × 2 × 3 design, with 12 conditions, shown in Table 4.2. This 12-cell design is much more complex than the original 2 × 2. It is triple the size and, therefore, either requires three times as many subjects or spreads the same number of subjects thinner, with one-third the number in each condition. It also introduces not just one additional factor that may produce effects but three additional interactions.

To describe an interaction, we shall examine a 2 × 2 design like that shown in Table 4.1 (Costrich, et al., 1975). The actors were confederates of the experimenter—persons who pretended to be regular participants like the subjects but who actually played preassigned parts. Each actor was a member of a discussion group with four to eight other people, who were the subjects. An experimenter had instructed the actors to take either an assertive or submissive role in the group discussion, but no one else in the group was aware of this backstage plan. One-fourth of the groups had an assertive male confederate, one-fourth had a submissive male confederate, one-fourth had an assertive female confederate, and one-fourth had a submissive female confederate. At the end of the discussion hour, each member of the group rated each other person on a number of qualities, including popularity.

Notice that the variable "actor's gender" in this study refers not to the gender of the subjects who participated but to the confederates or actors whom the subjects rated. This is an important distinction. Subjects' age and gender are characteristics they bring with them rather than experimental conditions to which people can be randomly assigned. The portion of a study that examines such subject variables is, therefore, technically not a true experiment because it does not feature random assignment. The gender of an actor or stimulus person to whom subjects respond is an experimental variable, however, because subjects can be randomly assigned to interact with or observe a male or female actor.

The experimenters combined two independent variables—actor's behavior and actor's gender—because they were particularly interested in the effect of the combination. The dependent variable was observers' ratings of how popular they thought the actor was. The experimenters believed the effects of an actor's behavior on popularity would depend not only on how the actor behaved but also on stereotypes of how a man or woman should behave. Therefore, it was important to look at all four combinations of behavior and gender. The margins of Table 4.3 contain the average popularity ratings for male and female actors who behaved assertively or submissively.

We have transferred these results to graphs to discuss the varieties of effects that you can examine with a factorial design. You can examine the separate *main effects* of each independent variable and the *interaction effect*. The *main effect* shows whether one independent variable has an effect when you average across the conditions of any other variable. The average values that appear around the margins of Table 4.3 show the main effects. The *interaction effect* is the combined effect of two or more independent variables acting together. The values inside the four cells of Table 4.3 show the interaction effect.

Figure 4.1 shows the main effect of the actor's behavior. Overall, submissive behavior and assertive behavior received the same average popularity rating—medium. You can see this in the horizontal line of Figure 4.1 and in the values that appear on the right side of Table 4.3. There is no difference between the popularity ratings of submissive and assertive actors when we ignore the actor's gender and look at the overall average. This means there is no significant main effect of the actor's behavior.

TABLE 4.3   Popularity of Male and Female Actors Who Behaved Assertively or Submissively

Actor's Behavior	Actor's Gender		
	Male	Female	
Assertive	High Popularity	Low Popularity	Average for Assertive: Medium
Submissive	Low Popularity	High Popularity	Average for Submissive: Medium
	Average for Male: Medium	Average for Female: Medium	

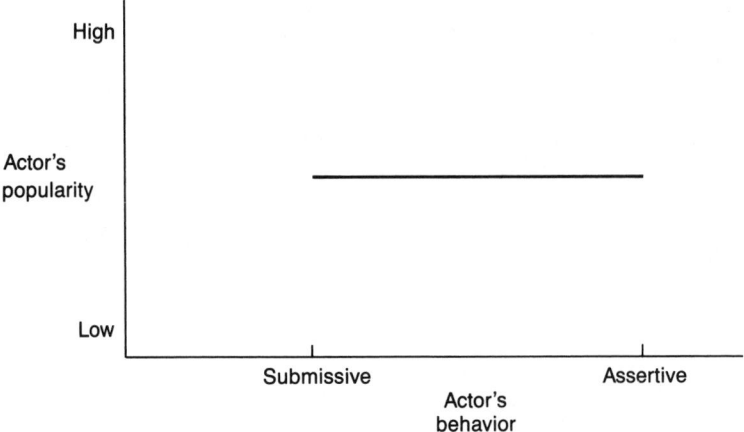

FIGURE 4.1   No effect of actor's behavior on popularity ratings in a discussion group

To see whether there is a main effect of the actor's gender, look at Figure 4.2. You will see the same horizontal line, which shows that the average popularity ratings of male and female were the same—medium. This also appears at the bottom of Table 4.3, where the overall average for male and female actors is listed. There is no significant main effect of the actor's behavior.

Does this mean that neither behavior nor gender had an effect? It means that neither one alone explains the actor's popularity, but we can look further to see whether they had an effect in combination. Figure 4.3 shows the *interaction effect* of actor's gender and behavior on popularity.

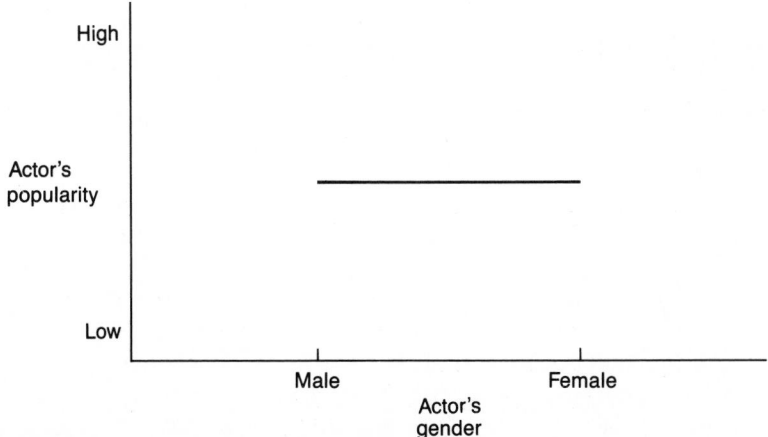

FIGURE 4.2   No effect of actor's gender on popularity ratings in a discussion group

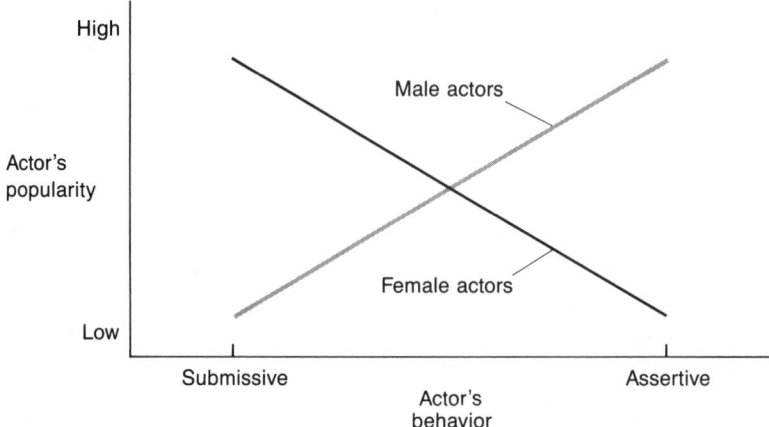

FIGURE 4.3 **Effect of the interaction of actor's gender and behavior on popularity ratings in a discussion group**

It is clear now that these variables did affect popularity, not alone, but in combination. Being assertive or submissive affected popularity in different ways depending on whether the actor was male or female. For men, being assertive caused them to be more popular than being submissive. For women, the opposite was true; being submissive caused them to be more popular than being assertive.

Interaction effects require more-complex theoretical explanations than main effects. In the preceding example, the explanation for the inter-action introduces a new concept: out-of-role behavior. Both men and women are less popular in groups if they violate the stereotypes of their gender and step out of role (Costrich et al., 1975). The researchers designed this study because they had a hunch that out-of-sex-role behaviors would cause people to be less well liked. They used a factorial design because they were specifically interested in the combined effects of gender and assertiveness. One reason to use factorial designs is to look for inter-action effects. Another reason is to be able to generalize the effects of one variable across several levels of another variable. For instance, if you wanted to study the effects of being able to control noise (variable 1) on people's ability to solve puzzles, you might vary the type of puzzle as a second independent variable. This would enable you to demonstrate that people perform better on not just one but two types of puzzles (variable 2) when they can control the noise in their environment. You add the second variable not because you expect it to make a difference but to demonstrate that it makes no difference. A third reason to include more than one inde-pendent variable in an experiment is to study the separate effect of that variable. You may design a factorial study even if you expect to find only two main effects and no interaction.

Factorial designs, with two or more independent variables, therefore, have several advantages over single-factor designs. They permit the investigator to discover interactions as well as main effects. And if there are no interactions, they enable the researcher to generalize the main effect of one factor across two or more values of another factor. If we were interested in the effects of assertiveness training on career advancement, we might not expect any interaction between assertiveness training and the trainee's race, age, or gender; but it would still be wise to include trainees of more than one sex, race, and age. Only then could we generalize and draw conclusions about the effects of assertiveness training that are not limited to men or whites or young people. If we included only young white men in the study, we would not know whether the results hold true for others.

In the past, some social science theories that were thought to be true of people in general were, in fact, true of only one group. For instance, much of the early research on achievement motivation predicted achievement behavior in men but not in women (McClelland et al., 1953). Only later did researchers point out that the same laws did not explain women's behavior (e.g., Alper, 1974). Subsequent research showed that women sometimes feared success, something McClelland had not predicted (e.g., Horner, 1972). Other research, varying both the gender of the subjects and the gender-appropriateness of the task, has found both men and women anticipate negative consequences for someone who succeeds at a task that is generally reserved for a person of the opposite sex (Monahan, Kuhn, & Shaver, 1974). Both men and women fear the consequences of violating sex-role stereotypes. Only when the gender of the subjects and the gender-appropriateness of the tasks were included as variables in the research design could the researchers discover these effects. Note that age and race of the subjects were not included as factors. To know whether black as well as white and old as well as young people avoid opposite-sex-labeled tasks, researchers must include these factors as independent variables.

Repeated Measures Designs: One Solution to the Numbers Problem

Repeated measures designs are also called *within-subjects* designs. Rather than assign different people to different treatments, the experimenter exposes the same persons to multiple treatments. Each subject is repeatedly treated and tested, and the variations caused by different treatments appear within the same person's performance rather than between different groups of people.

The independent variables we have presented in the preceding examples are of two types: manipulated variables and subject variables. Manipulated variables are designed by the experimenter, and any subjects can be randomly assigned to manipulated treatments. Subjects can be randomly assigned to groups with assertive or submissive confederates; they can be randomly assigned to work on sex-appropriate or sex-inappropriate tasks; they can be randonly assigned to receive visitors whose visits are predictable or unpredictable. Subject variables, on the other hand, come with the subject, such as age, height, personality traits, gender, race, and so on.

Subject variables impose restrictions on research design as well as analysis because they cannot be used as within-subjects or repeated measures factors. It is a rare and ingenious researcher who can have the same group of subjects experience being both old and young or both male and female or both black and white. If an experimenter could do this, it would mean that these subject variables had become manipulated variables. A white novelist did this as a personal experiment (Griffin, 1962). He used medications to darken his skin and wrote about his experiences as a white man and then a black man. People who have undergone surgery to change their gender have also experimented with their own subject characteristics. Aside from these personal experiments, however, we have no instances in which a researcher manipulated such subject variables. Subject variables, therefore, cannot be used as within-subjects or repeated measures factors.

When factors can be varied within subjects, experimenters can use a design that requires fewer subjects. Repeated measures designs are more efficient because they require fewer subjects and provide more sensitive measures of the effects of a variable. For instance, if we wanted to study how quickly men and women can solve puzzles that are labeled "masculine problem" and "feminine problem," we could study this as a between-subjects or within-subjects design. The subjects' gender is a subject variable and must be a between-subjects factor. The label on the puzzle could be either a between-subjects or within-subjects factor. If it were between subjects, we would have to recruit 20 subjects for our study, using a rule of thumb that there be 5 observations in each cell of the design. The 20 observations would come from 20 different people. (See Table 4.4.)

We could, however, make the sex labeling of the task a within-subjects factor and have each subject solve both a "masculine"- and "feminine"-labeled puzzle. In this case, we would need only 10 subjects, 5 men and 5 women, to get the same number of observations in each cell because each person would solve two puzzles. (See Table 4.5.)

TABLE 4.4 Illustration of the Number of Subjects Needed for a Between-Subjects Design

| | | Sex-Labeling of the Task | |
		Masculine	Feminine
Subjects' Gender	Male	5 men	5 men
	Female	5 women	5 women

Total = 20 subjects

TABLE 4.5 Illustration of the Number of Subjects Needed for a Within-Subjects Design

		Sex-Labeling of the Task	
		"Masculine"	"Feminine"
Subjects' Gender	Male	5 men -------	--------- (5)
	Female	5 women -----	--------- (5)

Total = 10 subjects

The other efficient feature of repeated measures designs is the precision gained by using each subject as his or her own comparison. Like the pretest observations of the before-and-after, two-group design, the repeated measures give us individual base lines for each subject. The five men who solve the "masculine" puzzle in Figure 4.5 may vary widely in the time they require. One may solve the puzzle in 10 seconds and another may take 10 minutes. If each person takes one minute longer to solve the "feminine" than the "masculine" puzzle, this would not appear as a noticeable difference between the two puzzle groups if we used a between-subjects design, but it would appear as noticeable in a within-subjects design.

Subject variables cannot be used with repeated measures; not even all manipulated variables are suitable as within-subjects or repeated measures variables. Some manipulated variables would arouse the subjects' suspicions about the purposes of the experiment. For instance, suppose we tried to use the race or gender of job applicants as a within-subjects variable. If we presented prospective employers with two hypothetical job applications and résumés in which everything was identical except the race or gender of the applicant, the prospective employers could see immediately that we were testing to see if they practice race- or sex-discrimination in hiring. Other variables are not suitable if they produce long-lasting effects that would carry over from one testing to the next. For instance, if we tried to compare the effects of alcohol and hallucinogenic drugs on drivers' reaction times, we would not have them drink a large dose of alcohol, give them a driver's test, and then give them hallucinogenic drugs an hour later for a second test. In addition to the obvious ethical problems of administering drugs to experimental subjects (see Chapter 18 on ethics), we also run into practical problems. If we use repeated measures designs, we must be sure the effects of the first level of a treatment are gone before we try to administer the second. A third limitation is that we must be careful not to confuse the effects of a treatment with the sequence in which the treatments are administered. If each subject receives treatment A before treatment B, we cannot tell whether the difference in reactions to the two treatments is a result of the treatments or of their sequencing—subjects may show fatigue or practice effects by the time they receive the second treatment. Any repeated measures design should include at least two sequences: treatment A before B for half the subjects and treatment B before A for the other half.

The Strengths and Weaknesses of
True Experiments

We have emphasized the strengths of true experiments. By randomly assigning people to experimental conditions, experimenters can be reasonably confident that the subsequent differences are caused by the treatments and not preexisting differences among groups of people. Manipulated experimental variables, unlike subject variables, enable experimenters to conclude, "This caused that." No experimenter can be 100 percent sure that "this" experimental treatment was the cause of "that" effect, but experimenters can rule out many rival explanations, with the exception of a special set known as experimental *artifacts*.

Experimental Artifacts

By using random assignment, experimenters can rule out many of the extraneous variables that might affect the results. There is one set of extraneous variables that remain to plague experimenters in particular, however. These are called *experimental artifacts*. Even with selection, history, maturation, instrumentation, and the other threats to internal validity taken care of, some experimenters worry that the results of their research may not be true effects of the experimental treatment but may be *artifacts*, effects of some extraneous variables. For instance, experimenters may unwittingly influence their subjects to behave in ways that confirm the hypothesis, particularly if the subjects want to please the experimenter.

Randomized laboratory experiments are especially vulnerable to such artifacts when subjects know they are being studied and want to create a good impression and when experimenters are in direct communication with their subjects and can communicate their expectations verbally and nonverbally (Rosenthal, 1966, 1976; Rosenthal & Rosnow, 1969; Rosnow & Rosenthal, 1976; Rosnow & Davis, 1977). Laboratory experiments have the virtue of eliminating many extraneous sources of stimulation to study the effects of one or two isolated stimuli or treatments. This virtue, however, presents its own dangers. One danger is that the subjects who enter this rarefied atmosphere will be paying particular attention to subtle nuances of the experimenter's behavior or experimental setting, trying to discover the purpose of the study and trying to respond "correctly." The greater the subjects' anxiety about how they will appear, the greater the likelihood that they will try to give "correct" or socially desirable responses (Rosenberg, 1969). Such anxiety and need for approval are called *evaluation apprehension*. People who volunteer for experiments generally have a high need for approval and are more anxious to please than people who are required to participate. Experimental research that relies on volunteers, therefore, is biased by the subjects' willingness to conform to what they believe the experimenter wants to demonstrate (Rosenthal & Rosnow, 1975). Experimental subjects may not always be correct about what the experimenter's wishes are, but they try nonetheless to be "good subjects."

Experimenters wittingly and unwittingly give subjects cues about how they are supposed to behave. Such cues are called *demand characteristics* (Orne, 1969; Rosnow & Davis, 1977). Experimenters do not always know what cues or demand characteristics their subjects perceive. For instance, in a laboratory study of obedience to authority, subjects were placed in front of a board with electric switches; numbers indicated that if the subjects pushed switches at the far right side of the board they would be shocking another person with 450 volts, and the words on the board said "Danger . . . Severe Shock . . . XXX." These obvious cues told the subjects that they should not continue to press the switches. On the other hand, the experimenter who urged the subjects to press the switches and administer shocks told them that although the shocks may be "painful," they were not "dangerous." Almost all the subjects administered what seemed to be high shock levels (Milgram, 1964). There are two possible interpretations of these results. One is that the subjects were very obedient and willing to endanger the life of another person (if we take the words of the shock panel seriously). Another interpretation is that the subjects took more seriously the words of the experimenter, who assured them that the shocks were painful but not dangerous. Movies made of subjects who participated in these experiments show them to have been under severe stress, not knowing which set of cues to take more seriously. Multiple demands were placed on these experimental subjects, which make it more difficult for us to interpret their actions (Kidder, 1982).

In another study subjects also behaved in ways that appeared to be destructive, and these can be interpreted as the result of demand characteristics. They were asked to endanger their own safety by picking up a poisonous snake or taking a penny out of an acid solution that would presumably burn their bare hands. They were willing to follow the experimenters' instructions because they believed, correctly, that the experimenters would not truly endanger the subjects' lives. The experimental setting, therefore, contained demand characteristics which conveyed to the subjects, "do it, it's really all right" (Orne, 1969).

Nonexperimental research is also susceptible to artifacts, but the potential is greater in randomized laboratory experiments because the isolation, the absence of normal constraints on behavior, and the awareness that "this is an experiment" all heighten subjects' sensitivity to clues from the experimenter or the setting. Subjects who volunteer to be in experiments are particularly likely to respond to signals and demands they perceive in the experimental setting (Rosenthal & Rosnow, 1975). Nonvolunteers are generally less eager to participate and therefore less sensitive to the experimenters' intended and unintended cues.

In addition to paying attention to details of the experimental procedure that may have unintended effects, experimenters must pay attention to the *external validity* or generalizability of their results. This is the other point for which experiments have been criticized.

External Validity

Experimental designs and procedures maximize the internal validity of research—they enable the researcher to rule out most rival explanations or threats to internal validity. There is a tradeoff, however. Experimenters maximize internal validity often at the expense of the external validity or generalizability of the results. Do the findings extend beyond the laboratory? Can the experimenter talk about these phenomena in the world outside, or do they appear only in seemingly sterile conditions?

A common criticism of laboratory experiments in particular is that they are poor representations of natural processes. Babbie (1973) lists three disadvantages of controlled experiments: (1) They provide "an artificial test of the hypothesis. The relevance of the experiment to the real world is always subject to question" (p. 33). (2) They may not be generalizable to other segments of the population. Many psychology experiments use college sophomores as subjects, yet they are not intended to be studies of the psychology of college students but studies of people in general. Unless we repeat those experiments with middle-aged people, noncollege-educated people, working people, elderly people, or other segments of the population, we do not know whether the findings are generalizable. (3) Experiments provide no useful descriptive data. For instance, if 20 percent of the people in the treatment group agree with a statement about the usefulness of therapy, this tells us nothing about the percentage of people who agree with this statement in the larger population *unless* we have recruited the subjects for our experiment by selecting a *representative sample* from the larger population. In theory, this can be done; in practice it is rare. These are important criticisms, but they are not inevitable condemnations of experimental designs because not all experiments contain these limitations and not all nonexperimental research is beyond reproach on the same grounds.

Some laboratory experiments, like Glass and Singer's studies of noise, use remote analogs of real-world variables, like urban stress. The artificial conditions in those experiments may be more effective ways to study the problem than are some more realistic conditions. For instance, the unpleasant intermittent laboratory noise may produce realistic effects, more like the urban stresses that Glass and Singer want to generalize to, than would intermittent traffic sounds. The latter are realistic but relatively mild, and they may have negligible effects. Glass and Singer wanted to re-create in a short time in the laboratory the same effects that are created over weeks, months, or years of living with unpredictable and uncontrollable urban stresses, including city traffic but also including bureaucratic harassment and the other physical and social stresses of urban living. They chose laboratory-generated noise not because they thought it sounded like urban stressors but because they thought it would produce the effects of urban stress, condensed in a short time and a small space. The laboratory noise and laboratory measures of physiological and cognitive effects are all substitutes for the real phenomena—they are analogs and, therefore, artificial. Being artificial is not necessarily a disadvantage, however. Some laboratory analogs are more effective than their realistic but mundane counterparts and, therefore, make the research more persuasive.

Field experiments are less likely to seem artificial. Schulz's study of residents in a retirement home introduced experimental variations that were not part of the daily routine in the home and in that sense may seem artificial, but having visitors is a normal occurrence in retirement homes, and the only abnormal feature was that these visitors had been asked to go there by the researcher. Even this is not entirely artificial, however, because social agencies and volunteer organizations also send visitors to rest homes, hospitals, and other institutions. How generalizable any treatments and effects are can be discovered only by trying to replicate the findings in another setting.

The second criticism of experiments questions the representativeness of the research subjects. Are college students representative of the larger population? For some research questions, yes; for others, no. For much psychological research college sophomores are no different than anyone else. For instance, to study the effects of a variable like amount of piano practice on level of performance in a piano recital, we can assume that what is true for 18-year-old college students is also true of 6-year-old elementary school students and 40-year-old workers. To study the effects of a more socially situated variable, however, like the effects of politicians' campaign styles on people's support for candidates, we would be wise to include a more heterogeneous group of people. Or to study the effects of an economic variable like tax incentives for installing solar energy systems, it is necessary to include people with a range of incomes. Often the subjects of research are not individuals but groups or aggregates, such as classrooms, nations, businesses, or price indexes. There are many instances where college sophomores are not the appropriate subjects of a study, but this does not preclude conducting an experiment. If the units, be they classrooms, schools, commercial districts, or housing units, can be randomly assigned to treatment conditions, we can conduct a true experiment.

For many social science questions, the subjects in the research must be more heterogeneous than college students—they must vary in age, income, education, or occupation if these are variables in the research. Sociological research usually raises questions about various groups or types of people—people of different economic, ethnic, educational, and cultural backgrounds. Or if not different groups of people, sociologists study the effects of different types of situations and social structures. Sociological questions, therefore, cannot usually be studied with college sophomores alone. There is nothing about experimental designs, however, that requires studying college sophomores. Schulz's study of residents in a retirement home was a true experiment with a noncollege population. The only requirement of a true experiment is random assignment; and with manipulable variables, with ingenuity, and with tact, experimenters have been able to use random assignment in many places outside colleges.

The third criticism—that experiments provide no useful descriptive data—like the first two, is often true but need not be. An important difference between experiments and surveys is that surveys contain a random sample of respondents who are *representative* of some larger population. Therefore, if 80 percent of the people in a representative sample say they believe cigarettes cause cancer, we can generalize this to the population. Because the sample is a random selection of people from a population, the distribution of beliefs and preferences in that sample is approximately the same as the distribution in the population. The survey, therefore, provides descriptive data about the population. An experiment, on the other hand, usually does not contain a representative or random sample because the purpose of the experiment is not to provide descriptive data about percentages of people in the population who profess certain beliefs. The purpose of an experiment is to provide information about causes and effects.

If an experimenter wanted first to select a random sample of people from a particular population and then randomly assign people in the sample to treatment groups, there is nothing to prevent this. Nothing in the design or logic of experiments would rule against random sampling in addition to random assignment. Experimenters usually have no incentive to select random samples, however, because their purpose is not to describe the frequency with which people say or do one thing versus another. Their purpose is to discover *why* people say or do one thing under some set of circumstances—to discover the causes rather than the frequencies of events.

Summary

Randomized experiments are the method *par excellence* for examining causal relationships and concluding "this caused that." They enable a researcher to test and rule out the primary threats to internal validity: maturation, history, instrumentation, mortality, and selection. Experiments that contain more than one independent variable provide tests of both the main effects and the interaction effects of those variables. The high internal validity of randomized experiments is sometimes achieved at the cost of external validity. The control that experimenters have over their research subjects and conditions occasionally introduces unwanted experimental artifacts. The decision to conduct a randomized experiment depends, therefore, on one's purposes and priorities—what one wishes to achieve and what one is willing to sacrifice.

The different research methods we describe in this book—experiments, surveys, participant observation—are not logically incompatible with each other. Experiments can be performed with representative samples and can include a survey; surveys can include experiments embedded within the interview. Experimenters can do some participant observation, and participant observers can introduce some experimental manipulations. Seldom are these strategies combined, however, either for lack of time and resources or for lack of knowledge. Researchers often become specialists in one method and use that exclusively. We hope the readers of this book will develop an understanding of and appreciation for various methods. We do not expect the readers to combine all these methods in all their research. Instead, we expect them to become adept at choosing the most appropriate methods to answer the questions rather than trying to do everything all at once.

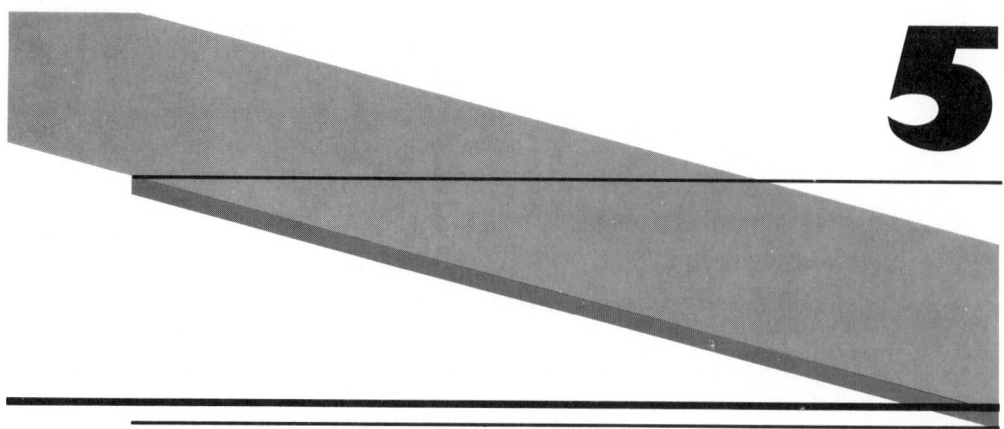

5

Quasi-Experimental Designs

Science does not begin and end with the randomized experiment. Science is a process of discovery, in which you use the best tools available to answer your questions. When random assignment and laboratory control are unavailable, you may choose from a large assortment of other techniques. The term *quasi experiments* covers a wide range of other research designs. The term first became popular with the publication of a small but influential book by that name, written by Campbell and Stanley (1963), later revised and expanded (Cook & Campbell, 1979; also Judd & Kenny, 1981).

Quasi experiments are research designs that do not have randomly assigned treatment and comparison groups. Instead, the comparisons between treatment and nontreatment conditions must always be made with nonequivalent groups or with the same subjects prior to treatment. If you cannot randomly assign people or groups to treatment conditions, you lose the ability to control what happens to whom. You can still *observe* what happens, when, and to whom, however; and by deciding what and when to measure, you can design one of several quasi experiments. You forfeit control when you do not use random assignment, but you can still conduct research and analyze cause-effect relationships without a true experiment. By judiciously gathering data from additional times and places, you can create a quasi experiment. For instance, Lawler and Hackman (1969) studied the effects of participative decision making on the work attendance of janitors. They could not randomly assign men to participative decision-making groups or control groups and, therefore, had no equivalent control group with which to make comparisons. The researchers did, however, have a long series of absenteeism records from the men prior to their new participatory decision making and could compare absenteeism rates before and after the participatory procedures were introduced. This was not a true experiment because there was no random assignment. It was a quasi experiment, called a *time-series design.*

In this chapter, we show how you can do research in which you assess causes and effects even if you cannot randomly assign people to conditions. Well-conceived quasi experiments permit you to rule out many of the threats to internal validity that we discussed in Chapter 4. Ill-conceived pre-experiments do not. We begin our discussion with examples of pre-experimental designs so that you can then appreciate what quasi experiments do by the contrast. Pre-experiments are research designs that lack random assignment and that contain few data points or O's in our experimental notation. The following are three pre-experimental designs, which are examples of how *not* to do research.

Pre-Experimental Designs

The One-Shot Case Study

X   O

Suppose you have a hunch that practicing yoga makes people serene. For the moment we will not worry about how we measure or define serenity. We will assume that can be done. To test this idea, you interview people who practice yoga. This is a one-shot case study. The *X* is practicing yoga; the *O* is your assessment of each person's serenity. Imagine that the interviews reveal a high level of serenity among men and women yoga devotees. Will you conclude that practicing yoga makes people serene? You cannot—not without some comparisons. The one-shot study, with only one *X* and one *O*, includes no comparisons.

This design is so weak that your conclusion is vulnerable to at least three rival explanations. The level of serenity you observed could be the result of

1. **Selection**   People who study yoga may be serene to begin with, and had they not been able to find yoga instruction, you may have observed the same levels of that attitude. You cannot rule out this very plausible alternative because you have no preyoga measures.
2. **History**   The level of serenity you observe may be a reflection not of those people but of a political and historical climate of the time. Perhaps everyone is becoming more relaxed. Without a comparison you cannot rule out this possibility.
3. **Mortality**   Perhaps other people who once practiced yoga but then discontinued would not show such serenity; the remaining people whom you interview could be a select group of yoga students. Had you been able to interview the others, you might have found no great level of serenity.

With this one-shot, one-group design, the level of serenity you observe is meaningless without some comparison level, and the pre-experimental one-shot case study includes no comparison. If you developed a serenity scale that had a low score of 0 and maximum of 75, and if the yoga students averaged 50 on the scale, you would not know whether that was a relatively high or low score because you had no data or standards with which to compare it in this one-shot design.

The One-Group Pretest-Posttest Design

O_1 *X* O_2

The one-group pretest-posttest design adds one more data point, the pretest O_1, and that permits you to rule out selection as a rival explanation. If the yoga practitioners have a higher score after they studied yoga than before, you know that the high score was not a preexisting characteristic of this group. But can you attribute it to the practice of yoga? No. There are five other rival explanations or threats to the internal validity of this design.

1. **History** If the posttest observation is made after considerable time, the difference between it and the pretest may be the result of different social climates—the nation may have ended a war, a new presidential candidate may be talking about Eastern philosophies, or popular culture may be advertising new forms of meditation. Any historical changes like these could be rival explanations if they occurred in the time between pretest and posttest.
2. **Maturation** If the people you were studying became older, more relaxed, or retired with the passage of time alone, this would be a rival explanation. The longer the time between the pretest and posttest, the more likely it is that such developmental changes could explain the difference.
3. **Testing** If the first interview sensitized the people you were studying and made them believe they should relax or slow down, the pretesting alone could have produced higher scores on the posttest. The shorter the time between pretest and posttest, the more plausible are testing effects.
4. **Instrumentation** If you changed your interview questions or scoring system between the first and second observation, these changes in the measuring instrument could account for a difference between pre- and postlevels of serenity.
5. **Interaction of selection and maturation** (or selection and any of the other threats to internal validity). Even if none of the preceding threats are plausible explanations for the population in general, they may be plausible explanations for the select group of people who study yoga or for that specific group of practitioners whom you interview. For instance, you may decide it is implausible that maturation makes all people serene; some people may become more anxious with age. Nonetheless, you may find it plausible that the kind of people interested in yoga would naturally become serene as they matured even if they did not practice it, and this represents an interaction between selection and maturation. Similarly, you may decide that not all people would be sensitized by the pretest interview and try to be calmer on the posttest; but for the group of people you have selected, testing may have that effect. This would be an interaction of selection and testing.

These five rival explanations are potential threats for any pre-experiment of this design. You may be able to rule out one or more of these for any particular case because either the results or the context make that threat implausible. For instance, if you used unobtrusive measures of yoga students' state of tension or relaxation—such as the amount of lip biting or nail chewing they exhibited—you could regard *testing* as an implausible explanation of any changes you observed because the students would have been unaware of, and therefore unaffected by, your testing. Whether a study is vulnerable to these threats depends on both the design and the details of the procedures and results. Any one-group pretest-posttest study is *potentially* vulnerable to the five threats discussed, however, until proved otherwise. This is a generally weak design that you should avoid if you can design something better. The third pre-experimental design has two sets of observations, but instead of observing one group of people twice, it observes two groups once.

The Static-Group Comparison

Group 1	X	O_1
Group 2	not $-X$	O_2

The dashed line separating the two groups indicates that people were not randomly assigned to group 1 and group 2; instead, these are either naturally occurring groups or groups to which people are assigned for some reason. If we apply this design to our question about yoga, we would interview one group of people who practiced yoga (group 1) and another group who did not (group 2). The treatment, yoga, is signified by the X for group 1. If you conducted this study using the static-group comparison pre-experiment, you would have to contend with the following threats to validity:

1. **Selection**   Selection is the major threat to this design. Because you did not randomly assign people to group 1 and group 2, it is very likely that the two groups are different in many ways apart from practicing yoga. You can imagine that if you had interviewed the people in group 1 just before they learned yoga, they would have scored higher on your serenity scale than the people in group 2. Such preexisting differences may, in fact, be the cause of learning yoga. Their serenity may have caused them to become yoga students rather than vice versa.
2. **Mortality**   If you conducted your study by interviewing yoga students who belonged to a particular meditation group and found they were different from nonpractitioners, you may err in concluding that yoga makes a person serene. Membership requirements in the meditation group may have caused less-serene people to drop out because they did not meet the standards required. Any such differential dropout rates are threats to internal validity.
3. **Selection by history interaction**   Although historical events that both groups are exposed to cannot account for a difference between them, differential exposure to such events would be a threat to validity. If you have reason to suspect that one group experienced some event

that the other group did not experience, you have a rival explanation for any difference you observe.

The static-group comparison is a correlational design. The X is a characteristic of people that they bring into the study—such as practicing yoga or attending private school or going to a therapist. The static-group comparision shows what the relationship is between that characteristic (X) and another characteristic (O), such as feeling serene, having academic aspirations, or showing insight into oneself. A correlational study shows whether there is a positive or negative relationship between two characteristics and whether the relationship is strong or weak. A positive relationship appears when people have simultaneously high scores or simultaneously low scores on both characteristics. For instance, a positive relationship between going to a therapist and having insight into one's motives means that people who go to a therapist (have a positive score on that variable) also have insight, and those who do not go to a therapist do not have insight into their motives. A positive relationship between attending private school and having academic aspirations means that those who attend have high aspirations and those who do not have low academic aspirations. This would appear as a positive correlation between those two variables.

A positive correlation does not mean that the variable labeled X causes the variable labeled O. It is just as likely that the causal relationship goes in the opposite direction: Having insight into one's motives can cause one to go to a therapist, and having academic aspirations can cause a person to attend private schools. It is also possible that there is no direct causal relationship between the two variables in spite of their positive relationship. Both could be the result of a third variable—being raised in a family that puts great emphasis on education could cause people to attend private schools and to have academic aspirations. If you conduct a correlational study, like the static-group comparison, you often cannot determine which of these three explanations accounts for the positive relationship. The impossibility of disentangling these and other rival explanations is expressed in the adage "correlation does not prove causation." This third pre-experimental design is correlational.

The three pre-experimental designs are examples of how *not* to do research if there are alternatives. Quasi-experimental designs provide an alternative. When you do not have the power to assign people randomly to treatment conditions, you can still gather data and rule out many of the threats to validity by using carefully chosen quasi-experimental designs. There are several books written about quasi experiments (e.g., Campbell & Stanley, 1963; Cook & Campbell, 1979; Judd & Kenny, 1981) which you can consult to see the full range of designs. In this chapter we discuss three types of quasi experiments, each of which is an extension of a pre-experiment. Each of these achieves its greater interpretability through the addition of more data points or observations to the pre-experimental base.

Quasi-Experimental Designs

With some forethought and planning it is often possible to turn a nonuseful pre-experimental design into a usable quasi-experimental design. The chief difficulty with the pre-experiments is that either we do not know how much two comparison groups differed before one of them received the treatment or we do not know how much a single group would have changed between pretest and posttest even in the absence of a treatment. For instance, with the one-group, pretest and posttest design we do not know how much the group might have changed from pretest to posttest simply as a result of the passage of time, in the absence of any treatment. With the two-group static comparison we do not know how much the two groups differed before the treatment was introduced. The quasi-experimental designs solve these problems by including additional observations. The additional observations are gathered in two ways: (1) across time for a single group and (2) across groups for a single time. These observations allow the researcher to determine how much a group changes simply by the passage of time and how much two or more groups differed even before a treatment was introduced. The three quasi-experimental designs that we discuss next are vast improvements over the pre-experimental designs.

Interrupted Time-Series Designs

$$O_1 \; O_2 \; O_3 \; O_4 \; X \; O_5 \; O_6 \; O_7 \; O_8$$

Time-series designs are an extension of the pre-experimental one-group pretest-posttest design ($O_1 \; X \; O_2$). Although that pre-experimental predecessor is subject to many threats to internal validity, the time series, with its long sequence of O's, provides information to rule out several threats, particularly maturation and testing. If you find a marked difference between O_4 and O_5 and wonder whether the difference is truly a result of the treatment (X) or of maturation, you can inspect all the intervals before and after that point to look for maturation trends. Presumably, if maturation were occurring, it would show up as a long-term trend, producing similar differences between O_1 and O_2, O_2 and O_3, and so on, along the entire series. If none of the other intervals show such a trend and the only difference lies between O_4 and O_5, maturation is not a very plausible explanation, unless, of course, you are studying some phenomenon that happens to coincide with a particular maturational change such as puberty and that could also plausibly be affected by puberty. Only under such a special set of circumstances and coincidences would maturation pose a threat to the validity of a time-series study.

    The same reasoning applies to testing as a rival explanation. If you suspected that the difference btween O_4 and O_5 resulted not from the treatment but from the sensitizing effects of the pretest (O_4), you could examine all the preceding and succeeding intervals to see whether the repeated testing produced similar differences along the entire series. If there were no differences at any other points, it would be highly implausible that the testing at O_4 alone would have created an effect at O_5.

Sometimes the X occurs only once, and its effect is presumed to persist forever or for some specified time. A measles innoculation should last forever; a flu shot may have a limited period of effectiveness. Sometimes the X signals a permanent change in the situation—as when a state changes its divorce laws to permit no-fault divorce or when the federal government introduces new air pollution standards. In cases like these, when the treatment occurs not only at a single time but continues in force, the time-series is more rightly diagrammed as follows:

$$O_1 \, O_2 \, O_3 \, O_4 \, XO_5 \, XO_6 \, XO_7 \, XO_8$$

In either case, with a one-shot treatment or a continuing treatment, the virtue of time-series designs is that you can examine the *trends* in the data before the treatment, at the time of intervention, and after the treatment. This allows you to assess the plausibility of maturation as a rival explanation. If maturation is a cause, it should appear as a trend before the treatment as well as afterward.

How easily you can interpret a time-series and rule out rival explanations depends not on the formal features of the design alone but also on the pattern of results. Some results are relatively easy to interpret—you can rule out most of the threats to validity and conclude the treatment caused the effect. Other patterns are more vulnerable to rival interpretation.

The two features that researchers examine in results from an interrupted time-series design are the slopes of the lines for the pretest and posttest observations and the intercept—the point at which either line would intersect the vertical axis. For instance, Figures 5.1 to 5.3 show a variety of results plotted for interrupted time-series designs—the first (5.1) is readily interpretable and shows an effect of the treatment; the second (5.2) is ambiguous; the third is a clear case of no effect of the treatment (5.3).

With results like those in Figure 5.1, there are not many rival explanations. It is quite obvious that the treatment caused the shift in scores from the pretest level to the posttest level. There are no maturation trends in either the pretest or posttest observations; so maturation alone or maturation by selection interaction are not persuasive alternative explanations. The most problematic and plausible threat is history—some event that coincided with the treatment. How plausible this is depends entirely on the problem under study. If we were studying the effects of a foreign relations film on American students' attitudes toward people of other countries and if the showing of the film coincided with international

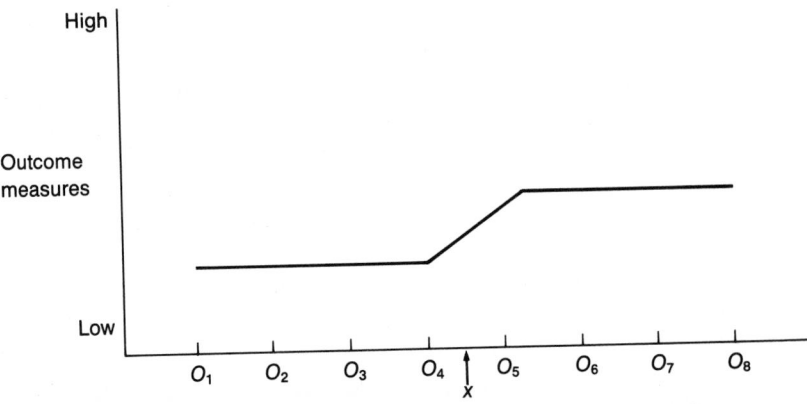

Temporal intervals when outcome measures were taken, with treatment introduced between O_4 and O_5.

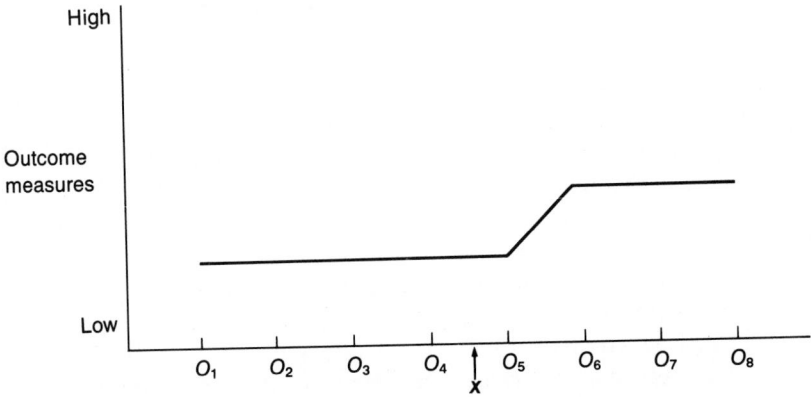

Temporal intervals when outcome measures were taken, with treatment introduced between O_4 and O_5.

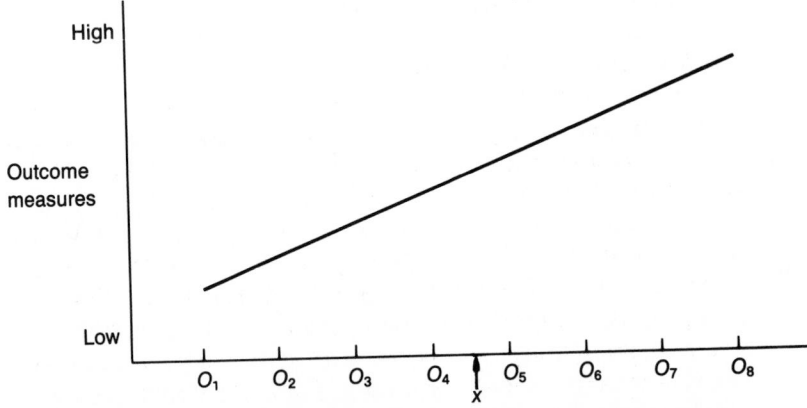

Temporal intervals when outcome measures were taken, with treatment introduced between O_4 and O_5.

FIGURES 5.1, 5.2, 5.3 Some possible outcomes resulting from the introduction of a treatment (X) into a time series of measurements

agreements about sharing the world's energy resources or with an international incident in which Americans were suddenly held hostage by another country, these historical events would be plausible rival explanations. If there are no obvious external events that coincide with the treatment and could have produced the same effects, history presents no problem.

With results like those in Figure 5.2, it is not clear that the treatment caused the shift upward because the shift does not coincide with the treatment; it lags behind by one time interval. In some cases, there may be reason to expect such a lag and, therefore, to attribute the effect to the treatment. For instance, a rise in the world's petroleum export prices would not be felt immediately in domestic gas prices at the pumps because there is a six-month oil reserve that was bought at lower prices. Therefore, if you were studying the effects of world export oil price increases on American car pooling, the effect may lag six months behind the cause. If the time-series observations were made quarterly, at three-month intervals, the effect would appear not in the first observation following treatment but in the second, and the pattern in Figure 5.2 would be a convincing demonstration of the effect of the price increase on car pooling. If there is no such plausible storage mechanism and, therefore, no plausible lag for the cause to have its effect, Figure 5.2 is more difficult to interpret, and other rival explanations may be causes. These alternative explanations would probably fall under the heading of history—other events that followed the treatment and produced the effect.

Figure 5.3 is the clearest case of no effect. The higher levels of O after the treatment merely reflect the prevailing trend that also produced increasingly higher levels of O before the treatment. This figure also shows most clearly why the time-series design is far superior to the preexperimental one-group pretest-posttest design. If the pattern seen in Figure 5.3 were studied with only one pretest and one posttest (points O_4 and O_5), the researcher would be tempted to conclude that the treatment had an effect—causing O_5 to be higher than O_4. Without the other data points, it would be impossible to distinguish between a real effect and the prevailing trend that we see in Figure 5.3.

By the addition of a series of pre- and posttest observations, the time-series design is much more interpretable than the one-group pretest-posttest design. Even though it lacks random assignment and lacks a control group, it is a useful quasi-experimental design because the additional observations allow the investigator to test the plausibility of several rival explanations—maturation, testing, instrumentation, and mortality. The chief threat to internal validity with this design is history.

The interrupted time-series design has several variations. It may include more than one group or subject, making it a multiple time-series design:

$$O_1 \quad O_2 \quad O_3 \quad O_4 \quad X \quad O_5 \quad O_6 \quad O_7 \quad O_8$$
$$\overline{}$$
$$O_{1'} \quad O_{2'} \quad O_{3'} \quad O_{4'} \qquad O_{5'} \quad O_{6'} \quad O_{7'} \quad O_{8'}$$

This design provides identical information about a second group or subject and permits you to test the most troublesome threat to internal validity that a single time-series design is heir to—*history*. If the treatment coincided with some historical event and if the two groups were presumably exposed to the same historical conditions, the effect of that historical incident should appear in both time series as a difference between O_4 and O_5. For instance, suppose we had tried to assess the effect of a film called *The Death of a Princess* on American and European attitudes toward Saudi Arabians. The film was a fictionalized account of a true story—a Saudi Arabian princess was executed by a firing squad after she had been accused of committing adultery. Saudi government officials protested the showing of this film in Europe and America because they said it misrepresented Arab society and would arouse hostility in viewers. Nonetheless, the film was shown on American and European television. If we had studied its effects—by measuring the anti-Saudi sentiment expressed in newspaper editorials or counting the number of anti-Saudi bumper stickers on cars, we might have found an effect like that in Figure 5.1. Suppose, however, that the showing of the film coincided with a rise in oil prices or an act of terrorism. Any such event that occurred at approximately the same time could account for the rise in hostility as recorded in the media or in our bumper sticker count. How could we determine whether it was the film or the other historical events that produced the effect? If we could find a locale that had been exposed to the same rise in oil prices or had heard of the same act of terrorism but had not been exposed to the film, we could assess the rival explanations. Two towns that had both experienced the rise in oil prices, one of which had received the film broadcast and one of which had not, would provide a test of the rival explanation. If the anti-Saudi sentiment expressed in the former town's newpapers or bumper stickers rose after the film broadcast, whereas the level remained constant in the other, we would rule out the rival explanations of *history* and conclude that the film produced the effect.

This example presents a hypothetical quasi experiment but a real dilemma. Sometimes the questions that quasi experiments are designed to answer are important political questions with serious implications, but the measures available to answer them are sorely inadequate. A time-series design, in particular, is often based on archival data—such as sales records of the numbers of bumper stickers sold—that were never intended to be sensitive indicators of a social variable—such as attitudes toward another nation. Nonetheless, such data may be the only measures available in a long enough series to use in a quasi experiment like the time series. Chapter 12 on observational and archival data discusses the strengths and weaknesses of such available archival data.

Regression-Discontinuity Designs

Group 1 ◯ O_1

———————

Group 2 ◯ O_2

———————

Group 3 ◯ O_3

———————

Group 4 ◯ XO_4

———————

Group 5 ◯ XO_5

———————

Group 6 ◯ XO_6

The regression-discontinuity design is an extension of the pre-experimental static-group comparison $\dfrac{X}{\text{not} - X} - \dfrac{O_1}{O_2}$. It has many rank-ordered comparison groups, both with and without the treatment. It also has a phantom pretest because the groups differ on some known criterion which is used to determine whether or not they receive the treatment. For instance, students who received scholarships on the basis of their academic performance (a standardized test or course grades) can be rank-ordered on the basis of their qualifications. Above a certain grade or test score they receive the scholarship; below that cutoff they do not. Therefore, the groups differ before the treatment in a way that is measureable and known to the researchers. Researchers can use this information about the preexisting differences to make a projection, extending the line as shown in Figure 5.5. We have, therefore, depicted this information about the prior differences as a phantom pretest observation, or ◯ (in dashed lines).

The static-group comparison is weak because *selection* is an ever-present plausible rival explanation for a difference between the two O's. The regression-discontinuity design, with its long series of comparison groups, provides information about the *plausibility* of such preexisting group differences and enables the researcher to rule out selection as a rival explanation. A researcher can examine the differences between the various nontreated groups to see what the naturally occurring groups' differences are. The groups in a regression-discontinuity design are all ranked or ordered on a criterion, such as financial need or test scores, and those above or below a cutoff point receive the treatment, such as a scholarship award.

The regression-discontinuity design is a cross-sectional design; it allows one to examine the effects of the treatment by looking *across* many groups of persons and compare those below the cutoff point with those above. The time-series designs are longitudinal designs; they allow one to examine the effects of the treatment by looking *along* a single group or

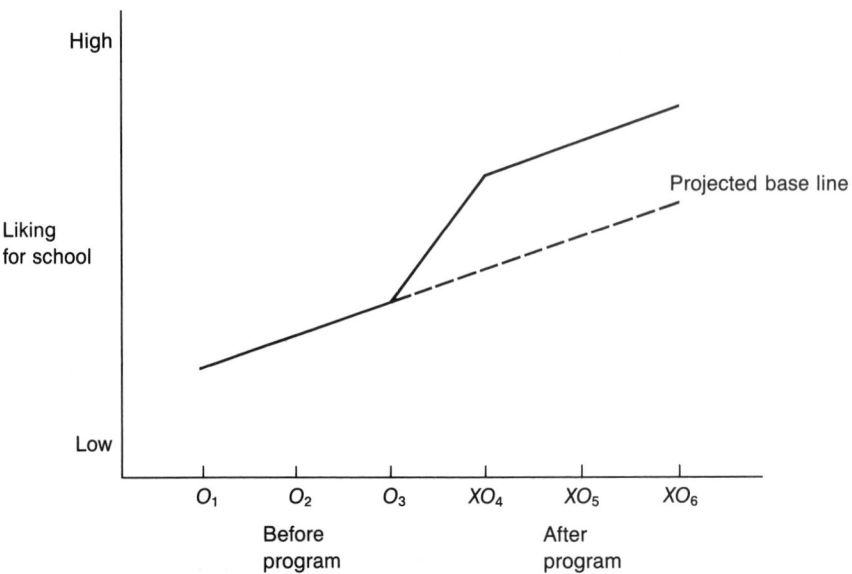

FIGURE 5.4 Time series for one group of children. Effects of academic enrichment program on children's liking for school.

person's time line and comparing the observations made before the treatment with those after. As diagrammed earlier, the two types of designs look very different. As graphed in Figure 5.4 and 5.5, the two look similar.

   Although the statistical analyses are different (the interested reader can consult Cook & Campbell, 1979, and Judd & Kenny, 1981, for details), the logic underlying the interpretation of these two designs is similar. In both cases we can project the point just before the treatment and compare the projected estimate with the observed results. If the observed results differ from the projection, that is evidence of an effect of the treatment. In both cases, we assume that if there is a preexisting trend, that trend would normally continue and should not be confused with a treatment effect. For instance, if the children whose time series we show in Figure 5.4 liked school more with each passing year, we expect that trend to continue. The change in the intercept shows that the liking increased to a new level after the academic enrichment program; the program gave the children a boost. The regression-discontinuity design shows the same effect (Figure 5.5). If children who receive higher test scores naturally like school more and if children are selected for an enrichment program on the basis of their test scores, we would expect the trend to continue along the projected line even if there were no real effect of the program. The upward shift of the line, the change in intercept, demonstrates the effect of the program over and above the natural trend.

   The time-series design and the regression-discontinuity design achieve their interpretability by the addition of observations. Time series

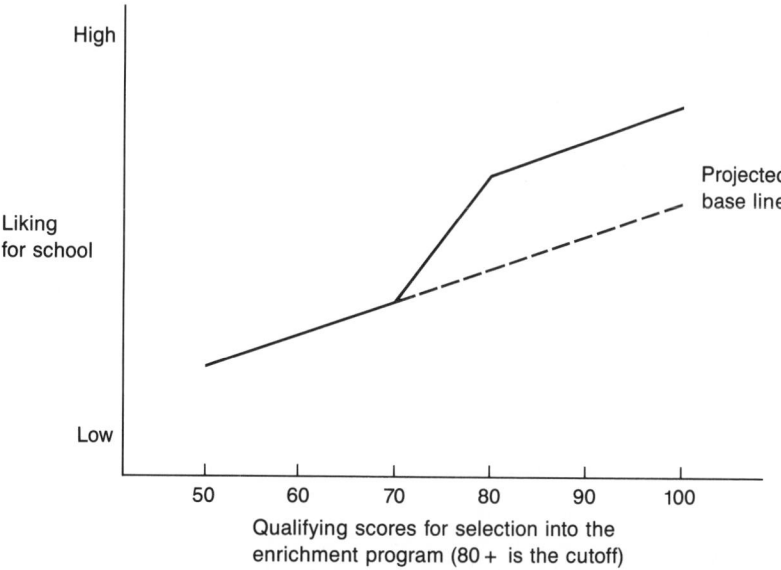

FIGURE 5.5 **Regression-discontinuity for groups of children below and above the cutoff. Effects of academic enrichment program on children's liking for school.**

add observations over time—taking the long view forward and backward. The regression discontinuity adds observations across different groups, all at one time. The added observations in both cases permit us to compare the difference between observations immediately adjacent to the treatment with the differences between pairs of observations before the treatment and pairs after the treatment. The series also permit us to examine naturally occurring trends and to compare those projected trends with the actual results.

Pretest-Posttest Nonequivalent Control Group Design

This design does not include a long series of observations either over time or across groups.

Group 1 O_1 X O_2
_____
Group 2 O_3 O_4

It is not an extension of any of the pre-experimental designs; rather, it is a combination of the static-group comparison and the one-group pretest-posttest pre-experiment. By combining the features of both, it is more interpretable than either of those. It includes pretest information about the existing group base-line levels, and it provides a comparison group. The comparison group is not formed by random assignment, however. It is a preexisting or preselected group, which we choose because it is similar, but it is not equivalent. Nonetheless, the simple addition of a comparison group and a pretest lets us possibly rule out a number of threats to internal validity.

A major advantage of this design over the static-group comparison is that we can measure preexisting differences between groups. Figure 5.6 illustrates results that are fairly interpretable, thanks to the added pretest. It is quite likely, as Figure 5.6 shows, that people who install solar panels use energy more sparingly than other people to begin with. Their interest in solar energy is a further expression of their preexisting inclinations. Therefore, if we had only the posttest information, we would not know whether the difference reflected the natural conservation tendencies of the people who installed solar panels or whether it reflected the savings produced by the panels. When we look at the pretest differences, we see that those who installed the panels were conservers to begin with. They used less electricity even before they installed the panels. This difference became even larger after the treatment, however, which suggests that the solar installations had an effect.

Are there any rival explanations? You might suspect that the people who became interested in solar energy would naturally have decreased their electric consumption even if they had not installed the panels—because they were conscious of the need to conserve energy, they may have naturally used less hot water in January 1985. This design does not provide the information necessary to rule out this possibility—a selection by maturation interaction. Only if we had a longitudinal series of observations could we see whether the treated group was on a natural downward trend both before and after the solar installation.

This example illustrates how you must consider not only the design but also the content of a study and the pattern of results when ruling out

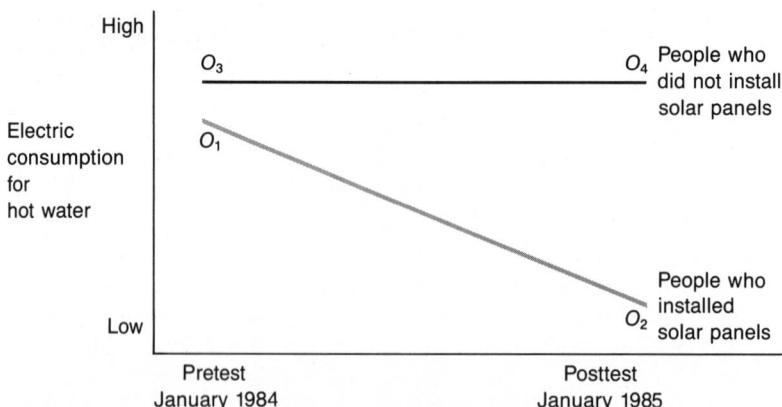

FIGURE 5.6   **Effects of solar heating panels on electric use**

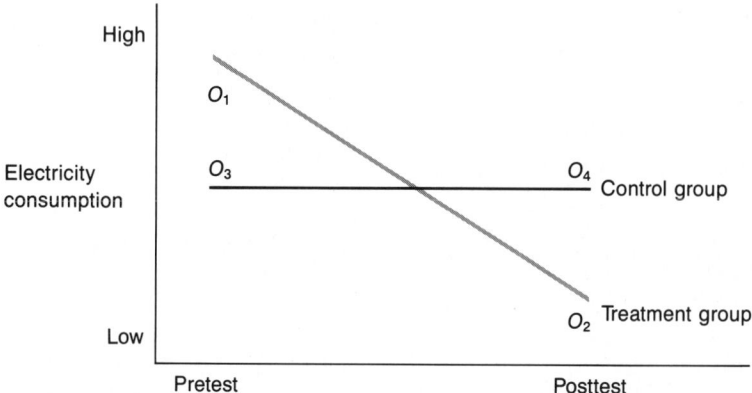

FIGURE 5.7 **Electric consumption levels by people living in treatment and control states**

rival explanations. For some topics you may not consider it plausible that the treated group would have changed so as to become increasingly different from the control group without the intervention of the treatment.

For some patterns of results, the most plausible explanation is that the treatment produced the effects. Imagine an energy conservation program imposed on people who live in states that use the most air conditioning. Suppose the imposed conservation program consisted of higher electric rates for people in the high-consumption states. To study the effects of this program we could compare the electric consumption by people in those states with consumption by people in neighboring states who had not consumed as much electricity for air conditioning. We know that the treatment group initially consumed more electricity than those in the comparison states, so their pretest levels would look like O_1 and O_3 in Figure 5.7. If the posttest showed that the treatment group reduced their consumption below the level of the control group, the most plausible explanation is that the program worked. A crossover like that in Figure 5.7 is more difficult to explain with any of the rival explanations, like a maturation by selection interaction. In this example, the constant trend of the control group we may consider the normal trend; the downward trend of the treatment group we can reasonably attribute to the treatment. To explain away the apparent treatment effect by calling it differential maturation (or differential development of energy consciousness), we would have to regard the people in the formerly high-electric consumption states an extraordinary group of late-blooming conservationists who not only met but also surpassed the conservation levels of the people in the neighboring states. This is so unlikely for this case, and most others, that the crossover pattern shown in Figure 5.7 is usually interpreted as a treatment effect.

Matching as a Mistaken Strategy in Quasi Experimentation: Regression to the Mean

All three quasi-experimental designs gain an advantage over the pre-experiments by providing pretest information about groups. These pretests show us what the differences are between groups in the case of the regression-discontinuity and nonequivalent control group designs, and they show us what the differences are over time for a single group in the case of interrupted time series. In each case, the quasi experimenter inspects these differences but does not try to eliminate them. Occasionally a researcher may try to eliminate preexisting group differences by "matching" otherwise nonequivalent groups on their pretest scores. We warn you against trying to match groups unless you can subsequently randomly assign people from your "matched" pairs to a treatment and control group. Even when it appears that you have matched perfectly on a pretest, the preexisting group differences are likely to reappear on the posttest and make it impossible for you to decide whether the differences you observe after the treatment are the result of the treatment or are the resurgence of the preexisting difference.

To show you how this can happen, we must introduce another threat to internal validity—*regression to the mean*. Regression to the mean appears whenever two sets of scores are not perfectly correlated (i.e., correlated less than 1.00). Two sets of scores are never perfectly correlated if there is any error in the measurement of either one. There is always error in measurement (recall Chapter 3). Therefore, there will always be regression to the mean. This is a tidy syllogism that we will now elaborate for you.

Let us imagine giving a midterm and a final exam to a class of 58 people. The midterm we shall call our "pretest" and the final our "posttest." In general, the people who scored in the upper half of the class on the pretest score in the upper half on the posttest, and the people who score in the lower half score there again, but there is some shifting of scores from the first to the second test. The correlation is not perfect. This means that the people who received the highest pretest scores do not all receive the highest posttest scores, and those who received the lowest pretest scores do not all receive the lowest posttest scores. Figure 5.8a shows what scores these people received on the pretest and posttest. Of the four people who scored 100 on the pretest, only one received 100 again on the posttest. The other three people obtained scores of 90, 80, and 70. Therefore, the *average* posttest score of those people is *closer* to the mean than their pretest scores were. A similar movement toward the mean appears for the people who received the lowest pretest scores. They all received 40 on the pretest, but on the posttest their scores ranged from 40 to 70. At

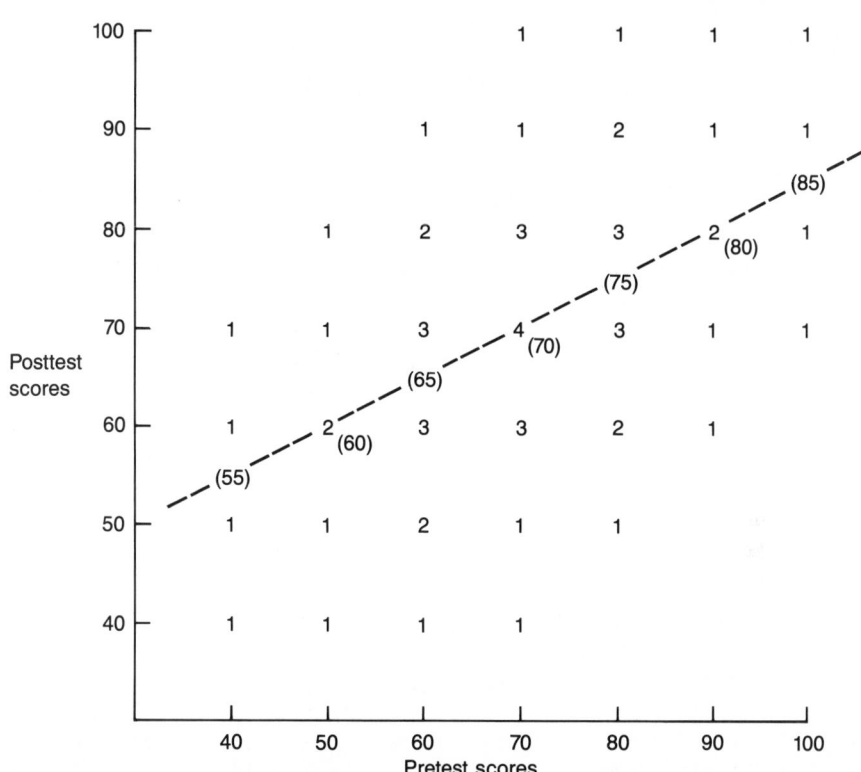

FIGURE 5.8a Scatterplot showing regression toward the posttest mean from pretest scores. The numbers inside the graph (1s, 2s, 3s, and 4) indicate how many students received each score on the two tests. The dashed line represents the average posttest score for each group of students who received a particular pretest score. The figures in parentheses are those averages. Turning the figure on its side shows the average pretest score for each group of students who received a particular posttest score. The regression toward the mean operates in both cases.

both extremes of the pretest, we find the group's average posttest scores are closer to the mean. This is what we mean by *regression toward the mean.*

Regression toward the mean occurs whenever there is an imperfect correlation. To see this, compare Figure 5.8a, which shows two measures that are imperfectly correlated, with Figure 5.8b, which shows two measures that are perfectly correlated. There is no regression toward the mean in Figure 5.8b because everyone who received the highest score on the pretest also received the highest score on the posttest, and everyone with the lowest pretest score has the lowest posttest score. You will never find a perfect correlation like this in reality because all our measurements contain a random error component—which means that their observed

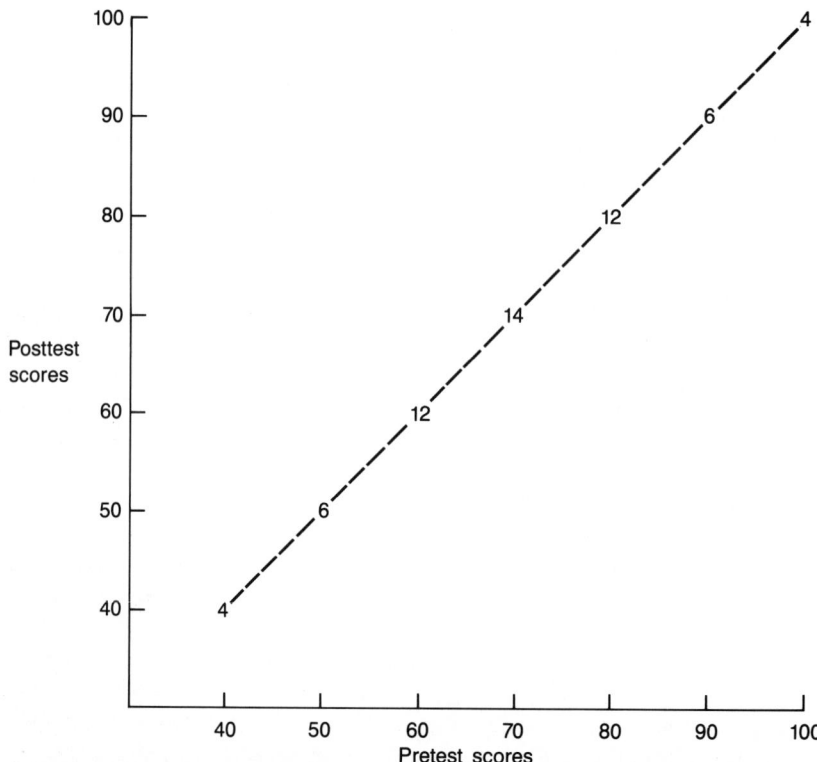

FIGURE 5.8b Scatterplot showing no regression toward the mean when there is a perfect correlation between pretest and posttest scores. The numbers along the dashed line indicate how many students received each score on the two tests. The dashed line with all scores falling exactly on the line has no "scatter" of points around it. Therefore, there is no regression toward the mean. The posttest score is the same as the pretest score for each group of people.

scores are not perfectly reliable and will show fluctuations from one test-ing session to the next. Such fluctuations reduce the correlation, and the lower the correlation the more you will find regression toward the mean as it appears in Figure 5.8a.

The fact that extreme scores regress toward the mean does not imply that students become more homogeneous over the course of a semester. If we work backward and begin with final exam scores, we find the same regression effect of final exams on midterm scores. The students who received the highest scores on the final exam would not all receive iden-tical midterm scores, and those who received the lowest scores on the final would not all receive the lowest scores on the midterm. If we turn Figure 5.8a one its side, we can see that the same regression toward the mean occurs when we look first at posttest scores and second at pretest scores.

Regression toward the mean occurs, therefore, not as a result of a homogenization process but as a result of scores being less than 100 percent reliable. Any change of the most extreme scores is of necessity a regression toward the mean.

When we apply this logic to the quasi-experimental study of compensatory programs like Head Start, regression artifacts can make a program look detrimental in the following way. If children are not randomly assigned to the treatment and control groups but are selected on the basis of some qualifications, we cannot assume that the children in the two groups come from the same population. In fact, the more reasonable assumption is that they come from two different populations or social groups, those who qualify and those who do not. In the case of a compensatory program, those who qualify must usually demonstrate a disadvantage, such as having a low income. The children who qualify for the program come from a group considered disadvantaged; the comparison children come from a group considered advantaged. These two groups obviously differ in their income levels and in the many other advantages that accompany income. They also differ in their average pretest achievement levels, a difference that the evaluators may try to remove by "matching" on pretest scores. In the process of matching, a researcher sets the conditions for regression artifacts to operate. Figure 5.9 shows the distributions of pretest scores for two hypothetical groups—one an advantaged comparison, the other a disadvantaged treatment group. The distributions overlap but they have different means or averages. In an attempt to "match" individuals from the two groups, the researcher draws from opposite ends of each group—from the upper end of the disadvantaged group and the lower end of the advantaged group. The darker region of Figure 5.9 shows the "matched" portion of each group.

These two "matched" groups represent extreme scorers from their respective populations. Because the pretest scores are not 100 percent reli-

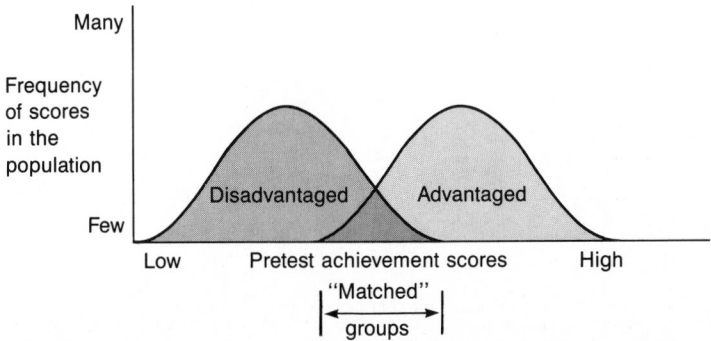

FIGURE 5.9 **Hypothetical distributions of pretest achievement levels of two populations, one considered disadvantaged and one advantaged. The darker region represents the "matched" groups from the two populations.**

able, we know that the posttest scores of these children will not be equally extreme—they will regress in opposite directions, toward their population means. The advantaged group's posttest scores will be slightly higher, for they represent the bottom end of their population; the disadvantaged group's posttest scores will be slightly lower, for they represent the upper end of their population. Figure 5.10 illustrates these regression effects and shows how regression artifacts alone can create a difference on the posttest even if no compensatory program had actually been implemented. Regression effects can make a program look detrimental if the treatment and comparison groups are selected in such a way that they represent opposite ends of two preexisting social groups. The same regression artifacts can also make a program look mistakenly beneficial if the treatment is given to the advantaged group and a presumably "matched" comparison group is drawn from a disadvantaged group.

Matching, therefore, is inadequate for removing preexisting group differences. Unless we randomly assign individuals from a common pool to treatment and control groups, it is always likely that the two groups represent different populations with different means. Attempts to match on either pretest scores or other variables are destined to be imperfect, and regression toward the mean is a potential explanation for subsequent differences. Critics of Head Start preschool programs have said that compensatory education does not work; critics of the Head Start evaluation have said that evaluation was in error. The nonequivalent control group made the program look ineffective; and "matching" did not remove the bias (Campbell & Erlebacher, 1970).

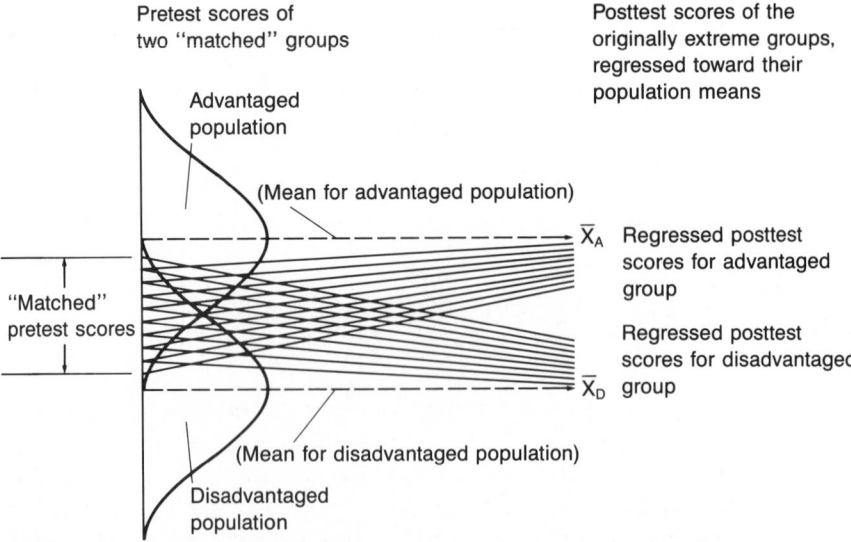

FIGURE 5.10 Regression toward the mean of posttest scores from the extremes of two populations' pretest scores

Researchers may try to match nonequivalent groups either on pretest measures of the dependent variable or on other variables known to correlate with the dependent variable. Both of these strategies fail to eliminate preexisting group differences. Matching on variables known to correlate with the dependent variable always errs in the direction of undermatching and, therefore, fails because we can never know when we have matched on enough variables to be sure the two groups represent the same population. For instance, the Head Start evaluators matched the treatment children with a comparison group on the basis of age, sex, race, kindergarten attendance, and parents' social status. The children may still have differed in the kinds of television programs they watched, in their grandparents' education levels, in numbers of books in their homes, in the achievement levels of their friends, and so on. The numbers of variables on which they were not matched is infinite. As compensatory social programs are usually designed for populations that are defined as disadvantaged, the children from the treatment group had fewer natural "head starts" than the comparison group on many other variables (Campbell & Erlebacher, 1970). Therefore, because they were not matched on grandparents' education, kinds of television programs watched, and many other variables, the treatment group probably would have scored lower on these unmatched variables. The two groups were undermatched, with the advantage probably going to the control group. Therefore, matching on variables known to correlate with the dependent variable is inadequate because it is always incomplete. The resulting undermatching will usually favor the control group and make compensatory social programs look harmful solely as a result of the failure to equate groups.

In the Head Start evaluation, the negative results are not convincing because there is a rival explanation—regression artifacts alone could have made the program look ineffective. It may be the evaluation research rather than the social program that failed in this case. An experiment with randomization makes it possible for an evaluator to assess a program with greater confidence that the results represent true program effects. Randomization, however, remains a controversial procedure. We shall consider the case for and against random assignment in Chapter 16.

When to Do Quasi Experiments

We have said in this chapter and the previous one that if you want to make causal statements, you should conduct an experiment and avoid pre-experiments. If you cannot use random assignment, a quasi experiment is the second-best choice. A quasi experiment is a fallback position, not as good as a randomized experiment but far superior to pre-experiments.

Many social interventions—housing programs, school programs, drug programs, taxation programs—are important to study but are not

administered with random assignment. To study the effects of such innovations, we must fall back on some quasi-experimental design. Which
quasi-experimental design you choose depends on what kind of data are
available. The time-series and regression-discontinuity designs require a
large number of data points and are most easily used when studying archival data—data that have been regularly collected, like census data, annual
price index data, monthly weather reports, and so on. Although these data
were originally collected for other purposes, you can use them to test
hypotheses about the effects of new social programs. Sometimes, however,
archival data gathered for one purpose are not suitable for answering
other questions. For instance, if we wished to study the effects of a rape-
prevention program on the incidence of rape, we might try using a time-
series quasi experiment to study the effects of a new preventive program
on the number of rapes reported to the police over a 15-year period. We
would expect to find a decrease in the number after the program began.
In theory this sounds like a good time-series design with useful archival
data. In practice, the data would be difficult to interpret because the actual
incidence of rape is much higher than the number of rapes reported to
the police. The archival data, therefore, would underestimate the overall
number of rapes. Also, it is conceivable that the number of rapes reported
to the police would increase rather than decrease as a result of the program if part of the program consisted of encouraging rape victims to
report the crime.

When existing archival data are unavailable or unsuitable, a
researcher could still design a time series and gather data over a number
of weeks, months, or years. The longer it would take to gather such data,
the less likely it is that you or anyone would want to conduct a time-series
quasi experiment because it would be costly in time and effort. The advantage of the time-series design is that it includes a large number of observations to test rival explanations; the disadvantage is that it is costly to
gather so much data if they do not already exist in archives.

The same is true for the regression-discontinuity design. It is best
suited for studying social programs for which data are regularly available.
For instance, school records exist for a large cross section of students. It
is possible, therefore, to study the effects of scholarship awards or special
admissions or enrichment programs even though students are not randomly assigned to such treatments. The large number of data points available from a wide cross section of students lets you design a regression-
discontinuity study that is far better than a simple two-group static-group
comparison.

The pretest-posttest nonequivalent control group design is not so tied
to the availability of archival data. Because it requires fewer data—fewer
observation points—it is a design that you can use when you gather your
own data. It can be less costly than either of the other two quasi-experimental designs because you must locate only two groups and observe
them only twice.

Internal Validity, External Validity, and Quasi Experiments

Quasi experiments are a compromise—between a true experiment with random assignment and a pre-experiment, which is often uninterpretable. They also represent a compromise between maximizing internal validity and external validity. What true experiments achieve in drawing causal inference and maximizing internal validity they sometimes sacrifice in external validity. Laboratory experiments sometimes bear no surface similarity to the real-world phenomena they are intended to mimic, and even field experiments sometimes lose external validity simply because the subjects know they are experimental guinea pigs subject to random assignment. Quasi experiments often avoid these drawbacks. A time-series analysis of the effects of rape-prevention programs does not create guinea-pig effects because the victims are not even aware of being studied. Quasi experiments can be less intrusive than true experiments because they permit the natural selection processes to occur. People are accustomed to choosing their own treatments or being selected for treatments by some criterion measure such as scholastic promise. They are not accustomed to being randomly assigned to treatments except in the case of an announced lottery.

The subject assignment processes that quasi experiments include are the naturally occurring biased selection processes that exist in the world. These nonrandom sorting processes make it difficult for us to disentangle the treatment effects from other rival effects, particularly selection, but they also give quasi-experimental studies an element of external validity that true experiments lack. They enable us to study the effects that treatments have on that segment of the population that is most likely either to choose or to be chosen for the treatment. Not everyone would choose to attend an experimental college or enter psychotherapy or work a four-day week. For treatments like these that people are able to choose for themselves, it does not make sense to rule out the self-selecting bias that would normally exist. We would not want to assign all people randomly to some level of these treatments. We could devise a true experiment from among those people who would normally choose such treatments if we recruited more volunteers than each program could accommodate. If we randomly selected the entrants from among the self-selected applicants, we could devise a true experiment. Most people are not accustomed to entering a lottery for such programs, however, and it would require either deception or education to make a lottery acceptable. We do not advocate deception. We would like to see some public education to make lotteries possible for evaluating some programs—though this would raise people's awareness that they were guinea pigs and may thereby lower the external validity of a study.

Summary

Quasi-experimental designs provide a way to study some naturally occurring social treatments. They are a compromise between a true experiment that has high internal validity and the poor pre-experiments that have almost no internal validity at all. Quasi experiments enable us to rule out some threats to validity because they include more data points than the pre-experiments. The number of quasi-experimental designs that a creative researcher can construct is limitless. We have presented three types that are extensions of pre-experiments to show how the additional data points make a previously uninterpretable design interpretable. A determined researcher can design yet unthought-of quasi experiments by gathering data from enough subjects at enough times to rule out many threats to internal validity, so that even without random assignment, it will be possible to infer causes and effects.

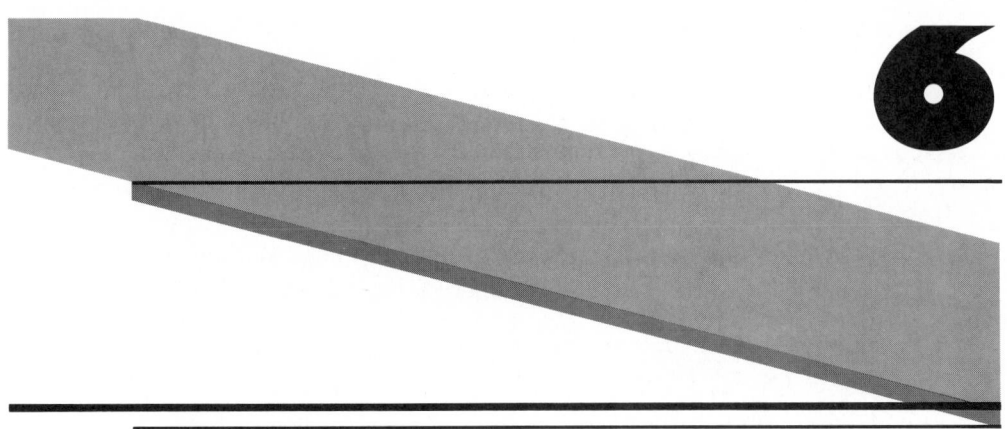

Survey Research Designs

The focus in the last two chapters has been on internal validity. That is, we have been concerned primarily with designing research that enables us to conclude that one variable causes or affects another. We have seen that we can make such causal conclusions most confidently with randomized experiments. Such experiments, however, frequently must be conducted in laboratory settings so that the researcher is precisely able to control who is exposed to the various levels of the independent variable, that is, who is in the treatment group and who is in the control group. In addition, as we have discussed, randomized experiments may be particularly subject to demand characteristics and experimenter expectancies. They may yield results that are difficult to generalize because subjects find themselves in unusual settings and search out clues, from the experimenter, about appropriate behavior.

Because of these drawbacks, researchers frequently make use of quasi experiments. Quasi experiments, as we have seen, require much less control on the part of the experimenter than do randomized experiments. As such they can be used in a wider variety of circumstances to examine the effects of independent variables that we are not able to control. With multiple observations, quasi experiments can be used to eliminate many of the threats to internal validity, although there always remain ambiguities in reaching causal conclusions from quasi-experimental designs. For instance, as we saw in the last chapter, history remains a threat to internal validity when we use the quasi-experimental design that we have called the interrupted time-series design.

As also discussed in the last chapter, a number of pre-experimental research designs have particularly poor internal validity and should generally be avoided when conclusions about the causal effect of one variable on another are important. In these pre-experimental designs we generally gather observations from subjects only a single time, and ruling out threats to internal validity is extremely difficult, if not impossible.

Nonetheless, there are a wide variety of circumstances when these pre-experimental research designs are adequate. When our primary goal in research is not to describe causal effects but rather to answer questions about the distribution of and relationships among characteristics of people as they exist in their natural settings, pre-experimental designs suffice. We might ask, for example, "What is the distribution of candidate preferences among the voting-age population of the United States?" Or "What variables are associated with differences among young people in how well they do in school or how much schooling they receive?" Or "How does family background or peer group processes relate to educational performance?" In such cases, where our primary goal is description rather than causal inference, pre-experimental research designs can be enormously useful because they are relatively easy to implement and because they permit us to gather data from people in their natural settings. Research that uses such pre-experimental designs to gather data about the distribution of variables and the relationships among variables is known as **survey research.**

In doing survey research, one collects data from all or part of a population to assess the relative incidence, distribution, and interrelations of naturally occurring phenomena (Kerlinger, 1964). The term **population** here refers to the aggregation of people to which we wish to generalize. For example, if we ask, "What is the distribution of candidate preferences among voting-age populations in the United States?" the relevant population is all potential voters in the United States. If we ask, "What accounts for differences among young people in how well they do in school?" the relevant population might be people in the American population who have reached an age beyond which they are unlikely to seek further education. The relevant population for "How do family background or peer group processes relate to educational performance?" could be the same as that for the second question. The phrase **naturally occurring phenomena** refers to the processes of life as they occur. This is in contrast to the "manipulated" variables of experiments discussed in Chapters 2 and 4. Many variables measured in surveys are what were referred to as subject variables in Chapter 4.

Survey researchers typically gather their data as verbal responses to predetermined questions asked of most or all the research subjects. This is in contrast to the unstructured interviewing done in participant observation. The participant observer's questions at one point may be determined by respondents' answers to previous questions (see Chapter 8). It is because survey respondents answer the same questions that the incidence and distribution of characteristics can be studied. In the planning of surveys, careful attention is given to both the wording of questions and the way questions are presented to repondents. These important topics are covered in Chapters 10 and 11. As survey questionnaires are planned before the data collection begins, surveys cannot explore feelings or interpretations of individual respondents in great depth as could be done in participant observation. On the other hand, the systematic data collected from each respondent allows the exploration of relationships among variables that are measured (for example, education related to income). Such relationships cannot be explored if each respondent or situation is not measured in the same way.

Some survey research attempts to go beyond the reporting of distributions and relationships to their interpretation. In some cases the researcher wants to *explain* a phenomenon in addition to describing it. For instance, the survey researcher may wish to explain what accounts for the distribution of occupations among men and women in the United States. Such attempts at explanation, because they rest on correlational rather than experimental data, are subject to the various threats to internal validity that arise when we make causal assertions. Suppose in attempting to explain what accounts for the differential distribution of occupation by sex, we discovered that males and females differed in their average level of education and further that educational achievement was related to what occupation one had. We might then be tempted to conclude that it was differences in education that accounted for differences between sexes in typical occupations. Clearly this sort of conclusion, based on survey research, is subject to a host of threats to internal validity. For instance, in addition to having different educational backgrounds, males and females receive different amounts of encouragement and face different forms of discouragement in selecting occupations.

Nevertheless, in cases like this, we may be forced to rely on the results of survey research since randomized experiments or even quasi experiments are not feasible. Randomized experiments demand that subjects be randomly assigned to levels of the independent variable. When the independent variable is sex or educational attainment, we clearly cannot use a randomized experimental design. Quasi experiments demand that we measure subjects before they are exposed to the treatment whose effects are being evaluated. How are we supposed to measure subjects' occupations before they are enrolled in school? There simply is no way. Hence, for many sorts of questions, attempts at causal explanation must rely on survey research, using pre-experimental research designs, subject to all the pitfalls of interpretation that were discussed in the last two chapters.

The wide variety of situations and purposes for the application of survey research can be seen in the following examples of its use:

1. Sociologists collect data on a representative sample of male members of the U.S. labor force to study their training and occupational attainments.
2. Public opinion polling organizations conduct studies of the popularity of various presidential candidates among potential voters.
3. Market research organizations conduct studies of smokers to find out what they want cigarettes to be like.
4. Medical researchers survey the nation's population to determine the incidence of disease-related characteristics.
5. Political scientists interview members of the U.S. House of Representatives to understand why reorganization reform was adopted.
6. A national women's magazine asks its readers to answer a questionnaire that solicits information about their occupational aspirations.
7. Political sociologists survey a sample of students in large universities to

determine whether they support or are against reinstitution of a military draft in the United States.

8. A national broadcast-rating organization (using mechanical recording devices instead of questionnaires and interviewers) measures the distribution of television watching each week.

9. A housing researcher surveys mortgage lenders to determine the proportions of their mortgage loans made in poor versus middle class and wealthy neighborhoods.

Some Survey Designs

The most straightforward design in survey research seeks to establish the incidence and distribution of characteristics or the relationships among characteristics. Where survey researchers have these limited goals, they only concern themselves with whether their study populations are representative of the populations to which they wish to generalize and that they have accurately measured the characteristics on which they wish to report. The national public opinion polling organizations like Lou Harris, Associates, and the Gallup Poll frequently conduct studies that fit this model. These organizations often are commissioned by the news media to study public reaction to current issues. For example, studies reported in the daily newspapers have covered people's views on nuclear power, the gasoline shortage, whether the military draft should be reinstituted, and what adults consider to be the most pressing problems facing the country. The report of a typical study done by one of these organizations will consist of respondents' opinions tabulated successively by such personal characteristics as race, region of the country, and kind of occupation. Although such studies require careful planning and execution, they do not raise complex problems of statistical analysis or interpretation. All data are collected in a single interview for each respondent, and very simple tabulations are presented. No explanation of *why* people hold different opinions is attempted. Such studies provide useful information about the bare essentials of public opinions and preferences.

Static-Group Comparison Designs

Where more than distributions and simple tabulations are needed, a research design must be conceptualized. A common design for survey research that attempts explanation and interpretation of relationships is very close to one of Campbell and Stanley's pre-experimental designs, the "static-group comparison":

$$
\frac{X \quad O}{\quad O}
$$

If we imagine this design with a naturally occurring X with several levels (e.g., sex—female/male; socioeconomic status—low/medium/high), it becomes the following:

$$\begin{array}{cc} X_1 & O_1 \\ \hline X_2 & O_2 \end{array}$$

The design depicts two or more comparison groups defined by their value on X. One would compare the O scores of the comparison groups to assess whether there is a relationship between X and O.

Suppose X in the preceding diagram represents occupation (blue collar, white collar) and O represents income. If the comparison groups differ in income, it is tempting to interpret this difference as the effect of occupation on income. Such an interpretation would be analogous to our interpretation of the effects of X in a randomized experiment. The difficulty with interpreting the results of a static-group comparison is the possibility that there are other differences between two occupation groups that might also affect income. Such differences are alternative plausible explanations for any differences in income between groups. There are three criteria for inferring causation: (1) that X and O covary, (2) that X precedes O in time, and (3) that there are no alternative explanations of the group differences in O. To say that two variables covary means that certain values of or levels of one variable occur with particular values of or levels of the other variable. For example, to say that education and income covary (or that they are correlated) is to say that lower levels of income tend to occur with lower levels of educational attainment and that higher levels of income tend to occur with higher levels of educational attainment. The basic correlational design of survey research can almost always meet the first of these three criteria. Readers who have taken statistics courses may recall the uncompromising dictum of statistics teachers: "Correlation does not demonstrate causation." To that truism should be added the statement that causation does imply **correlation.** Thus, the demonstration of a correlation between two variables using different populations and different research conditions certainly lends credence to a causal hypothesis involving the two variables. Each such instance is a test of the hypothesis that could disconfirm it (Campbell & Stanley, 1963, p. 234). In addition, each such instance has to be examined for plausible alternative explanations before even tentative causal interpretation is suggested.

A comment should be made about the assumption of time order in this design. It is actually the case that X and O are measured at approximately the same time; that is, each is likely to be measured by responses in a questionnaire. In this sense it cannot be said that X comes before O in time. The survey researcher must assume that X as measured in the survey has influenced the respondent as part of her or his prior life processes. Sometimes it can be determined in survey research problems that X preceded O in time. For example, for most Americans, the end of schooling comes before the beginning of their first full-time employment. If we used survey data to study the occupational attainments of American workers, we could say that, for most male Americans, educational attainment came before occupational placement. Even so, this time order does not describe part of the population. Some people who ultimately attain college degrees work on a full-time basis at a job they consider to be permanent before they attend or complete college. To the extent that respondents are not uniform regarding the ordering of education and the first job, there is ambiguity in the interpretation of the relationship between them. Such ambiguity is one reason for survey researchers to exercise caution in making causal inferences from survey research.

If one's purposes are limited to assessing the incidence or distribution of characteristics, say, the number or proportion of men and women in a given occupation, the design is perfectly adequate for providing the answer. Even when one wishes to assess the degree of covariation among variables, this design is adequate to the task. Thus, using this design, one could readily gather data from which to calculate the degree of correlation between family background measures (income, parents' educational attainments) and performance in school (grades, grade point average). It is when one wishes to go beyond the calculation of relationships to the interpretation of them that the limitations of the research design are met.

Panel Design

To meet the time order criterion for establishing causation, we can use a second common survey design, namely, the **panel survey design.** This design takes into account time and changes over time by collecting data on the X's and the O's at two or more points in time from the same subjects at each time:

Interview 1	Interview 2	$\cdots$	Interview K
$X_{11}\ X_{12}\ X_{13}\ O$	$X_{12}\ X_{13}\ O$	$\cdots$	$X_{12}\ O$
$X_{21}\ X_{22}\ X_{23}\ O$	$X_{22}\ X_{23}\ O$	$\cdots$	$X_{22}\ O$

The first of the two subscripts on the X's indicates the level of the variable, for examples, for sex, female and male. A particular variable might take on more than two values, of course. If the variable were age when first surveyed, it could take on as many values as were represented in the range of ages among the respondents surveyed. The second subscript represents the variable identification. In the preceding diagram, information on variables X_1, X_2, and X_3 was gathered on the first interview; X_2 and X_3 on the second; and so forth. What is implied in this diagram is that data on a number of X's and perhaps a number of O's are collected at a number of points in time. Some of the X's are variables whose values are not expected to change, like those of sex and race. Others are X's whose values may change for some people, as in employment status and educational attainment. Finally, some of the variables are like O's from experimental research, whose values would be expected to change where values of X's have changed, as for income level. One of the early studies of voting behavior in this country used this design to look at such X's as class background, religion, and exposure to political campaign appeals and such O's as intention to vote and candidate preference (Berelson, Lazarsfeld, & McPhee, 1954).

Studies using panel designs have come increasingly into use for following complex processes like changes in employment and changes in consumer expenditure patterns. For example, the National Longitudinal Surveys of Labor Market Experience is a study using annual or biennial interviews of several groups in the U.S. population. Different groups are being studied because they encounter different kinds of labor market problems. "For the two cohorts of youth, these problems revolve around the process of occupational choice, and include both the preparation for work and the frequently difficult period of accommodation to the labor market and when formal schooling has been completed. The special problems of the middle-aged men stem in part from skill obsolescence, from the increasing incidence of health problems, and from employment discrimination, all of which are reflected in declining labor force participation rates and in longer-than-average duration of unemployment, if it occurs. For the women, the special labor market problems are those associated with re-entry into the labor force by married women who feel that their children no longer require their continuous presence at home" (Center for Human Resource Research, 1977). This study is funded by the U.S. Department of Labor and is intended to provide a basis for understanding more general issues affecting workers in the U.S. labor force as well as the specific problems facing the groups being studied. Even questions that were not part of the original study design can be included in the annual reinterviews to give flexibility to the research design. Some of the results of the continuing study are used by policy makers in the Department of Labor to formulate changes in the economic policies of the federal government and to evaluate present policies.

Another panel study with comparable national scope and importance is the Panel Study of Income Dynamics carried out by the Institute for Survey Research at the University of Michigan (Morgan et al., 1974–79). Based on annual interviews with 5000 American families, this study has collected economic and social data on families and their individual members since 1969. The study has produced massive amounts of data, including information on such things as short-run and long-run unemployment, work hours of family heads, use of food stamps, home ownership, residential mobility, child care, shifting family composition, taxation, income inequality, trends in food expenditure, and the economic effects of higher gasoline prices. Like the National Longitudinal Survey of Labor Market Experience, the Panel Study of Income Dynamics is funded by federal government agencies who are interested in the data to help them make and evaluate economic policy.

In panel design surveys special kinds of detailed analyses of changes in the level of some of the variables can generate useful insights about change processes. However, ruling out alternative hypotheses remains problematic. There are two major problems. First, it may be that the time between interviews in the panel study does not correspond to the time period necessary to tell whether one variable affected another. For example, suppose one were reinterviewing at one-year intervals and found that both consumer debt (for the purchase of a new car) and the number of adults from the household who are employed had increased since the last interview. It would not be clear whether the additional household member had gone to work so that they could buy a new car or whether the new car had been purchased to allow the household member to go to work (or, perhaps, both). The second problem is that there may be other important differences between comparison groups defined by the X's that have not been taken into account.

Cross-Sectional, Pseudopanel Design

Sometimes survey researchers are unable to gather data by using a panel design, but they nonetheless have a definite idea about which variables precede which others in temporal sequence. They then may gather all their data at the same time, or cross-sectionally, but act as if those data had been gathered longitudinally. Such a pseudopanel design can be represented as follows:

$$X_{11}\ X_{12}\ X_{13}\ X_{14}\ X_{15}$$
$$X_{21}\ X_{22}\ X_{23}\ X_{24}\ X_{25}$$
$$\cdot$$
$$\cdot$$
$$\cdot$$
$$X_{i1}\ X_{i2}\ X_{i3}\ X_{i4}\ X_{i5}$$

As always, X's stand for measured variables. The first subscript represents different survey respondents or groups of respondents who are expected to differ, and the second subscript represents the presumed temporal ordering of the variables. A number of variables may be presumed to occupy the first temporal position. Similarly, at later times in the pseudopanel (in other words, values of the second subscript greater than 1), there also may be numerous variables. That is, variables having a second subscript of 1 are presumed to have "happened" earliest, even though all variables regardless of their subscripts have been measured at the same time. Variables having a second subscript of 2 are presumed to have "happened" somewhat later, and so forth.

An example will clarify this design. Blau and Duncan (1967) studied the effects of a large number of variables on the level of occupational placement of American males during the early and middle 1900s. Their theory placed the key variables in a time-ordered sequence as depicted in Table 6.1. This table presents an interpretation of their theory that was derived from the data analysis presented in their book. The first set of variables (the X_{i1}'s) summarizes influences on the lives of young men before they begin to make the crucial decisions that determine how much education they will receive and what kind of work they expect to do as adults. Next come the respondents' educational attainments (the X_{i2}'s). The next two variables are the prestige level of the respondents' first jobs and their marital status at that time (the X_{i3}'s). Finally come the prestige level of the respondents' 1962 jobs and their places of residence in 1962 (the X_{i4}'s). Blau and Duncan argued that family background determined educational level and that family background and educational attainment together determined level of attainment in the first job. They further

TABLE 6.1 Theoretical Time Sequence of Variables Measured in a Pseudopanel Design

X_{i1}'s	Race, ethnicity Sex Father's education Type of school attended before age 16 Birth order and number of siblings Composition of respondent's family when he was 16 Size of city of residence when he was 16 Decade respondent was 16 Oldest brother's educational level Father's occupation when respondent was 16
X_{i2}	Respondent's educational level
X_{i3}'s	Respondent's first job Respondent's marital status
X_{i4}'s	Respondent's residence in 1962 Respondent's job in 1962

SOURCE: P. M. Blau and O. D. Duncan, *The American Occupational Structure* (New York: Wiley, 1967).

argued that family background, educational attainment, and the first job determined level of occupational attainment at the time of their study (1962). In none of their analyses were independent variables manipulated, or for that matter, manipulatable. Their research was aimed at discovering and understanding the patterns of educational and occupational attainments of males in the U.S. labor force over the first half of the twentieth century. It is hard to imagine how any important part of that process could have been studied in the laboratory under experimental conditions.

In the preceding pages we have outlined the most common models in survey research. The survey researcher seeks to understand and generalize from "natural" processes that have occurred (e.g., educational or occupational attainment) or are occurring (e.g., a preelection opinion poll). Frequently, the processes of interest occur over the course of a generation or several generations. A multitude of influences, recognized and unrecognized, many impinge on the processes being studied. This is in contrast to the situation faced by experimental researchers who, with laboratory isolation and control over exposure to stimuli, can greatly simplify the influences affecting the processes they study.

Introduction to Survey Analysis

Survey research covers a broader range of purposes than experimental and quasi-experimental research. In these kinds of research, the major problem is to establish whether X caused Y. Whereas most social research, including surveys, aims at establishing the kind of understanding of social processes that ultimately will lead to general laws explaining the processes, much survey research is aimed at establishing facts and relationships prior to the elaboration of causal laws. In many cases survey research is aimed at establishing whether X and Y covary or under what conditions they covary. To take an example, the studies of voting behavior in the United States conducted at the University of Michigan Survey Research Center (A. Campbell et al., 1954, 1960, 1966) have, as a total research program, generated a wealth of understanding about the attitudes, social processes, and structural conditions affecting political behavior in the United States. No one of the many studies that has been part of that research program constitutes a test of whether X caused Y. Clearly, however, the aim of the program is to establish the causes of voting choice—party identification, support for extremist candidates and third parties, and so on.

Assessing the internal validity of such a program of research is a complex task. Many of the specific pieces of research in that program were aimed at establishing that socioeconomic status (SES) and party identification covary, assessing what the conditions are under which they covary, whether they covary with other relevant variables taken into account, and so on. Where the intention is merely to establish relationships and to establish the conditions under which they hold, internal validity is not an issue. As the pieces of research are put together to go beyond just establishing relationships to interpreting them, internal validity becomes an issue. Internal validity of research conclusions may be more meaningfully assessed in reviewing an area of research than in reviewing individual pieces of research. However, internal validity cannot be established on the basis of individual pieces of research that themselves have no validity. Statistical control is a strategy for enhancing the internal validity of individual pieces of research.

Statistical Control

To rule out alternative explanations of variation or change in the dependent variable, survey researchers use statistical procedures. For example, suppose we found, by examining records of fires in some city (note that surveys don't have to be of people!), that there is a positive and strong relationship between the number of fire trucks called to a fire and the amount of damage in dollars resulting from the fire (i.e., the more trucks, the higher the monetary damage). Does this correlation represent a causal connection between trucks and cost of damage? Your intuition would probably tell you that it does not, but let us examine the situation closely. First, we do have a situation where X and Y covary. Second, one could argue that in modern times, when fire insurance requirements for urban fire coverage demand that every covered building by reachable by fire equipment within a specified time limit after an alarm, trucks arrive before the damage is done. (We wouldn't want the reader to reject our point on the basis of disagreement with this dubious assumption.) Thus, the time precedence of a possible causal relationship is satisfied. The most problematic question is whether there are alternative explanations of the observed correlation, such as the effects of a third variable. One such variable is the size of the fire. Figure 6.1 depicts these two alternative explanations. Alternative A says the number of fire trucks present is the cause of the monetary damage. Alternative B suggests the following three propositions:

1. The severity of fires determines how much damage is done.
2. The severity of fires determines how many fire trucks are called to the scene.
3. These two propositions taken together imply that there will be a correlation between amount of damage and number of fire trucks called.

Intuition compels us to prefer alternative B. A statistical procedure can help us decide whether our intuition is supported by evidence. The pro-

A. number of fire trucks ⟶ amount of monetary damage

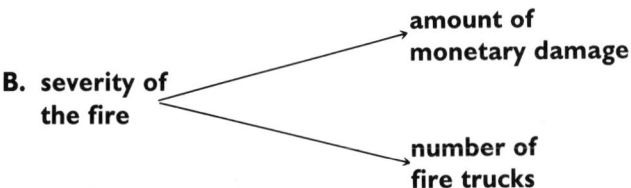

**B. severity of
   the fire**

amount of
monetary damage

number of
fire trucks

FIGURE 6.1 Two explanations of the relationship between number of trucks at fires and the amount of damage done by the fires

cedure is to examine the relationship between number of trucks and amount of damage while taking into account the severity of fires. One way to do this would be to classify fires into two categories, those that are of average or less severity and those that are greater than average in severity. We then calculate the relationship between number of trucks and amount of damage for fires classified as less severe and for those classified as more severe. If alternative B is correct, there should be very little relationship between trucks and damage when the severity of the fire is taken into account. This is because most of the fires with few trucks and little damage should be among those that are of less severity. Likewise, most of the fires with many trucks and lots of damage should be among those of greater severity. The same point is illustrated in Figure 6.2.

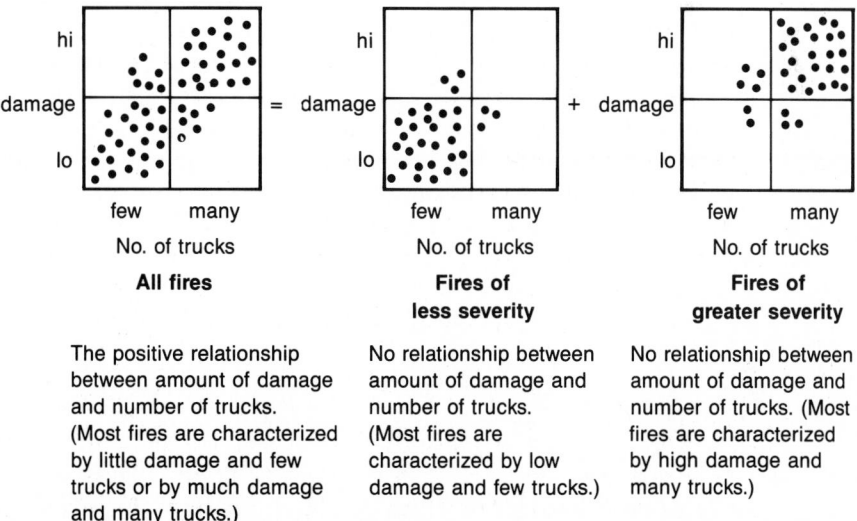

All fires	**Fires of less severity**	**Fires of greater severity**
The positive relationship between amount of damage and number of trucks. (Most fires are characterized by little damage and few trucks or by much damage and many trucks.)	No relationship between amount of damage and number of trucks. (Most fires are characterized by low damage and few trucks.)	No relationship between amount of damage and number of trucks. (Most fires are characterized by high damage and many trucks.)

FIGURE 6.2 Controlling for severity of fires to reduce a positive relationship between amount of damage and number of trucks called to fires—hypothetical data

A correlation like that between number of trucks and amount of damage is called a **spurious correlation** because it does *not* represent a direct causal connection between the variables. Calling a correlation "spurious" does not imply that it does not exist or that it has a value of zero. It means the correlation is created by the common dependence of the variables on an antecedent variable. The correlation simply does not represent a direct causal connection between the two variables. In survey analysis, before we can assert causal connection between two variables, we must be sure their correlation is not spurious. To do this, we take into account other variables that could cause a spurious correlation. In our preceding example, severity of fire was an uncontrolled third variable: When we took it into account, it became a controlled variable, and it explained the spurious correlation.

Examining correlations between variables and what happens to those correlations as third variables are controlled is the central procedure for analyzing data from survey research. This process has been called **elaboration** (Glock, 1967; Kendall & Lazarsfeld, 1950; Lazarsfeld & Rosenberg, 1955). Only by going through this process can we begin to seek explanations for the relationships we observe in survey data. In Chapters 14 and 15 we explain in much greater detail the steps involved in analyzing survey data and detecting spurious relationships. There, we show how the tables presented in Figure 6.2 are derived and how we compute indices from the tables to assess the extent to which two variables are correlated.

There are two important points from the preceding discussion that ought to be underlined. First, although surveys, based on pre-experimental research designs, are unlikely to be as internally valid as randomized or quasi experiments, they nevertheless are extremely important research tools. For many kinds of variables and relationships, they may be the only feasible research design. So in spite of the difficulties of reaching conclusions about causal effects from survey data, it may nevertheless be important to try to do just that.

In this chapter and the previous two we have described a series of research designs that represent a continuum in their susceptability to threats to internal validity. As we have seen, randomized experiments are the least susceptible to such threats. Ouasi experiments come next, followed by survey research designs. Because surveys generally involve pre-experimental research designs, their internal validity is particularly poor. At the same time, however, through survey research we are often able to gather data and conduct interviews with subjects and in settings where randomized experimental and quasi-experimental designs are not feasible. As a result, we may be in a stronger position to generalize our results based on survey data than on experimental or quasi-experimental research. In other words, although surveys generally have lower internal validity than do randomized experiments and quasi experiments, they may be more externally valid. In surveys it is often easier to collect data from randomly drawn samples of subjects instead of from captive volunteers, who are our usual subjects in laboratory experimental research. In this sense, then, this chapter forms a bridge with the next two, where we consider procedures for increasing the external validity of social relations research. Although survey research may be criticized for its internal validity, it is often the only feasible research to be done when generalization to a population and across diverse settings is desired.

Second, the process of elaboration can indeed be useful in discriminating among causal hypotheses with survey data. As a result, although survey data may not be as internally valid as data generated from experimental and quasi-experimental research designs, they nevertheless can be useful in discriminating among competing causal hypotheses through the process of controlling for third variables that may induce spurious correlations. Ultimately, however, the success of this endeavor depends on whether we have chosen the right third variables to examine as controls. We must have hypotheses or hunches about the variables that may be most responsible for causing a spurious relationship in the data we observe, and we must have the foresight to have measured those variables. Ultimately, therefore, the success of elaboration, or of explaining relationships in survey data, depends on the strength of the theory that guides the research. No amount of survey data, in the absence of good theory, can ultimately enable us to figure out why it is that we observe relationships between the things we measure.

Summary

The strength of survey research lies in answering questions of fact and in assessing the distributions of the characteristics of populations. In uses of this kind, issues of internal validity are not raised, and hence the pre-experimental research designs that are typically used do not cause problems. There are no causal inferences to be made. Because survey designs lend themselves easily to extensive data collection over large geographical areas, they typically obtain data that are more externally valid than data gathered in laboratory settings. Sampling procedures to enhance external validity are more easily implemented in survey research than in experimental research. Likewise, many naturally occurring phenomena can be observed in survey research, whereas those same phenomena might not be amenable to experimental simulation and manipulation.

When the aims of survey research are broadened to include interpretation and causal analysis of correlations, internal validity becomes important. Because survey research deals primarily with naturally occurring variables that cannot be randomly assigned and manipulated, both the time order of occurrence and alternative explanations of relationships become problematic. On the other hand, many interesting and important social science research problems are not amenable to simulation in the laboratory. No experimentally oriented social scientist has yet found a way to simulate the lifetime effects of being reared in poverty versus wealth, of being born female versus male, of being born a black American versus a white American, or of having high versus low education. Where processes such as occupational attainment take place over a lifetime, they cannot reasonably be studied by research techniques other than survey.

Many of the research areas where survey research is the logical choice are areas where the researcher wishes to make causal inferences. Such inferences can never be made with the same certainty as in some experimental research. Certain strategies can be employed to enhance the internal validity of survey research, however. In some research problems, the time order of variables can be determined by collecting data over a period of time. In other research problems, alternative hypotheses can be rendered less tenable through statistical controls. The internal and external validity of *research programs* or long traditions of research can more readily be assessed than the results of single instances of survey research.

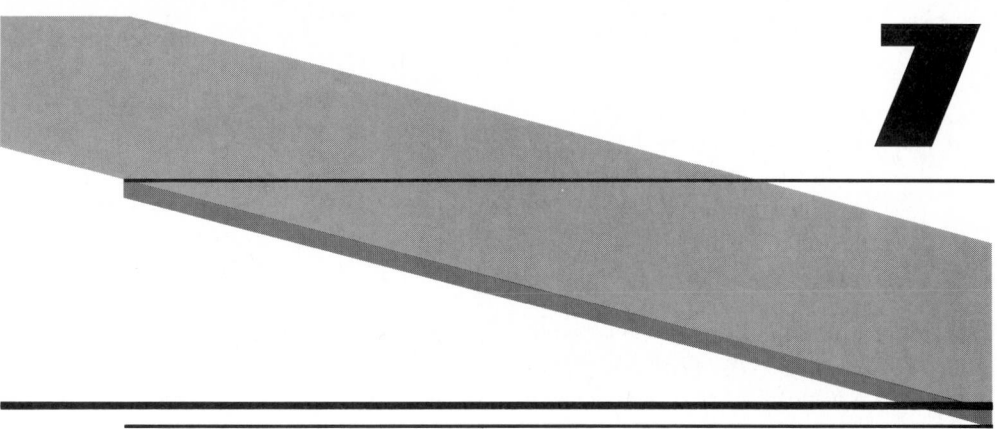

7

An Introduction to Sampling

In every piece of research a crucial issue is whether the conclusions can be generalized beyond the immediate settings and samples that have been studied. In the second chapter we labeled this issue *external validity*. A piece of research that has high external validity is one from which we can confidently generalize the results to the population and settings that are of theoretical interest.

The purpose of this chapter and the next one is to provide an introduction to procedures that can be used to increase the external validity of a piece of research. In this chapter we give a nontechnical introduction to sampling: We show how the process of selecting a sample from a population affects the degree to which generalizations to the population can be confidently made. This chapter is not a manual of sampling procedures, nor does it review the statistical theory that underlies much of what we know about sampling. Rather the goal is to provide a sufficient introduction to the topic so that you can appreciate the considerations involved in sampling. In Chapter 8 we discuss a kind of research, called **participant observation**, in which we study people in their natural settings so we can more confidently reach conclusions about those settings and conditions that we are most interested in.

A few general remarks about external validity may be helpful here, before we plunge into the details of sampling and participant observation. The first point to be made is really a reiteration of one already made in Chapter 2. A necessary condition for external validity is that the hypothesis or theory that motivates the research must specify the theoretically desired limits of generalization. That is, before we can ever worry about generalization, we need to know beforehand to whom and where we want to be able to generalize. If a theory or hypothesis is vague about populations or settings of interest to which generalization is sought, all the techniques discussed in this chapter and the next are not very useful.

Second, there are times when external validity is very important and there are other times when it is less important. In most survey research, external validity is quite important. For instance, a national public opinion polling organization that conducts a survey to estimate the proportion of voters who favor one candidate or another in an election is naturally very concerned about external validity. It is not efficient for this organization to interview all voters, and hence only a relatively small sample of voters is surveyed. Whether or not the sample is well chosen affects the success of the entire enterprise. On the other hand, for most laboratory experimental research in psychology, for instance, external validity may not be that important. When one conducts randomized experiments, one is usually quite concerned about internal validity, for that is the strong suit of randomized experimental research designs. Based on this concern, every effort is made to control extraneous variables that might affect the results. That is why randomized experiments are frequently conducted in laboratories. But not everyone is interested in spending his or her time coming to a laboratory to be a subject in research. Hence, experimental researchers must frequently make do with whatever subjects are available. For instance, subjects may come from a pool of students who must participate in research as a course requirement. Because of the researcher's primary focus on internal validity, it may not be possible to engage in the kind of sampling procedures that lead to externally valid research.

In addition, many experimental psychologists would argue that external validity need not be an important consideration for their work because they are studying basic psychological processes—like memory, attention, or how the perceptual systems work—that are universal phenomena. In other words, experimental psychologists might argue that subjects' characteristics (things such as their age or sex or educational background) do not affect how memory works or how the eye codes colors. If this is the case, studying a few subjects, regardless of their characteristics, may be all that is necessary. Elaborate sampling plans to ensure external validity may serve little purpose.

As we have argued earlier, in doing research a variety of purposes can be served. For some purposes, internal validity may be crucially important. For other purposes, as illustrated by political polling, external validity may demand the utmost attention. The relative priority of the various research validities depends on what you are trying to accomplish.

Having made these points, we are now ready to begin our introduction to sampling. This chapter is organized in three parts. First we provide some basic definitions and concepts that will be used throughout. Then the remaining two sections are devoted to two fundamentally different kinds of sampling: nonprobability and probability.

Some Basic Definitions and Concepts

A **population** is the aggregate of *all* the cases that conform to some designated set of specifications. Thus, by the specifications *people* and *residing in the United States*, we define a population consisting of *all* the people who reside in the United States. We may similarly define populations consisting of *all* the shop stewards in a factory, *all* the households in a particular city district, *all* the boys in a given community under 16 years of age who deliver newspapers, or *all* the case records in a file.

By certain specifications, one population may be included in another. Thus, the population consisting of all the *men* residing in the United States is included in the population consisting of all the *people* who live in the United States. In such instances, we may refer to the included population as a *subpopulation*, a *population stratum*, or simply as a **stratum** (pl. *strata*). A stratum may be defined by one or more specifications that divide a population into mutually exclusive segments. For instance, a given population may be subdivided into strata consisting of males under 21 years of age, females under 21 years of age, males from 21 through 59 years old, and so on. Similarly, we may specify a stratum of the U.S. population consisting of white, male, college graduates who live in New England and who have passed their 75th birthday; or we may have some reason for regarding this group of individuals as a population in its own right—that is, without reference to the fact that it is included in a larger population.

A single member of a population is referred to as a population *element*. We often want to known how certain characteristics of the elements are distributed in a population. For example, we may want to know the age distribution of the elements, or we may want to know the proportion of the elements who prefer one political candidate to another. A **census** is a count of all the elements in a population and/or a determination of the distributions of their characteristics, based on information obtained for each of the elements.

It is generally much more economical in time, effort, and money to get the desired information for only some of the elements rather than for all. When we select some of the elements with the intention of finding out something about the population from which they are taken, we refer to that group of elements as a **sample.** We hope, of course, that what we find out about the sample is true of the population as a whole. Actually, this may or may not be the case; how closely the information we receive corresponds to what we would find by a comparable census of the population depends largely on the way the sample is selected.

For example, we may want to know what proportion of a population prefers one candidate to another. We might ask 100 people from that population which candidate they prefer. The proportion of the sample preferring Jones may or may not be the same as the corresponding proportion in the population. For that matter, even the actual distribution of votes in an election may not correctly represent the distribution of preferences in the population. Unless there is a 100 percent turnout, the actual voters constitute only a sample of the population of people eligible to vote. A very high proportion of the people who prefer Smith may be overconfident with respect to their candidate's chances and neglect to come to the polls; or they may be living in a rural area and be discouraged from coming to the polls by a heavy downpour. The election results may properly determine which candidate will take office, but they will not necessarily indicate which candidate is preferred by a majority of the population.[1]

[1] It has been a common practice to predict the outcome of an election on the basis of a preelection sample survey, which at best answered only the question of preferences. The results have occasionally been disastrous. The fiascos are by no means attributable simply to the failure of the samples to represent the distribution of preferences in the population

Similarly, the early returns in an election may be taken as a sample of the population of returns; and as everyone knows, they can be thoroughly deceptive.

In the case of elections and in the case of early returns in a national election, there probably is not much we can do to guarantee that the samples will correctly represent their populations. We usually accept on faith that the outcome of an election does reflect the popular will. And if we are misled by the early returns with respect to the final outcome, then at least our errors are soon corrected. There are, however, situations in which we can to some extent control the properties of the sample. In these situations, the way we go about drawing the sample can, if not guarantee, then at least increase the likelihood that the sample returns will not be too far from the true population figures for our purposes. We can never guarantee that the sample returns do reflect the population for the characteristics we are studying unless we have simultaneously conducted a complete comparable census. We can, however, devise sampling plans, which if properly executed can guarantee that if we were to repeat a study on a number of different samples selected from a given population, our findings would not differ from the true population figures by more than a specified amount in more than a specified proportion of the samples.

For instance, suppose that we frequently want to know what percentage of the population agrees with certain statements. On each of these occasions we might put such a statement to a sample, compute the per-

---

at the time the polls were taken. In one instance (the U.S. presidential election of 1948), the preelection surveys showed that a large proportion of people were undecided, and there are clear indications that an unanticipated consolidation of opinion in this group helped to confound the predictors. As already indicated in the text, the fact that different proportions of those who prefer different candidates may actually vote complicates the translation of preference estimates into election forecasts.

There are also measurement problems involved. Preferences measured one way may or may not correspond to preferences measured another way. Thus, behavior in the voting booth does not necessarily correspond to preferences expressed to an interviewer. The former is generally accepted at face value as the more valid measure, but we have no certainty that this is the case. An 18-year-old voting for the first time may, for instance, follow his or her parents' preference rather than his or her own, at the last moment, and it is possible that there may be enough of such instances to affect materially the outcome of an election. Similarly, other kinds of subjectively felt pressures or momentary impulses may take effect in the election booth. Practical politicians seem to feel that the position of their candidate's name on the ballot affects his or her chances, as do the names of other candidates running for other offices on the same ticket; such effects may have a bearing on voting behavior without affecting preferences.

Further complications arise from the gerrymandering of election districts and other factors (e.g., the electoral college system), which have the effect of giving different voters different weights in determining the outcome of an election. Perhaps the moral of this footnote will be clear: The usefulness of findings obtained from a sample may depend in large measure on factors that are extraneous to the sampling issues per se. Nor is it easy to draw a hard and fast dividing line between the factors that are extraneous and those that are not. Thus, what is extraneous to the sampling of one population (e.g., eligible voters) may be intrinsic to the sampling of another (actual voters); the ambiguity arises when we sample one population with the intention of learning something about the other.

centage who agree, and take this result as an estimate of the proportion of the population who agree. We can devise a number of sampling plans that will carry the insurance that our estimates will not differ from the corresponding true population figures by, say, more than 5 percent on more than, say, 10 percent of these occasions; the estimates will be correct within 5 percentage points (the **margin of error** or *limit of accuracy*) 90 percent of the time (the probability or confidence level). We can similarly devise a number of sampling plans that will produce correct results within 2 percentage points 99 percent of the time or within any other limits of accuracy and any assigned probability. In practice, of course, we do not repeat the same study on an indefinite number of samples drawn from the same population. But our knowledge of what would happen in repeated studies enables us to say that with a given sample, there is, say, a 90 percent probability that our figures are within 5 percentage points of those that would be shown by a census of the total population using the same measures. Having set our level of aspiration for accuracy and confidence in the findings, we would select from the available alternatives the sampling plan that could be most economically carried through. Needless to say, the higher the level of aspiration, other conditions being equal, the higher the cost of the operation.

A sampling plan that carries such insurance may be referred to as a *representative sampling plan*. Note that in this usage the word *representative* does not qualify *sample* but *sampling plan*. What a representative sampling plan can do is to ensure that the odds are great enough so that the selected sample is, for the purposes at hand, sufficiently representative of the population to justify our running the risk of taking it as representative.

The use of such a sampling plan is not the only kind of insurance that can decrease the likelihood of misleading sample findings. Another involves taking steps to guarantee the inclusion in the sample of diverse elements of the population and to make sure (either by controlling the proportions of the various types of elements or by analytical procedures in the handling of data) that they are taken account of in the proportions in which they occur in the population. We shall consider this type of insurance at greater length in our discussion of quota sampling and of stratified random sampling.

It should perhaps be emphasized that the dependability[2] of survey findings is affected not only by the sampling plan and the faithfulness with which it is carried out but also by the measurement procedures used. This is one reason why sample surveys of a large population can, in practice, produce more dependable results on some matters than can a census. There simply are not enough highly skilled interviewers available to get anything beyond the most superficial information in a national census; a

[2]Throughout this chapter, the terms *accuracy, dependability,* and *precision* are used interchangeably. Although technical distinctions are sometimes made among these words, in most discussions of sampling they are used as synonyms.

survey on a smaller scale puts less of a drain on the available supply of interviewers and also more readily permits a relatively intensive training program. Similarly, a smaller-scale survey may make it economically feasible to spend more time with each respondent and, hence, make it possible to use measurement devices that could not be seriously considered for a census of a large population.[3]

The basic distinction in modern sampling theory is between **probability** and **nonprobability** sampling. The essential characteristic of probability sampling is that one can specify for each element of the population the probability that it will be included in the sample. In the simplest case, each of the elements has the same probability of being included, but this is not a necessary condition. What is necessary is that for each element there must be some specifiable probability that it will be included. This point will be considered more fully in connection with the discussions of simple random samples and stratified random samples. In nonprobability sampling, there is no way to estimate the probability each element has of being included in the sample and no assurance that every element has *some* chance of being included.

Probability sampling is the only approach that makes possible representative sampling plans. It makes it possible for the investigators to estimate the extent to which the findings based on their sample are likely to differ from what they would have found by studying the population. Conversely, if they use probability sampling, they can specify the size of the sample (or the sizes of various components of complex samples) that they will need if they want to have a given degree of certainty that their sample findings do not differ by more than a specified amount from those that a study of the total population would yield.

The major advantages of nonprobability sampling are convenience and economy—advantages that may outweigh the risks involved in not using probability sampling. Precise comparisons of the relative costs of the two approaches to sampling are, however, not available. Moreover, the comparative costs will vary depending on the number of surveys contemplated. Thus, if a number of surveys of the same population are to be carried out, the cost of preparing and maintaining lists from which to sample (generally a necessary step in probability sampling) can be distributed over all of them.

---

[3]There is another reason why sampling surveys may produce more dependable information than censuses. In practice, no census ever reaches all the population elements; in effect, what is supposed to be a census is actually a sample, albeit a sample that includes a very high porportion of the population elements. If the unreached elements differ markedly from those that are reached, the result may be quite different from the true population value even though the unreached elements may be a relatively small proportion of the population. Not all those unreached are inaccessible; they vary along a continuum of accessibility, depending on the amount one is prepared to invest in trying to reach them. In a relatively small-scale survey, one may be able to afford a greater investment in trying to reach the comparatively inaccessible elements.

Major forms of nonprobability samples are accidental samples, quota samples, and purposive samples. Major forms of probability samples are simple random samples, stratified random samples, and various types of cluster samples.[4]

Nonprobability Sampling

Accidental Samples

In accidental sampling, one simply reaches out and takes the cases that are at hand, continuing the process until the sample reaches a designated size. Thus, one may take the first hundred people one meets on the street who are willing to be interviewed. Or a college professor, wanting to make some generalization about college students, studies the students in his or her classes. Or a television station, wanting to know how "the people" feel about a given issue, interviews conveniently available shoppers, store clerks, barbers, and others who are presumed to reflect public opinion. There is no known way (other than by doing a parallel study with a probability sample or with a complete census) of evaluating the biases[5] introduced in such samples. If one uses an accidental sample, one can only hope that one is not being too grossly misled.

Quota Samples

Quota sampling (sometimes misleadingly referred to as "representative" sampling) adds insurance of the second type referred to earlier—provisions to guarantee the inclusion of diverse elements of the population and to make sure that they are taken account of in the proportions in which they occur in the population. Consider an extreme case: Suppose that we are sampling from a population with equal numbers of males and females and that there is a sharp difference between the two sexes in the characteristic we wish to measure. If we did not interview any females, the

---

[4]The reader should be warned that *accidental sampling* and *random sampling* are technical terms, as defined in the text. The words *accidental* and *random* may have quite different connotations in ordinary, everyday usage. These meanings should not be confused with those assumed in the technical usage. Thus, it may be no "accident" (everyday usage) that a sampler picks the cases he or she does in an "accidental sample" (technical usage). In everyday usage a "random sample" may not connote any nonpurposive sample or what is technically defined as an accidental sample. The justification of the technical usage would take us too far afield and will not be attempted here.

[5]*Bias* refers to the difference between the *average of the estimates* of a population value that would be obtained from a very large number of samples selected by a given procedure and the *actual* population value, assuming identical measurement processes.

results of the survey would almost certainly be an extremely misleading picture of the total population. In actuality, females and minority-group members are frequently underrepresented in accidental samples. In anticipation of such possible differences among subgroups, the quota sampler seeks to guarantee the inclusion in the sample of enough cases from each stratum.

As commonly described, the basic goal of quota sampling is the selection of a sample that is a replica of the population to which one wants to generalize—hence the notion that it "represents" that population. If it is known that the population has equal numbers of males and females, the interviewers are instructed to interview equal numbers of males and females. If it is known that 10 percent of the population lies within a particular age range, assignments are given to the interviewers to assure that 10 percent of the sample will fall within that age range.

The question of the kinds of characteristics that must be taken into account will be considered in more detail in the course of our discussion of stratified random sampling. It is enough, for the moment, to say that in the sampling of preferences, opinions, and attitudes, experience indicates that it is wise to take into account such bases of stratification as age, sex, education, geographical region of residence, socioeconomic status, and ethnic background. Not all these are equally visible; the usual practice is to *set* the quotas for the interviewers in regard to the more manifest traits and to get information in the course of the interviews on the less manifest ones. The latter information permits correction of the inadequacies of the sample by adjustments introduced during analysis, a procedure that will be illustrated in the following paragraphs. It also calls attention to omissions, if any should occur, of important segments of the population.

It often happens, in practice, that the various components of the sample turn out not to be in the same proportions as the corresponding strata are in the population. The interviewers may not have carried out their instructions exactly; instead of interviewing equal numbers of males and females, 55 percent of the people they interviewed may have been males. Disproportions between the sample and the population are most likely to occur, of course, in the less manifest traits that have not been included as part of the specifications for the interviewers' quotas. Suppose it is known that in a given population, 40 percent have not gone beyond grammar school; suppose, however, that only 20 percent of the people interviewed fall in this category. The inadequacy in the sample can be corrected in the analysis by weighting the different strata on the basis of their proportions in the population. This may be done by multiplying or dividing the obtained results by the appropriate figure.

Let us say that the total sample consisted of 1,000 persons, of whom 800 had attended college and 200 had not. Suppose we asked this sample whether they had seen a certain television program, and they responded as follows:

	No College	Some College Attendance	Total
Yes	20	400	420
No	180	400	580
Total	200	800	1000

In other words, one-tenth of the people without a college education and half of those with such education said they had seen the program. If we wished simply to report the figures for the educational groups separately, no adjustment would be needed. But if we wanted to estimate the proportion of the total population that had seen the program, our sample findings would be misleading. The program had been seen by 42 percent of the people in our sample. But our sample underrepresented people in the lower educational category and overrepresented those with a college education. To derive an estimate of the correct figure for the total population, we must calculate what the responses would have been if 40 percent of the people in the sample had had only a high school education and 60 percent had at least attended college (the proportions we have assumed for the population). One way of doing this is to multiply the responses of the no-college group by two (to bring the 20 percent in the sample up to 40 percent) and of the college group by three-fourths (to reduce the 80 percent to 60 percent). This would give 40 yeses in the no-college group and 300 in the college group, or 340 for the total group; thus we would estimate that 34 percent of the population had seen the program, rather than the 42 percent we would have estimated if we have not weighted the strata.

From this example it should be clear that the critical requirement in quota sampling is not that the various population strata be sampled in their correct proportions, but rather that there be enough cases from each stratum to make possible an estimate of the population stratum value, and that we know (or can estimate with reasonable accuracy) the proportion each stratum constitutes in the total population. If these conditions are met, the estimates of the values for the various strata can be combined to give an estimate of the total population value.

However, despite these precautions in the selection of the sample and the corrections in the analysis, quota sampling remains basically similar to the earlier described accidental sampling procedure. The part of the sample in any particular class constitutes an accidental sample of the corresponding stratum of the population. The males in the sample are an accidental sample of the males in the population; the 20-to-40-year-olds in the sample constitute an accidental sample of the 20-to-40-year-olds in the population. If the instructions received by the interviewers and their execution of these instructions produce correct proportions of the compound classes (e.g., white males in the 20 to 40 age range), the sample cases in these classes are still accidental samples of the corresponding compound strata in the population. The total sample is thus an accidental sample.

There is by now, however, enough experience with quota sampling to make it possible to minimize the risks of at least certain types of unfortunate accidents. It is known that interviewers, left to their own devices, are especially prone to certain pitfalls. They will interview their friends in excessive proportion. But their friends are likely to be rather similar in many respects to themselves. Now consider the possibility that in certain matters, people who do interviewing and others like them are atypical of the population at large. If these matters are included in the survey, the sample results are likely to be inaccurate. Once we are aware of the danger, however, we can take steps to discourage the practice.

If interviewers fill their quotas by stopping passersby and inviting them to be interviewed, they will tend to concentrate on areas where there are large numbers of potential respondents: the entertainment centers of cities, college campuses, business districts, bus and air terminals, entrances of large department stores and factories. Such samples will overrepresent the kind of people who tend to gravitate to these areas. A concentration on many varieties of such areas will presumably be better than a concentration on only one, but even so, such samples will underrepresent the kind of people who seldom leave their immediate neighborhoods and especially those who seldom leave their homes. Often this will make no difference, but it is conceivable that on some matters at some times, there may be sharp differences between the overrepresented and the underrepresented population segments. When this is the case such a sample would, of course, yield misleading results. Again, to be forewarned is to be forearmed.

If the interviewers fill their quotas by home visits, they will tend to proceed along lines of convenience and striking appearance. Thus, concentrating on certain times of the day, they will tend to miss the kind of people who are not at home at such times (e.g., working men and women during the daytime). Similarly, they will tend to avoid the upper stories of buildings without elevator service! They will tend to favor corner buildings and to avoid dilapidated buildings and buildings situated behind others. Such sampling tends to build in a systematic socioeconomic bias (i.e., in each residential area to overrepresent those people living in nicer-looking homes) and possibly other biases as well.

The point to be noted about selective factors such as these is that they are not easily corrected during the analysis of the data. For many populations we know in advance the true relative proportions of the two sexes and of the various age groups and so can correct for disproportions in the sample, but what true proportion of what definable population is most likely to be found at an airport terminal during the course of a survey? The major control investigators have available in connection with such variables is in the sampling process itself. They can try to make sure that important segments of the population are not entirely unrepresented in their sample, try to benefit from their experience and sample in such a way that many possibly relevant variables are not too grossly distorted in their sample, and hope that whatever disproportions remain will not have an undue bearing on the opinions, preferences, or whatever it is that they seek to know.

Purposive Samples

The basic assumption behind purposive sampling is that with good judgment and an appropriate strategy one can handpick the cases to be included and thus develop samples that are satisfactory in relation to one's needs. A common strategy of purposive sampling is to pick cases that are judged to be typical of the population in which one is interested, assuming that errors of judgment in the selection will tend to counterbalance each other. Experiments on purposive sampling suggest that without an objective basis for making the judgments, this is not a dependable assumption. In any case, without an external check, there is no way of knowing that the "typical" cases continue to be typical.

Purposive samples selected in terms of assumed typicality have been used in attempts to forecast national elections. One such approach is as follows: For each state, select a number of small election districts whose election returns in previous years have approximated the overall state returns, interview all the eligible voters in these districts on their voting intentions, and hope that the selected districts are still typical of their respective states. The trouble with the method is that when there are no marked changes in the political atmosphere, one can probably do as well by forecasting the returns from previous years without doing any interviewing at all; when changes are occurring, one needs to know how the changes are affecting the selected districts in comparison with other districts.

Probability Sampling

Probability samples involve the first kind of insurance against misleading results that we discussed earlier—the ability to specify the chances that the sample findings do not differ by more than a certain amount from the true population values. They may also include the second kind of insurance—a guarantee that enough cases are selected from each relevant population stratum to provide an estimate for that stratum of the population.

Simple Random Samples

Simple random sampling is the basic probability sampling design; it is incorporated in all the more complex probability sampling designs. A simple random sample is selected by a process that not only gives each element in the population an equal chance of being included in the sample but also makes the selection of every possible combination of the desired number of cases equally likely. Suppose, for example, that one wants a simple random sample of two cases from a population of five cases. Let the five cases in the population be *A, B, C, D,* and *E.* There are ten possible pairs of cases in this population: *AB, AC, AD, AE, BC, BD, BE, CD, CE,* and DE. Write each combination on a disc, put the ten discs in a hat, mix them thoroughly, and have a blindfolded person pick one. Each of the discs has the same chance of being selected.[6] The two cases corresponding to the letters on the selected disc constitute the desired simple random sample.

There are, in the tiny illustrative population of five cases, ten possible samples of three cases: *ABC, ABD, ABE, ACD, ACE, ADE, BCD, BCE, BDE,* and *CDE.* Using the same method, one can select a simple random sample of three cases from this population.

In principle, one can use this method for selecting random samples from populations of any size, but in practice it could easily become a life-time occupation merely to list all the combinations of the desired number of cases. The same result is obtained by selecting each case individually, using a list of random numbers such as may be found in most textbooks of statistics. These are sets of numbers that after careful examination have shown no evidence of systematic order. Before using the table of random numbers, it is first necessary to number all the elements in the population to be studied. Then the table is marked at some random starting point (e.g., with a blind pencil stab at the page), and the cases whose numbers come up as one moves from this point down the column of numbers are taken into the sample until the desired number of cases is obtained. The selection of any given case places no limits on what other cases can be selected, thus making equally possible the selection of any one of the many possible combinations of cases. This procedure is, therefore, equivalent to selecting randomly one of the many possible combinations of cases.[7]

---

[6]In this illustration, each of the discs (i.e., each combination of two cases) has one chance in ten of being selected. Each of the individual case also has the same chance of being selected—four in ten because each case appears on four of the discs. There are, however, very many ways of giving each case the same chance of being selected without getting a simple random sample. For example, suppose we were arbitrarily to divide an illustrative population of ten cases into five pairs as follows: *AB, CD, EF, GH, IJ.* If we write the designations for these pairs on five discs, blindly pick one of the discs, and take as our sample the two cases designated on this disc, then every case has one chance in five of being picked, but obviously not every possible combination has the same chance of being selected as every other—in fact, most of the combinations (for example, *AC*) have no chance at all as they have not been included on the discs.

[7]The procedure of selecting a random sample should not be confused with the procedure of sampling from a list or a file of cases by taking every *k*th (for example, every 14th or every 63rd) case. The latter procedure is called *systematic* sampling. Systematic samples may be either probability or nonprobability samples, depending on how the first case is selected. Suppose one wants to select every 60th case. To get a probability sample, the first case has to be selected *randomly* from the first 60, and every 60th case thereafter is selected. If the first case is not selected randomly, the resulting sample is not a probability sample

Without going into the mathematical argument, it is possible only to illustrate the underlying principles of probability sampling. Consider, for this purpose, a hypothetical population of ten cases as follows:

Case	A	B	C	D	E	F	G	H	I	J
Sex	F	F	F	F	F	M	M	M	M	M
Age	Y	O	Y	O	Y	O	Y	O	Y	O
Score	0	1	2	3	4	5	6	7	8	9

The first five cases are females; the last five, males. The cases designated Y are younger, and the O's are older. Age and sex will be considered later, in relation to stratified sampling. The score represents some attribute of the individual, such as his or her performance on a test of mechanical aptitude.

The mean score for this population of ten cases is 4.5. Assuming that this were not known, the problem would be to make an estimate of the population mean on the basis of the scores of the elements in the sample that is drawn. According to the definition of simple random sampling, the method of selecting the sample must give equal probability to every combination of the desired number of cases; in other words, over the long run, with repeated sampling, every combination should come up the same number of times. We can, therefore, figure out what will happen in the long run in our illustrative population by the simple device of considering all the combinations; that is, we take every combination of the desired number of cases and compute a mean for each combination. What results

---

because most of the cases have a zero probability of being included in the sample. Although to the uninitiated, systematic sampling seems to be the most natural and rational way to go about sampling from a list, it involves complications not present in a simple random sample. When the first case is drawn randomly, in a systematic sample, there is in advance no limitation on the chances of any given case to be included in the sample. If we are selecting a sample of 100 cases from a population of 6000, before the first case is selected each case has one chance in 60 (100 in 6000) of being included in the sample, whether we are using simple random or systematic sampling. But in a systematic sample, once the first case is selected, the chances of other cases are altered. Suppose the first case drawn is number 46. Selecting every 60th case thereafter means that numbers 106, 166, 226, and so on will be drawn; the cases between these numbers now have no chance of being included.

This means that a systematic sampling plan does not give all possible combinations of cases the same chance of being included; only combinations of elements 60 cases apart in the list have any chance of being selected for the sample. The results may be quite deceptive if the cases in the list are arranged in some cyclical order. Suppose, for example, that the 6000 cases are houses in a community that was built according to a systematic plan and that they are listed in order of streets and numbers. Corner houses would then appear at regular intervals throughout the list; say, the first house and every 20th house thereafter is a corner dwelling. A sample consisting of cases 1, 61, 121, and so on would be made up entirely of corner houses; one consisting of cases 2, 62, 122, and so on would contain no corner houses. But corner houses are usually larger and more expensive than those within the block, and their occupants may accordingly differ systematically in certain characteristics. Thus, any sample made up entirely of corner houses or entirely lacking in corner houses would give misleading results if the study concerned characteristics in which occupants of the two types of dwellings differ.

TABLE 7.1   Mean Scores of Samples from Illustrative Population of Ten Cases with Population Mean Score of 4.5 (Simple Random Samples)

| Sample Means* | Number of Samples | | |
	Samples of 2 Cases	Samples of 4 Cases	Samples of 6 Cases
.5	1		
1.0	1		
1.5–1.75	2	2	
2.0–2.67	5	10	2
2.75–3.25	3	25	10
3.33–4.00	8	43	52
4.17–4.83	5	50	82
5.00–5.67	8	43	52
5.75–6.25	3	25	10
6.33–7.0	5	10	2
7.25–7.5	2	2	
8.0	1		
8.5	1		
Total no. of samples	45	210	210
Mean of sample means	4.5	4.5	4.5
Percent of sample means greater than 4.00 and less than 5.00	11	24	39
Percent of sample means greater than 2.67 and less than 6.33	60	89	98

*With the small number of different scores in the illustrative population, there are only a limited number of possible sample means. Thus, for samples of two cases, there is no combination that can yield a mean of 2.25; but there are three samples of four cases (*ABDF, ABCG, ACDE*) with a mean of 2.25. Similarly, a mean of 2.67 is not possible for one sample of six cases. For convenience of tabulation and in order to help bring out the characteristics of the sampling distributions, the means of the samples have been grouped.

is a distribution of sample means—known as a **sampling distribution.** For example, there are 45 possible combinations of two cases in our hypothetical population of ten cases. One, and only one, combination (cases *A* and *B*) will yield a sample mean of .5; there are 5 combinations (*A* and *J*, *B* and *I*, *C* and *H*, *D* and *G*, *E* and *F*) that will yield sample means of 4.5; and so on. Similarly, there are 210 possible samples of four cases. One of these combinations (*A, B, C,* and *D*) will yield a sample mean of 1.5; one (*A, B, C,* and *E*), a sample mean of 1.75; and so on.

Table 7.1 shows the sampling distributions for sample means based on simple random samples of two, four, and six cases from our illustrative population.

Notice that for samples of any given size the most likely sample mean is the population mean;[8] the next most likely are values close to the pop-

[8]This point is obscured in Table 7.1 for the case of samples of two, by the grouping of means. Actually, there are five possible samples of two cases with means of 4.5; there are four possible samples with means of 4.0; and so on.

ulation mean; the more a sample mean deviates from the population mean, the less likely it is to occur. Also, the larger the sample, the more likely is it that its mean will be close to the population mean.

It is this kind of behavior on the part of probability samples (not only with respect to means but also with respect to proportions and other types of statistics) that makes it possible to estimate the population characteristic (e.g., the mean) as well as the likelihood that the sample figure differs from the true population figure by a given amount.

One interesting feature of simple random sampling ought to be mentioned, even though it is hard for most people to believe it without mathematical proof. When the population is large compared to the sample size (say, more than ten times as large), the variabilities of sampling distributions are influenced much more by the absolute number of cases in the samples than by the proportion of the population that is included; that is, the magnitude of the errors that are likely depends more on the absolute size of the sample than on the proportion of the population it includes. Thus, the estimation of popular preferences in a national preelection poll, within the limits of a given margin of error, would not require a substantially larger sample than the estimation of the preferences in any one state where the issue is in doubt. Conversely, it would take just about as large a sample to estimate the preferences in one doubtful state with a given degree of accuracy as it would to estimate the distribution of preferences in the entire nation. This is true despite the fact that a sample of a few thousand cases obviously includes a much larger proportion of the voters in one state than the same-size sample does of the voters in the nation.

Stratified Random Samples

In stratified random sampling, as in quota sampling, the population is first divided into two or more strata. Again, the strata may be based on a single criterion (e.g., sex, yielding the two strata of male and female) or on a combination of two or more criteria (e.g., age and sex, yielding strata such as males under 21, males 21 and over, females under 21, females 21 and over). In stratified random sampling, a simple random sample is taken from each stratum, and the subsamples are then joined to form the total sample.

To illustrate how stratified random sampling works, we may return to the previously described population of ten cases. Consider samples of four with equal proportions of males and females (e.g., samples made up by combining subsamples of two males with subsamples of two females). To satisfy this last condition, many samples of four that were possible under the conditions of simple random sampling are no longer possible—for example, samples consisting of cases *A*, *B*, *C*, *D* or of cases *A*, *B*, *C*, *F* or of cases *D*, *F*, *G*, *I*—because they do not have two males and two females. In fact, there are now exactly 100 possible samples as compared to the 210 previously possible. As before, we have computed the mean score for each of the possible samples and thereby obtained the sampling distribution of the mean. Table 7.2 compares the sampling distribution for samples of four obtained on the basis of simple random sampling, stratified sampling using sex as a criterion for stratification, and stratified sampling using age as a criterion.

It will be noted that there is a marked improvement over simple random sampling when the sampling is based on a stratification of our hypothetical population by sex; with this kind of stratification we get a marked increase in the number of samples that give means very close to the population mean and a marked reduction in the number of sample means that deviate widely from the population mean. When the population is stratified by age, however, there is no such marked improvement in the efficiency of sampling; in fact, the means of individual samples are somewhat less likely to be very close to the population mean.

In general, stratification contributes to the efficiency of sampling if it succeeds in establishing classes that are internally comparatively homogeneous with respect to the characteristics being studied—that is, if the differences between classes (e.g., between males and females) are large in comparison with the variation within classes (among the males and

TABLE 7.2 Mean Scores of Samples of Four Cases from Illustrative Population of Ten Cases with Population Mean Score of 4.5 (Simple and Stratified Random Samples)

Sample Means*	Number of Samples		
	Simple Random Samples	Samples Stratified by Sex	Samples Stratified by Age
1.50–1.75	2		1
2.00–2.50	10		7
2.75–3.25	25	3	8
3.50–4.00	43	25	26
4.25–4.75	50	44	16
5.00–5.50	43	25	26
5.75–6.25	25	3	8
6.50–7.00	10		7
7.25–7.50	2		1
Total no. of samples	210	100	100
Mean of sample means	4.5	4.5	4.5
Percent of sample means greater than 4.00 and less than 5.00	24	44	16
Percent of sample means greater than 2.50 and less than 6.50	89	100	84

*Again, the means of the samples have been grouped. See note to Table 7.1.

among the females). In our illustrative population, the difference in scores between the sex groups is relatively large and that between age groups relatively small; that is why stratification by sex is effective in this case and stratification by age ineffective. The general principle is that if one has reason to believe that stratifying according to a particular criterion or set of criteria will result in internally homogeneous strata, it is desirable to stratify. If the process of breaking the population down into strata likely to differ sharply from one another is costly, one has to balance this cost against the cost of a comparable gain in precision obtained by taking a larger simple random sample. The issues involved in the decision whether to stratify have, basically, nothing to do with trying to make the sample a replica of the population; they only have to do with the anticipated homogeneity of the defined strata with respect to the characteristics being studied and the comparative costs of different methods of achieving precision. Both simple and stratified random sampling involve representative sampling plans.

Except for a slight saving in arithmetic, there is no reason for sampling from the different strata in the same proportion; that is, even with respect to the criteria selected for stratification, it is not necessary for the sample to reflect the composition of the population. Thus, in sampling from a population in which the number of males equals the number of females, it is permissible (and may sometimes be desirable) to sample nine or five or two or some other number of females to every male. When this is done, however, it is necessary to make an adjustment in order to find the mean score (or the proportion of elements with a given characteristic or whatever measure is desired) for the sample that will be the best estimate of the mean score of the total population of males and females. This is accomplished by "weighting" the figure for each stratum in such a way that it contributes to the score for the total sample in proportion to its size in the population, as in the quota sampling illustration previously mentioned. When the various strata are sampled in constant proportion, one is spared this bit of arithmetic since the various strata are already properly weighted.

There may be several reasons for sampling the various strata in different proportions. Sometimes it is necessary to increase the proportion sampled from classes having small numbers of cases in order to guarantee that these classes are sampled at all. For example, if we are planning a survey of retail sales volume in a given city in a given month, simple random sampling of retail stores might not lead to an accurate estimate of the total volume of sales because a few very large department stores account for an extremely large proportion of the total sales, and there is no guarantee that any of these large stores would turn up in a simple random sample. In this case, we would stratify the population of stores in terms of some measure of their total volume of sales (e.g., the gross value of sales during the preceding year). Perhaps only the three largest department stores would be in the topmost stratum. We would include all three of them in our sample; in other words, we would take a 100 percent sample of this stratum.[9] Any other procedure in such a situation would greatly reduce the accuracy of the estimate, no matter how carefully samples were taken from other strata. Again, of course, figures from the various strata would have to be appropriately weighted in estimating the total volume of sales in the city.

Another reason for taking a larger proportion of cases from one stratum than from others is that we may want to subdivide the cases within each stratum for further analysis. Let us say that in our survey of retail sales we want to be able to examine separately the volume of sales made by food stores, by clothing stores, and by other types. Even though these classifications are not taken into account in selecting the sample (i.e., the sample is not stratified on this basis), it is clear that we need a reasonable number of cases in each volume-of-sales stratum to make possible an analysis of different types of stores within each stratum. If a given stratum has relatively few cases, so that sampling in the proportion used in other strata would not provide enough cases to serve as an adequate basis for this further analysis, we may take a higher proportion of cases in this stratum.

One of the major reasons for varying the sampling proportions for different strata cannot be fully explained without going into the mathematical theory of sampling, but the principle involved can be understood on a more or less intuitive basis. Consider two strata, one of which is much more homogeneous with respect to the characteristics being studied than the other. For a given degree of precision, it will take a smaller number of cases to determine the state of affairs in the first stratum than in the second. To take an extreme example: suppose that there is reason to know that every case in a given stratum has the same score; we could then determine how to represent that stratum in the total sample on the basis of a sample of one case. Of course, in such an extreme case we are not likely to have this information without also knowing what the common score is. But in less extreme cases we can often anticipate the relative degrees of homogeneity or heterogeneity of strata before carrying out the survey. For example, if with respect to certain types of opinion questions, men differ among themselves much more than women, we would accordingly plan our sample to include a larger proportion of men. If it is the case that women may be expected to be more alike than men in these matters, they do not have to be sampled as thoroughly as do the men for a given degree of precision.

---

[9]Note that in such a procedure, the cases in the total population do not all have the same chance of being included in the sample. Each of these three largest stores has a 100 percent chance of being included, whereas each of the stores in another stratum may have only one chance in ten. But the probability of inclusion of each case can be specified, thus meeting the basic requirement for probability sampling.

In general terms, we can expect the greatest precision if the various strata are sampled proportionately to their relative variabilities with respect to the characteristics under study rather than proportionately to their relative sizes in the population. A special case of this principle is that in sampling to determine the proportion of cases possessing a particular attribute, strata in which we can anticipate that about half the cases will have the attribute and half will not should be sampled more thoroughly than strata in which we would expect a more uneven division. Thus, in planning a stratifed sample for predicting a national election, using states as strata, we should not plan to sample each state in proportion to its eligible population; it would be wiser to sample most heavily in the most doubtful states.

Cluster Sampling

Except when dealing with small and spatially concentrated populations, there are enormous expenses associated with simple and stratified random sampling—for example, in the preparation of classified lists on population elements and in sending interviewers to scattered localities. The more widely scattered the interviews, the greater are the travel expenses, the greater is the proportion of nonproductive time spent in traveling, and the more complicated—and hence expensive—are the tasks of supervising the field staff. There are also other factors that often make it difficult or impossible to satisfy the conditions of random sampling. For example, it may be easier to get permission to administer a questionnaire to three or four classes in a school than to administer the same questionnaire to a much smaller sample selected on a simple or stratified random basis; the latter may disrupt the school routines much more. For such reasons, large-scale survey studies seldom use simple or stratified random samples; instead they use the methods of cluster sampling.

In cluster sampling, one arrives at the ultimate set of elements to be included in the sample by first sampling in terms of larger groupings *(clusters)*. The clusters are selected by simple or stratified methods; and if not all the elements in these clusters are to be included in the sample, the ultimate selection from within the clusters is also carried out on a simple or stratified random-sampling basis.

Suppose, for example, that we want to do a survey of seventh-grade public school children in some state. We may proceed as follows: Prepare a list of school districts, classified perhaps by size of community, and select a simple or stratified random sample. For each of the school districts included in the sample, list the schools and take a simple or stratified random sample of them. If some or all the schools thus selected for the sample have more seventh-grade classes than can be studied, we may take a sample of these classes in each of the schools. The survey instruments may then be administered to all the children in these classes or, if it is desirable and administratively feasible to do so, to a sample of the children.

Similarly, a survey of urban households may take a sample of cities; within each city that is selected, a sample of districts, within each selected district, a sample of households.

Characteristically, the procedure moves through a series of stages—hence the common term **multistage sampling**—from more-inclusive to less-inclusive sampling units until we finally arrive at the population elements that constitute the desired sample.

Notice that with this kind of sampling procedure it is no longer true that every combination of the desired number of elements in the population (or in a given stratum) is equally likely to be selected as the sample of the population (or stratum). Hence, the kinds of effects we noticed in our analysis of simple and stratified random sampling of our hypothetical population of ten cases (the population value being the most probable sample result and larger deviations from the population value being less probable than smaller ones) cannot develop in quite the same way. Such effects do, however, occur in a more complicated way, provided that each stage of cluster sampling is carried out on a probability sampling basis. One pays a price, however, in terms of sampling efficiency. On a per-case basis, effective cluster sampling is much less efficient in obtaining information than comparably effective stratified random sampling; that is, for a given number of cases, the probable margin of error is much larger in the former case than in the latter. Moreover, the correct statistical handling of the data is apt to be more complicated. These handicaps are, however, more than balanced by the associated economies, which generally permit the sampling of a sufficiently larger number of cases at a smaller cost. The comparison of cluster sampling with simple random sampling is somewhat more complicated. Stratified sampling principles may be used to select the clusters, and what is lost in efficiency because of the clustering effects may be regained by this stratification. Depending on the specific features of the sampling plan in relation to the object of the survey, cluster sampling may be more or less efficient on a per-case basis than simple random sampling. But again, even if more cases are needed for the same level of accuracy, the associated economies generally favor cluster sampling in large-scale surveys.

Concluding Remarks on the Two Kinds of Sampling

Throughout the preceding discussion, we have made it clear that only by using probability sampling do we have any basis for estimating how far sample results are likely to deviate from the true population figures. At the same time, we have noted that the major advantages of nonprobability sampling are its convenience and its economy. It is likely, therefore, that many investigators will continue to use nonprobability methods and to justify their use on the ground of practical experience, even while conceding the superiority in principle of probability sampling. Moreover, many will argue that in some cases at least, this superiority exists only on paper. They will point out that there is a difference between the sampling plan and its actual execution; there can be many a slip in the carrying out of the plan that would nullify its theoretical advantages. Interviewers, for instance, may fail to follow their instructions in selecting respondents, or they may omit some of the questions in interviewing some of the respondents (and thereby produce samples of somewhat different and not strictly comparable populations in relation to the various questions in the same interview schedule); some of the selected cases may refuse to be interviewed or not be available; compromises may be made by allowing interviewers to substitute other respondents when those designated for the sample are not found at home; and so on. The sample actually obtained may, hence, not be the probability sample it was planned to be.

Moreover, there are circumstances in which probability sampling is unnecessary or inappropriate. One such circumstance arises from the fact that one does not necessarily carry out studies of samples only for the purpose of being able to generalize to the populations that are being sampled. If one uses samples for other reasons, ability to evaluate the likelihood of deviations from the population values is irrelevant. For example, if the goal is to obtain ideas, good insights, and experienced critical appraisals, one selects a purposive sample with this in mind. The situation is analogous to one in which a number of expert consultants are called in on a difficult medical case. These consultants—also a purposive sample—are not called in to get an average opinion that would correspond to the average opinion of the entire medical profession. They are called in precisely because of their special experience and competence. Or the situation may be viewed as analogous to our more or less haphazard sampling of foods from a famous cuisine. We are sampling not to estimate some population value but to get some idea of the variety of elements available in this population.

Another example of sampling for ideas rather than for the estimation of population values is provided by the field of market research known as *motivation research*. The typical problem of motivation research is to find out something about motives, attitudes, and associations evoked by certain products, brand names, and package designs that may not be obvious even to the respondents themselves. The results of such studies are turned over to advertising agencies, which use them in developing advertising campaigns. Characteristically, the motivation researchers are quite happy with accidental samples or with purposive samples selected in such a way as to maximize the likelihood of differences among the elements in the sample. They are looking for ideas to transmit to the advertising people, not for correct estimates of population distributions. One might argue that they would be better off if they could establish not merely the variety of motives that are likely to become associated with certain products but also the precise distribution of these motives. At present, however, it seems to be problematical whether the additional information would be worth the extra cost of getting it. At any rate, as long as these researchers deceive neither themselves nor their clients into believing that they are getting the second kind of information, no one can take exception to their application of accidental sampling.

Sometimes there is no alternative to nonprobability sampling. If one is trying to find out something, for example, about the attitudes of people in the People's Republic of China, one has no realistic choice but to rely on informants who have recently spent some time there (each of whom reports on the accidental sample involved in his or her contacts) and on immigrants, who are themselves far from typical. The choice here is between data that do not permit a statistical assessment of the likelihood of error and no data at all. Similarly, if one is trying to reconstruct a picture of a dying or recently deceased culture, one has no choice except to rely on relatively articulate informants for certain types of information. This does not mean that one is not concerned with the possibility of error, but one places one's reliance on the internal consistency of the data and their coherence with other things that one knows.

Another special case justifying the use of nonprobability samples arises from the fact that there are many important considerations in research in addition to the sampling design. In the introduction to this chapter, we discussed how in experimental psychology the need for experimental control may override sampling considerations. That is, experimental psychologists frequently trade some external validity for increased internal validity. There may also be times when the claims of construct validity and external validity conflict. That is, it may be necessary on occasion to decide whether we want a better sampling design or more-sensitive and generally more-informative measurements. Consider a study by Chein (1956) on the factors related to the use of drugs by boys in juvenile street gangs. Chein used group workers as informants (with complete protection of the anonymity of the individual gang member). These workers had spent months winning the confidence of the boys, convincing the latter that they were not confederates of the police, social reformers, or other things reprehensible in the eyes of the boys; and they had been working closely with the gangs for many more months—in some instances, for several years. As these informants were available only for the gangs that were being worked with, the sample of gangs—and hence of gang members— was an accidental sample. Assuming that (1) it would have been possible to get a probability sample of gang members and (2) the information obtained through the group workers was much more dependable than would have been information obtained through direct interview, what should the investigators have done?

The answer to such a question is not easy. The first thing to do, of course, is to assure oneself that the dilemma is real. If convinced that it is, one must then decide whether the problem is, under the circumstances, worthy of investigation at all. If the answer is still in the affirmative, one must decide, in terms of the research purpose, whether it would be better to gather more-adequate information based on a not very sound sample or less-adequate information based on a sounder sample.

Summary

The focus of this chapter has been on sampling as a vehicle for maximizing the external validity of research. We started by arguing that in order for a sampling procedure to be representative, the first thing that must be done is to specify the population to which one wants to generalize. Then one can proceed to use either probabilistic or nonprobabilistic sampling procedures. In the former, every element in the population has a known, nonzero probability of being included in the sample. In the latter, we do not know the probability of inclusion for each element and many of the elements may have zero probability of inclusion. Only in probability sampling do we have a basis for estimating how far sample results are likely to deviate from the true population figures.

Three types of nonprobability sampling were defined: accidental, quota, and purposive samples. The first is defined by interviewing whomever is convenient, accessible, or otherwise accidentally encountered. Quota samples are also accidental samples; the only difference is that in quota samples we specify strata from each of which accidental samples are to be gathered. Finally, in purposive samples, one uses one's best judgment to decide which elements are most representative of the population and includes them in the samples.

Three types of probability sampling procedures were defined: simple random sampling, stratified random sampling, and cluster sampling. In the first every element has the same probability of being included in the sample. With stratified random sampling, one first breaks up the population into strata and then proceeds to collect data from a simple random sample within each stratum. If one defines strata optimally, stratified random samples are more precise than simple random samples. In cluster sampling, one draws random samples at a number of different levels of aggregation. Thus, to cluster sample schoolchildren, one might first draw a random sample of school districts; then within chosen districts, another random sample of schools; and then within chosen schools, another random sample of children. Cluster sampling tends to be more efficient than simple random or stratified random sampling, although it may be less precise in its population estimates.

   In the concluding part of the chapter, we discussed some special situations in which nonprobabilistic sampling may be recommended over probabilistic sampling. One of these occurs when other validities are judged more important and when the need to engage in probabilistic sampling conflicts with precise measurement or experimental control.

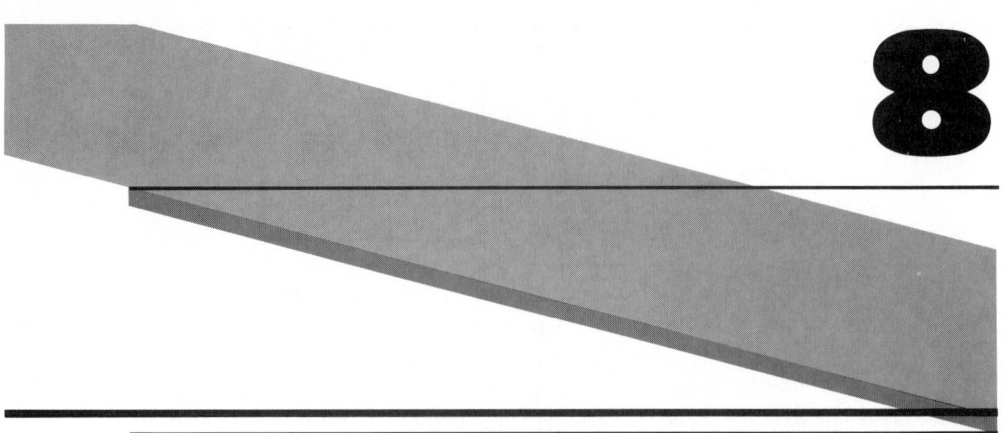

8

Field Work and Participant Observation: Studying Particular People and Places

Research has external validity when its conclusions are true of people and places beyond those studied. In the preceding chapter you learned how survey researchers sample subjects and settings to obtain data that will allow them to generalize their conclusions to other people and places. In this chapter we will examine a research strategy that is almost diametrically opposed to sample survey methods. It is the strategy used by field researchers and participant observers, who immerse themselves in a group or location and record in detail the lives and experiences of particular people. Rather than sample people or places to be representative of some wider population, they select particular people and places. It appears on the surface, therefore, as though survey researchers seek generalizability and field workers seek specificity. Specificity, however, need not preclude generalizability.

Specificity and Generalizability

Experimenters frequently use college students as their subjects even though they are not trying to study the mental or social life of college students. Instead, they wish to make observations about psychological processes that occur in all or most people. They wish to generalize beyond the college laboratory and say something about "people in general."

Participant observers who study college students do so very deliberately—to learn about their experiences. They may observe the behaviors and attitudes of medical students, for instance, to draw conclusions about becoming a doctor (e.g., Becker et al, 1961). Participant observers, like anthropologists, record in detail how people live, feel, and work in particular locales. Rather than go to foreign shores, however, they study places closer to home—a neighborhood street gang, a parole office, an assembly line, or an Appalachian community. Like anthropologists, they provide rich detail on the lives of particular people in a particular place.

Such specificity, however, does not preclude generalizing beyond the particular study. Participant observers do not generalize by claiming that their locale is representative of others. Instead, they generalize by asserting that the people they observed behaved as anyone would if placed in that situation. For instance, McCleary (1978) studied two parole offices in one American city. He did not conclude that all parole offices in all American cities operate the same way, but rather, that anyone placed in such an office would do the things he observed those parole officers doing. He made general statements about how *any person* would act in such circumstances without making statements about *all*, or even most, parole offices. (We describe McCleary's study in more detail later.)

Field workers, therefore, draw conclusions about general social processes beyond the confines of the people and places they studied. They generalize beyond their data just as much as survey researchers generalize beyond their sample, but their generalizations have a different form, and their methods of doing research are dramatically different. In the sections that follow we examine the form of the participant observer's generalizations and also the methods on which the generalizations are based.

Generalizations from Field Work

Field researchers study how people behave in specific organizations, communities, or circumstances and conclude that anyone would behave similarly in those situations. For instance, in a study of how people become hypnotized, Kidder (1972) observed workshops in one city during one month. She did not sample hypnosis workshops and did not conclude that what she saw is true of all workshops or hypnotic inductions. Instead, she analyzed how hypnotists and their subjects "negotiated reality" until both were satisfied that the subject had gone into a trance. They negotiated over how "deep" the trance had been, how voluntary the process was, and who was responsible for whether or not the subject went into a trance. Kidder did not conclude that all hypnotists and their subjects negotiate this way. Instead she concluded that the negotiations worked because the hypnotists used a number of techniques to change their subjects' behaviors and attitudes and that these techniques would have worked on anyone. Though the people in the workshop were special because they sought out the experience, what worked with them would also work on people in general. The hypnotists used techniques of attitude and behavioral change known to work on other people in other circumstances. In this case the techniques were used to make people act and feel hypnotized.

Unlike a survey researcher, a field researcher rarely asks, "What percent of persons in the population would respond this way"? Instead she or he says, "What I have found true of the people in this study is likely to be true of any people placed in this situation." Field researchers are like laboratory experimenters in this respect. Both assume that the environmental forces or situational constraints they have studied would affect most people the same way. Experimenters and field researchers share this assumption even though they conduct their research in dramatically different ways and places. Experimenters rarely do their research on street corners; they request or require college students to volunteer as subjects. Field researchers rarely study college students; they conduct their research in nonacademic places. They study people in real-world situations, which seem to give the research an a priori claim to external validity. Real-world settings do not automatically confer external validity, however.

Although field work might seem to have a priori external validity simply because it takes place in the external world, field researchers must demonstrate that their conclusions are valid beyond the confines of their study. They are rarely content to say that the processes observed are true only for the people and places named in the study. If they set such limits, few readers would be interested in their conclusions. Field researchers, as much as experimenters and survey researchers, need to demonstrate that their research has wider validity.

External validity is acquired by gathering and analyzing field data so that the similarities to other persons or situations become clear. We say more about this when we examine the methods of field research. In the remainder of this chapter we describe the methods of data gathering and analysis and show how conclusions drawn from studying particular people and places can be extended to other persons and situations.

Field Research Methods

Degrees of Participation

Some field workers participate fully in the lives of the people they study, by either being or becoming members of the group. Others remain outsiders, purely observers. Between these two end points are countless possibilities, with more or less emphasis on being a *participant*.

The decision about how much to participate in the lives of the people one studies usually depends on nonscientific considerations. For instance, in studying men who had been convicted of embezzlement, Cressey (1953) did not try to become one. In studying foreign sojourners in India, Kidder (1977) could not help but be one. The degree of participation is often foreordained—either because the observer is already part of the situation or because he or she *cannot* become part of it. There are instances, however, when the observer cannot be a bona fide member of the group but can become accepted as a trusted friend and confidante. The following example illustrates how Carol Stack, a white woman, became accepted in a family and circle of friends in a black community. She studied how family and friendship networks helped residents of that community cope with illness, unemployment, and housing evictions. The following description of how she became a participant observer is from her book, entitled *All Our Kin:*

> I first came by the Walters' home in the summer of 1968 . . .[the family] were sitting in the living room on a red velvet couch, which Magnolia had covered herself. The eight were methodically folding several piles of newspapers for Lenny's five evening paper routes. . . . After a lesson from a seven-year-old on how to make the fold, I joined in. . . . I told them I would like to begin a study of family life in The Flats. . . . Several months later Magnolia told me that she had

been surprised that I sat with them that first day to fold papers, and then came back to help again. "White folks," she told me, "don't have time, they's always in a rush, and they don't sit on black folks' furniture, at least no whites that come into The Flats" [1975, p. 10].

Stack got to know Magnolia's daughter, Ruby, who introduced her to life in The Flats and taught her much by example.

Ruby and I enjoyed comparing our attitudes and approaches toward everything. Although she asked me to bring my white friends over to her house, she was always hypercritical in assessing whether they were anti-Black or whether they "put on airs." Some of my friends she liked very much, yet she encouraged me to break up some friendships, especially if she had reason to doubt a friend's loyalty to me. It seemed at times, by the circumstances and demands that she contrived, that she was testing the loyalty of my friends—using her own standards, of course—just as she tested her own friends. For example, she insisted that I ask my friends to take care of Kevin [Stack's son] or to loan me money. She was in fact teaching me how to get along [p. 14].

Such immersion in the lives of the people one studies is very different from the distance maintained by experimenters and survey researchers. The latter often do not know or ask for the names of their research subjects, trying instead to assure them of anonymity and to treat all persons alike. Participant observers do the opposite; they become well acquainted with the people they study and consequently treat no two people alike. Moreover, participant observers are also drawn into interactions by the people they study, as the preceding and following examples illustrate.

Ruby had a quick, affirmative way of letting others know my presence was acceptable to her, and that it "damn well better be acceptable to them." At one large family gathering, relatives came from out of town to see Ruby's stepfather, who was sick. Ruby sensed their hostility and insecurity toward me. She turned to me and said, "What is your white ass doing sitting down when there is so much cooking and work to do in my kitchen?" I responded, "My white ass can sit here as long as your black ass can." With that, we both got up, went into the kitchen and got to work [pp. 15–16].

This degree of immersion in the research setting is at odds with the distance and anonymity of experiments and surveys. Does it make participant observation more vulnerable to distortion? Not necessarily; in fact, the lack of anonymity of repondents may ensure that the researcher observes phenomena as they are and not as the respondent or the researcher wishes they were. Subjects in laboratory experiments and anonymous respondents in surveys may be freer to distort reality than are people whose identities are known and whose actions are observed in their natural setting (Becker & Geer, 1957). The people studied by participant observation are constrained to act as they normally would, particularly if the research continues over many weeks or months. They cannot put on an act and continue to function with their friends, families, or fellow workers. Even if a participant observer could not recognize an act or a distortion, the actor's associates would, and the participant observer would probably hear about it. We have a paradox: The more time a participant observer spends with the people he or she studies, the less influence the observer exerts as a researcher because although the research subjects may wish to appear a particular way in the researcher's eyes, they cannot act in unnatural ways if the observer stays with them very long. The more the participant observer is immersed in the research setting, therefore, the less likely the research subjects are to distort the research.

By participating in the lives of people in the study, a field worker is vulnerable to criticism that she or he is not objective. Sherif, a social psychologist whose own work was mainly experiments, wrote about bias in supposedly "objective" research. She said that by separating ourselves from the people we study, not seeing them as whole persons but dissecting them into "parts, elements, or variables," we risk ignoring much that should be included in our research to understand adequately what is going on (1979). The strategy of field researchers is not to isolate variables but to try to record everything, to not miss anything. This becomes a staggering task and can never be totally accomplished, but by writing long and detailed field notes, a researcher creates a record of events that can be read and checked by others who were present.

Field Notes

A field worker must make detailed records, called *field notes*, of everything he or she hears and sees. This requirement may strike the beginning field worker as an impossible task, which it is, because the term *everything* sets no limits. It can include endless details about the time and location of an interview or observation, with descriptions of the building, the furnishings, the decor, the level of cleanliness, the amount of noise, the numbers of other people present, the facial expressions of the persons being observed, their appearance and dress styles, their behaviors, and so on. Only some of these details will be relevant to the analysis, but when the participant observer begins, he or she does not know what the final analysis will be. The rule, therefore, is to try to remember "everything" and write notes that are as complete as memory allows.

Recording everything that is said is an equally arduous task. Participant observers generally do not record conversations on tape because a tape recorder would inhibit the researcher's participation in many situations. For instance, if Stack had carried a tape recorder into Ruby's home whenever she went to visit, she probably would not have developed the rapport described earlier. Occasionally a tape recorder may not intrude; Kidder (1972) studied how people became hypnotized by attending a series of hypnosis workshops where she tape-recorded the hypnotic inductions and the posthypnotic discussions between hypnotists and their subjects. Many of the other participants in the workshop also had tape recorders, which they used to record the lectures that preceded and followed the hypnotic inductions, so Kidder's use of a tape recorder was not unique or obtrusive.

When a tape recorder would interfere with participant observation, the researcher must rely on memory to write the field notes as soon after the observations as possible. The following excerpt of field notes from McCleary's study of parole officers (POs) illustrates how a participant observer selects, remembers, and records the materials that become the data from which illustrative examples can be drawn.

A Day in the Life

(What follows is an actual interview written up in the first week of June, 1976. Naturally, the interview as presented here has been edited so as not to include any identifiers. I prefer making notes during the actual conversation. The notes are then used as a mnemonic device for reproducing the conversation. This is not always possible because some POs are annoyed or bothered by note taking. Other POs seem not to mind, or at least, understand the necessity. Bob, the PO who speaks in this interview, has told me this explicitly. Because I was able to take notes, my conversations with Bob are of a better quality than the average. I have shown him this particular interview and he agreed that this is more or less what he said.

(I can give a brief description of Bob here without identifying him. He is a "typical" PO—at least demographically. He has an undergraduate degree in a social science and is currently enrolled in a psychiatric social work graduate program. His future plans are uncertain, but after the M.S.W., he would like to stay with the DC [Department of Corrections], "if possible." By this, Bob means that he expects the DC to promote him to a position where he can utilize his academic credentials.

(Bob is in his late twenties, black, and has lived most of his life in the city. His parole district coincides roughly with the neighborhood he grew up in. Not surprisingly, a number of his childhood friends are now his parolees. Bob has commented on this fact a number of times. He attributes his relative success in life to a positive family, religion, and fortune: "I was one of the lucky ones."

(On the evening of this conversation, I met Bob in a restaurant near his office. We talked for less than an hour about his workday. We then went out into the field, and after two hours, adjourned to a tavern. The conversation at that time was more general. The conversation begins at approximately five in the afternoon, and counting the interruption, lasts until ten at night. Bob speaks:)

"My vice is letting things go until the last minute. You know, never do today what you can put off until tomorrow. Well, today was tomorrow.

"First I had a site investigation report to file. The deadline was today. I got down to the office about nine and Terry was already waiting for the report. His deadline was tomorrow. I gave him my standard excuse and asked him to give me a hand with it. He complained about it, you know how he is, but he agreed to help. Everybody in the office does. So we split the report up. I took the home investigation and he took the employment investigation. He can handle that by phone. All he has to do is call the employer and verify the job. The home investigation is different. You usually can't do that by phone, and even if you could, Terry wouldn't let you. He's a pretty liberal supervisor but that's one rule he won't bend. If he even suspects you didn't visit the home, he'll make you do the report over."

(The PO training manual is explicit on this point: "The PO must conduct this investigation in the residence where the client plans to reside." Supervisors enforce this rule to the letter. The reason for this is that, or so supervisors believe, a knowledge of the home environment often gives the PO some control over his parolee.)

"I had my car this morning. The address was on _____ street, near the el tracks. I couldn't find a parking place nearby, so I parked in front of a loading zone sign. I've got a little Sheriff's Department card that says "Official Vehicle." I put that on my dash and I usually don't get a ticket. The house was a lower flat, kind of depressed looking. There were vacant lots on both sides and a lot of trash. It was fairly nice looking on the inside, though. The hallway corridor was clean.

"The dude I was investigating planned to live at that address with his sister and brother-in-law. You get problems with those arrangements. Sometimes the relatives don't want the dude but they're either afraid to tell him so or else the dude won't take No for an answer. I get some cases where relatives tell the dude No right out but then the dude thinks they'll change their minds after he moves in. Well, you have to make sure the relatives want the dude."

These field notes read like the script of a play. They contain descriptions of the time, the setting, and the actor; they have an aside by the narrator, McCleary; and they contain the lines spoken by the main actor, Bob. The lines spoken by Bob are approximations because the researcher wrote them from memory rather than from a tape recording. As readers we must generally trust that the quotations and descriptions are fairly accurate. In this case, McCleary tells us that he showed the written interview to Bob, who agreed it was accurate.

Not all the details in these notes became usable data in McCleary's analysis. Nonetheless, it was important for him to have recorded them for two reasons. First, by trying to write down as much as possible, the researcher stands a better chance of having useful data available for analysis later on; deciding which data are useful should be done during the analysis rather than during the writing of the field notes. Second, writing even those details that seem irrelevant at the time helps the researcher recall other details that are clearly relevant; each piece of information acts as a cue for recalling other pieces of the setting and is, therefore, worth recording as a device to activate memory. If you doubt that you could recall and write from memory an hour-long interview, try it. You will probably be surprised by how much you can remember if you try to write "everything."

The Use of Numbers

With data in the form of field notes instead of answers to uniform questions, field researchers do not make much use of numbers. The questions they ask people change continually throughout their research, and the answers they receive are usually long descriptions or explanations that do not fit into simple coding categories. Their analyses are not numerical. The following examples show how some field researchers have used or tried to use numbers.

Sample Sizes and Numbers of Observations

In a book called *The Making of Blind Men* (R. Scott, 1969) we find some references to sample sizes, but they are very inexact compared with numbers reported in survey research or experiments. The book is a study of socialization into the world of the blind. The author argues that agencies designed to help people with visual impairments can make people become helpless and dependent. Some agencies also make visually impaired clients "blinder" than they were by encouraging them to depend on a specially accommodative environment rather than teaching them to maneuver in the world outside. In telling the reader about the samples of people and agencies he studied, the author gave approximations rather than exact numbers, as in the following excerpts (emphasis added):

> I spoke with *perhaps a hundred* blind people . . .[p. 12].

> I conducted *nearly one hundred* interviews with professional workers in the field of work for the blind . . .[p. 12].

> . . . I have analyzed the records and reports of *many* public and private organizations for the blind [p. 11].

> I also spent *much time* visiting and observing a representative sample of other organizations, programs and agencies in the blindness system [pp. 12–13].

The use of numbers here is different from their use in quantitative research. Experimenters and survey researchers tell us exactly what the sample size or number of observations is. No surveys or experiments or quasi experiments refer to "perhaps" or "nearly" 100. They tell us whether there were 99 or 100 or 101 interviews because these figures enter into the statistical analysis and they must be exact. Participant observers do not usually perform statistical analyses, and therefore it makes little difference whether they interviewed 99 or 101 people. It is conceivable that if there were 99 observations that fit the hypothesis, the 100th or 101st would be a negative case, but the larger the number of cases observed, the less likely it is that an additional case would contradict and therefore change the conclusions. Scott reported that he spoke with "perhaps a hundred" blind people, because he wished to inform the reader that his sample was approximately 100 and not approximately 10 or 20.

A large sample size serves the same purpose in all kinds of research—it makes the results more reliable because it is less likely that additional observations would change the outcome. A large sample size does not always mean that many people were studied. It could mean that a small number of people were studied over a long period of time. This is analogous to a within-subjects or repeated-measures design in experimentation, in which case the researcher reduces the number of people and increases the number of observations obtained from each person.

Measurement

Participant observation need not be all qualitative work; it can include quantitative measures, too. In a participant observation study of parole officers, McCleary (1977, 1978) observed that the officers did not always report parole violations. In fact, he found they "ignore most of the crimes, incidents, and violations that they observe in their caseload" (1977, p. 576). They reported incidents only when the report would benefit them by enabling them to transfer a troublesome parolee from their caseload, threaten a parolee, or protect their own careers. Otherwise, the amount of paperwork that they would create by full reporting would be too costly. It would take an inordinate amount of time, it would limit the PO's ability to counsel men and give them a "second chance," and it would jeopardize the PO's own job because he or she may have to defend the decisions in a hearing. McCleary used his own observations and reports from parole officers to document that many violations go unreported. He tried to supplement these qualitative data with a quantitative measurement of paperwork. The following excerpt describes his efforts "to collect 'crucial' quantitative data" (1978, p. 39).

> . . . It occurred to me that I could test a number of hypotheses simply by measuring the *quantity* of writing done under certain conditions. This seemed to be a simple task when conceived but later proved to be nearly impossible. I first tried measuring the amount of time POs spent on paperwork in the office writing reports. I discovered what I already knew, however: That POs spend little or no time in the office writing reports. Most of this work is done at home. Office time is spent answering phones, interviewing clients, and socializing with office-mates and supervisors. I next considered going into the files in each office and simply counting the number of pages in each dossier. This figure could then be correlated with the predicted aspects of each case. Given the volume of records in each office, however, there was no way I could do this unnoticed. I settled finally on "use of the Xerox machine" as the best quantitative indicator. Certain types of reports are always copied. Furthermore, the Xerox machines in each office have accounting sheets which each user must sign. It was a simple matter to copy these sheets and then code them as data. This method was both unobtrusive and precise. After a few weeks, I knew how much Xeroxing each PO in every branch

office had done. I then attempted a simple statistical analysis, with "use of the Xerox machine" as my dependent variable. The analysis failed to confirm my theories, however. The independent variables that I believed would predict how much report writing each PO would do all proved statistically insignificant. At that point I had two options. I could discard or modify my theories about report writing or I could discredit my quantitative indicators. I was reluctant to discard my theories because, first, I "knew" that they were correct, and second, they were based on a common-sense notion of human nature. The second alternative, discrediting my quantitative indicators, was more attractive. According to Cook and Campbell (1975), a threat to construct validity occurs whenever there is a discrepancy between the construct variable and its operationalization. In this case, I searched for a discrepancy between the "amount of report writing" and "use of the Xerox machine," its operationalization. I knew that Xerox copying was an imprecise measure of report writing because supervisors, POs and secretaries make personal use of the Xerox machine. I had thought that the personal use was minimal, however. To investigate this assumption, I observed the Xerox machines in a few branch offices for an entire day. I discovered that many of the POs who were full-time students copied books, journal articles, and class assignments on the office Xerox machines. In one branch office, over 80 percent of the copying done during my observation period was for personal use. I admit to some pleasure at making this discovery. Had I not been able to discredit this quantitative indicator, I would have been forced to discard a number of theories. The displeasure in this would have come about simply because I "knew" the theories were correct. "Knowing" and quantitative data come together when one "proves" the other [p. 41].

Had it worked, the quantitative measure of "amount of Xerox machine use" would have been a simple, unobtrusive, and objective measure of report writing. As it turned out, it was more a measure of personal copying than of report writing and was, therefore, not a valid indicator for McCleary's purposes. We present this example not to suggest that quantification cannot work in participant observation but to demonstrate that it is not guaranteed to succeed. Numerical data are no freer from errors than are qualitative observations. They can each be biased. The use of the Xerox machine was an *unintentionally* biased measure. The POs were not purposely inflating the Xerox machine records to make it seem as though they were writing more reports—had they known someone was checking on their Xerox machine use, they probably would have reduced their use since they used it for nonofficial purposes.

Negative Case Analysis and Hypothesis Generation

Rather than design a study to test a hypothesis, field researchers gather data to generate hypotheses. Hypothesis testing is called *deductive* research. Experimenters generally work deductively, beginning with a theoretical framework, formulating a hypothesis, deducing what the results should be if the hypothesis is correct, and gathering data to test the hypothesis. Field researchers work in the opposite direction—generating rather than testing hypotheses. Theirs is called *inductive* research. They begin with observations and generate hypotheses that fit the data. In practice, no one works either purely deductively or purely inductively. Most researchers use a combination of inductive and deductive logic. Nonetheless, we can still characterize research methods as being predominantly deductive or inductive, and field work is predominantly inductive. Field workers may begin their research with some preliminary hunches and crude hypotheses, but as they proceed, they *revise* their hypotheses by the method of *negative case analysis,* a procedure that takes the place of statistical analysis in field work.

Negative case analysis requires the researcher to look for data that would disconfirm the hypothesis. When a single negative case is found, the participant observer revises the hypothesis so that it accounts for that case. Cressey's study of embezzlers illustrates how negative case analysis works (1953). He revised his hypothesis five times before he completed his analysis of what leads embezzlers to use other people's money. The following excerpts show how he used negative case analysis to generate his final hypothesis.

> The first hypothesis . . . was that positions of financial trust are violated when the incumbent has learned in connection with the business or profession in which he is employed that some forms of trust violation are merely technical violations and are not really "illegal" or "wrong," and on the negative side, that they are not violated if this kind of definition of behavior has not been learned [p. 27].

Cressey developed this hypothesis from previous work on white-collar crime. After he had interviewed only a few inmates convicted of embezzling, however, he revised his hypothesis because the men told him they had known all along that embezzling was illegal. His revised hypothesis was that

> positions of trust are violated when the incumbent defines a need for extra funds or extended use of property as an "emergency" which cannot be met by legal means . . . [p. 27].

Although some embezzlers admitted this was true, others said that there had been no financial "emergency," and they had still taken the money. Yet others said that when there had been financial emergencies earlier in their lives, they had resisted taking other people's money. Both these cases contradicted the second hypothesis, so Cressey developed a third:

> It shifted the emphasis from emergency to psychological isolation, stating that persons become trust violators when they conceive of themselves as having incurred financial obligations which are . . . non-socially sanctionable and which . . . must be satisfied by a private or secret means [p. 28].

When qualitative researchers revise their hypotheses, they test them not only in light of new data gathered in subsequent days or weeks but also in light of the data already recorded. Each day's observations become recorded on tape or on paper (and tape-recorded data are usually transcribed so that they, too, appear on paper) in the form of field notes, and these notes provide the basis for hypothesis revision and rejection and confirmation. When Cressey developed his third hypothesis, he checked it not only against subsequent interviews but also against previous ones. He found "that in a few of them there was nothing which could be considered as financial *obligation*, that is, as a debt which had been incurred in the past and for which the person at the present time felt responsible. Also, in some cases there had been non-sanctionable obligations at a prior time, and these . . . had not been alleviated by means of trust violations" (p. 28). So Cressey revised his hypothesis again:

> . . . emphasizing this time not financial obligations . . . but non-shareable *problems* not only because of an acknowledged responsibility for past debts, but because of present discordance between his income and expenditure as well [p. 29].

This included men who had not developed debts but who have been living above their means and had been afraid to admit this to their families or friends, and it included some who had been maintaining separate households without telling their family and friends. Again, however, there were exceptions, men who said they had had the nonshareable problem for a long time before they embezzled—"some stated that they did not violate the trust at the earlier period because the situation was not in sharp enough focus to 'break down their ideas of right and wrong'" (p. 30). This led to Cressey's final revision:

> Trusted persons become trust violators when they conceive of themselves as having a financial problem which is non-shareable, are aware that this problem can be secretly resolved by violation of the position of financial trust, and are able to apply to their own conduct in that situation verbalizations which enable them to adjust their conceptions of themselves as trusted persons with their conceptions of themselves as users of the entrusted funds or property [p. 30].

Cressey developed and tested this hypothesis with all cases of embezzlement found in one state prison. He then tested the hypothesis in three additional ways. He searched the literature on embezzlement to see if his hypothesis was consistent with other studies. He examined 200 cases of embezzlement collected by another researcher, E. H. Sutherland. And he went to a federal penitentiary and interviewed people convicted of federal bank and post office embezzlement. In each of these sources he looked for negative cases that would contradict his hypothesis and concluded the following:

> In all of the cases interviewed the process was found to be present, and when cases were examined with a view to answering the question: "Why did these men

not violate their trust in an earlier period?" it was seen that in earlier periods one or more of the events in the process had not been present [p. 31].

Cressey's book is atypical because few other published reports reveal so clearly the process of forming, revising, and retesting hypotheses. It is typical, however, in its use of negative case analysis to revise and generate hypotheses.

What makes qualitative research systematic is not standardization but negative case analysis. Cressey revised and developed his hypotheses and his conclusion by testing each revision against data he had already gathered and subsequent data that he continued to gather. Each time he found a negative case, he revised his hypothesis to incorporate the new evidence. He did this until there were no more disconfirmations. To conduct systematic qualitative research, therefore, means making a thorough search for cases that might disconfirm the hypothesis. The search and the data collection are not routinized; in fact, they usually require asking new and different questions in each search. The measurements are not standardized, the data are not uniform, and they do not yield numbers that can be added or averaged. But the *procedure* is systematic.

Negative case analysis, with its continual revision and retesting of hypotheses, is more like what experimenters do when they design subsequent studies. Participant observers in effect do a series of consecutive studies, but do them all within the same piece of research because there is no rule that says they cannot change the hypotheses or questions in midstream. The technique, in fact, requires changing the questions to take account of the unanticipated answers and observations that come along.

Negative case analysis is what the field worker uses in place of statistical analysis. In some respects, it is a more stringent analysis because it tolerates no deviations from the rule. Statistical analysis is necessary when there are deviations from the rule, as there always are in studies with quantitative measures. Not everyone receives the same score, and statistical tests become necessary to see whether group averages adhere to the predicted pattern in spite of individual deviations from the average (see Chapter 13). When negative case analysis has been completed, there are no deviations. This, of course, assumes that the researcher is capable of setting aside all personal or theoretical biases and conducting a tireless and objective search.

Participant observers are not gifted with any greater skills of objectivity than are experimental researchers, and some critics of qualitative research suspect that the social sciences in which participant observation predominates, such as anthropology, are also fields that recruit "countercultural romantics and displaced creative novelists" (D. T. Campbell, 1973, p. 3). Experimental social psychologists warn that most people err by believing vivid personal testimonials more than dull statistical information, which can make participant observation sound truer than it might be (Borgida & Nisbett, 1977). Participant observers are more vulnerable to criticism on these grounds than are experimenters. The ulitmate test of the believability of any kind of research, however, is not its seeming objectivity but its replicability. If no one can replicate or repeat the research and reach the same conclusions, the research is not believable, no matter how vivid the data.

Causal Analysis of Careers

Negative case analysis does not tell us whether a treatment produced an effect or whether two groups differ significantly from one another. It does not produce conclusions like those of an experiment or survey, but it does tell us something about causal processes, particularly about processes of becoming. Becoming a marijuana user, becoming an embezzler, becoming hypnotized—these are the topics and in some cases titles of some field studies. Field research often analyzes socialization into roles or "careers," both standard occupational careers and deviant careers. The causal analysis of field work consists of the delineation of the steps involved in becoming a marijuana user, parole officer, embezzler, or hypnotized subject.

A field researcher generally does not look for *single* causes but rather seeks *multiple* causes of social events. There are two different approaches: One, the *disjunctive* model, assumes there may be many alternative causes, any one of which may be sufficient to produce effect Y. For instance, "X or Z or W is sufficient to account for Y." The negative case analysis used by Cressey did not follow this model. The second approach, a *conjunctive* model, assumes there are multiple causes that work in combination. For instance, "X and Z and W are necessary *in combination* to account for Y." The negative case analysis used by Cressey follows the conjunctive model, identifying a combination or series of links in a causal chain.

There is nothing to prevent a field researcher from using negative case analysis with a disjunctive model. The analysis would try to show that in every case of Y (e.g., embezzling) the embezzler had *either* experienced a financial loss *or* incurred debts *or* been tempted to lead a higher life-style, and so on. Typically, however, field researchers who analyze careers use a conjunctive model, seeking a series of steps in a causal chain. Only when all the links are present does a person become a marijuana user, embezzler, or whatever the "career" may be. In his study of embezzlers, for instance, Cressey identified four conditions a person must meet before becoming an embezzler:

1. Be in a position of financial trust.
2. Have a nonshareable financial problem.

3. Recognize embezzlement as a possible solution to the problem.
4. Develop a way to rationalize embezzlement to make it seem like a "loan" or justifiable use of other people's money.

A participant observation study of becoming a marijuana user describes three conditions that lead to marijuana use for pleasure (Becker, 1963):

1. Learning the technique of smoking to produce effects.
2. Learning to perceive the effects.
3. Learning to enjoy the effects.

This series of conditions must occur in the order listed, and no one condition alone is sufficient to cause marijuana use. Learning to smoke to produce physical symptoms is necessary but not sufficient because the physical symptoms are not always obvious; the novice must learn to perceive them. The following quotation illustrates the learning that takes place:

> I didn't get high the first time. . . . The second time I wasn't sure, and he [smoking companion] told me, like I asked him for some of the symptoms or something. . . . So he told me to sit on a stool. I sat on—I think I sat on a bar stool—and he said, "Let your feet hang," and then when I got down my feet were real cold, you know.

> And I started feeling it, you know. That was the first time. And then about a week after that, sometime pretty close to it, I really got on. That was the first time I got on a big laughing kick, you know. Then I really knew I was on [pp. 49–50].

Without all three conditions present, people do not continue to use marijuana for pleasure. The following quote is from someone who learned to smoke marijuana to produce and perceive effects but did not enjoy them.

> It was offered to me and I tried it. I'll tell you one thing. I never did enjoy it at all. I mean it was just nothing that I could enjoy. [Well, did you get high when you turned on?] Oh, yeah, I got definite feelings from it. But I didn't enjoy them. I mean I got plenty of reactions, but they were mostly reactions of fear [p. 54].

Even people who have been regular users may discontinue use if one of the necessary conditions no longer occurs, as in the following instance:

> It was too much, like I only made about four tokes, and I couldn't even get it out of my mouth, I was so high, and I got real flipped. . . . I walked outside, and it was five below zero, and I thought I was dying. . . . I fainted behind a bush. I don't know how long I laid there . . . all weekend I started flipping, seeing things there and going through hell, you know, all kinds of abnormal things. . . . I just quit for a long time then [p. 57].

Participant observers frequently revise not only their hypotheses but also their topic of study. For instance, in Becker's analysis of becoming a marijuana user, he ultimately narrowed his topic to people who use marijuana for pleasure. The three steps he identified are the conditions that lead to the use of marijuana for pleasure. There are also other reasons why people may use marijuana, and Becker's analysis would not apply to them. For instance, some people may use marijuana to become or remain members of a social group, and they may smoke even if they perceive no effects. Others may use marijuana not for pleasure but for the thrill of doing something illegal or experiencing terror. In such cases, the fear reported by the people in the preceding quotations might not prevent further marijuana use. In revising their hypotheses, participant observers also redefine their topic of study.

When Kidder (1977) went to India to study the acculturation of foreign sojourners, she began with the idea that Western visitors would gradually learn to see India through the eyes of Indians who had become their "best friends." She revised this idea when she began interviewing sojourners and found that when she asked them for the names of Indians with whom they spent the most time, many had no answer. The friends with whom many sojourners spent time and talked about India were not Indians but other foreigners. The research topic, therefore, changed—from a study of how foreigners become acculturated into Indian society to a study of how they become socialized into a society of sojourners. Kidder interviewed foreign sojourners and recorded her own experiences as a Westerner in India to analyze the process of becoming socialized into the society of sojourners. She found sojourners acquired an identity that they had not anticipated if they had not lived abroad before: They quickly learned that they were wealthy and alien. They adapted to that identity by learning to bargain for goods and select among foods to protect both their wealth and their health. Their newly acquired wealth derived from the difference in cost of living at home and in India; their fragile health derived from their lack of immunity to a new variety of ailments. The final accommodation made by most of the sojourners was to recreate a Western life-style in India. They learned this from other sojourners, who taught them how to shop, eat, and socialize. Therefore, the study changed its focus—from an examination of how sojourners become "Indianized" to an observation of how they became "foreignized."

The Use of Analogy: Generalizing beyond the Specifics

In analyzing social institutions or relations, researchers often draw analogies between the phenomenon they have studied and other phenomena that readers are already familiar with. Field researchers do this as a means of showing that the particular people and places they studied tell us something about social relations in other settings. The analogies and comparisons provide a means of generalizing beyond the particulars. An analogy works in both directions. It gives a new perspective from which to understand the people in a particular study, and it suggests that people in general would probably behave the same way because there are analogous behaviors to be found among other people in other settings.

For instance, in her analysis of how people became hypnotized in the workshops she attended, Kidder (1972) showed how the process she observed is similar to attitude change; the workshop participants changed their attitudes about their own behaviors and experiences and learned to redefine hypnosis. The hypnotists brought about the change in several stages. First they convinced the subjects that they had acted as though they were hypnotized. For instance, when a subject asked after the first hypnotic induction:

> " . . . how do you know if you were in a trance or not? I mean, I know I did some things, but I think they were all under conscious voluntary control," the hypnotist replied, "I think you can tell if someone is in a trance by looking at them . . . the facial expressions. I could walk around the room and tell who wasn't and who was, by how they responded. I thought you were, but maybe you didn't *think* you were" [p. 317].

A second hypnotist concurred:

> You were actually the one that I thought went into trance the quickest [p. 317].

In addition to direct persuasion, the hypnotists used other techniques known to produce attitude change. They pointed out that the subjects were not coerced to behave as they had during the trance inductions; therefore, they must have done so because they wished to become hypnotized. When some subjects protested that they had behaved as though they were hypnotized and felt as though they were just "playing the game," the hypnotists pointed out that there must have been some reason for their doing so:

> . . .*Why* did you feel that you wanted to play the game? [p. 319].

The hypnotists negotiated responsibility by persuading the subjects that a hypnotic trance would not be forced on them but that they could enter a trance if they chose to cooperate:

> Well, let me say this. Earlier hypnosis was done in an authoritarian fashion—now it is much more permissive and we conceive of hypnosis as the achievement of the subject, in which the hypnotist helps . . . [p. 319].

The workshop participants who became hypnotized changed their definitions of their own behaviors and of hypnosis. They agreed that hypnosis was not so different from some relaxed waking states, and they conceded that they had behaved in ways that a hypnotist would call trance-like. The techniques that the hypnotists used are like techniques used in attitude change experiments. Therefore, becoming hypnotized is like changing one's attitude. The analogy makes hypnosis understandable in other terms. It may also seem like an irreverent debunking of hypnosis. Participant observation research sometimes has an air of debunking, as when a researcher compares mental hospitals with refuges for unwanted persons or schools with prisons. Reasoning by analogy is risky because it may draw comparisons between two processes that have never before been described in similar terms or even in the same sentence, and it may identify similarities between the sacred and the profane. Analogies are useful, however, because they enable us to understand new phenomena in familiar terms.

Ethical Issues

Field work raises some unique ethical issues precisely because the researcher is often a participant in the lives of the people under study. This gives the members of the group under study considerable scrutiny over the observer, but it also makes it difficult for them to know exactly when they are and are not serving as the objects of study. Is there ever any "time off"? Is a field worker obliged to announce whenever he or she is making mental notes, later to be recorded as field notes?

Shils (1959) takes a strong stand against observers masquerading as participants when they are really observers: "It is wrong for an inquirer ostensibly to take up membership in a community with the intention of conducting a sociological inquiry there without making it plain that that is what he is doing. His self-disclosure might occasionally hamper the research he is conducting, but the degree of injury suffered does not justify the deviation from straightforwardness implied by withholding his true intentions" (p. 128). This sounds like a reasonable request, but the problem is not so straightforward. For instance, Kidder lived and conducted research in India among other Americans and Europeans. She interviewed over 100 ex-patriots who consented and knew she was studying sojourners. In addition to conducting formal interviews, Kidder wrote field notes from her observations and participation as a sojourner among other ex-patriots. Would it be necessary, under Shils's requirement, that she announce her intention of making mental notes and later writing field notes every time she met someone on the street, at dinner, or wherever two foreigners might meet? She never knew whether a social encounter or chance meeting would yield data, and she did not carry a clipboard to announce when she was "on-" or "off-duty." Had she prefaced every social encounter with a warning that she might remember what was said and write it in her field notes, she would probably have been excluded from the social life of her compatriots. She had a bona fide membership in that community; how was she to draw the line between being a participant and being an observer?

Shils (1959) tries to draw a distinction between the observations of everyday life and the observations of field research: "The observations of everyday life are conducted in relationships which have arisen out of intentions other than observation. The observer has not created the relationship merely for the purpose of observing the other person" (p. 129). What happens, however, when observations from everyday life, where there is no intention of "doing research" later acquire significance for research? In a long author's note describing the methodological and ethical dilemmas of writing about a rape survivor in a hospital emergency room, Fine presents the problem of "what to do with information gathered in a context in which research was not being conducted, in which the assumption is one of privacy, from which a publishable article evolves two years later" (1984, p. 260). She had been working as a volunteer with rape survivors when it became clear that what some of the women said contradicted current psychological theories about coping and taking control. Could she use this information? The organization for which she volunteered had no objection. The women with whom she had talked had not been informed she was doing research "because at the time there was no research to be informed of" (p. 260). The notes Fine had were from relationships she had entered as a volunteer, not researcher. If we use Shils's criterion, Fine's were like the observations of everyday life. Does that preclude writing about them?

In deciding whether or not to publish her observations, Fine says, "a central consideration, here, is the issue of risk" (p. 261). Would writing about one rape survivor's reactions, her decision not to prosecute, and her fears for her family put her at greater risk? If the woman had chosen to prosecute the rapist (an option that Fine recommended but the woman rejected, for reasons reported in the article), Fine writes, "the potential risk would be enormous and publication out of the question" (p. 261). The survivor might not want to say the same things in a court of law.

Field researchers' participation in the lives of the people they study raises yet other issues. For instance, Stack, a white researcher, participated extensively in the lives of the black women she studied in a neighborhood she calls "The Flats." She provided some services: "Once I had the car, people continually asked me to run errands—taking children, goods and gossip between households. For a while all I seemed to be doing was taking half a pot roast from one house to another, picking up the laundry from a home with a washing machine, going to the liquor store for beer, or waiting with mothers in the local medical clinics for doctors to see their sick children" (Stack, 1974, p. 18). She also developed genuine friendships, not for the purpose of observing but as a consequence of being there. Did her services and her friendship make her observations more ethically correct, or less so?

Some writers have examined the role of the white researcher in black society (Cedric X, 1973) and have asked whether white people should study black people, particularly since that has been done for many years without clear benefits to the observed. Ladner (1971) says, "the relationship between the *researcher* and his *subjects,* by definition, resembles that of the oppressor and the oppressed, because it is the oppressor who defines the problem, the nature of the research, and, to some extent, the quality of the interaction . . ." (p. 6). Participant observation is clearly not free of ethical problems. This particular problem, however, defining the questions and issues solely from the researcher's perspective, is one that participant observers handle better than many other researchers. By being actors as well as observers, recording rather than manipulating events, and listening to people's explanations rather than forcing them to select from multiple-choice answers, field workers give the people they study a more equal voice (cf. Cicourel, 1964).

Summary

Participant observation differs from the other forms of research discussed in earlier chapters in several notable ways. The data are usually qualitative rather than quantitative and are recorded as field notes written largely from memory. Participant observers immerse themselves in the research setting and in the lives of the people they study. Although the field notes and research reports use fictitious names, the research subjects are not anonymous to the participant observer. They each become known to the other. Participant observers generate and revise their hypotheses as they gather data, and they use negative case analysis to arrive at conclusions that hold true for every observation, without exception.

The similarities are more subtle and difficult to detect. Like quasi experiments and surveys, participant observation is used to study naturally occurring phenomena. Participant observers do not manipulate treatments or randomly assign people to situations, but they occasionally attempt causal analysis. Studies of careers and adult socialization are causal analyses. They contain descriptions of necessary steps or conditions for becoming an embezzler, a marijuana user, a hypnotic subject, or whatever else the end point may be. Quasi experimenters, survey researchers, and participant observers each gather and analyze their data in different ways, but they face similar problems when they try to perform causal analyses of naturally occurring phenomena.

PART III

Data Collection

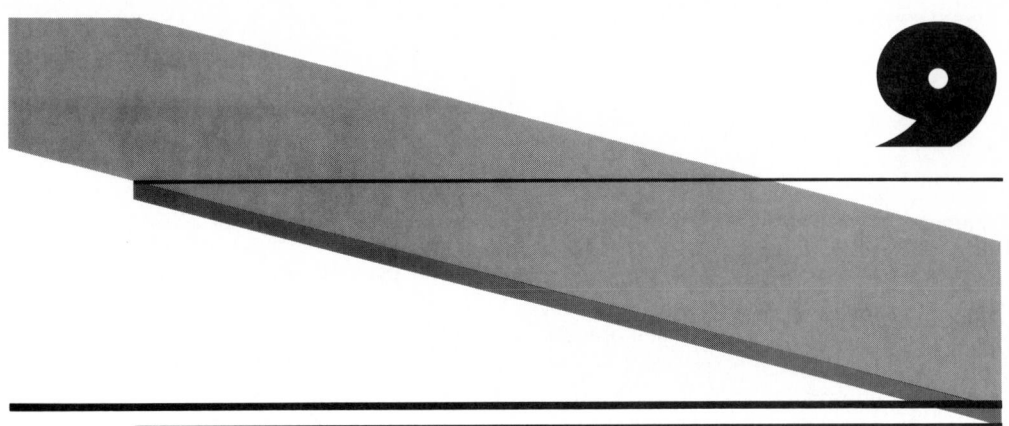

Scaling

Chapters 9–12 were written by Eliot R. Smith.

As noted in Chapter 3, a *construct* (such as attitude toward the Equal Rights Amendment, general political liberalism or conservatism, or the closeness of supervision found in a work place) is generally not considered to be directly observable. The researcher must assign scores to people, work places, or other objects to use as measures of the construct by referring to one or more observable attributes that are somehow related to the construct. So we might infer an attitude toward the ERA on the basis of a person's response to several questions that indicate favorability toward it or measure the closeness of supervision by asking workers to judge closeness based on observable criteria, such as the amount of time the supervisor spends nearby.

The set of categories or range of scores on a variable is called a *scale* (see Chapter 3), and the process of assigning scores to objects to yield a measure of a construct is called *scaling*. Scaling is always both a theoretically and empirically based activity. The use of observable characteristics to generate a scale that will reflect an underlying construct requires, first, a clear theoretical specification of the identity of the construct and, second, empirical results that document the reliability and validity of the obtained measurement.

Scaling techniques are of two basic types, which define the two major subdivisions of this chapter. Some scaling methods use *judgments*— by the individual in question or by observers—to assign scores to individuals or other objects to reflect the underlying construct. For example, individuals may rate their own liberalism or conservatism in response to a question like "Do you consider yourself to be very liberal, liberal, middle of the road, conservative, or very conservative?" The response places the individual in a particular position on the scale, which may meaningfully predict other attitudes, for example, voting choices. As another example, raters or judges may rate news stories as "favorable, neutral, or unfavorable" (Holsti, 1969, p. 107) with respect to a controversial issue. The raters evaluate the content and style of presentation of the story based on a standardized set of rules that they have been trained to use, assigning scores that locate the stories along a scale from favorable to unfavorable.

Other scaling methods use *multiple responses* or measurements of some type—often responses to questions—and combine the responses into a single scale score. For example, a congressional representative's positions on a number of roll-call votes might be combined to give a single score measuring the representative's overall liberalism or conservatism. Each individual response (each vote in the example) is assumed to be related to the underlying construct, and scaling techniques can combine them into a single overall measure of the construct. As another example, to measure a white person's attitudes toward racial integration, one might construct items like "I would prefer to have blacks as well as whites in school classes," "Property values do not decline when black people move into a neighborhood," and so on. An overall measure of favorability toward integration might be formed by summing the total number of *agree* responses. The total score would represent a *general* attitude toward integration, even though each individual item refers to a different specific aspect of the issue.

Advantages of Multiple-Item Scaling

In common with rating scales, multiple-item scales serve the basic function of providing a usable measure of a theoretical construct. However, multiple-item scaling procedures offer additional advantages to the researcher. First, scaling can reduce the complexity of data. Creating a single score to summarize several observed variables in a meaningful way can simplify the analysis. For example, it would be simpler to make predictions or test hypotheses about congressional representatives based on one total liberalism or conservatism score than based on a large number of individual roll-call votes.

Second, some scaling methods allow the researcher to test hypotheses about the nature of a construct; for example, to test whether liberalism or conservatism constitutes a single dimension or several different dimensions. The *dimensionality* of a construct that one wishes to measure is one of its most important attributes. If a series of variables all measure a single general characteristic of an attitude or other construct, the variables should all be highly interrelated. The construct is then said to be *unidimensional*. However, low relationships among some variables imply that several dimensions may exist. Perhaps political liberalism or conservatism is not a unidimensional construct, for we may find that representatives who are liberal on social welfare issues are not particularly likely to be liberal on civil rights issues. That is, the pattern of relationships among the variables might reveal high correlations among variables within each of the dimensions (e.g., between two votes on social welfare issues) but lower correlations between variables across dimensions (between a social welfare vote and a civil rights vote). We would then need to take account of at least two dimensions of overall political ideology, attitudes toward social welfare and civil rights.

The dimensionality of a construct is a research hypothesis that like any other is subject to empirical testing as well as theoretical consideration. In fact, dimensionality may change over time or vary with the subject population. For example, consider political efficacy, defined as the individual's sense of power or weakness about his or her relations to government and the formation of public policy. Four political efficacy items were found to form a single dimension in several studies conducted on a variety of populations during the 1950s and early 1960s (Campbell et al., 1954, 1960). Thus, it was assumed that efficacy constituted a fairly immutable, general, and unidimensional attitude, and it was found to be useful for explaining several aspects of political participation. Later, more-refined analyses of the same items with data collected during the 1960s revealed that the four items had split apart so that they represented *two* distinct dimensions rather than one. One dimension appeared to reflect attitudes about one's personal power to affect political life, whereas the other dimension was related to attitudes about politicians' ability to bring about change (Balch, 1974). The set of items no longer measured what they once had because the interrelationships of the items had changed. The dimensionality of the scale had changed from one to two dimensions.

Finally, the most important advantage of multiple-item scaling techniques is improved reliability and validity of measurement. A scale formed by combining multiple items or variables can (under specified circumstances) have better reliability and validity than the individual variables that make it up. A short example can illustrate this concept, which will be discussed in detail later in this chapter. Say that we are considering a set of roll-call votes from the U.S. Congress, all related to issues of social welfare. If we want to determine which representatives are generally liberal and which are conservative on social welfare issues, this might best be done by assigning each representative one scale score based on how he or she voted on all the roll calls. The votes could be combined in a meaningful way, using one of the multiple-item scaling techniques to be described later in the chapter. This would provide a simplified description, one scale value for each representative instead of the long list of individual votes. More important, the scale value might be more reliable and valid as a measure of liberalism or conservatism than any single vote. Any particular vote is surely influenced by many things besides the representative's underlying liberalism or conservatism, such as the impact of the specific issue on the home district, lobbyists' influences, or pressure from party leadership to vote a particular way. But across a large number of votes, such varying influences might be expected to roughly cancel out, leaving the scale formed from all the votes as a purer measure of the underlying construct, the representative's liberalism or conservatism.

In the remainder of this chapter, we discuss first the use of single-item rating scales and then the various techniques of combining multiple items to assign scores to individuals or other objects. For simplicity of presentation, most of our examples will focus on measuring attributes of individuals (such as attitudes) and therefore on the use of questionnaire responses as the basis for scaling. However, it is important to remember that *any* type of measurement—including observational and archival measures (Chapter 12) as well as questionnaire items (Chapter 11)—can be used as raw material for scaling procedures to improve the reliability and validity of measurement.

Rating Scales for Quantifying Judgments

The proper use of rating scales rests on an understanding of exactly what demands they place on the judge. Most commonly, the judgment task is viewed as consisting of two steps: forming a subjective impression or *judgment* of the position of the stimulus object along the desired dimension, and then translating that judgment into an overt *rating*, using the scale provided. "In scaling, the job of the judge is to map a domain comprising the subjective representations of a set of stimuli onto a range of responses" (Upshaw, 1984, p. 246).

As to the first step, researchers often simply assume that judges can be made aware of the desired dimension for judgment and can form an impression of each stimulus that corresponds to the object's position on that dimension, possibly with some degree of random error added. As we shall see later (in discussions of "halo bias," for instance), this assumption is not always justified. The judge's impression of the object on other dimensions may affect the judgment on the desired dimension. To the extent that this occurs, the ratings will be invalid, reflecting something other than the intended construct.

The second step is also problematic, because the correspondence of a particular subjective impression (of the favorability of a newspaper article toward a particular policy, for instance) to a particular point on the rating scale cannot be explicitly defined for the judge. Therefore, the way the judge uses the rating scale to reflect his or her subjective impressions, and hence the rating the judge assigns to any given stimulus, may vary from judge to judge or from time to time. That is, the judge's *frame of reference* for using the rating scale will affect his or her ratings. The frame of reference may depend on the particular set of objects that are being rated at the moment, the set of objects that the judge recalls having seen in the past, or particular salient stimuli or reference points (such as the judge's own attitude or a neutral point of the scale) that serve to "anchor" the scale. Such *context effects* in judgment have been widely investigated (Birnbaum, 1982; Sherif & Hovland, 1961; Upshaw, 1984) and lead to the conclusion that *"all judgment tasks ultimately refer to entire sets of objects, rather than isolated stimuli"* (Upshaw, 1984, p. 245; italics in original). That is, we cannot understand the rating given to a single object without knowing something about the range of objects with which the judge is implicitly comparing it.

Classic studies by Sherif and Hovland (1961) on ratings of attitudes illustrate this principle. They demonstrated that individuals' own attitudes influence their ratings of attitude statements on a dimension of favorability versus unfavorability to an attitude object (e.g., civil rights). People tend to place items with which they disagree in a more extreme category than items with which they agree. In effect, the individual's own attitude is used as an anchor, a reference point with which other attitude statements are compared in order to rate them.

Selltiz, Edrich, and Cook (1965) and Dawes, Singer, and Lemons (1972) applied this basic finding to develop an indirect or disguised attitude assessment procedure. Respondents either rate the extremity of statements provided by the researcher or write attitude statements characterizing the positions of people with varying positions on the issue. The extremity of the ratings or of the generated statements (as rated by judges) indicates the subjects' own attitude. For example, Dawes, Singer, and Lemons (1972) asked subjects who supported either the conservative George Wallace or the liberal Eugene McCarthy in 1968 to write statements characterizing the views of both candidates' supporters. A McCarthy supporter wrote "More law and order" and "Prosecute all dissidents and revolutionists" as positions of Wallace backers, as opposed to "Provide the American public with leaders chosen by the public instead of by political party machinery" and "Defend American freedom to dissent and disagree" as positions of McCarthy backers (Dawes, 1972, p. 127). The positions attributed to the opposition were generally more extreme than those attributed to the writer's own group, and judges' ratings of statement extremity could correctly classify over 90 percent of the subjects as Wallace or McCarthy supporters. This procedure, then, can be used to assess subjects' attitude in a disguised form. (Note that the disguise is only partial: Subjects are obviously aware of the attitude domain in which the investigator is interested, though they may remain unaware that their responses give clues to their own attitudes.)

However, despite their possible usefulness in indirectly assessing attitudes, for the most part such context or anchoring effects on ratings have been viewed as an important problem in research, a barrier to obtaining reliable and valid ratings. Several different types of rating scales have been used, which take different approaches to the issues of reliability and validity.

Graphic Rating Scales

One of the most widely used is the graphic rating scale. The judge or rater indicates his or her rating by placing a mark at the appropriate point on a line that runs from one extreme of the attribute in question to the other. Scale points with brief descriptions may be indicated along the line, but their function is to serve as a guide to the judge in locating the rating on the scale rather than to provide discrete categories. Figure 9.1 shows an example, a "feeling thermometer" graphic rating scale. This can be used by respondents to rate their feelings toward some object, such as a political candidate, along a dimension from warm (favorable) to cold (unfavorable).

One of the major advantages of graphic rating scales is their ease of use. To use them effectively, though, one should take several precautions. For example, one should avoid end statements so extreme that they will

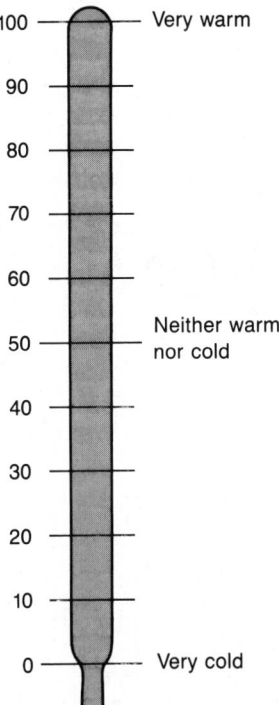

FIGURE 9.1 "Feeling thermometer" graphic rating scale

rarely be used (e.g., "hot" and "freezing" on a feeling thermometer scale or "best job imaginable" and "worst job imaginable" on a scale of feelings about one's job). Guilford (1954) presents a detailed discussion. Graphic rating scales do not explicitly take account of the frame of reference problem, simply assuming that most judges will use the scale in the same way.

Itemized Rating Scales

Itemized rating scales are also called *specific category scales* (Krech & Crutchfield, 1948) and *numerical scales* (Guilford, 1954). In this type of scale, the rater selects one of a small number of categories that are ordered by their scale position. The number of scale positions or categories varies, depending on the research problem and the type of judgments required, but 5 to 11 categories are typical.

For example, a respondent might be asked to rate his or her own liberalism or conservatism by choosing from categories such as "extremely liberal," "liberal," "moderate; middle of the road," "conservative," and "extremely conservative." The respondent is instructed to choose the category that best describes his or her own political viewpoint.

The resulting rating may be used to predict voting behavior, preferences on specific political issues, and so on.

The verbal descriptions used to specify the categories may be brief statements indicating only degrees of the attribute (like the example just given) or may be elaborate descriptions including illustrations of behavior appropriate to the category. As an example of detailed descriptions, Sherif, Sherif, and Nebergall (1965) labeled categories on their scale of political attitudes with such descriptions as "The election of the Republican presidential and vice-presidential candidates in November is absolutely essential from all angles in the country's interests" at one extreme, and "From the point of view of the country's interests, it is hard to decide whether it is preferable to vote for presidential and vice-presidential candidates of the Republican or the Democratic Party in November" as a neutral position. In general, it has been assumed that more clearly defined categories should decrease interjudge variability in the use of the scale and hence give greater reliability. It is likely that relatively vague categories like "liberal" or "conservative" will be used in different ways by judges with different frames of reference. For example, someone who associates mainly with relatively liberal college professors may rate his or her political attitudes as moderate, whereas another individual, whose daily contacts are mostly with conservative businesspersons, might rate the identical position as somewhat liberal—due to a different frame of reference. However, even the use of extensive and precise descriptions for rating categories cannot completely eliminate context effects.

Comparative Rating Scales

Graphic and itemized rating scales do not require the rater to make *explicit* comparisons of the rated individual or object with others, though, as argued previously, all ratings are inherently comparative because of the effects of frames of reference on the use of rating scales (Upshaw, 1984). Comparative rating scales—as their name suggests—explicitly require the judge to make comparisons. The positions on the rating scale are expressly defined on the basis of a given population or social group or in respect to people of known characteristics. For example, a questionnaire used in selecting applicants for admission to a graduate school may ask the rater for an estimate of the given applicant's ability to do graduate work, "as compared with the total group of graduate students you have known." Is the applicant more capable than 10 percent of them? 20 percent? 30 percent? Or the rater may be asked to indicate, for example, whether an individual's leadership skill most closely resembles that of person A, of person B, or of person C (all of whom are known to the rater and all of whom have been assessed in terms of their leadership skill). In the first example given earlier, in order to make a valid rating, the judge must have a clear conception of the range and distribution of the abilities of the total graduate student group. Scales of the second type are often difficult to con-struct, for there may not be sufficient variation in leadership behavior (or whatever attribute is being rated) among the people known to the judges for them to serve as examples for the various points on the scale.

Another comparative or relative rating procedure is the *rank-order scale.* Here the judge is required to rank individuals specifically in relation to one another; the judge indicates which person is highest in regard to the characteristic being measured, which is next highest, and so on, down to the one who is lowest. Ranking in this fashion is used only when the investigator is concerned with a limited group of individuals. The rating an individual receives indicates simply his or her relative rank or position in the group being studied; it would not necessarily be of any usefulness apart from the specific group whose members are being compared.

Self-Ratings Versus Ratings by Others

All these types of scales may be used to secure individuals' ratings of them-selves or someone else's rating of each of them. It seems reasonable to assume that individuals are often in a better position to observe and report their own beliefs, feelings, and fears than anyone else is. This assumption is valid, however, only if individuals are aware of their own beliefs and feelings and are willing to reveal them to others. If a man is unaware, for example, of the fact that he has hostile feelings toward a particular minor-ity group or if he is aware of such feelings but is afraid of the consequ-ences of revealing them, the self-rating procedure is of little value. Another difficulty arises from the fact that even if individuals are capable of reporting their beliefs or feelings objectively, their concept of what con-stitutes a moderate or an extreme position may be quite different from those of others making comparable self-ratings. That is, since in most self-rating procedures each judge rates only one stimulus (i.e., him- or herself), it is difficult to ensure that the frame of reference and hence usage of the response scale is comparable across judges.

Despite the hazards involved, self-ratings have proved useful in the measurement of social attitudes and other attributes. For beliefs and feel-ings that the individual can be expected to know and be willing to report— for example, attitudes toward specific television programs—self-ratings are probably the most useful source of information. In fact, self-ratings have been shown to be equal or superior to other types of assessments in predicting a wide range of criteria, including how the person is viewed by friends on personality dimensions, the career the person will enter, and how the person will function in school or in psychotherapy (Shrauger & Osberg, 1981).

Several precautions must be taken, however, to obtain reliable and valid self-ratings. The individuals should be told explicitly and specifically what attribute is to be rated, should be given an opportunity and incentive to recall their behaviors in past situations that are relevant to the judgment, and should be motivated to give accurate (rather than socially desirable) ratings (Shrauger & Osberg, 1981). The latter point is probably the most important. It is often assumed that when ratings are to be used to distribute valued resources (such as jobs or positions in training or therapy programs), self-raters will distort their responses rather than convey their honest assessments. However, evidence for this assumption is limited, and studies of alcoholics and other drug abusers even suggest that these people are usually accurate in reporting their drinking and drug use—an area where one might expect dishonest responses (Petzel, Johnson, & McKillip, 1973). The researcher should attempt to enlist the subject's cooperation and active involvement in the rating task and should stress that accuracy is highly valued and will be checked (Jones & Sigall, 1971). With precautions like these, self-ratings can give reliable and valid measures of a variety of constructs.

Construction and Use of Rating Scales: Some Cautions

Since a large element of subjective judgment enters into the use of rating scales, both random and systematic errors may influence the measurement. A common form of systematic error is *halo bias* (W. H. Cooper, 1981). This refers to the tendency for overall positive or negative evaluations of the object or person being rated to influence ratings on specific dimensions. For example, Thorndike (1920) found that supervisors' ratings of teachers yielded a very high correlation of 0.80 between rated intelligence and rated ability to discipline. Since the actual correlation (based on intelligence test scores) is probably only around the modest level of 0.30, Thorndike concluded that the raters were unable to judge each dimension independently. Instead, their global evaluations of the teacher influenced their ratings of both "intelligence" and "ability to discipline," increasing the correlation. Another type of error, related to halo bias, is the *generosity error*, where the rater overestimates the desirable qualities of people that the rater likes.

Other types of error are related to the general frame of reference problem described earlier—that is, they reflect differences among raters in the translation of subjective judgments into overt rating scale responses. Some raters seem to *avoid extreme response categories* and assign ratings to only the more moderate categories. The *contrast error* (Murray, 1938), a tendency for raters to see others as opposite to them on a trait, arises from the use of one's own position on a dimension as an anchor for rating others. For example, raters who are very orderly tend to rate others as relatively disorderly, and vice versa.

Besides systematic errors or biases like these, random errors can enter into any ratings and reduce their reliability. The most obvious source of random error is simple *mistakes* caused by rater fatigue, inattention, or improper training.

A number of steps can be taken in the construction and use of rating scales to minimize the impact of such biases and errors. Obviously, training and motivating the raters will play an important role. The use of multiple raters and computation of a mean rating for each ratee will almost always reduce the impact of random errors (unreliability), since the independent errors will tend to balance each other out in the averaging process. The use of multiple raters also reduces halo bias, compared to the use of a single rater (Kenny & Berman, 1980). Of course, combining multiple independent ratings is generally more feasible when the rating is being done on the basis of recorded material or by people observing a sample of behavior. It is often impossible to have more than one rater present to observe live social interaction.

Increasing the rater's familiarity with the ratee also reduces halo bias (E. M. Brown, 1968), though it may increase generosity errors (Guilford, 1954). This may account for the fact that self-ratings (which are obviously made by a familiar rater) are less subject to halo than are ratings by others (Thornton, 1980). Ratings made concurrently with observation of behaviors are less subject to halo than are ratings made from memory after witnessing the behaviors (Shweder & D'Andrade, 1980). On the other hand, one frequently used technique does *not* seem to be effective in reducing halo bias: rating all ratees on one category before going on to the next category instead of rating each ratee on all categories in succession (W. H. Cooper, 1981).

In terms of the construction of the rating scale itself, as opposed to the procedures involved in its use, certain precautions can reduce error and bias. Many precautions amount to efforts to give all the raters a common frame of reference so that they use the rating scale in the same way. For example, all raters may be asked to rate a common set of practice stimuli before proceeding to the actual ratings required by the research. Their ratings on the practice stimuli can be compared and training can be provided until the ratings are made in similar ways. Raters' tendency to avoid extreme positions may be counteracted by giving less-extreme labels to these positions. People may be more likely to check, for example, "I am well satisfied with my job" than "I am completely satisfied with my job," and may be more likely to check "There are many things about my job that I do not like" than "There is nothing about my job that I like."

The use of a common frame of reference is also more likely if the scale (or the training procedure) provides clear, concrete definitions of the characteristic being measured, preferably including illustrations of behaviors or other responses that exemplify the various rating categories. (Many of the principles of clarity and precision in question writing from Chapter 11 apply here.)

The labeling of response categories should also take account of generosity biases. For example, in rating their instructors, college students rarely use any category worse than "good." Therefore, on a five-category scale, with "average" as the middle category, almost all the responses would fall in the upper two categories. Some universities therefore use asymmetrical wording, with "good" at the center of the scale, in order to obtain a more symmetrical response distribution: "superior," "very good," "good," "average," and "poor" (Dawes, 1972, p. 115). This example also points out the common fallacy of interpreting rating scale response *literally* (Dawes, 1972). On a scale like this one, 80 percent to 90 percent of the responses may be above the "average" category, though it is obviously impossible for 90 percent of the instructors to be above average in their teaching effectiveness. The information in a rating scale response is not literally contained in the specific category label that the rater chooses (such as "good" or "average") but is implicit in the scale's demonstrated relationships to other measures (its validity).

Finally, the number of categories on the response scale can influence reliability. Providing fewer than five to seven categories seems to limit reliability, though increasing the number of categories over this number helps little if at all (Masters, 1974).

Summary

The apparent simplicity of rating scales often recommends their use, though the time and effort involved in scale construction, rater training, and the use of multiple raters to achieve adequate reliability should not be underestimated. Rating scales can provide convenient measures of many characteristics (such as effectiveness of leadership or emotionality of facial expressions), and rating scales have the advantage of flexibility. They can be used to code communication content, observed behavior, questionnaire responses, or almost any other form of data.

The use of rating scales, like any method of gathering data, demands attention to reliability and validity. Some relevant considerations in scale construction and use have been mentioned. However, there is no substitute for actual checks on reliability and validity, such as the examination of relationships between ratings and external criteria. Not all ratings can be assumed to be valid, particularly when the raters' differing frames of reference influence the ways in which judgments are reported on the rating scale, as they will when the characteristics to be rated is vague and ill-defined. Intuitive judgments of vague concepts—even by trained and experienced people, such as clinical psychologists (Kelly & Fiske, 1950)—sometimes show little evidence of measurement reliability or validity. However, properly constructed rating scales with specific, concrete referents often have acceptable reliability and validity.

Multiple-Item Scales

When an individual indicates his or her own attitude or a judge rates an object on some scale, a large element of intuitive judgment is involved, no matter how precise the rating instructions and no matter how well trained the rater. This fact brings both benefits and costs. First, judges can meaningfully rate objects even when they have no idea of what specific properties of the objects underlie the ratings; for example, judges could rate the emotionality of facial expressions in photographs or the physical attractiveness of the faces. Such ratings must be done on an intuitive basis because we do not presently know how else to do them. Second, ratings by judges are often easy and inexpensive to obtain and may be the best way to measure some constructs, even if alternative methods are available, for example, in assessing the favorability of newspaper articles toward some issue.

However, as noted, the subjective judgment in the use of rating scales makes the ratings vulnerable to bias—different judges making ratings with different frames of reference, using different criteria, or even no criteria at all—and hence unreliability or invalidity of measurement. If we wanted ratings of the "honesty" of a series of faces portrayed in photographs, it is possible that judges' ratings might instead be most influenced by their attractiveness. We then would have a set of measurements that did not validly reflect the dimension in which we were interested, and in real life we would often not have any way to *know* that this was the case.

For these reasons, particularly for measuring attitudes, procedures have been devised that do not depend on single judgments or ratings of the construct of interest, either by the individual or by observers. Instead, individuals respond (usually with agreement or disagreement) to *multiple* statements relevant to the attitude under study, and scores are assigned by numerically combining the responses. The process of constructing the standardized set of items establishes that the combined scale score is a reliable and valid measure of the underlying attitude.

Item Construction

A number of considerations are important in constructing items for use in multiple-item scales. First, the items must be empirically related to the construct that is to be measured; otherwise, they can contribute nothing (except random error) to the measurement. The different types of scaling techniques to be discussed all ensure that this condition is met, though in different ways.

Second, the items must differentiate among people who are at different points along the dimension being measured. In order to discriminate not only between extreme positions but also among individuals near the midpoint of the scale, items that tap different points along the scale are generally included. Thus, a test of opinions about child-rearing practices to measure strictness versus permissiveness would contain some items representing a very strict approach, a very permissive approach, a position of moderate strictness, and so on. However, items representing the most extreme positions are often not worth including. For example, if a particular item elicits 97 percent agreement and only 3 percent disagreement, it would not be of much value in discriminating among people with different positions on the attitude dimension (especially considering that many of the 3 percent may simply represent random errors).

Third, it is important to avoid items that are "double-barreled" or otherwise ambiguous (Dawes, 1972, pp. 114–15). Consider the item "Most people don't realize the extent to which their lives are governed by secret plots hatched in hidden places" (drawn from the authoritarianism scale of Adorno et al., 1950). Does a person who disagrees with this statement mean that most people *do realize* the extent to which their lives are controlled by secret plots, or does disagreement mean that secret plots *do not govern* people's lives? Obviously, interpreting responses to such double-barreled items is problematic. Other types of ambiguity can create similar interpretive problems, for example with items that use intrinsically vague words such as *often, most, frequently, many,* and so on. (Many points in Chapter 11 on questionnaires, particularly concerning clarity and precision in question writing, are relevant to the construction of attitude scale items.)

Finally, it is important to include items worded in both positive and negative directions, so that the attitude being measured is expressed by a "yes" or "agree" response approximately half the time and by "no" or "disagree" half the time. This avoids confounding the measure of the attitude itself with *acquiescent response style,* the tendency to generally agree with statements regardless of their content. If a scale were composed of all positively-worded items, a person who just tended to agree a lot would be wrongly classified as having a high level of the attitude. However, Rorer (1965) and others have argued that much of the evidence traditionally regarded as demonstrating response styles such as acquiescence is better interpreted in terms of subjects' reactions to the content of the items, and that content-independent response styles are not a major contaminant of questionnaire responses. Still, since it often requires little extra effort in the scale construction process, it is a worthwhile precaution to create balanced scales with roughly equal proportions of "agree" and "disagree" items.

Three Types of Multiple-Item Scales

Three general procedures for developing mutliple-item attitude scales have been widely used. They differ most fundamentally in their assumptions about the relationship between the person's underlying attitude and the responses that will be given to the individual items that make up the scale. Other differences (in the types of item used, the way the individual responses are combined to produce a scale score, and so on) follow from this fundamental difference. All three scaling methods assume that attitude items can be thought of in terms of their position along the attitude dimension, that is, that "The Equal Rights Amendment should be passed immediately" represents a position favorable to the ERA, whereas "The ERA will contribute to the breakdown of the traditional family" represents a position of opposition.

The fundamental assumptions of the three scaling methods are as follows. *Differential scales* or *Thurstone scales* are based on the assumption that people with a particular position on the attitude dimension will agree only with items that express positions near their own and will disagree with items that differ in either direction (both more favorable and less favorable items). *Cumulative* or *Guttman scales* involve the assumption that people with a particular position will agree with items on one side of their own position and will disagree with items that fall on the other side. Finally, *summated* or *Likert scales*, the most commonly used, rely on the assumption that the probability of agreeing with each item either increases or decreases steadily depending on the individual's own position on the attitude dimension. These statements will be elaborated as each type of scale is discussed in turn.

Thurstone Scales

Differential scales, developed initially by L. L. Thurstone (1929), include items that represent known positions on the attitude scale. Subjects are assumed to agree with only those items whose position is close to their own and to disagree with items that represent distant positions.

Construction and example   The scale is constructed by a complex multi-step procedure. A large number of statements related to the attitude are gathered or constructed, and they are submitted to judges. Working independently, the judges classify the statements into categories (usually 11) on the basis of the statement's favorability toward the attitude object (or position on a dimension such as liberalism-conservatism). The first category includes the statements that the judge considers most favorable to the object, the second the next most favorable statements, and so on. The *scale value* of each item, ranging from 1 to 11, is then calculated as its average category placement by the judges. Table 9.1 shows an example of Thurstone-type items with their scale values, drawn from Thurstone's study of attitudes toward the church (1929). Items on which judges fail to agree are discarded as ambiguous or irrelevant. Finally, items representing a wide range of scale values are selected to form the scale. They are presented to subjects, usually in a random order (i.e., not ordered by scale value), with instructions to check each statement with which they agree. The subjects' attitude is calculated as the mean of the scale values of the items with which they agree.

Monotone and nonmonotone items   In contrast to other scale types, Thurstone scales require items that have a definite position on the scale— that is, items that will elicit agreement from people with positions near

TABLE 9.1 Example of a Thurstone Scale

Scale Value	Item
1.2	I believe the church is a powerful agency for promoting both individual and social righteousness.
2.2	I like to go to church for I get something worthwhile to think about and it keeps my mind filled with right thoughts.
3.3	I enjoy my church because there is a spirit of friendliness there.
4.5	I believe in what the church teaches but with mental reservations.
6.7	I believe in sincerity and goodness without any church ceremonies.
7.5	I think too much money is being spent on the church for the benefit that is being derived.
9.2	I think the church seeks to impose a lot of worn-out dogmas and medieval superstitions.
10.4	The church represents shallowness, hypocrisy, and prejudice.
11.0	I think the church is a parasite on society.

Note: On the actual questionnaire the items would appear in a random order, not ordered by scale value as shown here.

the item's scale value but disagreement from others whose attitudes are *either* more favorable or less favorable. For example, "Affirmative action is a necessary evil" will obtain agreement from people with a particular attitude position near the midpoint of the scale, but people who either strongly favor or strongly oppose affirmative action will disagree with the item. This is an example of *nonmonotone* item of the sort that Thurstone scales use. Guttman and Likert scales, in contrast, require *monotone* items: items that are either clearly favorable or unfavorable to the object. The probability of agreeing with such items should increase (or decrease) consistently as subjects move from one end of the attitude dimension to the other. For example, "Affirmative action programs increase the overall fairness of our society" would presumably elicit consistently more agreement from people who favor affirmative action than from those who oppose it.

Advantages and disadvantages The Thurstone scaling method offers certain advantages. For one thing, the responses offer a check on the scale's assumptions. Subjects are supposed to agree with only a narrow range of items around their own position (such as items with scale values of 6.7, 7.1, and 8.0). If a subject checks a wide range of noncontiguous items (e.g., scale values of 3.3, 7.1, and 9.4), it may mean that the subject does not have an attitude on this issue at all or that the attitude is not organized along the dimension assumed by the scale. For subjects who meet the assumptions of the scale, the *latitude of acceptance* (defined as the range of scale values that the subject agrees with) can be calculated from the responses. This measure is related to the degree of the subject's involvement with the issue or the attitude: Those who are more involved in an issue tend to agree with a narrower range of positions (Sherif & Sherif, 1969).

However, the Thurstone scaling technique is little used today because of several disadvantages. Most obviously, the construction procedure is lengthy and cumbersome. Though the use of judges' ratings may allow the discarding of items that are ambiguous or meaningless, other scaling techniques achieve similar results with less effort. And there is much evidence that the attitudes of the judges themselves influence their assignment of scale values to the items, which is undesirable in the context of this measurement technique (Hovland & Sherif, 1952). Finally, and perhaps most important, Thurstone scales have generally lower reliabilities than Likert-type scales with the same number of items (Tittle & Hill, 1967). Since reliability is the first requirement of any scaling technique, this disadvantage is crucial.

Guttman Scales

Cumulative scales are also made up of a series of items with which the subject indicates agreement or disagreement. The special feature of cumulative or Guttman scales (Guttman, 1944) is that items are related in such a way that a subject with a particular attitude will agree with all items on one side of that position and disagree with other items. As noted, Guttman scales thus require each item to be monotone: either clearly favorable or unfavorable to the object.

Construction and examples An analogy with a test of ability may make the basis of Guttman scales clear. Imagine a mathematical ability test composed of three items: a simple addition problem like $3 + 4 =$, a long-division problem involving four- and five-digit numbers, and a complex problem in calculus. We would expect anyone who passes the long-division problem to pass the first problem as well, and anyone who passes the calculus problem to pass both others also. That is, a person's level of mathematical ability can be thought of as a point on a scale, and the person is expected to pass all items below his or her ability level but to fail all items above it. With "agree" and "disagree" substituted for "pass" and "fail," this is exactly the pattern expected in a Guttman scale. The scale score is simply defined as the total number of items passed or agreed with.

In the field of social attitudes, one of the earliest scales was intended to have this cumulative pattern: the Bogardus Social Distance Scale (1925, 1928). The scale lists a number of relationships and asks which would be acceptable with members of a particular social or ethnic group. Table 9.2 illustrates the scale.

TABLE 9.2   Bogardus Social Distance Scale

	To Close Kinship by Marriage	To My Club as Personal Chums	To My Street as Neighbors	To Employment in My Occupation	To Citizenship in My Country	As Visitors Only to My Country	Would Exclude from My Country
English	1	2	3	4	5	6	7
Black	1	2	3	4	5	6	7
French	1	2	3	4	5	6	7
Chinese	1	2	3	4	5	6	7
Russian and so on	1	2	3	4	5	6	7

Directions: For each race or nationality listed in the scale, circle each of the classifications to which you would be willing to admit the average member of that race or nationality (not the best members you have known or the worst). Answer in terms of your first feeling reactions.

Note that the items are monotone, and the expected cumulative pattern seems logical. That is, a person who circles number 4 in respect to some group, indicating willingness to accept them to employment in his or her occupation, should also be willing to allow them as citizens in the country (number 5) and should *not* circle 6 and 7 (since these two items are worded negatively). If the subject did not circle 3, we would not expect them to circle 2 or 1.

Response patterns that allow the formation of cumulative scales occur in other domains as well, including the economic liberalism and favorability to civil rights of Supreme Court justices (Spaeth, 1965) and the conditions under which physicians will recommend abortions (Koslowski, Pratt, & Wintrob, 1976). The items range from those conditions in which most physicians sampled would recommend abortion, such as the pregnancy constituting a threat to the mother's life (77 percent accept abortion), to those in which most would reject abortion, such as the pregnancy disrupting the mother's career or education (only 40 percent accept). For the most part, the physicians' acceptance of abortion under the 11 different circumstances studied followed the cumulative pattern of a Guttman scale. For example, physicians who accept abortion if the pregnancy disrupts the mother's career also accept abortion if the pregnancy threatens the mother's life.

Advantages and disadvantages   The most important advantage of a scale with this cumulative pattern is that a single number (the person's scale score) carries complete information about the exact pattern of responses to every item—under the crucial assumption that there is no random error in responses. For example, anyone with a score of 2 on the preceding ability test would be assumed to have passed the addition and division items and failed the calculus problem, rather than any of the other possible patterns of two passes and one failure. Anyone with a score of 5 for a particular group on the social distance scale would be known to favor allowing them to his or her street as neighbors, and into his or her country and occupation, but not to a social club or to close kinship by marriage. Thus, the scale score from a cumulative scale is unusually informative.

Another advantage is that the scale provides a test of the unidimensionality of the attitude. Items that reflect more than one dimension generally will not form a cumulative response pattern; indeed, Guttman (1944) originally proposed his technique as a means of examining unidimensionality rather than constructing scales. However, this advantage is tempered by the fact that simple random error in responses may destroy the perfect cumulative response pattern, making it difficult to determine whether the attitude domain is "really" unidimensional when error is present (as it usually is). Various measures of the "scalability" or "reproducibility" of a set of items have been developed in an attempt to answer such questions (Guttman, 1944; Green 1956). Figure 9.2 illustrates some possible response patterns for a hypothetical four-item Guttman scale. The first five rows show the expected response patterns; if all subjects give these patterns, the scale has perfect reproducibility, indicating perfect unidimensionality. However, error in responses may produce patterns like the examples in the last three rows, which do not fit the cumulative pattern. Measures of reproducibility use various assumptions to estimate the proportion of error responses and hence the degree of departure of the scale from unidimensionality.

Other disadvantages of the Guttman scaling technique are related to its limitation to unidimensional domains. First, unidimensionality should not be assumed to be a property of a set of *items;* rather, it is a pattern of an attitude within a given population of individuals. A particular set of items may show a unidimensional pattern for one group of individuals but not for another, or it may be unidimensional at one time but not later (as the example of a political efficacy scale at the beginning of this chapter illustrates).

Subject Number	Items				Scale Score
	1	2	3	4	
Expected Response Patterns					
1	−	−	−	−	0
2	+	−	−	−	1
3	+	+	−	−	2
4	+	+	+	−	3
5	+	+	+	+	4
"Error" Response Patterns: Examples					
6	+	−	−	+	
7	−	−	+	+	
8	−	+	−	−	

FIGURE 9.2 Patterns of responses on a Guttman scale (+ means agree, − means disagree)

Second, it is hard to find domains that are unidimensional. Consider attitudes toward government, for example. People may have attitudes toward government regulation of business that are distinct from their attitudes toward taxation, civil rights enforcement, and so on. No one of these dimensions would completely index the attitude toward the complex concept of *government* or provide the sole basis for predicting voting or other behaviors. The best approach in such cases is to accept the fact that the attitude of interest may be multidimensional and to measure it with Likert-type scales, which do not require strict unidimensionality, rather than with Guttman-type scales. For these reasons, Guttman scales are less frequently used today than Likert scales to measure complex social attitudes.

Likert Scales

Summated scales of the form developed by Likert (1932) are the most widely used in the social sciences today. Like Thurstone and Guttman scales, a Likert scale consists of a set of items to which the subject responds with agreement or disagreement. However, there are a number of differences. Only monotone items are used in Likert scales, that is, items that are definitely favorable or unfavorable in direction, not items that reflect a middle or uncertain position on the issue. Respondents ordinarily indicate a *degree* of agreement or disagreement to each item rather than simply checking those items with which they agree. For example, subjects may respond to an item like "A working mother can establish just as warm and secure a relationship with her children as a mother who does not work" with (1) strongly disagree, (2) disagree, (3) agree, or (4) strongly agree. The set of response choices may or may not include a middle (neutral, undecided) position.

Finally, the scale score is derived by summing the numerically coded agree and disagree responses to each item (with sign reversals for negatively worded items) rather than by averaging the scale values of the items with which the subject agrees, as in a Thurstone scale. As with any scaling method, the scale score is interpreted as representing the subject's attitude or other construct being measured. The basis for the interpretation is that the probability of agreeing with favorable items (and disagreeing with unfavorable ones) increases directly with the degree of favorability of the subject's attitude. (This is the definition of monotone items.) Thus, a subject who is highly favorable will respond favorably to many items and be given a high score, a subject who is ambivalent or holds a middle position will respond favorably to some items and unfavorably to others and be given an intermediate score, and a subject who is unfavorable will respond unfavorably to many items and be given a low score. As noted in Chapter 3, the measured response to any single item is considered to reflect in part the error-free underlying attitude or other construct and in part measurement error (i.e., $X = T + E$). The summation of many item responses into a single scale score allows the error components (some of which are positive, some negative) partially to be cancelled out, while preserving and strengthening the common core of the "true" underlying attitude reflected in each item.

Construction and example The Mach IV scale of Christie and Geis (1970), a measure of "Machiavellianism" or the desire to manipulate other people, is a Likert scale. The items from this scale include those shown in Table 9.3. There, (+) and (−) indicate the direction of the item's relationship to the total scale; they are included for the reader's information but would not appear on the scale as administered to subjects. Subjects indicate agreement or disagreement with each item on a four-point scale ranging from strong agreement to strong disagreement. The sum of responses to the items labeled (+), minus the sum of responses to the items labeled (−), constitutes the scale score.

The procedure for constructing a Likert-type scale involves several steps: (1) Based on a theoretical conception of the attitude or other construct to be measured, the investigator assembles a large number of items that are relevant to the attitude and that are either clearly favorable or unfavorable (i.e., are monotone). (2) The items are administered to a group of *pilot subjects* drawn from a population that is similar to that in which

TABLE 9.3   Example of a Likert-Type Scale (Christie & Geis, 1970)

Item	(Circle One)			
	Strongly Agree	Agree	Disagree	Strongly Disagree
2. The best way to handle people is to tell them what they want to hear. (+)	SA	A	D	SD
10. When you ask someone to do something for you, it is best to give the real reasons for wanting it rather than giving reasons which might carry more weight. (−)	SA	A	D	SD
15. It is wise to flatter important people. (+)	SA	A	D	SD
17. Barnum was very wrong when he said there's a sucker born every minute. (−)	SA	A	D	SD
18. It is hard to get ahead without cutting corners here and there. (+)	SA	A	D	SD

the scale will eventually be used. The subjects indicate their agreement on a multipoint response scale. (3) The subjects' scale scores are computed, taking into account the direction in which each item is worded (as illustrated with the Mach scale). (4) Finally, the responses are analyzed to determine which items contribute the most to the reliability and validity of measurement.

This *item analysis* stage is the most important in the development of a scale. There are several available techniques. A simple approach is to calculate the correlation of the response to each item with the total scale score. Items that do not correlate highly with the scale score are not doing a good job of measuring the desired attitude dimension and should be discarded. More sophisticated and complex approaches are also available, using the data-analytic technique of *factor analysis*. A discussion of this technique is beyond the scope of this book, but the interested reader should consult Harmon (1967) or Rummel (1970).

Use of "subtle" items   Though any scaling technique requires the use of items that are empirically related to the construct being measured, there is no requirement that the relationship be obviously based on the item's content. For example, the anti-Semitism scale of Adorno et al. (1950) contains the item "Anyone who employs many people should be careful not to hire a large percentage of Jews," which is obviously related to the construct being measured. On the other hand, Adorno et al.'s measure of authoritarianism (or antidemocratic ideology) includes the item "When a person has a problem or worry, it is best for him not to think about it, but to keep busy with more cheerful things." This is an example of a "subtle" item having no *apparent* content relationship to the desired construct, though it is related in terms of an underlying theory linking a lack of psychological insight into oneself or others to personality structures (including repressed hostility and a weak ego) that predispose people to antidemocratic ideology. Of course, this item was not included in the scale simply because of this theoretical assumption; its empirical relationship to the construct was demonstrated in the scale construction process (e.g., the item analysis process in forming a Likert scale).

There are a number of issues to be considered with regard to subtle items. The most important argument for using them is that they can disguise to a degree the researcher's purpose and therefore limit faking or distortion of responses. People who are unwilling to reveal antidemocratic ideology in response to items with obvious content might give their true responses on subtle items, allowing the researcher to assess their ideology correctly.

However, gaining this advantage may require two types of tradeoff. First, it is much harder to find subtle items that correlate well with a construct to which they bear no obvious content relationship than to find or write items that are obviously related to the construct. The construction of such scales often requires large-scale empirical investigations starting with pools of hundreds of diverse items. Second, recent evidence shows that the use of subtle items does not improve measurement over the use of obvious items (Burisch, 1978; Lanyon, 1984, p. 674). In fact, Jackson and Paunonen (1980) report studies showing that undergraduates with no special training can write items based on the definition of a construct that give better reliabilities than elaborate empirical methods of scale construction. In short, unless disguise of the purpose of a scale is of the utmost importance, the use of subtle items is neither necessary nor desirable.

Dimensionality   Besides being based on the analysis of data from pilot subjects, item analysis also calls on the investigator's theoretical conceptions of the construct to be measured. The most crucial issue is dimensionality. If the domain is considered to be unidimensional, all the scale items should correlate moderately to highly, and all at about the same level. On the other hand, the domain might be multidimensional. For example, political liberalism or conservatism is sometimes considered to be composed of somewhat independent dimensions of economic liberalism and favorability to civil rights. The scale items should then divide into two subsets (called *subscales*), corresponding to the two content domains. Within each subset one would find high interitem correlations because each subset forms a small scale measuring its single dimension. Between subsets the interitem correlations would be lower, though probably still positive. (Factor analytic techniques are statistical procedures for detecting this type of pattern, so the researcher does not need to look for them by eye.)

Thus, there is a strong interplay among the theoretical conception of the construct to be measured, the process of writing items to reflect the theoretically expected dimensions, and the analysis of the data from pilot subjects to verify the presence of the expected patterns. The final scale generated by this process may be unidimensional or multidimensional (incorporating two or more subscales) depending on the informed decisions of the researcher. Even if several dimensions emerge, however, they should all be positively correlated to some extent, as otherwise the concept of a single overall scale score makes no sense.

Advantages and disadvantages   The advantages of Likert scaling methods are several. First, a Likert scale is usually simpler to construct than a Thurstone scale. Second, Likert scales can be used in many cases (e.g., multidimensional domains) in which Thurstone or Guttman scales cannot be created. Since many attitudes, such as favorability toward racial integration or political liberalism or conservatism, seem to be complex and multidimensional, this is a major advantage. Third, a Likert scale is generally more reliable than a Thurstone scale of the same length (Tittle &

Hill, 1967). Finally, the range of agreement-disagreement responses permitted with Likert items may make subjects more comfortable in indicating their position than the simple "agree" versus "disagree" choice forced by Thurstone items. The graded responses may also give more precise and reliable information about the subject's opinion.

On the other hand, Likert scales also have disadvantages. Unlike Thurstone scales, they do not yield information about the subject's latitude of acceptance to measure the degree of issue involvement. (However, with a Likert scale one could calculate the number of responses of *strong* agreement or disagreement for a rough measure of involvement.)

Unlike Guttman scale scores, those from a Likert scale do not carry information about the exact pattern of responses to all the individual items. The same scale score might be based on quite different combinations of responses to individual items. However, it is not clear that this should be seen as a disadvantage. The individual items in a unidimensional Likert scale are considered to be basically interchangeable; their individual identity is not as important as the fact that each reliably reflects the underlying attitude. Some differences in response patterns that lead to a particular scale score may derive from simple random error, which it is desirable to ignore. The fact that the scale contains a number of items means that random variations on individual items may cancel each other out when the variations are unrelated to the construct being measured.

On the other hand, when a scale is considered to be multidimensional, the same total score may derive from different response patterns in ways that are conceptually meaningful rather than simply due to random error. For example, two people may receive the same total liberalism score on the two-dimensional scale given as an example previously, one by being high on economic liberalism and average on civil rights attitude, and the other by being quite favorable to civil rights and average on economic liberalism. These are meaningfully different response patterns which might yield the same total score. In such cases the researcher could use the subscale scores (i.e., civil rights liberalism and economic liberalism) as well as the total scale score. The subscale scores would differentiate these two patterns of responses. This point illustrates the advantages of the Likert scale construction technique, where multiple correlated dimensions can be included within a scale when it is empirically and theoretically meaningful.

The Semantic Differential

One specialized scaling method, which has been applied to the measurement of social attitudes, shares the basic characteristics of summated scales but also has some unique features. The subject is asked, in effect, to make a series of ratings on multiple-point response scales. A total score is then derived from the individual item responses by statistical techniques that may include factor analysis. In these ways the *semantic differential* resembles other summated scales.

Osgood, Suci, and Tannenbaum (1957), who developed the semantic differential, described it as a method for measuring the meaning of an object to an individual. It may also be thought of as a series of attitude scales. The subject rates a given concept (e.g., "Irish," "Republican," "me as I am") on a series of seven-point bipolar rating scales, of the type shown in Figure 9.3. Any concept—a political issue, a person, an institution, a group—can be rated. The bipolar scales include the following: (1) fair-unfair, clean-dirty, good-bad, valuable-worthless; (2) large-small, strong-weak; (3) active-passive, fast-slow, hot-cold. Factor analyses have demonstrated that these scales generally group together into three underlying attitude dimensions: (1) the individual's *evaluation* of the object, corresponding to the favorable-unfavorable dimension of traditional attitude scales; (2) the individual's perception of the *potency* or power of the object or concept; and (3) the individual's perception of the *activity* of the object. The subject's responses to the individual bipolar scales can be summed to give scores that indicate his or her position on these three underlying dimensions of attitude toward the object being rated. This usage of semantic differential ratings thus resembles a Likert-type scale with three subscales (the three dimensions).

Semantic differential scales have also been used in a somewhat different way, not to measure underlying attitude dimensions but to measure the similarity or difference between an individual's concepts of different objects. For example, does the person's picture of "me as I am" coincide with the picture of "me as I would like to be," or are the two quite differ-

Me as I Am

fair	1	2	3	4	5	6	7	unfair
clean	1	2	3	4	5	6	7	dirty
light	1	2	3	4	5	6	7	heavy
large	1	2	3	4	5	6	7	small
passive	1	2	3	4	5	6	7	active
strong	1	2	3	4	5	6	7	weak
slow	1	2	3	4	5	6	7	fast
bad	1	2	3	4	5	6	7	good

Note: The subject is instructed to circle a number from 1 to 7 on each scale to rate the given concept.

FIGURE 9.3 Example of semantic differential

ent? Such measurements might be used to track a patient's progress during psychotherapy. Similarly, one could compare two different individuals' concepts of the same object by measuring the similarity of their ratings of the object.

This usage of the semantic differential is illustrated by Figure 9.4, drawn from Osgood, Suci, and Tannenbaum (1957, p. 244). It shows the "conceptual structure" for a number of concepts derived from a patient's semantic differential responses before, during, and after psychotherapy. In the figure, the closeness of two concepts represents their conceptual similarity for the patient. The position of a concept reflects its meaning in the three-dimensional scheme: Good is up, bad down; active is left and passive right; and strong is away from the viewer in perspective, weak toward the viewer. The therapist who treated this patient noted in the pre-treatment diagram the "extreme polarization (evaluative dimension) between concepts like GOD, MOTHER, and ME, on the one hand, and SIN and FRAUD on the other" (p. 246). During therapy the concepts of MOTHER, FATHER, and ME dropped noticeably in evaluation, but by the end of therapy the self-evaluation was higher again. The therapist noted, "One of the

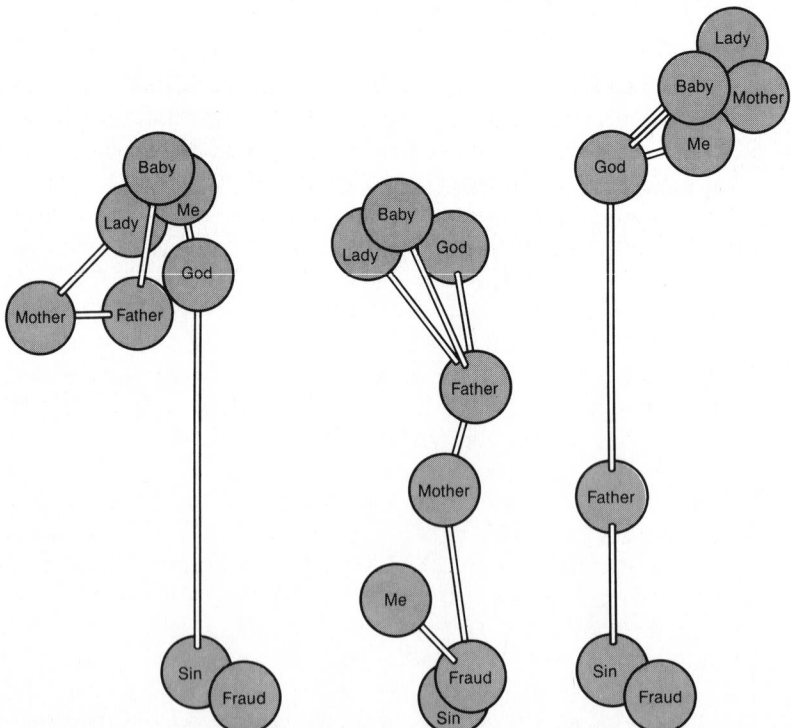

FIGURE 9.4 **Semantic space for female patient at beginning of therapy** *(left),* **middle of therapy** *(center),* **and shortly after termination of therapy** *(right)*

(female) patient's main difficulties had been her 'alliance' with her father against her mother. . . . During therapy this situation was explored and repudiated" (p. 247). The figures clearly show the shift in parental identification that the patient experienced during therapy.

Osgood and his associates suggested that the semantic differential allows the measurement and comparison of diverse objects by diverse subjects. They implied that the measuring instrument is not greatly affected by the nature of the object being measured or the type of person using the scale. Though some of their results, including several cross-cultural studies, support this claim, other evidence indicates that the measuring instrument is not completely comparable across concepts. The meanings of scales and their relation to the other scales vary depending on the concept being judged. What is good, for example, depends on the nature of the concept: "Strong" may be good in judging athletes but bad in judging odors. The implication is that the rating scales may not provide consistent measurements of the underlying dimensions independently of the concepts being judged.

Scaling and "Levels of Measurement"

Scaling methods are undergoing rapid development, and major contributions have been made by Coombs (1964), Torgerson (1958), Dawes (1972; Dawes & Smith, 1984), and others. This situation results in occasional disagreement among experts on particular issues. In particular, some authorities claim that particular scale construction methods necessarily give rise to data representing different "levels of measurement" (Stevens, 1968). Usually, Guttman and Likert scales are said to provide only ordinal data, whereas Thurstone scales produce interval scale data (because the judges are asked to rate the scale values of the individual items in terms of "equal appearing intervals"). Some authorities even hold that certain useful methods of data analysis ("interval" statistics such as correlation, factor analysis, and so on) can in principle be meaningfully applied only to interval scale data.

However, other authorities disagree with all these claims (e.g., Anderson, 1961; Dawes, 1972, pp. 81–83; Hays, 1963). Their basic argument is that the "level of measurement" of a particular set of data is an *empirical* question, to be settled—like other issues of scale validity—by examining the relationships of the data to other measurements. If the relationships are essentially linear, the data may be treated as interval scaled, and powerful data-analytic methods may be used.

The statement that this is an empirical issue means that the level of measurement is not an intrinsic property of data that is guaranteed by the use of a particular scaling method. Thus, any of the rating scale or multiple-item scaling techniques discussed in this chapter may be found to produce data that meet the requirements of an interval scale. There is no theoretical assumption that Thurstone scale data will be "better" than any other type. Empirical investigations by Dawes (1977) and others have shown that even single rating scales often approach linear relationships with physical measurements (such as height) remarkably well, and multiple-item scales do even better. These authorities, then, provide empirical and logical justification to the common practice in social research of treating rating scales or Likert scale data with powerful "interval" statistics.

Summary

In this chapter we have discussed various methods of scaling that distinguish among individuals (or other objects) in terms of the degree to which they possess a given characteristic, or their position on an underlying construct. The methods range from the simple use of judgments quantified along rating scales to the complex multiple-item scaling techniques associated with Thurstone, Guttman, and Likert. Here, as with other measurement techniques, we have raised issues related to reliability and validity, which are crucial determinants of the quality of any measurement. Investigating the validity of data is often difficult, posing both theoretical problems of determining what would be appropriate criteria for validity and empirical problems of gathering the necessary data. However, many thousands of investigations using ratings and multiple-item scales have demonstrated meaningful empirical relationships between such data and other constructs. Each such relationship constitutes evidence for the general usefulness and validity of these measurement techniques, when properly applied.

Most of the examples in this chapter have concerned the scaling of attitudes rather than other individual, group, or organizational characteristics. This does *not* mean that scaling techniques are applicable only to attitudes—only that a way was needed to present examples that are brief and clear. The references on measurement and scaling in this chapter give many examples of scaling objects other than individual attitudes, as well as examples of more sophisticated scaling techniques.

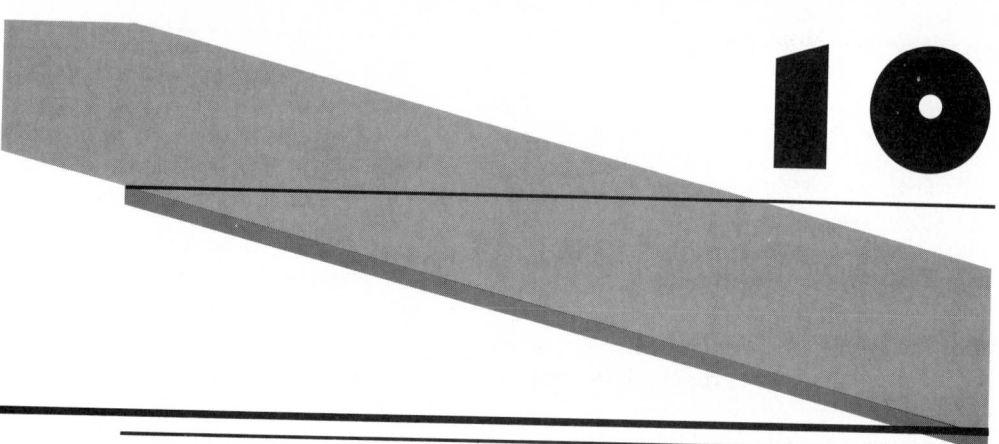

Questionnaires and Interviews: Overview of Strategies

In our daily lives as well as in social research, when we want to know something about another person's beliefs, attitudes, behaviors, feelings, perceptions, motivations, or plans, our first recourse is often simply to ask them an outright question. Verbal responses to direct questions—whether a highly constrained choice from a small set of alternative answers or a lengthy, open-ended description of the respondent's thinking—are the most widely used source of data in social research. The most obvious reason is the flexibility of verbal communication. Human language is a powerful and precise medium for phrasing and answering questions about attitudes, behaviors, experiences, or virtually any other topic, real or imagined, past, present, or future. In comparison, observations and archival data tap a narrower range of constructs, though they may be essential when the study requires detailed observation of actual interactions or the use of historical data, for example.

Our everyday reliance on people's reports of their experiences, beliefs, or behavior underlines the general usefulness of questionnaires and similar approaches for research. For example, if we ask a friend how he likes his job and he responds, "It's pretty boring," we ordinarily assume that the statement accurately represents his feelings. However, everyday experiences also make us aware of the potential for unreliable or invalid responses to questions. Though we ordinarily accept verbal reports as valid indicators of the speaker's beliefs, we are aware that the speaker's beliefs themselves may at times be inaccurate. This suggests that questionnaire approaches are sometimes less useful for determining concrete facts than individual perceptions or reactions. Also, we may doubt verbal reports if we suspect that they are self-serving, that the speaker is attempting to create a positive impression or would risk embarrassment by telling the truth. We often judge the credibility of verbal statements by attempting to assess the speakers' *motivations:* Are they telling the truth or are they trying to impress me? Similar considerations apply in judging the validity of verbal responses in research.

Besides factual errors in speakers' knowledge and motivational biases, there is one other major limitation on the use of direct questions: the limitations of verbal responses themselves. Language is a powerful and flexible system of communication, yet it fails in certain situations, as even a skillful poet realizes when trying to describe the color of a sunset or the feelings involved in love or despair. We can have fleeting or powerful reactions to people or situations without being able to verbalize them. For example, we may immediately like or dislike someone we meet without being able to say quite why. Finally, on some topics we may not have an attitude that is well formulated enough to be verbalized, so that when we are asked for our attitude we have to say honestly, "don't know" or else answer at random. Even such a seemingly simple question as "Are you shy with strangers?" may require people to make complex inferences or judgments about themselves based on many past events. People do not always have complete self-knowledge that would permit ready, valid answers to such questions.

In sum, there are limitations of the use of verbal reports in research: The respondent may not know the answer, may be unwilling to give it, or may be unable to express it verbally. Nevertheless, our reliance on verbal communication in everyday life as well as in social research suggests that the boundaries set by these limitations are quite broad. Within these limits, questions can elicit information that otherwise either could not be obtained at all or could be obtained only with great difficulty and by more fallible methods. For example, people's reactions to hypothetical policy proposals, such as a new type of taxation system, are routinely elicited by survey questions, and it is difficult to imagine how observation or any other method could gather this type of information. Or a person's feelings toward his or her employer could be directly assessed by questioning (with proper precautions related to the sensitive nature of the issue) but could be assessed, if at all, only with great difficulty and problematic validity by close observation of the person at work.

In this chapter and the next, we consider a number of issues related to the use of interviews and questionnaires as data-gathering tools. The use of a *structured questionnaire* is the most common method of data collection. The researcher must consider whether the data are best gathered by written questionnaires, personal interviews, or telephone interviews, and the basis for making this decision is discussed in this chapter. The next chapter will take up a number of issues that must be considered as topics are chosen, specific questions are written, and interviewing procedures outlined, to ensure that valid responses are collected.

Modes of Data Collection

Data can be gathered with a structured questionnaire in three ways: by using a *written questionnaire,* by *personal interviews,* and by *telephone interviews.* The choice among these modes is the researcher's initial concern once the basic decision to use a structured questionnaire has been made. Each mode has specific advantages and disadvantages which the researcher needs to evaluate for their suitability to the research question and the specific population being studied, as well as relative cost. As one might expect, written questionnaires are the least expensive, followed by telephone interviews, and face-to-face personal interviews are the most expensive. The three modes of data collection will be discussed in turn, followed by a summary of their relative advantages and disadvantages.

Written Questionnaires

Advantages *Low cost* is the primary advantage of written questionnaires, whether they are mailed—the most common means of distribution—or handed out in other ways. It might appear that printing and the postage or other costs of distributing and collecting the questionnaires are all that need to be taken into account, suggesting a very low cost figure, perhaps one dollar or less per respondent. However, as will be discussed shortly, this is certainly an underestimate if the steps needed to obtain high-quality data are included. Still, written questionnaires are the least-expensive means of data gathering, and cost is not a trivial consideration. Cost often determines whether research can be done at all, and low cost may mean that responses can be obtained from more people, increasing the sample size.

A second advantage of written questionnaires is the avoidance of potential *interviewer bias*. Research has shown that the way the interviewer asks questions and even the interviewer's general appearance or vocal qualities may influence respondents' answers. Although these biases can be minimized in interviews, they can be completely eliminated only with a written questionnaire.

A third advantage is that written questionnaires may place less pressure for *immediate response* on the subject. This may be important, for example, when the subject has to look in personal records for the information to answer a question. Responses to attitude questions may also, at times, benefit from the subject taking ample time to consider each question carefully rather than giving the response that springs immediately to mind. The latter is more likely under the social pressure of long silences in an interview. However, subjects must also be *motivated* to give such extensive, careful consideration to their responses, and interviewers can generally motivate subjects more than a written questionnaire can.

Written questionnaires are sometimes credited with another advantage—giving respondents a greater *feeling of anonymity* and therefore encouraging open responses to sensitive questions. However, the merits of this claim are uncertain, given recent research and the development of new techniques for handling sensitive questions in interviews. At present, there is no evidence of large differences between the quality of responses to sensitive questions in written questionnaires versus interviews.

Disadvantages The written questionnaire also has important disadvantages, particularly in the *quality of data* that can be obtained. This includes at least two considerations. The first is the *response rate*, defined as the percentage of respondents in the initial sample from whom complete responses are obtained. Response rate is the chief index of data quality in a survey because it defines the extent of possible bias from nonresponse. Nonrespondents may differ in important ways from respondents, so that if only 25 percent or 50 percent of the sample actually responds, there is no way of knowing if their characteristics can be generalized to describe the whole sample (let alone the population the sample is intended to represent). Therefore, a low response rate calls into question *any* conclusions based on the data. A response rate of 80 percent or 90 percent, on the other hand, means that even if the nonrespondents differ substantially from those who respond, the overall estimates will not be badly biased.

It is important to remember, though, to ask the question "90 percent of what?" That is, even a high response rate is meaningless unless the sample design itself is strong. One might hand out questionnaires to 20 of one's friends and acquaintances and achieve a near-perfect response rate—but the results would not be meaningful (except as a description of that particular set of people) because they do not constitute a representative sample of any larger population (see Chapter 7 on sampling). Therefore, response rate is not the only consideration in evaluating the quality of data from a survey; it is only meaningful when the initial sample is properly designed.

Mail surveys generally have the lowest response rate of the three modes of questionnaire data collection, often less than 50 percent when the target population is the general public. This fact alone limits the usefulness of mail samples because the unknown bias from extensive nonresponse makes the sample estimates quite untrustworthy. On the other hand, when specialized populations are sampled (such as members of a particular profession or alumni of a particular college) response rates from mail surveys can reach respectable levels.

Data quality has another aspect besides response rate—the *accuracy and completeness of responses* to questions. Here the key issue is the motivation of the respondent, and there are problems in creating and maintaining motivation with a written questionnaire. A personal or telephone interview makes it easier to build rapport between interviewer and respondent, motivating the respondent to give full and accurate answers. On this dimension of data quality as well as on response rates, written questionnaires generally fall short.

Other, less serious disadvantages also characterize mail surveys. One is the requirement to use a *short questionnaire.* Dillman (1978) found that questionnaires up to about 12 pages or 125 individual responses produced response rates that did not depend on length. But over that level, which represents a relatively short questionnaire, increasing length decreased response rate.

Another problem is a *lack of control over question order.* It is often important that the respondent answer one question before seeing another. For example, a questionnaire might start by asking what the respondents see as the most important problem facing their community and then go on to ask numerous questions about the availability of parks and recreation facilities. It is safe to assume that if the respondent were aware of this focus of the questionnaire, it would bias their response to the initial open-ended question. With a written questionnaire, the respondents are likely to glance through the entire questionnaire before starting to answer, so there is no way to control question order.

Another problem is the inability to control the *context of question answering*, and specifically, the presence of other people. Respondents may ask friends or family members to examine the questionnaire or comment on their answers, causing bias if the respondent's own private opinions are desired.

A certain number of potential respondents, particularly the least educated, will also be unable to respond to written questionnaires because of *illiteracy or other difficulties in reading or writing* (e.g., poor vision). Complex questions or instructions for some respondents to skip certain questions may lead to confusion, errors, or complete nonresponse. For everybody, not just the uneducated, writing long responses to open-ended questions is more work than giving them orally, and this factor may reduce response rates.

Finally, written questionnaires do not allow an interviewer to *correct misunderstandings or answer questions* that the respondent may have. The respondent might answer incorrectly or not at all out of confusion or anger, often without the researcher being able to tell that a question has been misinterpreted.

If the researcher accepts these secondary disadvantages, which are intrinsically part of mail surveys, steps can be taken to reduce the primary disadvantage of low response rate and hence low data quality. Dillman (1978) and others have developed techniques for carefully following up mail surveys with multiple waves of letters, postcards, and the like to attain as high a response rate as possible, sometimes reaching 70 percent or higher in samples of the general public with a short questionnaire. However, these techniques increase cost and may substantially reduce the cost advantage of a mail survey over a telephone interview, the next most costly alternative.

Mass administration to a captive population   Sometimes the desired population for a particular questionnaire study is "captive" (e.g., students in a school, employees in a business, clients of an organization). Written questionnaires can then be mass administered to large groups simultaneously in a lecture hall, cafeteria, or work place. This is a low-cost method of data collection, response rates can approach 100 percent of defined populations, and the usual restrictions on length need not apply since the respondents are captive and forced to respond. However, the restriction to specific populations is severe, and this method is not widely used. Mass administration to self-selected volunteers is not an appropriate sampling method since those students or clients who show up to fill out the questionnaire differ in unknown ways from those who do not. Though the "response rate" in such a situation may be 100 percent, the figure is meaningless because the sample is not representative.

Personal Interviews

Advantages Personal interviews are the most costly form of data collection in general, but they also offer important advantages, some of which are shared by telephone interviews. The ability of the interviewer to *notice and correct the respondent's misunderstandings*, to *probe inadequate or vague responses*, and to *answer questions and allay concerns* are important in obtaining complete and meaningful data. The interviewer can control the *order in which the respondent receives the questions*, which is not possible with written questionnaires. And in general the interviewer can control the *context of the interview*, including the possible biasing presence of other people.

Other advantages are specific to the personal interview. *Visual aids* (photographs, maps, or cards with possible responses printed on them) can be used. Such aids are useful in a number of contexts; for example, in surveys of prescription drug use it is helpful to show illustrations of different types of pills and capsules to aid the respondent's memory for medications that he or she might have used but forgotten the name of.

The most important advantage, though, is in *data quality*. Personal interviews can attain the highest response rate of any survey technique, sometimes over 90 percent. Their advantage is particularly marked with special populations, such as low-income minority populations, who may not have telephones or respond to mail surveys. Moreover, a face-to-face interviewer can best *establish rapport and motivate the respondent* to answer fully and accurately, again improving the quality of data. Personal interviews also allow the greatest *length* in interview schedules. An hour or so is typical, and interviews two to three hours long with samples of the general public are not unknown. The additional length permits extensive in-depth questioning about complex or multifaceted issues.

Disadvantages Related to the potential rapport between interviewer and respondent is the possibility of large *interviewer effects*. The interviewer's expectations or personal characteristics (such as race or sex) can influence responses. Consistent with the idea that face-to-face situations create the strongest rapport—and hence the strongest tendency for respondents to give invalid, socially desirable answers to suit the interviewer's expectations or desires—scattered studies have found larger interviewer effects in personal than in telephone interviews (Bradburn & Sudman, 1979; Dillman, 1978).

The primary disadvantage of personal interviews is their *high cost*, which depends heavily on the geographic coverage required by the study. For a city or other limited area, costs for personal interviews may not greatly exceed those for telephone interviews. However, for larger geographic areas, travel and subsistence costs for interviewers in the field are large, and personal interviews typically cost two to three times as much as telephone interviews of equivalent length (Groves & Kahn, 1979).

Telephone Interviews

The use of telephone interviews in social research has expanded rapidly in recent years. In the 1940s and 1950s, a sizable proportion of households did not have telephones, and some studies seemed to show that only short interviews on simple topics could be adequately done by phone. However, these conclusions have been decisively overturned by recent research, and cost and other advantages of telephone interviews have greatly increased their use more recently.

Advantages Today, telephone interviews permit a *high response rate*, on the average just five percentage points lower than personal interviews (Groves & Kahn, 1979). Other studies (Bradburn & Sudman, 1979) even find that higher response rates are attainable by telephone than by personal interview in special situations such as urban-area samples. Telephone response rates average ten to fifteen percentage points higher than even the best conducted mail surveys, with a much larger advantage over more typical mail response rates (Dillman, 1978).

Telephone interviews do not impose strict limits on *interview length*, though they generally do not extend much over an hour, as do some personal interviews. It was once believed that five minutes or so was an upper limit to the length of telephone interviews, but this belief is thoroughly discredited by recent research (Groves & Kahn, 1979; Quinn, Gutek, & Walsh, 1980). For example, Dillman (1978) reports that in one survey of the general public with phone interviews averaging over 30 minutes, only 4 percent of the respondents broke off after the interview started. Another large-scale study was successful in using interviews that averaged nearly an hour in length, covering such topics as beliefs about opportunity for racial minorities (Kluegel & Smith, 1982) and women (Smith & Kluegel, 1984). Special populations may allow even longer interviews without major problems.

All the other advantages of personal interviews, except the ability to use visual aids, are also available in telephone interviews. These include the interviewer's ability to correct misunderstandings, motivate the respondent, and probe for more detail when answers are vague. Though the ability to motivate the respondent may not be as great with telephone interviews as in person, this is compensated for by the somewhat smaller interviewer bias and tendency toward socially desirable responses that may characterize telephone interviews (Bradburn & Sudman, 1979). Carefully designed studies comparing personal and telephone interviews using the same questions have found few if any differences in overall data quality (Groves & Kahn, 1979; Quinn, Gutek, & Walsh, 1980). The conclusion of a review of 25 different comparisons is that "researchers have not found consistent support for the contention that telephone interviewing yields less reliable or less valid data than face-to-face interviewing" (Quinn, Gutek, & Walsh, 1980, p. 139).

Telephone interviews, then, seem to offer response rates and data quality comparable to personal interviews. They also have several advantages over personal interviews, besides the obvious one of *substantially lower cost*. The cost advantage, as mentioned, is generally a factor of two to three, depending mainly on the geographic coverage needed. Larger areas give greater cost advantages to the telephone, since long-distance toll charges actually depend little on distance (or depend not at all if special WATS phone lines are used). One advantage that is sometimes overlooked is the *supervison of interviewers*. Since interviewers can all work from a single room equipped with a bank of telephones, their supervisors can be constantly available to answer questions, resolve problems, or even talk to difficult respondents. The problem of a dishonest interviewer faking data, which does occasionally occur with personal interviews performed in distant geographic areas, is virtually ruled out by this type of arrangement for telephone interviewing. This arrangement also allows errors in the questionnaire or interviewing procedures to be corrected immediately upon discovery, which is usually impossible with personal interviewing. All these factors contribute significantly to higher data quality as well as lower cost (Groves & Kahn, 1979).

Another advantage of telephone interviews is *speed*. A questionnaire can be put together quickly and hundreds of interviews conducted almost overnight to assess public responses to a disaster, assassination, television program, or some other event. Mail or personal interviews would reach respondents only many days after the event, greatly reducing the likelihood of valid immediate responses.

Finally, telephone interviews make possible the use of *computer-assisted interviewing techniques*, which promise to become more widely used in the near future. The interviewer sits with the telephone in front of a computer display and keyboard, reads questions displayed one at a time on the screen, and types in codes for the respondent's answer. The computer can check for valid data and signal the interviewer to recheck implausible responses, eliminating most coding and data-entry errors. Furthermore, the computer controls the sequence of questions, preventing interviewer errors in sequencing questions or in asking questions of the wrong subgroup of respondents (e.g., asking unmarried respondents about their spouses' occupation). Finally, biases deriving from question order can be reduced or eliminated by having a set of questions asked in a different randomly selected order for each respondent; this would be difficult if not impossible for interviewers to do manually. Computer assistance is currently limited to telephone interviews, but the development of powerful portable computers may allow personal interviewers to take advantage of the technique as well (Quinn, Gutek, & Walsh, 1980).

Disadvantages With these advantages as well as low cost, why have telephone interviews been less used than personal interviews in the past? Several widespread concerns about telephone interviews, which recent results show to be unfounded, seem to be responsible. These concerns center on interview length and sampling. As noted, recent research shows that telephone interviews can last up to an hour without major problems. Sampling poses more-significant issues. Since the notorious 1936 *Literary Digest* survey, which wrongly predicted the presidential election of that year by using a mail survey of names and addresses drawn from telephone directories, researchers have been wary of directories as sources from which to draw samples. It is argued, first, that not all households have telephones, and second, that not all those who have phones have listings in the directory (because they are new arrivals in an area or because they choose to be unlisted).

The first point is often exaggerated. Data from the U.S. census show that nationally, only 6 percent of households do not have access to a phone (Dillman, 1978), and this number is shrinking. Personal interviews cannot reach 100 percent of the national population either; small percentages of the population do not have fixed addresses or other characteristics that allow interviewers to locate them. However, possession of a phone is not uniform; it varies by state and area (low-income and rural areas have more households without telephones).

The second point, that telephone directories may yield inadequate samples of phone subscribers, is more important. To overcome this problem, *random digit dialing* techniques have been devised. The interviewer dials a three-digit area code and a three-digit telephone exchange code, followed by four randomly chosen digits (drawn from a random number table). This technique gives unlisted phone subscribers and new arrivals an equal chance of being called with those listed in the directory. Unfortunately, it also gives nonworking numbers and businesses and other non-household subscribers an equal chance. At times, five numbers must be dialed to get one that is a working household number, though newly developed techniques can greatly reduce this wasted effort by taking advantage of regularities in the ways telephone companies assign numbers (Sudman, 1973). The use of random digit dialing avoids the potential biases in sampling from telephone directories, at the cost of some extra effort in screening out nonworking and nonhousehold numbers.

Telephone interviews do have a few more serious disadvantages. Interviewer effects are possible, though they may be smaller than with personal interviews. The inability to use drawings, maps, or other visual aids means that some types of questions must be reworded for telephone use. Some questions are difficult to ask on the phone because of their complexity; if the respondent misses even a single word the entire question may become unintelligible. The interviewer does not have visual cues (a puzzled look, a shake of the head) that a misunderstanding has occurred. As a result, more attention probably needs to be paid to question wording with telephone interviews than with other techniques. Finally, there are technical problems in the computation of response rates in random digit-dialed telephone surveys because numbers that are never answered on repeated calls are of uncertain status. If they are nonworking numbers, they should not be counted in the response rate calculations, but if they represent households where nobody was at home at the time of any of the calls, they should be counted as nonrespondents.

Combined Methods

More than one of these techniques can be combined in a single study to lower cost, improve data quality, or both. One frequent combination is the use of a more-expensive method to interview people who do not respond to an initial less-expensive method. For example, one may use the telephone to interview those who do not return mail questionnaires or send personal interviewers to question people who cannot be reached by telephone. The result should be both a higher response rate and lower average costs because a major proportion of the interviews should be accomplished by the less-costly method. However, response differences (e.g., different interviewer effects) between the portions of the data collected by different modes are a potential source of problems.

It is also possible to leave a written questionnaire with a respondent in a personal interview, with instructions to complete it and mail it back.

In this situation, motivation is usually high and the other advantages of mailed questionnaires (anonymity, lack of time pressure to answer) can be gained.

Finally, in surveys requiring repeated contact with respondents (to assess attitude change, improvement following medical treatment, or other phenomena studied over time) the use of telephone follow-ups to personal interviews is growing in popularity. The respondent's phone number and promise of cooperation can be obtained during the initial personal interview, so subsequent phone contacts are inexpensive and usually achieve a response rate of 90 percent or better.

Modes of Data Collection: Summary

The only completely defensible answer to the question "What is the best way to collect questionnaire data?" is, of course, "It depends." Table 10.1 presents a schematic summary of the strengths and weaknesses of the diferent methods that were presented in more detail, so readers can weigh specific considerations as they choose. Nevertheless, to give a general guideline, for surveys of the general population that cover more than a local geographical area, the older conventional wisdom favoring personal interviews is probably outdated, and today, *telephone interviews are the method of choice.* Quinn, Gutek, & Walsh (1980, p. 152) summarize their review of relevant research and their own findings as follows: ". . . the generally favorable comparison with face-to-face interviewing in terms of response rates, overall quality of data, and quality of data on sensitive issues should make telephone interviewing the most efficient, inexpensive, and methodologically sophisticated form of collecting survey data."

Exceptions to this generalization include a number of specific situations. Mail surveys should be considered (1) for homogeneous groups—such as alumni of a specific college or members of an organization—if they are widely scattered geographically; (2) if mailing lists are available, to minimize sampling costs; or (3) if cost constraints are maximal and low data quality is acceptable for the specific research purpose. With mail surveys, the techniques of Dillman (1978) should be used to improve response rate at some additional cost.

Personal interviews should probably be chosen (1) if maximal data quality is required and cost is no object; (2) if the study calls for special populations difficult to reach in other ways (e.g., low-income rural residents who may not have phones and may be too uneducated to respond well to mail questionnaires); or (c) if the population to be studied is geographically concentrated, making personal interview costs comparable to telephone costs or only somewhat higher.

In general, though, properly conducted telephone surveys (using precautions discussed by Groves & Kahn, 1979, and Dillman, 1978) offer, figuratively speaking, 90 percent of the data quality and other advantages

TABLE 10.1   Summary Comparison of Different Data-Collection Methods

Dimension of Comparison	Mailed Questionnaire	Personal Interview	Telephone Interview
Cost	Low	High	Moderate
Data Quality			
Response rate	Low	High	Moderate to high
Respondent motivation	Low	High	High
Interviewer bias	None	Moderate	Low
Sample Quality	Low, unless high response rate	High	Moderate to high, if directory; high, if random digit dialing
Possible interview length	Short	Very long	Long
Ability to clarify and probe	None	High	High
Ability to use visual aids	Some (e.g., maps)	High	None
Speed	Low	Low	High
Interviewer supervision	—	Low	High
Anonymity	High	Low	Low
Ability to use computer assistance	None	Possible	High
Dependence on respondent's reading and writing ability	High	None	None
Control of context and question order	None	High	High

of personal interviews for approximately 50 percent of the cost, a combination that is proving compelling to more and more researchers.

Outline of Procedures in Questionnaire Research

A step-by-step guide for planning and carrying out questionnaire research may help organize the decisions and issues that the researcher must consider, which are discussed in this chapter and the next. This outline begins after the investigator weighs possible alternative methods of data collection and decides that a questionnaire (rather than archival data, written records, observation, or some other technique) is the most appropriate method to obtain all or part of the desired information.

1. The most basic choice is among *modes* of data gathering: written questionnaire, personal interview, or telephone interview. Advantages and disadvantages of each were discussed earlier in this chapter. However, this decision also overlaps with issues surrounding *sampling* (Chapter 7) and with the nature of the population that is to be investigated. For example, the existence of a list of names and addresses of the relevant population makes mail surveys or personal interviews more feasible and random digit dialing unnecessary; the geographical area covered by the population affects the relative costs of personal versus telephone interviews and so on.

2. The next decisions involve the *specific content areas* to be covered by the questionnaire. Obviously the purpose of the study will dictate certain central areas. For example, if the study is to determine attitudes toward the location of a toxic waste disposal site near a particular city, questions on that specific issue would be included. However, related topics may also be important, perhaps including the respondent's perception of risks from toxic waste, beliefs about the causes of cancer and other diseases, general optimism or pessimism, attitudes of trust or distrust toward the authorities who will make the decision about the site, and attitudes about the chemical industry in general. The investigator should consult other social scientists as well as experts in areas specifically related to the survey topic to decide what related issues should be included in the questionnaire.

3. Given a list of specific content areas to be covered, several other decisions need to be made before questions can actually be written. On some topics, *existing questions or scales* may be used, saving the work of writing new questions and preserving some comparability with earlier research. In addition, it should be decided what content areas are central to the research and warrant coverage with a scale (Chapter 9) or a series of related questions, including follow-up questions or open-ended probes (questions allowing the respondent to answer in his or her own words), and what topics are less important and only require a question or two.

4. Finally, the process of *writing questions* starts. Wording decisions must be made on a host of detailed issues, as discussed in the next chapter. At this point, a number of questions may be written in open-ended form, to be converted to closed-ended questions (those with a fixed set of alternative responses) after pretesting.

5. The questions (newly written or drawn from prior studies) are put together into a complete draft of the questionnaire. A number of guidelines on question sequence and transition should be observed and a bal-

ance of open-ended and closed-ended questions maintained (though there may be more open-ended questions at this stage than in the final questionnaire).

6. At this stage the draft questionnaire should be circulated to experts and consultants for comments and suggestions and revised accordingly to eliminate obvious problems even before the pretest stage. As much as possible, the experts should represent different theoretical approaches or social orientations to maximize the chance of identifying biases and blind spots due to the researcher's personal values as well as simple technical defects.

7. The questionnaire is now pretested. This stage is absolutely essential in questionnaire research and should not be confused with the informal examination of the questionnaire by experts (step 6). A proper pretest involves respondents from the same population as the actual study, not just a sample of students, secretaries, researcher's friends, or whoever happens to be conveniently accessible. The interviewers should also be those who will be conducting interviews in the main study. Even if the main study is to involve a mailed or other written questionnaire, it is wise to do some personal interviews as part of the pretest so that respondents' immediate verbal reactions or expressions of difficulty with some questions can be noted.

The interviewers in the pretest should be aware of the overall purposes of the study and the aim of every individual question, so they can note whether the question is understood and answered as intended. The comments and reactions of the respondents should be recorded as clues to questions that may be misunderstood or cause difficulties in other ways. After the interview is complete, the interviewer should go back over the questionnaire topic by topic and ask the respondents for their overall reactions: what difficulties they had, how the questions were interpreted, what further topic-related ideas were not tapped by the questions, and what the respondents' thoughts were when they responded "don't know." The interviewers as well as the pretest respondents should critique the questionnaire, pointing out difficulties they had in following the sequence, explaining particular questions, holding the respondent's interest, or maintaining rapport.

The pretest serves a number of purposes. (a) It will identify unforeseen problems in question wording or respondents' comprehension, question sequence, or questionnaire administration, so that they can be eliminated before the actual study. No researcher, no matter how experienced, avoids such unforeseen problems. (b) It may indicate the need for additional questions on some topics or the elimination of others. (c) It can gather data for item analysis for any scales included in the questionnaire (see Chapter 9). (d) The length of the interview can be determined (and possibly, the necessity for shortening it). (e) Open-ended responses can be collected to permit the phrasing of closed-ended response alternatives for the final questionnaire. Finally, (f) the pretest may constitute part of the interviewers' training if the study involves interviewers.

8. The pretest results are analyzed and any necessary changes made in the questionnaire. If the changes are major, further pretesting should be done; few experiences in research are more common or more frustrating than changing a questionnaire to correct a problem revealed by a pretest and then taking it immediately into the field for the final study, only to discover that the change introduced a new problem that was worse than the first. Since problems with wording or respondent comprehension can vitiate the worth of the entire study, pretesting is low-cost insurance against such potential disasters.

9. With the final version of the questionnaire, final interviewer training can proceed (if interviewers are used). More pretesting may be done in conjunction with training, or interviewer training may begin in conjunction with the pretest of step 7. The content and form of the questionnaire and associated interviewer instructions (e.g., to skip certain questions for certain respondents, to probe if the respondent answers "don't know," or to accept such a response when given) should be reviewed for clarity and completeness.

10. Finally the actual administration of the study begins. Supervision of interviewers and continuous monitoring of completed interviews as they come in are essential in order to detect problems as soon as they appear and get out corrections if possible. The administration of the survey must include standard procedures for tracking down members of the sample who cannot easily be reached, screening out ineligible respondents, sending out repeated reminders (in a mail survey), or making several callbacks (in personal or telephone interview studies) to maximize the response rate, and so on.

11. Finally the data are coded and analyzed, and (if all is well up to this point) conclusions are drawn about the issues that were the focus of the research. All the preceding steps are justified by their contribution to the validity of these conclusions.

Summary

Some fundamental methological issues must be addressed when interview or questionnaire research is planned and conducted. First is the appropriateness of the method to the study topic: Are verbal reports theoretically capable of giving the desired information, or should observation or some other method of data collection be used instead? Second, individuals' self-reports of facts, beliefs, attitudes, or behaviors can be elicited in many different ways. In deciding whether to use a written questionnaire, personal interviews, or telephone interviews, researchers should consider the advantages and disadvantages of each mode as they relate to the purposes of the study. The nature of the target population and the sampling design chosen for the study also have implications for the mode of data collection (e.g., the potential use of random digit dialing with telephone interviews).

Finally, the decision concerning the mode leads into many more detailed decisions on question content, wording, sequence, and interview practices. These issues are taken up in the next chapter.

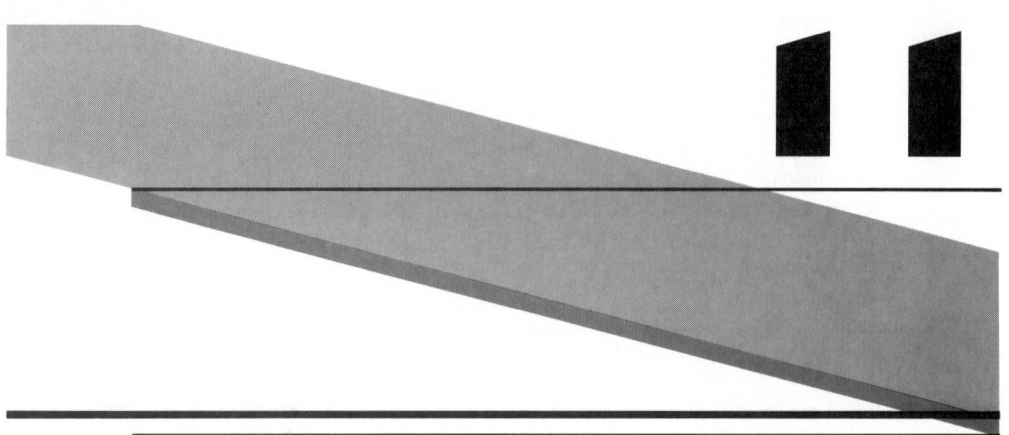

Questionnaires and Interviews: Asking Questions Effectively

Once the basic decision about the mode of data collection has been made, following the considerations listed in the previous chapter, a number of detailed issues remain. To obtain reliable and valid answers, question content, wording, and sequence must all work together to convey to the respondents what information is desired and motivate them to provide it. The interviewer's behavior may also contribute to these goals (except, of course, in the case of a written questionnaire). This chapter also includes some discussion of special procedures used to obtain information that is socially undesirable or sensitive when respondents may be unwilling to provide it in response to a direct question.

Question Content

In questionnaire-based research, the goal may be to learn what the respondents know (facts); what they think, expect, feel, or prefer (beliefs and attitudes); or what they have done (behaviors). A questionnaire will generally include questions referring to more than one of these categories, and at times a single question has aspects of more than one category. However, these distinctions are convenient for discussing the issues involved in selecting content.

Questions Aimed at Facts

Often the simplest and most economical way of ascertaining facts is to approach people who know them and ask. We expect people to know a variety of facts about themselves and their situation, and a major proportion of any questionnaire is ordinarily devoted to obtaining factual information, such as the respondent's age, education, religion, income, marital status, and occupation. Questions about events, circumstances, or conditions known to the respondent, such as details of recent illness or medical treatment, are also common.

The possibility of error in reported facts must always be taken into account. Errors can arise from memory problems or from response biases of various forms. For example, respondents may overstate their incomes in an effort to impress the interviewer with their prestige, or they may understate them if they fear that the interviewer is connected with the taxing authorities. Parry and Crossley (1950) found several examples of inaccuracy in facts reported in interviews. Comparisons of respondents' answers with official records showed that approximately 40 percent of the respondents inaccurately reported on whether they had contributed to the United Fund, 25 percent erred concerning whether they had registered and voted in a recent election, and 17 percent misstated their age. These inaccuracies may be due either to a need to give socially desirable responses (e.g., saying that one has contributed to the United Fund makes one look good) or to lapses of memory (e.g., contributing to the United Fund may not be a highly salient or memorable event for many people, so they do not remember whether they actually contributed and are forced to guess).

Memory failures are more likely for events that are farther in the past or that are more trivial and routine for respondents. The structure of the questionnaire itself may ease the respondent's task of remembering the desired facts; for example, fertility, occupational, or medical history data are often collected in a chronological format. Remembering temporally related events may aid recall of more of the desired details. Reinterviews also increase the probability of recall. Cannell, Fisher, and Bakker (1965) found that in a first interview, respondents failed to report about 30 percent of hospitalizations that had occurred a year earlier. In a second interview, after the interviewer urged the person to remember, a higher proportion was reported.

In reporting their ages, people tend to round off (to 30, 40, 50, and so on) rather than reporting exactly (R. J. Myers, 1940); we could also expect some older people to understate their ages. To avoid both of these problems, survey researchers have learned to ask for the year of the respondents' birth rather than their current age.

Specificity is important in factual questions, to give precise information about what response is desired and to avoid respondents' interpreting questions in terms of their own frame of reference. Mauldin and Marks (1950) asked farmers whether they had any fruit or nut trees or grapevines. A large proportion answered no, but when more specific follow-up questions were used (asking whether they had even one or two trees, or any that were not producing fruit) over half the farmers who originally said no now said they did. The researchers concluded that the farmers were not intentionally deceptive but were simply answering in terms of a frame of reference in which one or two trees, particularly if they were not producing, were not worth mentioning. The more specific questions did elicit the desired information.

On the whole, specific facts from the recent past that are nontrivial and therefore memorable should be reported relatively well—if they are nonthreatening to respondents. This is particularly true if question wording, questionnaire forms, and interviewing techniques are properly designed. But even such major events as hospitalizations can be substantially underreported just a year later; memory cannot be completely trusted.

Questions Aimed at Beliefs or Attitudes

A frequent focus of questionnaire research is on relatively *subjective* phenomena, such as the respondent's belief that the President is managing the economy well or poorly, attitude toward one's job, or feelings about abortion. For convenience, in this section we will refer to all such subjective questions as attitudes except where finer distinctions are necessary.

Questions about attitudes are probably the most difficult type to write, for a number of reasons (Moser & Kalton, 1972). First, there is always the possibility that respondents *may not have an attitude* because they never thought about the issue until the interviewer asked about it. One cannot count on the respondent saying "I don't know" in this situation; many people simply respond with a "doorstep opinion" that is not well thought through (Schuman & Presser, 1979). Recent research in social cognition, however, has shown that at least in the laboratory, people who have formed an attitude toward an object can be distinguished from those who have not by the *shorter time* they take to answer an attitude question (Fazio, Powell, & Herr, 1983; Powell & Fazio, 1984). The amount of time between a question and response could be unobtrusively measured in telephone interviews (or less unobtrusively in personal interviews), possibly helping to overcome the problem of "doorstep opinions."

Second, attitudes are often *complex and multidimensional.* A person may not have a single overall attitude toward abortion, but may favor it in some circumstances and reject it in others or favor it on medical grounds but disapprove of it on moral grounds. Third, attitudes have a dimension of *intensity.* People who have the same attitude (e.g., opposing busing for school desegregation) may differ widely in intensity, with some viewing the issue as relatively trivial and others feeling very strongly, actively writing letters, attending demonstrations, and so on.

The result of all these factors is that *expressed attitudes are dependent on details of question wording, question sequence, and interviewer effects* to a greater extent than are responses involving facts, for instance. There are numerous examples of this phenomenon, which has been recognized for over 30 years (Payne, 1951). Two questions used by the Gallup and Harris polls just three or four months apart in 1969 produced estimates of support of President Nixon's Vietnam War policy of 29 and 49 percent, undoubtedly because of differences in wording rather than because popular opinion actually changed that much in such a brief period (Schuman & Duncan, 1974).

Besides the necessity to word attitude questions carefully, a number of other considerations are significant. It may be important to measure the attitude's *intensity.* The respondent may be asked to directly rate the intensity of the attitude with a question like "How strongly do you feel about this issue?" Alternatively, an attitude question may be followed up with questions about related behaviors: After asking "How well did you like the book?" one could ask whether the respondent has recommended it to other people or sought out other books by the same author. Still another approach is to point out difficulties or costs implicit in the respondent's position and ask if he or she stands by it. For example, those who favor improved protection of the environment could be asked whether they would be willing to pay $5, $50, or $500 more in taxes per year to attain that goal. Whatever approach is taken, the measurement of attitude intensity is an important adjunct to the measurement of attitude position.

The *level of specificity* of questions about attitudes is as important as it is with questions about facts or behaviors. General and specific questions often will not obtain the same responses, as when a person expresses a negative attitude toward a particular racial group in general but a positive attitude toward individual members of the same group. Usually, specific questions obtain more valid responses than general ones. For instance, simply asking people whether they favor more educational television programs would not reveal whether they wanted them for themselves or simply generally thought they would be good for other people. It would be preferable to ask whether they would *watch* more educational programs if they were available. On the other hand, answers to seemingly specific questions may sometimes reflect general attitudes, making the response subject to misinterpretation by the researcher. For example, people might be asked, "Do qualified black teachers have just as good a chance as qualified white teachers to be hired in the schools in this city?" Unless the respondent has some specific knowledge about practices in the school system, it is very likely that the question will be answered on the basis of a general opinion that blacks are (or are not) treated fairly. The answer will not actually refer to the specific issue, though it may seem to. It is always important to frame questions at an appropriate level of specificity, avoiding both questions that are so general as to be meaningless and questions that are too specific to be answered.

Attitudes can best be measured (at the cost of using more interview time) by using multiple related questions and constructing an attitude *scale*, as discussed in Chapter 9. A properly constructed scale will have better reliability and validity than a single item. Scales generally use closed-ended questions, though coded open-ended responses could also be included.

Sociometric questions   One specific focus of content is on attitude toward other people in a group. *Sociometric* studies focus on positive and negative attitudes or actual interactions among people in a group. The interactions may be of various kinds, including talking to, sitting next to, lending to, visiting, buying from, or playing with. Sociometric studies commonly use questionnaires, though observational or archival data may also be used when actual interaction (rather than attitudes or preferences for interaction) is the point.

A sociometric questionnaire asks each member of a group to indicate which other members he or she would like to have as a partner in some interaction (for example, "eat lunch with") and which group members he or she would not like to have as a partner. Respondents may be allowed to name as many others as they wish or may be restricted to naming three or some other specific number. It is often assumed that preferences will be stated more honestly if the subject believes they will really determine subsequent social arrangements (e.g., that seating arrangements or work partnerships will actually be assigned on the basis of the questionnaire). Therefore sociometric questionnaires are sometimes given with the statement that the investigator will arrange circumstances to fulfill the participant's preferences if possible. Of course, ethical problems arise if any statement of this sort is made without the promise being carried out.

Sociometric data can provide information about an individual's position in the group, the social subgroups or "cliques" within the group, the relationships among subgroups, the group's cohesiveness, the leadership structure, and other matters. Data of this type have been used in studies of leadership, peer relationships in racially mixed schools, the effects of experimental treatments on group structure, and so on.

In a study of friendship choices among members of the Wisconsin state legislature, for example, Patterson (1959) found that legislative leaders tended to be selected as friends by Assembly members more frequently than did nonleaders. Patterson interviewed (or contacted by mailed questionnaire) 87 percent of the members of the Assembly in a study of informal organization in the legislature. Mailed questionnaires were used as a supplement to personal interviews when legislators could not be reached in person. Each member was asked to nominate his or her closest personal friends in the Assembly. Patterson found that the structure of friendships in the Wisconsin Assembly tended to parallel voting patterns there. Expressions of friendship that were directed toward leadership in the Assembly were concluded to be helpful in mitigating political conflicts.

Among the earliest applications of sociometric techniques to the study of relations between racial or ethnic groups were the studies of Criswell (1937). She asked children in mixed black and white classes from kindergarten through the sixth grade in a public school to choose two classmates beside whom they would like to sit. She found that in this school and within this age range, cleavage between the sexes was far more marked than cleavage between blacks and whites. The white children did not begin to form a "racial" group until the fifth grade—a finding previously reported by Moreno (1934).

Although such studies are extremely useful in revealing interrelationships among members of a given group, one must be cautious about interpreting cleavages as evidence of prejudice. Preference for members of one's racial or ethnic group may simply indicate greater familiarity. For example, the white students in a racially mixed class may live in the same neighborhood and know one another well, but they may have little acquaintance with the black students, who live in a different neighborhood. If this is true, a nonrandom choice (more white students choosing other white students than would be expected by chance) does not necessarily indicate an avoidance of black students. This is not to deny that prejudice may be involved somewhere, historically, in the chain of causation—as in the creation of the segregated neighborhoods. But this is different from asserting that the nonrandom choice patterns of the children are necessarily indications of prejudice among them.

Questions Aimed at Behavior

People are in a uniquely favorable position to observe their own behavior, so questions often concern the respondent's present or past behaviors. The most important guideline for asking about behaviors is that the question should be *specific*. For example, "What brand or brands of coffee do you have in the house today? Do you usually buy that brand?" is preferable to a more general question like "What brand of coffee do you usually use?" A telephone survey on television viewing should ask, "Is your television on right now? What program is it tuned to?" rather than "What television programs do you usually watch?" In each case the first question offers better cues for recall by anchoring the respondent to the concrete instance. Similarly, in the study of prejudice, questions about specific past behaviors are likely to elicit more valid reports than general questions. It would be preferable to ask, "For whom did you vote in the last mayoral election? What made you vote for this person? Did you know the religion of any of the candidates? Were you influenced for or against any candidate by knowledge of that person's religion?" rather than "Do you usually tend to consider a candidate's religion in deciding for whom to vote?"

As with questions about facts, the length of time elapsed since the behavior will influence the accuracy of responses. The shorter the interval, the better. Because of the problems of memory, studies of behavior often use techniques like *diaries* in which respondents log their behavior as it occurs rather than relying on recall after the event. (See, e.g., LoSciuto, 1971.)

Question Content: General Issues

A number of considerations apply to questions regardless of their specific content category (facts, attitudes, or behaviors). One crucial decision is the *number of questions* to devote to a topic. Given the ever-present pressures on interview time, it is important to avoid unnecessary questions and unnecessary levels of detail. For example, instead of asking the age of each child in a family, it might be sufficient for the research purposes to know the number of children under age 16.

On the other hand, particularly for the central topics of a study, enough questions should be included to permit full understanding of the responses. Often this principle implies using multiple-item scales (Chapter 9) for high reliability and validity in the measurement of key attitudes, but it has other implications as well. For example, asking for the respondent's opinion of a particular racial group should be done in the context of parallel questions about other groups. Otherwise, one would not know whether a negative opinion was specific to this group or reflected a negative view of all racial outgroups or even of all people in general. It is also valuable to ascertain how important the respondent considers a particular issue or condition. A respondent may say that he or she favors the provision of more parkland in the community but may perceive the issue as relatively unimportant in the context of other pressing problems. People can be asked directly to rate the importance of different issues or can be asked an open-ended question like "What two or three problems do you consider to be the most important ones facing our community today?" (Obviously, such a question should be asked before any mention of specific issues, to avoid biasing the responses.)

Often, question content needs to differ for different subsets of respondents, and such situations should be anticipated. Those who watch a television program "regularly," for example, may be asked about their attitudes toward the program, whereas those who watch "occasionally" or "never" might be asked instead about what other programs they watch, what they know about this program, and so on.

Finally, the sensitivity or level of threat posed by the question content needs to be carefully considered. If the response might be viewed as private or personal by the respondent, special precautions in wording and interview technique can be applied to maximize the chance of obtaining valid answers instead of misinformation or refusals to answer. Techniques for measuring opinions on sensitive topics will be discussed later in this chapter.

Question Wording

The wording of questions is perhaps the most difficult and important task in questionnaire construction. Improperly worded questions can only result in biased or otherwise meaningless responses, and, as noted, attitudes are particularly subject to biases caused by wording. An essential prerequisite for developing properly worded questions is to have a clear conceptual idea of just what content is to be measured. It is then important to pretest the questions to revise and improve them, as was outlined in the previous chapter.

Prior decisions about question content dictate some aspects of wording. The specification of the desired content must be detailed enough to provide guidance. For example, a researcher may want to measure someone's "income." This is too vague, for it could mean (1) the respondent's earnings from his or her occupation, (2) the respondent's total income (including interest or other payments besides earnings), or (3) the respondent's total family or household income; it could mean before-tax or after-tax income; and so on. The question would have to be worded differently in each case. As another example, consider these questions: "Are working conditions satisfactory or not satisfactory in the plant where you work?" and "Are you personally satisfied or dissatisfied with working conditions in the plant where you work?" The general thrust of the questions is similar, but the second will probably elicit a more individual expression of feelings and the first a judgment more tempered by what the respondent supposes other people think, what comparable work places are like, and so on. Conceptual clarity is therefore the essential starting point of wording adequate questions.

At times, wording decisions may be bypassed. The overall research purpose may involve the replication of a question or an entire study that was conducted earlier. This eases decisions about question wording, because wordings should be repeated exactly when this goal is important. Even seemingly minor wording changes—such as the use of the term *forbid* instead of *not allow*—can result in large differences in responses, so they should be avoided. A similar situation arises when information derived from the questionnaire is to be compared to other sources of data (e.g., U.S. Census data, personnel records, or directory listings); again, the question and the response categories should follow those used in the other data source. Often, the goals of the research involve both the exploration of new areas and the partial replication of an existing study, creating a conflict between the desire to replicate questions that were used before and the desire to improve them. An attempt to compromise and maintain both goals is often unsatisfactory because wording improvements will interfere with comparability. "In a serious replication one will repeat faithfully the 'errors' of the original study as well as adhere to its 'good ideas'" (Duncan, 1969).

Even when replication is not a primary purpose of the research, the ability to compare results from a study with those of earlier research often greatly increases the meaningfulness of the results by placing them in context. It is therefore common for researchers to search out earlier questions on the topic of their interest and repeat them exactly in a new study. This also allows one to avoid "reinventing the wheel," spending time and effort developing a usable measure of a construct that other researchers have measured in the past. Survey archives (discussed in Chapter 12) and compilations of questions and scales by Robinson and Shaver (1969) and Shaw and Wright (1967) are useful sources in which to locate previously used questions.

This section on question wording is divided into discussions of a number of specific issues, including terminology, or the choices of individual words to identify concepts in questions; question structure; the proper expression of alternatives in questions; the avoidance of unwarranted assumptions; the choice of response categories; and the assessment of "no opinion" or "don't know" responses. A final section discusses differences among the three modes of data collection (written questionnaires, personal interviews, and telephone interviews) that influence decisions on wording.

Terminology

The choice of specific terms to convey the question's concepts is often the most difficult part of question wording. As noted, the use of terms like *earnings* versus *income* can completely change the meaning of a question. The first guideline, therefore, is that terms should be *exact*, reflecting just what the question content is intended to mean. A second guideline, of equal importance but often conflicting with the first, is that terms must be *simple:* comprehensible even to the least-educated respondents. Many commonly used terms are frequently misunderstood, including personal characteristics like "nationality," "marital status," or "unemployed" and attitude objects such as "affirmative action," "guaranteed wage," or "mass media." Such terms should be avoided and simpler equivalents substituted, or else they should be spelled out and clarified in detail. For example, instead of asking, "What is your marital status?" (which might elicit reports of marital problems, plans for the future, opinions about marriage, or feelings about personal fitness for marriage), it is best to ask, "Are you currently married, widowed, divorced, or separated or have you never been married?" This recommendation cannot be followed in all cases, however, since the substitution of simple words for difficult ones often turns simple *sentences* into difficult ones. Dillman (1978) gives an example: "Should the state sales tax on prescription drugs be reduced from 5 percent to 1 percent?" (difficult words) could be rewritten as "Should the state sales tax on those medicines that can only be bought under a doctor's order be lowered so that people would pay 1 cent tax instead of 5 cents tax for every dollar spent on such medicine?" (difficult sentence).

Ambiguous or vague words are frequent sources of trouble. Even familiar, simple words can give rise to ambiguity: In "What kind of headache remedy do you usually use?" the word *kind* may be understood by some respondents to refer to a *brand* and by others to mean *pills versus powder*. Quantifying words (e.g., *frequently, often, sometimes, almost never, usually*) are intrinsically vague and should be avoided in favor of numerical ranges when possible. In "Do you attend religious services regularly?" one respondent may take "regularly" to mean weekly, whereas for another it may mean once a month.

Finally, *biased words* in questions can produce biased responses. Terms that produce powerful emotional responses, like *freedom, equality, justice, communism, boss, bureaucrat,* or *big business,* should be avoided if possible. Two people with opposite viewpoints might word questions about wage and price controls in two different ways: "Do you think that government bureaucrats should be involved in regulating workers' wages and the prices charged by businesses?" versus "Do you think that big business and powerful union leaders should be able to set prices and wages at whatever levels they choose, or should the government step in to protect consumers from increases in the cost of living?" The second version is likely to elicit more procontrol responses. These examples of biased questions, although extreme, are not fanciful; newsletters sent by congressional representatives to their constituents often contain "surveys" that use equally biased questions. One suspects that the purpose of such questions is as much to persuade voters of the wisdom of the representative's position as to determine the voters' true opinions.

On the other hand, Schuman and Presser's (1981) research points to an interesting conclusion: The more blatant an attempt at influencing the respondent by biased wording, the less likely it may be to succeed. If this conclusion is correct, the preceding examples may not influence responses as much as seemingly innocuous wording changes, such as the choice between the terms *forbid* and *not allow*. These terms seem to mean exactly the same thing, but a question about whether the government should *allow* public speeches by a Communist elicits up to 25 percentage points fewer pro-free-speech responses than an otherwise identical question using the term *forbid* (Schuman & Presser, 1981). Such effects of wording remind us that questions drawn from a previous study should be repeated exactly if complete comparability is to be maintained.

Question Structure

Complex and lengthy sentences are particularly likely to be misunderstood by respondents, so questions should be *short and simple*. As previously noted, however, the need to use simple words often results in lengthy sentences, and compromises sometimes must be struck. One guideline is that the *key idea in the question should come last* to avoid the respondent's beginning to formulate an answer prematurely. Qualifications and conditional clauses should come first. For example, researchers ask, "If your party nominated a woman for President, would you vote for her if she were qualified for the job?" instead of "Would you vote for a woman for President if . . . " and even the standard wording might be improved by moving the phrase about qualification for the job to the beginning.

Finally, questions should *simplify the respondent's task* as much as possible. For example, instead of asking what percentage of income the respondent spends on rent, it is preferable to ask for both the respondent's monthly income and monthly rent payments. Instead of asking about the average length of recent vacation trips, ask for the length of the three most-recent trips. The researcher can calculate the desired percentage or average from the respondent's answers.

Expressing All Alternatives

Questions should *make the alternatives clear* unless they are totally unambiguous (like favoring versus opposing some policy proposal). Even when the implied alternative is reasonably clear, stating it explicitly can make it more vivid and salient and hence place the two possible answers on a more equal footing. Payne (1951) gives a striking example of the effect of failing to state alternatives explicitly. To the question "Do you think most manufacturing companies that lay off workers during slack periods could arrange things to avoid layoffs and give steady work right through the year?" 63 percent said companies could avoid layoffs, and 22 percent said they could not (the rest had no opinion). An equivalent sample of respondents was asked the question with the alternative made explicit: The phrase "or do you think layoffs are unavoidable?" was simply added at the end. To this question, only 35 percent said companies could avoid layoffs and 41 percent said they could not.

Omitting some alternatives or not treating them equally in the question actually constitutes a form of bias. The question "In the mayoral election, do you plan to vote for Mayor Jones or the challenger?" is blatantly biased; the names of both candidates should be given, and perhaps the fact that one is the incumbent should be omitted (" . . . do you plan to vote for Jones or Brown?"). Another example is "How do you generally spend your free time, watching television or what?" (Warwick & Lininger, 1975, p. 143).

Finally, one fairly common practice is to describe a policy by introducing it with "Some people say we should . . . " to lead in to a question about "Do you agree or disagree?" or "What do you think?" The result can be a biased question unless care is taken to treat the opposing position equally, as in "Some people say that women should have an equal role with men in running business, industry, and government. Others say that women's place is in the home. What do you think?" Without the second sentence the question might be biased. On the other hand, Schuman and Presser's (1981) research finds that wording changes like this have relatively little effect on responses. Nonetheless, they recommend avoiding questions that present a statement (with or without the preface "Some people say . . . ") and ask for the respondent's agreement or disagreement, in favor of the use of a forced-choice format. For example, one would not use "[Some people say that] individuals are more to blame than social conditions for crime and lawlessness in this country" with an agree or disagree response scale. A preferable question, according to Schuman and Presser, would be "Which in your opinion is more to blame for crime and lawlessness in this country—individuals or social condtions?" This forced-choice wording seems to elicit more valid responses than the agree or disagree wording, perhaps because the latter is more susceptible to response biases such as a general tendency to agree with statements regardless of their content.

Avoiding Unwarranted Assumptions

The question "What is your occupation?" assumes that the respondent has an occupation. "For whom did you vote in the last presidential election?" assumes the respondent voted (Warwick & Lininger, 1975, p. 145). Such examples of the "Have you stopped beating your wife?" type annoy respondents and are likely to produce invalid data. The general solution to this problem is to ask a preliminary question about whether the respondent is working, did vote, or whatever is appropriate and then ask the question of interest for only those respondents who fall into the relevant category. For other respondents the interviewer is instructed to skip around the irrelevant question.

Another way unwarranted assumptions can be introduced into questions is with *double-barreled questions*, which inappropriately combine two separate ideas and require a single response. Asking about the attitude of one's "parents" is inappropriate, for the father's and mother's attitudes may be different. Other examples are "Do you think taxes on corporations should be increased and taxes on individuals lowered?" "Do you think that the government's policy on inflation is fair and effective?" and "Do you plan to sell your house and move away in the next year?" (the respondent might plan to sell without moving or move without selling).

Response Categories: Open-Ended Versus Closed-Ended Questions

The primary decision about the form of the respondent's choices is between *open-ended*, or free-response, versus *closed-ended*, or fixed-alternative questions. Open-ended questions allow the respondent to answer in a relatively unconstrained way, either writing the response (in the case of a written questionnaire) or telling it to the interviewer, who is instructed to record the response verbatim. Later, the researcher will code the response in terms of a system of categories. Closed-ended questions, on the other hand, present two or more alternatives, and the respondents select the choice closest to their own position.

Open-ended and closed-ended questions have complementary strengths and weaknesses. Open-ended questions allow respondents to convey the fine shades of their attitude to their own satisfaction instead of forcing them to choose one of several statements that may all seem more or less unsatisfactory. For this reason, open-ended questions may be more motivating to respondents. Also, they can be used even when the researcher does not know the full range of attitude positions in the population under study, whereas construction of a closed-ended question requires such knowledge in advance.

Open-ended questions also have disadvantages, however. The most important are the cost and difficulty of adequately coding the responses. They are frequently self-contradictory, incomprehensible, or irrelevant, and a major proportion of them will usually defy all efforts at meaningful categorization. Open-ended responses are functions of the respondents' attitude position, but also of their intensity, knowledge about the issue, involvement, education, general verbal fluency, communicative style, and other factors. To code such responses meaningfully requires a major effort and is sometimes simply impossible. Closed-ended questions are easily coded to produce meaningful results for analysis.

Another advantage of closed-ended questions is that the provision of response categories may help clarify the intent of the question for the respondents, or help their memory. For instance, a respondent may be unable to recall the name of his or her preferred political candidate before a primary election but may be able to pick the name out of the list of candidates if it is provided. Or people may not be able to remember all the state parks they have visited in the past year without the aid of a list of their names and locations. At times, though, providing a list of possible responses is unnecessary, and an open-ended format will be satisfactory, as when the respondent is asked, "In which state were you born?" Often open-ended questions are asked about the respondent's reasons or explanations for a response. The follow-up might be worded, "Just how do you mean?" "Why do you feel that way?" or "Would you tell me a little more about your thinking on that?" Full information often requires the use of more than one question, however. For example, the question "Why do you feel the way you do about abortion?" may elicit answers involving personal or educational experiences, beliefs about legal restrictions, political attitudes, moral or religious values, or beliefs about when human life begins. (This variety of possible frames of reference for responses illustrates the difficulties of coding open-ended responses in ways that permit comparisons across respondents.) The goals of the research might be best served by asking each respondent about each of these different aspects of the issue, requiring a series of questions. This will take valuable interview time and much effort in coding (unless closed-ended questions are used), so that relatively few variables can be explored in such depth in a single study.

Researchers often seek to obtain the benefits of both open-ended and closed-ended questions. One approach is to give a set of fixed response alternatives and also an open-ended "other" category, allowing people who do not fit any of the given alternatives to fill in their own. However, this type of question rarely obtains enough "other" responses to warrant analysis. Most respondents will choose one of the offered response categories rather than create their own, perhaps because the former involves less effort. This type of question remains useful in identifying situations where important response alternatives are not included among the fixed set: A relatively large number of "other" responses indicates that the set of responses is unsatisfactory and should be revised.

Perhaps the best way to combine the advantages of open- and closed-ended questions is that suggested by Schuman and Presser (1979, 1981). Initially, open-ended questions are asked with a relatively small pretest sample of the population that is to be studied. On the basis of their responses a closed-ended question can be constructed that represents the most common response categories found in the pretest sample. This approach saves work (for only the open-ended responses from the pretest, not from the whole study sample, need to be coded) while ensuring that the closed-ended question that is finally used adequately represents the range of opinions on the issue. The approach avoids both the danger of using a large number of open-ended questions in a survey (and ending up with largely uncodable data) and the danger of writing closed-ended questions that fail to reflect the diversity of opinion that exists in the population. Schuman and Presser (1981) conclude that closed-ended questions constructed in this way generally have equal or superior validity to the open-ended questions from whch they were constructed. Most researchers today use mainly closed-ended questions in attitude measurement, but with a sprinkling of open-ended questions to obtain reasons or illustrations for attitudes on key issues. The open-ended responses can help in the formulation of new hypotheses and are often quoted to lend interest and concreteness to reports of research results.

Response Categories: Other Issues

If closed-ended questions are used, a number of further decisions remain. The question may call for a *response scale* along a single dimension; for example, "How frequently do you attend religious services: never, a few times a year, about once a month, about two to three times a month, about once a week, or more often than once a week?" A common response scale involves the dimension of agreement versus disagreement, sometimes using just those two categories, other times using qualified categories like "strongly agree," "agree," "disagree," and "strongly disagree." However, note the caution raised by Schuman and Presser's research (1981, chs. 7, 8) and mentioned previously: There is some evidence that forced-choice questions produce more valid responses than agree or disagree questions. Questions using response scales are appropriate when the dimension of the desired response is known and the respondents are to classify themselves along it, a procedure discussed under the heading of self-ratings in Chapter 9. These are usually among the easiest types of questions for respondents to answer, since the response dimension is so clearly identified.

Closed-ended questions can also involve *unordered response choices* that do not fall along a single dimension; for example, "To what social class do you belong: middle class, working class, upper class, or lower class?" "If the election were being held today, which presidential candidate would you vote for: Ronald Reagan or Walter Mondale?" "Which of these things will influence you most when it comes to choosing your next car: appearance, gas mileage, comfort, pickup, dependability, safety, ease of driving, smoothness, cost, or speed?" or "Would you say the group most responsible for causing inflation is business, labor unions, government, or some other group?" As the last example illustrates, a residual "other" category may be included in a set of responses. One danger with lists of unordered response categories is that they may fail to include the preferred choice of some respondents, but this possibility can be reduced by pretesting as described. Another problem is that generally each of the given response alternatives must be individually considered by the respondent, and this makes the question difficult to answer. With personal interviews, a lengthy set of response choices can be printed on a card which is handed to the respondent to reduce the memory burden of answering such questions. A final problem is that the categories may fail to be mutually exclusive, forcing respondents to choose between equally true alternatives; for example (Dillman, 1978), "How did you first hear about the proposed freeway: from a friend or relative, at a meeting of an organization to which I belong, at work, from my spouse, over television or radio, or from a newspaper?" What if the respondent heard about it from a friend at work? Poorly constructed sets of response categories are among the most common faults in questionnaires.

Response categories must strike the appropriate balance between vagueness and overprecision. Most respondents would find it hard to answer a question like "How many meals did you eat at restaurants last month: _____ meals," for too much precision is implied by the request for a specific number. On the other hand, "very many, quite a lot, not too many, just a few, none" would be too vague. *Ranges of numbers* are usually the best solution in cases like this. An example is "none, 1–2 meals, 3–5 meals, 5–10 meals, 11–20 meals, over 20 meals." Income is generally measured with numerical categories, since respondents are often more comfortable placing their income in a category like $15,000–$19,999 than giving an exact figure. As with any set of response categories, the ranges should be mutually exclusive so they should not overlap. Income categories, for instance, should not be given as $15,000–$20,000, $20,000–$30,000, and so on. The point may seem minor (not many respondents will have an income of exactly $20,000), but such details create an overall impression of sloppiness or care in question construction and therefore indirectly influence the respondent's motivation to take the task seriously.

Finally, response categories should be properly *balanced*. Consider this example: "Do you think that judges should sentence criminals to prison terms that are much longer than at present, longer than at present, about the same as at present, or shorter than at present?" With more response categories on the "longer" side than on the "shorter" side, the set of categories is biased rather than balanced. Of course, sometimes balance is unnecessary and unwise, as in "Over the next few years, do you hope to obtain large pay raises, moderate-size pay raises, or only small pay raises?" Categories involving decreases in pay seem unnecessary in this context.

Filters and the Assessment of No Opinion

People responding to surveys have an unfortunate tendency to answer questions like "Do you agree or disagree with the governor's policy on layoffs for state employees?" or "Do you favor or oppose the extension of the Agricultural Trade Act?" even if they do not know what the governor's policy or the act in question is. Unless the purpose of the research includes the measurement of such top-of-the-head, uninformed reactions, the assessment of "no opinion" or "don't know" (DK) responses should be allowed for in question construction.

The most common approach is to list DK as one response alternative. Usually this option is not mentioned in the question read to the respondent, but the interviewer is instructed to check DK on the questionnaire if the respondent gives that answer. Sometimes the DK response is explicitly mentioned in the question, as in "Do you favor or oppose . . . or haven't you thought much about it?" A variant of this approach is to include a neutral point in a response scale, for example, "strongly agree," "agree," "no opinion," "disagree," or "'strongly disagree." Of course, more DK responses are obtained when the possibility is explicitly mentioned than when it is not.

Sometimes the substantive opinion question is preceded by a separate *filter question* intended solely to screen out respondents who do not have any knowledge or opinion on the issue. One might ask, "The governor has recently taken a position on the issue of layoffs for state employees. Have you heard or read enough about this to have an opinion on the matter?" Respondents who answer affirmatively may even be asked to state what the governor's position is, to verify that their understanding is correct. Finally they would be asked about their opinion. Respondents who claim not to have an opinion are never asked the opinion question; their interview simply proceeds from the filter to the subsequent question. The use of filter questions produces an increase in DK responses of as much as 25 percentage points over the standard (unfiltered) version of the same question (Schuman & Presser, 1979).

If different techniques of assessing DK responses merely change the proportion of respondents who choose that response, the issue would not be very important. But in fact recent research shows that different approaches to DK responses (using filtered versus unfiltered questions) can change the *distribution* of substantive responses—that is, the relative balance of agreement versus disagreement on an issue (Bishop, Oldendick, & Tuchfarber, 1983). For example, in a 1978 survey, one question concerned cutting federal taxes even if it meant that some public employees would lose their jobs. Although 48 percent of the respondents who gave an opinion favored the tax cut with the standard (unfiltered) form of the question, 58 percent had a favorable opinion when a separate filter question was used—a substantial difference in support.

Using filtered versus unfiltered questions can also change the relationships among different attitude measures (Schuman & Presser, 1979). Interestingly, Schuman and Presser did not find evidence that filtering materially affected relationships of attitude items to the respondents' background characteristics, but it would be premature to conclude that such relationships will never be affected. The research seems to show that there is a substantial number of people, perhaps as many as 25 percent of the population, who will give a DK response when a filter question invites it but will give a substantive opinion to an unfiltered question. Schuman and Presser (1979) call these respondents *floaters*. Using unfiltered questions and therefore including the floaters' responses can seriously affect conclusions drawn from attitude surveys. An overall recommendation is to use filters to screen out uninformed respondents if the measurement of only informed opinion on the issue is the goal but to use standard (unfiltered) questions if basic values, ideologies, or general attitudes are desired (Schuman & Presser, 1981, p. 312).

Special Considerations for Different Modes

Written questionnaires, personal interviews, and telephone interviews have somewhat different requirements for question wording, telephone interviews being perhaps the most different. One obvious consideration is that the use of visual aids and printed materials (such as lists of response categories) is impossible over the telephone. Photographs, line drawings, or maps can greatly clarify certain types of questions, and they have been used in research on such topics as interracial attitudes (Helgerson, 1943; Horowitz, 1936) and attitudes about work (Whyte, 1957). Particularly when children or people of limited literacy are being studied, visual techniques are valuable, for they reduce the demands placed on verbal comprehension. However, even with general populations, pictures, diagrams, or maps can help communicate some types of situations or concepts. As previously noted, printed lists of response categories are also useful when the lists are long and would pose a burden on the respondent's memory. The inability to use visual aids of either the pictorial or the list type frequently makes it necessary to reword questions for telephone interviews.

These questions need to be carefully constructed especially for brevity and clarity. Respondents to a written questionnaire have the question in front of them and can reread it if necessary, and in a personal interview the interviewer can detect nonverbal signs of incomprehension or confusion. But the telephone interviewer faces special problems since question content that is often complex and abstract must be communicated completely by voice, without the respondent having much chance to control the pace of the interview. The maxim "keep it short and simple" applies with even more force to questions that will be asked over the telephone. If questions are necessarily complex (e.g., summarizing a complex program to ask a respondent's opinion of it), they should include considerable redundancy, and the key elements should be summarized at the end so that respondents can check their comprehension (Dillman, 1978). Sometimes complex questions can be divided into two or more parts, each of which is conceptually simpler.

Sets of response categories must also be kept simple for telephone use. Obviously large numbers of unordered categories (for which printed lists would be used in personal interviews) cannot be used. Neither can questions that ask respondents to rank order a number of choices; these should be replaced with a separate evaluation of each individual choice. Even response scales should probably be kept to no more than five or so categories (Dillman, 1978). It is tempting to request numerical responses (e.g., "on a scale from 0 to 10, where 0 means strongly disagree and 10 means strongly agree . . . ") in order to avoid giving respondents a list of possible responses, but Dillman reports mixed results with this technique. Some people understand the technique quickly and are comfortable using it, but others never seem to get the idea.

A number of special considerations for written questionnaires involve the use of page layout and typography to clarify and simplify the respondent's task; Dillman presents a detailed set of recommendations. One significant point is that written questionnaires cannot use skips and filter questions as freely as questionnaires administered by trained interviewers because respondents frequently have trouble comprehending instructions to skip over one or more questions depending on their response to a previous question.

Question Sequence

The sequence of the questions in a questionnaire has two major implications. First, an appropriate sequence can *ease the respondent's task in answering*, which is particularly important at the very beginning when one must capture the respondent's interest and motivate completion. Second, the sequence of questions can either *create or avoid biases* that influence responses to the later questions. *Context effects* (the effects of preceding questions on the response to later questions) have been much studied in recent years, and they pose the same sorts of issues as effects of question wording, though they seem to be less powerful. The following guidelines should be followed to produce questionnaires that are as free from bias as possible and seem natural to respondents.

Overall Sequence

Respondents often begin an interview or questionnaire with some doubts about whether they can perform the task. After all, they are not experts on the topic or (perhaps) even highly educated. Will they simply embarrass themselves by not knowing the answers at all? To overcome these doubts, every questionnaire should begin with a few easy and unchallenging questions (probably closed-ended questions with only two or three response categories). At the same time, the initial questions should be interesting to the respondent, possessing clear social importance and clear relevance to the stated study purpose (Dillman, 1978). Therefore, one common practice, beginning the questionnaire with easy-to-answer background items like age, marital status, or education, is unwise. Examples of reasonable opening questions (assuming that the stated study topic involves household financial matters) are "There's been a lot of talk about inflation. How much would you say you and your family have been hurt by inflation recently: a great deal, somewhat, not too much, or not at all?" or "We are interested in how people are getting along financially these days. During the last few years, has the financial situation of you and your household been getting better, staying about the same, or getting worse?" Questions like these should be both interesting for respondents and easy to answer, building up their confidence that they can successfully complete the questionnaire or interview.

Following a few initial questions of the sort just described, the main questions follow; they may be concerned with the respondent's beliefs, behaviors, attitudes, or whatever is entailed by the purpose of the study. Questions about respondents' social and demographic background should be put at the end. At that time the respondents are ordinarily more willing to give such personal information, and in case they are not, at least the replies to the belief and attitude questions will not be affected by the suspicion or resentment that personal questions occasionally arouse.

A final consideration is to keep topically related questions together. Respondents are frequently confused and angered if questions skip around from topic to topic, as when one question asks about tax policy, the next about the number of children respondents have, and the next about their satisfaction with their job. Both the respondents' comprehension and ability to answer the questions will be facilitated by keeping topically related questions together. Moreover, each topic area in turn should be linked in the respondent's mind to the overall purpose of the study. Questions with no evident connection to the topic are bound to arouse suspicion and resentment, for example, if a questionnaire about "how people feel about the Social Security system" suddenly turned to a series of questions on drinking and drug use. Even background items such as income and education will often be resisted by respondents if their purpose is not understood. This is another reason for putting such items at the end of the questionnaire; the implicit or explicit message is then that they will be used to compare the beliefs or opinions of people with different characteristics. Thus the respondent can see their relevance.

Clear and meaningful transitions between topics that point out the relevance of the new topic to the study purpose are essential. At a minimum, transitional statements signal that one topic has been completed and a new one is coming up. These statements might be as simple as "The next few questions are about the upcoming election" or "We've been talking so far about your general feelings about your neighborhood. Now I'd like to ask a few questions about your family." Beyond this level, transitions can explain—though not with great technical detail—the rationale for the succeeding questions in terms of the study purpose or their relationship to the preceding topic. Examples are "An important part of understanding people's attitudes toward Social Security has to do with their feelings about retirement from work. So next we would like to ask some questions about your plans and thoughts about retirement" or "Finally, we would like to ask some questions about yourself, to help interpret the results" (to introduce the personal background items at the end of the questionnaire). Well-written transitions are indispensable for smoothing the flow of a questionnaire, thereby easing the respondent's task and motivating them to continue by showing the inquiry to be meaningful and relevant. Sensitive questions demand particular attention to transitions, to ensure that respondents understand the relevance of the questions to the research purpose.

Sequence within a Topic Area

Within a specific topic area, two general guidelines relate to question sequence. The first is the "funnel" principle: General questions should come first, followed by increasingly specific and detailed questions, with the sequence "funneling down" to the most detailed questions at the end. This sequence has several points in its favor. The more general questions (e.g., satisfaction or dissatisfaction with one's work in general) are most easily justified in terms of their relevance to the study purpose. They then serve as a natural lead-in to more specific questions about, for example, the activities involved in the job, working conditions, feelings about co-workers, wages, and so on. In addition, the general-to-specific sequence should produce less bias than the reverse. For example, if a series of specific questions about satisfaction with wages preceded the general question about satisfaction with the job as a whole, the focus of the respondent's attention on wages would undoubtedly lead to wages being overweighted in the overall judgment. Such biases are probably less frequent when general questions precede specific ones.

The second general principle is to avoid context or question sequence effects by looking out for possible relationships among questions that might produce bias if two or more questions are close together in the questionnaire. For example, one would not want to ask a series of questions about strikes and labor troubles before a question about attitudes toward unions.

Schuman and Presser (1981) summarize their extensive research on question order effects by noting that they can be large (as much as 15 percentage points in some cases). For example, a 1979 survey used a general question on abortion: "Do you think it should be possible for a pregnant woman to obtain a *legal* abortion if she is married and does not want any more children?" When this question was asked before any other abortion-related questions, 60.7 percent of the respondents said "yes." However, when it was asked (with an equivalent subsample of respondents) after a separate, more-specific question about abortion in the case of a defect in the unborn child (to which 84 percent said "yes"), the general question obtained only 48.1 percent "yes" responses, a decrease of 13 percentage points. A second survey used the same questions and obtained a slightly larger decrease, 17 percent in "yes" responses. In neither case did responses to the specific question differ much depending on whether it was asked first or second.

Question sequence effects are more likely to occur with general or summary questions than with others. However, there are instances of order effects influencing specific attitude questions and even factual responses. In a crime victimization survey, respondents reported that they had been the victims of more crimes if a series of crime-related attitude items preceded the factual questions, perhaps because the attitude questions aided recall (Schuman & Presser, 1981). Our ability to predict what questions may be influenced by order effects is not complete, but common sense must be applied in questionnaire construction to avoid obvious problems. One possibility arising from the new technology of computer-assisted telephone interviewing is to ask a series of questions in a different random order for each respondent, thereby avoiding any systematic order effects. (Interviewers could vary question order manually, but without computer assistance the task is likely to be troublesome and error-prone.)

Perhaps the most serious implication of order effects involves the replication of questions between different surveys to assess changes over time. Though researchers have long known that even seemingly minor wording changes can greatly influence responses, confounding intended replications, it now appears that the context of a question, and particularly the few preceding questions, can have similar effects. Perhaps replications should carry over a whole sequence of questions, rather than just a single question, for maximum interpretability.

Researchers like Schuman and Presser (1981) have used *split-ballot experiments* within surveys to determine the effects of differences in question wording and sequence; some of their results have already been cited. In a split-ballot experiment, two (or more) versions of a questionnaire that use different wordings or sequences are used for different randomly chosen subsets of respondents. Since the random choice means that the respondents receiving the different forms will be equivalent (on the average), any differences in response can be attributed to the wording or sequence variation. Split-ballot experiments are useful not only for methodological investigations like those previously cited; they also can be valuable in any survey where the researcher wishes to rule out question wording effects as a major influence on the results. For example, one could use two different wordings of a crucial question in a split-ballot survey. If the results were identical or similar in the two halves of the sample, one would conclude that question wording effects probably did not play a major role in the results. This approach can be an important tool in showing that survey results are not specific to one particular wording or question order, and it deserves to be more widely used.

Special Techniques for Sensitive Content

When the content of interest might prove embarrassing or threatening to the respondent or is viewed as private or personal, direct questioning may elicit deceptive responses or refusals to answer (or even cause the respondent to break off the interview completely). Questions about illegal behaviors (shoplifting, marijuana use), sexual practices, and racial attitudes pose obvious problems, and even questions about income and political affiliation are viewed as threatening by some respondents. A number of techniques have been developed in an effort to maximize the proportion of truthful answers on such topics. The basis on which valid responses to all sensitive questions (and nonsensitive questions as well) depends is, however, the interviewer's rapport with the respondent. Skilled interviewers encounter remarkably few refusals to reply; the projection of a professional attitude and the confident expectation of a reply rather than embarrassment and doubtfulness will usually gain cooperation. It is also important that sensitive topics be fully introduced by transition statements in the questionnaire and their relationship to the study topic made clear.

Respondents will be more willing to respond if they understand the need for the information than if the questions seem gratuitous or unnecessary.

Standard Precautions

For topics of only marginal sensitivity, certain precautions in wording are typical. As mentioned, it is wise to ask for the year of the respondents' birth rather than their age and to ask how many years of school they completed rather than whether or not they graduated from high school. Income is typically requested with a set of broad categories rather than an exact figure.

When one possible response is marginally socially undesirable, the wording can "explain away" the behavior and make respondents more comfortable in giving that reply. Examples are "Did you vote in the presidential election last November, or didn't you find the time to vote?" and "Do you favor or oppose the program of . . . or haven't you happened to hear much about this?" Not having voted or not knowing enough to have an opinion are implicitly excused in the wording to encourage respondents in those categories to answer truthfully.

Other practices involving wording also seem effective in encouraging reporting of threatening behavioral items. Bradburn and Sudman (1979) found that wording variations had little effect on yes or no responses to simple "Have you done it?" questions about various socially undesirable behaviors, but had major effects on quantitative responses to questions about how much or how often. The most valid results seemed to come (1) with long questions instead of short ones and (2) with open-ended rather than closed-ended formats. There were some indications that another practice also helped: (3) the use of the respondent's own preferred word for the behavior, ascertained in a prior question, rather than some standard term. Dillman (1978) recommends that a threatening behavioral question should be embedded in a connected sequence of questions. That is, one should ask about how frequently the respondent thinks other people perform the behavior, how much the respondent approves or disapproves of it, whether anyone the respondent knows personally has done it, and so on, before asking whether the respondent has done it.

One special issue of sensitivity which arises in the majority of questionnaire studies is the assessment of racial or ethnic identification. Some respondents object to terms such as *Negro* or *Mexican-American* whereas others object equally strenuously to alternatives like *black*. The term *Native American*, if used without further clarification, is selected by many white people as well as by American Indians (whom it is intended to denote). The best solution may be the liberal use of alternatives in each response category (Dillman, 1978): *Black (Negro), Chicano (Mexican-American), Native American (American Indian), White (Caucasian), Oriental (Asian-American),* Other (*specify:* _____).

Beyond the consideration of question wording and sequence, some interviewing practices can help overcome response biases on sensitive questions. A self-administered written questionnaire on a few topics can be given to the respondent during a personal interview, which the respondent can return by mail or seal in an envelope before handing back to the interviewer. This technique has been found to be effective in reducing overstatements of socially desirable behaviors but ineffective in reducing understatements of undesirable acts (Bradburn & Sudman, 1979; Weiss, 1968). The use of telephone rather than personal interviews in general may help increase respondents' feelings of anonymity and hence encourage accurate reporting on sensitive topics. Bradburn and Sudman (1979) compared face-to-face and telephone interviews and found the former to be slightly better with low-threat topics, but telephone interviews obtained fewer response distortions with highly threatening questions, particularly reducing overstatements of desirable acts.

Indirect Questions

Indirect measurement techniques fall into two categories. *Projective methods* involve the presentation of ambiguous or unstructured stimuli to respondents, who interpret them in a way that theoretically reveals their inner characteristics. Other, *more-structured indirect methods* involve questions or objective measurements of attributes that are inferentially rather than directly related to the attribute of interest. For example, tests of knowledge or memory and judgments of attitude statements have been used as indirect measures of attitudes. These indirect methods have conceptual similarities to the use of "subtle" items on attitude scales, discussed in Chapter 9.

The fundamental assumption of *projective measures* is that the inner characteristics of the perceivers (such as their attitudes) are reflected in the ways they perceive and respond to relatively unstructured stimulus materials. For example, the Thematic Apperception Test (TAT) consists of several pictures about which the subject is asked to tell stories; the task is usually presented to subjects as a "test of creativity." Many of the pictures are somewhat ambiguous, so a variety of meanings could be read into them. Various scoring systems have been developed that formalize inferences about the individual's personality, needs, attitudes, or self-concepts based on the content of the stories. It is assumed that the individuals are unaware of the inferences that can be made about them, so that the responses can serve to measure even sensitive characteristics that they might not wish to reveal. Examples of techniques, their uses in research, and the frequent problems with their reliability and validity will be presented here, divided into two broad categories by their use of visual (pictorial) versus verbal stimuli.

Visual projective techniques   Among visual techniques, the TAT and related techniques have been the most popular but have often fallen short on measurement reliability and validity. One project (Burwen & Campbell, 1957) attempted to measure attitudes toward authority with TAT-like pictures but found that the results showed strong evidence of invalidity. They correlated more strongly with another TAT-based measure of a seemingly unrelated concept (attitude toward peers) than with a direct measure of the same concept (attitude toward authority). This pattern of results is the opposite of what one would find with a valid measure of a particular attitude, as discussed in Chapter 3.

Other investigators have attempted to use pictures including members of minority groups as stimuli to assess subjects' racial attitudes, with similar difficulties. In addition, the necessity to use pictures that are clearly identifiable as to race probably cues virtually all subjects to the purpose of the test, eliminating the supposed advantage of nonobviousness of indirect over direct measurement. The indirect measurement of social attitudes by means of pictorial projective tests may be a dead end. Repeated efforts to develop such measures, over at least three decades, have met with failure.

Despite this negative conclusion about the general usefulness of visual projective stimuli for attitude measurement, there are some more-specific issues, such as conceptions of "personal space," on which similar tests can be useful. Little (1968) asked subjects from several different cultures to arrange dolls representing people on a paper background so that they would "look natural" in a number of different situations. The situations varied on a number of dimensions, including affective tone, authority relationships, and intimacy. The results showed consistent differences between both the different types of situation and the different cultures, and Little interpreted them in terms of different cultural conceptions of appropriate personal distance in relationships. The good fit between the specific research question faced by Little and the use of visual projective measurement techniques contributed to the success of the research.

Verbal projective measures   Verbal projective techniques, like pictorial ones, present incomplete or ambiguous stimuli to which subjects must respond. They also have been most widely used for tasks related to personality assessment, but some applications to the measurement of social attitudes have appeared.

Sentence completion is perhaps the simplest verbal projective technique. The individual is given incomplete sentences and is asked to complete them. Sentence-completion tests have generally been found to have better validity as measures of personality characteristics than have pictorial projective tests. For example, Loevinger's sentence-completion tests of ego development (Loevinger, Wessler, & Redmore, 1970) have been extensively evaluated for validity (Loevinger, 1979). Perhaps the better record of verbal as opposed to pictorial techniques for personality assessment is due to the greater specificity of focus they allow; the sentence stem limits the subject's response to the issue of concern much more effectively than in the case of a story told in response to a vague picture. However, this same advantage points to a possible disadvantage: The intent of the test may be as clear to the subject as it would be with direct questioning.

Sentence-completion tests have also been used in studies of social attitudes. For example, in a study of national stereotypes among the English, Kerr (1943) used such sentences as "When I think of the Russians I think of . . ." and "If you invite an American to your home he may. . . ." Though this technique has face validity as a measure of stereotypes, it is possible that direct questioning might be able to get at the same constructs.

Other forms of indirect verbal questioning have been used. One technique is to ask the respondent about what "other people" think on an issue. It is assumed that people might find it easier to express their own opinions on a sensitive issue in answer to such an indirect and impersonal question. Again, this argument has some plausibility, but the technique has a danger that direct questioning would avoid, illustrated by this marvelous example from Maccoby and Maccoby (1954):

> . . . a young woman being interviewed about her attitudes toward her job situation was asked: "How do most of the girls [sic] in the office feel about the supervisor?" She answered, "They think he's wonderful. They'll do anything for him." At which point the interviewer followed with: "And how about you—how do you feel about him?" She made the reply: "I really detest him. I'm trying to transfer out of the unit."

In summary, verbal projective techniques show more promise than visual ones. However, in many cases, even when indirect techniques are found to have adequate reliability or validity, they have not been compared with well-designed direct measures, so the possibility often exists that direct measurement would have equal or superior quality. In addition, as mentioned, many of the better projective techniques (such as sentence-completion tests) cannot be assumed to disguise adequately the purpose of the test from the respondent; thus, one often-claimed advantage of indirect measurement is lost.

More-structured indirect methods   Measurement techniques that avoid the disadvantages of projective measurement but still disguise the purpose of testing have long been sought by social researchers. Some more-structured indirect measures are based on the fundamental assumption that attitudes influence perception, memory, and judgment; thus, tests that directly tap these psychological processes may be able to measure attitudes indirectly.

Unfortunately, a number of attempts to measure attitudes indirectly with tests of knowledge, judgment, and memory have not succeeded. Some researchers have constructed tests, presented to the subject as multiple-choice tests of knowledge, in which all the presented alternatives are actually wrong and the respondent's choice among equally wrong alternatives is taken to indicate an attitude. This technique has face validity (Dawes & Smith, 1984): Giving the answer that heavy cigarette smoking reduces one's life expectancy by 5 years seems to indicate a more favorable attitude toward smoking than answering 15 years (the true answer, by the way, is about 10). However, research findings on the validity of measures of this type are mostly negative: Direct measures are generally superior (Kidder & Campbell, 1970).

Conceptually similar techniques, some with long histories of use (e.g., Watson, 1925), include those in which subjects are asked to judge the correctness of logical arguments (syllogisms) in which the conclusions actually do not follow from the given premises. Judging such a syllogism as correct is taken to indicate that the subject substantively agrees with the conclusion. However, some evidence (S. W. Cook, 1968; Kidder & Campbell, 1970) shows little or no validity of the results. Other investigators have attempted to use bias in learning or memory: Subjects are presumed to learn more rapidly or remember better when the materials they study agree with their own attitudes than when they disagree. However, again, the evidence is that this presumption is largely false (Brigham & Cook, 1969; Greenwald & Sakumura, 1967).

In general, efforts to construct indirect measures disguised as tests of knowledge, judgment, or memory have foundered on the problem that relationships between these psychological processes and attitudes are not simple or straightforward. Therefore, the inference from patterns of performance on such tests to the attitude is quite problematic or is valid only under limited but unknown circumstances. The result is that such indirect tests are generally inferior to direct measures of the attitude of interest.

Randomized Response Techniques

To handle sensitive questions where projective or other indirect techniques are unsuitable or unavailable, *randomized response techniques* (Warner, 1965) can be employed. A variety of techniques have been used, but they have similar characteristics, which may be illustrated by an example (Bradburn & Sudman, 1979). In a personal interview study, interviewers handed respondents a small box that contained 70 red beads and 30 blue beads and was constructed so that when it was tipped, one bead appeared in a small window on the box. The respondent was also given a card with two yes or no questions on it. Opposite a red dot was the sensitive question, for example, "I have been arrested and charged with drunken driving." Opposite a blue dot was an innocuous question, such as

"My birthday is in the last half of the year, from July to December." The respondents were told to tip the box and answer the first question if a red bead appeared and the second question if a blue bead appeared, saying only "yes" or "no" in either case. They were assured that the interviewer could not tell which question was being answered and was only recording the "yes" or "no" response.

The key characteristic of any randomized response technique is that the interviewer does not know whether the answer pertains to the sensitive question, so the respondent's privacy is protected in some measure. A randomizing device (the throw of a die, flip of a coin, or a special device as in the preceding example) is used to tell the respondent privately whether to answer the sensitive question or give a nonsensitive response (either a preprogrammed response or an answer to a nonsensitive question). However, because the properties of the randomizing device are known (e.g., 70 percent of the time a red bead will appear), the results can be statistically analyzed to reveal meaningful variations in the sensitive answer, such as differences among population subgroups.

A particularly simple version of the technique, suitable for use even in telephone interviews, was developed by Dawes and Moore (1979). Subjects are asked to flip a coin and either answer the yes or no question if it is heads or simply respond "yes" if it is tails. (The use of a threatening behavioral question, where "yes" is the sensitive answer, is assumed.) The calculation of the true response probabilities is also simple in this case. If a particular subgroup (say female respondents) give 60 percent "yes" responses, it is known that 50 percent of them (on the average) are due to the coin falling tails. Of the other 50 percent, who answered the question because the coin fell heads, 10 percent must have said "yes." Therefore, 20 percent of all females (10 percent divided by 50 percent) are estimated to have the characteristic in question. Subgroups can also be compared: If 70 percent of males say "yes," it is clear that a larger proportion of males than females have the characteristic.

Other randomized response techniques (Himmelfarb & Edgell, 1980) are suitable when numerical responses are required (e.g., for questions about how many times a behavior was performed).

Research has shown that in general people are more likely to admit to socially undesirable behaviors with randomized response techniques than with an anonymous questionnaire (Bradburn & Sudman, 1979; Dawes & Moore, 1979; Greenberg et al., 1969). However, the results are not completely consistent. Bradburn and Sudman found that randomized response gave the least distortion in response to very high-threat questions (arrests for drunken driving) but was ineffective for questions posing little threat (e.g., voting in a primary election). The latter, however, seem innocuous enough to be asked directly without much problem. In general, randomized response techniques promise to add greatly to researchers' ability to elicit sensitive information.

In summary, there is probably a relatively small number of topics for which standard precautions in question wording and interviewer rapport are insufficient to obtain valid responses. For such topics, anonymous written questionnaires used in an interview or randomized response techniques may be the most useful approaches. As noted, which of these techniques is preferable depends in part on whether the problem is the overstatement of socially desirable behaviors or the understatement of undesirable ones. Projective and other indirect questioning techniques and the use of attitude scales made up of subtle items (Chapter 9), though often plagued by unreliability and invalidity, may also be useful in some specific circumstances.

Interviewing

Any questionnaire study has the dual goals of motivating the respondent to give full and precise replies, which may take effort (e.g., searching memory for specific details or dates), and avoiding biases stemming from social desirability, conformity, or other sources. In general it is the interviewer who must attempt to fulfill these goals in interaction with each individual respondent (though written questionnaires, when used alone, must take over these motivating and bias-avoiding functions; Dillman, 1978). The ability of the interviewer to gather valid data depends first on proper study design and questionnaire construction. But given a well-designed questionnaire, proper training and proper interviewer behavior can help greatly in attaining the goals.

Interviewing is part art, part science. Some of the recommendations given are based on little more than research folklore and common sense, whereas others have been developed and tested in repeated empirical studies (e.g., Bradburn & Sudman, 1979; Cannell, Miller, & Oksenberg, 1981; Dillman, 1978). Detailed discussions and further recommendations can be found in Hyman (1975), Cannell and Kahn (1968), and (for telephone interviews) Dillman (1978) and Groves and Kahn (1979).

As an overall framework for thinking about interviewing, it is useful to examine the processes needed to generate good (i.e., complete and valid) data in the interview. These processes include the respondent's comprehension of the questions and response alternatives and the accessibility in memory of the information that is requested as well as the respondent's motivation to make the necessary effort. Comprehension and accessibility largely depend on the design of the questionnaire, and the interviewer's task centers on motivation. This term is meant to include both creating and maintaining motivation to answer fully and correctly and avoiding creating motives to give socially desirable, conforming, or other biased responses. The specific tasks of the interviewer which contribute to these overall goals involve *creating a positive atmosphere, asking the questions properly, obtaining an adequate response, recording the response,* and *avoiding biases.* In some research designs the interviewer also has responsibility of some aspects of *sampling.*

Sampling

Sampling—selection of the designated respondent—may be a part of the interviewer's job, as discussed in Chapter 7. No matter how precise and valid the original sampling plan, it may be undermined if the interviewers do not carry it out properly. Biasing errors have been observed even in the "objective" process of listing dwelling units for an area sample and randomly selecting households and individuals within those households. Both the sample design and interviewer training must be carefully planned to avoid such biases.

Creating a Friendly Atmosphere

The first few moments of contact between the interviewer and respondent are crucial. Motivational forces that encourage the respondent to participate in the study must be mobilized and negative forces counteracted (Cannell & Kahn, 1968). The positive forces available to the interviewer are the respondent's liking for the interviewer, any prestige or positive feelings attached to the research sponsor, the respondent's self-image as a dutiful citizen, and perhaps curiosity or loneliness. The negative forces include the press of competing activities and demands for time, worries about appearing ignorant or becoming embarrassed, dislike for the interview content, and perhaps fear of the consequences of participating.

To take advantage of the positive forces and suppress the negative ones, the interviewer's introduction should be brief and positive. The goal is for interviewers to introduce themselves, identify the sponsoring agency, and give the general topic of the study in an interesting way, for example (Cannell & Kahn, 1968):

> I'm from the Survey Research Center of the University of Michigan. We're doing a survey at this time, as we have for a number of years now, on how people feel things are going financially these days. The study is done throughout the country, and the results are used by government and industry. The addresses at which we interview were chosen entirely by chance, and the interview will take only about a half hour. All information is entirely confidential, of course.

For many respondents, this will suffice; many people are flattered and interested at the prospect of being singled out for an interview. Once the actual questions begin, a properly designed questionnaire will quickly remove respondents' lingering doubts, for example, about their ability to answer the questions. Other respondents will have questions to which the interviewer will need to respond or will need to receive a fuller account of the research and its value or the tasks and topics involved in the interview. A personal interviewer will be prepared to show credentials (a card or letter on official stationery identifying the interviewer by name) and a personal or telephone interviewer will have a phone number that the respondent can call to verify the sponsor's identity.

Recent research suggests that the task of responding to a questionnaire is sufficiently unfamiliar to many respondents that explicit *instructions*, stressing completeness and accuracy of response, are helpful. The beginning of the interview, therefore, could include a paragraph like this:

> In order for your answers to be most helpful to us, it is important that you try to be as accurate as you can. Since we need complete and accurate information from this research, we hope you will think hard to provide the information we need.

Cannell, Miller, & Oksenberg (1981) find that this procedure does yield fuller reports of past events.

Once the interview begins, the interviewer's manner should be friendly, courteous, conversational, and unbiased. The idea is to put respondents at ease so that they will talk freely and fully. The opportunity to talk to a good listener and to have one's ideas taken seriously and noted down is the chief positive outcome of the interview for most respondents, and a major part of the interviewer's task is to use this reward to maintain cooperation. For interviewers, maintaining a conversational tone depends on a thorough mastery of the questionnaire. They must be familiar enough with the questions to ask them conversationally rather than reading them stiffly, and they should know what questions are coming next so that awkward pauses do not occur.

The interviewer's job is fundamentally that of a reporter, not an evangelist, a curiosity seeker, or a debater. Interviewers should take all opinions in stride and never show surprise or disapproval of a respondent's answer. They should assume an interested manner toward the respondent's opinions and never divulge their own. If the interviewers should be asked for personal views, they should laugh off the request with the remark that the job at the moment is to get opinions, not to have them.

Interviewers must keep the direction of the interview in hand, discouraging irrelevant conversation and endeavoring to keep the respondent on the point. Fortunately, they will usually find that the rambling, talkative respondents are the very ones who least resent a firm insistence on attention to the actual business of the interview.

Asking the Questions

Unless the interview is unstructured or only partially structured, interviewers must be impressed with the importance of *asking each question exactly as it is worded*. Each question has been carefully pretested to express the precise meaning desired in as simple a manner as possible. Interviewers must understand that even a slight rewording of the question can so change the stimulus as to provoke answers in a different frame of reference or bias the response.

Any impromptu *explanation* of questions is similarly taboo. Such an explanation again may change the frame of reference or bias the response, and it is easy to see that if each interviewer were permitted to vary the questions, the survey director would have no assurance at all that responses were in comparable terms. If any respondent gives evidence of failing to understand a particular question, the interviewer can only repeat it slowly and with proper emphasis, offering only such explanation as may be specifically authorized in his or her instructions and, if understanding is still lacking, noting this fact on the schedule.

For similar reasons, the questions must be asked in the same *order* as they appear on the questionnaire. Each question sets up a frame of reference for succeeding questions, and it is assumed that each respondent will be exposed to the same stimulus.

The interviewer, finally, must ask *every* question, unless the directions on the questionnaire specifically direct skipping certain ones. It may sometimes seem that respondents have already, in answering a prior question, given their opinion on a subsequent one, but the interviewer must nevertheless ask the later question in order to be sure, perhaps prefacing the inquiry with some such phrase as "Now you may already have touched on this, but. . . . " Similarly, even if the question seems foolish or inapplicable, the interviewer must never omit asking it or take the answer for granted. Again, the inquiry may be prefaced with some such remark as "Now I have to ask. . . . "

Obtaining the Response

It might be thought a simple matter to ask respondents the required questions and to record their replies, but interviewers will soon find that obtaining a *specific, complete* response is perhaps the most difficult part of their job. People often qualify or hedge their opinions; they answer, "Don't know" in order to avoid thinking about the question; they misinterpret the meaning of the question; they launch off on another discussion; they contradict themselves—and in all these cases, the interviewer usually has to *probe.*

Alertness to incomplete or nonspecific answers is perhaps the critical test of a good interviewer, and as no one can foresee all the possible replies that may call for probes, each interviewer must understand fully the overall objective of each question, the precise thing it is trying to measure. Both the written instructions and the oral training should emphasize the purpose of the question and should give examples of inadequate replies that were commonly encountered during the pretest. When asking open-ended questions, interviewers should form the habit of asking themselves, after each reply, "Does that completely answer the question I just asked?"

When the first reply is inadequate, a simple repetition of the question, with proper emphasis, will usually suffice to get a satisfactory response. This is particularly effective when the respondent has seemingly misunderstood the question or has answered it irrelevantly or has responded to only a portion of it. If the respondent's answer is vague or too general or incomplete, an effective probe is this: "That's interesting. Could you explain that a little more?" or "Let's see, you said. . . . Just how do you mean that?"

Throughout, the interviewer must be extremely careful not to *suggest* a possible reply. People sometimes find the questions difficult, and sometimes they are not deeply interested in them. In either case, they will welcome any least hint from the interviewer that will enable them to give a creditable response. Interviewers must be thoroughly impressed with the harm that results from a "leading probe," from any remark that "puts words in their mouth." To be safe, the interviewer should use repetition of all or part of the actual question or such innocuous nondirective probes as are suggested in the preceding paragraph.

The "Don't know" reply is another problem for the interviewer. Sometimes that response represents a genuine lack of opinion; but at other times it may hide a host of other attitudes: fear to speak one's mind, reluctance to focus on the issue, vague opinions never yet expressed, a stalling for time while thoughts are marshaled, a lack of comprehension of the question, and so on. It is the interviewer's job to distinguish among all these types, and when appropriate, to repeat the question with suitable assurances. In one case, for example, one might say, "Perhaps I didn't make that too clear. Let me read it again"; in another, one might say, "Well, lots of people have never thought about that before, but I'd like to have your ideas on it, just the way it seems to you." Or again, the interviewer might point out, "Well, I just want your own opinion on it. Actually, nobody really knows the answers to many of these questions."

Qualified answers to questions that have been precoded in terms of "yes-no," "approve-disapprove," or similar dichotomies are an interviewing problem that is actually in the domain of the study director. As far as possible, the most frequent qualifications of opinion should be anticipated in the actual wording of the question. If very many people find it impossible to answer because of unspecified contingencies, the question is a poor one. Most qualifications can be foreseen as a result of the pretest, and those that are not taken care of by revisions of the wording should be mentioned in the instructions to interviewers, with directions on how to handle such answers. In some cases, special codes may be provided for the most frequent qualifications; in other cases, the interviewer may be instructed to record them as "Don't know" or "Undecided." In avoiding many qualifications inherent in the response to almost any opinion question, the interviewer may find it helpful to use phrases such as, "Well, in general, what would you say?" or "Taking everything into consideration" or "On the basis of the way things look to you now."

Sometimes the interviewer may react to respondents' answers by providing evaluative *feedback*. The interviewer can convey that the respondent's behavior is adequate by such phrases as "Uh-huh, this is the kind of information we want" or "Thanks, we appreciate your frankness." Or the interviewer can convey that the answer is inadequate by "You answered that quickly" or "You only mentioned two things." Such feedback helps respondents understand what is wanted in the interview and motivates them to perform well. Cannell et al. (1981) found that careful training is important so that the interviewer supplies feedback appropriately. Interviewers who are not specifically trained have been found to give the most positive feedback (e.g., "That's OK") after respondents *refuse to answer* a question, the worst possible respondent behavior. Interviewers do this to maintain a positive atmosphere despite the refusal, but the comments may reinforce inadequate answers.

Recording the Response

There are two chief means of recording responses in the interview. Closed-ended questions require only that the interviewer check a box or circle a response code. Errors and omissions are possible even in this relatively simple task, but they can be reduced by clear questionnaire design, including appropriate use of typography and page layout (see Dillman, 1978).

The better the interviewer, the fewer the mistakes made, but even the best interviewers will occasionally be guilty. The unforgivable sin is to turn in the interview as complete when it contains errors and omissions. The only certain way for the interviewer to avoid this is to form a habit of *inspecting each interview* immediately after its completion, before going on to another respondent, to make sure it has been filled in accurately and completely. If any information is lacking, interviewers can go back and ask the respondent for it; if the questionnaire contains any errors or omissions, they can correct them on the spot; if the interviewer's handwriting is illegible in places or if they have recorded verbatim replies only sketchily, they can correct the weakness right there. If they wait until later in the day or until they return home at night, they will have forgotten many of the circumstances of the interview, or perhaps the prospect of editing the whole day's work will seem so forbidding that they will skip the matter completely.

In reporting responses to free-answer questions, interviewers should be aware of the importance of *complete, verbatim* reporting. It will often be difficult to get down everything the respondent says in reply, but aside from obvious irrelevancies and repetitions, this should be the goal. Interviewers should be given some idea of the coding process so that they can see the dangers of summarizing, abbreviating, or paraphrasing responses.

Unless coders can view the *whole* answer, just as the respondent said it, they are likely to classify it improperly or lose some important distinctions.

Interviewers should be instructed to quote the respondent directly, just as if they were news reporters taking down the statement of an important official. Paraphrasing the reply, summarizing it in their own words, or "polishing up" any slang, cursing, or bad grammar not only risks distorting the respondent's meaning and emphasis but also loses the color of his or her reply. Frequently, the verbatim responses of individuals are useful in the final report as illustrations of the nuances of attitudes, and they should not be abbreviated or distorted.

Even with closed-ended questions, if the respondent says anything to explain or qualify the coded response, the interviewer should note it verbatim. Such remarks by respondents often help the researcher evaluate the meaning of results and warn of any commonly held qualifications or differences in intensity of opinion.

Avoiding Bias

From the earliest days of survey research it has been known that interviewers can influence the data that are gathered. Rice, in a study reported in 1929, had two interviewers collect data from people living in poverty. In one interviewer's data, overindulgence in alcohol emerged as the most-common cause of poverty, whereas the other interviewer's results showed social and economic conditions to be the most frequent cause. It turned out that the first interviewer was a prohibitionist and the second a socialist.

More recently, research on the interview has revealed several ways interviewers can influence responses. Besides the interviewers' own *attitudes* (as illustrated in the Rice example), they may have *expectations* about what a particular category of respondents may say or think, which may bias the data. Rosenthal's work (1966) on experimenter effects in the laboratory, referred to in Chapter 4, is relevant to this issue. The respondents' perceptions of the interviewer's *characteristics* (age, sex, race, apparent social status, and so on) may also bias their answers; it is known, for example, that blacks reveal less-hostile attitudes toward whites when interviewed by white interviewers than by black. Such effects can occur no matter how conscientiously the interviewer attempts to be "unbiased." However, it is likely that they are smaller in magnitude with telephone than with personal interviewing; fewer cues about the interviewer are available over the telephone. Indeed, several studies have found only small interviewer effects with telephone interviews (Singer, Frankel, & Glassman, 1983; Tucker, 1983).

Not all interviewer effects operate through the respondent's perception of the interviewer, however. Indeed, some respondents appear to be totally immune to even the most flagrant biasing characteristics of the interviewer. Fully as important a source of bias are the interviewer's perceptions of the respondent. No matter how standardized the questionnaire may be and no matter how rigidly interviewers may be instructed, they still have much opportunity to exercise freedom of choice during the actual interview, and it is often their perception of the respondent that determines the manner in which they ask the question, probe, classify equivocal responses to precoded questions, and record verbatim answers.

Interviewers do not approach each new respondent in an identical fashion: Indeed, they often have strong expectations and stereotypes, which are more and more likely to come into play as they continue interviewing. On the basis of their past judgments or of prior answers received from other respondents, they may, for example, quite unconsciously come to associate lack of education with ethnic or religious prejudice; or they may come to anticipate a large number of "no opinion" responses from the housewives they interview. Such expectations will almost inevitably affect their performance. Thus, given the same "no opinion" response from a wealthy businessman and from a housewife, they may probe the former's reply, in the belief that an opinion must be lurking there somewhere, whereas they will routinely accept the latter's reply without probing and go on to the next question.

A final source of bias arises from interviewers' perception of the *situation*. If they see the results of the survey as a possible threat to personal interests or beliefs, for example, they are likely to introduce bias. Or if they regard the assignment as impossible, they are almost bound to introduce bias. Such difficulties can best be overcome by proper motivation and supervision.

Because interviewers are human beings such biasing factors can never be overcome completely, but their effects can be reduced by standardizing the interview procedures. Thus, the use of standard wording in survey questions aims to prevent the bias that would result if each interviewer worded the question in his or her own fashion. Similarly, if interviewers are given standard instructions on probing procedure, on the classification of doubtful answers, and so on, their biases will have less chance to operate.

Of course, as interviewers' freedom is restricted, the opportunity for effective use of their insight is correspondingly reduced. Cannel and Kahn (1968, p. 577) observe that "the universal tendency of interviewers to introduce flexibility into rigid procedures probably has the effect of saving some distant question writers from the fate they prescribe for themselves." Nevertheless, the reduction in bias from standardized interviewing technique is probably the most important consideration here, and increased attention should be paid to the construction of a clear and precise questionnaire so that interviewers do not have to make on-the-spot adjustments to get responses to inadequate or confusing questions. Recent research (Cannell et al., 1981) also underlines the importance of standardizing interviewer behavior in order to reduce bias. The findings also suggest that the procedures mentioned earlier (giving respondents instructions at the beginning of the interview and making feedback contingent on the quality of their performance) reduce social desirability biases in responding and produce fuller and more-accurate answers. There is clearly room for more research on ways to minimize bias in the interview.

Many critics tend to exaggerate the significance of interview bias—overlooking the fact that social scientists are universally dependent on data that have been collected by means of oral or written reports and that these reports, no matter how collected, are invariably subject to essentially the same sources of error and bias as are those collected by survey interviewers. The clinician and, frequently, the experimenter depend on oral reports of feelings, perceptions, behavior, and so on; and they, as well as the sophisticated "participant observer" in another type of investigation, are just as likely to bias their subjects' responses as are the interviewers participating in an attitude survey. The major difference is that when social scientists have to depend on other people as interviewers, they are themselves one step removed from the data. This can make them more aware of potential interviewer bias.

Less-Structured Interviews

So far we have been discussing standardized interview or questionnaire research, where the questions are predetermined. The possible answers are also largely predetermined, with the general use of more closed-ended than open-ended questions. All questions are presented in the same order and with the same wording to all respondents, in order to ensure comparability of responses. Although most surveys today follow this pattern, there are exceptions in which the interviewers—generally the investigators themselves rather than someone hired for the job—use only an outline of topics (if anything) and the questions and answers are completely free. Such interviews take various forms and go under various names—the "focused" interview, "clinical" interview, "nondirective" interview, and so on. Like participant observation methods, these interviewing techniques are used in an effort to obtain a more-intensive study of perceptions, attitudes, and motivations than a standardized questionnaire permits. This type of interview is useful in scouting a new area of research, to find out what the basic issues are, how people conceptualize the topic, what terminology people use, and what their level of understanding is.

The flexibility of the unstructured interview, if properly used, helps us to bring out the affective and value-laden aspects of respondents' responses to determine the personal significance of their attitudes. Not only does it permit the subject's definition of the interviewing situation to receive full and detailed expression, it should also elicit the personal and social context of beliefs and feelings. This type of interview achieves its purpose to the extent that the subject's responses are spontaneous rather than forced, are highly specific and concrete rather than diffuse and general, and are self-revealing and personal rather than superficial.

The freedom that the interviewer is permitted is, at once, both the major advantage and the major disadvantage of interviews of this type. As a *measurement device* such a procedure is inadequate, for its flexibility results in lack of comparability of one interview with another. Moreover, analysis is more difficult and time-consuming than that of standardized interviews. There can be little doubt, however, of the usefulness, in the hands of a skilled investigator, of such interviews as a source of hypotheses, as is done in participant observation (see Chapter 8). Partially structured interviews are also used, on occasion, in studies that test hypotheses. However, the lack of comparability from interview to interview and the complexity of analysis usually make them less efficient for this purpose than standardized interviews.

Let us briefly discuss several of the major types of partially structured and unstructured interviews.

Focused interview   In the focused interview (as described by Merton, Fiske, & Kendall, 1956) the main function of the interviewer is to focus attention on a given experience and its effects. Interviewers know in advance what topics or what aspects of a question they wish to cover. This list of topics or aspects is derived from a formulation of the research problem, from an analysis of the situation or experience in which the respondent has participated, and from hypotheses based on psychological or sociological theory. This list constitutes a framework of topics to be covered, but the manner in which questions are asked and their timing are left largely to the interviewer's discretion. Interviewers have freedom to explore reasons and motives and to probe further in directions that were unanticipated. Although respondents are free to express completely their own line of thought, the direction of the interview is clearly in the hands of the interviewer. Lane (1962) is a classic example on the topic of political ideology.

Merton, Fiske, and Kendall (1956) have described this type of interview.

> First of all, the persons interviewed are known to have been involved in a *particular situation:* they have seen a film, heard a radio program, read a pamphlet, article or book, taken part in a psychological experiment or in an uncontrolled, but observed, social situation (for example, a political rally, a ritual or a riot). Secondly, the hypothetically significant elements, patterns, processes and total structure of this situation have been provisionally analyzed by the social scientist. Through this *content or situational analysis,* he has arrived at a set of hypotheses concerning the consequences of determinate aspects of the situation

for those involved in it. On the basis of this analysis, he takes the third step of developing an *interview guide*, setting forth the major areas of inquiry and the hypotheses which provide criteria of relevance for the data to be obtained in the interview. Fourth and finally, the interview is focused on the subjective experiences of persons exposed to the pre-analyzed situation in an effort to ascertain *their definitions of the situation*. The array of reported responses to the situation helps test hypotheses and, to the extent that it includes unanticipated responses, gives rise to fresh hypotheses for more systematic and rigorous investigation.

The focused interview has been used effectively in the development of hypotheses about which aspects of a specific experience (a television program, a moving picture, a lecture, and so on) lead to changes in attitude on the part of those exposed to it. The interviewer, being equipped in advance with a content analysis of the stimulus experience, can usually distinguish the objective facts of the case from the subjective definitions of the situation. Thus, the interviewer is alerted to the possibility of **selective perception** and is prepared to explore its implications. Suppose, for example, that one is concerned with reactions to a series of newspaper pictures portraying housing conditions in a slum neighborhood, intended for use in connection with a campaign for more stringent housing laws or for urban development. The pictures show broken stairs, wallpaper peeling off, holes in walls through which rats are reported to enter—in general, conditions that may reasonably be attributed to inadequate maintenance on the part of the landlord rather than slovenliness on the part of the tenants. A respondent, in discussing the pictures, may say, "They show how these low-class people do not take care of their places; there is no use trying to give them decent housing; they just knock it to pieces anyway." The interviewer, knowing that the content of the pictures is not intended to give this impression, can follow up the respondent's interpretation, trying to discover whether there are unconsidered aspects of the pictures that form a basis for this impression or whether it stems from the subject's stereotyped views.

The definition of a focused interview may be broadened to include any interview in which interviewers know in advance what specific aspects of an experience they wish to have the respondent cover in their discussion, whether or not the investigator has observed and analyzed the specific situation in which the respondent participated. For example, in a study of the functioning of a program of part-time work for high school students, we might prepare a set of questions to be covered even though we are not familiar with the specific job of each of the students. We might include questions such as the following: "Does the student feel that he or she was given an adequate picture of the job before starting it? Does he or she feel that the job is at a level appropriate to his or her skills?"

Market researchers have used an approach similar to focused interviews to elicit the "images" that people have of a particular product. In one example (Haire, 1950), the researchers were concerned with attitudes toward Nescafé, one of the first brands of instant coffee to be introduced. Respondents who did not use Nescafé were asked directly, "What do you dislike about it?" but the researchers believed that the responses (citing its flavor and so forth) did not truly reflect the reasons for not buying instant coffee. Using a more unstructured approach, they showed respondents a short "shopping list" which included, for different respondents, either "Nescafé instant coffee" or "Maxwell House Coffee (drip ground)" (as well as a half dozen other items). Respondents were asked to write a brief description of the personality of the woman who had made out the shopping list. The results showed that the author of the list with Nescafé was often described as lazy, a spendthrift, and a poor wife, whereas such characterizations were almost completely absent when the respondents read the list with the drip ground coffee. The researchers concluded that buying instant coffee was as much influenced by attitudes about what constitutes good housekeeping (keep in mind the date of this study) as by concerns about flavor and so forth. In a check on the validity of this projective measure, they looked in the respondents' kitchens and found that those who described the Nescafé buyer unfavorably were less likely than others to have instant coffee in the house. It might be possible for more-structured questions to assess such "product images" equally effectively, but this type of unstructured interviewing technique does seem to possess predictive validity.

Clinical interview Somewhat similar to the focused interview is the clinical interview, the primary difference being that the latter is concerned with broad underlying feelings or motivations or with the course of the individual's life experiences rather than with the effects of a specific experience. In this type of interview, too, interviewers know what aspects of feeling or experience they want the respondent to talk about, but again the method of eliciting the information is left to their discretion. The "personal history" interview, used in social casework, prison administration, psychiatric clinics, and in individual life histories in social research, is perhaps the most common type of clinical interview. The specific aspects of the individual's life history that the interview is to cover are determined, as in all data-collection instruments, by the purpose for which the information is gathered.

For example, Lee (1957) was interested in the possibility that adolescents who become heroin addicts may be predisposed to addiction by family experiences that lead to certain personal characteristics. On the basis of earlier work with juvenile addicts, Lee and colleagues conducting related studies hypothesized that among boys living in the same neighborhood, and thus exposed to roughly the same opportunities for using heroin, addicts are likely to differ from nonaddicts in the following ways: They have relatively weak ego functioning, defective superego functioning, inadequate masculine identification, lack of realistic middle-class orientation, and distrust of major social institutions. Next, the investigators asked themselves what types of family environment might be expected to stimulate or enhance such characteristics. On the basis of theoretical considerations, largely drawn from psychoanalytic thinking, they constructed a list of circumstances or events of family life that might be expected to contribute to each of the five characteristics. For example, it was considered that factors such as the following might be conducive to weak ego functioning: inappropriate handling of childhood illnesses, discordant relationship between parents, the mother figure either passionate or hostile toward the boy, either parent's having unrealistically high or low aspirations for the boy, and so on.

It seemed clear that relatively unstructured interviews would be a more appropriate method of getting the needed information than would a standardized series of questions. Accordingly, the interviewers visited the parents of the boys included in the study—a sample of addicts and a control group of nonaddicts—and encouraged them to talk freely about their sons. The interviewers had no set questions to ask. They were instructed to cover the following major topics: the physical characteristics of the neighborhood and the house, the composition of the family and the household, the health history of the family, the present and early adolescent life situation of the subject, childhood training and socialization, relationships within the family, and relationships between the family and the "outside world." The interview guide indicated a number of subtopics to be covered under each of these major ones; for example, under "childhood training and socialization," the interviewer was to get information about early development, discipline and patterns of handling by parents, early socialization experiences, and early school experiences. Under each of these subtopics, the interview guide listed more specific points to be covered.

Nondirective interview   In the nondirective interview, the initiative is even more completely in the hands of the respondent. The term *nondirective* originated from a type of psychotherapy in which patients are encouraged to express their feelings without directive suggestions or questions from the therapist. In a more-limited sense, nondirection is implicit in most interviewing; that is, although interviewers are expected to ask questions about a given topic, they are instructed not to bias or direct the respondent to one rather than another response. In nondirective interviewing, however, the interviewer's function is simply to encourage the respondent to talk about a given topic with a minimum of direct questioning or guidance. The interviewer encourages the respondent to talk fully and freely by being alert to the feelings expressed in the statements of the respondent and by showing warm, but noncommital, recognition of the subject's feelings. Perhaps the most typical remarks made by the interviewer in a nondirective interview are these: "You feel that . . . " or "Tell me more" or "Why?" or "Isn't that interesting?" or simply "Uh-huh."

The nondirective interviewer's function is primarily to serve as a catalyst for a comprehensive expression of the subject's feelings and beliefs and of the frame of reference within which the subject's feelings and beliefs take on personal significance. To achieve this result, the interviewer must create a completely permissive atmosphere in which subjects are free to express themselves without fear or disapproval, admonition, or dispute, and without advice from the interviewer.

Summary

In investigating individuals' self-reports of facts, beliefs, attitudes, or behaviors, careful attention must be paid to questionnaire construction and the interviewing process. There is much accumulated experience available to a researcher today, in the form of guidelines and recommendations based on research, for decisions on question content, wording, and sequence. Often there is a need for multiple-item scales, or multiple questions, both closed-ended and open-ended, on key variables in the study. No one item is likely to be reliable enough or multifaceted enough to stand alone, especially if one is dealing with beliefs and attitudes rather than facts. Interviewing procedures must also be carefully designed and standardized to avoid error and bias, with careful training of interviewers. The structured, standardized questionnaire has been emphasized in this chapter because of its suitability for a wide range of topics and its consequent popularity in practical use. However, for some purposes, such as providing a basic description of a new topic or generating hypotheses, less-structured interviewing techniques are appropriate.

Whatever data-collection techniques are used, individual questions, no matter how carefully constructed, cannot exactly match or completely cover the conceptual definition of a construct. The variables that are actually measured in any study are only approximations to abstractions or constructs like "attitudes toward democracy"; they are the answers to the specific questions that have been formulated to measure the abstractions, nothing more.

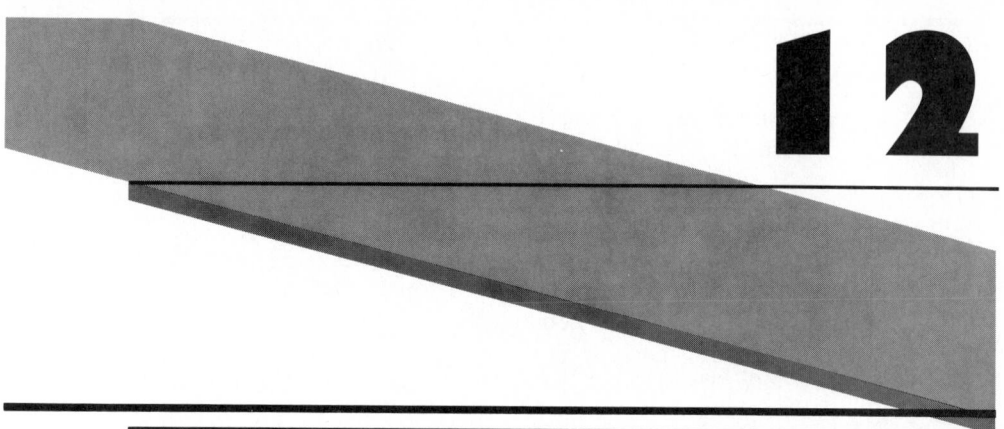

12

Observational and Archival Data

Despite the wide usefulness of questionnaire and interview techniques in social research and their popularity in practice, many research questions are not well suited to study by these methods. For example, one might want to draw conclusions about Thomas Jefferson's political ideology, about the links between social integration and suicide, or about the prevalence of gazing into each others' eyes during conversations between lovers. Observational techniques and the use of archival data often provide the only avenues of approach to such issues. For example, one may observe couples to record the frequency and duration of eye-gazing during conversations, examine government-kept statistical records to determine suicide rates in social groups with differing levels of social integration, or examine Jefferson's writings to note the relative frequency of references to different ideological themes.

In addition, observational and archival methods often carry advantages of their own. The data are often "there for the taking," easily accessible to the researcher without great physical or financial costs. Archives often provide aggregated measurements of significant constructs drawn from millions of individuals, hundreds of organizations, or dozens of different societies—data that would be difficult to obtain in any other way. And archives provide our only access to the thinking of people who are dead or otherwise unavailable for direct questioning.

Finally, and perhaps most important, some forms of observation and most archival research avoid potential problems caused by the respondents' awareness of being studied: They can be unobtrusive measures. Laboratory research and questionnaire studies inevitably run the risk that respondents may behave in unnatural ways, give socially desirable or otherwise biased responses rather than valid ones, attempt to guess the research hypothesis, or otherwise respond to the very *fact of being studied* rather than acting as they normally would. Concern about these possibilities has led to an emphasis on naturalness in research, which involves several issues that will be discussed in the first section of this chapter. The remainder of the chapter is organized into two major sections, the first concerned with observational methods and the second with the use of archival data and other records.

Naturalness in Research

Observational and archival research, in different ways, emphasize unobtrusiveness or nonreactiveness (Webb et al., 1981) of research procedures. With these methods, subjects either are unaware of being observed (with unobtrusive observation or the use of archival data) or are thought to habituate quickly to the presence of open observers. The researcher therefore hopes that subjects' responses will not be shaped by such considerations as a desire to impress the researcher or a belief that certain behaviors will help support the research hypothesis. The general assumption is that subjects are more likely to behave in the same way that they would in "real life" (i.e., outside the research context) if they can be studied in the circumstances in which they are ordinarily found. In contrast, experimental and questionnaire-based research may be more likely to elicit behaviors that are specific to the unnatural research context, such as socially desirable responses (e.g., questionnaire answers that conceal the respondent's racially prejudiced attitudes).

This emphasis on the advantages of nonreactive forms of research for the external validity (Chapter 2) or generalizability of results leads to a strategy of seeking *naturalness* in research. Of course, the very presence of an observer prevents the attainment of complete naturalness, but three dimensions of naturalness have been generally emphasized (Tunnell, 1977). Different researchers have stressed different dimensions, and the three do not always go together. The purest conception of natural research might involve all three dimensions (Kraut & Johnston, 1979): for example, unobtrusive observation of a *natural behavior* (e.g., smiling) as it happened in its *natural setting* (e.g., a bowling alley) as the result of a *natural event* (e.g., getting a strike).

Natural behaviors are those that are "not established or maintained for the sole or primary purpose of conducting research" (Tunnell, 1977, p. 426). They reflect a concern with naturalness in the *dependent variable* in research. For example, committing suicide, gazing into one's lover's eyes, or smiling upon bowling a strike are natural behaviors because they would have occurred without the researcher's presence. Conversely, questionnaire or interview responses occur only as a result of the researcher's questions and would not be considered natural behaviors. Neither would specific behaviors that subjects are aware are being observed, for subjects might shape the responses in ways that depend on the presence of the observer. Ethologists (Blurton Jones, 1972; Rajecki, 1977) have mainly been interested in natural behavior. An example of a study of a natural behavior but neither a natural setting nor a natural treatment is one by Byrne, Ervin, and Lamberth (1970). Subjects, paired on the basis of high or low similarity of responses to an attitude questionnaire, spent 30 minutes together on a "Coke date." When they returned from the date to the laboratory, interpersonal attraction was assessed by observing a natural behavior, the physical distance between the two persons as they stood together in front of the experimenter's desk. Closer distances were taken to indicate greater attraction, caused in turn by greater initial similarity of the individuals' attitudes.

Natural settings are contexts that are not established for research purposes (Tunnell, 1977), such as shopping centers, private homes, race-tracks, commercial aircraft, churches, or hospitals. For example, observation in the Kraut and Johnston (1979) study mentioned earlier took place in a bowling alley, a natural setting. Ecological psychologists and advocates of participant observation (Bogden & Taylor, 1975; Garfinkel, 1967) have been primarily concerned with natural settings. Barker (1968), an ecological psychologist, has attempted to identify and describe all the publicly available natural behavior settings in a number of small towns.

Finally, a *natural treatment* is an event or incident that is not arranged for research purposes and that has some human consequences: a natural *independent variable* in research. Examples whose effects have been studied include natural disasters, economic fluctuations, heat waves, and surgery. Analysts of archival data (e.g., Holsti, 1969) have often been interested in the effects of natural treatments or events. In an archival study of the impact of a natural event, Carlsmith and Anderson (1979) examined the "long, hot summer" hypothesis to see if there was a relationship between temperature (a natural treatment) and the incidence of urban riots. Comparing newspaper reports of weather conditions and of urban rioting, they found that the probability of a riot increased with increases in air temperature.

Benefits and Costs of Naturalness

Natural behaviors, settings, and treatments are three distinct facets of naturalistic research, though they may go together in various combinations in practice. Naturalness in any of these forms may bring advantages. In particular, studying natural behaviors in natural settings may lead to greater generalizability (external validity) of research results because subjects will not shape their behavior to take account of being studied. Naturalness can also contribute to construct validity because unobtrusively observed behaviors (such as racially integrated seating patterns in a lunchroom) are likely to reflect the desired construct (unprejudiced attitudes) to a greater extent than questionnaire or other responses obtained for obvious research purposes, which might be more subject to response biases.

Nevertheless, naturalness is not the sole criterion—or even the most important one—by which to evaluate research. Every study, not just those using observational or archival methods, must meet the fundamental criteria of reliability and validity of measurement, and naturalness in research may have costs in these and other respects. Conducting research in a natural setting often limits the researcher's ability to control extraneous factors that introduce error into observations and hence reduce reliability. Some research topics, such as the examination of eye-gazing, may require the use of an unnatural laboratory setting, where precise measurement (e.g., carefully placed video cameras, observers behind one-way glass, freedom from outside interruptions) can be arranged.

The relative importance of the advantages and disadvantages of naturalness in research depends on the type of research question. Questions that concern rates or patterns of natural behaviors in natural settings obviously require naturalistic research to answer them. For example, one may wonder about sex differences in the practice of "civil inattention" (aversion of one's gaze from the other person's face) when strangers pass each other on the sidewalk. Results from laboratory research on this behavior might not generalize to real street settings. However, one must remember that nonlaboratory settings differ among themselves also. Results obtained on Broadway in New York City—however natural that setting—may not generalize to other locales (e.g., side streets of small towns), any more than results obtained in a laboratory might. Ultimately, whether results obtained in one setting (natural or unnatural) will generalize to another setting is an empirical question, not one that naturalness in research can answer automatically.

Research questions concerned with causal relationships among constructs or with hypothetical ("if-then" or "what-if") questions often require specifically *un*natural research settings and treatments (Berkowitz & Donnerstein, 1982). To estimate the causal effects of watching violent television shows on aggressive behavior among adolescents requires the subjects to be given unnatural treatments (some caused to watch, others prevented from watching, violent television). Attempts to answer this research question with nonexperimental methods (e.g., simply correlating people's reports of their television viewing with their aggressiveness) have low internal validity. One cannot be confident of the *causal* nature of the relationship unless random assignment to an experimental manipulation—unnatural by definition—is used (Chapter 4). In short, advantages of natural research in external validiity are often counterbalanced by costs in internal validity.

As an example of a hypothetical or "what-if" question, to determine whether extensive experience cooperating with a black person on some task would reduce antiblack attitudes among initially prejudiced whites, one would probably need to create an unnatural setting. Waiting for a prejudiced person to show such cooperative behavior naturally might take a long time. Although answering questions about the natural prevalence or patterning of behavior calls for natural settings, answering causal or hypothetical questions usually calls for the creation of an unnatural setting or treatment (manipulation).

The importance of naturalness also depends on the target population of individuals, settings, or behaviors to which one wishes to generalize. The goal of drawing conclusions about a *particular* situation—for example, determining whether goal setting will improve the productivity of workers at the Acme Widget Co. factory—is best attained by studying those particular workers performing their natural tasks in their natural setting. However, many research questions do not so narrowly specify the target population or setting. For example, researchers who study helping behavior often have in mind a very broad intended target of generalizations (i.e., any humans in any settings). For such research, naturalness is often simply irrelevant, and since it often interferes with experimental control and other important goals, it is often absent. The chief requirement in such research is *experimental realism* (defined by Carlsmith, Ellsworth, & Aronson, 1976, as the meaningfulness and impact of the situation for the subject) rather than *mundane realism* (the resemblance of the situation to some aspect of everyday life). Thus, helping has often been studied in an artificial laboratory setting with unnatural behaviors, by the staging of accidents or emergencies that occur while the subject is working on some task (e.g., Clark & Word, 1972; Latané & Darley, 1968). The researchers observe the subject's behavior of leaving his or her task and seeking to provide help to the victim of the bogus accident. The subjects in such research *believe* that they are seeking needed help for another person, so the treatment is high on experimental realism despite its thorough unnaturalness. The researchers assume that the *subject's interpretation* of his or her behavior, setting, and surroundings, rather than their naturalness per se, influences generalizability. That is, it is argued that the theories supported by this research should apply in other situations in which people think that help is required despite differences in the setting, type of accident that necessitates help, and so on.

In summary, naturalness has an important place in the design of research to answer certain types of questions. For other questions it is irrelevant. Just as it might be a mistake to create an unnatural setting for research if one's goal were to assess a target behavior as it naturally occurs in everyday life, it would be a mistake to view naturalness as an overriding criterion for the validity of all research. Dipboye and Flanagan (1979) reviewed hundreds of laboratory studies and field studies (i.e., studies using natural settings and usually natural behaviors) in industrial-organizational psychology and concluded that the ability to generalize from research is not related to its degree of naturalness. "Too often the assumption is made that because a study was conducted in a field setting, it is inherently more externally valid than a laboratory study" (Dipboye & Flanagan, 1980, p. 388). The generalizability of any research finding is ultimately an empirical question, to be settled only by replication of the research with different subjects, behaviors, and settings. No specific feature of a study (e.g., neither a laboratory setting nor a natural setting) can *guarantee* generalizability.

Though we have focused on external and construct validity, which are usually the chief concerns of advocates of natural research (either observational or archival), other important goals may also be served by natural research. It may generate new hypotheses (which might then be tested in more internally valid ways, perhaps by laboratory experimentation). It may reveal previously unsuspected empirical relationships, and it may identify limitations of theories. All these purposes are important for the advancement of knowledge about social relations.

Observation

Some of the observations made by social scientists appear to be mundane at first glance. For example, it has been noted that some restaurant diners salt their food before tasting it and others salt only after they have had a first bite (McGee & Snyder, 1975); that some house owners construct fences around their property whereas others leave their grounds unmarked (Edney, 1972); and that some billiard players show their tongues while making difficult shots whereas others keep them out of sight (Smith, Chase, & Lieblich, 1974). These observations become scientific when the data are gathered systematically and are related to other data also systematically gathered for the purpose of uncovering a general principle of human behavior. As to salting food, McGee and Snyder predicted that the more individuals ascribe stable traits to themselves, as opposed to seeing their behavior as varying with context, the more likely they are to salt their food before tasting it. Results confirmed their prediction. People who see their behavior changing with the situation are more likely to taste the food before seasoning it. In a comparable fashion, Edney found that people who lived in "defended" houses, with fences and "No Trespassing" signs, had lived there longer than those in undefended houses and expected to continue to live there longer. And finally, Smith, Chase, and Lieblich observed that tongue showing occurs when one is engaged in some demanding activity and signals an unwillingness to interact. Good billiard players showed their tongues more often on hard than on easy shots and showed the tongue less than did unskilled players overall.

Observation thus becomes scientific when it (1) serves a formulated research purpose, (2) is planned deliberately, (3) is recorded systematically, and (4) is subjected to checks and controls on validity and reliability.

Observational techniques can be roughly classified on the basis of the types of operations involved in the research. *Unobtrusive measures involving physical traces* rely on "pieces of data not specifically produced for the purpose of comparison and inference but available to be exploited opportunistically by the alert observer" (Webb et al, 1981, p. 5). Examples include tallying fences around houses (previously cited); examining dirt smudges, fingerprints, and underlining on pages of an encyclopedia to determine which articles are most often referred to (Mosteller, 1955, cited in Webb et al., 1981, p. 9); or sampling graffiti in public restrooms to draw inferences about shifting concerns on sex, politics, and other graffiti topics

(Jorgenson & Lange, 1975). *Systematic observation* involves the use of relatively objective measures of behavior or other observable phenomena (such as checklists or detailed coding systems for movements), often in conjunction with a systematic procedure for sampling time intervals or other units for observation. The observer may be open or hidden but usually makes an effort to avoid interfering in any way with the ongoing behavior that is being observed. In contrast, participant observation, discussed in Chapter 8, involves unstructured recording techniques, such as open-ended verbal descriptions of behavior, and the observer's participation in the ongoing behavior is accepted. It is considered to be a method of hypothesis generation rather than of structured data collection.

Reliability, Validity, and Ethics of Observation

Observation, like any data-collection technique, must meet the requirements of reliability and validity of measurement and must be consistent with general standards of research ethics. The special considerations that obervational research requires under these headings will be briefly mentioned here.

Reliability Reliability entails consistency and freedom from random error of the scores obtained by a measurement technique, as noted in Chapter 3. The reliability of observational measures is usually assessed in two ways. One is the extent to which two or more independent observers agree in their ratings of the same events or objects, often measured by the percentage of scored units on which the observers agree. Of course, low reliability (disagreement among observers) precludes validity; if two or more observers do not even agree on what they see, we cannot assess the meaning of their observations.

Reliability is also assessed by looking at the repeatability of observations over time (Mitchell, 1979), usually by means of test-retest comparisons. If we assume that a particular behavior pattern is *stable* (e.g., that the proportion of time that lovers spend gazing into each other's eyes is similar today and tomorrow), disagreement among observations at different times points to unreliability in the observation process.

Validity Validity refers to the extent to which the recorded observations accurately reflect the construct they are intended to measure. Two observers may agree in their concrete observations, indicating good reliability, but the measurements might still be irrelevant to the intended construct. For instance, the construct of interpersonal attraction might be measured by how close together two people stand (in inches). Such a measure is valid if it accurately reflects the underlying construct (attraction) and does *not* systematically reflect other things, such as varying cultural norms for interpersonal distance. Validity is assessed by examining how well the observations agree with alternative measures of the same construct and how well they can be differentiated from measures of alternative, potentially confounding constructs, as outlined in Chapter 3.

In observational studies where the subjects are aware of observation, as in reactive experimental or questionnaire studies, the subjects' awareness of the research may threaten the validity of measurements. For example, when observers are visible, subjects are known to suppress negative behaviors (Samph, 1976), increase desired behaviors (Zegiob & Forehand, 1978), and reduce overall activity (White, 1977). Questionnaire measures seem to underestimate whites' negative attitudes toward blacks, compared to observational measures involving aggression, helping, and nonverbal behavior (Crosby, Bromley, & Saxe, 1980). These reasons sometimes motivate researchers to use unobtrusive measures or hidden observation techniques.

Ethics Observations made without the awareness of the participants pose special ethical problems. The subjects usually have not given permission for the recording, nor do they have access to the information or veto power over its use. The ethical issues are complex and need to be considered whenever unobtrusive means are employed; Webb et al. (1981, ch. 5) give a detailed discussion. Among the considerations are whether individual subjects are personally identifiable, whether subjects would refuse consent if given the opportunity, and what effects are likely to result for these or similar people if the data are made public. For example, a study of graffiti in public restrooms might show a high level of homosexual content in one particular building. Though the individual identity of the writers of the graffiti is not known, the research may pose a risk to identifiable groups of people. One must always consider whether the subjects' privacy is invaded by naturalistic research and whether such invasion is warranted (Diener & Crandall, 1978).

Unobtrusive Measures Involving Physical Traces

Physical traces, changes such as erosion or accretion that can show the frequency or extent of some behavior, have not been widely used as unobtrusive measures of social constructs. However, imaginative researchers have used such measures on occasion, and Webb et al. (1981) argue that they have much potential. One often-cited example is the finding (p. 7) that floor tiles around a museum exhibit featuring live, hatching chicks had to be replaced about every six weeks, whereas tiles around other exhibits in the same museum went months or years without replacement. This measure of erosion appears to show differences in the popularity of the exhibits. Note, however, that this inference might be in error. For example, viewers, possibly children, might move around and scuff their feet more at the chick-hatching exhibit, wearing out the tiles. Thus, the exhibit might not be seen by more people or for a longer time than other exhibits; it might just be seen by people whose feet are more active.

This sort of inferential problem is characteristic of many physical-trace measures. Consider the collection of graffiti to index the topics of concern at a campus or other area (e.g., Jorgensen & Lange, 1975). Without knowing the identity of the writers, one cannot be certain whether a large and representative proportion of the population contributes to the graffiti, or whether just a few people write most of it. On the other hand, some accretion measures, such as the examination of fingerprints and pencil marks on pages to see which sections of a reference work are most frequently read (Mosteller, 1955, cited in Webb et al., 1981, p. 9), seem to be largely free of such interpretive problems. Phsyical-trace measures occasionally even possess enough validity to be used to correct misinformation obtained by other measurement techniques. Rathje and Hughes (1975) compared estimates about beer consumption obtained by interviews and by sampling the household's garbage and counting beer cans. The "front door" interview data estimated that beer was consumed in only 15 percent of the homes, whereas the "back door" data found evidence of consumption in 77 percent.

In summary, physical-trace measures such as erosion and accretion generally involve low data-collection costs but require imagination and often pose validity problems. They may be most useful when they are used in conjunction with other, perhaps more-reactive measurement techniques, for then convergence of the different measures can help establish construct validity.

Systematic Observation

Systematic observation has often been used in the field of interpersonal interaction, but applications in other areas are also found. For example, eye contact by dating couples (observed from behind one-way mirrors in a laboratory setting) is positively related to self-reports of love (Rubin, 1970). In the field of nonverbal communication, there is evidence that several types of subtle but observable behaviors signal whether the speaker is being deceptive (Ekman & Friesen, 1969a) and whether the speaker likes or dislikes an object. Hess and Polt (1960) found that dilation of the pupil of the eye is related to the subject's interest in a photograph, under some circumstances. Friedman, DiMatteo, and Mertz (1980) even found that observers' ratings of the "positivity" of facial expressions of television newscasters during the 1976 election campaign differed reliably between stories about candidates Carter and Ford. Observational techniques for nonverbal behavior range from global ratings of positivity versus negativity to highly detailed systems for scoring minute facial movements from film or videotape (Ekman & Friesen, 1978).

Beyond interpersonal interaction, systematic observation has been used to measure such constructs as conservatism of social attitudes (by observing clothing styles; McGovern & Holmes, 1976), political preferences (by noting automobile bumper stickers; Wrightsman, 1969), interest in movies (by measuring body movements in theater audiences; Kretsinger, 1952), and attitudes toward time in different cultures (by noting the accuracy of people's watches; Levin, West, & Reis, 1980). It seems that both public clocks and watches in Brazil are less accurate than those in the United States, and that Brazilians with watches are less accurate in reporting the time than North Americans. Further examples can be found in Webb et al. (1981, chs. 7 and 8).

An Example of Systematic Observation

A person's posture can indicate a stance taken toward someone or something. The following describes one study on postural arrangements in a group in considerable detail to illustrate some of the elements in systematic observation. In this investigation (LaFrance, 1979), an effort was made to test a notion put forward by Scheflen (1964) that people who share similar postures in an interaction usually share a similar viewpoint as well.

The study involved videotaping a number of college classrooms twice during a six-week summer session, once during the first week of the course and again during the final week. At both times, students filled out a self-report questionnaire assessing their attitudes toward the class. Two questions guided the study: (1) Would similar postures by students and instructors relate to their feelings of involvement in the class? (2) What was the nature of this relation; that is, does posture sharing affect involvement or is the reverse relation true?

Courses were selected for small class size (maximum 20 students) so that all participants could be videotaped simultaneously from an overhead wide-angle camera. The videotapes were then coded by two trained observers working independently. The observational procedure entailed noting separately each person's body position at ten equally timed intervals in an hour of class time, resulting in one observation every six minutes. Three body areas (left arm, right arm, and torso) were coded, using graphic symbols derived from a master sheet depicting the range of possible postures. For example, if a student's right arm were bent at the elbow such that the elbow was resting on the desk and the right hand was touching or supporting the person's head, the coded symbol was ⋏⋋ . The second step of the coding procedure involved placing each student's noted body position alongside the body positions noted for the instructor and scoring whether or not each body part was a mirror image of the other person's body part. For example, a student's left arm was scored as sharing if it were in the same position as the right arm of the facing instructor.

The third step included correlating each student's posture-sharing score with the rating of his or her involvement in the class on a seven-item bipolar scale.

Definition of systematic observation   Systematic observation involves the selection, recording, and encoding of a set of natural behaviors or other naturally occurring phenomena. The study investigating the relation between posture sharing and feelings of involvement exemplifies each of these components. In the first place, the study entailed *selection*. Postural arrangements were selected for observation, and other elements of the situation such as smiling or gazing were ignored. The selection was deliberate and settled on before the investigation began.

Next the researchers had to make decisions about *recording* and *encoding*. Once a set of behaviors has been selected for investigation, the researcher needs to establish *when* the observations are to be made and in *what form* they are to be gathered. Both decisions are implicated in the recording of the observations. In the posture-sharing study, the initial decision was to videotape-record the whole class period twice for each course. The choice of videotape rather than in vivo recording was based on the desirability of obtaining a permanent record that could be repeatedly examined. This enhances the accuracy of the observations and allows discrepancies between observers to be resolved. In addition, the videotap-

TABLE 12.1   A Sampling Coding System for Arm Posture Used in Study of Participants in College Classrooms from LaFrance (1979)

Symbol		Verbal Description
Right Arm	Left Arm	
		arm straight, extended downward
		arm straight, extended forward
		arm straight, extended laterally
		arm bent at elbow, lower arm forward and parallel to floor, perpendicular to upper arm
		arm bent at elbow 45° angle across front of body
		arm bent at elbow, forearm across body
		arm bent at elbow, forearm upward
		arm bent at elbow, forearm up and hand touching head
		arm bent at elbow, hand behind head or neck
		arm bent at elbow, elbow out from body with hand at waist or hip

ing was done according to the principle of nonintervention. No attempt was made to impose any particular sort of narrative on the shooting. A comprehensive wide-angle overhead position was chosen and sustained throughout each class. The taping began before the class began and finished after it was over.

The videotape was then systematically examined, and a record was made of the postures displayed by all participants in each class. Instead of recording every posture for every student for every second, a decision was made to record the postures according to a method of *time sampling*. The aim was to obtain records of posture sharing that could be compared across classes (because each was observed the same number of times according to the same schedule) without the greater time investment required of continuous and hence complete recording.

The latter method of coding is called **continuous real-time measurement** (Sackett, 1978a). Continuous measurement occurs when every onset of a behavior (frequency) or elapsed time of a behavior (duration) is recorded during the observational session. For example, had continuous measurement been used in the posture-sharing study instead of time sampling, a judgment would have been made every time there was mirroring between each student's posture and his or her respective instructor's posture. A judgment of sharing would start a stopwatch, which would be stopped when the mirroring temporarily ceased. When mirroring again occurred, the timing would restart.

The posture-sharing study used *time sampling* instead of continuous measurement to record postures for the classroom participants. More specifically, that study used **time-point sampling** as contrasted to **time-interval sampling.** In the first of these, recording is done instantaneously at the end of set time periods, such as every ten seconds or every sixth minute or every hour on the hour, with the number and spacing of points selected to be appropriate to the session length. This is like freezing time and recording then whether or not a particular behavior is present. Through the use of film or videotape, the time point is literally accomplished through stop action on one frame. In contrast, time-interval sampling, like continuous measurement, records behavior in real time; but as in time-point sampling, each observed behavior, such as posture sharing, is scored once and only once during successive intervals of the session (for example, 60 seconds) regardless of the number of actual occurrences in each interval. Both time-sampling methods are particularly apt when there is a large number of behaviors to code or long observational sessions to be recorded or quick changes in the relevant behaviors. Time sampling tends not to be appropriate for behaviors that occur infrequently or that may be missed or when the sequence of the behavior amid other behaviors is significant or when actual frequencies or durations are important to know. Consequently, continuous recording in real time is the method of choice when these concerns are paramount in the research.

Following recording, the next step entails encoding the observations. Encoding is the process of simplifying the observations through some data-reduction method, such as categorization, and quantifying the categories so that statistical analysis can be done. In our present example, the actual postures displayed were compared (each student to his or her instructor) to determine whether they were sharing posture or not. The presence or absence of posture sharing thus constituted the category for the simplification of the data. A count was then taken of how much sharing each student showed by adding the number of occurrences across the ten observation points. This was correlated with how much involvement they had reported feeling in the class, which was the average rating given on six seven-point scales. That is, each student had two scores: the mirroring score and the average self-report score. The values for all students in one class were statistically correlated to yield the degree of relationship between posture mirroring on the one hand and self-reported involvement on the other hand.

Sometimes recording and encoding can involve a single operation, as when an observer counts whether or not a specific, preestablished behavior has occurred when making a "live" observation. The data are thus already encoded by virtue of being recorded. Sampling according to time-point procedures in vivo would yield this type of situation. In contrast, the recording of a single or multiple behavior through continuous time measurement would allow different types of encoding to be done, such as frequency, rate, duration, percentage duration, and sequential analysis. The distinction between recording and encoding is a critical one in that the same recorded observations may be encoded according to different systems. In this at least, observations do not speak for themselves. The question that the researcher has in mind will guide the encoding of the observations. Take gaze behavior; for example, two pairs may look at each other for comparable total duration, thus looking very similar; however, the first pair may have accomplished this through one or two relatively extended periods of eye contact, whereas the second pair brought it about through frequent but brief looks.

Types of systematic observation   Systematic observation studies differ considerably in how the behaviors or observations of interest are recorded and encoded. At one end of the continuum are methods that are relatively unstructured and open-ended. The observer tries to provide as complete and nonselective a description as possible. On the other end of the continuum are more structured and predefined methods that itemize, count, and categorize behavior. Here the investigator decides beforehand which behaviors will be recorded and how frequently observations will be made. The investigator using structured observation is much more discriminative in choosing which behaviors will be recorded and precisely how they are to be coded.

Relatively Unstructured Methods: Natural History Approaches. The most unstructured and nonselective method of observation would be a complete descriptive account of everything that surrounded an event. This is not only an impossible goal but also not a desirable goal. The basic principle of any observational technique is that it summarize, systematize, and simplify the representation of an event rather than provide complete replay of it. Even films and videotapes do not provide exact reproduction, for they are subject to biases introduced by camera angle, lighting, microphone placement, and lens used (Michaelis, 1955). Nor is a "complete" description ever a perfect carbon copy owing to investigators' expectations, language structure, or other cultural biases that may unintentionally affect what is recorded. These issues will be discussed further but are noted here to alert the reader to the fact that all observational techniques involve selection and editing. The issue is to make one's techniques as explicit and available as possible.

Yet natural history and ethological approaches opt for as little prior categorization as possible. Ethologists attempt to enter a scene to discover what is there. The object is to derive as detailed and comprehensive a description as possible about the nature of an animal's or person's behavioral repertoire. A basic assumption for ethologists is that the natural world is best approached through careful exploratory studies aimed at the generation of hypotheses rather than the testing of them (Blurton Jones, 1972).

Consequently, ethologists concentrate on molecular behaviors, that is, behaviors tied to specific motor or muscular phenomena, and avoid descriptions that involve inference. For example, ethologists would *not* describe someone as looking "very pleased." That would entail too much interpretation. They would instead describe such details as facial expression, body movement, speech content, and the behavioral results of such a display rather than allude to some underlying state or intention. For example, Eibl-Eibesfeldt (1970) has used a camera with a right-angle lens, which allows a film to be taken of a person while the camera is apparently orienting 90 degrees in the other direction. Such observations led to the discovery of the "eyebrow flash" that occurs during greetings, wherein both eyebrows are raised maximally and simultaneously, and that is completed within one second. Other ethological observations have discriminated between different types of smiles and the occasions for their use (Brannigan & Humphries, 1972) and the natural "fidgetiness" by patients in dentists' waiting rooms (Barash, 1974).

Structured Methods: Checklists. The major difference between unstructured and structured observational methods is that in the latter investigators know what aspects of social activity are relevant for their purposes before starting and deliberately set forth a specific and explicit plan to record these activities.

Most structured observational methods require an observer to be present to code the appearance of the behavior, but some newer technological devices can record even in an observer's absence. For example, television meters note how many and what television programs are turned on, pedometers calculate the territory covered by people on foot during any given day, and clap meters gauge the level of an audience's reaction (Schwitzgebel, 1968). Pressure-sensitive floor mats have been used to record the differential use of space in public areas such as art galleries (Bechtel, 1967), and ultrasonic motion detectors attached to chairs have been used to record subjects' spontaneous movements in reactive situations (Dabbs, 1975).

Checklists or category systems can range from simply noting whether or not a single behavior has occurred to multiple behavior systems. As an example of the first, Bryan and Test (1967) recorded whether or not individuals donated money to a Salvation Army kettle in a study dealing with donations and modeling behavior, and Strayer and Strayer (1976) classified initiation of antagonistic behavior by children in a playground into one of several categories: bite, chase, hit, kick, push-pull, and wrestle. The construction of a reliable and valid checklist is crucial to its usefulness as an observational tool. First, a critical feature of a good checklist is the explicitness with which the behavior is defined. For example, in observing antagonistic behavior, observers would need to know when a friendly tap becomes a "hit." This is accomplished more easily when the behaviors are classifiable on objective grounds rather than on inferential ones. The observer would code a behavior as a "hit" only if it actually met the explicit description for the act and not if it only appeared that the child "wanted" to hit. Second, each behavior of interest must be able to be classified into one and only one category. A behavior would be either a "push-pull" or "wrestle" but not both. Third, the total set of categories for classifying a particular kind of behavior such as fighting or greeting should be exhaustive of the type but limited in distinctions. The code should cover the sphere of interest but be sufficiently finite to allow meaningful assessments to be made.

Group process and classroom interaction are enduring targets for checklist observational systems. Two such systems are Bales's (1970) Interaction Process Analysis for studying group interaction and Flanders' (1970) system for analyzing teacher behavior. In the former, each act by a group member is categorized into 1 of the 12 categories (p. 92) shown in Figure 12.1.

In Flanders' system, classroom behavior is classified according to the 10 categories shown in Figure 12.2.

Bales's checklist system uses a modified version of continuous time sampling, that is, each act by a person is coded into 1 of the 12 possible types, and an act is defined as "a communication or an indication, either verbal or nonverbal, which in its context may be understood by another

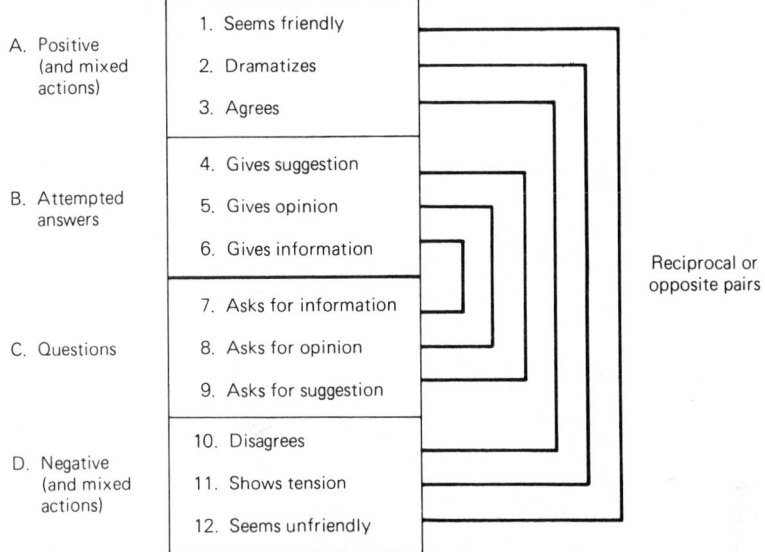

FIGURE 12.1   Category system for interaction in groups

member as equivalent to a single simple sentence (p. 68)." Flanders, in contrast, uses very small interval time-point sampling in order to maintain a rendering of the original behavioral sequence in the classrooms. An observer codes ongoing behavior into one of Flanders' 10 categories every three seconds. (See Figure 12.2.)

Structured methods such as checklists are particularly appropriate for testing specific hypotheses after the behaviors have been described and hypotheses generated, perhaps by less-structured observational methods. Of course, the relative specificity of checklists means that a single coding system will not be equally appropriate to all situations. Researchers sometimes become so attached to a particular system that they apply it in contexts where it is not particularly useful. On the other hand, an

	Response	1. Accepts Feeling 2. Praises or Encourages 3. Accepts or Uses Ideas of Pupils
Teacher Talk		4. Asks Questions
	Initiation	5. Lecturing 6. Giving Directions 7. Criticizing or Justifying Authority
Pupil Talk		8. Pupil-Talk Response 9. Pupil-Talk Initiation
Silence		10.

FIGURE 12.2   Category system for classroom behavior

existing checklist or other category system may well be found to be appropriate for a particular research purpose. For example, at least 73 systems for observing young children are available in the literature (Boyer, Simon, & Karafin, 1973).

Ecological Observation. One particular type of systematic observation, *ecological observation,* specifically emphasizes the setting of behavior. Ecological psychologists assume that all behaviors depend heavily on settings. In their view, the best way to predict a person's behavior is to know where he or she is: "In a post office, he behaves post office, at church he behaves church" (Willems, 1969, p. 16). Thus, these researchers are centrally concerned with characterizing behavior settings in terms of such dimensions as their geographical character (rural, urban), practical functions (drugstore, garage), typical objects (chairs, blackboards), primary behavioral displays (singing, discussing), and temporal domain (morning, evening).

Ecological studies by Barker and those of his students (Barker, 1968; Barker and Schoggen, 1973; Bechtel, 1977; Wicker, 1979) comprehensively described all the behavior settings of a particular community, which were then organized in hierarchies of types and subtypes. The final step in this **behavior setting survey** is the description of the settings in terms of whichever of their many attributes and characteristics may be of interest. Individuals are known then by the settings they inhabit as they conduct their daily lives. For the ecological psychologist, the life-style of an individual can be accurately grasped by listing the behavior settings that he or she inhabits. Listing the behavior settings is a technique called **behavior range.** For example, the behavior range for a particular person or group of persons is informative about how active the person or persons are in community life, what interests they have, and where they spend most of their time.

Another method used by ecological psychologists is called a **specimen record.** In specimen records, a skilled observer provides a narrative account of specific actions of one person, such as a child in a noncontrived setting, over a substantial time period. The record is made of everything that happens in the behavior and situation of a person. This includes whatever he or she says and does and whatever is done or said to him or her, including the manner in which actions are carried out (Wright, 1967). The observer's task is to capture in plain language a full word picture of the goal-directed behaviors of the child along with those concrete aspects of the situation relevant to the child's behavior (Schoggen, 1978). The most desirable method for doing this is dictation during the observation into a shielded microphone attached to a portable recorder.

An excerpt from an observation of *One Boy's Day: A Specimen Record* (Barker & Wright, 1951, p. 147) illustrates the type of data captured by this method.

10:47 [A.M.]	Placing his hands straight ahead of him on his desk, he folded them properly for a moment.
	Relaxing somewhat, he picked up the ballpoint pen from the trough and peered at it curiously.
	Then he scanned the roman numerals which the teacher had written on the blackboard.
	Mrs. Logan brought a piece of plain white paper and put it down on his desk.
	Children were moving all around him, *some whispering and talking.*
	Raymond bit on the end of his pen and gazed around the room absently.
10:48	Leaning forward and grasping his pen very tightly, he began drawing numerals with care on the piece of paper.

The amount of detail available in a specimen record of a full day is almost overwhelming.

Ecological observation is thus a type of systematic observation that emphasizes full and impartial recording of behaviors in their specific setting and context. As in participant observation (Chapter 8), the goal is the discovery of ecologically valid base-rate information rather than hypothesis testing. In contrast to participant observation and like other forms of systematic observation, though, the emphasis is on the objective observation of specific actions rather than the inference of underlying processes. Although ecological psychology has not yet had a major impact on researchers in other areas, the theoretical emphasis on the influence of the setting on behavior is certainly well placed.

Steps in Conducting an Observation

Any study using observation will follow a general sequence of steps, which will be outlined here as a summary of the considerations that affect the research.

Step 1: Find an observable measure of the desired construct(s) This step may be the most difficult, as it can require considerable imagination or creativity on the part of the researcher to decide to observe "fidgetiness" in doctor's waiting rooms as a measure of nervousness or floor-tile wear to measure an exhibit's popularity in a museum. The selection of the behavior or physical trace to observe is guided both by the focus of interest and by practical and ethical concerns that limit what is observable. It is also important that the target of observation should be unambiguously definable, so that reasonable reliability and validity in measurement can be attained.

Step 2: Select the setting and mode of observation Since settings exert a powerful influence on behavior, one must choose a setting in which the trace or behavior can be expected to occur with sufficient frequency to make observation worthwhile. The setting should, if possible, also permit relatively unobtrusive but reliable observations by an in-person observer or recording instrument (such as videotape equipment). For example, if fine, small behaviors are to be coded, the setting should permit the observers to be physically close to subjects or else permit the use of binoculars or telephoto lenses. The choice between live coding of behaviors and permanent recording for later coding is crucial. Videotaped or other recorded data facilitate the use of multiple coders for each behavior and therefore the reliability of measurement.

Step 3: Select a sampling strategy Continuous real-time observation allows the determination of the actual frequency or duration of particular behaviors, whereas time-sampling strategies require less coding effort and allow estimation of total frequencies and comparisons of subgroups. Sampling considerations also include issues of who is to be observed, what locations are to be examined for physical traces, and when and for how long the observers or coders should make records. If more than one subject is to be observed at a time with live coding, multiple observers may be necessary.

Step 4: Train the observers Like raters and judges in general (Chapter 9), observers are not all alike (Yarrow & Waxler, 1979), and they need to be trained to code objects or events similarly and to avoid errors of commission and omission in scoring. Training may proceed in conjunction with the development of coding categories or checklists. Before actual coding begins, observers practice on sample behaviors until they reach acceptable levels of agreement (i.e., high reliability). If adequate reliability cannot be attained, the coding system or checklist needs to be revised, probably in the direction of more specificity in the definitions of the coding categories. Furthermore, *observer drift*, a decline in observer reliability or validity over time, is a common phenomenon. Because of fatigue or habituation, the use of coding categories may vary randomly or systematically over time so that behaviors are not coded in the same way. One cannot assume that high reliability at the beginning of a study implies high reliability at the end.

Observers are also subject to a number of biases (such as halo) that are characteristic of raters in general (see Chapter 9) and that can only be reduced, not totally eliminated, by careful training. The best control of such biases, as well as of sequence effects related to observer drift or fatigue over time, involves the use of videotaped records of behavior. Taped records can be shown to different observers in different sequences, so that some observers will see a particular behavior segment early in the sequence and others late. Thus, observer drift will be approximately canceled out. In addition, it is sometimes possible to edit videotapes to remove information that identifies the condition under which the observation was made and thus remove halo and other potential biases. For example, if the research hypothesis is that male subjects smile more while conversing with females than with males, and if the observers can see the other party to the conversation, their ratings of the subject's smiles might be influenced by their knowledge of the circumstances of the observation. This bias might even falsely lead to a seeming confirmation of the hypothesis (Rosenthal, 1976). On the other hand, it might be easy to record or edit videotaped observations so that the coders could see and hear only the subject, not the partner, removing any possibility of this form of bias. This is a form of *blind coding*. As this example makes clear, it is often easier to arrange for blind coding when videotape or other recording techniques are used than with live observers.

Step 5: Analyze the data   After the coding system has been found or created, good reliability and validity have been achieved, and observations have been recorded on the research subjects, analysis of the data is the final step. Chapter 13 on data analysis describes the organization of data to give maximal information. A number of special data-analytic techniques are available for the investigation of behavior streams and sequences (e.g., Bakeman, 1978; Gottman, 1978). The conceptual questions that guided the data collection will continue to determine exactly what types of analysis are appropriate.

Summary of Observation

Like other methods of data collection for social research, observation of physical traces, naturally occurring behaviors, or other phenomena demands rigorous training of observers, careful construction of checklists or coding schemes, careful sampling, and caution in interpreting results. The special strengths of observational research are its ability to describe naturally occurring events in natural settings, avoiding problems that may arise with questionnaire measures or other methods that make respondents aware of participating in research. This means that observations may be particularly informative about activities that cannot be talked about because of ignorance or inability (such as nonverbal behaviors) or will not be talked about because of fear or embarrassment (such as drivers' compliance with traffic laws).

Archival Data

Statistical archives and written records are kept by all literate societies for a variety of purposes, of which research is by no means the most important. However, such archives can be used by imaginative researchers for purposes that were never envisioned by the originators of the archives or documents, often in a way that takes advantage of the strengths of archival data. These strengths are the potential for (1) spanning long periods of time (including the ability to look *back* in time, which is not possible with other research methods); (2) covering large populations of people or other units of observation; and (3) quantifying reactions to events, such as earthquakes, riots, or factory closings, that researchers cannot intentionally impose for practical or ethical reasons.

This section of the chapter will be divided into three parts, based on the nature of the archive that is the data source. First we will consider *statistical records* and other government or institutional records, such as those on hospital admissions, unemployment rates, daily temperatures, or population growth. Next *survey archives* of data collected for research purposes by standard survey methods (usually by telephone or personal interviews) will be considered; they generally include a range of sociodemographic information as well as attitudes on social and political topics, drawn from a sample of one to two thousand individuals. Finally, the research use of *written records*, ranging from private diaries to mass-circulation newspapers, and the associated techniques of content analysis will be presented.

Statistical Records

Many available statistical data refer to socioeconomic information about age, sex, family size, occupation, residence, and other characteristics. Health statistics give birth- and death rates and the like; federal, state, municipal, and private economic institutions collect and publish data on wages, hours of work, productivity, absenteeism, strikes, financial transactions, and so on. Many voluntary organizations have records not only of their own membership but also of groups of people whom they serve. In addition, a small but steadily increasing body of data is being collected by various institutions on psychological characteristics such as IQ, personality, anxiety, and attitudes. For example, schools, hospitals, social service agencies, personnel departments in businesses, and similar institutions nowadays frequently administer psychological tests of various kinds to their entire populations.

Brenner (1973) used available statistics to examine the relation between economic factors and mental health. He found a positive correlation between rates of unemployment and mental hospital admissions and concluded the state of a country's economy can affect the state of its citizens' mental health. Kasarda (1976) has argued that the data provided in various national censuses offer opportunities for secondary analyses that are limited only by the imagination of the researcher. Among these opportunities Kasarda has mentioned the chance to analyze educational attainment, ethnic and racial segregation, poverty, marriage and divorce, social mobility, and commuting patterns.

Available statistical records are now being used as **social indicators** to chart the status and change in the quality of life (Andrews & Withey, 1976). The U.S. government has published reports (U.S. Office of Federal Statistical Policy and Standards, 1976) detailing various social indicators of human well-being, including employment levels, housing availability, and crime rates. These reports are compiled to monitor present social conditions and to chart societal changes. Therein lies one of the singular advantages of using existing records. Many of these are collected regularly, thus enabling the user of archival data to measure relations between social variables across time. For example, is the socioeconomic standing of various racial or sex groups declining, rising, or sustaining the status quo, and to what other social factors is there a systematic tie?

Examples Data from available records were used in a series of studies by Gurr (1968) to explain violence in modern societies. The hypothesis guiding this archival study was that violence results from feelings of relative deprivation, which occurs when there is a discrepancy between what people expect to receive and what they actually do receive. The challenge for this study was to find, in existing records, indices that could be translated into signs of relative deprivation (natural treatment) on the one hand and magnitude of violence on the other.

Eleven hundred observations of strife collected on 114 nations from 1961 to 1965 were drawn primarily from reports in the *New York Times Index, Newsyear* (the annual volumes of *Facts on File*), and the *Africa Digest.* These sources were supplemented by reports of incidents of strife in the *Annual Register of Events in Africa*, and *Hispanic-American Report* as well as country and case studies. All these are publicly available reports.

In addition to deriving quantitative measures of strife, including the number of participants involved, the number of casualties suffered, and the number of days the strife lasted, Gurr developed several quantitative measures of relative deprivation, including economic downturns and increases in political suppression. Economic downturns and political suppression are "natural" treatments in the sense of happening without any intervention by social science researchers. Gurr found that these natural events were associated with increases in civil strife.

Another creative use of existing records was made by Durkheim (1951) in his study of suicide. Durkheim's primary hypothesis was that a basic cause of suicide is lack of integration into a social group. He examined three major kinds of social group integration: religious, familial, and political. He found suicide rates were lower among Catholics than among Protestants, lower among married people than among single people, lower among those with children than among those without children, and lower during periods of national fervor. All these findings, he argued, supported the hypothesis that belonging to a cohesive social group is a deterrent to suicide.

The range of research topics to which archival records are applicable is extremely broad (see Webb et al., 1981, chs. 4 and 6). Carlsmith and Anderson (1979) correlated newspaper reports of the occurrence of urban riots and daily temperature records to test the notion (the "long, hot summer") that these two variables would be related. The probability of riots did increase with rising temperatures. Simonton (1977) used archival data to analyze the determinants of eminence among classical composers. And Schwartz and Barsky (1977) examined records of thousands of major-league sports contests to investigate the extent of, and possible explanations for, the home team advantage.

Characteristics Archival studies such as these have a number of common characteristics. First, they rely entirely on the analyses of data collected for purposes other than those of particular studies in social relations. Consequently, they require familiarity with known sources of data such as the *New York Times Index* and skill in uncovering less well-known material such as cemetery records. Second, archival studies often call for ingenuity in translating existing records into quantifiable indices of some general concepts. For example, objective public records of relative deprivation and social integration do not exist. Gurr's and Durkheim's resourcefulness is evident in using existing material as indicating more general social psychological processes. Third, archival studies are particularly susceptible to alternative interpretations for the natural events and/or their effects. What is required then is care in using multiple measures or ruling out other explanations. For example, Durkheim examined a number of alternative hypotheses—that suicide is the result of psychopathic states, of imitation, of racial or hereditary factors, or of climate. He then demonstrated that the statistics are not in accord with any of these hypotheses. For example, in considering the hypothesis that suicide is influenced by climate, he started with the observation that in all countries for which statistics are available over a period of years, the incidence of suicide increases regularly from January until June and then declines until the end of the year. This observation had led other writers to conclude that temperature has a direct effect on the tendency to suicide. Durkheim examined this possibility in great detail and demonstrated that the data did not support it. He argued, for example, that if temperature were the basic cause, suicide would vary regularly with it; but this is not the case. There are more suicides in spring than in autumn although the temperature is slightly lower in spring. Moreover, suicide reaches its height not in the hottest months (July and August) but in June. By a series of such analyses. Durkheim demonstrated that the seasonal regularities in suicide rates could not be accounted for by temperature and suggested the alternative hypothesis that social activity is seasonal and that the rate of suicide is related to the extent of social activity.

Census data The U.S. Census, a truly massive data collection undertaken every 10 years, produces a variety of statistical records that are suitable for some research purposes. The variables include a fairly narrow range, being limited to basic characteristics of people (such as age, sex, race, ethnic background, education, occupation, and income) and housing units (such as location, value, inclusion of indoor plumbing, and occupants per room). The Census Bureau publishes a number of tabulations of data (e.g., income broken down by race and sex) for the United States as a whole and for states and smaller areas, and using these data for research is as simple as looking up the appropriate table.

However, often the particular relationships in which a researcher is interested are not among those tabulated by the government, so the researcher must turn to the raw data. Public Use Microdata samples of a tiny percentage of the actual census responses are released by the government, coded in relatively gross geographical areas so that individual respondents' privacy is not threatened by the release of the actual data. From the raw data, any desired tabulation or analysis of the existing variables can be prepared by an appropriate computer program.

Despite their unparalleled coverage of the U.S. population, census data have important limitations for research. Though the repetition of the census every 10 years provides a good basis for research over time, the researcher must be wary of changing definitions and operationalizations that render some year-to-year comparisons problematic. For example, the entire scheme for coding occupations changed between 1970 and 1980; some change is necessary as new occupations appear and old ones vanish, but the changes can make comparisons over time inexact. The boundaries of census areas within which data are accumulated (tracts and metropolitan areas) also change over time as population patterns shift. Again, examining social or economic changes within a city or other area can be difficult because of these noncomparabilities. Finally, social change can affect the way people respond to the questionnaire, even when data-collection procedures remain unchanged. Between 1970 and 1980, it appears that a large number of people of Spanish origin shifted from indicating "White" to "Other" on a question about race; in 1970, 90 percent of this group indicated "White" compared to 58 percent "White" and 38 percent "Other" in 1980. Racial breakdowns across years would be confounded unless special precautions were taken because the "White" and "Other" groups would contain varying proportions of Spanish-origin respondents.

The relatively small number of variables collected by the census has already been mentioned, and it poses the most important limitation on research content. No attitude or belief variables are included. However, for whole fields within the social sciences, including the study of fertility, educational and occupational differences in income, or characteristics of different areas within cities (e.g., residential segregation by race or income), the census is the single most valuable data source (see Kasarda, 1976).

Survey Archives

One recent innovation in social research is the easy accessibility of data archives created specifically for research. Several organizations (including the Roper Center of the University of Connecticut and the Interuniversity Consortium for Political and Social Research, ICPSR) maintain and distribute data files drawn from large-scale surveys, often based on high-quality probability samples of the general U.S. population.

One data series, the General Social Survey (Davis, 1982), illustrates the types of data that are available. This survey has been conducted with a new representative sample of about 1,500 respondents yearly from 1972 through 1978 and every two years from 1980 to the present. Many of the questions remain the same from year to year and others appear in rotation every two or three years, offering valuable opportunities to make comparisons over time. The questions cover a range of standard social and demographic characteristics of the respondent, including age, sex, education, income, religion, urban or rural residence, occupation, and marital status. In addition, many questions about beliefs, attitudes, and behaviors relevant to social and political topics are included, for example, reported vote in the most recent presidential election, preferences for government spending on a range of programs, interracial attitudes, political alienation, attitudes toward labor unions, gun ownership and attitudes toward gun control, and attitudes on political issues such as the Equal Rights Amendment and abortion.

The use of such archives for research has obvious advantages and disadvantages. The advantages include the availability of extensive data drawn from high-quality samples over time, which would be beyond the ability of any researcher to collect for him- or herself. Low cost is also a benefit; in many colleges and universities such data sets are available through the campus computing center or otherwise, and the cost to obtain them is typically low ($50 to $500) if they are not already available. Finally, in contrast to most archives, these survey data sets are created and maintained for research use, so that they do not have many of the problems that must be faced by the user of government or institutional archives, where research use is often a mere afterthought.

The main limitations are, of course, those imposed by the method (sample surveys, clearly not an unobtrusive or nonreactive form of data gathering) and the topics. Though the questions cover a wide range of topics, a researcher who is interested in an issue that is not included is simply out of luck. In addition, some older data sets have annoying problems, such as incomplete or inaccurate codebooks (the documentation describing what variables are recorded where and what codes are used in the data; see Chapter 13) and obsolete recording methods (such as "multiple punched columns" in punched cards). More-recent data sets are largely free from these problems.

A number of excellent studies have been conducted with the General Survey or other archival survey data sets. Recent examples are analyses of symbolic versus group-interest influences on whites' interracial attitudes (Bobo, 1983), changes in sex-role attitudes among men and women from 1972 through 1978 (Cherlin & Walters, 1981), the effects of education on psychological well-being and life satisfaction (Glenn & Weaver, 1981), and tests of various claims about the political mobilization of a "new religious right" or "moral majority" (Mueller, 1983).

Written Records

Public and private documents Verbal documents also provide a rich source of data. For example, public documents such as the inaugural addresses of U.S. presidents can be analyzed to detect prevalent motivational themes. Donley and Winter (1970) determined the degree to which achievement and power themes were present in each of the inaugural addresses of presidents. Presidents' motives, as shown by their first official statement, corresponded to the subsequent accomplishments of their administrations. Similarly, Tetlock (1979) drew material from public speeches pertaining to policy decisions by the U.S. government. The speeches associated with decisions later judged to have been faulty were contrasted with speeches associated with well worked out policy decisions. An existing coding scheme was applied to assess the degree to which less-differentiated and less-integrated modes of information processing prevailed in the poor decisions as opposed to the good decisions. Results showed speeches in the former case were more simplistic and biased.

Personal documents, including autobiographies, letters, diaries, school essays, and the like are also open to social scientific observation once obtained. For example, Schneidman (in Gerbner et al., 1969) used the thinking, reasoning, and cognitive maneuvering in suicide notes to understand better the mental processes of suicide victims. A classic study by Thomas and Znaniecki (1918) used letters sent between Poland and the United States, along with other data sources, to draw conclusions about Polish peasants who immigrated to the United States and, more broadly, the effects of culture on beliefs and attitudes.

Potentially, the research use of personal documents can achieve for inner experiences such as beliefs and attitudes what observational techniques can achieve for overt behaviors: reveal them to the social scientist without the mediation of reactive questionnaires or other research instruments. However, personal documents are relatively rare and often pose problems for the researcher. Their authenticity can be uncertain—were the letters from Polish peasants actually written by the person in question or by somebody else (such as a village scribe)? If the latter, that person might influence the content. In addition, available samples of documents might be biased. If not all peasants are literate, conclusions about their thinking based on letters probably pertain to a biased sample of individuals, underrepresenting those who do not write.

Mass communications In addition to statistical records and autobiographical documents, every literate society produces a variety of material intended to inform, entertain, or persuade the populace. Such material may appear in the form of literary productions, newspapers and magazines, or—more recently—film and radio and television broadcasts. Mass communications provide a rich source of data for investigating a variety of questions. They may be used to throw light on some aspects of the culture of a given group, to compare different groups in terms of some aspect of culture, or to trace cultural change. For example, Scott and Franklin (1972) investigated the way that sex has been portrayed in seven high-circulation periodicals in 1950, 1960, and 1970. Analyzing each sentence that referred to sex in a sample of issues of *Reader's Digest, McCall's, Life, Look, Saturday Evening Post, Time,* and *Newsweek,* the authors concluded that few changes in liberal (or permissive) references to sex occurred during the period. A slight increase in the total number of references to sex was revealed by the analysis, and although conservative (or restrictive) references to sex declined from 1950 to 1960, no further decrease in the proportion of references that were conservative occurred between 1960 and 1970.

A similar analysis of magazines was conducted to assess the inclusion and portrayal of blacks in advertisements (Cox, 1971). Five magazines (*Life, Saturday Evening Post, New Yorker, Ladies Home Journal,* and *Time*) were analyzed for all their issues in 1967 and the first half of 1968 and compared with the issues of these same magazines during 1949 and 1950. Only one-half of 1 percent of the ads in 1949 and 1950 included blacks, and that portion in 1967 and 1968 had increased to slightly over 2 percent. Gains were more apparent with respect to portrayal. In the 1949–1950 period, 95.5 percent of blacks were presented as having occupations below skilled labor, whereas the proportion had dropped to 30.9 percent in the 1967–1968 period.

Both the preceding studies document trends in content in the mass media. Other questions susceptible to this kind of analysis include tracing the development of research ideas, disclosing international differences, comparing different media, assessing coverage against objectives, exposing propaganda techniques, uncovering stylistic features, identifying psychological motivations, and assessing responses to events or ideas (Berelson, 1952; Holsti, 1969; Webb et al., 1981).

All utilize a technique called **content analysis,** which is "any technique for making inferences by systematically and objectively identifying specified characteristics of messages" (Holsti, 1969, p. 601). This is similar to the definition of systematic observation of natural behavior. Both techniques require objectivity of coding categories in order to assure reliability, systematic application of these coding systems across a representative sample of material in order to control observer bias, and consistency in theoretical aims so that the findings can be related to some relevant variable or variables.

The steps of content analysis are very similar to the steps in conducting a systematic observation of a natural behavior. (1) The phenomenon to be coded, such as the presence and portrayal of elderly people in the print media, must be chosen. (2) The media from which the observations are to be made must be selected. The issue here, as in systematic observation, is the selection of media that are typical or representative of what is available and with which people have contact. The issue is to find out what is out there and not to select so as to enhance or inhibit the possibility of obtaining particular findings. (3) Deriving the coding categories is a third step. As was the case with systematic observation, content analysis categories can range from a simple binary system, in which the presence or absence of people of a certain age are noted, to multicategory systems using mutually exclusive and exhaustive categories in which distinctions are made on a range of phenomena, such as the status of the portrayed character (e.g., high, middle, or low), background physical attractiveness (attractive, neutral, unattractive), or evaluation of context (positive, neutral, negative). (4) Deciding on the sampling strategy is another step. The distinctions here again are roughly comparable to the decisions involved in systematic observation. The task is to choose among strategies that code every reference to the phenomenon in question or to select a discontinuous though regular method of sampling, such as every other issue of several magazines over a year's period. (5) A fifth step is training the coders. Reliability of content analysis is an important consideration and particularly so when inferences are required in order to decide, for example, whether the portrayal of an elderly person is cast positively or negatively. (6) Lastly, we have analyzing the data. Sometimes with content analysis the most straightforward analysis is the straightforward representation of the data in summary form, such as numbers represented and percentage representation.

One type of category system for content analyzing newspapers has been used by Laswell and his associates (1949). Lasswell developed a system of "symbol analysis," which was employed during World War II in several branches of the U.S. government. In this system, newspaper content was studied for the appearance of certain symbols, such as *England, Russia, democracy, Jews, Stalin*, and so on. The frequency with which these symbols appeared was noted, as well as whether their presentation was favorable, unfavorable, or neutral (or "indulgent," "deprivational," "neutral"). Favorable references were sometimes further divided into those stressing "strength" and those stressing "goodness" or "morality"; negative references were divided into "weakness" and "immorality" categories.

Sampling material from mass communications is a step requiring much time and thought. The first task is to define the universe—newspapers, magazines, radio, or television. But even if we limited ourselves to newspapers, it would not be satisfactory to list all the newspapers published in a given country and draw every tenth or twentieth one. Even if we were also to introduce controls to ensure that newspapers representing different geographical areas, political orientations, economic groups, and ethnic groups were included in the proportion in which they are represented in the total population of newspapers, there would be a problem. The difficulty arises from the fact that newspapers vary tremendously in size and influence, and a realistic sample should not weigh an obscure journal equally with a metropolitan daily. The situation is not the same as that of drawing a representative sample of a voting population, each member of which has equal influence at the polls—namely, one vote.

Graber (1971) wished to represent a cross-section of the newspapers used by the general public as sources of information in the study previously mentioned. She developed a complex sampling scheme that reflected where these newspapers would be found. First, it was decided that newspapers in each of the major regions in the country should be included in the sample. Cities in each region were then divided into three groups by population: over 1 million, 500,000 to 1 million, and fewer than 500,000. It was decided to draw three-fourths of the sample from the most-populous states in each region and the remainder from the less-populous states to reflect "voting power" on the basis of population.

Further decisions narrowed even more the potential newspapers that could be included in the sample. Half the newspapers were selected from states in which the Democratic party was stronger; half, from states in which the Republican party was stronger. Newspapers were selected, moreover, to represent monopolistic as well as competitive newspaper market situations. Finally, two types of newspapers, appealing to either special or general audiences, were included in the sample. Graber then coded all the campaign stories in the newspapers included.

Frequently, then, the sampling procedure in communication analysis consists of three stages: sampling of sources (which newspapers, which radio stations, which films, and so on are to be analyzed), sampling of dates (which period is to be covered by the study), and sampling of units (which aspects of the communication are to be analyzed). With respect to the sampling of units, decisions are often arbitrary and based on tacit assumptions about which feature of a medium best characterizes it. For example, is it the headline, the human interest story, the editorial, or some other feature that best indicates the policy of a newspaper?

To avoid such arbitrariness, content analysts frequently follow one of two possibilities: They analyze on the basis of several different units (e.g., they take samplings of headlines, of human interest stories, and of editorials and then count how many times a given subject is mentioned in each); or they disregard these "natural" units completely, dividing the issues of a newspaper mechanically into lines or inches of space from which they draw a sample. Note here the similarity to the distinctions among types of time sampling.

In summary, content analytic methods applied to written records, either personal communications or derived from the mass media, constitute an underused resource for social research. Content coding schemes for a variety of psychological states (such as anxiety, positive and negative feelings, and hostility) already exist and have been shown to have adequate reliability and validity (Viney, 1983). Future advances in content analysis may include the use of computers to perform the analyses, with benefits of both lower cost and higher objectivity and reliability compared to human coders. As the previous examples illustrate, the range of issues that can be approached by content analytic techniques is wide indeed.

Issues in Archival Research

Archival records give the opportunity to assess the impact of natural events and investigate many other issues. They are obviously strong on external validity because of the subjects' unawareness of the research or its aims. However, they also characteristically offer certain problems of interpretation, centering on internal and construct validity. For example, records are available on the two variables of ice-cream sales and crime rates, which turn out to have a positive relationship (Kasarda, 1976). Can we conclude that eating ice cream increases the propensity to commit crimes? Obviously not, and this is an example of a spurious relationship: The two variables are related because they are both influenced by a third variable. Here, the variable is probably weather conditions—increasing temperature increases both ice-cream sales and crime, but the latter two variables probably do not affect each other. When using archival records, one must control for the possibilities of internal invalidity or spurious relationships (caused, for instance, by common influences of increasing population, inflation-induced price rises, or weather or other seasonal effects). This can require the collection of additional data, such as temperature records in this example, to rule out threats to internally valid causal inferences.

Another major issue for the user of archival data is the construct validity and reliability of the data for research purposes (see Webb et al., 1981, ch. 3). The researcher does not control the collection of archival data, so they may be subject to various sources of unreliability, bias, or invalidity. For example, organizations may keep records haphazardly, with little attention to consistency in recording similar events in the same way over time. Records may also be subject to systematic biases; for example, crime records collected and maintained by a new police administration might be suspected to underreport crimes, or samples of written documents from some societies might overrepresent the literate (and therefore those with higher status) and underrepresent the illiterate. Even the *Congressional Record*, a rich source of archival data on speeches and official proceedings in government, is edited after the fact by the speakers, so that what appears in the record may not be what was spoken on the floor.

Finally, archives are subject to gaps and incompleteness that make it difficult to determine whether the available data adequately represent the population of interest. A demographer interested in the lifespan of ancient Romans investigated tombstones to find birth- and death dates—but found biases. Tombstones that survive to the present are more likely to represent the middle and upper classes than the poor, and it even appeared that "a wife was more likely to get an inscribed tablet if she died before her husband than if she outlived him" (Durand, 1960). Researchers have examined suicide notes for clues to the mental states of suicide victims, but the majority of suicide victims do *not* leave notes. Are their mental states the same as those of note writers? And archives may contain data that are simply wrong. The 1979 *World Almanac* gives a number of characteristics of major cities in the United States, including the existence of a symphony orchestra, but Kansas City, Chicago, and Los Angeles are not reported as having orchestras (Webb et al., 1981)! Such difficulties must always be kept in mind by the user of archival data, and checks against alternative sources of data and alternative explanations of data patterns should be built in to the research plan.

However, archival data offer important advantages for some research questions. The use of archives is often economical, for the researcher is spared the time and cost involved in data collection and recording. This may be offset, though, by the effort involved in finding the relevant information as well as the search for materials that would allow one to rule out alternative interpretations. Another important advantage is that much information is collected by governments and other organizations as part of their everyday operations, and it is often collected repeatedly. This helps to avoid the difficulties associated with people's awareness of being subjects in research (reactivity) and often makes possible the analysis of trends over time. Finally, archival data are particularly well suited to the investigation of large-scale or widespread social or natural phenomena that are not amenable to study in other ways.

Summary

A concern with naturalness is the main defining feature of most of the research methods considered in this chapter. In contrast to questionnaire data gathering, many forms of observation and archivally based research stress natural behaviors, treatments, and settings, so that some of the potential problems stemming from the respondent's awareness of being a research subject can be avoided. Of course, this generalization must be modified in the case of survey data archives, which share the characteristics of other questionnaire techniques, and in the case of obtrusive observation, in which the subject is aware of being studied.

For certain types of research questions, particularly those dealing with the naturally occurring rates or patterns of behaviors, methods like those described in this chapter are the most appropriate. The use of one or more of the dimensions of naturalness may increase the generalizability of findings. Observational methods give particular stress to natural behaviors and settings, though the specific methods vary in their emphasis. Archival methods (with the exception of survey archives) also emphasize the use of records that are kept by or about individuals in the natural course of their activities, so they similarly offer access to natural behavior that is unaffected by the research process. Archival data may be particularly well suited for the analysis of the effects of natural treatments, such as natural or human-created disasters or social changes.

In this chapter, as elsewhere in the book, we emphasize the use of appropriate research techniques to improve the validity of findings. The specific technique that is most appropriate depends on the nature of the question as well as other factors, but for a wide range of research questions, observational and archival methods are certainly strong candidates for adoption. Naturalness in research may increase the external and construct validity of results, as many examples cited indicate, especially with respect to subjects' awareness of research and associated problems like social desirability biases in responding. However, these methods are characteristically weaker on internal validity and other aspects of construct validity; we often cannot be certain that a measure is affected by only the single desired construct rather than multiple possibilities. It is when a research hypothesis has been tested, with converging results, by both observational or archival methods *and* questionnaire or other more reactive methods that we can be most confident of its validity.

PART IV

Data
Analysis

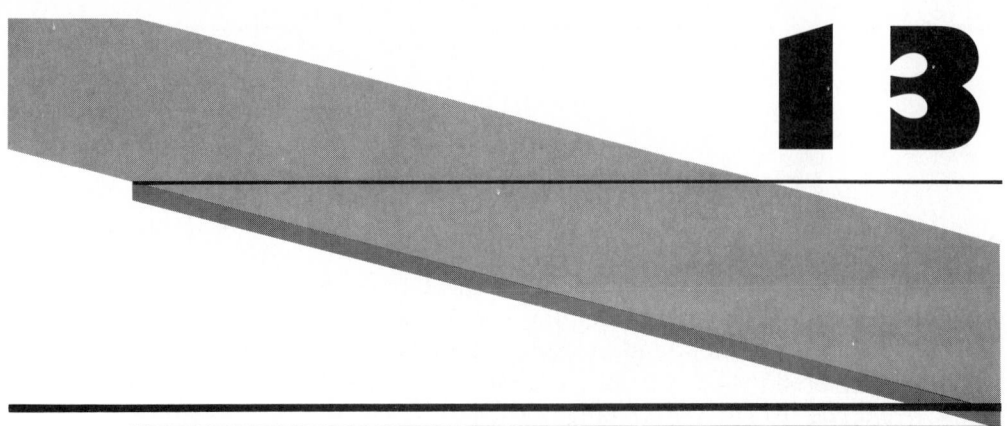

Coding Data and Describing Distributions

Social relations research generates information that must be coded, analyzed, and interpreted. By coding, we mean that the information generated by research must be put into a form that makes analysis possible. That is, the information must be turned into data that can be subjected to statistical analyses of one sort or another. In addition, coding means that records are kept and the data are stored in such a way that they can be referred to and used in the future. Once the data are coded, analysis proceeds. In analysis we attempt to describe the data, explore relationships that exist in them, and generally see if the data are consistent with our hypotheses and theories.

This chapter and the next two cover the important issues in data coding and analysis. In this chapter we discuss coding and statistical procedures for describing data on a single variable.

The Data Matrix

It is useful to view a set of information collected in a study as being arranged in the form of a large matrix, or to use a more ordinary illustration, in a form that resembles the layout of mailboxes in a campus post office. A set of boxes is arranged along a wall in a large rectangular shape so that a number of rows and columns appear. People find their mailboxes by ascertaining the appropriate row and column among the boxes, although we rarely think of "finding our mailbox" in this way because we have become so accustomed to walking right up to the same place each day, perhaps checking the number on the front of the box and then dialing the correct combination to open it.

Now let us step back from the set of mailboxes for just a moment. Each box in the large, rectangular wall of boxes can be located by specifying the column and row in which the box occurs. We call such a configuration of mailboxes a *matrix* of mailboxes. Now let us imagine how we could put social science data in the same matrix form. Suppose we have interviewed 1000 individuals from a cross section of the adult electorate in the United States regarding their attitudes on current social and political issues. On our survey we asked 100 questions, including many about attitudes on a variety of topics ranging from abortion to school busing to local and national political candidates. We have asked about the respondent's age, education, background, income, occupation, past voting record, and political party preference.

Let us place each of the people interviewed along the rows of the matrix so that each person is assigned one and only one row. The rows represent the *units of analysis,* which in this case are individuals whom we have interviewed. The first case (or individual in this instance because we are discussing the results of a survey) is placed in the first row, the second case in the second row, the third case in the third row, and so on until the thousandth case is placed in the thousandth row of our data matrix. If we were assigning each person a row of mailboxes, we would require a post office that had mailboxes stacked 1000 rows high, possibly stretching the post office analogy a bit far.

We now assign one and only one column to each of the characteristics that we have collected in our survey. Because information on 100 different aspects of each individual was collected, we need 100 columns to accomodate all the information. We call each different piece of information a *variable.* Each column in the data matrix represents one variable. Let us say that the first variable concerns the report of which candidate the respondent voted for in the 1984 presidential election. Thus, information about respondents' votes would be placed in column 1 for each case. Column 2 is assigned information about the respondents' age. Each variable is assigned one column in this manner until the hundredth variable, let us say, the respondents' income level, is assigned column 100.

We have now defined the rows and columns of the data matrix. The next thing we need to specify are the values that fill the cells of the matrix. These values represent a particular piece of information gathered from a particular individual (row of the matrix) on a particular variable (column of the matrix). For instance, the first individual may have voted for Walter Mondale in the 1984 presidential election. Assuming that the first variable was the respondent's reported presidential vote in 1984, the first cell of the data matrix (i.e., row 1, column 1) contains a value that stands for or means Walter Mondale. Similarly, if the third individual's reported income was $15,000 and if reported income was the 100th variable, the cell in the 3rd row, 100th column of the matrix would contain a value representing $15,000.

To construct the data matrix, three questions need to be addressed. First, the variables, or columns, of the matrix need to be defined. Defining the variables in a study amounts to deciding on how the theoretical constructs of interest are to be measured. This topic was thoroughly covered in Chapter 3. The second question concerns the definition of the rows of the matrix: What is the unit of analysis in this particular study? Answering this question raises a number of complex issues that have not been dealt with in previous chapters. The final question concerns how the values on specific variables are defined—what values are used to represent different responses to each variable. These latter two questions, concerning definition of the unit of analysis and the values of variables, are discussed briefly in the following paragraphs.

Unit of Analysis

In the example we have been using, where 1000 people are interviewed about their political attitudes and behaviors, the question of defining the unit of analysis is apparently easily answered. Individuals naturally constitute the rows of the data matrix, since each individual presumably has a value on each of the variables. However, there is no requirement that individuals always be the unit of analysis. In fact, there are many studies in which the unit of analysis is at some level other than the individual. For instance, in cross-cultural or cross-national research, the unit of analysis is quite likely to be a nation (e.g., Firebaugh, 1983). Likewise, smaller groupings of individuals can be the unit of analysis, as Eulau and Eyestone's (1968) 77 different city councils. In looking at how informal groups that are structured in different ways interact, Bales (Bales & Cohen, 1979) has treated groups as the unit of analysis. In all these examples, the unit has been defined as aggregates or groupings of individuals. The unit might also be defined in any particular study within individuals. For instance, a psychophysicist might be interested in examining how different temperatures are perceived when different parts of the body are exposed to them. In such a study, all the data might be collected from a single individual, and the unit of analysis becomes "body part." Similarly, in time series designs, a single individual may be repeatedly observed over time and then the unit of analysis is defined as different times.

All these examples illustrate the fact that there is no single appropriate unit of analysis that should be used in any and all studies. Rather, the choice of the unit of analysis should depend on the research questions that are being addressed and the level at which the researcher wishes to generalize. If generalization to individuals is sought, the individual is most appropriately the unit of analysis. If we are interested in group processes, generalization across groups may be desired, and groups are the appropriate unit.

Errors of generalization often occur when the unit of analysis is not at the same level as the unit to which one seeks to generalize. For instance, assume that a set of data about voting trends and income is gathered from different counties. Here counties are the unit of analysis. Assume further that we find that wealthier counties tend to be on average more Republican and less Democratic. If we attempt to generalize these results, found for counties, to the individual level, we may well commit what is called the **ecological fallacy.** It is inappropriate to assume, on the basis of these "group level" data, that the individuals within the counties necessarily behave in a way that is analogous to the way that their counties behave. Wealthier individuals may well be inclined to cast Republican ballots, and less-affluent individuals may well be inclined to cast Democratic ballots. But the individual and the ecological (group) associations are by no means necessarily the same. Typically, associations that are found when the unit of analysis consists of a group of individuals are larger than the same associations would be if the individual were the unit of analyses. So for instance, in this example the relationship between counties' wealth and voting trends is likely to be considerably stronger than that between individuals' wealth and voting records.

Sometimes it makes sense to employ multiple levels of analysis within the same study. Suppose, for instance, that we measured party preference and income for individuals. If we wanted to generalize about the relationship between these two variables to other individuals, we would want to treat individuals as the unit of analysis. However, we might also want to generalize the relationship to counties: Are wealthier counties more likely to vote Republican on average? In that case, we would want to compute the average income and party preference for each county, averaging across all the individuals within a county, and then relate the county averages of income and party preference, treating counties as the unit of analysis.

In fact, the issue of what is the appropriate unit of analysis is a much more complex subject than we have portrayed it, for it raises statistical issues that are beyond the scope of this book. The important point for our purposes is that generalization should always be at the same level as the unit of analysis. Hence, to define what constitutes the rows of the data matrix, we need to think about whether we wish to generalize to individuals, groups, nations, or whatever.

Defining Values for Variables

The cells of the data matrix contain the data that are to be analyzed. Returning to our example in which 1000 individuals were asked about political preferences, each cell contains information about an individual's response to a given question. Normally, those responses are coded in numeric form. Thus if the first question is which presidential candidate the respondent voted for in 1984, a response of "Reagan" might be coded as a "1," a "Mondale" response might be coded as a "2," and so forth, reserving a particular number, say a "9," for no response or missing data. Responses are coded numerically rather than as "Reagan," "Mondale," and so forth, because computerized analysis of the data is easier if they are in numeric form.

For some variables, the choice of numbers for different responses is arbitrary. For other variables the choice is not at all arbitrary. In the example of the previous paragraph, where the variable is presidential vote, the choice of numbers to represent the different candidates is purely arbitrary. A "Reagan" response might be coded as a "1" or a "2" or whatever, as long as we were consistent in our use of the values assigned to different responses. By consistent, we mean that if the "Reagan" response is coded as a given number, it is always given that value and no other response is given that value.

A consistent but arbitrarily defined coding scheme is used whenever the variable is measured on a nominal scale. Recall from Chapter 3 that measurement by a nominal scale means that responses can be sorted into different groups but that they cannot be rank ordered. Thus variables such as sex of respondent, hair color, and presidential vote can all be coded with arbitrary values.

Variables measured on ordinal, interval, or ratio scales cannot be coded arbitrarily. Since all these scales contain information about the rank order of different responses, at the least, that rank order must be preserved in the values used for coding responses. In addition, for interval and ratio scales, the units of measurement have meaning. Thus coding schemes must preserve not only the rank order of responses for variables measured on these scales but also the relative differences among responses. In addition, for ratio scales, zero has a meaningful definition, and hence the scale values are fixed or anchored there. Table 13.1 summarizes the types of numerical coding schemes that can be used for variables measured with different scales of measurement.

Let's illustrate each one. If we measure respondent's sex (a nominal variable), we could code males as 0 and females as 1. We could also code females as 0 and males as 1. As long as we use a coding scheme consistently, it makes no difference which numbers we use. For an example of a variable measured on an ordinal scale, suppose we had the rank order of the heights of 10 individuals. Thus we knew that a given person was, for instance, the third tallest, but we did not know how much taller he was than the fourth tallest individual. We could code the tallest person as 1 and the shortest as 10. We could also code the tallest as 100, the next tallest as 97, the next tallest as 86, and so forth. The only thing that matters is that we preserve the rank order in our coding scheme.

TABLE 13.1 Scales of Measurement and Permissible Coding Schemes

Variable's Scale of Measurement	Coding Scheme Requirements
Nominal	None: values arbitrary
Ordinal	Values must preserve rank order
Interval	Values must preserve rank order and unit differences
Ratio	Values must preserve rank order, unit differences, and fixed zero point

Now, suppose we knew how many inches separated everyone even though we did not know their actual heights. Our coding scheme would then have to preserve the *relative* differences between people as well as the rank order. Finally, when we know their height in inches, we have a ratio scale at our disposal and height should be coded as actual inches, with a fixed zero value and a meaningful unit of measurement.

The Code Book

As coding schemes are decided on and as the values in the data matrix are entered, it is essential that the researcher keep a record of the organization of the data matrix and of all coding decisions. This record, called the **codebook,** is needed to guarantee that in the future the coded data can be interpreted. All too often researchers fail to maintain an adequate and detailed codebook. As a result, when they attempt to return to a set of data after some interval, perhaps as short as a few days or weeks, they have a difficult time reconstructing what the numbers in the data matrix actually mean. Codebooks should therefore be complete and detailed. Further, multiple copies of them should be made and they should be stored in safe places.

To illustrate the essential ingredients of a codebook, we return to the data matrix example used earlier, where 1000 people were interviewed about their political opinions and actions. The codebook contains information about the columns of the data matrix. More specifically it identifies the variable that occupies each column and then defines the values used to code that variable. Suppose the first variable in the matrix is presidential vote in 1984; the next variable is respondent's age; the third variable is respondent's sex; the fourth is his or her party preference. Table 13.2 illustrates the essential components of the codebook for these four variables.

There are a number of things in this table that deserve comment. First, notice that variables can occupy more than a single column in the matrix, once a column is redefined as just a single digit wide.[1] Thus because age takes two digits it must occupy columns 2 and 3 in the matrix. If a respondent were only 9 years old, his or her age would be recorded as 09 to preserve the column location of all other variables.

Second, wherever there is the possibility of missing data, one or more missing data values are included. For most variables, only a single missing

---

[1] Earlier we said that a column was a variable wide, that is, that each variable occupied one and only one column. Now that we are actually coding the data, we have redefined a column of the data matrix as a single digit wide. Since some variables are coded with multiple digits, variables may now occupy multiple columns under this new definition.

TABLE 13.2   Codebook Example

Column	Variable	Values
1	1984 presidential vote	1 = Reagan 2 = Mondale 3 = Other 7 = Don't know 8 = Didn't vote 9 = No response
2–3	Respondent's age	18–95 99 = No response
4	Respondent's sex	1 = Male 2 = Female
5	Respondent's party preference	1 = Democrat 2 = Republican 3 = Independent 4 = Don't know or No response

value is necessary. However, there may be times when it is helpful to preserve information about why respondents failed to answer a question. Thus, for the first variable in Table 13.2, three missing data values are defined to differentiate between respondents who don't know for whom they voted, respondents who say they did not vote, and respondents who fail to answer for any other reason.

Third, it is important that the values used to code missing values be numbers or responses that could not occur naturally as legitimate responses on the variable. Notice that for the missing value on the age variable, this is not the case. The value of 99 is used to represent any missing data, and yet it is possible that a respondent may in fact be 99 years old. The value of 99 was chosen here as the missing value because it is sufficiently unlikely that a respondent would be that old. Should one be encountered, his or her age will be recorded as 95 rather than as 99. Thus the value of 95 in fact stands for any one whose reported age is 95 or more.

Once all the coding decisions have been made and a detailed codebook constructed, the data are then ready to be analyzed. Usually this means that the data are read into a computer, and computer programs to analyze the data are run. The data matrix may be read by the computer and stored by it in many forms. It may be key punched onto computer cards and then read via a card reader. However, key punching is relatively inefficient given recent advances in computer technology. More typically, the data are entered directly onto a computer disk (a part of the computer that stores data) from a computer terminal.

However the data are entered, it is essential that they be checked thoroughly and repeatedly for errors. To do this, it is sometimes most efficient to enter the data twice and then use the computer to check for inconsistencies between the two versions of the data matrix. Another way of checking for some types of errors is provided by most of the popular statistical analysis packages. Most of them permit specification of the possible values for each variable. The package then flags any values in the data matrix that do not conform. Of course, this type of checking will not flag a value that is an error but nevertheless is a valid value for the variable (e.g., a 3 entered as a 4, where both 3 and 4 are legitimate values for a variable).

Once the data are entered into the computer, analysis proceeds. Storage of the data on the computer is usually on disks or computer tapes, the latter being cheaper but also less efficient if continued access to the data is necessary. In addition to computer storage of data, the raw data (e.g., questionnaires or observational records) should be kept by the researcher in a safe place. Above all, the researcher should know where the data are, how they can be read by others, and what the values in the data matrix mean. Once again, we emphasize the need for a detailed and complete codebook.

Describing the Distributions of Variables

After the data have been collected and coded, social scientists turn their full attention to analysis and interpretation, a process consisting of a number of closely related operations. It is the purpose of analysis to summarize the completed observations in such a manner that they yield answers to the research questions. It is the purpose of interpretation to search for the broader meaning of these answers by linking them to other available knowledge. Both these purposes, of course, govern the entire research process; all preceding steps have been undertaken to make them possible.

However, one should not regard analysis and interpretation as simply the final steps of a linear process that beings with hypothesis generation, research design, and data collection. Research is actually a circular process, so that data analysis usually serves to stimulate further hypotheses to be tested. Data analysis is not necessarily a final boring task at the conclusion of a stimulating research project (although many people treat it that way). It can be a very creative and exciting enterprise, particularly when one encounters interesting and unanticipated results.

In the remainder of this chapter and the next two, we discuss data-analysis procedures, with the hope of not only teaching what those procedures are but also conveying to the reader why data analysis can be a creative and exciting enterprise. In the remainder of this chapter, procedures to describe the data for a single variable are discussed: What does the distribution of variable X look like? In Chapter 14, we discuss techniques used to explore relationships between two variables: How is variable X related to variable Y? Finally, in Chapter 15, we discuss techniques to examine the effect of third variables on the relationship between two others: What happens to the X: Y relationship when we hold a third variable, Z, constant? In all three cases, we attempt to explain why and when one would be interested in using the techniques described. That is, our goal is not only to describe the statistical procedures but also to discuss what kinds of questions the procedures can answer. By making clear how these procedures can be used to answer interesting questions about a set of data, we hope to convey to the reader an appreciation of the inherent interest that lies in data analysis. Analysis is fundamentally like a bit of detective work. Many potential answers to many interesting questions lie hidden in a set of data. The goal of analysis is to figure out what those data can tell us, what those answers may be, as well as to get them to pose new and interesting questions.

Data Displays

Table 13.3 presents a data matrix that we will be analyzing in this and the next two chapters. In these data, the unit of analysis is the state. For each of the 48 contiguous states we have values for each of three variables: 1979 birthrate (number of live births per 10,000 residents), 1979 marriage rate (number of marriages per 10,000 residents), and 1979 divorce rate (number of divorces per 10,000 residents). Obviously these three variables are measured on a ratio scale. Most of the techniques that we discuss in the remaining pages of this chapter assume ratio or interval measurement scales. These demographic data were gathered from the 1983 *Statistical Abstract of the United States,* compiled by the U.S. Bureau of the Census.

Suppose we had collected these data because we were interested in how birth-, marriage, and divorce rates varied across states and how they related to each other. The first thing we might want to do is look at the data themselves and see what they could tell us. Look at the data in Table 13.3. What impressions do you get from them? Other than seeing that marriage rates seem to be higher than divorce rates, and birthrates higher than the other two, it is hard to conclude much about these data just by scanning them.

A more useful procedure for examining a set of data is to draw a picture of them or, equivalently, to graph them. To do this for the divorce rate variable, we must first reorder the data so that they go from the lowest divorce rate to the highest. We then count the number of times each value occurs. Table 13.4 presents all the divorce rates that were in Table 13.3, reordered from lowest to highest, along with how frequently each divorce rate was observed in a state. Thus, for instance, only a single state,

TABLE 13.3 Marriage, Divorce, and Birthrates for 48 Contiguous States

State	Marriage	Divorce	Birth	State	Marriage	Divorce	Birth
Maine	109	56	149	W. Vir.	94	53	159
N.H.	102	59	145	N.C.	80	49	150
Vt.	105	46	152	S.C.	182	47	173
Mass.	78	30	122	Ga.	134	65	172
R.I.	79	39	128	Fla.	117	79	137
Conn.	82	45	124	Ky.	96	45	167
N.Y.	81	37	134	Tenn.	135	68	156
N.J.	75	32	132	Ala.	129	70	166
Pa.	80	34	135	Miss.	112	56	189
Ohio	93	55	156	Ark.	119	93	167
Ind.	110	77	162	La.	103	38	197
Ill.	97	46	164	Okla.	155	79	170
Mich.	97	48	157	Texas	129	69	190
Wis.	84	36	155	Mont.	104	65	179
Minn.	91	37	161	Idaho	148	71	221
Iowa	96	39	161	Wyo.	144	78	217
Mo.	109	57	157	Colo.	118	60	170
N. Dak.	92	32	179	N. Mex.	131	80	206
S. Dak.	130	39	189	Ariz.	121	82	191
Nebr.	89	40	167	Utah	122	56	301
Kans.	105	54	165	Nev.	1474	168	176
Del.	75	53	153	Wash.	120	69	164
Md.	111	41	140	Oreg.	87	70	165
Va.	113	45	148	Calif.	88	71	167

Massachusetts, had a divorce rate of 30 per 10,000 residents. Three states, however, had a divorce rate of 39 (namely, Rhode Island, Iowa, and South Dakota). The third column of Table 13.4 adds up the frequencies as we go from the lowest to highest values. Naturally the last number in this column must be the total number of states from which we have data. Rearranging the data from the lowest value to the highest and counting the frequency of each value is called a **frequency distribution.**

From frequency distributions it is easy to graph the data into what are called **frequency histograms.** We put the values along the horizontal axis, we put the frequencies along the vertical axis, and we draw a vertical bar or panel for each value to indicate how frequently it occurs. If we did this from the frequency distribution of Table 13.4, we would observe a lot of bars one unit high (i.e., one frequency), some two units, and a few three. In other words, the frequency histogram would consist of a bunch of small bars all spread out across the possible values. A more informative frequency histogram might result if we grouped values together in some way. Suppose, for instance, that we grouped together values from 30 to 39, 40 to 49, 50 to 59, and so forth. Such a grouping results in the fre-

TABLE 13.4 Frequency Distribution of 1979 Divorce Rate

Value	Frequency	Cumulative Frequency
30	1	1
32	2	3
34	1	4
36	1	5
37	2	7
38	1	8
39	3	11
40	1	12
41	1	13
45	1	14
46	3	17
47	2	19
48	1	20
49	1	21
53	1	22
54	2	24
55	1	25
56	3	28
57	1	29
59	1	30
60	1	31
61	1	32
65	2	34
68	1	35
69	2	37
70	2	39
71	1	40
77	1	41
78	1	42
79	2	44
80	1	45
82	1	46
93	1	47
168	1	48

quency distribution of Table 13.5 and the frequency histogram of Figure 13.1.

Notice that the horizontal axis in this graph is discontinuous at one point. In these data there is one very extreme value: Nevada has a divorce rate of 168 per 10,000, whereas no other state's rate exceeds 100. To include this extreme case in the histogram without this discontinuity, we could have drawn a very long horizontal axis, including all the possible values between 99 and 160, all with zero frequencies.

Instead, we chose to show a discontinuity in the axis. A case with an extreme value on a variable, such as Nevada on this variable, is known as an **outlier**. As we will see later on, outliers can have a disproportionate

TABLE 13.5 Grouped Frequency Distribution of 1979 Divorce Rate

Value	Frequency	Cumulative Frequency
30–39	11	11
40–49	10	21
50–59	9	30
60–69	7	37
70–79	7	44
80–89	2	46
90–99	1	47
160–169	1	48

and unfortunate effect on certain statistics that are computed on the data as a whole. Therefore, it is important to look for outliers and realize if they are unduly influencing the results of any analysis.

Frequency distributions and their associated histograms are useful for looking at the shape of a distribution of data on a variable. For instance, by examining the graphed frequency distribution, we can easily form some impressions about the variable. It seems as if the typical rate is somewhere in the range of 50 to 60. In addition the distribution appears to be sloping downward to the right. That is, there are a lot of states in the 30 to 50 range, fewer in the range of 50 to 80, still fewer from 80 to 100, and only a single one after that. Most of the states seem to be bunched in the 30 to 80 range, and those that do not lie in that range are all above it.

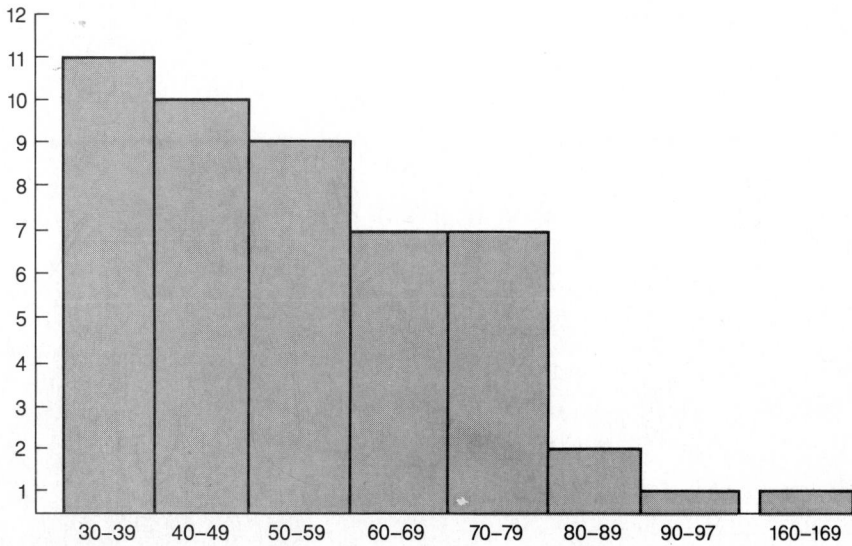

FIGURE 13.1 Grouped frequency histogram of 1979 divorce rate

Another procedure for graphing the data, invented by John Tukey, gives the same sort of information as a grouped frequency histogram, and in addition, it presents the actual raw data at the same time. This procedure is called a **stem-and-leaf diagram** and is illustrated for the divorce rate data in Table 13.6. A stem-and-leaf diagram is constructed as follows for these data. First, the first digits for all observed values are written in a column on the left side of the diagram. This column is called the *stem*, and in this case the numbers represent increments of 10 units. For each case, the second digit of that case's value on the variable is written to the right of its stem. This digit is called the *leaf*. Thus, the numbers in the first row in Table 13.6 tell us that one case had a value of 30 (stem of 3 and leaf of 0), two cases had the value 32 (stem of 3 and leaf of 2), and so forth. In this way, all the actual raw data for all 48 cases are contained in the diagram. In addition if we turn the diagram on its side, it has exactly the same shape as the frequency histogram of these data that was presented in Figure 13.1. Thus we can graphically examine the shape of the distribution from this diagram, while presenting all the raw data as well.

Descriptive Statistics

Although frequency distribution, histograms, and stem-and-leaf diagrams are useful in forming impressions about the shape of a distribution of data, we would like some more-precise ways of characterizing this shape.

TABLE 13.6   Stem-and-Leaf Diagram of 1979 Divorce Rates

3	0 2 2 4 6 7 7 8 9 9 9
4	0 1 5 6 6 6 7 7 8 9
5	3 4 4 5 6 6 6 7 9
6	0 1 5 5 8 9 9
7	0 0 1 7 8 9 9
8	0 2
9	3
.	
.	
.	
16	8

Central tendency of a distribution The first way we might like to characterize a distribution of data is by identifying what seems to be a typical value. In other words, we would like to find a single value that is in some sense the most typical or representative of all the observed values. Such a typical value is also called the *central tendency* of a distribution.

There are a variety of ways to define the central tendency. The two most frequently used definitions are the mean and the median. The **mean** is the average value of the variable, computed across all cases. It is defined by the following formula:

$$\overline{X} = \sum_{i=1}^{N} X_i/N$$

In this formula, $\overline{X}$ is the mean. the Σ simply means that we add up the values on variable X_i for each case, adding from the first case ($i = 1$) to the last case ($i = N$). We then divide that sum by the total number of cases, N. Using this formula for our divorce rate data, we compute the mean as

$$\overline{X} = 2748/48 = 57.25$$

where 2,748 is the sum of all the divorce rates contained in Table 13.3, and 48 is the number of states for which we have data. Thus, one way of identifying the central tendency of the distribution of the divorce rate variable is to say that the average or mean divorce rate is 57.25 per 10,000 residents.

Whereas the mean is defined as the average value of a variable, the **median** is defined as the middle-most value in a set of data. It is the value that separates the top half of the cases on the variable from the bottom half. The median is easily determined by counting cases, using the stem-and-leaf diagram of Table 13.6. To do this, we first have to divide the number of cases (N) by 2 and then take the number that the result of this division "grows to." *Grows to* is a fairly simple idea suggested by Tukey, the inventor of the stem-and-leaf diagram. Any number that is not an integer (e.g., 10.5, 10.01, 12.9) grows to the next highest integer. So 10.5 grows to 11 as does 10.01, and 12.9 grows to 13. Any integer grows to that number plus one-half, so 15 grows to 15.5, 20 grows to 20.5 and so on. Do not confuse *grows to* with *rounding* because they are slightly different.

In our example, when we divide 48 by 2, we get 24, which "grows to" 24.5. We now want to count cases in the stem-and-leaf diagram until we get to the 24th case. The median is the value that is halfway between the values of the 24th and 25th case. In the divorce rate data, using Table 13.6 and counting from the lowest value, we find that the 24th case has a value of 54; the 25th case has a value of 55. So the median for this distribution of data is 54.5.

So now we have two different ways to identify a typical value or central tendency for this distribution of data. The median value is 54.5 and the mean value is 57.25. You might wonder why these values differ, and since they differ, which one better represents the central tendency of the distribution. The answer to the first question is that they differ because they are two alternative definitions of the central tendency. The median is the "middle-most" value, obtained by counting cases. In finding this value, we don't care by how much cases are above it or below it; we simply want to find the value that separates the top and bottom 50 percent of the cases. The mean, on the other hand, is the average value. One way to think about what this average value means is as follows. Suppose we took all the cases that have values above the mean, and we added up how far they were above the mean. Suppose now we did the same thing for all cases below the mean: We added up how far they were below the mean. By the definition of the mean, it turns out that these two sums must exactly equal each other. So whereas the median is defined by counting cases, the mean is defined by taking into account not the number of cases above it or below it but the amount by which cases are above it or below it.

Which of these two measures of central tendency is preferable? The answer is that they are both useful. The mean is used more frequently, perhaps, primarily because it can be manipulated algebraically with greater ease than the median. As a result, the mean is used in computing many other useful statistics. A disadvantage of the mean, however, is that it is relatively less **resistant** than the median. That is, the mean is affected more than the median by relatively extreme values or outliers in a distribution of data. A single extreme case in a distribution can have a dramatic effect on the mean, whereas it may have little or no effect on the median. To illustrate, let's drop the outlier in the divorce rate data that we have been examining and recompute the mean and median. Recall that the state of Nevada, with its divorce rate of 168, was a clear outlier, that is, considerably different from all other states. If we delete Nevada from the distribution and recompute the mean and median, they turn out to be 54.89 and 54 respectively. Compare these values with the mean and median computed earlier and based on the full data set, including Nevada:

Including Nevada	Deleting Nevada
$\overline{X} = 57.25$	$\overline{X} = 54.89$
Median = 54.5	Median = 54

Clearly the presence of the outlier has a much larger effect on the mean than on the median. With the outlier deleted, the mean and median are in fairly good agreement about where the central tendency of the distribution lies.

Spread of a distribution   A second characteristic of a distribution that we might like to describe is how spread out it is. In other words, we might like to know whether the values are bunched all together around the central tendency or are relatively spread out and variable.

There are two ways to assess how spread out a distribution of data is. The first way is based on counting cases, just as the median is based on counting cases. This measure of spread, called the *interquartile range,* is defined as how far apart the 25th and 75th percentile scores are. What is a percentile score? The median is the 50th percentile score: It separates the bottom 50 percent of the distribution from the top 50 percent. So the 25th percentile score is that score that separates the bottom 25 percent of the cases from the remaining 75 percent, and the 75th percentile score is that score that separates the top 25 percent of the cases from the remaining ones. The difference between these two percentile scores is the interquartile range.

To compute the interquartile range on the divorce rate data, we need to compute the 25th and 75th percentile scores. To do this, we divide the total number of cases by 4 and then take the number that this result "grows to." In this case, $48/4 = 12$, which grows to 12.5. To get the 75th percentile score, we count down from the top of the distribution of data in the stem-and-leaf diagram and average the 12th and 13th values from the top. The 75th percentile score is thus 69—that is, $(69 + 69)/2$. The 25th percentile score is obtained analogously by counting up from the bottom of the distribution of data and averaging the 12th and 13th scores from the bottom. For these data, the 25th percentile score is 40.5—that is $(40 + 41)/2$. The interquartile range is the difference between these two values:

$$69 - 40.5 = 28.5$$

Since 25 percent of the cases have values less than 40.5 and since 25 percent of the cases have values greater than 69, the interquartile range defines the range within which lies the middle 50 percent of the distribution of scores. Clearly, if one distribution of scores is more spread out than another, the interquartile ranges will differ.

Notice that like the median, the interquartile range is a relatively resistant measure of spread. Since we are only counting cases in computing it, it makes no difference whether Nevada has a divorce rate of 100, 168, or 2000. It is still the case with the highest value and would appear in the highest 25 percent of the cases, regardless of its actual value. Hence, the interquartile range is unaffected by the extremity of such outliers.

The second way to assess the spread of a distribution of data is to ask how far, on average, the typical or average case is from the central tendency of the distribution. If, on average, cases have values quite discrepant from the center of the distribution, the distribution is more spread out or variable than if the cases are, on average, tightly bunched around the center.

To compute the average distance of cases from the center of the distribution, we might add up, for all cases, how far they are from the mean and then divide that total by the total number of cases:

$$\sum_{i=1}^{N} (X_i - \overline{X})/N$$

The resulting number would seem to be the average distance of cases from the mean of the distribution. Unfortunately, this nice intuitive measure of spread doesn't work. It will always equal zero for every distribution. Why? Think about cases that have values less than the mean. For them the difference $(X_i - \overline{X})$ will be negative. Cases with values above the mean will have positive difference scores. Recall that one way to think about the mean is as follows: If we took all cases above the mean and added up how far they are above the mean, that total would exactly equal the sum of how far the cases below the mean are from the mean. Hence, it is true that

$$\sum_{i=1}^{N} (X_i - \overline{X}) = 0$$

We still would like a measure of how far cases are, on average, from the mean, so we might decide to take the average of the *absolute* difference between each case's value and the mean:

$$\sum_{i=1}^{N} |X_i - \overline{X}|/N$$

where the vertical lines mean that we add up all the $(X_i - \overline{X})$ after having deleted all the negative signs. This, in fact, is a very adequate measure of how spread out a distribution of data is. It is the average *absolute* difference between the value of the typical case and the mean of the distribution. However, it suffers from one major shortcoming: Absolute value operators (i.e., the vertical lines) are not easily manipulated algebraically. Hence, we typically adopt another strategy to get rid of negative signs for those cases whose values are below the mean. What we do is compute the average *squared* difference between each case's value and the mean of the distribution. The result is called the **variance** of a distribution:

$$\sum_{i=1}^{N} (X_i - \overline{X})^2/N$$

Let's compute the variance for the divorce rate data, using the raw data from the stem-and-leaf diagram. We know that the mean value for all 48 cases is 57.25. For each case, we want to take the difference between that case's value and this mean, square the difference, and then total all those squared differences. Finally, we will divide the sum total by the number of cases:

variance $= (30 - 57.5)^2 + (32 - 57.5)^2$

$+ (32 - 57.5)^2 + \cdots + (168 - 57.5)^2/48 = 505.64$

What does this number mean as a measure of how spread out this distribution is? By definition, the variance is the average squared difference between the cases in a distribution and the mean of the distribution. It is how far, in squared units, the average case is from the mean. Because most of us have trouble thinking in terms of squared units, the square root of the variance is frequently used as a measure of spread. The square root of the variance is known as the **standard deviation** and is defined as

$$\sqrt{\sum_{i=1}^{N} (X_i - \overline{X})^2 / N}$$

For the divorce rate data, the standard deviation equals 22.49.

We now have two measures of how spread out a distribution of data is: the interquartile range and the variance (or equivalently, the standard deviation). The former is based on counting cases, much like the median is as a measure of central tendency. The variance, on the other hand, is based not on counting cases but on *how far* cases are on average from the middle of a distribution. Which of these two measures is preferable?

There is no simple answer to this question, as there was none in choosing between the mean and median as measures of central tendency. Like the mean, the variance or standard deviation is used as a measure of spread more frequently than the interquartile range. As we will see in the next chapter, the variance is used in computing other statistics concerning relationships between variables. However, the variance suffers from the same problem as the mean does: Relative to the interquartile range, it is not a very resistant statistic. It tends to be affected by outliers more than does the interquartile range. To illustrate, let's compute the interquartile range and the standard deviation for our data, first including and then deleting Nevada because of its relatively extreme divorce rate.

Including Nevada	*Deleting Nevada*
Standard deviation = 22.49	Standard deviation = 15.81
Interquartile range = 28.50	Interquartile range = 29.00

Clearly the effect of deleting the outlier is much greater on the standard deviation than on the interquartile range.

Other characteristics and other distributions One of the things we noticed earlier about the divorce rate distribution is that it generally sloped down and to the right when we examined the shape of the frequency histogram or the stem-and-leaf diagram. Whether or not a distribution has an especially long tail in one direction or another is referred to as the **skewness** of the distribution. A distribution that is skewed upward has more extreme high values than extreme low values. Its long tail is at the upper end. A distribution that is skewed downward has more extreme low values than high values. Hence its tail is at the lower end. A distribution that is completely symmetrical, with equally long tails at both its upper and lower ends, is not skewed. Figure 13.2 shows the shape of skewed and symmetrical distributions.

Although there are measures of degree of skewness in one direction or another, they are beyond the scope of this book. What is important to know is not how to measure skewness but how to label a distribution as skewed or not.

We have now discussed three major characteristics of distributions: their central tendency, their spread or variability, and their skewness. All three of these can be determined by examining the stem-and-leaf diagram for any distribution of data. So far, we have relied on the divorce rate data to illustrate these characteristics. You should now return to Table 13.3 and generate stem-and-leaf diagrams for the marriage rate and birthrate data.

As you do this, one thing will become immediately clear. If the state of Nevada is an outlier in the divorce rate data, it is even more so in the marriage rate data. Although the majority of the states have marriage rates per 10,000 residents in the range of 80 to 180, Nevada's marriage rate is 1474. Interestingly, however, Nevada is not relatively extreme on the birthrate variable.

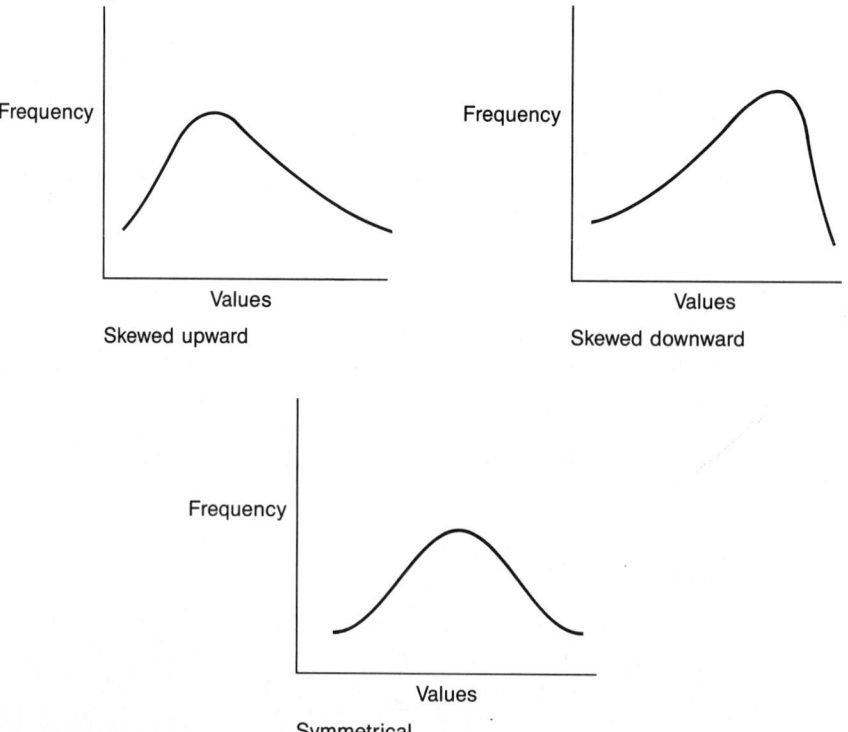

FIGURE 13.2   Distributions illustrating skewness

TABLE 13.7   Descriptive Statistics of States' Marriage, Divorce, and Birthrates per Ten Thousand Residents

Including Nevada

	Marriage Rate	Divorce Rate	Birthrate
$\overline{X}$	135.94	57.25	166.35
Median	105.00	54.50	164.00
Interquartile range	30.50	28.50	23.50
Variance	38,614.60	505.64	860.60
Standard deviation	196.51	22.49	29.34

Excluding Nevada

	Marriage Rate	Divorce Rate	Birthrate
$\overline{X}$	107.47	54.89	166.15
Median	105.00	54.00	164.00
Interquartile range	32.00	29.00	23.00
Variance	531.82	249.88	876.89
Standard deviation	23.06	15.81	29.61

Table 13.7 presents descriptive statistics for all three of the variables, both including Nevada in the distributions and deleting it. Using the stem-and-leaf diagrams that you have made for the marriage and birthrate data, you should make sure that you know how to compute all the statistics in Table 13.7.

Examining these statistics makes clear the undue influence a single case can have on some mesures of central tendency and spread when it is an extreme outlier. The effect of including Nevada in the marriage rate distribution is to increase the mean rate from 107.47 to 135.94. The effect on the variance is even more marked: from 531.82 to 38,614.60. Clearly, these two statistics are not resistant to the presence of this outlier. Notice, however, that the median and interquartile range are hardly affected. This should teach us a lesson: Look for outliers! When they are present, rely on the median and interquartile range rather than the relatively less-resistant mean and variance. If for other reasons, the mean and variance are to be used to assess central tendency and spread, then do so only after extreme outliers have been deleted from the distribution of data.

Summary

Once data have been collected, they must be put in a form to permit analysis. To do this a data matrix is constructed, the columns of which are variables, the rows of which are the units of analysis, and the cells of which are the coded raw data. All coding decisions should be recorded in a codebook. Above all, careful records should be maintained of the data matrix and how it was constructed. This permits the researcher who collected the data, as well as others, to use them in the future.

In describing distributions of data, we discussed how frequency histograms and stem-and-leaf diagrams permit us to form impressions about the shape of a distribution. The median is a measure of central tendency based on counting cases: It is the value that separates the top and bottom 50 percent of the cases. The mean is the average value of a distribution and, as such, takes into account not how many cases are below it or above it but by how much cases are below it or above. Measures of spread include the interquartile range, the variance, and the standard deviation. The interquartile range tells us the range of values within which the middle 50 percent of a distribution lies. The variance tells us how far on average cases are from the mean of the distribution, measuring distances in squared units. The standard deviation is simply the square root of the variance.

Throughout this chapter we have paid particular attention to the undue influence that outliers can have on particular statistics. We will continue to underscore that point in the next chapter as well.

Now that we have discussed procedures to describe the distribution of a single variable, we turn to procedures for examining the relationship between two variables.

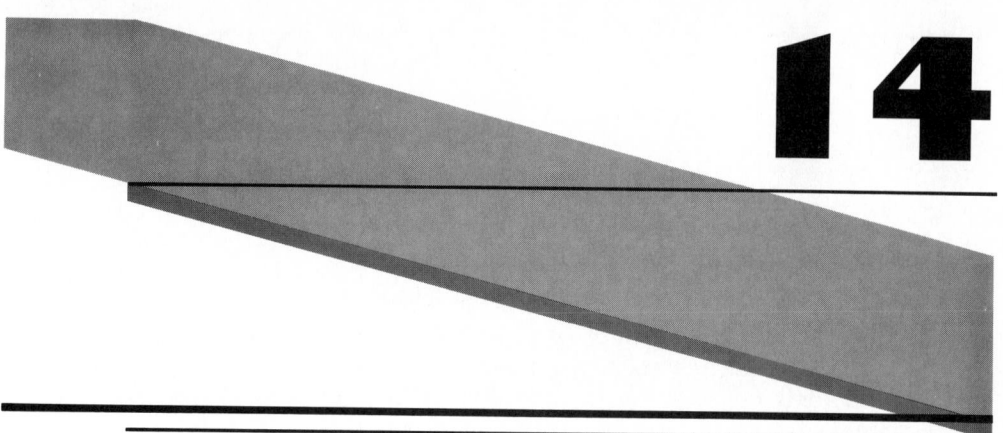

14

Describing Relationships between Variables

Most of the interesting hypotheses that social relations researchers examine concern relationships between variables. For instance, we may want to know whether political party affiliation is related to age; whether educational attainment is associated with subsequent earnings; whether birth-, marriage, and divorce rates are interrelated; or whether one personality trait is associated with another. When we analyze our data, then, not only do we want to describe the distributions of single variables, but we also want to describe relationships between two or more variables. In this chapter we discuss procedures for describing relationships between two variables. In the next chapter we bring in the further complicating factor of third variables.

Relationships between Dichotomous Variables

When we say two variables are related to each other, what exactly do we mean? What does it mean to hypothesize that marriage and divorce rates are related across states? To answer this question initially, let's simplify things considerably. Rather than having a whole range of possible values for marriage and divorce rates, let's make the simplifying assumption that these two variables can each take on only two values: high and low. In other words, the marriage and divorce rate data for any particular state will be recoded as simply relatively high or relatively low rather than as specific numbers per 10,000 residents. After we define what it means for two variables to be related in this simplified case, we will return to the original raw data.

In order to make our simplifying assumption that these variables have only two values (high and low), we have to translate the raw data from Table 13.3 into these new values. Since the median is the measure of central tendency that divides the cases in half, let us use the median to define the new values: Any state whose marriage or divorce rates exceeds the median will be coded as high on that variable. Any state with a value below the median will be coded as low. When there are states whose value is right at the median, we will arbitrarily decide to assign them to the high group.

Table 14.1 presents the recorded marriage and divorce rate data for all 48 states. With only two possible values for each of our variables, the variables may be called *dichotomous*. Now, how might we tell if the marriage and divorce variables are related?

TABLE 14.1   Dichotomous Marriage and Divorce Data for 48 Contiguous States

State	Marriage	Divorce	State	Marriage	Divorce
Maine	high	high	W. Vir.	low	low
N.H.	low	high	N.C.	low	low
Vt.	high	low	S.C.	high	low
Mass.	low	low	Ga.	high	high
R.I.	low	low	Fla.	high	high
Conn.	low	low	Ky.	low	low
N.Y.	low	low	Tenn.	high	high
N.J.	low	low	Ala.	high	high
Pa.	low	low	Miss.	high	high
Ohio	low	high	Ark.	high	high
Ind.	high	high	La.	low	low
Ill.	low	low	Okla.	high	high
Mich.	low	low	Texas	high	high
Wis.	low	low	Mont.	low	high
Minn.	low	low	Idaho	high	high
Iowa	low	low	Wyo.	high	high
Mo.	high	high	Colo.	high	high
N. Dak.	low	low	N. Mex.	high	high
S. Dak.	high	low	Ariz.	high	high
Nebr.	low	low	Utah	high	high
Kans.	high	low	Nev.	high	high
Del.	low	low	Wash.	high	high
Md.	high	low	Oreg.	low	high
Va.	high	low	Calif.	low	high

An examination of Table 14.1 reveals that states that have a low value on the divorce variable tend also to have a low value on the marriage variable. Similarly, states with a high divorce rate tend also to have a high marriage rate. Clearly, there are exceptions to this generalization: New Hampshire, Vermont, Ohio, South Dakota, Kansas, Maryland, Virginia, South Carolina, Montana, Oregon, and California are all high on one of the two variables and low on the other. But out of the 48 states, 37 of them are either high on both or low on both.

An easy way to display these dichotomous data for the two variables is by putting them into what is called a **contingency table.** To construct such a table, we lay out all the possible pairs of values that states might have on these two variables: high-high, high-low, low-high, and low-low. We make one variable, say divorce rate, the columns of the contingency table, and one variable the rows. There are thus two columns and two rows to the table, since each variable has only two possible values. We then count the number of states that fall into each of the four possible cells of the table. For instance, Maine is in the high-high cell, New Hampshire is in the low-high cell, and so forth. The resulting contingency table is presented in Table 14.2.

TABLE 14.2 Marriage by Divorce Contingency Table

		Divorce		
		Low	High	
Marriage	Low	18 37.5%	5 10.4%	23 47.9%
	High	6 12.5%	19 39.6%	25 52.1%
		24 50%	24 50%	48 100%

Eighteen states, or 37.5 percent of the total 48 states, are low on both variables. Five states (10.4 percent) are high on divorce and low on marriage. Six states (12.5 percent) are low on divorce and high on marriage. And finally 19 states (39.6 percent) are high on both. The other numbers in the contingency table, outside the numbers in the four cells just described, are called the *marginal frequencies*. They tell us how many states have a given value on one of the variables, forgetting about what their value is on the other. Thus, for instance, 23 of the 48 states, or 47.9 percent, are relatively low on marriage. The grand total number of states, 48, is indicated at the bottom right of the table.

The question of whether marriage and divorce rates are related in the 48 states is really a question about our ability to predict a state's value on one of the two variables from knowledge of its value on the other. In terms of the contingency table, the question of relationship between the two dichotomous variables is whether we can predict which column a state falls into once we know which row of the table it is in. Or equivalently, can we predict which row a state is in given that we know which column it is in?

If the two variables were perfectly related to each other, we should be able to predict perfectly columns from rows or vice versa. Thus states might all be low on both variables or high on both variables, and the low-high and high-low cells would have zero frequencies. A hypothetical perfect relationship between two dichotomous variables is illustrated in Table 14.3.

TABLE 14.3 Hypothetical Perfect Relationship between Dichotomous Variables *X* and *Y*

		X		
		Low	High	
Y	Low	10 50%	0 0%	10 50%
	High	0 0%	10 50%	10 50%
		10 50%	10 50%	20 100%

If two variables were completely unrelated to each other, it would mean that we could not predict rows from columns at all. Knowing which column a state falls in does not give us any information that can be used in predicting rows. A hypothetical set of data showing no relationship between two dichotomous variables is illustrated in Table 14.4.

Most contingency tables constructed with real data, such as our marriage by divorce contingency data in Table 14.2, show relationships in between the two extremes exemplified by the perfect relationship of Table 14.3 and the total absence of a relationship of Table 14.4. What we would like, therefore, is some way to index or assess *how much* of a relationship there is between two variables in a contingency table. If a perfect relationship means that we can predict perfectly rows of a table from columns, and if no relationship means that knowing columns gives no aid in predicting rows, it would seem that a measure of how much two variables are related might be developed by examining *how much* our predictions of rows improve when we know columns or vice versa. This is the rationale underlying a measure of relationships for contingency tables known as **lambda** (λ), developed by Goodman and Kruskal (1954).

To understand what lambda is, suppose in our data of Table 14.2 we wanted to predict whether some state, chosen at random from the set of 48 states, was high or low on marriage. If we knew nothing about that state's divorce rate, what is our best prediction about its marriage rate? Looking at the marginal frequencies on marriage, our best prediction is that a state chosen at random is in the high group. If we made this choice we would be right 52.1 percent of the time and wrong 47.9 percent of the time. Knowing nothing about a state's divorce rate, then, our best prediction about a randomly chosen state's marriage rate would be wrong 47.9 percent of the time.

If the two variables are related to each other, our ability to predict a state's marriage rate should improve once we know where it stands on the divorce variable. Suppose we again picked a state at random and tried to predict whether its marriage rate was high or low. This time, however, we know whether it is high or low on the divorce rate. What happens to the accuracy of our prediction? Looking at the table, if the state's divorce rate is low, we would obviously predict that its marriage rate is low since the

TABLE 14.4 Contingency Table Illustrating No Relationship between Dichotomous Variables *X* and *Y*

		X		
		Low	High	
Y	**Low**	5 25%	0 25%	10 50%
	High	5 25%	5 25%	10 50%
		10 50%	10 50%	20 100%

majority of the states in the "low" column are in the "low" row. On the other hand, if the randomly chosen state's divorce rate is high, we would obviously predict that its marriage rate is also high since the majority of states in the "high" column are in the "high" row. Given that these are our predictions, how accurate are they? By adding up the percentages in the cells of the table, we can see that we would be correct in our predictions 77.1 percent of the time and wrong 22.9 percent of the time. (These two percentages result from adding up the percentages in cells that we predict correctly, i.e., 37.5 percent + 39.6 percent = 77.1 percent, and the percentages in those cells that we incorrectly predict, i.e., 12.5 percent + 10.4 percent = 22.9 percent.)

To return to the question of how highly related these two variables are, we want to assess how much our predictions about where a state is on the marriage variable improve by knowing where it is on the divorce variable. Or alternatively, how much do our errors of prediction decrease when we know where a state is on the divorce variable? We have seen that if we do not know whether it is high or low on the divorce variable, our best prediction about whether it is high or low on the marriage variable will be wrong 47.9 percent of the time. If we do know its status on the divorce variable, however, our marriage prediction will be in error only 22.9 percent of the time. So our prediction error rate has decreased from 47.9 percent to 22.9 percent. Is this reduction a lot or a little? Well, it all depends on the magnitude of the original error rate, that is, the error rate when we don't know a state's status on the divorce variable. What we might like to answer is the following question: By what *proportion* does the prediction error rate decrease when we know a state's status on the divorce variable as compared to when we don't have that information? The answer is that our error rate decreased from 47.9 percent to 22.9 percent, and that decrease (47.9 − 22.9 = 25) is .522 of the original error rate (i.e., 25/47.9 = .522). This proportional reduction of errors of prediction is what is known as *lambda*. For our dichotomous divorce and marriage data, the lambda for predicting marriage category (high versus low) from a state's divorce category is .522. In other words, our best predictions about a state's marriage category are 52.2 percent better if we know its divorce category than if we don't.

Since lambda is a proportion, it varies between 0 and 1. The value of 0 indicates that knowing the value on variable X does not at all improve our predictions about variable Y. A lambda of 1 indicates that our predictions of Y are perfect when we know X. In between these two extremes, lambda tells us by what proportion our predictions of Y improve as a function of knowing X.

Let us review the general point here. We have argued that two variables are related to each other if we can use knowledge of one to predict the other. A little more exactly, we say that two variables, X and Y, are related if our prediction of a case's value on Y gets better when we know its value on X than when we don't. For contingency tables, lambda is a measure of degree of relationship since it tells us by what proportion our predictions improve or by what proportion our errors of prediction decrease. It is important to realize that lambda is not necessarily a symmetrical statistic. That is, the lambda for predicting Y from X is not necessarily the same number as the lambda for predicting X from Y. Nevertheless, its interpretation as the proportional reduction of errors of prediction holds in either case. You just have to be clear about what is being predicted from what.

Table 14.5 presents the three possible contingency tables among all possible pairs of our marriage rate, divorce rate, and birthrate data, having recoded states as high or low on each variable by whether their actual rate is above or below the median rate. For each table two lambdas are

TABLE 14.5 Bivariate Contingency Tables among Dichotomously Coded Marriage Rate, Divorce Rate, and Birthrate Data

		Divorce Low	Divorce High	
Marriage	Low	18 / 37.5%	5 / 10.4%	23 / 47.9%
	High	6 / 12.5%	19 / 39.6%	25 / 52.1%
		24 / 50%	24 / 50%	48 / 100%

lambda predicting marriage = .522
lambda predicting divorce   = .542

		Birth Low	Birth High	
Marriage	Low	15 / 31.3%	8 / 16.7%	23 / 47.9%
	High	8 / 16.7%	17 / 35.4%	25 / 52.1%
		23 / 47.9%	25 / 52.1%	48 / 100%

lambda predicting marriage = .304
lambda predicting birth   = .304

		Birth Low	Birth High	
Divorce	Low	16 / 33.3%	8 / 16.7%	24 / 50%
	High	7 / 14.6%	17 / 35.4%	24 / 50%
		23 / 47.9%	25 / 52.1%	48 / 100%

lambda predicting divorce = .375
lambda predicting birth   = .348

presented, one for predicting X from Y and the other for predicting Y from X. As we can see, all three variables seem to be related to each other at least moderately highly in dichotomous form. The strongest relationship of the three is between states' divorce and marriage rates.

In arriving at these conclusions, we have made the simplifying assumption that the variables each had only two values: low and high. This was done to simplify the explanation of what it means for two variables to be related. Now let's return to the actual raw data of Table 13.3 (p. 325) for these three variables and look at analogous procedures for assessing relationships between variables measured on interval or ratio scales. Bear in mind, however, that the preceding discussion of lambda was included not merely as preparation for what is to come in the next section of this chapter. Many, many variables in social and behavioral sciences are measured with nominal, or at best, ordinal scales of measurement. In such cases, relationships between variables are best assessed by examining contingency tables, as we have just done, rather than by using the techniques we are about to describe.

Relationships between Continuous Variables

Regression: Deriving Predictions of One Variable from Another

One way to think about a contingency table is that it is like a plot or a two-dimensional graph. To construct a contingency table we lay out the possible values of one of our variables horizontally and the possible values of the other variable vertically on a sheet of paper, and then we put each case in the appropriate cell of the table according to its values on the two variables. We can do the same thing with variables measured on interval scales. The only difference is that there is a very large, indeed infinite in theory, number of possible values a variable can take, and as a result, it is unlikely that any two cases have exactly the same values on the two variables. Hence, rather than counting frequencies in the cells of the table, we construct a table where each case is represented by a single point in a dimensional graph, positioned according to its values on the two variables. Such a graph is called a **scatterplot.**

Let's make such a graph for the raw data on states' divorce and marriage rates from Table 13.3. We will make the possible values on the divorce variable the horizontal axis of the scatterplot and the possible values on the marriage variable the vertical axis. To do this we must identify the lower extreme and upper extreme of the values that we need to include in order to represent all cases in the scatterplot. For the divorce variable, the lowest rate is 30 (Massachusetts) and the highest is 168 (Nevada). For the marriage variable, the lowest rate is 75 (both New Jersey and Delaware) and the highest is 1474 (again Nevada). Hence our horizontal axis needs to go from 30 to 168 and the vertical axis from 75 to 1474. Once the two axes are laid out, we draw a dot for each state in the graph, positioned so that its divorce rate is indicated by where it is on the horizontal axis and its marriage rate by where it is vertically.

In Figure 14.1, we have begun the process of making this scatterplot. You should take the data from a few states from Table 13.3 and attempt to plot them in this graph. It will quickly become apparent that the axes as presently drawn are not very useful for visually examining the relationship between the two variables. All the points, representing states, will be clustered in the lower left-hand portion of the graph, with one exception. The state of Nevada is positioned far away from the other points. What has happened is that when we include Nevada in the graph, the scale values of the axes must be so compressed that differences among the other states look to be inconsequential. An extreme outlier, such as Nevada is on

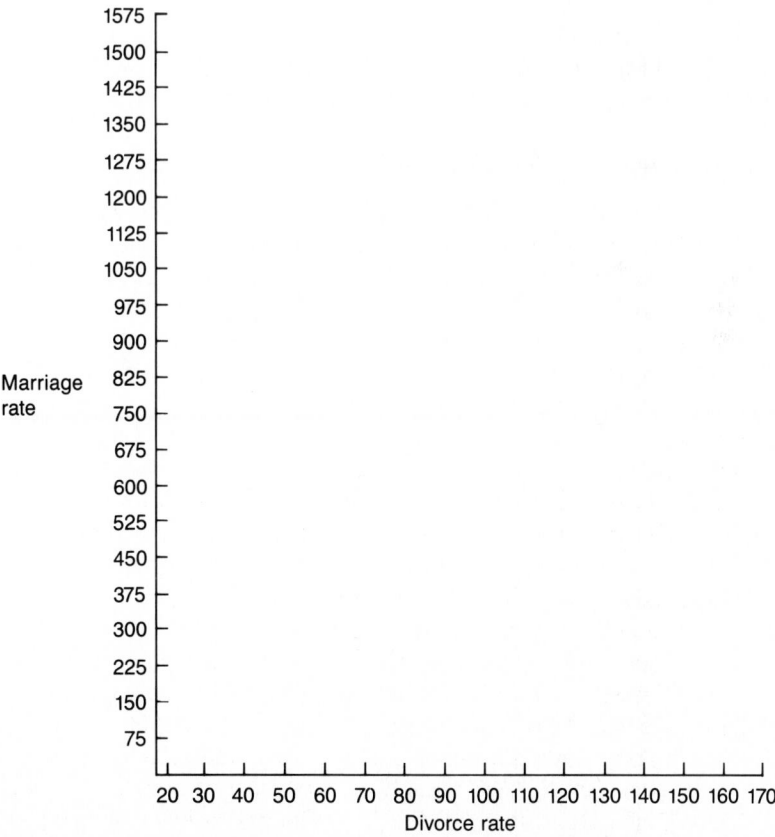

FIGURE 14.1 Scatterplot of divorce and marriage rates

these two variables, may make a scatterplot useless in examining relation-ships between variables and, as we will see, may greatly distort measures of association.

Why didn't this issue come up earlier when we were examining the relationship between these two variables with a dichotomous contingency table and lambda? The answer is that under the dichotomous recoding of the variables, Nevada appeared simply in the high category on both vari-ables. The fact that its raw values were considerably different from the raw values of other states in the high category was lost. The implication is that measures of relationship between variables are relatively more resistant to the effect of outliers when those variables are treated as if they were measured on a nominal or ordinal scale rather than an interval or ratio scale. In Figure 14.2 we have redrawn the scatterplot for these data, omitting the state of Nevada. Each point in this scatterplot represents a different state (if you count them, there are 47 points), and all the infor-mation about states' divorce and marriage rates that was presented in

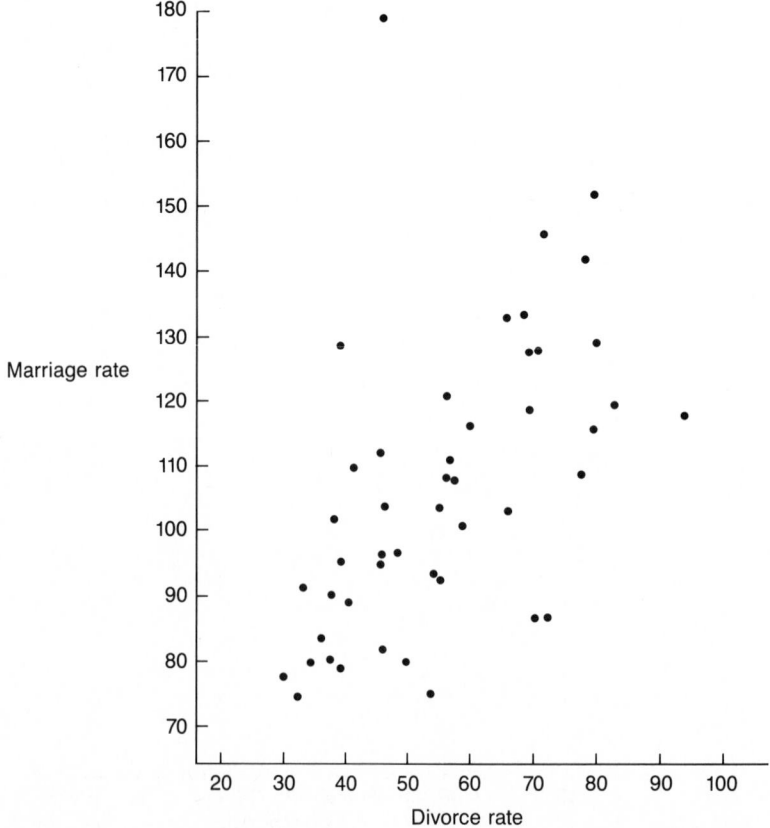

FIGURE 14.2   Scatterplot of divorce and marriage rates deleting Nevada

Table 13.3 is included. A relationship between two variables means that we can predict one from the other, so it would appear from this scatterplot that a relationship between the two variables exists. The points have a clear upward trend from the lower left of the plot to the upper right. Higher marriage rates seem to be found with higher divorce rates, and at the opposite end of the scatterplot, lower marriage rates seem generally to go with lower divorce rates.

In order to be more precise about predicting values on one variable from the other, we might draw a straight line through the points in the plot, so that the line summarizes the relationship between the two variables. We then could use this straight line to generate predictions of one variable from the other. In other words, once we had a straight line that summarized the relationship between the two variables, we could then predict a given marriage rate from a given divorce rate by seeing where points on that line were located on the vertical axis.

In Figure 14.3 we have taken the scatterplot for these data and drawn in a line by eye that seems to capture the relationship. To see how

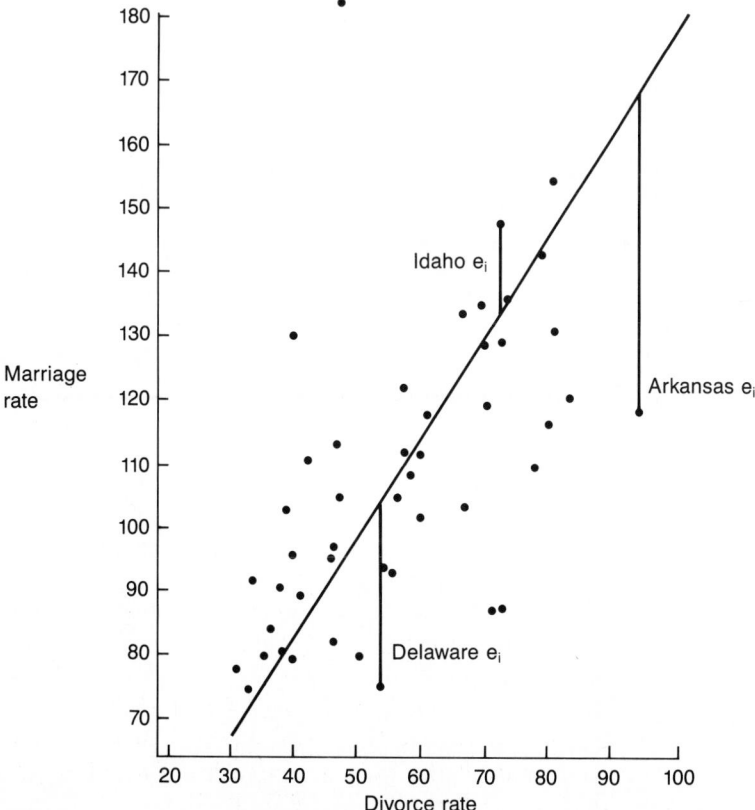

FIGURE 14.3 **Scatterplot and linear predictive function fit to the data by eye**

such a line can be used to predict values of one variable from the other, suppose we wanted to predict, in light of these data, what value on the marriage rate variable seems to go with a divorce rate of 60 per 10,000. We would go up from the horizontal axis at 60 until we hit our prediction line and then see at what value on the vertical axis we found ourselves. As this table shows, our predicted marriage rate would be about 115 per 10,000.

Of course a line is just one possible form that a prediction function could take. For some data, when we look at a scatterplot, it might appear that a curved rather than a straight line best summarizes the relationship between the two variables. By convention, however, we normally use a straight line as the prediction function, and thus we normally refer to relationships between variables as *linear* relationships.

Fitting a linear prediction function to a set of data by eye is not always an easy task. If you did so for these data, your line would probably agree fairly closely with the line we have fit by eye in Figure 14.3. However, for other data sets, where the relationship between two variables might not be as apparent, there might be much less agreement on where the line should go. One way of looking at how highly related two variables are, then, is to see how easy it is to draw a line by eye to fit the data points in a scatterplot.

Since there is potential for disagreement about where the line should be drawn, it would be nice if we could agree on a criterion for deciding what the best line would be to summarize a relationship. The essence of a relationship is predicting values on one variable from values on the other, so the best line would seemingly be the one that yielded the best predictions. Suppose, for instance, that we took the 47 states represented by points in the scatterplot of Figure 14.3 and attempted to predict each one's marriage rate from its divorce rate, using the line we have fit by eye to make our predictions. For instance, the state of Idaho has a divorce rate of 71. Using the line we have fit by eye to the data, what do we predict Idaho's marriage rate to be? Verify for yourself that we would predict the marriage rate to be about 130.

But of course, Idaho's marriage rate per 10,000 residents isn't 130; it is 148. Hence our prediction is in error. Using the prediction line of Figure 14.3, we have underestimated Idaho's marriage rate by 18 per 10,000 residents. Eighteen is the number of units on the vertical axis between the marriage rate we predict for Idaho, knowing that its divorce rate is 71, and Idaho's actual marriage rate. This difference represents an error in our prediction. It is also called a **residual.**

In Figure 14.3 we have shown the size of the residuals for three different states: Idaho, Delaware, and Arkansas. All these errors of prediction are vertical distances in the graph, representing the difference between the state's actual marriage rate and our prediction of its marriage rate, given the prediction line that has been fit to the data. If we define Y_i as the

ith state's actual marriage rate and $\hat{Y}_i$ as our prediction of the ith state's marriage rate, our error of prediction for this ith state, or its residual (e_i), is

$$e_i = Y_i - \hat{Y}_i$$

which is the difference between the actual marriage rate and our prediction of it from its divorce rate. Notice from this formula that these residuals, or errors of prediction, may be either positive or negative. For instance, for the state of Idaho, our predicted marriage rate ($\hat{Y}_i$) is less than Idaho's actual marriage rate (Y_i), so Idaho's residual is positive. On the other hand, for Delaware, our predicted marriage rate ($\hat{Y}_i$) is considerably higher than the state's actual rate, and hence the error of prediction, or residual, is negative.

To decide what might be the best line to describe the data in the scatterplot, it makes sense to pick the line that makes our errors of prediction for those data, that is, the residuals, as small as possible. To show what that means, we need to be slightly more formal. Recall from high school geometry that the equation for a straight line is

$$\hat{Y}_i = a + bX_i$$

In this equation we are saying that our prediction of marriage rate ($\hat{Y}_i$) is a linear function of the state's actual divorce rate (X_i), where b represents the **slope** of the line and a represents the **intercept.** The slope tells us how many units our prediction of Y changes for each unit increase in X. The intercept is the value of $\hat{Y}_i$ when X_i is zero. Hence it is the point on the vertical axis where the line crosses it. These two coefficients, the slope and the intercept, are all that are necessary to describe completely a straight line and hence to describe our linear prediction function.

As we said before, we want to pick a line that gives us the best possible prediction of Y from X. Therefore we need to choose as values of a and b, the intercept and the slope, those that make our predictions ($\hat{Y}_i$) for the 47 states as close as possible to the states' actual Y_i. In other words, we might choose values for a and b to make as small as possible the errors of prediction, or residuals, summed up across all 47 states. Hence, a rule for defining the best line might be

$$\text{Choose } a \text{ and } b \text{ so as to minimize } \sum_{i=1}^{N} (Y_i - \hat{Y}_i)$$

Unfortunately, although this seems like a nice idea, it doesn't work as a criterion for picking the best line. The reason it doesn't work is that some of the residuals are negative and some positive, as you recall. As a result, there are lots of possible lines where the sum of these residuals is zero. As we move the line around (i.e., change the values of a and b) the negative residuals may get more negative and the positive ones more positive, but their sum may still equal zero.

To avoid this problem, we might decide to choose a line so that the sum of the residuals is as small as possible, having gotten rid of any negative signs attached to these residuals. In the last chapter, when we were discussing how spread out a distribution was, we met a very similar problem. There we eliminated the negative signs by squaring the differences from the mean before adding them up to compute the variance. Here, we might follow a similar tack and decide to pick a prediction line that makes as small as possible the total *squared* errors of prediction or the total squared residuals:

Choose a and b so as to minimize $\sum_{i=1}^{N} (Y_i - \hat{Y}_i)^2$

This rule gives us a single line, and it turns out to be a very useful prediction function. When a and b are chosen in this way, the line

$$\hat{Y}_i = a + bX_i$$

is known as the **least squares regression line.** The word *regression* in this name is confusing, but the *least squares* part of it should not be. A prediction line chosen by this criterion gives us the "least" total of "squared" errors of prediction.

It is quite easy to show (although we will not do so) that the following formulas for a and b give us the least squares regression line for any set of data:

$$a = \overline{Y} - b\overline{X}$$

$$b = \frac{N\Sigma X_i Y_i - (\Sigma X_i)(\Sigma Y_i)}{N\Sigma X_i^2 - (\Sigma X_i)^2}$$

The value for a is easy to calculate once we find b ($\overline{Y}$ is simply the mean of the Y values; $\overline{X}$ is the mean of the X's). Calculating b may look difficult, so you should do it one part at a time. The first term, $N\Sigma X_i Y_i$, means that you should take each case, multiply its X and Y values, sum all these products, and then multiply the sum by N (the number of cases). The second term of the numerator, $(\Sigma X_i)(\Sigma Y_i)$, is very easy: Just add all the X values; then add all the Y values; then multiply these two sums. Subtract the second term $(\Sigma X_i)(\Sigma Y_i)$ from the first term $(N\Sigma X_i Y_i)$, and that is the numerator.

Now all that is left is the denominator. The first part, $N\Sigma X_i^2$, is calculated by taking each X value, squaring it, summing all the squared values, and then multiplying this sum by N. The second term, $(\Sigma X_i)^2$, is easy: Take the sum of the X's you calculated in the numerator and square it. Again subtract the second term from the first term, and that is the denominator. Divide the numerator by the denominator and that is b.

A simple example of this procedure is provided for the data shown in Table 14.6. As we show there, the linear prediction function

TABLE 14.6 Fitting a Least Squares Regression Line

Data

Case	X_i	Y_i	X_iY_i	X_i^2
1	5	1	5	25
2	4	3	12	16
3	3	2	6	9
4	2	5	10	4
5	1	5	5	1
Sum	15	16	38	55

$$b = \frac{N\Sigma X_iY_i - (\Sigma X_i)(\Sigma Y_i)}{N\Sigma X_i^2 - (\Sigma X_i)^2} \qquad a = \bar{Y} - b\bar{X}$$

$$= \frac{5(38) - (15)(16)}{5(55) - 15^2} \qquad = \frac{16}{5} - (-1.0)\frac{15}{5}$$

$$= 3.2 + 3.0$$

$$= \frac{-50}{50} = -1.0 \qquad = 6.2$$

Calculating Residuals

$\hat{Y}_i = 6.2 - 1.0X_i$

Case	$\hat{Y}_i$	$Y_i - \hat{Y}_i$	$(Y_i - \hat{Y}_i)^2$
1	1.2	−.2	.04
2	2.2	.8	.64
3	3.2	−1.2	1.44
4	4.2	.8	.64
5	5.2	−.2	.04
Sum		0	2.80

$$\hat{Y}_i = 6.2 - 1.0X_i$$

best fits the data in the table, according to the least squares criterion. Note that in this case, the slope is negative: As the values of X go up, the predicted values of Y go down. At the bottom of the table we have calculated the predicted Y for each case, by substituting X for each case in turn into the prediction function and solving for $\hat{Y}$. We then calculated the error of prediction or residual for each case $(Y_i - \hat{Y}_i)$, as well as the squared residual $(Y_i - \hat{Y}_i)^2$. The least squares criterion means that the sum of these squared residuals (in this case 2.80) is as small as possible. There is no other prediction line or values for a and b that will give us a number smaller than 2.80 for the sum of the squared residuals.

You should now try calculating a least squares regression line for some small set of data. Make up some values on X and Y for some small number of cases, just as we have done in Table 14.6. By the way, the least squares regression line that can be used to predict states' marriage rate from their divorce rate is

$$\hat{Y}_i = 61.90 + .83X_i$$

In other words, based on these data, we predict that as a state's divorce rate goes up 1 unit, its marriage rate increases .83 units, and if there were a state with no divorces, our best guess, based on these data, is that its marriage rate would be 61.90 per 10,000.

Remember that we left Nevada out of these data because, as an outlier, it might unduly influence our assessment of the relationship between these two variables. To make the point clear, the following least squares prediction function results if Nevada is included in these data:

$$\hat{Y}_i = -243.80 + 6.63X_i$$

Clearly, a single case, when its values are very different from the other cases, can have a major impact when it comes to examining relationships between variables.

Correlation: How Good Are the Predictions?

As we saw in the first part of this chapter, when dealing with dichotomously coded variables, in order to assess how related or associated two variables are, we need to examine how well we can predict the values of one of the variables given knowledge of the other variable. The least squares regression line gives us the "best" possible predictions of the values of one variable from those of the other. In order to measure how strongly related the two variables are, we want to examine how good those "best" predictions are.

With dichotomously coded variables, the measure of how highly related two variables are is called *lambda*. This statistic, we saw, has an intuitively appealing definition. Suppose we wanted to predict values on the variable Y from the variable X. With dichotomously coded data, lambda compares the predictions of Y we make with and without X. More specifically it tells us by what proportion our errors of prediction of Y are reduced when we take X into account, compared to the errors of prediction we would make ignoring X.

The same sort of statistic can be defined for measuring how related two variables are that have been measured on interval or ratio scales. What we want to do is compare errors of predicting Y when we do and do not use X to predict Y. Earlier, we defined the least squares regression line as the line that made as small as possible the sum of the squared residuals, or the sum of the squared errors of prediction:

$$\sum_{i=1}^{N} (Y_i - \hat{Y}_i)^2$$

These residuals are squared in order to eliminate the negative signs for those cases with values on Y below their predicted values. By definition, this sum measures the errors of prediction we continue to make, even when we make our "best" prediction of Y based on knowledge of X. Actually, because of the need to eliminate the negative sign, this sum measures the total *squared* errors of prediction we continue to make when we take X into account.

How large are the errors of prediction if we don't take X into account? To answer this question we need to figure out what would be the "best" prediction of Y for each case, given no information about X. In order to be right in the long run or on average, what value of Y would we predict each case to have, given that we possessed no knowledge of any other variable? In order to be right "on average," the answer is that our best prediction, given no information about the cases' values on X, is the mean of Y, $\overline{Y}$. Suppose, for instance, that we knew nothing about the states' divorce rates, and we simply wanted to predict each state's marriage rate. Clearly, in order to be right on average, we would want to predict the average marriage rate for each individual state, given no other information.

How good are these average predictions of Y given no knowledge of X? Let's add the errors of prediction across all cases:

$$\sum_{i=1}^{N} (Y_i - \overline{Y})$$

which is the sum of differences between each individual case's actual Y value and our "best" prediction, given no knowledge of X. Of course, as we have made clear, this sum is invariably zero, since by the definition of the mean, the negative values that are added are as large as the positive values. Hence once again, we square the difference between each case's Y and the mean before adding them:

$$\sum_{i=1}^{N} (Y_i - \overline{Y})^2$$

This sum represents the total squared errors we would make in predicting Y if we did not take X into account.

By how much do our squared errors of prediction decrease when we do base our predictions on X? Obviously, the answer is the difference between the squared errors of prediction without knowledge of X and the squared errors of prediction given X:

$$\sum_{i=1}^{N} (Y_i - \overline{Y})^2 - \sum_{i=1}^{N} (Y_i - \hat{Y}_i)^2$$

To make the final analogy to lambda, we now want to convert this difference to a proportion. By what proportion are the errors of prediction reduced when we base those predictions on X compared to not using X to predict values of Y? The answer is given by dividing the previous difference in squared errors of prediction by the sum of the squared errors of prediction given no knowledge of X:

$$r^2 = \frac{\sum_{i=1}^{N} (Y_i - \overline{Y})^2 - \sum_{i=1}^{N} (Y_i - \hat{Y}_i)^2}{\sum_{i=1}^{N} (Y_i - \overline{Y})^2}$$

As we indicate in this formula, this statistic is known as *r-squared*. It is a measure of how related two variables, X and Y, are, and its meaning is exactly analogous to the interpretation we earlier gave for lambda with dichotomous data. It tells us by what proportion our predictions of one variable improve when we base those predictions on knowledge of the other variable. As a proportion, like lambda, *r*-squared varies between 0 and 1.

Look at the preceding formula for *r*-squared. When will it exactly equal zero? Clearly only when the numerator equals zero. This will come about only if

$$\sum_{i=1}^{N} (Y_i - \overline{Y})^2 = \sum_{i=1}^{N} (Y_i - \hat{Y}_i)^2$$

In other words, *r*-squared will only equal zero if our "best" predictions based on knowledge of X are only as good as our predictions without knowledge of X.

When will the formula for *r*-squared equal 1? Another way to write the formula is as follows:

$$r^2 = 1 - \frac{\sum_{i=1}^{N} (Y_i - \hat{Y}_i)^2}{\sum_{i=1}^{N} (Y_i - \overline{Y})^2}$$

Clearly this will equal 1 only when the numerator of the fraction that is to be subtracted from 1 equals 0. That is to say that *r*-squared equals 1 if and only if our "best" predictions given knowledge of X are in fact perfect. That is, if all the residuals, and hence all the squared residuals or squared errors of prediction, exactly equal zero:

$$\sum_{i=1}^{N} (Y_i - \hat{Y}_i)^2 = 0$$

In Table 14.7 we show how to calculate *r*-squared for the data used as an example in Table 14.6. As you can see, once we have calculated the

TABLE 14.7   Computing r-squared: Data from Table 14.6

Case	X_i	Y_i	$\hat{Y}_i$	$(Y_i - \hat{Y}_i)^2$	$(Y_i - \bar{Y})^2$
1	5	1	1.2	.04	4.84
2	4	3	2.2	.64	.04
3	3	2	3.2	1.44	1.44
4	2	5	4.2	.64	3.24
5	1	5	5.2	.04	3.24
Sum	15	16	16	2.80	12.80

$$\hat{Y}_i = 6.2 - 1.0X_i \qquad \bar{Y} = 16/5 = 3.2$$

$$r^2 = \frac{\Sigma(Y_i - \bar{Y})^2 - \Sigma(Y_i - \hat{Y}_i)^2}{\Sigma(Y_i - \bar{Y})^2}$$

$$= \frac{12.80 - 2.80}{12.80}$$

$$= 10/12.80 = .78$$

sum of the squared errors of prediction given the least squares regression line, calculating r-squared is quite easy. For these data, r-squared tells us that our predictions of Y, based on X, improve 78 percent compared simply to predicting the mean of Y for each case.

Another way of thinking about what r-squared means is as follows. Suppose we divide both the numerator and denominator of r-squared by N, the number of cases. Of course, doing this doesn't change r-squared, since it amounts to multiplying r-squared by 1:

$$r^2 = \frac{\sum\limits_{i=1}^{N}(Y_i - \bar{Y})^2 - \sum\limits_{i=1}^{N}(Y_i - \hat{Y}_i)^2}{\sum\limits_{i=1}^{N}(Y_i - \bar{Y})^2} \times \frac{1/N}{1/N}$$

$$= \frac{\dfrac{\sum\limits_{i=1}^{N}(Y_i - \bar{Y})^2}{N} - \dfrac{\sum\limits_{i=1}^{N}(Y_i - \hat{Y}_i)^2}{N}}{\dfrac{\sum\limits_{i=1}^{N}(Y_i - \bar{Y})^2}{N}}$$

The denominator and the first term in the numerator of this new way of writing r-squared should look familiar. These terms are the variance of Y, that is, the average squared deviation of values on Y from the mean of Y. The second term in the numerator is also a kind of variance. However, instead of calculating the average squared deviation from the mean of Y, in this term we are calculating it from the predicted values of Y based on the least squares regression line.

It follows from this new expression for r-squared that another interpretation of r-squared is as follows: It tells us what proportion of the variance of Y can be predicted from or is associated with X. This interpretation for r-squared is used very frequently and will, in fact, be used in the next chapter extensively.

The square root of r-squared is what is commonly known as the **Pearson product moment correlation coefficient.** Although the correlation coefficient, r, is in fact reported more frequently than its square, r-squared, we prefer r-squared as a measure of strength of relationship between two variables. As we have seen, r-squared has a direct intuitive meaning based on the definition of a relationship between two variables as the ability to predict one from the other. The correlation coefficient, r, has no such intuitive definition. The following formula can be used to compute the correlation coefficient:

$$r = \frac{N\Sigma X_i Y_i - (\Sigma X_i)(\Sigma Y_i)}{\sqrt{N\Sigma X_i^2 - (\Sigma X_i)^2}\sqrt{N\Sigma Y_i^2 - (\Sigma Y_i)^2}}$$

Of course, if you have calculated r-squared, as we have recommended, then r is just the square root of r-squared:

$$r = \sqrt{r^2}$$

The only trick in calculating r this way is that r-squared has two roots: a positive root and a negative one. The sign of r, like the sign of the slope b, tells us whether X and Y are positively or negatively related. When b and r are positive, the points in the scatterplot tend to go upward to the right. With a negative relationship and negative values for b and r, the points tend to go downward to the right. So, although r-squared has a more intuitive meaning than r, the correlation coefficient does tell us about the direction of the relationship, whereas r-squared does not. But, then, if you've calculated the least squares regression line, as we have recommended, you already know the direction of the relationship by looking at whether the slope has a positive or a negative sign.

Returning once again to the states' data on birth-, divorce, and marriage rates, we can calculate the correlation, and r-squared, between each pair of variables:

Relationship between marriage and divorce rates: $r = .567$

$r^2 = .321$

Relationship between marriage rates and birthrates: $r = .504$

$r^2 = .254$

Relationship between birth- and divorce rates: $r = .347$

$r^2 = .120$

All three relationships were calculated by using the data from only 47 states, since Nevada's position as an outlier distorts things considerably, as we have seen. Notice that all three relationships are positive: States with higher values on one of the variables tend to have higher values on the others.

Relationships between a Continuous Variable and a Dichotomous One

We frequently encounter the case in which the two variables that are to be related are measured on different sorts of scales. For instance, one of the variables may be continuous and the other may be dichotomous, having only two values. In the example we have been exploring, suppose we had full information about states' marriage rates, that is, we knew the exact numbers, but for divorce rate we knew only whether a given state was relatively high or low. In this case we might think that the procedures we have presented for examining whether two variables are related might not work. Using a contingency table and calculating lambda clearly would not work since we cannot create a contingency table when one of the variables is continuous. We also might think that the use of regression and correlation for examining the relationship between two variables would not work, since those procedures are used when both variables are measured continuously. In fact, however, regression and correlation generalize to the case of one continuous variable and one dichotomous variable quite easily, as we will show in this section. In other words, the procedures developed in the last section of this chapter for assessing relationships between two continuously measured variables are also perfectly appropriate when only one of the two is measured continuously and the other is a dichotomy.

We want most frequently to examine the relationship between one continuous and one dichotomous variable in experimental and quasi-experimental research, so let us develop a new example with new data to illustrate the process. Suppose we were interested in different leadership styles in small working teams, and we wanted to see whether those different leadership styles affected the team's productivity (Lewin, Lippitt, & White, 1939). Suppose we had 10 teams, and in 5 of them leaders tended to be quite autocratic and directive, telling team members what they should work on, telling them how they should work, and setting work goals and schedules for the team members with little or no consultation. In the other 5 teams, leaders operated much more democratically, asking team members how they thought the work should be structured, who should work on what, and so forth. Now suppose each team worked for some number of hours at a given task, for instance, attempting to solve a series of logical puzzles, and at the end of that time we had a measure of how successfully each team had accomplished its task, that is, the number of puzzles correctly solved by each team. In Table 14.8 some hypothetical data that might have resulted from this study are presented.

Obviously we are interested in whether the teams who had one type of leader were more- or less-productive than the teams with the other type of leader. Another way of saying this is to say that we are interested in whether a dichotomous variable, namely, leadership style, is related to a continuous one, namely, team productivity in these data. Or to phrase the same question yet again in the language of prediction developed in this chapter, we want to know whether we can predict a team's performance with any success based on knowledge of that team's leadership style.

To answer this question, we can use the regression and correlation procedures developed in the last section. That is, we are going to calculate the least squares regression equation for predicting team productivity from leadership style in these data and then we will calculate r-squared to examine the question of whether our predictions are any better because we have based them on knowledge of leadership style. The only difficulty in using this approach is that we must code our leadership style variable numerically in order to compute the intercept and slope in the regression equation. A frequently used convention for coding a dichotomous variable like leadership style is to use **dummy variable** coding. We arbitrarily assign a value of 1 to one level of the variable and a value of 0 to the other level. For instance, in the example, we would create a variable representing leadership style. Let us call it X since it is the variable we will be predicting from. If leadership style is democratic, we will define X equal to 1. If leadership style is autocratic, we will define X equal to 0.

For each of our 10 teams we now have values on two variables, productivity and leadership style, with the former continuously measured and the latter being a dummy variable that codes a dichotomous distinction. We can now proceed to use the formulas presented in the last section of this chapter for predicting one variable from another, in this case for

TABLE 14.8 Hypothetical Data from Study of Leadership Styles and Team Productivity

	Number of Puzzles Solved by	
Autocratic Teams		**Democratic Teams**
8		10
10		12
7		9
11		11
12		13
Mean 9.6		11.0

TABLE 14.9 Computation of Least Square Intercept and Slope for Team Example: Predicting Productivity from a Dichotomous Leadership Style Variable

	Y_i (Productivity)	X_i (Leadership style: 0 = autocratic 1 = democratic)
	8	0
	10	0
	7	0
	11	0
	12	0
	10	1
	12	1
	9	1
	11	1
	13	1
Mean	10.3	0.5

$$b = \frac{N\Sigma X_i Y_i - (\Sigma X_i)(\Sigma Y_i)}{N\Sigma(X_i^2) - (\Sigma X_i)^2} = \frac{10(55) - 103(5)}{10(5) - 25} = 1.4$$

$$a = \overline{Y} - b\overline{X} = 10.3 - 1.4(.5) = 9.6$$

predicting team productivity from the dummy coded leadership style variable.

If we solve for the slope and the intercept with the two formulas presented earlier, we get the following least squares regression equation:

$$\hat{Y}_i = 9.6 + 1.4X_i$$

The data, including values on X, and the formulas used to compute the values in this regression equation are all contained in Table 14.9. Look over the computations there to refresh yourself on the formulas used.

Recall for a minute what this regression equation tells us. What we are doing here is generating a predicted value for each team's productivity, based on knowledge of that team's leadership style, in such a way that our squared errors of prediction are made as small as possible. The value 9.6 is the intercept in this regression equation and it tells us what the predicted productivity level is when leadership style, X, is set equal to 0. The value 1.4 is the slope, and it tells us by how much our prediction of productivity changes as X changes one unit, from 0 to 1.

According to this regression equation, for teams with an autocratic leadership style, when X equals 0, our best prediction of their productivity is 9.6:

$$\hat{Y}_i = 9.6 + 1.4(0) = 9.6 \text{ for autocratic teams}$$

For democratically led teams, our best prediction of their productivity is 11.0:

$\hat{Y}_i = 9.6 + 1.4(1) = 11.0$ for democratic teams

Notice that these two values are the means or averages for the two groups of teams presented in Table 14.8. That is, our best prediction for the productivity of the autocratic teams based on knowledge of their leadership style is the mean productivity of those teams. Likewise, our best prediction for the democratic teams is the mean productivity for the five teams with a democratic leadership style. This is a very important conclusion that bears repeating. When we are predicting the values of a continuous variable based on knowledge of a dichotomous variable, the least squares predicted values will always be the two group means on the continuous variable, where the groups are defined by the dichotomous variable that is the basis of prediction. If we want to predict team productivity from knowledge of two kinds of leadership style, our best predictions are the mean productivities of the two groups of teams.

Our next task is to evaluate how good these predictions are. Recall that we do this by examining relative errors of prediction. That is, we ask the following question: By what proportion are our errors of prediction reduced when we use X to predict Y as compared to the case where our predictions are not made on the basis of X? The statistic that we have labeled r-squared gives us the answer to this question. Once again, r-squared is defined by the following formula:

$$r^2 = \frac{\sum\limits_{i=1}^{N} (Y_i - \overline{Y})^2 - \sum\limits_{i=1}^{N} (Y_i - \hat{Y}_i)^2}{\sum\limits_{i=1}^{N} (Y_i - \overline{Y})^2}$$

In the case at hand, the predicted values of productivity given knowledge of leadership style, that is, the $\hat{Y}_i$'s in this equation, are the two means on productivity from the two types of teams ($\overline{Y}_t$). So this formula for r-squared in this case where we are predicting from a dichotomous X variable takes on the following equivalent form:

$$r^2 = \frac{\sum\limits_{i=1}^{N} (Y_i - \overline{Y})^2 - \sum\limits_{i=1}^{N} (Y_i - \overline{Y}_t)^2}{\sum\limits_{i=1}^{N} (Y_i - \overline{Y})^2}$$

The value of r-squared for our example is computed in Table 14.10. The interpretation of the resulting value is as follows: By knowing whether a team has an autocratic or a democratic leadership style, we can improve our predictions of the team's productivity by 15 percent over our

TABLE 14.10 Computing r-squared: Team Example

Case	X_i	Y_i	$\hat{Y}_i$	$(Y_i - \hat{Y}_i)^2$	$(Y_i - \bar{Y})^2$
1	0	8	9.6	2.56	5.29
2	0	10	9.6	.16	.09
3	0	7	9.6	6.76	10.89
4	0	11	9.6	1.96	.49
5	0	12	9.6	5.76	2.89
6	1	10	11.0	1.00	.09
7	1	12	11.0	1.00	2.89
8	1	9	11.0	4.00	1.69
9	1	11	11.0	0.00	.49
10	1	13	11.0	4.00	7.29
Sum	5	103	103	27.20	32.10

$$\hat{Y}_i = 9.6 + 1.4X_i \qquad \bar{Y} = 103/10 = 10.3$$

$$r^2 = \frac{\Sigma(Y_i - \bar{Y}_i)^2 - \Sigma(Y_i - \hat{Y}_i)^2}{\Sigma(Y_i - \bar{Y})^2}$$

$$= \frac{32.10 - 27.20}{32.10} = .15$$

best predictions if we do not know the team's leadership style. Since our best prediction given knowledge of leadership style is the mean productivity for each of the two types of teams, this interpretation can also be made as follows: Suppose for each team we predicted its productivity as the mean productivity for teams having the same kind of leadership style. The resulting predictions would be 15 percent better than simply predicting for each team the overall mean productivity for teams, not taking into account their different leadership styles.

It should be apparent from these interpretations that as the difference between the two means for the two groups of teams increases, other things held constant, the value of r-squared will increase. That is, as the two kinds of teams are more and more different in their average productivity, the value of r-squared will increase; r-squared in this case then tells us about the difference between the two mean values of productivity for the two groups of teams. As the two groups of teams differ more and more in their mean productivity, other things held constant, we would expect the value of r-squared to increase since relative to the overall mean the two means from the two groups of teams would be much better predictions.

The other thing that affects the value of r-squared in this case is the variability of productivity between different teams all having the same leadership style. Holding constant the difference between the two means of these two groups of teams, as the productivity of teams within each

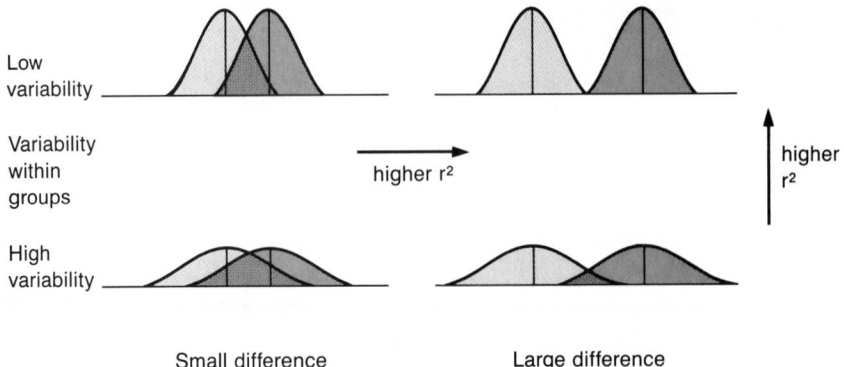

Differences in Means between Groups

FIGURE 14.4 Illustrating factors that effect r^2 in the case of the relationship between continuous and dichotomous variables

group is more and more variable, using the mean from the two groups of teams as our best prediction does not result in particularly good predictions. We still may miss the productivity of individual teams by a fair margin, even knowing the kind of leadership style a team has.

Thus, the value of r-squared in this case is affected by two things: the difference between the means for the two groups of teams and the variability in productivity between teams having the same type of leadership style. As the mean productivity for the autocratic teams increasingly differs from the mean productivity for the democratic teams, r-squared will get larger, other things held constant. As the variance of productivity within the two groups of teams increases, that is, as productivity becomes more variable among teams having the same leadership style, r-squared gets smaller, again with other things held constant. Figure 14.4 presents four cases in which the value of r-squared would be either relatively high or low, as defined by these two factors.

Inferring Relationships in Populations from Sample Data

We now have discussed procedures for examining how highly related two variables are in three different cases. In all three cases, our strategy has been to talk about the magnitude of relationships by asking how well we can use one variable to predict values on the other. The three cases have been defined by how the variables were measured. With two dichotomously measured variables, we calculate our relative ability to predict one from the other by using lambda. With two continuous variables, we use r-

squared, which although different computationally from lambda, is identically interpreted as the proportional reduction in errors of prediction. Finally, in the case of one continuous and one discrete variable, we can continue to use r-squared in talking about our ability to predict the continuous variable from the dichotomous one. In this case, we can think of the dichotomous variable as defining two groups of observations. When we predict values on the continuous variable from knowledge of the dichotomous one, our predictions are the means from the two groups of observations. Hence r-squared tells us in this case about the relative difference between the two group means. A large r-squared tells us the two group means on the continuous variable are relatively more different than a smaller r-squared.

Beyond simply calculating the magnitude of a relationship in some sample of data, we frequently want to ask questions about what that relationship tells us about the population of observations from which we have drawn a sample. This brings us back to some fundamental notions of sampling that were introduced in Chapter 7. Recall that the population consists of all those objects, elements, or individuals that we would like to be able to talk about or generalize our results to. In the case of political opinion polling, the population is likely to consist of all voting age citizens of the country. Because it is inefficient to gather data from the entire population, we proceed to use a sample, gathering data from a sample of respondents drawn from the population of interest.

In light of this need to generalize from our samples to populations of interest, we frequently want to know whether an observed relationship between two variables in a sample of data can be generalized to the population from which that sample has been drawn. In other words, just because we calculate in some set of data that X and Y are related and that the value of r-squared is, perhaps, .42, does that mean we can necessarily conclude that if we gathered data on X and Y from the entire population, we would continue to find a relationship in the population? Can we infer a population relationship from the observation of one in a sample of data? That is the question to be answered in this section. We will confine ourselves to inferences about relationships that have been calculated by using r-squared. We will not discuss inferences from sample relationships to populations with lambda, although such procedures are routinely covered in introductory statistics textbooks.

The logic of statistical inference starts with what is called a **null hypothesis**, a hypothesis that specifies what we hope is *not* true in the population. In the case of a relationshp between two variables, we usually want to argue for theoretical reasons that two variables are related to each other. That is, based on an r-squared that we calculate from some sample of observations, we hope to be able to conclude that the two variables are related not only in the sample but also in the population from which the sample was drawn. Therefore our null hypothesis would be that the two variables are unrelated in the population or, in other words, that the value of r-squared in the population, if we could measure X and Y for everyone, is zero. By looking at our sample data we hope to be able to conclude that this null hypothesis is in error.

It probably seems odd that when interested in one hypothesis (that two variables are related), we start with its opposite in statistical inference (that they are unrelated). But the reason is not too difficult to follow. There is a direct analogy with criminal trials. A jury must make a decision whether or not a defendant is guilty of the crime of which he or she is accused. Before the trial begins and any arguments or evidence is heard, the defendant is entitled in the U.S. legal system to a "presumption of innocence," that the defendant did not commit the crime. The prosecutor would like the hypothesis of "guilty" confirmed by the jury, but the prosecutor must provide enough evidence to overrule this presumption of innocence beyond a reasonable doubt. Our legal system recognizes that it is not possible to prove the lack of innocence (i.e., the guilt) of a defendant conclusively, without any doubts whatsoever. So the requirement is that the prosecution must prove guilt beyond a reasonable doubt.

Social scientists are engaged in a task quite analogous to that of the prosecutor. When they collect data from a sample, they wish to conclude that the hypothesis that motivated the research is correct (i.e., that two variables are related). So they start out with the presumption that their hypothesis is not true (the null hypothesis). They must then demonstrate, based on their sample of data, that this presumption is unlikely to be true in the population. Only then can they have reasonable confidence that their research hypothesis is in fact true in the population. Just as in the courtroom analogy, there will always remain the possibility that they have reached the wrong conclusion.

The null hypothesis of no relationship between two variables is either in fact true in the population or it is not. That is, if we could gather data from everyone in the population we would either find a relationship or we would not. In the latter case the null hypothesis would be true; in the former it would not. Based on our sample data we are going to attempt to decide whether or not the null hypothesis ought to be rejected as false. That is, we are going to attempt to distinguish between the two states of reality in the population (null hypothesis in fact true or false) on the basis of our sample data. The two states of reality and the two possible conclusions we can reach based on our sample data set up the decision matrix presented in Table 14.11. The columns of this matrix represent the states of reality. The rows of the matrix represent the decision we will reach. The cells of the matrix, defined by the intersections of rows and columns, inform us about the quality of our decision. Two cells, the upper left and lower right, tell us that we have made the correct decision. In the former, the null hypothesis is in fact true; that is, the two variables are not in fact related, and on the basis of our sample data we have decided not to reject

TABLE 14.11   Statistical Inferences Decision Matrix

	Null Hypothesis in Fact True	Null Hypothesis in Fact False
Decide not to reject null hypothesis	correct	Type II error
Decide to reject null hypothesis	Type I error	correct

the null hypothesis. In the lower right-hand cell, the null hypothesis is in fact false; that is, the two variables are in fact related in the population, and we have decided, based on the sample data, to reject the null hypothesis.

If we wind up in the other two cells of the decision matrix we have reached an erroneous conclusion. In the lower left-hand cell we have made what is called a **Type I** error. As defined by the row and column of this cell, we can see from the matrix that we have decided to reject the null hypothesis of no relationship in the population erroneously when in fact there is no relationship. In other words our sample data have led us to conclude that there probably is a relationship when in fact there is none. The other erroneous cell of the matrix defines what is called a **Type II** error. Here, if we wind up in the upper right-hand cell, we have failed to reject the null hypothesis based on our sample data when in fact that null hypothesis is false and should have been rejected. In other words, we fail to realize that X and Y are related in the population when in fact they are. We fail to realize that the hypothesis that motivated the research in the first place is right when in fact it is.

Now that we have defined the decision to be made and the possible outcomes of that decision, let us proceed to examine how the decision is to be made. Remember we start with the null hypothesis as the presumption, much like the jury is supposed to start with the presumption of innocence. Only if the evidence encountered subsequently is sufficiently compelling or surprising will we want to abandon this presumption. Let us then assume that the presumption of no relationship in the population is correct. Under this presumption, what would constitute compelling or surprising evidence in our sample? In other words, what sort of results in our sample would be sufficiently compelling to cause us to abandon the null hypothesis? If we drew out a random sample of 10 cases and we observed a value of r-squared of .01 (the correlation, r thus equals .10), would that constitute sufficiently compelling evidence to cause us to abandon our presumption of no relationship? What if we drew out a random sample of size 10 and the sample value of r was .80; would that be sufficiently compelling?

Fortunately, the answer to this question of what constitutes surprising sample results if the null hypothesis of no relationship is true has been worked out by statisticians. They have told us that if there is no relation-ship between X and Y in the population from which we draw a sample of size n, the probability of observing sample values of the correlation coef-ficient, r, is given by what is called a t distribution. Such a distribution for the case when n equals 100 is given in Figure 14.5. For this t distribution, values of t greater than 2.00 or less than -2.00 are obviously quite unusual. In fact they occur less than 5 percent of the time. Such values are probably sufficiently surprising or compelling to cause us to reject the null hypothesis. In other words, if the null hypothesis were true and we observed a correlation coefficient from a sample that was way out in the tails of the t distribution, we would certainly think that such an extreme value was quite surprising. In fact we might even decide that it was suf-ficiently surprising to cause us to doubt the null hypothesis, since such an extreme value for the sample correlation coefficient is much more likely to occur if the relationship in the population is something other than zero.

In order to make use of the t distribution, we need to convert the sample correlation coefficient, that is, the square root of the sample r-squared, to a t statistic. The following formula does just that:

$$t_{n-2} = \frac{r\sqrt{N-2}}{\sqrt{1-r^2}}$$

If the t statistic that results is larger than 2 or smaller than -2, given a sample size greater than about 50, the sample value of r-squared is gen-erally considered sufficiently surprising to cause us to doubt the null hypothesis. In other words, in such cases, since the sample value of r-squared would occur only less often than 1 time in 20 if the null hypothesis of no relationship were true, we generally conclude that such a sample value constitutes evidence sufficient to reject the null hypothesis "beyond a reasonable doubt."

Let us illustrate the procedure here with two examples used earlier in this chapter. First, we saw that the value of r-squared when we looked at the relationship between states' marriage and divorce rates is .321, and the square root of this value, the correlation coefficient, equals .567. The

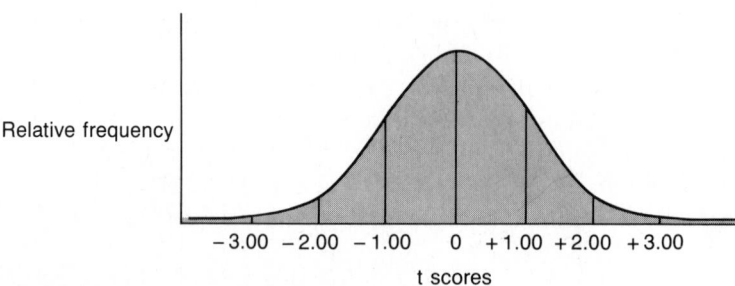

Relative frequency

-3.00 -2.00 -1.00 0 $+1.00$ $+2.00$ $+3.00$

t scores

FIGURE 14.5 A t distribution

data for this correlation came from all 47 contiguous U.S. states, with the exception of Nevada, from the year 1979. We now want to know whether we can conclude from this correlation that the relationship between marriage and divorce rates is a statistically reliable one. In other words we want to determine if from this sample of data we can conclude that the two variables are related in the population.

The notion of a population in this case is admittedly a little strange since the data from the 47 states constitute nearly the complete set of data for that given year. Nevertheless, we can still ask the question about whether this relationship is different from zero in the population, recognizing that this population is in some sense a hypothetical entity. Our real question here is whether this correlation between the two variables would hold up if we did the study over and over again, from many different years and conceivably using different subsamples of states. In a formal sense the population remains undefined, yet we still want to know whether the relationship between the two variables we observe in our data is a reliable one, one we can count on and expect to see again, using data from future years and other samples of states.

To decide whether we can reject the null hypothesis of no relationship, we need to convert the sample correlation coefficient, .567, to a t statistic. Using the previous formula, we get

$$t_{45} = \frac{.567 \sqrt{45}}{\sqrt{1 - .567^2}} = 4.62$$

The resulting t is clearly greater than 2. Hence if the null hypothesis of no relationship in the hypothetical population were true, we would expect to observe a sample correlation coefficient this large substantially less often than 1 time in 20. Since we have defined a surprising bit of evidence against the null hypothesis as evidence that would occur less often than 1 time in 20 if the null hypothesis were true, this constitutes surprising evidence and we decide that the null hypothesis of no relationship probably is not true.

Just as in the criminal trial analogy, there is, of course, no guarantee that we have reached the right verdict. It is entirely possible that the null hypothesis is in fact true and that we have simply observed a rare or unusual sample value of the correlation coefficient, one that converts to a t statistic greater than 2.00. Since we have defined a surprising sample result as one that would occur less often than 1 time in 20 if the null hypothesis were true, the probability that in fact such a surprising bit of evidence occurs when the null hypothesis is true is 1 in 20. In other words, once we decide to reject the null hypothesis as a result of observing a sample value of the correlation coefficient, or equivalently, r-squared, that would occur less often than 1 time in 20 if the null hypothesis were true, we are risking a 1 in 20 probability of a Type I statistical error. The odds are in fact 1 in 20 that such an unusual or surprising sample value of r-square would occur when the null hypothesis of no relationship is in fact true in the population.

In the other example, we examined the relationship between a dichotomous variable and a continuous one. Using hypothetical data, we found that the value of r-squared when predicting team productivity from whether teams had an autocratic or democratic leader was .15. In other words, our predictions of productivity were 15 percent better when we predicted for each team the mean productivity for the group of teams having a similar leadership style than when we predicted simply the overall mean productivity, forgetting about style of leadership. As we discussed at the time, the value of r-squared gives us information concerning how different the two means are for the two groups of teams, other things held constant. As the mean productivity for the autocratic teams differs from the mean productivity of the democratic teams, the value of r-squared will increase.

We now want to examine whether the relationship between productivity and leadership style that we have found in these data is a statistically reliable one. That is, we want to know whether the difference in productivity between these two groups of teams can be expected to be observed if we had access not simply to our sample of ten teams but to all such teams. Again, the population that we wish to generalize to is a hypothetical one of all similar teams that we might encounter now and in the future. In reality, seeking generalization to the population of such teams amounts to seeking generalization to future studies, using other samples, that we might conduct. We want to know whether we would continue to find the difference in productivity by leadership style if we did this study over and over again.

Once again our null hypothesis is that the two variables of productivity and leadership style are unrelated in the population. In this case, since the magnitude of the relationship between the two variables tells us about the difference in the mean productivity for the two groups of teams, the null hypothesis is that in the population the mean productivity for autocratically led teams does not differ from the mean productivity for democratically led teams.

To test this null hypothesis, we convert our sample value of r-squared to the simple r, or the correlation coefficient, by taking the square root of r-squared. The resulting correlation coefficient is .39. We now need to convert it to a t statistic, with the same formula used in the last example, to examine whether a correlation of .39 in a sample of 10 teams is sufficiently surprising or unusual to cause us to doubt the null hypothesis. The conversion of the correlation coefficient to a t statistic is done as follows:

$$t_8 = \frac{.39\sqrt{8}}{\sqrt{1 - .39^2}} = 1.20$$

The resulting t value of 1.20 does not meet the criterion adopted in the previous example for deciding whether the sample correlation coefficient was sufficiently surprising to reject the null hypothesis. Recall that that criterion was defined by a resulting t statistic greater than 2.00 or less than -2.00. Such a t statistic means that our sample correlation coefficient would occur less often than 1 time in 20 if the null hypothesis is true. Since in this example the t value is only 1.20, we cannot regard this sample correlation coefficient as sufficiently compelling evidence to cause us to reject the null hypothesis. In other words, based on these sample data, we cannot reject the null hypothesis that team productivity and leadership style are unrelated. To state our conclusion somewhat differently, we cannot conclude, based on these sample data, that there is a reliable difference between the mean productivity of autocratically led and democratically led teams. In most statistics textbooks, the t statistic for testing the difference in two means is usually given as follows:

$$t_{n_1 + n_2 - 2} = (\overline{Y}_1 - \overline{Y}_2) \bigg/ \sqrt{S_p^2 \left(\frac{1}{n_1} + \frac{1}{n_2} \right)}$$

Let us interpret this formula by using our example. $\overline{Y}_1$ and $\overline{Y}_2$ are the mean productivities for the two groups of teams. Similarly, n_1 and n_2 are the number of teams having each of the two kinds of leadership styles. S_p^2 represents the average or pooled variance of productivity, computing the variance in productivity from within each of the two groups of teams and then averaging or pooling those two variances together. As we show in Table 14.12, this formula for t gives us the exact same t value that we obtained by using the much-simpler formula for converting the correlation coefficient to a t statistic. We prefer using the formula for computing t from the correlation coefficient not only because we think it is easier to use but also because we know how to interpret the correlation coefficient, or equivalently, r-squared, in a manner that is consistent with our inter-

TABLE 14.12 Testing the Difference in Mean Productivity by Leadership Style

Autocratic Teams	Democratic Teams
$\overline{Y} = 9.6$	$\overline{Y} = 11.0$
variance $= 4.3$	variance $= 2.5$
$n = 5$	$n = 5$

$$t_{n_1 + n_2 - 2} = (\overline{Y}_1 - \overline{Y}_2) \bigg/ \sqrt{S_p^2 \left(\frac{1}{n_1} + \frac{1}{n_2} \right)}$$

$$= (11.0 - 9.6) \bigg/ \sqrt{3.4 \left(\frac{1}{5} + \frac{1}{5} \right)} \qquad S_p^2 = (4.3 + 2.5)/2 = 3.4$$

$$= 1.4 / \sqrt{1.36} = 1.20$$

pretations whenever we are examining the relationship between two variables.

Returning to our test of the null hypothesis for this example, because our t statistic was not as large as 2.00, we concluded that we could not reject the null hypothesis. This conclusion, of course, does not mean that the null hypothesis, that team productivity and leadership style are unrelated, is correct. Whenever we fail to reject the null hypothesis, there is always the danger that we are committing a Type II error, namely, failing to reject the null hypothesis when in reality it is false. Based on our sample data we can only conclude that we do not have evidence for a relationship between team productivity and leadership style. That does not mean that there is in fact no relationship.

Interpreting Relationships

Now that we have the tools to describe relationships between variables and to infer from sample data whether those relationships are reliable, a few warnings are in order about how these statistical tools are used and interpreted.

First, as we have seen, a few unusual and extreme cases can distort measures of relationship, particularly when the variables are assumed to be measured on interval or ratio scales. In examining relationships between variables, it always makes sense to examine scatterplots of the data. Doing so may well point to unusual cases that exert undue influence on our statistics. Recall that when we drew a scatterplot of states' divorce and marriage rates, the state of Nevada stuck out like a sore thumb.

Second, it is important to emphasize once again that a relationship between two variables does not mean that one of them causes the other. As we have said before, a necessary condition for a causal relationship between two variables is that they be related. But it certainly is not true that because two variables are related we can infer that one causes the other. As we have seen, states' birthrates and divorce rates are reliably related. But this result does not mean that higher birthrates result in higher divorce rates. Similarly, in our hypothetical example, we saw that democratically led groups were somewhat more productive than autocratically led ones. By itself, this result does not necessarily mean that a group's style of leadership affects its productivity.

In the presence of a simple relationship between two variables, for instance states' birth- and divorce rates, there are at least three causal alternatives that are consistent with the observed relationship. First, it may be in fact that birthrates affect divorce rates:

birthrate ———→ divorce rate

It may also be that the effect is in the opposite direction:

divorce rate ⟶ birthrate

Finally, and most probably for these data, there may be other variables that affect both birth- and divorce rates and are therefore responsible for the relationship we observe between the two. In other words, if these two variables share one or more common causes, we may observe a relationship between them that is uninformative about the causal effect of one on the other. For instance, it is quite likely in these data that states with higher marriage rates have both higher divorce rates and higher birthrates. States' marriage rates are a cause of both their divorce rates and birthrates and the relationship that we observe is not a causal one; rather it is a *spurious* one.

There is nothing in these data that can be used to prove definitively any one of these various causal possibilities. Likewise in the hypothetical example of the relationship between team leadership styles and productivity, there is nothing in the data to clarify whether leadership styles cause productivity, whether productivity causes leadership styles, or whether the relationship between the two variables is a spurious one.

The question of whether one variable causes another is not a statistical question. Rather, to argue for a causal relationship, we must rely on research design considerations. As we have often said at earlier points in this book, a relationship between two variables can be interpreted as causal only if subjects have been randomly assigned to levels of the independent variable. In such cases, we have used a randomized experimental design. In our hypothetical example, if teams had been randomly assigned to one style of leadership or the other, the relationship between the two would indicate a causal effect. In the absence of random assignment, conclusions about causal effects are likely to be erroneous.

In quasi-experimental or correlational data, we can often look at how the relationship between two variables changes as we hold constant or "control for" third variables. As we will see in the next chapter, techniques for examining relationships between two variables while controlling for a third may give us some insights about the various causal possibilities, or at least about which causal possibilities are unlikely. Whenever we have data collected from a quasi-experimental or correlational research design, such procedures are useful.

A third warning that we need to issue in interpreting relationships between two variables concerns the so-called *ecological fallacy*, discussed briefly in the last chapter. Birth- and divorce rates are correlated when measured at the state level. That is, the unit of analysis is states, not individuals. It may be totally misleading to take these data and attempt to infer from them anything about how births and divorces go together in individual lives. It may be that the same relationship exists on the individual level as on the aggregate level, but one cannot be sure without collecting data on individuals.

So, you might say, why have we bothered with analyzing the aggregate data at all? Why don't we always just deal with data on individuals? There are several reasons. Aggregate data are generally cheaper and easier to obtain. Often they are already collected in easily obtainable sources. Individual data can only be obtained in surveys, which can be very expensive. Additionally, one may be interested in aggregate data, such as the behavior of nations or state governments. Finally, conclusions can be drawn about individual behavior from aggregate data if particular precautions are taken. The issues involved in this type of inference are too complex to be discussed here, but the interested reader is referred to Langbein and Lichtman (1978), who present a fairly detailed analysis.

Finally, it is important to realize that statistical significance and theoretical importance are not the same thing. In other words, just because a relationship between two variables yields a t statistic greater than 2.00, that by itself does not mean that the relationship is theoretically important. Concluding that a relationship exists in a population on the basis of sample data is rather different from concluding that a relationship is theoretically or practically important. To illustrate, imagine if we collected data on two variables, X and Y, from 3000 cases, and suppose we observed a correlation between these two variables of .04. Because our sample is so large, we would conclude from the resulting t statistic that this relationship is reliable in the population from which we have drawn the sample. At the same time, however, we know from the value of r-squared, that is, .0016, that our predictions of Y when we take X in account are only about 0.16 percent better as a result of taking X into account. So although the relationship is statistically reliable or significant, it is unlikely to be of theoretical or practical importance.

Summary

In this chapter we have considered procedures for describing relationships between two variables, X and Y. We started with the simplifying assumption that X and Y were both measured on dichotomous scales, with only two values each. The data from the two variables could then be displayed in a 2 by 2 contingency table.

A relationship between two variables is said to exist whenever we can predict a case's value on one of the variables, given knowledge of that case's value on the other variable. In the case of two dichotomous variables, the statistic lambda measures how well we can predict one variable from the other compared to predicting a variable without information about the other.

With data measured on interval or ratio scales, a relationship between two variables is best seen by drawing a scatterplot rather than a contingency table. What we then do is find a line to represent the points in the scatterplot so that we can predict values on one variable from the other. The least squares regression line is the line that gives us the "best" predictions according to the criterion of minimizing the sum of the squared errors of prediction.

A measure of the degree of relationship between the two variables, based on the least squares regression line, is r-squared. Exactly analogous to lambda, it tells us by what proportion our predictions of one variable are improved when we make those predictions conditional on the other variable. The square root of r-squared is known as the *correlation coefficient.*

In the case of one dichotomous variable and one measured on an interval or ordinal scale, we can assess relationships by using the same procedures of regression and correlation. In this case, r-squared tells us about the relative difference between the means of two groups of observations on the continuous variable, where the two groups of observations are defined by their values on the dichotomous variable.

Beyond calculating whether or not two variables are related in a sample of data, we usually want to know what that relationship tells us about the population from which we have drawn the sample. This is the domain of inferential statistics. By converting a sample correlation coefficient to a t statistic, we showed how one can evaluate the null hypothesis that says that the two variables under consideration are unrelated in the population from which a sample of data has been collected. In the case of a relationship between a dichotomous and a continuous variable, this test amounts to testing whether the observed difference in the means of the two groups in the sample permit us to conclude that the two groups also differ in the population.

Finally, we discussed pitfalls in interpreting relationships between two variables. More specifically we warned about the dangers in interpreting a relationship as indicative of a causal effect of one variable on the other. We cautioned against using standard measures for assessing relationships when there are extreme outliers in the data. We warned about the dangers of interpreting relationships at different levels of aggregation than the level at which the data were collected. And finally, we offered the advice that a statistically reliable relationship is not necessarily the same thing as a theoretically or practically important relationship.

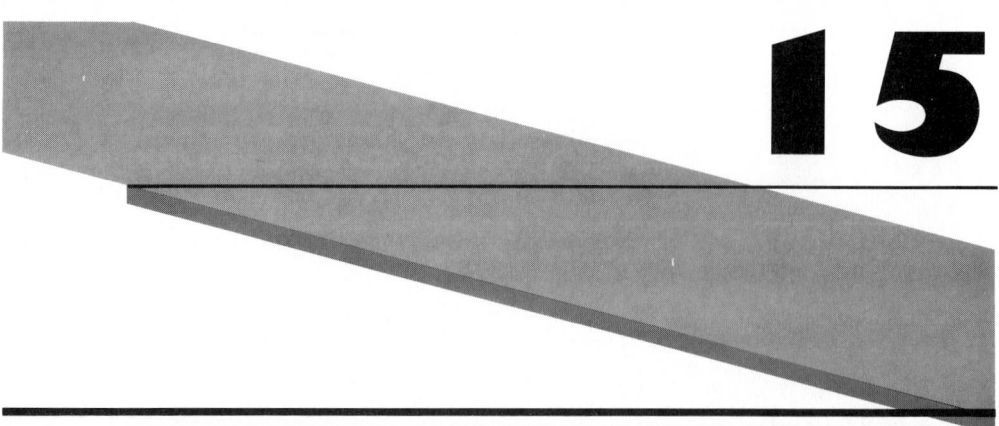

Controlling for Third Variables

In much of the research that we do as social scientists, it is not enough simply to examine relationships between pairs of variables. To critically evaluate theories and hypotheses, we must usually probe the data more deeply and ask *why* two variables are related. As we saw in the first chapter, many social relations hypotheses concern causal relationships between theoretical constructs. With most research designs, simple relationships between variables are consistent with, but certainly do not demonstrate, causal relationships. Hence, further probing is necessary. The purpose of this chapter is to discuss some techniques for such probing. More specifically, we present ways for seeing what happens to a relationship between two variables when a third variable is "controlled," or held constant statistically.

Why is this sort of further probing important? Or alternatively, why would we want to look at a relationship between two variables when we statistically hold a third variable constant? Let's use our data on states' birth-, divorce, and marriage rates to answer this question. In the last chapter, we saw that states' birth- and divorce rates were positively related: States that had higher birthrates also tended to have more divorces for every 10,000 residents. As suggested, this relationship is consistent with a variety of causal explanations. Suppose someone believed that children are a great stress to marriage, and therefore, couples who have more children run a greater risk of getting divorced. This hypothesis, although it may sound a little suspect, is an entirely adequate explanation for the observed relationship between the birth- and divorce rates. The observed correlation may in fact have been produced by the hypothesized causal link between births and divorces.

At the same time, we certainly know that a variety of other causal processes may also have produced the observed relationship. For instance, the relationship may be a *spurious* one, where there is no causal link at all between the two variables but rather they share some common cause. It certainly seems reasonable, for instance, that in those states where there are relatively more marriages, there are also relatively more divorces and births. Usually births and divorces occur only after marriages. (For divorces we can obviously be more confident about this sequence than for births.) Therefore, for a state to have a lot of births and divorces, it must also necessarily have had a lot of marriages.

The point is that there is nothing in the observed relationship between the divorce and birth variables that can be used to discriminate among a variety of different causal possibilities; that is, the relationship is equally well explained by a variety of causal hypotheses. Once again we emphasize that the results of research may well support a given causal hypothesis, but there always remain alternative explanations for exactly the same research results.

Although the two causal explanations we have discussed are equally consistent with the observed relationship, they have rather different implications for other studies and other variables. Suppose, for instance, that we could conduct a randomized experiment, randomly assigning married couples to different numbers of children. Of course such a study couldn't be done. But just for a moment, what do the two competing explanations for the birthrate and divorce rate relationship imply about the results of such an experiment? If we believed that the birth- and divorce rates were related because having lots of babies increases the probability of divorce, we would expect that couples who were randomly assigned to have more children would be more likely eventually to get a divorce. On the other hand, if we believed that the relationship between the birth- and divorce rates was spurious—that is, that it only happened because both births and divorces are generally preceded by marriages, and therefore, that higher divorce rates and higher birthrates are found wherever there are higher marriage rates—our expectations about the results of the randomized experiment would be quite different. Since all couples who were assigned to have differing numbers of children were married, we would not expect them necessarily to differ later on in whether or not they got divorced. The two causal explanations for why states' birth- and divorce rates are related, then, have rather different implications for this hypothetical further bit of research.

Assuming that such a study could not in fact be done for the purpose of discriminating between the two hypotheses, what other implications follow from the two that could in fact be examined? Suppose we found some states that differed in their birthrates but not in their marriage rates? What do the two competing causal explanations imply about their divorce rates? Well, if births cause divorces, states with more children per couple should have more divorces, even if marriage rates were the same across states. On the other hand, if we believed that birth- and divorce rates were related only because of varying marriage rates from state to state, if we found states that had the same marriage rate but different birthrates, we would not expect their divorce rates to differ. In other words, since this second explanation argues that states' divorce rates and birthrates go together only because they both are partly affected by marriage rates, if we found states that had the same marriage rate, we wouldn't necessarily expect them to differ on the divorce rate variable, regardless of whether their birthrates were the same or different.

Hence, the two explanations for why birth- and divorce rates are related have rather different implications if we looked only at states that were similar in their marriage rate. Holding marriage rate constant, if we could, the first explanation, that births result in divorces, suggests that we would still find a relationship between birthrates and divorce rates. On the other hand, the second explanation, that birthrates and divorce rates are related only because states' marriage rates affects them both, suggests that the relationship would vanish if we held marriage rates constant.

By the techniques that are illustrated in this chapter, we can examine what happens to a relationship between two variables when we hold constant or control for a third variable. As we have just seen, different causal explanations for why two variables are related may have rather different implications for what the relationship would look like if we held constant some third variable. Hence, controlling for third variables is a way of discriminating between competing hypotheses in social scientific research. As such, it is a widely used and potentially powerful tool. Of course, the most powerful tool for discriminating among competing causal explanations is the randomized experiment. But as in our example, it is frequently impossible to conduct an experiment that would reliably discriminate between the two competing explanations. In such cases, we can often begin to discriminate between them by using the techniques discussed in this chapter.

In general, whenever we have a causal hypothesis that X causes Y, and whenever we are unable to do a randomized experiment, randomly assigning subjects or units to levels of the independent variable, X, it always makes sense in quasi-experimental and correlational designs to see if X and Y continue to be related when we control for or hold constant third variables. If the X:Y relationship is in fact a causal one, not a spurious one produced by the common cause Z, X and Y (i.e., birth- and divorce rates) should continue to be related even when Z (i.e., marriage rate) is controlled or held constant. Because of this, the techniques that we discuss in this chapter are widely used in social relations research, particularly when examining those causes of human behavior that cannot be experimentally manipulated effectively.

Partial Relationships with Contingency Tables

Examining a relationship between two variables while controlling for a third is also known as examining a **partial** relationship between the two. In this section, we return to our dichotomously coded data in order to give an intuitive explanation for what it means to control for a third variable.

Let's look at the relationship between birth- and divorce rates by using the dichotomously coded data of Table 14.1 (p. 339). In Table 14.5 (p. 343) we presented the contingency table for data along with the resulting lambda for predicting divorce rates from birthrates. Those results are reproduced in Table 15.1. The lambda of .375 means that we reduce our

TABLE 15.1   Bivariate Birth by Divorce Contingency Table

		Divorce Rate		
		Low	High	
Birthrate	Low	16 33.3%	7 14.6%	23 47.9%
	High	8 16.7%	17 35.4%	25 52.1%
		24 50%	24 50%	48 100%

Lambda predicting divorce = .375.

errors of predicting whether a state is high or low in its divorce rate by 37.5 percent if we know whether it is high or low in its birthrate. Now what we want to do is see what happens to this relationship if we hold constant or control for whether a state is high or low in its marriage rate. If the partial relationship is considerably smaller than the simple relationship between the two, we have evidence that the causal explanation that having children results in divorce is at least partly in error.

How might we hold constant whether or not a state has a high or low marriage rate? A rough approximation might be to look at the relationship between birth- and divorce rates twice: once looking only at states that are relatively low on the marriage rate variable and once looking only at states with relatively high marriage rates. In Table 15.2 we present two seperate birth by divorce contingency tables, one for the low marriage rate states and one for the high marriage rate states. We can now assess the relationship between birth- and divorce rates within each of these groups of states.

As Table 15.2 makes clear, our ability to predict whether a state is high or low on its divorce rate from its birthrate completely disappears when we control for whether the state is high or low in its marriage rate. The lambdas in both of the contingency tables are .000, indicating the absence of any predictive power. Comparing these two tables with the one in Table 15.1, where we are not controlling for marriage rate, it is clear that in Table 15.1 the vast majority of the states that are low on both birth- and divorce rates are also low on marriage rate. Similarly, the high-birth states of Table 15.1 also tend to be high on the marriage variable. Hence, when we look at the birth and divorce relationship within levels of the marriage variable, the states seem to be clustered in only a single cell of each of the two contingency tables of Table 15.2.

Rather than two lambdas (one for each of the two contingency tables) to measure the partial relationship between birth- and divorce rates, controlling for marriage rate, let's come up with a single measure of the partial relationship. Recall that lambda tells us by what proportion

TABLE 15.2 Two Birth by Divorce Contingency Tables

LOW MARRIAGE RATE		*Divorce Rate*		
		Low	**High**	
	Low	13	2	15
		56.5%	8.7%	65.2%
Birthrate				
	High	5	3	8
		21.7%	13.0%	34.8%
		18	5	23
		78.3%	21.7%	100%

Lambda predicting divorce = .000.

HIGH MARRIAGE RATE		*Divorce Rate*		
		Low	**High**	
	Low	3	5	8
		12%	20%	32%
Birthrate				
	High	3	14	17
		12%	56%	68%
		6	19	25
		24%	76%	100%

Lambda predicting divorce = .000.

the prediction error rate decreases in predicting one variable from another. More specifically, if we are predicting divorce rate from birthrate, lambda tells us by what proportion our error rate in predicting divorce is decreased if we know where a state is on the birthrate variable. From Table 15.1, the simple lambda between these two variables is

$$\frac{.50 - (.167 + .146)}{.50} = .375$$

When we control for a third variable, a single lambda that assesses the partial relationship becomes only slightly more complicated. Now, instead of comparing our prediction error rates with and without information about birthrate, we are also going to take the marriage rate variable into account. More specifically, we are going to compare the error rate in predicting divorce, given information about marriage rate, with the error rate in predicting divorce, given information about *both* marriage rates and birthrates. In this way, we will see if the birthrate variable continues to be useful in making predictions even when we have knowledge of or look within levels of the marriage rate variable.

From Table 15.2, what is the total prediction error rate in predicting divorce rates if we know whether a state is high or low in marriage rate but we have no information about its birthrate? Looking at the marginal frequencies of the columns, if we know a state has a low marriage rate, we will predict that the state has a low divorce rate, and we will be wrong 5 times. If we only look at the high marriage rate states, our best prediction is that a state has a high divorce rate. And we will be wrong in that prediction for 6 states. So given knowledge of only a state's marriage rate, what is our error rate in predicting whether a state is high or low on divorce? Well, of the 48 states, we will be wrong for 11 of them, so our error rate is $11/48 = .229$.

Now, to assess the partial relationship between divorce and birth, controlling for marriage, we want to ask by what proportion does this error rate decrease if we also take a state's birthrate into account. Looking at Table 15.2, if a state is low on both marriage rates and birthrates, we would predict a low divorce rate as well, and we would be wrong for 2 states. For low marriage rate, high birthrate states, our best prediction is that a state is again low on divorce, and we would be wrong 3 times. In the case of high marriage, low birth states, our best prediction is that a state is high on divorce, and we would make an error for 3 states. Finally, for states that are high on both birth and marriage, our prediction would be that they are high on divorce as well, and we would err in the case of 3 states. Hence, in sum, if we know both marriage rates and birthrates, we erroneously predict divorce rates for $2 + 3 + 3 + 3 = 11$ out of the 48 states. Hence, the *partial lambda* is the proportional reduction in our error rate if we take into account where a state is on birthrate in addition to or over and above knowing where it is on the marriage rate variable.

$$\text{Partial lambda} = \frac{11/48 - 11/48}{11/48} = 0$$

As this statistic makes clear, we gain absolutely nothing in predicting divorce rate by knowing a state's birthrate, given that we already know the state's marriage rate. Or to put it another way, if we are predicting divorce rates, within levels of or holding constant the marriage rate variable, we gain no predictive power whatsoever by taking into account whether a state is high or low on the birthrate variable.

Since we would expect birthrates and divorce rates to continue to be related even within levels of the marriage rate variable if there was a causal relationship between birth- and divorce rates, finding that the partial relationship equals zero suggests that the causal hypothesis is in error. We then have discriminated among two competing explanations for why birth- and divorce rates are related by examining the partial relationship between the two, controlling for marriage rates. The resulting partial relationship, or more accurately, the absence of a partial relationship, lends support to the hypothesis that birthrates and divorce rates are spuriously related.

Partial Relationships with Continuous Variables

Now that we have the general notion of what it means to control for a third variable, let's return to the original data for the three variables and attempt to do the same thing with continuous variables. It may seem a little strange with such data to talk about examining the relationship between birth- and divorce rates within levels of the marriage rate variable since there are so many levels of the original marriage rate variable. But in fact we will use exactly the same principles here that we did with dichotomously coded data to examine partial relationships.

Recall from the last chapter that when we assessed the simple relationship between two variables measured on interval scales, we used r-squared. This statistic was conceptually identical to the simple lambda that was used to assess relationships between two dichotomously coded variables in a contingency table. Namely, both lambda and r-squared are measures of the proportional reduction of errors in predicting some variable Y, with and without information about some variable X. With partial relationships we also generalize the notions underlying the partial lambda to assess partial relationships with continuously measured variables. The resulting statistic, naturally enough, is known as a **partial r-squared.**

As we saw in the previous section of this chapter, the partial lambda between X and Y controlling for some Z compares the magnitude of errors in predicting Y from knowledge of Z alone to the magnitude of prediction errors when both X and Z are known. In the specific case of our data, the partial lambda tells us by what proportion our errors in predicting divorce rate from marriage rate are reduced when we also base our predictions on knowledge of a state's birthrate. In other words, does knowledge of birthrate help our predictions of divorce rate over and above knowledge of simply the marriage rate variable?

In the case of variables measured on interval scales, we saw in the last chapter that we derive predictions of one variable from another by using least squares regression. Specifically, if we want to predict some variable Y_i, based on another variable X_i, we compute the least squares regression line:

$$\hat{Y}_i = a + bX_i$$

where a is the intercept and b the slope. Our errors of prediction are thus the differences between each individual Y and the Y we predict for each case based on knowledge of X. Across all cases, we use as an index of errors the total *squared* errors of prediction:

$$\sum_{i=1}^{N} (Y_i - \hat{Y}_i)^2$$

since the sum of the simple or unsquared errors of prediction will always equal zero. Based on this least squares regression line, the simple r-squared tells us by what proportion our total squared errors of prediction are reduced when we take X into account, compared to simply predicting the mean of Y, $\overline{Y}$, for every case. When assessing the partial relationship between X and Y controlling for some Z, we want to compare total squared errors in predicting Y based on Z alone with errors of prediction using both X and Z. This will tell us whether X helps predict Y over and above Z or within levels of Z. To do this, we need to come up with two sets of predictions of Y, one based on Z alone and the other based on both X and Z. We will then compute the partial r-squared as the proportional difference between the two total squared errors of prediction.

We already know how to predict Y based on only the third variable Z. Namely, we derive the least squares regression line for predicting Y from Z:

$$\hat{Y}_z = a_z + b_z Z$$

so to minimize the total squared errors of prediction:

$$\sum_{i=1}^{N} (Y_i - \hat{Y}_z)^2$$

Notice that we have deleted the subscript i in these expressions, and the slope, intercept, and predicted values of Y now have a subscript of Z. This is to indicate that these predictions of Y are based on knowledge of Z.

To compare the total squared errors of prediction based on Z to the total squared errors based on both Z and X, we need to derive predictions based on both Z and X. Again we will use a least squares criterion to choose the best linear prediction function, but this time we will use two predictors in the equation rather than just one:

$$\hat{Y}_{xz} = a_{xz} + b_1 Z + b_2 X$$

Again, the coefficients of this equation, specifically a_{xz}, b_1 and b_2, are chosen to minimize

$$\sum_{i=1}^{N} (Y_i - \hat{Y}_{xz})^2$$

We need not be bothered with the formulas for these coefficients. They are readily available in statistics books, and in addition it turns out that they are not actually needed to compute the partial r-squared, as we will show.

Once we have our predictions of Y based on Z alone and on X and Z, we want to compare the relative magnitude of the two total squared errors of prediction. To do this, we take the difference between the two total squared errors:

$$\sum_{i=1}^{N} (Y_i - \hat{Y}_z)^2 - \sum_{i=1}^{N} (Y_i - \hat{Y}_{xz})^2$$

We then want to convert this difference to a proportion since we want to know by what proportion the total squared errors of prediction are reduced when we base our predictions not only on Z alone but also on X. To convert this difference to a proportion, we will divide it by the total squared errors of prediction based on Z alone:

$$\text{partial } r^2 = \frac{\displaystyle\sum_{i=1}^{N} (Y_i - \hat{Y}_z)^2 - \sum_{i=1}^{N} (Y_i - \hat{Y}_{xz})^2}{\displaystyle\sum_{i=1}^{N} (Y_i - \hat{Y}_z)^2}$$

As can be seen, this is the definition of the partial r-squared. It tells us by what proportion our prediction errors are further reduced by using X, over and above Z, to predict Y. As we saw in the case of dichotomously coded data, this is equivalent to knowing whether X can be used to predict Y within levels of Z or holding Z constant. The partial r-squared that we have just derived is known as the partial relationship between Y and X controlling for Z.

There is a relatively simple way to compute this partial r-squared based on knowledge of all the simple correlations between pairs of the three variables, X, Y, and Z. Using the procedures discussed in the last chapter, we can compute three correlations between pairs of these three variables: the correlation of X with Y, r_{xy}; the correlation of X with Z, r_{xz}; and the correlation of Y with Z, r_{yz}. Once we know these three correlations, the partial r-squared between X and Y, controlling for Z, can be computed as

$$\text{partial } r^2 = \frac{(r_{xy} - r_{xz}\, r_{yz})^2}{(1 - r_{xz}^2)\,(1 - r_{yz}^2)}$$

Returning finally to the divorce, birth-, and marriage rate data, let's compute the partial r-squared between birth- and divorce rates controlling for marriage rates. Given in Table 15.3 are the three simple correlations between all pairs of these three variables, which have been taken from Chapter 14. Make sure that you remember how they were computed and what they mean. As is indicated in the table, these correlations are based

TABLE 15.3 Correlations among States Birth-, Divorce, and Marriage Rates ($N = 47$)

	Birth	Divorce
Divorce	.347	
Marriage	.507	.567

on only 47 of the 48 states, deleting Nevada. As we saw in the last chapter, correlations can be dramatically affected by an outlier, and hence we are basing our analysis here on the 47 contiguous states excluding Nevada.

We will use the preceding equation to calculate the partial r-squared, defining states' birthrate as variable X, divorce rate as variable Y, and marriage rate as variable Z. Thus, just as we did when the data were dichotomously coded, we are computing the partial relationship between birth- and divorce rates, controlling for or within levels of the marriage rate variable. The partial r-squared is

$$\text{partial } r^2 = \frac{[.347 - (.507)(.567)]^2}{(1 - .507^2)(1 - .567^2)}$$

$$= \frac{.0035}{.5041}$$

$$= .007$$

Thus, when we attempt to predict states' divorce rates, given knowledge of their marriage rates, our errors of prediction are reduced by less than 1 percent by knowing, in addition, birthrates. Or alternatively, when we examine the relationship between birth- and divorce rates, controlling for marriage rates, the two are essentially unrelated. Holding marriage rate constant, there remains almost no relationship between birth- and divorce rates.

Based on this analysis with the original data, we reach exactly the same conclusion as we did with the dichotomously coded data. Let us review the argument here. The simple r-squared between states' birth- and divorce rates was found to be .12 in the previous chapter. Thus, errors in predicting divorce rates are reduced by about 12 percent by taking into account a state's birthrate. At least two causal interpretations exist for this relationship. It may be that having lots of children increases the probability of divorce, and hence the relationship may be a causal one. It also may be that the relationship is a spurious one, resulting from the fact that states with higher marriage rates would tend to have higher birth- and divorce rates. The two explanations have rather different implications for the partial relationship between birth- and divorce rates, controlling for marriage rates. If births produce divorce, the two should be related even when we control for marriage rates. On the other hand, if the relationship is a spurious one, it should vanish when we hold marriage rates constant. The partial r-squared strongly suggests that the simple relationship is not due to a causal connection between birth- and divorce rates. Since we are unable to conduct a randomized experiment, randomly assigning states to different birthrates, we can use partial relationships to help us choose among alternative causal explanations.

One final comment before we leave the subject of partial relationships. In the last chapter when we discussed simple relationships, we noted that r-squared is the measure of association between two variables, measured on interval scales, that is most easily interpreted. At the same time, many people simply report the square root of r-squared, which is known as the *correlation coefficient*. So too, when dealing with partial relationships, many people report the square root of the partial r-squared, which is known as the **partial correlation coefficient.** The formula for the partial correlation coefficient is simply the square root of the formula for the partial r-squared:

$$\text{partial } r = \frac{r_{xy} - r_{xz}r_{yz}}{\sqrt{1 - r_{xz}^2}\ \sqrt{1 - r_{yz}^2}}$$

We recommend, however, that the partial r-squared be routinely used, since like r-squared, it is much more easily interpreted than its square root.

Partial Relationships with Continuous and Dichotomous Variables

In the last chapter we saw that the procedures used to assess relationships between two continuous variables can be simply generalized to the case where one of the two variables is measured dichotomously. When we are predicting a continuous dependent variable wtih a dichotomous independent variable, we code the dichotomous distinction by using a *dummy variable.* This means that we assign the value of 1 to some observations and the value of 0 to others, according to whether observations are grouped together on the dichotomous independent variable; r-squared can then be computed between this dummy variable and the continuous dependent variable, just as it was in the case of two continuous variables. With a dichotomous independent or predictor variable, we have an additional interpretation for r-squared. Not only does it tell us about the proportional reduction of errors of prediction that results when we use the dichotomous variable to predict the continuous one, but also it equivalently informs us about the relative difference between the two group means on the dependent variable, where groups are defined by the dichotomous independent variable.

The generalization from the case of two continuously measured variables to that of one continuous and one dichotomous variable continues with partial relationships. Specifically, we can use partial r-squared to assess the relationship between a continuous variable and a dichotomous one when controlling for a third variable. Such a procedure is used with great regularity in the analysis of data from quasi-experimental research designs.

Consider an expanded version of the example discussed in the last chapter. Using hypothetical data, we explored the relationship between team leadership style and productivity. In those data, there were five teams under an autocratic leadership style and five that were run democratically. We found that there was a small, although not statistically significant, relationship between leadership style and productivity, with democratic teams showing higher productivity. If those data had been collected from a randomized experimental research design, where teams had been randomly assigned to one of the two leadership styles, that small difference in productivity could have been interpreted as a causal effect of leadership style had it been statistically reliable. Suppose, however, that a quasi-experimental design had been used, one that we defined in Chapter 5 as the pretest-posttest nonequivalent control group design. Under this design, teams would not have been randomly assigned to one or the other style of leadership, and hence differences observed in productivity may not have been due to the different leadership styles. Productivity differences, for instance, might have been due to differences in productivity levels between the different kinds of teams that existed long before their leaders ever assumed an autocratic or democratic leadership style. Recall from Chapters 2 and 5 that this kind of preexisting difference is called a *selection threat* to internal validity: The teams in the control and experimental conditions are found to differ not because the independent variable exerted a causal effect but because the two groups of teams differed before the start of the study.

In the pretest-posttest nonequivalent control group design, we attempt to overcome this selection threat by measuring the dependent variable as a pretest as well as a posttest. We then attempt to equate the two experimental and control groups on the basis of their pretest performance, so that any differences induced by the independent variable will be revealed over and above any differences that existed at the time of the pretest. This is the purpose, then, of controlling for third variables in quasi-experimental research designs. Given that we have an independent variable that is dichotomous—that is, autocratic versus democratic leadership style—and that subjects, or in this case, teams, have not been randomly assigned to the levels of this variable, we want to see whether the independent variable is related to the dependent variable, or the posttest, after we have equated the two groups of teams for any differences that existed at the time of the pretest. In the language of partial relationships that has been used in this chapter, we want to see whether the dichotomous independent variable is still related to the continuous dependent or posttest variable once we have controlled for or held constant the pretest variable.

We have all the tools necessary for this sort of analysis, based on procedures for assessing partial relationships with continuous variables. The only difference is that the dichotomous independent variable must be coded as a dummy variable to use these procedures, just as we were forced to do in the last chapter. Table 15.4 presents the hypothetical data from our leadership style study that was used in the last chapter. In addition, data have been included for each of the 10 teams from a pretest measure of productivity. That is, in addition to measuring productivity as a posttest, it was also measured as a pretest, prior to the team leaders assuming either an autocratic or democratic leadership style. The independent variable has once again been coded as a dummy variable, with autocratically led teams coded as 0 and democratically led ones coded as 1. Assuming these data came from a pretest-posttest nonequivalent control group design, our goal is now to determine whether the independent variable of leadership style is related to the posttest measure of productivity when we hold constant or control for the pretest measure. By equating teams on their pretest levels of productivity, we hope to remove the selection threat to internal validity in these data.

Recall from the last chapter that the value of r-squared between the posttest productivity and the independent variable leadership style is .15. If that relationship is not due to selection, it should not diminish when we control for pretest productivity. On the other hand, if the partial r-squared is substantially less than .15, we have evidence that the relationship between posttest productivity and leadership style was a spurious one or one that existed only because of the differences between the two groups of teams on the pretest. In addition to the raw data, Table 15.4 also presents the three correlations among all three variables: the correlation of the pretest with the posttest; the correlation of the pretest with leadership

TABLE 15.4 Data from Quasi-Experimental Hypothetical Example

Case	Pretest Productivity (Z)	Posttest Productivity (Y)	Leadership Style (X)*
1	9	8	0
2	10	10	0
3	8	7	0
4	9	11	0
5	11	12	0
6	10	10	1
7	11	12	1
8	8	9	1
9	11	11	1
10	12	13	1

$$r_{yz} = .8716$$

$$r_{xy} = .3907$$

$$r_{xz} = .3846$$

*Coded as 0 = autocratic style; 1 = democratic style.

style; and the correlation of the posttest with leadership style. Using the formula for the partial r-squared used earlier, we find that the partial r-squared between leadership style and the posttest controlling for the pretest equals

$$\text{partial } r^2 = \frac{[.3907 - (.8716)\,(.3846)]^2}{(1 - .8716^2)\,(1 - .3846^2)}$$

$$= \frac{.0031}{.2048}$$

$$= .015$$

This value is clearly less than the value of r-squared found in the last chapter for the relationship between leadership style and the posttest productivity when we did not control for the pretest. Hence, it would appear as if the relationship between leadership style and productivity disappears in these hypothetical data once we equate the two groups of teams on their initial pretest productivity level. In other words, the simple relationship between leadership style and productivity found earlier seems almost entirely due to the differences between the teams in their pretest productivity.

Recall from the last chapter that the relationship between a continuous dependent variable and a dichotomous independent variable tells us about the relative difference between the means of the two groups formed by the dichotomous variable. In other words, in the case at hand, the relationship between the posttest measure of productivity and style of leadership gives information about the relative difference in productivity between the autocratically led and democratically led teams. The partial relationship also gives us information about the mean difference, but this time it does so only after equating the two groups of teams on the pretest. In other words, the partial r-squared answers the following kind of question: By how much, in a relative sense, does the mean posttest productivity of the autocratic teams differ from the mean of the democratic teams if we act as if the productivity of the two groups of teams were the same on average at the pretest? In other words, if we force their pretest means to be the same, how much difference remains between their posttest means?

Although controlling for a pretest, as we have done, can be quite informative about the selection threat to internal validity in quasi-experimental research designs, it does not take care of the other threats to internal validity that one encounters in quasi-experimental research. Statistical procedures, such as controlling for third variables, are useful in helping to examine causal hypotheses with correlational and quasi-experimental data. Ultimately, however, the validation for causal hypotheses depends on experimental data.

Inferences about Partial Relationships

At the end of the last chapter we discussed how one can infer the presence of a relationship between two variables in a population from which one has randomly drawn a sample. To do this, we formulated a null hypothesis that stated that the two variables were unrelated in the population. We then converted the sample correlation between the two variables to a t statistic to determine whether our sample relationship was sufficiently surprising or compelling to cause us to reject this null hypothesis.

This general procedure, and indeed the formula for converting a sample correlation coefficient to a t statistic, generalizes in a very straightforward manner to the case of inferences about a partial correlation. Suppose we wanted to determine whether two variables, X and Y, are related in the population when we hold constant a third variable, Z. We start by formulating a null hypothesis that the two are unrelated in the population when Z is controlled. We then use the sample partial correlation between X and Y controlling for Z, $r_{xy.z}$, to determine whether it constitutes sufficiently compelling evidence to cause us to abandon this null hypothesis. Once again, we will convert our sample partial correlation to a t statistic. If the resulting t statistic is greater than 2.00 or less than -2.00 (given samples larger than approximately 50), we will then reject the null hypothesis since such a t value would occur less often than 1 time in 20 if the null hypothesis were true.

The formula for converting a simple correlation between X and Y to a t statistic is:

$$t_{N-2} = \frac{r\sqrt{N-2}}{\sqrt{1-r^2}}$$

The formula for converting a partial correlation to a t statistic is only slightly different:

$$t_{N-3} = \frac{r_{xy.z}\sqrt{N-3}}{\sqrt{1-r_{xy.z}^2}}$$

Let us return to the states' birth-, divorce, and marriage rate data to illustrate the inference process for partial relationships. The simple correlation between birth- and divorce rates in these data was .347. Using the first of the preceding two formulas, this correlation converts to a t statistic of 2.48:

$$t_{45} = \frac{.347\sqrt{45}}{\sqrt{1-.347^2}} = 2.48$$

Hence, we can conclude from this value that the null hypothesis of no relationship between the two variables in the population ought to be rejected. In other words the simple relationship between the birth- and divorce rates seems to be a reliable one. As we saw earlier, when we control for marriage rate, the partial r-squared between birth- and divorce rates was .007, and hence the partial correlation was .084 (i.e., the square root of .007). We now want to test the null hypothesis that this partial relationship does not differ from zero in the population. We do this by using the formula for converting partial correlations to t statistics. The resulting t statistic equals 0.56:

$$t_{44} = \frac{0.84\sqrt{44}}{\sqrt{1 - .084^2}} = 0.56$$

Clearly this t statistic is not greater than 2.00 and hence does not constitute evidence compelling enough to cause us to reject the null hypothesis. In other words, although we can conclude that birth- and divorce rates are related in the population, we cannot conclude that the partial relationship between them when controlling for marriage rate differs from zero in the population.

This statistical inference procedure can also be used when the predictor, or independent variable, involved in the partial correlation is dichotomous. For instance, we could also use this t statistic to test whether the leadership style dichotomous variable was reliably related to posttest productivity in our teams when we controlled for pretest productivity. Or in other words, the t statistic would tell us whether the difference in posttest productivity between the two groups of teams, when we equate them on pretest productivity, is a reliable difference, that is, one we might expect in the population as well.

Summary

In this chapter we have discussed how we can examine a relationship between two variables while controlling for a third. It is important to examine partial relationships in order to discriminate between competing causal hypotheses, particularly when randomized experiments cannot be used to help choose among different causal explanations. If a simple relationship between two variables is spurious, that is, if it is due to some common cause, the relationship should disappear when the common cause is controlled.

With dichotomously coded data, partial relationships are examined by seeing whether we can predict one variable from another within levels of a third variable that is held constant. We saw that the resulting partial lambda tells us the proportion by which errors of prediction are reduced when we make predictions of Y using X, within levels of Z, where Z is the variable being controlled.

We then generalized the notions underlying partial relationships from dichotomously coded data to variables that are measured on interval scales.

The partial r-squared was defined as the proportional reduction in total squared errors of prediction when we use X, in addition to Z, in predicting Y. These predictions were based on least squares linear prediction functions, as in the previous chapter when we dealt with variables measured on interval scales. To define the partial r-squared, we needed to derive predictions of Y based simultaneously on both X and Z. However, in computing the partial r-squared, we never need actually to compute these predicted values since the partial r-squared is easily computed from the three simple correlations between pairs of $X, Y,$ and Z. The resulting partial r-squared tells us whether two variables, X and Y, continue to be related when we examine that relationship within levels of a third variable, Z, or when we hold that third variable constant.

The procedures for computing partial r-squared generalize in a straightforward manner to the situation where our predictor variable, X, is dichotomous. Examining partial relationship with a dichotomous predictor, or independent variable, can be particularly informative when data are collected with a quasi-experimental research design. What we attempt to do in such cases is examine the partial relationship between the dichotomous independent variable and the posttest while controlling for or holding constant the pretest. Such a procedure helps us to overcome the selection threat to internal validity in quasi-experimental research designs. Although it is useful to try to overcome the selection threat, examining partial relationships with quasi-experimental data is not a panacea, for other threats to internal validity (e.g., selection by maturation) continue to be a problem.

The final topic considered in this chapter was inferences about the existence of partial relationships in the population based on observed sample partial relationships. The inference procedure was a straightforward extension of the procedure used in inferences about simple relationships that was developed in the last chapter.

PART V

The Application and Communication of Research

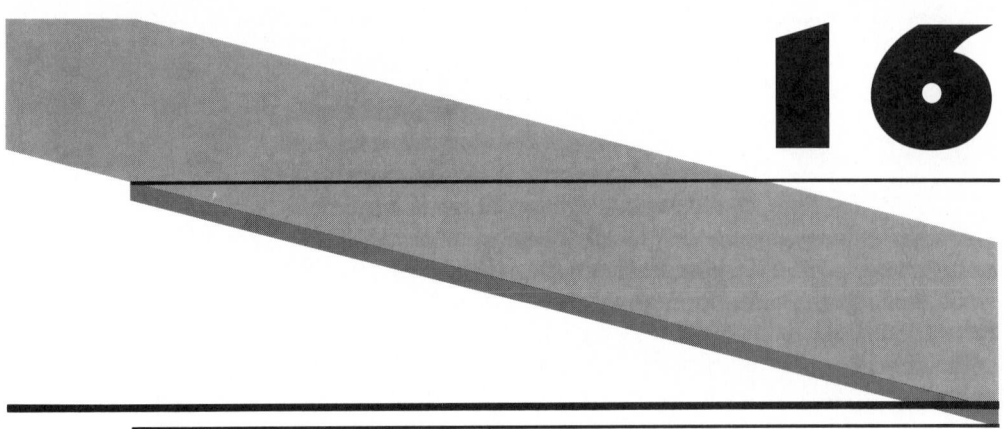

16

Applied and Evaluation Research

In this chapter we will examine both applied and evaluation research, although the distinction between the two is not always entirely clear. Applied research, which really subsumes evaluation research, is any social research designed to answer practical questions. Applied researchers may also be testing theories while they are answering practical questions, and they may be more or less directly involved in a practical or real-world setting, but ultimately they are interested in answering some question with practical implications. They are interested in gathering empirical data that can be useful in affecting, implementing, or changing some social policy. Ultimately, then, applied social researchers are interested in speaking to a somewhat different audience than are researchers who conduct more-basic social research. Applied social researchers ultimately wish their work to be used by those who make or change social policy. They are interested in affecting how legislators, judges, and administrators think about some social problem or issue. As they conduct their research, they must keep in mind this audience to whom they hope to appeal.

Evaluation research is best thought of as one type of applied research in the sense that it is designed to answer practical, real-world problems about the effects of some policy or program. Although applied research more broadly may serve to define a social problem or explore alternative policies or programs that might be implemented to solve some problem, evaluation research has as its primary goal the description and evaluation of some existing social policy or program.

The distinction between applied and basic research is not a distinction among different research methods and research designs. Applied and evaluation researchers use randomized experiments, quasi experiments, and surveys, just as basic researchers do. They collect data by using questionnaires, interviews, and observational methods. They are concerned with construct validity, internal validity, and external validity. All the issues discussed in this book are of concern to both applied and basic researchers. The distinctions between the two are more practical than methodological.

First, because applied research is typically conducted in the real world, real-world problems may intervene and make researchers change their plans and procedures. Subjects may not always be available when and where one would like. Data may be relatively hard to collect. Historical events may intervene and affect one's conclusions. An independent variable or treatment that is being evaluated may change during the course of the research because administrators decide that some change is necessary. In sum, practical problems may arise in carrying out a chosen research design and successfully collecting and analyzing the data.

Second, applied research differs from basic research in the audience it must appeal to. Applied researchers must often justify their claims and demonstrate the utility of their empirical work not to fellow social scientists, who usually take for granted the value of empirical research, but to policymakers and administrators who may be much more skeptical about the value of questionnaire, interview, or observational data. Since applied research takes place in a political world and ultimately seeks to affect policies that result from political processes, it must appeal to those processes in ways that more-basic research may not. One of the major frustrations in applied research is that researchers often feel that their work has been unappreciated or insufficiently utilized in policy formation. One of the hardest steps in conducting applied research is translating the empirical conclusions into a language and form so that their policy implications are both clear and useful.

Before considering applied and evaluation research in a relatively systematic fashion, we present two examples to give the flavor of applied research, the social problems and issues it occasionally addresses, and the political realities it inevitably must confront.

Environmental Impact: Social Research in Action

Psychologists and sociologists have become involved in court cases on behalf of persons who have suffered not just physical but also psychological and social damages from environmental disasters. In 1972, after a mining company dam burst and sent 100 million gallons of mud through a narrow mountain hollow of a community in West Virginia, sociologist Kai Erikson was asked by a law firm to recommend someone to assess the social and psychological damages. After going to the hollow, he was so struck by the damage and the need to report it that he volunteered to do the research. He went to Buffalo Creek, spoke with the survivors, read thousands of pages of legal transcripts, distributed questionnaires by mail (of which more than 90 percent were returned), and wrote his analysis in a moving book entitled *Everything in Its Path* (Erikson, 1976). This is a major piece of applied social research, which combines participant observation, surveys, and archival data.

Erikson first describes the past, the history of the mountain community and the people's adjustments to earlier adversity and disaster. The mining families had known evictions and beatings in the 1920s, when company owners feared the workers would unionize. The Depression was another disaster they had lived through, and automation in the 1950s caused about half the miners in Buffalo Creek to lose their jobs. The difference between these earlier hardships and the 1972 dam break was that although the earlier disasters had hurt large numbers of families, they had left the community intact; the flood that took "everything in its path" destroyed the community. Erikson documents how the destruction of community destroyed the people's resources for coping with disaster and left them economically, socially, and psychologically destroyed. People who had recovered from the earlier experiences did not seem able to recover from the dam break, which destroyed not only their personal property but also their community and social networks. Erikson's book weaves together his field work, surveys, and analysis of legal archives to piece together the story of their collective trauma. It is a major undertaking in applied social research.

After the nuclear reactor accident at Three Mile Island in Pennsylvania in March 1979, many research teams of psychologists tried to assess the psychological effects, particularly on people living near the reactor (Hartsough & Savitsky, 1984). That accident led lawyers and social scientists to ask whether psychological effects could also be considered environmental ones. If so, the future construction and operation of nuclear plants could be subject to environmental impact statements that include an assessment of potential psychological damage. Research on the psychological effects of disasters shows that sleep disturbances, anxiety, psychosomatic symptoms, fatigue, and depression are common short-term effects. The long-term effects are currently under investigation (Dew, Bromet, & Schulberg, 1985).

Many studies were conducted after the Three Mile Island accident using a great variety of measures and designs. Two telephone surveys of 2748 people compared the stress reactions of persons living close to the reactor and those living more than 40 miles away. The stress levels of those living near the reactor were very high the month following the accident and then began to decline; however, nine months after the disaster, about 15 percent of those people still reported higher than normal stress-related symptoms (Houts, 1980a, 1980b).

One group of investigators was particularly concerned about the psychological effects on mothers of preschool children, nuclear power plant workers, and clients in community mental health centers (Bromet et al., 1982; Bromet, Schulberg, & Dunn, 1982). Their study included comparison groups of people who lived near another nuclear reactor in a different part of the state. The researchers found that mothers of preschool children suffered greater effects than the nuclear power plant workers or mental health center clients. They were five times more likely to feel anxiety and depression immediately after the accident and also had higher levels of symptoms a year later. The power plant workers and mental health clients had higher stress symptoms than the comparison groups living near a distant reactor, but the effects were not as marked as those felt by the mothers of young children.

The authors of such "environmental impact" studies have encountered resistance from the courts, primarily on the grounds that psychological stress cannot be adequately measured. Judges and lawyers have argued that psychological claims can too easily be fabricated, and they fear a rash of fraudulent claims. Nonetheless, an appeals court decision (*Pane* v. *U.S. NRC*, 1982) did suggest that psychological stress could be a factor in environmental impact statements provided it (1) "is severe enough to threaten physical health" and (2) "can be reliably measured" (Hartsough & Savitsky, 1984, p. 1120). Therefore, the impact of applied social science research hangs on a basic principle of measurement—it must be *reliable*.

These examples represent only a small corner of the field of applied research. The content of applied social research is vast. A sampling of a recent volume of the *Applied Social Psychology Annual* (Oskamp, 1984) contains the following chapter titles: "Burnout in Organizational Settings" (Maslach & Jackson), "Organizational Work and the Overall Quality of Life" (Rice), "The Use of Power in Organizations and Interpersonal Settings" (Kipnis), "Research on the Social Impacts of Robotics" (Goodman & Argote), "Individual and Organizational Consequences of Computer-Based Office Information Technology" (Gutek, Bikson, & Mankin) and "Employee Ownership in the Restructuring of the American Economy" (Whyte & Rosen). These are academic pieces that test social science theories as well as reveal actual social facts and behaviors. Much applied social research is less exciting than these titles; much of it is purely practical and mundane. If you have ever answered consumer surveys on the phone, in person, or by mail, you have sampled the mundane variety.

Varieties of Applied Research

Applied research can take many forms. We will examine three examples chosen because each is relevant to some social problem. These examples are not representative of all applied social research because probably the greatest bulk of applied research is carried out by the marketing divisions of commercial organizations, or survey research companies hired by those organizations, to find out how to market products and increase sales. Much applied research is also conducted in industrial organizations to learn how to raise workers' morale and productivity. The military also has research divisions, in which social scientists conduct both basic and applied research to study group processes and assist military institutions. The examples of applied research we have chosen were conducted by academic researchers interested in social problems.

Academic researchers who conduct applied research occasionally study the same kinds of problems previously described; they might study advertising, industrial morale, or questions of interest to the military. Often, however, they study social problems, either because their funding comes from a source concerned with social issues or because they have no external funding and are not expected to provide answers that will be commercially or militarily profitable. The three examples of applied research that follow were conducted by academic social scientists addressing social problems in schools and prisons.

These examples illustrate three modes of studying social problems. The first is a simulation of prison conditions, the second an intervention in classrooms, and the third a set of interviews at an alternative high school for students who had dropped out of or been dropped from a traditional school. These examples are also instances of the experimental and survey research methods discussed in Chapters 4, 5, and 6.

When researchers simulate a real-life situation in a laboratory, they have more control over extraneous variables than they would if they conducted their work in the field. They can acquire an experimenter's control over third variables both by randomly assigning subjects to the simulated conditions and by holding other factors constant, as Zimbardo (1971) did in his study of a mock prison. The second study, an intervention in a classroom, is an experimental design that demonstrates that experimenters can also work in the real world. The intervention produced results that pleased both the teachers and the students, and many of the teachers decided to continue using the treatment after the research ended. The third example is a survey designed to answer questions about which students drop out of school and how they feel about themselves and the social and economic conditions that affect their lives. Unlike the second example, this survey does not examine students who were randomly assigned to their treatments. It reports the thoughts and feelings of students who were placed in alternative schools because they had dropped out or had been dropped from traditional schools. These survey results are nonetheless compelling and relevant for educators. This is the purpose of applied research—to affect decisions, inform policy, and make a difference in people's lives.

Simulation

Zimbardo designed a mock prison in the basement of a university building where he detained students as prisoners and guards. His study pits a dispositional explanation of prison behavior against a situational explanation. The former states that guards are "tough" or "callous" and prisoners are "rebellious" or "docile"; the latter states that being placed in the situation of being a prisoner or guard is sufficient cause to produce the behaviors and relationships found in prisons. He staged a surprise roundup of "prisoners" in the night. The men who became prisoners had volunteered to participate without knowing whether they would become prisoners or guards; they were randomly assigned to their positions and surprised by the police cars that picked them up in the night and delivered them to the prison. The men who became guards had also been randomly assigned to their roles; they had no choice but to be guards. Zimbardo summarized his findings as follows:

> At the end of only six days we had to close down our mock prison because what we saw was frightening. It was no longer apparent to us or most of the subjects where they ended and their roles began. The majority had indeed become "prisoners" or "guards," no longer able to clearly differentiate between role-playing and self. There were dramatic changes in virtually every aspect of their behavior, thinking and feeling. In less than a week, the experience of imprisonment undid (temporarily) a lifetime of learning; human values were suspended, self-concepts were challenged, and the ugliest, most base, pathological side of human nature surfaced. We were horrified because we saw some of the boys ("guards") treat other boys as if they were despicable animals, taking pleasure in cruelty, while other boys ("prisoners") became servile, dehumanized robots who thought only of escape, of their own individual survival, and of their mounting hatred of the guards [p. 3].

Zimbardo's results have clear implications for prison reform. They show that being placed in the position of a prisoner has a powerful effect on how a person acts and feels. The situation may be a greater factor than the person's preexisting character or personality. Reform efforts should, therefore, focus on the structure of social roles and relations in the prison rather than on the structure of inmates' personalities.

Although exceedingly compelling, Zimbardo's work also demonstrates some of the practical problems in conducting policy-relevant research. We suspect that those whom Zimbardo might like to influence, that is, those who make policy about how prisons are run, might be fascinated by Zimbardo's work but ultimately conclude that its relevance was minimal. They would base this conclusion on concerns about external validity and the general realism of the simulation. After all, they would argue, prison guards and prisoners aren't the same types of people as the college students who played the roles in Zimbardo's simulation. And after all, the basement of a university building that is converted into a prison really isn't the same as a real prison. Ultimately, the burden is on applied researchers to convince the policymaker that their research and conclusions are more than just interesting. They must convince those who make policy that those conclusions are useful and relevant for policy formation or modification.

Intervention

Research on education often takes place in the classroom rather than in a mock setting. Several researchers interested in finding ways to overcome competition and prejudice in classrooms devised a method they call the *jigsaw technique* (Aronson et al., 1978). They created an assignment for which students were each given only one small part of the solution. The students' job was to piece together the whole solution by learning from and teaching their classmates. For instance, in one assignment the students were expected to learn about the life of Joseph Pulitzer. His life story was divided into six periods, each described in a paragraph written by the researchers. They cut and distributed the separate paragraphs to fifth-grade students, who had been put into interdependent learning groups of six children each. Each child in the group had a different paragraph describing one of the six periods in Pulitzer's life, and they were not allowed to pass their paragraphs around or read one another's. Instead, they were to teach and learn from one another. This meant the other five needed to pay close attention to the one who was speaking because that person had valuable information and was an important resource. Each child was essential for the others' solutions; no one could be dismissed as unimportant or unintelligent. And no one could benefit from studying all alone, trying to be the "best," independent of the others in the group.

The students who were in these interdependent jigsaw groups liked each other and liked school better than children who were in traditional classrooms. They also came to like themselves better—they developed higher self-esteem. These positive effects went across racial and ethnic boundaries. For example, in some of the predominantly white classrooms there were Hispanic children who had previously remained silent in class. When they had been called on to speak in the traditionally competitive classrooms they had sometimes been embarrassed, so they and their teachers learned it was safest for them to be silent. With the jigsaw problem, these children had information essential for the solution, and what they said became valuable to others. The transition was not easy for them or their classmates, but their role in the class did change and so did their performance. The grades of children in minority groups went up almost a whole letter, as did their self-esteem and that of all the students who participated. Most of the teachers also liked what they saw happening in the interdependent groups, and many continued to use the technique after the intervention ended. The research had immediate practical implications for the lives of teachers and students.

This example illustrates one of the ways applied researchers can affect what actually occurs in the real-world settings they study. Teachers, to a large extent, set policy in their classrooms. They affect what goes on there, within the limits of broad guidelines defined by principals, administrators, and boards of education. Because the teachers themselves were involved in this research, and because the research was actually carried out in their classrooms, the teachers realized the effects of the intervention in a personal and direct manner. They were involved in the research and therefore they may have felt that its conclusions were their conclusions as well. As a result, those conclusions affected what subsequently happened in at least some of the classrooms.

On-Site Interviews and Observations

Eighty-eight students who had either dropped out or been dropped from New York City high schools were interviewed to learn how they felt about themselves and about fairness in school.

The researchers wanted to examine the popular image "that these students are lost, losers, and drifting" (Fine, 1983, p. 233). The students answered questions from a depression scale, a self-image scale, and several hypothetical stories about teachers' actions. One story read, "Let's say you expected a B in math class. The teacher gave you a C, which you felt you did not deserve. Would you do anything?" Another story described a student, Mary, who asked a classmate to lend her a pen and was promptly "yelled at" by the teacher and asked to leave the room. The students were to judge Mary as a "good student" or "not a good student" and the teacher as "right" or "not right."

The results of these interviews contradict the popular image. Two-thirds of the students said they would challenge the teacher, and the more likely they were to challenge the teacher the more positive were their own self-images. Students who were willing to say the teacher was wrong for scolding Mary and sending her from the room were less depressed. The results of these analyses made the researcher conclude that "recognizing unfair behaviors by teachers has a positive psychological payoff," and "being willing to challenge a teacher promises psychological and academic benefits for these adolescents" (p. 232). Moreover, the stereotype of the high school dropout as a "loser" or "drifter" is not borne out by the interviews. Compared with students who remained in the schools, those who dropped out were less depressed and more likely to take the initiative when they felt a teacher had been unfair. These results challenge both the stereotype of the dropout and the authority of teachers. As Fine concludes, "students who recognize injustice and are critical of their teachers tend to be among the least depressed and the most likely to drop out" (p. 234). Being a survey, this study cannot unequivocally identify causes and effects. Nonetheless it provides a new and useful portrait of students who drop out.

Simulations, interventions, and on-site observations are three very different forms of applied research. What they all have in common is the desire and perhaps the likelihood that their results have immediate practical implications for what gets done in prisons, schools, or wherever. As we have seen, many factors ultimately influence whether or not the research results will in fact have an impact. The first big step is simply to convince policymakers that the research is relevant or applicable to the problem at hand. Concerns about external validity and how true to life the research situation is may be paramount here. As we have seen, one way to convince policymakers of the relevance of applied research is to involve them directly in the research—in funding it or supporting it, in planning and executing it, and in drawing out its implications.

Evaluation research is applied research conducted when some group or agency asks a researcher to help design or evaluate a social program or policy. Because such research is instigated by the group or agency that has the ability to affect what program or policy eventually is carried out, presumably evaluation research is likely to have a more immediate practical impact than other types of applied research.

Varieties of Evaluation Research

Summative and Formative Evaluations

There are two general categories of evaluation research, *summative* and *formative* research, or *outcome* and *process* research. Summative or outcome evaluations examine the effects of a program and ask, "Does it work?" Formative or process evaluations ask, "What is it?" and "How does it work?" Outcome evaluations use experimental, quasi-experimental, and survey research designs. Process evaluations use techniques more like participant observation (see Chapter 8). Outcome research usually uses statistical analysis of quantitative data. Process research is usually qualitative research and uses case histories rather than statistics to make a point. Outcome evaluations are used to decide whether programs should continue or cease, and for this reason administrators may resist and evaluators find it difficult to implement an outcome evaluation. Process evaluations seem more benign because they are used to help the administrators form their programs, revise them, and improve them. Process evaluators provide feedback to the program director about how the participants react to the program, how the implementors are carrying out the program, and whether the actual program resembles the intended program. They define the program as it appears in action and describe how it works. This feedback often takes place during the early stages of a program, when there is still room for change and improvement—hence, the name *formative* evaluation. By contrast, summative evaluations are done at the end of a program or after it has been in existence long enough to have produced some measurable effects that provide a fair test of the program's success. This chapter focuses on summative evaluations; the chapter on participant observation describes the steps that can be used in formative evaluation research.

D. T. Campbell (1969) describes the inevitable conflicts that arise between administrators, whose careers depend on implementing successful programs, and evaluation researchers, whose careers require that they evaluate other people's programs. He urges program administrators to adopt an "experimental" attitude and use information from evaluators about whether the innovative programs they are administering achieve the intended goal. To have a truly experimental attitude, however, a program administrator would have to be in a position to administer two or more alternative programs, so that the evaluation could be an evaluation of programs rather than personnel. By evaluating programs rather than people, a researcher could gain cooperation from some of the people who would otherwise resist or distort program evaluation. Such social and administrative arrangements are unlikely, however, because it is not always possible to separate a program from its personnel or its administrators; so there may be no "pure" evaluations of programs detached from their directors or implementers.

Basic researchers often develop a "program" of research, which means they pursue a single issue or set of questions for months or years. Those who have such a research program revise their ideas and research designs to follow up questions raised by their previous studies. If evaluation and applied researchers were not dependent on one-shot grants to answer a burning question like "Does a guaranteed income destroy worker incentive?" they too could develop a research program that would help policymakers revise programs, test them again, and reformulate the questions and answers. This would be an ideal marriage between formative and summative evaluation research. If we lived in the experimenting society described by Campbell, evaluation researchers and program administrators could help one another. As it is now, they sometimes threaten one another. Program administrators, who feel their careers are based on running "successful" programs, cannot afford to have an evaluation show otherwise. And evaluation researchers, whose work is funded only until they have finished a particular evaluation, cannot afford to spend additional time and effort formulating ideas about new program designs and evaluations with policymakers or administrators. The political nature of evaluation research cuts short the cycle, the process of revising questions and answers. This makes it difficult for evaluation researchers to develop a sustained program, and they are more likely than basic researchers to change their focus from one issue to another. Put yourself in the position of a program administrator or policymaker. If you heard that a particular evaluation researcher had evaluated another program like yours and found it was "not working," you would probably be reluctant to employ the same research team.

Ideally, the evaluation researcher works with the program's staff, administrator, or policymaker in conducting both formative and summative evaluation simultaneously. Ideally, evaluation research is not a single, one-shot enterprise but a process that involves both summative and formative aspects, replications, reanalyses, and public criticism of research conclusions (T. D. Cook, 1985; Cook & Gruder, 1978). By working closely with both the program's staff and the concerned public, the goal is to make continual evaluation a part of the program or policy. If this happens, evaluation is continuous and changes in programs are made routinely, as needs and circumstances change.

Differences between Evaluation and Basic Research

Results with Immediate Impact

Because it is carried out to evaluate ongoing programs, evaluation research is designed with a shorter time span than basic research. The social problems are not solved immediately, but *decisions* about programs are made immediately because budget allocations and personnel decisions are frequently based on demonstrable "results." Lynn (1977) points out that "social problems are seldom solved by a single decisive act or policy declaration; rather, policies to deal with them are fashioned incrementally over time in a series of measures which are partial and not necessarily reversible" (p. 72). However, policymakers often have "short time horizons" and wish to see research results to justify continuing or terminating a program. The press for quick and definite answers makes most evaluation research different from basic research.

Although evaluation research is intended to produce immediate results and have an immediate impact, two circumstances often prevent this from happening. The first arises when results are equivocal or contradictory, so that it is not clear what the policy decision should be. There have been many evaluations of preschool Head Start programs, for instance, and they do not all agree about the program's success or failure (Campbell & Erlebacher, 1970; Cicerelli et al., 1969). Negative income tax or income maintenance programs have also been tried and evaluated in many places, and the results are contradictory (Kehrer, 1978; Kershaw, 1972). If the planners and decision-makers are to use these results, which set should they use?

The second circumstance that interferes with using the results of program evaluation arises when the real effects of social programs are not immediately visible. For instance, Head Start preschool education was originally introduced to "break the cycle of poverty" by educating three- and four-year-old children so that they would become achieving, self-sufficient adults. Today's educational planners do not intend to wait 20 or 30 years for an evaluation, however, before they decide whether to continue with the preschool programs. Instead, they use immediate outcomes—the children's subsequent academic achievement in elementary school—and assume that adult occupational achievement will follow from childhood scholastic performance. There is a positive but weak connection between the two.

Weiss (1972) calls these immediate or short-run effects "proximate" goals and the long-term desired effects "ultimate" goals. She says short-run effects suffice when previous research shows a direct and strong connection between proximate and ultimate goals. For instance, "in evaluation of a Smokers' Clinic, it is probably enough to discover that the program led participants to stop smoking. It is not essential to investigate the ultimate incidence of lung cancer" (p. 38). Many of our more-ambitious social programs, however, are designed to have long-range effects. Proximate outcomes in such cases are unsatisfactory, but they are all that we have. Later in this chapter we shall describe one evaluation that did assess the ultimate goals—a 30-year follow-up of men who had participated in a program as boys (McCord, 1978).

Vested Interests with Various Criteria for Success

The choice of dependent variables—the criterion for evaluating a program—makes evaluation researchers face this issue: In whose interests is the research? It is not sufficient to say "in the interests of science" because the outcome will influence more than science. Because the results of evaluation research are used to make funding decisions, there are vested interests in the criteria chosen for success. The evaluation may affect some people's jobs, education, or health; and the results may be in the interests of some people and perhaps to the detriment of others.

For instance, in negative income tax experiments across the United States, participants were given income subsidies, and the primary criterion (dependent variable) for evaluating the effect of the program was whether or not there was a decline in *work incentive*. The people and agencies that implemented and evaluated the income subsidy were concerned that the men and women who received a guaranteed minimum income would not stop working as a result. They judged the program successful or not on the basis of the number of hours the recipients worked and the amount of money they earned. The same programs could have been evaluated on a number of other grounds—the health of the participants, their increased enjoyment of leisure-time activities, their self-esteem, their participation in community activities, or their satisfaction with life. These other criteria were either ignored or deemphasized (Berk & Rossi, 1977). Work disincentive is a relevant criterion, as is the amount of money earned. Nonetheless, the other criteria could also have been used to judge the program's success or failure.

The scientific questions of selecting dependent variables become political questions in evaluation research. Whose criteria will prevail? It is not always clear that one set of criteria is "better" than another. All evaluation research must address the question of whose values, whose criteria for success or failure, will prevail in judging the outcome of a program. Different parties or participants in the research program have different perspectives and different goals. Evaluation researchers, therefore, even more than basic researchers, must ask themselves, "Whose side are we on?" (Becker, 1967).

Technical Decisions with Ideological Consequences

The technical issues involved in finding measurable criteria have ideological consequences. "Applied social researchers are more technically proficient in the study of individuals than in the study of organizations, and therefore, social research tends to be more social psychological than social structural" (Berk & Rossi, 1977, p. 81). For instance, we have scales for measuring the alienation of individuals but none for measuring the alienating features of work places that might produce the alienation in employees (Berk & Rossi). This critique applies to basic research as well as evaluation research, but its consequences are more immediate and apparent in research evaluating social progams.

Evaluation research affects more than a decision of whether a social program succeeded or failed. It also affects our definition of what the social problems and their solutions are. The technical ease with which we can measure problems and outcomes determines which ones we recognize or attend to: "Outcomes that can be counted easily tend to be listed as the outcomes desired" (Berk & Rossi). Crime-prevention programs provide a case in point. One criterion for success is reduction in crime rates. This can be accomplished or attempted in several ways. If we consider the events leading to crime as forming a long causal chain, we could intervene at any point along that chain to prevent or reduce crime (Kidder & Cohn, 1979). We could intervene in the childhood experiences of "potential delinquents" and try to prepare them for noncriminal careers (McCord, 1978). Or we could focus on adult employment problems and provide job skills for the unemployed. Or we could seek alternatives to unemployment and layoffs as industrial options. Or we could focus on the doorsteps of victims of crime and promote better home-security measures, such as locks and burglar alarms. All these are plausible starting points for explaining and preventing crime. They all suggest very different goals or solutions for crime-prevention programs, too, some of which would be much easier to implement successfully than others. Programs to install door locks and burglar alarms have higher success rates (if we simply count numbers of locks and alarms distributed) than do programs to restore community cohesion or job security; and as Berk and Rossi point out, "outcomes that can be counted easily tend to be listed as the outcomes desired" (p. 81). The technical decision—to count burglar alarms installed—has the ideological implications that the way to reduce crime is to prevent victimization.

Designs in Evaluation Research

If we put aside the uses or implications of the research and look only at the research design and measurement problems, evaluation research is very much like basic research. It includes all the same designs and threats to validity; it involves the same measurement issues and problems with operational definitions. We can find examples of evaluation research that use each of the designs or approaches we have discussed in the preceding chapters. There are over 200 evaluations that are "true experiments," with the treatment randomly assigned to recipients (Boruch, 1975). There are many evaluations that use quasi-experimental designs, with nonrandom assignment and comparisons made either with nonequivalent control groups or with the same groups' pretreatment measures. Some evaluations consist of surveys—these are often "needs assessment" studies to determine the demand for social programs such as community mental health centers. And some evaluations use qualitative methods and participant observation (see Chapter 8). In this section we describe two large-scale evaluations, one a true experiment and one a quasi experiment. Many evaluations are done on a much smaller scale, but we present these two because they magnify some of the issues previously discussed.

A True Experiment—The Cambridge-Somerville Youth Study

The Cambridge-Somerville Youth Study is a unique piece of evaluation research because it did what many social evaluations ideally should do. It examined the long-term effects of a childhood treatment program. In 1939 a social philosopher and physician named Richard Clark Cabot began a program that he hoped would prevent deliquency among boys in Boston. He located over 500 boys aged 5 to 13 through recommendations of teachers, clergy, police officers, and welfare agencies. Some of the boys were considered "difficult" or predelinquent, and others were identified as "average." Half were assigned to the treatment program, and the other half were designated "controls." The assignment was made by the toss of a coin, making this a true randomized experiment.

Boys in the treatment program had counselors visit them on the average of twice a month. The counselors worked with both the boys and their families and encouraged the families to seek assistance from the program. The assistance and counseling included tutoring for the boys, medical and psychiatric attention, summer camps, youth activities, and access to other community programs. Boys in the control group participated only by providing information about themselves. The program lasted five years.

Over 30 years later, in 1975 and 1976, Joan McCord and her research team traced 488 of the original 506 members of the experiment "through court records, mental health records, records from alcoholic treatment centers, and vital statistics in Massachusetts. Telephone calls, city directories, motor-vehicle registrations, marriage and death records, and lucky hunches were used to find the men themselves" (McCord, 1978, pp. 284–285). Both the program and the evaluation of the program are remarkable. The program is notable for its truly experimental nature with random assignment and its magnitude—506 boys were studied for five years. The evaluation is remarkable for its long-term follow-up and its thoroughness—95 percent of the men were located and their records traced 30 years after their original assignment to the treatment and control groups. In McCord's follow-up she compared the men who had been in the treatment group with "matched mates" from the control group. She used official records and statistics from courts, mental hospitals, and alcohol treatment centers, as well as the men's self-reports from a questionnaire, which was returned by 113 men in the treatment group and 122 in the control group.

The results of these comparisons are surprising and controversial. Many of the records show *no differences* between the men who received "treatment" and those who received none, and in those instances where there were differences, the differences often show the treatment to have been *harmful* rather than helpful. McCord divided the treatment and control samples into those who had been described as "difficult" and "average" at the beginning of the treatment to see whether treatment was more beneficial for boys who originally seemed "difficult"; she again found no beneficial effects. Instead, 34 percent of the "difficult" boys in the treatment group and 30 percent of the "difficult" boys in the control group had juvenile records.

Adult criminal records reinforced the finding of no difference. Equal numbers of both treatment and control group men had been convicted for crimes as adults. The one significant difference between the two groups' criminal records showed the treatment to have been harmful: "a higher proportion of criminals from the treatment group than of criminals from the control group committed more than one crime. . . . Among the . . . men with criminal records from the treatment group, 78% committed at least two crimes; among the . . . men with criminal records from the control group, 67% committed at least two crimes" (p. 286).

Comparisons of health statistics also made the treatment group look bad. In response to questionnaire items that asked whether they were alcoholic, 17 percent of the treatment group responded "yes," compared with 7 percent of the control group. On some other measures, the groups were equal: 21 men in each group had "received treatment in mental hospitals for disorders other than alcoholism" (p. 286). But the general mental and physical health of the treatment group appeared worse than the controls: (1) Of the 24 men in each group known to have died, those in the treatment group died at earlier ages, and (2) in response to questions about stress-related illnesses such as ulcers, asthma, high blood pressure, and the like, more men from the treatment group reported having had at least one of the ailments.

Comparisons of the family relations, occupations, and leisure-time activities of the treatment and control groups again showed few differences—and the differences that did exist made the treatment look harmful. Roughly equal percentages of the two groups were married, divorced, remarried, and never married. Approximately equal proportions were unskilled workers. They differed in their numbers of white-collar or professional workers, however: 43 percent of the control group and 29 percent of the treatment group had white-collar or professional jobs. A comparison of the prestige ratings of the occupations of the two groups with National Opinion Research Center ranks showed that the control-group men were in positions with higher prestige.

The *only* measure on which the treatment group indicated the program was successful was a questionnaire item that asked for their subjective evaluation of the program: "In what ways (if any) was the Cambridge-Somerville project helpful to you?" "Two-thirds of the men stated that the program had been helpful to them" (p. 287). They wrote comments such as, "helped me to have faith and trust in other people," "helped prepare me for manhood," and "better insight on life in general" (p. 287).

McCord's evaluation of the Cambridge-Somerville experiment has received much attention and comment, particularly because it contradicts many other beliefs about the value of social programs (e.g., Sobel, 1978). The only explanation McCord (1979) has found for the harmful effects of the experiment is that the men in the treatment group developed unrealistically high expectations. The unsolicited help and attention they received as boys may have led them to expect more of themselves and of other people than they were able to realize. Critics of McCord's conclusions warn against overstatement; they ask for further research before we decide that programs like the Cambridge-Somerville project be abandoned (e.g., Sobel, 1978).

Since the research design used a randomized experiment, with boys randomly assigned to treatment and control groups, we might be reasonably confident that the effects McCord reported were a result of the treatment and not preexisting group differences. However, as in all randomized experiments conducted in the real world, there are always questions about how successfully the experimental design was implemented. Was the treatment program as designed actually delivered to boys in the treatment condition and not in fact delivered to boys in the control condition? In real-world research, issues of treatment implementation, contagion or generalization of aspects of the treatment to the control group, and some sort of compensatory treatment of the control group (Cook & Campbell, 1979) are always threats. Overall, however, in spite of these potential threats, the evidence seems quite clear that the treatment hurt more than it helped. The only redeeming feature of the program appears in the men's subjective evaluations. We will return to this point when we consider the role of the client's satisfaction in program evaluation.

A Quasi Experiment—Head Start Preschool Education

To understand the evaluations of compensatory social programs it is helpful to examine the social philosophy underlying them. In a review of policy developments in improving education and training for low-income people, Levin (1978) notes two types of reasons given for why people who are capable of working are still poor: (1) that they are unwilling to work or incapable of working enough to earn enough to rise above the poverty level or (2) that there are not enough jobs. "The former explanation assumes that it is the low productivity of workers or their laziness that determines their low incomes. The latter explanation assumes that ... there just are not enough jobs with wages above the poverty level that are made available to such populations" (p. 523).

A decade of compensatory education programs in the United States began with the assumption that "if children of poor families can be given skills and motivation, they will not become poor adults" (Economic Report of the President, 1964). This assumption involved "blaming poverty on inadequacies of the poor versus blaming the poverty condition on the inadequacies of society" (Levin, 1978, p. 523). It reflected the personal theory of the program developers or perhaps the prevailing theory of the times. Social programs and their scientific evaluations are not neutral—they contain notions of blame and responsibility, and they represent someone's diagnosis of what the problem and the solution are. Head Start programs for preschool children focus on people instead of on societal conditions, and they are founded on the idea that poverty is caused by poor people's lack of education.

The actual evaluations of Head Start and other preschool programs did not, in fact, use measures of poverty to judge the programs' success or failure. They used children's subsequent academic achievement—a proximate rather than ultimate goal.

The evaluations of Head Start programs began within the agency that sponsored the programs, and they included three types: (1) summative evaluations of the overall effectiveness of all Head Start programs, (2) comparisons of different strategies and curricula within Head Start, and (3) on-site monitoring or process evaluations of individual programs (Williams & Evans, 1972). We will describe the first type of evaluation—summative evaluation of the overall effectiveness of the programs—and discuss some of the criticisms of it.

The first and most widely publicized evaluation of the overall effectiveness of Head Start was made by the Westinghouse Learning Corporation (Cicirelli et al., 1969). The evaluation included a sample of 104 Head Start centers from across the country and a sample of children from those centers who were then in first, second, and third grades. A comparison group was formed of children from the same grades and the same schools who had not been in preschool Head Start programs. These comparison children were selected to be similar to the Head Start children in age, sex, race, and kindergarten attendance. The evaluators tested both groups of children with a series of standardized tests to measure scholastic abilities and self-concepts. They also had teachers rate the children's achievement and motivation, and they interviewed the parents of both groups of children. The comparison group was not formed by random assignment, making this a quasi experiment rather than a true experiment. The researchers tried to match the children in terms of their backgrounds; we have already discussed in Chapter 5 how such attempts to "match" fail to eliminate group differences.

The results of this evaluation received wide attention because the findings were negative. The major conclusions were that (1) the summer programs were ineffective in producing gains that persisted in the elementary school years; (2) the full-year programs were marginally effective in producing cognitive gains and ineffective in producing gains in how the children felt about themselves; (3) Head Start children remained below national norms for standardized tests of language and scholastic achievement but approached national norms on school readiness in grade one. The most positive finding came from parents' testimonials: "Parents of Head Start enrollees voiced strong approval of the program and its influence on their children. They reported substantial participation in the activities of the centers" (pp. 7–8). The Westinghouse report concluded that "the Head Start children cannot be said to be *appreciably* different from their peers in the elementary grades who did not attend Head Start in most aspects of cognitive and affective development measured in this study, with the exception of the slight, but nonetheless significant, superiority of full-year Head Start children on certain measures of cognitive development" (pp. 7–8).

The criticisms of this study, even though it was not a true experiment with random assignment, include some of the criticisms made of randomized experiments: "the study is too narrow. It focuses only on cognitive and affective outcomes. Head Start is a much broader program which includes health, nutrition, and community objectives, and any proper evaluation must evaluate it on all these objectives" (Williams & Evans, 1972, p. 257). The authors of the evaluation answered that "in the final analysis Head Start should be evaluated mainly on the basis of the extent to which it has affected the life-chances of the children involved. In order to achieve such effects, cognitive and motivational changes seem essential" (p. 257).

Another criticism was that the test instruments used to measure the cognitive and motivational changes were not developed for disadvantaged children and were therefore insensitive and inappropriate. The evaluators conceded that this was possible, but they said that they "used the best instruments available" (p. 258).

A third criticism is that the study looked only for long-term effects by testing children in first, second, and third grades and ignored the immediate benefits that children may have derived from being in a pre-school program. "Rather than demonstrating that Head Start does not have appreciable effects, the study merely shows that these effects tend to fade out when the Head Start children return to a poverty environment" (p. 259). The evaluators admitted that this, too, may be true, but they said the program must be judged not by its short-term effects alone if those effects disappear in a year or two; ". . . the fact that the learning gains are transitory is a most compelling fact for determining future policy" (p. 259).

One other major criticism is the one we discussed in Chapter 5. The results were probably contaminated by a *regression artifact;* since the children were not admitted to Head Start by a lottery, the "control" group of comparison children was not equivalent, making this a nonequivalent control group design. The researchers tried to match the Head Start and comparison children on age, race, sex, kindergarten attendance, and parents' social status; but matching does not eliminate the effects of preexisting differences between two populations. Matching is a good strategy *only if* it is followed by random assignment. If the investigators had originally tried to match pairs of children and then from within each pair randomly assigned children to Head Start and the control group, they would have created equivalent groups. But matching alone is no substitute for random assignment.

The two examples of large-scale evaluations of social programs that we have discussed both showed negative results. In the first case, the results are difficult to dispute because the true experimental design makes most other explanations implausible. McCord's conclusion that the treatment in the Cambridge-Somerville experiment was harmful is persuasive. The question that remains unanswered about that evaluation is *why* did the treatment hurt more than it helped? In the Head Start evaluation, the negative results are not convincing because there is a rival explanation— regression artifacts alone could have made the program look ineffective. It may be the evaluation research rather than the social program that failed in this case. A true experiment, with randomization, makes it possible for an evaluator to assess a program with greater confidence that the results represent true program effects. Randomization, however, remains a controversial procedure. We shall consider the case for and against random assignment.

Randomization—Arguments Pro and Con

Critics have made the following arguments against randomized experiments:

1. They are not feasible.
2. They have a narrow scope and are limited because they "fail to include qualitative information . . . (and) are unable to recognize subtle human reactions to a social program" (Boruch, 1975, p. 122).
3. They are useless in providing information on how to make a program better.
4. They are unethical because they either deprive the control group of a desirable treatment or subject the experimental group to a questionable treatment.

In response, Robert Boruch, an evaluator, has addressed each of the criticisms as follows (1975).

1. Randomized social experiments are feasible because over 200 social programs have successfully used random assignment. This does not mean that it is easy to implement true experiments, but it is proof that they are feasible. Boruch's list of over 200 experiments shows a wide range of programs that include job training, education, mental health, social welfare, medical care, economic incentives, criminal justice, the mass media, and many others. Random assignment is possible in more places than the critics believe.

The critics may still have a point, however, if we ask whether there are some special conditions that make random assignment particularly difficult and other conditions that make it easy. Boruch gives us some insight on this: "The examples . . . serve as a basis for examining conditions under which controlled tests appear to be most readily mounted. For example, many such tests compare the effects of various material products, such as two different income subsidy plans, rather than the effects of social programs which are based heavily on personal skills or program staff, such as two rehabilitation programs for the mentally ill." It is conceivable that experimental tests of the latter sort are more difficult to conduct because we do not know enough about designing tests that are especially sensitive to staff skills or that do not threaten the status of program staff. Program administrators often resist random assignment and true experimental designs because they do not want an evaluation which looks foolproof—and they may be right. We may not know enough about designing treatments and measuring the effects of social as opposed to material programs to conduct a truly fair test of an idea; and well-intentioned program administrators do not want to jeopardize a good *idea* by having a rigorous evaluation conducted on an inadequate implementation of that idea.

2. Randomized experiments need not preclude gathering qualitative data, and gathering quantitative data need not preclude discovering "subtle human reactions to a social program." Data in true experiments can be either quantitative or qualitative; what matters is that they be systematic: "systematic and reliable information is essential for dispelling erroneous ideas generated by casual observation, dramatic anecdote, and unchecked impressions. That systematic information may be quantitative, or qualitative, or both" (Boruch, p. 122; Kidder, 1981).

Another part of the second criticism is that experiments are narrow and limited in scope because they are "one-shot affairs." Boruch replies that "nothing in experimental design methodology demands one-shot tests, and, for a variety of reasons, sequential assessment should ordinarily be the rule rather than the exception" (p. 125). Both the critics and the defenders of experiments are correct. Experiments and evaluations often are one-shot tests and do not follow the program or the participants over many months or years, but they need not be so limited. The 30-year follow-up evaluation of the Cambridge-Somerville experiment is a notable exception. The negative income tax experiments and many evaluations of mental health programs, remedial education programs, and job training programs, however, have not followed participants' progress long after the program. Most summative or outcome evaluations are not longitudinal studies because the answer to the question, "Does it work?" cannot wait for years.

3. The third criticism, that experimental evaluations are not useful because they provide little guidance on how to make the program better, also has a grain of truth to it. If we discover that job training programs do not succeed in getting higher wages for the trainees, we do not know what will succeed. All we know is that this attempt failed. Experiments do not necessarily provide ideas for innovations, but they do provide clear answers about whether a particular innovation worked or not. Whenever it is possible to compare two innovations, an experimental test will show which one is better. If we accept experiments for what they are—tests of effects—they do enable us to make decisions about whether a program is good and which of several alternative programs is the best.

Another part of the third criticism is that "rigorous evaluations of social programs, including experiments, can destroy any incentive to be creative in program development" (p. 128). Boruch answers that experimental design and evaluation cannot guarantee creativity but that there is also no reason why they must stifle it. The experimental mode is very compatible with creativity—people who are willing to experiment are innovative and creative. And those who experiment generally want to know the results of their experiments.

Barriers to innovation may arise when the results of the innovation threaten the innovator's career, and in this sense, experimental evaluations can stifle creativity. For this reason, Campbell (1969) says the ideal is to compare two innovations, with the program administrators' jobs guaranteed no matter what the evaluation reveals, so that administrators and evaluators can be impartial judges of the value of social programs. "This is a useful strategy to the extent that multiple comparisons inhibit premature emotional endorsement of what might be thought of as *the* solution to a complex social problem, and that they reduce the staff anxieties usually associated with a test of only one solution" (Bourch, p. 129).

4. The fourth criticism of randomized experiments concerns the ethics of experimentation, and it takes several forms. On the one hand, critics say that the untreated or control group is unfairly deprived of a potentially good program. On the other hand, critics also say the treated or experimental group (guinea pigs) are unfairly subjected to questionable treatments that may not help and may even harm them. Whether the treatment be helpful or harmful, experimentation is called unfair. Boruch has a simple answer: "failure to experiment ... [may be] unethical" (p. 135) because we will never know if a treatment is good or bad if we do not put it to experimental test.

In those cases where we know that a program will not be harmful and we doubt only whether it is helpful or simply ineffective, we ideally want to permit as many people as possible to participate. The limit on how many people can participate is usually determined not by any principle of experimental design but by budgets. If this is the case and if more people volunteer or express an interest in a program than can be served, randomization may be the fairest way of deciding who can participate in the program and who will be in the control or comparison group (Brickman et al., 1981; Wortman & Rabinovitz, 1979). Some people participate in lotteries for pleasure and profit. They may also be willing to participate in lotteries for access to social programs for which there are more volunteers or applicants than there are places available. Social psychologists who examined the fairness of lotteries found that people regard random assignment as fair when all the people in the pool are equally deserving (Brickman & Stearns, 1978). If prior screening of people's merits or needs still leaves a pool of people larger than the number who can receive a special program (e.g., scholarships), a lottery seems fair, and a lottery is random assignment.

Seligman's research on energy conservation is a good example of how it is possible to conduct randomized experiments in "the field" or in "the real world" (Becker & Seligman, 1978; Becker, Seligman, & Darley, Report No. 90; Seligman & Hutton, 1981). Seligman and his colleagues wanted to see whether homeowners would reduce their energy consumption if they were given feedback about how much energy they were consuming. They wanted to test this by randomly assigning homeowners to two groups; one received conservation feedback and the other did not. They first recruited a large number of potential participants, more than they could accommodate. The homeowners who were willing to participate were told that if they were selected for the experiment, they would have a small device installed in one wall of their home. They were also told that the experimenter might not have enough devices for everyone who was interested, in which case the devices would be allotted randomly. After the random assignment was made and the participants were informed of their luck, all remained willing to participate. Those who did not receive the feedback meters remained in the experiment as a control group. They were willing to answer questionnaires and have their energy consumption monitored because they shared an initial commitment to the goal of energy conservation. This, of course, makes the entire sample a special one, not a randomly selected sample. It limits the external validity of the experiment. Nonetheless, it gives the evaluation high internal validity. And it demonstrates the willingness of people in the real world to participate in randomized experiments.

The Political Uses of Evaluation Research

We started this chapter by saying that applied research, and particularly evaluation research, differs from basic research in the extent to which it can affect people's lives. The applied researcher gathers data with the ultimate hope of being useful in changing or affecting social policies and programs that have an impact on people's lives. Since policy change and formation are inevitably a political process, applied research must necessarily address the political realities within which it is conducted.

One of the most pressing political concerns in the conduct of evaluation research is the question of for whose benefit the research is conducted. Usually evaluation researchers are hired by program administrators or policymakers to evaluate a program or policy that affects some set of "clients." Ultimately, the program or policy ought to be judged perhaps as successful or not according to the extent to which it meets the clients' needs or helps them achieve their aspirations. All too often, however, the evaluation goals of the program administrator may simply be to document the program's successes in order to justify its continuation, and hence a continuation of the administrator's job, with less regard for whether the program truly is helping its clients in the desired ways.

The issue here is one of deciding what dependent variables the research should examine. What defines whether or not a program or policy is "successful"? Success in the eyes of a policymaker or program administrator may be defined very differently than it is for a client. If social programs are designed for the recipients or clients, it seems reasonable that the clients' evaluation of the program should be included in the criteria for judging its success.

Clients' Participation in Evaluations

Bush and Gordon (1978) valued client participation in their research on children's placements in foster homes, institutions, or their families of origin. In going through records, they came across the description of a woman described as a pyromaniac—a mother who set fire to her apartment and whose child was subsequently taken from her and placed in an institution as a ward of the state. When Bush and Gordon interviewed the child, they heard another version of that incident. The child said that during a cold winter, when the apartment heating was inadequate and the mother had repeatedly requested that it be repaired, the mother lit a fire in a wastebasket which tipped over and set fire to the apartment. From an agency's point of view, this was pyromania; from the child's point of view, it was an effort to keep warm. Whichever version of the story you believe, there are at least two—and one is the client's.

Bush and Gordon advocate including clients' preferences not only in the evaluation of social programs but also in the decision of what treatment they should receive. Letting clients choose their own treatments naturally obviates random assignment, but we present the case because it also tells us something about using clients' satisfaction as a criterion for program evaluation. Bush and Gordon make three points: (1) that clients have more information about their past and present needs and a greater stake in choosing the right treatment than do "outsiders"; (2) that clients who exercise such choice are more pleased with their treatments (in this case, foster placements for children) than clients who are denied the choice; and (3) that for the choice to be a *real* choice, it must be an "informed" choice. Two factors sometimes limit people's ability to make an informed choice: Relative deprivation may make small benefits look good to someone who has previously had no benefits at all, and restricted experience with alternative treatments in the past may limit people's ability to make an informed judgment about which treatment to choose. Some of the children in Bush and Gordon's study who could "only remember one kind of placement, institutions, were very reluctant to choose other forms of care when given a variety of options" (pp. 26–27). Only when the researchers made it clear to the children what the other placements were like were the children able to make an informed choice between living in an institution or a family.

Applying this logic to the McCord study casts doubt on the validity of the participants' subjective evaluations of the treatment. Would two-thirds of them still have said positive things about the treatment had they known about the subsequent criminal records, poor health, lower occupational standing, and earlier deaths of the treatment group? For clients' satisfaction to be a useful evaluation, it must be an *informed* evaluation, with hindsight about the objective consequences of the treatment and not a simple judgment of whether it made the clients feel good. It is fair and reasonable to include clients as judges and evaluators of the services they receive, but if they are not fully informed, they may err in their judgments. Like McCord's findings that clients' testimonials were contradicted by objective evidence, other researchers (McDill, McDill, & Sprehe, 1969) report inflated and sometimes misguided testimonials in evaluations of educational programs. "Studies of compensatory education programs have one 'universal finding': regardless of the type of program, duration, or actual results, parents are enthusiastic" (pp. 43–44). Perhaps the participants in the Cambridge-Somerville experiment and the parents of children in compensatory education programs are telling us that they appreciate the special attention—the investment of resources and the good intentions. Would they say the same if they knew the objective outcomes? We have yet to see the data from such "informed" subjective evaluations.

There are additional problems with subjective satisfaction ratings. Many surveys of satisfaction have generated extremely high levels of self-reported happiness with a variety of areas "in which it is 'common knowledge' that people are dissatisfied" (Gutek, 1978, p. 49). For instance, some survey data show 85 percent of assembly-line workers are satisfied with their jobs, whereas "researchers have concluded that assembly work is among the most powerless, meaningless, unchallenging, monotonous jobs around" (p. 49). Similarly, some survey data report that "a full 92% are satisfied with their marriages. Divorce statistics suggest that satisfaction rates should be lower . . ." (p. 48). Gutek concludes, "one reason for distrusting measures of satisfaction is simply that people seem to be satisfied with everything that social scientists ask them about" (p. 48).

Another reason to distrust satisfaction measures is that people's reports of their own satisfaction do not mesh with their reports of what they believe other people's satisfaction must be. For instance, "although 80% of subjects thought they were treated fairly in their encounter, only 42% thought that government agencies in general treat people fairly" (p. 49). This means that people regard their own experiences and perhaps their own satisfaction levels as exceptions to an otherwise bleak picture. Which is more accurate—their report of their own exceptional experiences or their assessment of what they think most people experience? And what does this mean for assessing satisfaction? Gutek describes the most drastic approach to the problem of using clients' satisfaction ratings— "abandoning the attempt entirely: better to assess organizational effectiveness in terms of objective factors, such as recidivism rate, number of cases handled, and the like" (p. 50).

We face a dilemma: We want to take into account clients' evaluations, criteria, ratings of effectiveness, and satisfaction; but those ratings do not always agree with objective indicators. If we resort to objective indicators, we face another problem: "the more any quantitative social indicator is used for professional decision making, the more subject it will be to corruption pressures and the more apt it will be to distort and corrupt the social process it is intended to monitor" (D. T. Campbell, 1975, p. 3). Moreover, objective indicators measure something quite different from satisfaction. The relationship between objective indicators such as absenteeism or job turnover and subjective ratings of satisfaction is weak (Gutek, 1978, p. 50). Gutek concludes, therefore, that we should *not* abandon subjective measures because "people live in a subjective world as well as an objective one. . . . Satisfaction may not take the place of objective indicators, but neither can objective indicators take the place of subjective indicators such as satisfaction" (p. 50).

Can We Afford Not to Do Applied Social Research? The Case of Nuclear Reactors

We have shown how complicated applied research conducted in the real world can be compared with basic research conducted under controlled laboratory conditions. Lest this tempt you to abandon applied research, we will describe an example that suggests we should continue to do this kind of work despite its complexities.

Dr. Rosalie Bertell, a mathematician and medical researcher, examined environmental influences on the survival of low birth weight infants in Wisconsin between the years 1963 and 1975 (Bertell, Jacobson, & Stogre, 1984). She and her colleagues chose Wisconsin because the state has routinely tested milk for radioactive materials, and these tests provide a measure of radioactive contamination of pasturelands. The researchers chose six regions based on their proximity to nuclear power plants. Three regions—Eau Claire, La Crosse, and Green Bay—are close to and downwind of nuclear power plants. The other three—Rice Lake, Wausau, and Madison—are distant from or upwind of nuclear power plants. They studied the effects on low birth weight infants (weighing less than 5½ pounds or 2500 grams) because those infants are very fragile and sensitive to environmental influences that might threaten human health or life.

To assess the health effects of nuclear power plants one must take into consideration not only proximity but also prevailing wind patterns. For instance, the three downwind regions were affected by the start-up of seven nuclear power plants, four in Wisconsin and three in Minnesota. The prevailing winds are from the west or northwest, so the residents of Eau Claire are downwind of the Minnesota nuclear plants.

The power plants whose effects Bertell and her colleagues examined were started up between 1969 and 1974. Therefore, the researchers compared the death rates of low birth weight infants for three time periods: 1963 to 1966, 1967 to 1970, and 1971 to 1975 (see Tables 16.1 and 16.2).

TABLE 16.1 Death Rates of Low Birth Weight Infants per 1000 Low Birth Weight Births for the State of Wisconsin and Three Regions Remote or Upwind from Nuclear Power Plants

| Year | State | Three Remote or Upwind Regions | | | $\bar{X}$ Rates for the Three Regions |
		Rice Lake	Wausau	Madison	
1963–1966	195.9	221.4	213.5	190.0	208.3
1967–1970	170.2	175.3	182.1	163.4	173.6
1971–1975	145.7	155.9	126.8	141.3	141.3
1971–1975 rate as % of the 1963–1966 rate	74.4%	70.4%	59.4%	74.4%	

NOTE: In 1963–1966 there were 348,142 total live births, with 20,974 or 6.0% low birth weight.

In 1967–1970 there were 305,227 total live births, with 18,010 or 5.9% low birth weight.

In 1971–1975 there were 332,932 total live births, with 17,829 or 5.4% low birth weight.

Source: Tables 16.1 and 16.2 are adapted from R. Bertell, N. Jacobson, & M. Stogre, Environmental influence on survival of low birth weight infants in Wisconsin, 1963–1975, *International Perspectives in Public Health*, Fall 1984, Vol. 1, Issue 2, p. 12. Reprinted with permission from International Institute of Concern for Public Health, Toronto, Canada.

They used the first two time periods to see whether there was an overall upward, downward, or level trend in the infants' death rates. They then compared the death rates in the third time period with the previous two to see whether there was a change after the start-up of the nuclear power plants.

Tables 16.1 and 16.2 show the death rates for low birth weight infants for the state and the six regions during the three selected time periods.

TABLE 16.2 Death Rates of Low Birth Weight Infants per 1000 Low Birth Weight Births for the State of Wisconsin and Three Regions Downwind of Nuclear Power Plants

| Year | State | Three Downwind Regions | | | $\bar{X}$ Rates for the Three Regions |
		Eau Claire	La Crosse	Green Bay	
1963–1966	195.9	207.7	184.1	203.7	198.5
1967–1970	170.2	153.2	175.3	178.7	169.1
1971–1975	145.7	183.6	157.4	186.5	175.8
1971–1975 rate as % of the 1963–1966 rate	74.4%	88.4%	85.5%	91.6%	

During the period from 1971 to 1975, which was after the start-up of the nuclear power plants, the death rates in two of the remote or upwind regions are below the state level (see rows 3 and 4 of Table 16.1). The death rates in the regions downwind and close to the nuclear power plants are all above the state level (see rows 3 and 4 of Table 16.2). The figures in the third row of each table also show that after the start-up of the nuclear reactors (1971–1975), death rates in all three downwind regions are higher than in the upwind regions.

Figure 16.1 summarizes the effects by showing the average death rates for infants in the downwind and the upwind or remote regions. Before the introduction of the reactors the death rates declined

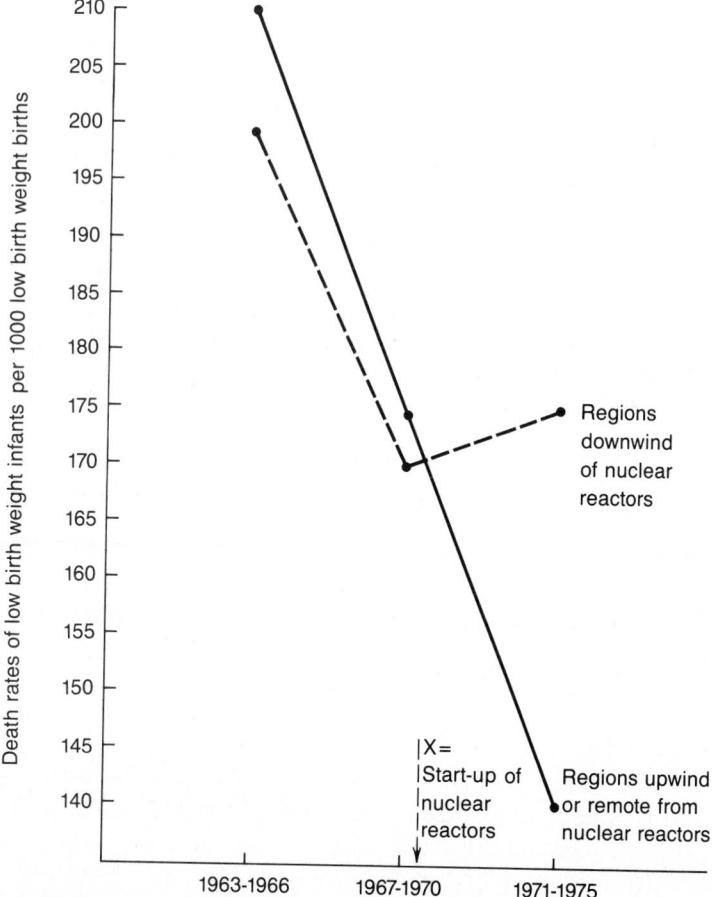

FIGURE 16.1 Average death rates of low birth weight infants per1000 low birth weight births for three downwind regions and three regions upwind or remote from nuclear power plants which were started up between 1969 and 1974

between the first and second time periods in both sets of regions. This decline probably resulted from advances in health care and medical technology. The decline in death rates continued in the remote or upwind regions from the second to the third time period because they were not affected by the start-up of nuclear reactors. In the downwind regions, however, the death rates rose again after 1970. This rise in deaths corresponds with the start-up of the seven nuclear reactors between 1969 and 1974.

The bottom rows of Tables 16.1 and 16.2 show the 1971–1975 rate as a percentage of the 1963–1966 rate. The patterns show that deaths in the downwind regions are higher than the state levels, and deaths in the remote or upwind regions are equal to or lower than the state level.

Before concluding that the increased death rates of these infants were caused by the nuclear power plants, Bertell and her colleagues examined some potentially confounding variables to see whether there were plausible rival explanations. The researchers were rightly concerned about the internal validity of their research, for the results could alarm people in Wisconsin and elsewhere and so must be carefully scrutinized before being made public. They considered several sets of potentially confounding variables. We will examine two here: (1) the existence of other environmental pollutants that could adversely affect the health of infants and adults, such as waste products from chemical plants and fossil fuel plants, and (2) the availability of quality medical facilities, particularly infant intensive care units, which are known to affect the survival rates of low birth weight infants.

In examining the effects of chemical plants and fossil fuel plants the researchers found no relationship between the existence or operation of those industries and the infant death rates. For instance, in Eau Claire, a downwind area where infant death rates increased, there are only two fossil fuel generators, whereas in Madison, where the infant mortality rates decreased, there are eleven fossil fuel generators. So fossil fuel plants cannot be implicated in the infants' deaths. The same pattern appears for chemical plants. In Eau Claire there are only 2 chemical companies and in Madison there are 28, but the death rates are higher in Eau Claire and lower in Madison.

The researchers also considered the second rival explanation—that the availability of medical facilities, particularly infant intensive care units, is the major determining factor in the infants' deaths. The evidence on the existence of perinatal care units shows that all three downwind regions, with the increased death rates, are served by perinatal care units, so the deaths cannot be attributed to lack of medical care. In fact, within one of the downwind areas, La Crosse, the highest rates of low birth weight deaths are occurring in those parts of the county with the best access to specialized medical care. In contrast, of the three upwind regions, two do not have perinatal or infant intensive care units, so their better survival figures cannot be attributed to better medical care.

As a final check on their data and interpretations, the researchers examined the relationship between reports of radioactive gases released and low birth weight infant death rates. They encountered several difficulties with this analysis. The first is that not all gaseous releases are reported by the operators of nuclear power plants. The Nuclear Regulatory Commission does not require operators to report the gases released during start-up and testing phases (Bertell, Jacobson, & Stogre, 1984). A second difficulty is that there are seasonal shifts in prevailing winds. Eau Claire, for instance, is downwind of one nuclear reactor about 50 percent of the year and downwind of another reactor 25 percent of the year, so the gaseous releases that affected Eau Claire came from different reactors at different times of the year. The researchers, therefore, had to proceed with the knowledge that not all gaseous releases were reported, and they had to combine seasonal wind factors with the timing of reported gaseous releases. They did find a relationship between gaseous releases and infant death rates and concluded,

> In spite of the many unknown factors, such as exact dates of "batch" releases of radioactive gases, wind direction at release times and probable doses to the downwind population, there is a discernible trend with greater excess in low birth weight infant deaths coinciding with years of larger radioactive gaseous releases, and fewer excess low birth weight infant deaths occurring during years with smaller radioactive gaseous releases [p. 19].

If this research had not been done, no one would know about the connection between infant deaths and the location of nuclear power plants. These deaths would still be attributed to other causes. It took the research to demonstrate that living downwind of nuclear power plants causes a rise in the deaths of these infants.

This research has not yet set off great alarms, perhaps because it is not widely known and perhaps because the persons most directly affected have not been informed.

Why use low birth weight infant death rates as the indicator of how nuclear power plants affect human health? These infants provide such sensitive indicators because they are very fragile. And being fragile, they are more vulnerable to respiratory infections that other infants survive. The radioactive gases and particles released into the atmosphere by nuclear power plants suppress the immune systems of the infants and make them more vulnerable to respiratory diseases than they already are. When these infants contract respiratory infections, they are more likely to die, and their death records usually state the cause of death as "pneumonia."

This scenario raises several questions. Does the fact that fragile low birth weight infants die when they are born downwind of nuclear reactors mean that hardy adults are also affected? Does the hospital record which says the cause of death is "pneumonia" accurately identify the cause? Might it not as well be said that the child died from "radioactive gaseous releases" or from "living downwind of a nuclear reactor"?

We will not say much more about this research or about the question of whether we can afford *not* to do applied research. But we want to come back to a question that we raised in Chapter 1 and that has been implied throughout other parts of this book. Is it possible to conduct social research—research that examines human relations and human welfare— without considering questions of social values? Does applied, and perhaps also basic, research not force us to consider whose purposes are served by an intervention or an evaluation or even a research question (cf. Becker, 1967)? And must we not usually choose sides?

Summary

Evaluation research has all the same problems and solutions in design and measurement as does basic research. It differs from basic research in its purposes and its connection with social policy. The relationship to policy and public welfare presents challenges to evaluation researchers that require personal, political, and philosophical decisions. The biases inherent in the questions asked and the criteria used to determine a program's success or failure do not simply get buried in libraries. They influence decisions and affect people's lives. This makes applied and evaluation research particularly relevant to social relations and human welfare.

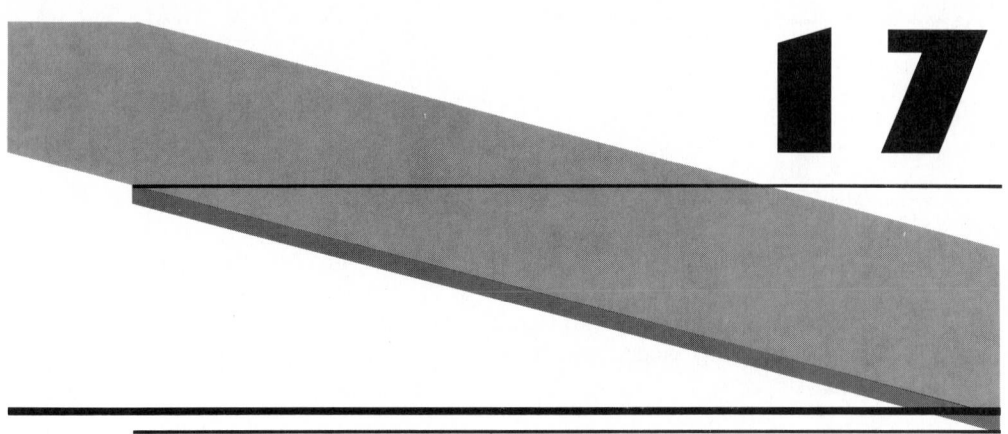

Writing the Research Report

This chapter was written by Daryl J. Bem.

You have conducted a study and analyzed the data. Now it is time to tell the world what you have learned, to write the research report. Even if your report is not for a professional audience, we suggest that you adopt the format used for research articles in the professional journals. This format permits readers not only to read the report from beginning to end, as they would any coherent narrative, but also to scan it for a quick overview of the study or to locate specific information easily by turning directly to the relevant section. Despite the standardized format, your individual style will find ample opportunity for expression.

The report is divided into the following sections:

1. Introduction (What problem were you investigating and why?)
2. Method (What procedures did you employ?)
3. Results (What did you find?)
4. Discussion (What do your findings mean? Where do we go from here?)
5. Summary or Abstract (A brief summary of points 1 through 4.)
6. References (An alphabetical list of books and articles cited in the report.)
7. Appendix (optional) (Copies of questionnaires, scales, or stimulus materials used in the research or tables of data too extensive or too peripheral to include in the body of the report.)

In this chapter we provide a step-by-step procedure for filling in the details of this outline as well as some stylistic suggestions for achieving maximum clarity in your report.

Some Preliminary Considerations

Which Report Should You Write?

There are two possible reports you can write: (1) the report you had in mind when you designed your study or (2) the report that makes the most sense after you have seen the results. They are rarely the same, and the correct answer is (2).

According to the popular view of the research process, an investigator begins with a formal theory, derives one or more hypotheses from that theory, designs and conducts a study to test these hypotheses, analyzes the data to see if they were confirmed, and then chronicles this sequence of events in the research report. If research actually proceeded according to this plan, most of the research report could be prepared before the data are collected. The introduction and method sections could be completely written beforehand, and the results section could be prepared in skeleton form, leaving spaces to be filled in by the specific numerical results obtained. The investigator could even prepare two possible discussion sections, one for positive or confirming results, the other for negative or disconfirming results. Research, however, does not usually go according to this plan—even when that was the plan the investigator had in mind to begin with. Accordingly, we suggest you begin thinking about your report by thinking about your data.

As we noted in Chapter 13, data analysis consists of more than simply checking to see if your original hypotheses were confirmed or disconfirmed. It also involves exploring the data thoroughly to see if there are any interesting results that may not have been originally anticipated. For example, by looking at the data separately for men and women, you might discover an unexpected sex difference. You may even find some results that are far more informative than the confirmation or disconfirmation of your original hypotheses. Statistical tests can help you decide just how much faith you should put in such discoveries. Perhaps you will only be able to mention these findings tentatively in your report and to suggest further research for following them up. On the other hand, you might be justified in deciding to center your report around these new findings and to subordinate or even ignore your original hypotheses.

This is not advice to suppress negative results or findings unfavorable to your theory. If your study was genuinely designed to test hypotheses derived from a formal theory or if the original hypotheses are of wide general interest for some other reason, the confirmation or disconfirmation of these hypotheses should remain the central focus of your report. In particular, the integrity of the scientific enterprise requires an investigator to report negative or disconfirming results no matter how personally disappointing this outcome might be.

But this requirement assumes that somebody out there cares about the disconfirmation of the hypotheses. Many, if not most, studies in social relations are launched from some personal speculations or idiosyncratic questions of the "I-wonder-if . . ." variety. If your study is of this type, nobody is likely to care if you were wrong. Contrary to the conventional wisdom, science does not care how clever or clairvoyant you were at guessing your results ahead of time. Your report should not be a personal history of your stillborn thoughts. Scientific integrity does not require you to lead your readers through all your wrongheaded hunches only to show—*voilà!*—they were wrongheaded.

Your overriding purpose is to tell the world what you think you have learned from your study about human behavior. That may or may not be the same as telling the world about what you used to think about human behavior when you began this investigation. If your results suggest an instructive or compelling framework for the presentation of your study, adopt that framework, making the findings that tell us the most about human behavior the centerpiece of your presentation. An appropriate metaphor here is to think of your data as a jewel. Your job is to cut and polish this jewel, to select the facets to highlight, and to craft the best setting for it. Good report writing is largely a matter of good judgment; despite the standardized format, it is not a mechanical process.

And so, think about your report by thinking about your data. You may even find that the easiest way to begin is to write the results section first.

The "Hourglass" Shape of the Report

An experimental report is usually written in the shape of an hourglass. It begins with broad general statements, progressively narrows down to the specifics of your particular study, and then broadens out again to more general considerations. Thus:

The introduction begins broadly:	"Humanity has long been thought of as basically evil."
It becomes more specific:	"Aggression has been seen as innate; altruism, as learned."
And more so:	"But studies of various animal species show that altruism often occurs . . ."
And more so:	"Indeed, Brewer reports that worker ants often sacrifice their own lives in order . . ."
Until you are ready to introduce your own study in conceptual terms:	"Two classes of behavior were selected, one antisocial, one prosocial . . ."
The method and results sections are the most specific, the "neck" of the hourglass:	(Method) Fifteen nursery school children were given M&M's and then observed. . . . (Results) Table 1 shows that 13 of the 15 children were more cooperative . . ."
The discussion section begins with the implications of your study:	"These results show that not all prosocial behavior needs to be learned . . ."
It becomes broader:	"Clearly we need a more symmetric approach to anti- and prosocial behaviors . . ."

And more so:
> "Humanity, then, can be viewed as both evil and good; both predestined and free; capable of great sin, but capable of great goodness as well."

This example may be a bit more grandiose in its opening and closing statements than would be appropriate for a professional journal article; but if your study is carefully executed and conservatively interpreted, you deserve to indulge yourself a bit at the two broad ends of the hourglass. Being dull only appears to be a prerequisite for publishing in the professional journals.

Introduction

What Is the Problem Being Investigated?

The first task of the research report is to introduce the background and nature of the problem being investigated. Even if your study were only asking a simple empirical question about human behavior or were directed toward a practical problem or policy issue, you must still place the question or issue into a larger context so that readers know why it is of any general significance. Here, for example, is an introduction to an article entitled "Does Sex-Biased Job Advertising 'Aid and Abet' Sex Discrimination?" (Bem & Bem, 1973):

> Title VII of the 1964 Civil Rights Act forbids discrimination in employment on the basis of race, color, religion, national origin—and sex. Although the sex provision was treated as a joke at the time—and was originally introduced in an attempt to defeat the bill—more than 40% of the complaints warranting investigation in the first year of the Act were sex discrimination complaints. Nearly 6000 charges of sex discrimination were filed in 1971 alone.

> Title VII extends as well to practices that aid and abet discrimination. For example, the Act forbids job advertisements from indicating a preference for one sex or the other unless sex is a bona fide occupational qualification for employment. In interpreting this provision, the Equal Employment Opportunities Commission (EEOC) has ruled that even the practice of labeling help-wanted columns as "Male" or "Female" should be considered a violation of the law.

> Nevertheless, a large number of employers continue to write advertisements that specify a sex preference, and many more write advertising copy clearly intended to appeal to one sex only. Moreover, many newspapers continue to divide their help-wanted advertisements into sex-segregated columns.

> Do these advertising practices aid and abet discrimination in employment by actually discouraging applicants of one sex or the other from applying for jobs for which they are otherwise well qualified? The two studies reported in this article

sought to answer this question empirically. Both were conducted and presented as part of legal testimony, the first in a suit filed by the EEOC against American Telephone and Telegraph Company, the second in a suit filed by the National Organization for Women against *The Pittsburgh Press*.

Note how this introduction conforms to the "hourglass" shape of report writing by beginning with the 1964 Civil Rights Act in general and then successively narrowing the focus to the sex provision of the act, the aiding and abetting clause, and finally to the specific practices that are the subject of the experiments to be reported.

The same reporting strategy is employed if your study was designed to contribute to some aspect of psychological or sociological theory. In this case, you need to summarize the theory or conceptual framework within which you are working. But no matter how theoretical or esoteric your study is, an intelligent nonprofessional—perhaps your neighbor—should still be able to grasp the nature of the problem and understand why he, she, or anyone should care. Here are four rules of thumb for helping that reader out:

1. Write in English prose, not psychological or sociological jargon.
2. Don't plunge the unprepared reader into the middle of your problem or theory. Take the time and space necessary to lead the general reader up to the formal or theoretical statement of the problem step by step.
3. Try to open with a statement about human behavior, not the behavior of behavioral scientists or their research. (This rule is almost always violated in the professional journals. Don't use them as a model here.)
4. Use examples to illustrate theoretical points or to help introduce theoretical or technical terms. The more abstract the theory, the more important such examples become.

The following are examples of opening statements:

> *Wrong:* Recent research in the forced-compliance paradigm has focused on the effects of predecisional choice and incentive magnitude.

> *Wrong:* Festinger's theory of cognitive dissonance has received a great deal of attention during the past 15 years.

> *Right:* The individual who holds two beliefs that are inconsistent with one another may feel uncomfortable. For example, the person who knows that he or she enjoys smoking but believes it to be unhealthy may experience a discomfort arising from the disharmony or inconsistency between these two thoughts or cognitions. This feeling of discomfort has been called *cognitive dissonance* by social psychologist Leon Festinger (1957), who suggests that individuals will be motivated to remove this dissonance in whatever way they can . . .

The Literature Review

After you have set the stage in your opening statement, summarize the current state of knowledge in the area of investigation. What previous research has been done on this problem? What are the pertinent theories of the phenomenon, if any? You should have familiarized yourself with previous work on the topic before you designed your own study, and hence most of your literature search should have been done by the time you are ready to write your report. Nevertheless, your results may have led you to recast your study in a slightly different framework or to introduce a new aspect of the problem. In this case, you may need to cite references you had not previously consulted. Suppose, for example, that you did discover an unanticipated sex difference in your results. You should then go back to the literature to see if other investigators have found such a difference or to see if there are any related findings that might explain your unexpected result. If you plan to make the sex difference a central feature of your report, you should discuss the topic of sex differences in the introduction, including citations to the relevant previous findings. If you plan to mention the sex difference only as a subsidiary finding, however, postpone any discussion of sex differences until the discussion section. (You should now begin to appreciate why you cannot really begin your report until you have a clear view of the results already in mind.)

In reviewing previous work, you need not describe every study ever done on your problem. Cite only articles pertinent to the specific issues with which you are dealing; emphasize their major conclusions, findings, or relevant methodological issues and avoid unnecessary detail. If someone else has written a review article that surveys the literature on the topic, you can simply refer your own readers to the review and present only its most pertinent points in your own report. Even when you must describe an entire study, try to condense it as much as possible without sacrificing clarity. One way of doing this is to describe one variation of the procedure in chronological sequence, letting it convey the overview of the study at the same time. Here, for example, is a description of a very complicated experiment on attitude change designed to test Festinger's theory of cognitive dissonance (Festinger & Carlsmith, 1959):

> Sixty male undergraduates were randomly assigned to one of three conditions. In the $1 condition, the subject was first required to perform long repetitive laboratory tasks in an individual experimental session. He was then hired by the experimenter as an "assistant" and paid $1 to tell a waiting fellow student (a confederate) that the tasks were fun and interesting. In the $20 condition, each subject was hired for $20 to do the same thing. Control subjects simply engaged in the tasks. After the experiment each subject indicated on a questionnaire how much he had enjoyed the tasks. The results showed that $1 subjects rated the tasks as significantly more enjoyable than did the $20 subjects, who, in turn, did not differ from the control subjects.

This kind of condensed writing looks easy. It is not, and you will have to write and rewrite such summaries repeatedly before they are both clear and succinct. The preceding paragraph is the eighth draft.

Books and articles are cited in the text of the report by giving the author's last name and the date of publication. For example: "According to L. A. Festinger (1957), people find cognitive dissonance uncomfortable. Not everyone, however, agrees with this conclusion (e.g., Abelson, 1968; Bem, 1967; Kermit, 1979). Nevertheless, direct evidence for internal discomfort has actually been demonstrated in at least one study (Zanna, Freud, & Theophrastus, 1977)." Note that footnotes are not used for references or citations.

Your Study

As you come to the end of the introduction, it is often useful to introduce your own study in brief overview. The purpose is not to discuss procedural details but to provide a smooth transition into the method section, which follows immediately. The following example could have ended the introduction to the previously cited sex-biased advertising study:

> The question, then, is whether or not such advertising practices discourage potential applicants from applying for jobs. The present study sought to answer this question by asking male and female high school seniors to read several telephone job advertisements and to rate their interest in each job. The interest ratings were analyzed to see if advertisements written in nonsexist language would increase the interest that men and women would show in jobs stereotyped for the "other" sex.

Method

What to Include

Readers need to know in considerable detail how the study was carried out. What was its basic design? If the study was an experimental one, just what were the experimental manipulations? (For example, was "threat" established by telling the subjects that they were about to take a very difficult test, which would determine their grades in a course, or by shouting "Fire!"?) At what point or points were the measurements taken?

If the data were collected by means of questionnaires or interviews, exactly what questions were asked? (The questionnaire or interview schedule is often given in an appendix.) How much and what kind of experience had the interviewers had, and how were they trained for this particular study? If the measurements were based on observation, what instructions were given to the observers?

Readers also need to know how the observations or replies to questions were translated into measures of the variables with which the study was concerned. (For example, which questions were taken into account in estimating "alienation"; or what kinds of bystanders' behavior were classified as "helping"?)

Regarding the sample used in the study, readers should be told the following: Who were the subjects? How many were there? How were they selected? These questions are crucial for estimating the probable limits of generalizability of the findings. Are elaborate conclusions being drawn on the basis of responses of ten college sophomores, selected because they happened to be friends of the investigator? Were only women interviewed? If so, is there any basis for extending the findings to people in general? Intensive study of a small number of cases that do not constitute a representative sample of any specifiable population may be quite valuable. Nevertheless, the number and characteristics of the participants on which the findings are based should be clearly stated so that readers can draw their own conclusions about the applicability of the findings to other groups.

If you conducted a fairly complex experiment in which there was a sequence of procedures or events, it is often helpful to describe the study as it was seen from the subject's point of view. First give an overview of the study, including a description of the subjects, setting, and the variables assessed; but then describe the sequence of events in chronological order so that the reader is carried through the experience as a subject was. Provide summaries or excerpts of what was actually said to the subject, including any rationale or "cover story" that was given. Show sample items from questionnaires, labels on attitude scales, pictures of apparatus or stimulus materials, and so forth, even if you also include the complete questionnaires or rating scales in an appendix to your report. If you administered a standard personality test, describe its general properties, and give a sample item even if it is a fairly familiar instrument; for example, "Subjects then filled out the Marlow-Crowne Social Desirability Scale, a true-false inventory that taps the degree to which a person describes him- or herself in socially desirable terms (e.g., 'I have never lied')." The purpose of all this is to give the readers a "feel" for what it was like to be a subject. This often bears importantly on the interpretation of your results, and readers should be in a position to arrive at their own judgments about your conclusions.

Name all operations and variables with easily recognized and remembered labels. Don't use abbreviations (The AMT5% group) or empty labels (Treatment 3). Instead, tell us about the sex-biased ads and the sex-neutral ads, the success group versus the failure group, the teacher sample versus the student sample, and so forth. It is also better to label groups or treatments in operational rather than theoretical terms. It is difficult to remember that it was the high dissonance group that was paid $1 and the low dissonance group that was paid $20. So tell us instead about the $1 group and the $20 group. You can remind us of the theoretical interpretation of these variables again later when it is necessary. And finally, it is often helpful in a complicated experiment to end your description with a one- or two-sentence summary of the procedure and its purpose.

An Example

The following example is excerpted from the method section of the sex-biased advertising study cited earlier.

METHOD

Subjects
One-hundred twenty seniors from a racially integrated high school in the San Francisco Bay area served as subjects. Half were male and half were female. Few planned to go on to any 4-year college. Students who were not planning to go on to college were purposely sought as subjects so that they might be both appropriate for and interested in jobs like those advertised by the telephone company. (As seniors, many would even be preparing for jobs like these in the near future.)

Procedure
Each student was given a booklet containing 12 job advertisements and was asked to indicate on a 6-point scale how interested he or she would be in applying for each job. The scale ranged from "very uninterested" to "very interested" and was labeled at each point. The 12 advertisements included four telephone jobs and eight nontelephone jobs. In order of appearance, the jobs were: appliance sales, telephone operator, photographer, travel agent, telephone frameman, dental assistant, taxicab driver, telephone service representative, assistant buyer, keypunch operator, telephone lineman, and public relations/advertising.

The cover sheet introduced all 12 jobs as follows: "All of the jobs have a starting salary of between $100 and $120 per week with regular raises after that. None of the jobs requires any previous training or experience beyond high school graduation; all of them provide paid on-the-job training." The phrase, "An Equal Opportunity Employer m/f," appeared at the end of every job advertisement.

Sex-Biased Job Advertisements
One-third of the booklets advertised the telephone jobs in the sex-biased format used by AT&T. In other words, these ads were copied verbatim from AT&T ads and brochures furnished to us by the EEOC. The four sex-biased telephone advertisements were worded as follows:

Telephone Operator

WHO SAYS IT'S A MAN'S WORLD?
Behind every man's telephone call, there is a woman. She's a smart woman. She's efficient. She has to be. She places the complex long distance calls people cannot place themselves or helps them locate telephone numbers.

Hers is a demanding job. But we make it worth her while. We can make it worth your while too. Not only do we pay a good salary to start, but also offer group life insurance, group medical coverage, good vacations with pay and free pensions.

A stepping stone to management positions.

Pacific Telephone

An Equal Opportunity Employer m/f

[The other advertisements and conditions were similarly described and illustrated.]

Summary of Procedure

The same four telephone jobs were thus presented in three different formats: the sex-biased format used by AT&T, a sex-unbiased format, and a sex-reversed "affirmative-action" format. All 8 nontelephone ads were worded in sex-unbiased fashion and remained constant in all booklets. In other words, only the wording of the telephone jobs changed from condition to condition. For purposes of analysis, a subject was defined as "interested in applying" for a job if he or she checked any of the following three categories: "slightly interested," "moderately interested," "very interested." A subject was defined as "not interested" if he or she checked "slightly uninterested," "moderately uninterested," or "very uninterested."

Ethical Issues

The subjects or participants in our studies are human beings and should be accorded respect and gratitude for their partnership in the research enterprise. Accordingly, after you have described your procedures, it is appropriate to tell us how you compensated them for their time and effort and how you dealt with any ethical problems. If the research design required you to keep subjects uninformed or even misinformed about the procedures, how did you tell them about this afterward? Did you obtain written consent from your subjects for their participation? Were they free to withdraw their participation at any time? Were they subjected to any embarrassment or discomfort? Were you observing people who were not aware of that fact? What steps were followed to protect the anonymity of your subjects or participants? If your study raises any of these ethical issues, you should be prepared to justify your procedures and to assure readers that your subjects were treated with dignity and that they left your study with their self-esteem intact and their respect for you and behavioral science enhanced rather than diminished.

Results

In short articles or reports of fairly simple studies, the results and discussion sections are often combined into a single section entitled "Results and Discussion." The results are discussed as they are presented, and the section ends with two or three paragraphs that state the conclusions reached, mention qualifications imposed by problems encountered in executing or analyzing the study, and suggest what further research might be appropriate. Most empirical studies can be handled in this fashion.

If, however, you need to present many different kinds of results before you can integrate them or draw any inferences or if you wish to discuss several different matters at length in the final discussion, you should separate the results and discussion sections. Even in this case, however, there is no such thing as a pure results section without any accompanying discussion. You cannot just throw numbers at readers and expect them to retain them in their memory until they reach the discussion section. In other words, the results section is still part of an integrated linear narrative about human behavior. It, too, is to be written in English prose, not numbers and statistical symbols.

Setting the Stage

Before you can present your main results, two preliminary matters must be handled. First, you need to present evidence that your study successfully set up the conditions for testing your hypotheses or answering your questions. If your study required you to produce one group of subjects in a happy mood and another in a sad mood, here is the place to show us that mood ratings made by the two groups were significantly different. If your study involved a mail survey, here is where you need to tell us how many people returned the survey and to discuss the possibility that those who did not respond differed in some important way from those who did. If you divided your subjects into groups, you need to assure us that these groups did not differ on some unintended variable that might bear on the interpretation of your results (e.g., social class, race, sex, age, intelligence). If your study required observers to record behavior or judges to score written materials, you should present quantitative evidence for interobserver agreement or interjudge reliability. If your study required that you misinform the subjects about the nature of the procedures, you should have some evidence that they were not suspicious, that subjects who participated earlier had not informed subjects who participated later, and that your "cover story" produced the state of belief required for the test of your hypotheses. If you had to discard certain subjects, either at the time of the study or later in the data analysis, you need to tell us why and how many and to discuss the possibility that this limits or qualifies the conclusions you can draw.

Not all these matters need to be discussed at the beginning of the results section. Some of them might already have been mentioned in the method section (e.g., interjudge reliabilities of scoring), and others might better be postponed until the discussion section, when you are considering alternative explanations of your results (e.g., the possibility that some subjects became suspicious). In some cases, you may not have any hard evidence to cite, and you may have to fall back on plausible argument: "The possibility that those who did not return the survey were politically more conservative than those who did seems unlikely because surveys were returned in approximately equal numbers from the dormitories, the cooperatives, and the fraternities. If the survey had alienated conservatives, we would have expected a smaller return from the fraternities; moreover. . . ."

The decision of what to include at the beginning of the results section to assure the reader that you have successfully set the stage for adequately testing your hypotheses or answering your questions is very much a matter of judgment. It is an important step, but don't overdo it. Get it out of the way as quickly as possible, and then get on with your story.

The second preliminary matter to deal with is the method of data analysis. First you need to describe any overall procedures you followed in converting your raw observations into analyzable data. How were the responses to your mail survey coded for analysis? How were observers' ratings combined? Were all measures first converted to standard scores? (Some of these, too, may have been discussed in the method section and need not be repeated. Similarly, data-combining procedures that are highly specific can be postponed. For example, if you combined three measures of anxiety into a single composite score for analysis, you can tell us about that later when you are about to present the anxiety data.)

Next you need to tell readers about the statistical analysis itself. If this is quite standard, it can be described in very few words (e.g., "All data were analyzed by two-way analyses of variance with sex of subject and mood induction as the independent variables"). If your analysis is unconventional or requires certain statistical assumptions that your data may not meet, however, you need to discuss the rationale for it, perhaps citing an article or book for the reader who wishes to check into it further.

And finally, this is the place to give readers an overview of the entire results section if it is complicated or divided into several parts. For example: "The results are presented in three parts. The first section presents the behavioral results for the men, followed by the parallel results for the women. The final section presents the attitudinal and physiological data for both sexes combined."

Presenting the Findings

 The general rule in reporting your findings is to give the forest first and then the trees. This is true of the results section as a whole: Begin with the central findings, and then move to more peripheral ones. It is also true within subsections: State the basic finding first, and then elaborate or qualify it as necessary. Similarly, discuss an overall measure of aggression or whatever first, and then move to its individual components. Beginning with one of your most central results, proceed as follows:

1. Remind us of the conceptual question you are asking (e.g., "It will be recalled that the men are expected to be more expressive than the women." Or "We turn first to the question: Are the men or the women

more expressive?"). Note that this is a *conceptual* statement of the question.

2. Remind us of the actual operation performed or the actual behavior measured (e.g., "Do the men produce more tears during the showing of the film than the women?"). Note that this is an *operational* statement of the question.

3. Tell us the answer immediately and in English. ("The answer is yes." Or "As Table 1 reveals, men do, in fact, cry more profusely than women.")

4. Now, and only now, speak to us in numbers. "Thus the men in all four conditions produced an average of 14 cc more tears than the women, $F(1112) = 5.79$, $p < .025$."

5. Now you may elaborate or qualify the overall conclusion if necessary: "Only in the father-watching condition did the men fail to produce more tears than the women, but a specific test of this effect failed to reach significance, $t = 1.58$, $p < .12$.

6. As shown in the preceding examples, every finding that involves a comparison between groups or a relationship between variables should be accompanied by its level of statistical significance. Otherwise, readers have no way of knowing whether the finding could have emerged by chance. But despite the importance of inferential statistics for deciding which results are to be presented as genuine findings, they are not the heart of your narrative and should be subordinated to the descriptive results. Whenever possible, state the result first and then give its statistical significance, but in no case should you ever give the statistical test alone without indicating its meaning in terms of the substantive results. Do not tell us that the three-way interaction with sex, esteem, and parent condition was significant at the .05 level unless you tell us immediately and in English that men are less expressive than women in the negative conditions if father watches—but only for men with low self-esteem.

7. In selecting the descriptive indices or statistics, your purpose should be to show us the behavior of people as vividly as you can, to be as descriptive of the actual behavior observed as possible. If children in your study hit a Bobo doll, tell us how many times they hit it or the percent of children who hit it. If an aggression score represents the mean on a 5-point rating scale, remind us that 3.42 lies between "slightly aggressive" and "quite aggressive." Just as the method section should give us a "feel" for the procedures employed, so, too, the results section should give us a "feel" for the behavior observed.

8. Every set of findings that is sufficiently important to be stressed should be accompanied by a table, graph, or figure showing the relevant data (unless the entire set of findings can be stated in one or two numbers). The basic rule here is that readers should be able to grasp your major findings *either* by reading the text *or* by looking at the fig-

ures and tables. This implies that tables and figures must be titled and labeled clearly and completely, even if that means constructing a very lengthy title or heading (e.g., "Mean number of tears produced in male and female subjects by the heart operation movie as a function of subject sex, parental observation, and self-esteem"). Within the text itself, you must lead the reader by the hand through the table to point out the results of interest: "As shown in column A of Table 2, men produce more tears (7.58) than women (6.34). . . . Of particular interest is the number of tears produced when both father and mother were watching (rows 3 and 4). . . ." Don't just wave in the general direction of the table and expect the reader to ferret out the information.

9. End each section of the results with a summary of where things stand. "Thus, except for the father-watching condition, which will be discussed later, the hypothesis that men cry more than women in response to visually depicted grief appears to receive strong support."

10. Lead into the next section of the results with a smooth transition sentence: "Men may thus be more expressive than women in the domain of negative emotion, but can we assume that they are also more willing and able to express positive emotions? Table 3 shows that we cannot. . . ." (Note, again, that you should give the reader the "bottom line" immediately.) As the results section proceeds, you should continue to summarize and "update" the reader's store of information frequently. The reader should not have to keep looking back to retrieve the major points of your plot line.

By structuring the results section in this way, by moving from forest to trees, by announcing each result clearly in prose before wading into numbers and statistics, and by summarizing frequently, you permit the readers to decide just how much detail they want to pursue at each juncture and to skip ahead to the next main point whenever that seems desirable.

After you have demonstrated that your quantitative results are statistically reliable, it is often useful to become more informal and to describe the behavior of particular individuals in your study. The point is not to prove something but to add richness to your findings, to share with the readers the "feel" of the behavior: "Indeed, two of the men used an entire box of tissues during the showing of the heart operation but yet would not pet the baby kitten owned by the secretary."

An Example

The following example is from the results section of the same sex-biased advertising study cited earlier.

RESULTS

Do sex-biased job advertisements discourage men and women from applying for "opposite-sex" jobs? As shown in Figure 17.1, our results clearly suggest this to be the case.

Consider first the results for women. When the jobs of lineman and frameman were advertised in a sex-biased format, no more than 5% of the women were interested. When these same jobs were advertised in a sex-unbiased format, 25% of the women were interested. And when the ads for lineman and frameman were specifically written to appeal to women, nearly half (45%) of the women in our sample were interested in applying for one or the other of these two jobs ($X^2 = 8.53$, $p < .01$, one-tailed). In other words, sex-biased advertisements do discourage women from applying for so-called male jobs; more women would be interested in applying for such jobs if the ad's sex bias were removed; and even more women would be interested if affirmative-action ads were specifically written to recruit them.

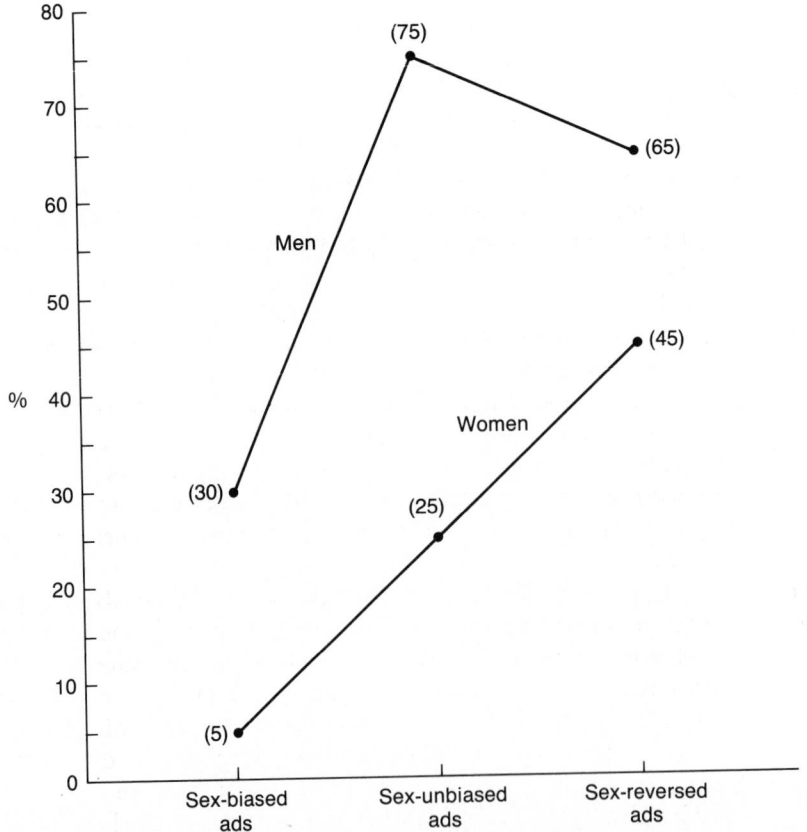

FIGURE 17.1 Percent of men and women who were interested in applying for either of the "opposite-sex" jobs (Each data point represents 20 subjects.)

The results for men show a similar, but not identical, pattern. As can be seen in Figure 17.1 men are generally more interested in the jobs of operator and service representative than women are in the jobs of lineman and frameman. (This difference may be due, in part, to the fact that Pacific Telephone does employ male operators in the Bay Area.) Despite this fact, the results clearly indicate that sex-biased job advertisements still tend to discourage men from applying for jobs as operator and service representative ($X^2 = 9.09$, $p < .01$, one-tailed). For when the sex bias is removed, the percentage of men interested in applying for one or the other of these jobs jumps from 30% to 75%. Wording these ads in sex-reversed "affirmative-action" format does not further increase the percentage of men who are interested. [Neither does it significantly reduce it, however ($X^2 < 1$, n.s.).] It may be that 75% is the maximum one can expect for any particular job and that a sex-reversed format *would* serve to further increase male interest for "female" jobs with lesser initial interest.

The results thus indicate that sex bias in the content of a job advertisement does serve to aid and abet discrimination by discouraging both men and women from applying for "opposite-sex" jobs.

Discussion

As we noted earlier, the discussion section is often combined with the results section; for more complex studies or studies with more extended or abstract implications, it often appears separately. In either case, the discussion forms a cohesive narrative with the introduction, and you should expect to move materials back and forth between the introduction and discussion as you rewrite and reshape the report. Topics that are central to your argument will appear in the introduction and possibly again in the discussion. Points you have decided to subordinate may not be brought up at all until the discussion section. The closing discussion is also the "bottom" of the hourglass-shaped format and thus proceeds from specific matters about your study to more general concerns (about methodological strategies, for example) to the broadest generalizations you wish to make.

Begin by telling us what you have learned from the study. Open with a clear statement on the support or nonsupport of the hypotheses or the answers to the questions you first raised in the introduction. Do not, however, simply reformulate and repeat points already summarized in the results. Each new statement should contribute something new to the reader's understanding of the problem. What inferences can be drawn from the findings? These inferences may be at a level quite close to the data or may involve considerable abstraction, perhaps to the level of a larger theory regarding, say, emotion or sex differences. What are the theoretical and practical implications of the results?

It is also appropriate at this point to compare your results to those reported by other investigators and to discuss possible shortcomings of your study, conditions that might limit the extent of legitimate generalization or otherwise qualify your inferences. Remind the reader of the characteristics of your sample, the possibility that it might differ from other populations to which you might want to generalize; of specific characteristics of your methods that might have influenced the outcome; or of any other factors that might have operated to produce atypical results. But do not dwell compulsively on every flaw! In particular, be willing to accept negative or unexpected results without a tortured attempt to explain them away. Don't make up long, involved, pretzel-shaped theories to account for every hiccup in the data. There is probably a $-.73$ correlation between the clarity of an investigator's results and the length of his or her discussion section. Don't contribute to this shameful figure.

But suppose that, on the contrary, your results have led you to a grand new theory that injects startling clarity into your data and revolutionizes your view of the problem. Doesn't that justify a long discussion section? No! In this case you should rewrite the entire report so that you *begin* with your new theory. As we noted earlier, your reporting task is to provide the most informative and compelling framework for your study from the opening sentence. If your new theory does that, don't wait until the discussion section to spring it on us. A research report is not necessarily a chronology of your thought processes.

The discussion section also includes a discussion of questions that remain unanswered or new questions that have been raised by the study along with suggestions for the kinds of research that would help to answer them. Indeed, suggesting further research is probably the most common way of ending a research report.

Common, but dull! If you are following the hourglass-shaped format of the research report, the final statements should be broad general statements about human behavior, not precious details of interest only to behavioral scientists. Consider: "Thus further research will be needed before it is clear whether the androgyny scale should be scored as a single continuous dimension or partitioned into a four-way typology." No, no! Such a sentence may well be appropriate somewhere in the discussion, but please, not your final farewell. Why not "Perhaps, then, the concept of androgyny will come to define a new standard of mental health, a standard that will liberate men and women rather than incarcerate them"? Yes, yes! End with a bang, not a whimper!

Summary or Abstract

A research report often concludes with a very brief summary that restates in barest outline the problem, the procedures, the major findings, and the major conclusions drawn from them. This is called the *summary*. Most journals have now replaced the summary with an **abstract,** an even briefer summary that appears at the very beginning of the article rather than at the end.

An abstract is only about 125 words or less. It permits potential readers to get a quick overview of the study and to decide if they wish to read the report itself. It is very difficult to write because it is so condensed, and it will require slaving over every word to attain clarity. You cannot summarize everything in an abstract—or even in a more extended summary at the end of your report if you choose that format. Instead, you must decide what you wish to highlight, and this implies that you should write the abstract or summary last, after you have a firm view of the structure and content of your complete report.

The title of your report itself serves as part of the abstract or summary. It, too, should convey the content of your study as accurately and as clearly as possible so that a potential reader can decide whether or not to go further. The most informative titles are those that manage to mention both the dependent and independent variables (e.g., "Emotional responses of men and women to visual stimuli as a function of self-esteem and being observed by parents"). Here is how the report of the sex-biased advertising study begins.

Does Sex-Biased Job Advertising "Aid and Abet" Sex Discrimination?

ABSTRACT

Two studies are reported which indicate that both sex-biased wording in job advertisements and the placement of help-wanted ads in sex-segregated newspaper columns discourage men and women from applying for "opposite-sex" jobs for which they might well be qualified. Both studies were originally conducted and presented as part of legal testimony in actual sex discrimination cases.

Title VII of the 1964. . . .

References

All books and articles cited in the text of a research report are listed at the end of the report under the heading "References." They are arranged alphabetically according to the author's last name, a format that parallels the way in which they are cited in the text.

The following three references are to journal articles cited in this chapter. The italicized numbers are volume numbers; they are followed by the page numbers.

Bem, S. L., & Bem, D. J. Does sex-biased job advertising "aid and abet" sex discrimination? *Journal of Applied Social Psychology,* 1973, *3,* 6–18.

Festinger, L., & Carlsmith, J. M. Cognitive consequences of forced compliance. *Journal of Abnormal and Social Psychology,* 1959, *58,* 203–210.

Martyna, W. What does "He" mean? *Journal of Communication,* 1978, *28,* 131–138.

The following references are to books cited in this chapter.

Festinger, L. A. *A theory of cognitive dissonance.* Stanford, Calif.: Stanford University Press, 1957.

Strunk, W., Jr., & White, E. B. *The elements of style* (3rd ed.). New York: Macmillan, 1979.

The following example, not cited in this chapter, illustrates a reference to an article by Zimbardo that appears in a book edited by Arnold and Levin.

Zimbardo, P. G. The human choice: Individuation, reason, and order versus deindividuation, impulse, and chaos. In W. A. Arnold & D. Levin (Eds.), *Nebraska symposium on motivation* (Vol. 17). Lincoln: University of Nebraska Press, 1969.

Appendix

The appendix to a research report contains copies of materials used in the research that would be too extensive to include in the report itself. These might include questionnaires, attitude scales, stimulus materials, or photographs and drawings of experimental apparatus or the research setting. These are materials that would help someone else duplicate your experiment in detail. A second appendix might contain tables of data or additional data analyses that are too extensive or too peripheral to include in the report itself. This is information that would enable an interested reader to explore your data in fine detail or to answer questions about your results that you omitted or that may not even have occurred to you.

Because journal space is at a premium, most journal articles do not have appendixes. Readers who have questions about the data or who wish to replicate the experiment themselves usually communicate directly with the original investigator. Dissertations, theses, and research reports done for class assignments, however, usually do include such appendixes. In fact, it is often useful in research reports done for class assignments to include an appendix containing the raw data themselves. Often an instructor will be able to spot findings in the data that may have been overlooked or to suggest alternative ways of organizing or analyzing data. In short, whether or not an investigator includes appendixes in a report depends a lot on who the readers will be and the likelihood that they will find the supplementary materials useful. But as we noted earlier, the report itself should still be self-contained; a reader should not have to consult an appendix to understand the methods or results. For example, even if your entire survey questionnaire is contained in an appendix, you should still provide a few sample items from it in the method section.

Some Suggestions on Procedure and Style

Accuracy and Clarity

The overriding criteria for good scientific writing are accuracy and clarity. If your report is interesting and written with flair and style, fine. But this is still a subsidiary virtue. First strive for accuracy and clarity.

Work from an Outline

Even though the standardized format we have described here will go a long way toward organizing your report, you will be able to produce a more coherent report with a minimum of rewriting if you first organize the main points in outline form, examine the logic of the sequence, check to see if important points are omitted or misplaced, and so forth. As we suggested earlier, it is sometimes helpful to begin with the results section, and it is also useful to think of your introduction and final discussion as part of the same conceptual narrative.

Write Simply. Use Examples. Use Friends as Reviewers

As we noted earlier, it should be possible for nonprofessionals to read your report and comprehend what you did and why—even if they know nothing about statistics, experimental design, or the substantive area of your research problem. This is achieved by writing simply, with a minimum of jargon, and using frequent examples to illustrate and introduce technical concepts. The more abstract the subject matter, the more you need examples to tie it back to the reader's own experience and previous level of knowledge.

Read over your own writing, trying to take the viewpoint of an intelligent but nonprofessional reader. Ask at each point, "Do I know yet what this concept means?" "Is this clear?" The ability to take the role of a "naive" reader or listener is the most important skill in writing or teaching. It is not easy. And because it is not easy, you should use your friends as reviewers, especially those who are unfamiliar with the subject matter. If they find something unclear, do not argue with them or attempt to clarify the problem verbally. If they have read carefully and conscientiously, they are always right: *By definition, the writing is unclear.* Their suggestions for correcting the unclarities may be wrong, even dumb. But as unclarity detectors, readers are never wrong.

Be Compulsive. Be Willing to Restructure

The best writers rewrite nearly every sentence in the course of polishing their successive drafts. The probability of writing a sentence perfectly the first time is vanishingly small, and good writing requires a high degree of compulsiveness and attention to detail. But whether or not one worries about writing style in the course of producing the first draft is to some extent a matter of individual taste. Some experienced writers spend a long time over each sentence, carefully choosing each word. But when the purpose is to convey information rather than to achieve a literary production, it is probably true for most people that time is saved in the long run by writing the first draft as quickly as possible. Once it is on paper, one can go back and rewrite sentences and paragraphs, fortified by the knowledge that at least a first draft of the report has already been produced.

In writing and rewriting, it is important to remember that a badly built building cannot be salvaged by brightening up the wallpaper. Rewriting often means restructuring, not just tinkering with sentences or paragraphs. Sometimes it is necessary to restructure totally an experimental report, even to go back and do more data analysis, just to iron out a bump in the logic of the argument. Don't get so attached to your first draft that you are unwilling to tear it apart and rebuild it. Rewriting often means restructuring.

Person and Voice

In the past, scientific writing employed the third person passive voice almost exclusively ("The experiment was designed by the authors to test the hypothesis that . . ."). This is dull and clumsy and is no longer the norm. It is now permissible to use the first person and desirable to use the active voice. Do not refer to yourself as "the author" or "the investigator." Do not refer to yourself as "we" unless there really are two or more authors or investigators involved. You may refer to yourself as "I" as long as you do it sparingly; constant use of the first person tends to distract the reader from the subject matter, and it is best to remain in the background. Leave the reader in the background, too. Don't say, "The reader will find it hard to believe that . . ." or "You will be surprised to learn. . . ."

Perhaps you are wondering what you *can* do. You can let people and their behavior serve as the subjects of sentences: "Individuals appear to cling to their prejudices even when. . . ." "Racial prejudice, then, diminishes when persons interact. . . ." You may also refer to the reader indirectly from time to time: "Consider, first, the results for men. . . ." You may also refer to yourself and the reader as "we" in some contexts: "We can see in Table 1 that most of the tears are produced. . . ." "In everyday life, of course, we tend to put great emphasis on a person's gender. . . ."

Tense

Use the past tense when reporting the previous research of others ("Bandura reported . . ."), how you conducted your study ("Observers were posted behind . . ."), and specific past behaviors of your subjects or participants ("Two of the group members talked . . ."). Use the present tense for results currently in front of the reader ("As Table 2 shows, the emotional film is more effective . . .") and for conclusions that are more general than the specific results ("Sex-biased advertising, then, leads qualified applicants to ignore . . .").

Gender

Because of the increased awareness that language can perpetuate stereotypes, authors of journal articles are now expected to avoid writing in a manner that reinforces questionable attitudes and assumptions about people and gender roles. The most awkward problems arise from the common use of masculine nouns and pronouns when the content refers to both genders. The generic use of *man, he, his,* and *him* to refer to both men and women is not only misleading in many instances but also research shows that readers visualize and think of male persons when these forms are used (Martyna, 1978). Sometimes the results are not only sexist but humorous in their naive androcentrism: "Man's vital needs include food, water, and access to females" (quoted in Martyna, 1978).

Unfortunately, the language has not caught up with this new awareness, and the available alternatives are not wholly satisfactory. In most contexts, the simplest alternative is the use of the plural. Instead of saying, "The individual who displays prejudice in his personal relations is probably . . ." substitute "Individuals who display prejudice in their personal relations are. . . ." If it is stylistically important to focus on the single individual, the use of *he or she, him or her,* and so forth is acceptable but clumsy if used very often or more than once in a single sentence: "The individual who displays prejudice in his or her personal relations is. . . ." Alternatives like *he/she* or *s/he* are unpronounceable and grate on the eye. They should be avoided. Eventually, our society will probably adopt one of the neutral forms currently being suggested (e.g., *e* or *tey*), but none of them has yet won wide acceptance. You may find it instructive to look back over this book for examples of how we have dealt with the pronoun problem during this time of transition.

Stylistic matters aside, however, you must be accurate in your use of pronouns when you describe your research or that of others. Readers must be explicitly informed about the gender of experimenters, observers, subjects, and participants. When referring to males, use male pronouns; when referring to females, use female pronouns. Under no circumstances should an investigator omit or hide gender identity in an attempt to be unbiased. Knowledge of gender is often critically important.

The problems of gender reference become easier when we move away from pronouns. Words like *man* and *mankind* are easily replaced by terms like *people, humanity, humankind,* and so forth. Instead of manning projects, we can staff them, hire personnel, or employ staff. The federal government has already desexed occupational titles so that we now have letter carriers rather than mailmen; in private industry we have flight attendants rather than stewardesses. And in life, children need nurturing or parenting, not just mothering. In all these cases, you will find it easy to discover the appropriate sex-neutral term if you simply think in terms of the activity or task rather than the person doing it.

And, finally, we come to plain old stereotyping, hidden assumptions about the roles that men and women play that can sneak into our prose. (The following examples are taken from the *Publication Manual* of the American Psychological Association [Change Sheet #2, 1977].) The author who notes that "research scientists often neglect their wives and children" fails to acknowledge that women as well as men are research scientists. Why not "Research scientists often neglect their families"? Or if the author specifically meant male research scientists, this should have been said explicitly. Often stereotypes show up in the asymmetry of the words used: *Man and wife* rather than *man and woman* or *husband and wife* assumes that the man is defined by his personhood, the woman by her relationship to a man. Referring to adult male persons as *men* and adult female persons as *girls* is another common sexist practice.

Adjective use can also connote bias. Thus, we have ambitious men and aggressive women or cautious men and timid women—where the use of different adjectives denotes not different behaviors on the part of men and women but our biased interpretations and evaluations of their behaviors.

Even verbs can carry hidden bias: "The client's husband lets her teach part time." Here the author intended to communicate the working status of the woman but inadvertently revealed a stereotype about husband-wife relationships. The author should have said, "The client teaches part time." If the bias is not the author's, but the client's or her husband's, that should be clearly indicated: "The client's husband 'lets' her teach part time." Or "The husband says he 'lets' the client teach part time." Or "The client says her husband lets her teach part time." Or "The client says sarcastically that her husband 'lets' her teach part time." The client and her husband are allowed to say such things. You are not.

And finally, try to avoid stereotyping when you select examples. Beware of your own unconscious assumptions about the gender of doctors, homemakers, nurses, athletes, and so forth. Why not "The athlete who believes in her ability to succeed . . ."? Let our writing promote the view that woman's vital needs are the same as man's: food, water, and access to equality.

Where to Find Additional Guidance

Two documents can provide additional information concerning the preparation of your research report. The *Publication Manual* (revised edition, 1974) published by the American Psychological Association provides highly specific information about the exact format used in the professional journals and general advice on format and style of the kind we have included in this chapter. If you are actually preparing a report for a journal, you should consult the *Manual*, as well as look at articles in the relevant journal itself.

There are many books on how to write expository prose, covering grammar, word usage, punctuation, and style. One of the best is *The Elements of Style* (3rd edition, paperback, 1979) by Strunk and White. It can be read in an hour and is highly entertaining as well. (But beware; it explicitly argues for continuing the use of generic masculine pronouns.)

Enough advice. Go write your report.

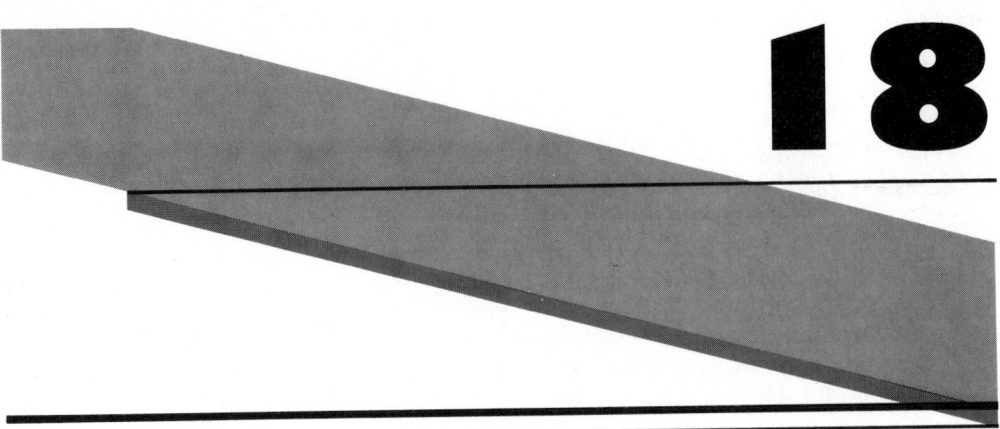

Ethical Implications

This chapter was written by Stuart Cook.

Why Ethical Issues Arise in Research with Human Beings

Other chapters of this book reflect the fact that research investigators have on occasion involved their subjects in research without asking them whether or not they wished to participate. Similarly, some investigators have withheld from their subjects certain information about the research in which they were taking part, at least until after the data had been collected. Others have given their subjects misleading information—sometimes to direct their attention away from the true purpose of the experiment and sometimes to create in them a psychological state, such as anxiety, that is required by the research plan. Still others have led their subjects to say or do things that violated their moral standards and about which they were later ashamed.

The fact that such things sometimes happen in research on social relations is a matter of great concern to social scientists, and scientific societies have formulated codes of ethics for the treatment of research participants (e.g., AAA, 1973; APA, 1973; APSA, 1968; ASA, 1971). In addition, individual social scientists have published books and articles on this topic (e.g., Barber et al., 1973; J. Katz, 1972; Kelman, 1968).

What happens to those who take part in research is of concern also to legislative bodies and government agencies. Federal and state legislatures have explored invasion of privacy, behavior control, and experimenting with humans in public hearings. The U.S. Department of Health, Education, and Welfare has issued regulations on the protection of human subjects that all recipients of federal research grants and contracts must follow. The White House, through its Office of Science and Technology, issued a set of ethical guidelines entitled "Privacy and Behavioral Research" (1967). In 1974 the U.S. Congress established a National Commission for Protection of Human Subjects of Biomedical and Behavioral Research, charging it with the responsibility to recommend needed legislative action.

It is important, on the one hand, to take seriously this concern about the possible mistreatment of human participants in research and, on the other, to keep it in correct perspective. An infamous historical event, that is, the so-called medical experiments carried out by Nazi German physicians in the concentration camps during World War II, sensitized the world to the general problem and gave rise to the Nuremberg code of medical ethics for human experimentation. The concern aroused by these medical "experiments" has been renewed by the wide publicity given to more recent experiments in which patients have suffered damage in the course of well-intentioned efforts to try out new drugs or new surgical procedures.

Although it is such developments in the medical sciences that have fueled the movement to protect research participants, the ethical issues in social research are no less real. They arise inevitably from the kinds of questions behavioral scientists ask and the methods used to obtain meaningful answers. They may be evoked by the research topic itself, the nature of the setting in which the research is conducted, the kinds of persons serving as research participants, the procedures required by the research design, the method of collecting data, the type of data collected, or the nature of the research report. As a matter of fact, certain types of ethical difficulties occur repeatedly in social relations research. Each type will be discussed in this chapter. As these discussions proceed, it will become clear that although a questionable practice may sometimes be eliminated, at other times to do so is tantamount to abandoning the proposed research. Hence, in a later section there will be found a discussion of the question of balancing the costs of questionable practices against the potential benefits of the investigation in which they occur.

Sometimes such an assessment will result in the research being abandoned. Such an action has serious implications. Although scientists have an obligation to protect the participants in their research, they also have an obligation to contribute to knowledge. The need for knowledge relevant to the promotion of human welfare and the solution of social problems is particularly acute. Scientists who are trained to provide such knowledge violate the trust placed in them by society if they do not take part in efforts to satisfy this need. Thus, when they consider abandoning a study (or using methods they think are not the best) they have a value conflict: They must choose between their obligation to conduct research and their obligation to protect the welfare of their subjects. This chapter discusses the latter obligation. *The reader should remember that the former is no less binding.*

Sometimes the balancing of costs and benefits of the investigation will result in a decision to carry it out. In this event the investigator incurs obligations to the participant following completion of the research. These obligations—for example, to clarify the nature of the research including the reasons for deception, to remove any harmful aftereffects of questionable practices used in the research, and to guarantee the subject's anonymity and the confidentiality of the data—together with suggestions for ways of meeting them are discussed in a later section of this chapter, Responsibilities to Research Participants after Completion of the Research.

In this chapter we show how social scientists have tried to balance the costs of using questionable practices and the benefits of conducting research. Before we proceed, however, we want to introduce a radical critique of how ethical issues are generally handled. A social psychologist with a different point of view from that represented in this chapter has made the following observations:

> The issues . . . can better be dealt with in terms of power than ethics. Professional ethics have a major function of regulating members of a profession so that successful criticism from outside the field is minimized. The apparent power balance in social research almost always lies with the social scientist. There is self-deception on our part about this. We do not like to realize the power differential. We prefer to think we are common partners in the scientific enterprise when, in fact, the people we study often would not be there at all if they did not need the money or were not required to be there or were aware of what we are doing. We can "remind participants of their autonomy and freedom," but this is self-deceptive for us. If others truly experience their autonomy, then reminding them of it is superfluous; if they are, in fact, at a disadvantage in the situation, then such a reminder is hypocritical. . . . We act as if there were not a question of power. We put our position in terms of defending freedom of inquiry. But its effect is often indistinguishable from defending privilege on more respectable terms. This is the same paternalistic assumption that those with greater power often make—to make their position more acceptable to themselves—that they are acting for the greater good. But we who have the power say what is the general good [Jack Sawyer, personal communication].

Although the remainder of this chapter does not address the issues as they are raised by Sawyer, we want to alert you that the question of who has power is a central macroethical issue, with several components. The ethical issues that we do address are formulated within a framework in which the researcher generally has the power to ask questions and determine the scope of the answers. As this is how most social science research is conducted, we want to inform you of the many ways researchers balance the costs and benefits of their work.

Balancing the Costs of Questionable Practices against the Potential Benefits of the Research

As noted, questionable practices with research participants come about partly because of the nature of the questions being asked about human behavior, partly because of the use of procedures designed to avoid misleading results, and partly because of the methods used to collect research data. Sometimes these practices can be avoided or minimized by the use of alternative procedures. Often, however, they cannot. When the latter is true, social scientists face a conflict between two values or rights. The first is the right of science and society to inquire and to know. The second is the right of the individual participant to have dignity, privacy, and self-determination. A decision not to conduct a planned project limits the first of these rights. A decision to conduct the research despite its questionable practices with participants limits the second.

Because the distinctive contribution of scientists to society is the development of knowledge and the informed application of that knowledge to human welfare, many feel an ethical obligation to conduct research and to defend it against attempts to censor it. One of the scientist's four commandments, according to a former president of the American Association for the Advancement of Science, is "fearlessly to defend freedom of inquiry" (Glass, 1965). The same thought is expressed by those who characterize scientific inquiry as the pursuit of knowledge for the sake of knowledge, regardless of its consequences.

Other scientists qualify this point of view extensively as it applies to research on human beings. The right to inquire and to know, they say, does not include the right to abridge individual dignity, privacy, and self-determination. Claims to the contrary are equivalent to saying that a good end (acquisition of knowledge) justifies the use of bad means (questionable practices with research participants). This price for knowledge, they argue, is too high.

In any investigation the initial obligation of the researchers is to weigh carefully the potential contributions of the proposed research against the costs to participants exposed to the questionable practices. If the researchers judge the theoretical or practical benefits too limited to justify the costs, they should not conduct the research. If they judge the converse to be true they should proceed; a decision not to act when the action is warranted is as morally reprehensible as a decision to act when action is not warranted.

Weighing the potential benefits of research against its anticipated costs is necessarily subjective. Though it is possible to enumerate many of the points to be considered, we believe that the balancing process itself must remain a matter for the individual investigator. Some argue that in reality, an investigator has no way to measure the value of a project against its costs to others who have not freely and knowingly consented to suffer those costs. However likely this may be, there seems no alternative to making the effort.

Among the potential benefits of a given research project are the following:

1. Advances in scientific theory that contribute to a general understanding of human behavior. An example might be a better understanding of the power of social influence to induce compliance and obedience.
2. Advances in knowledge of practical value to society. An example might be research on methods to increase the effectiveness of governmental leaders.
3. Gains for the research participant, such as increased self-understanding, satisfaction in making a contribution to science or to the solution of social problems, needed money or special privileges, knowledge of social science or of research methods, and so on.

The possible costs to the participant of various questionable practices in research include affronts to dignity, anxiety, shame, embarrassment, self-doubts, loss of trust in social relations, loss of autonomy and self-determination, and lowered self-esteem. In attempting to assess both the actuality and the seriousness of such costs, social scientists have turned to the research participants themselves. They have sought information in several ways. Some investigators, for example, have described studies involving questionable practices and asked respondents to judge the ethical quality of various aspects of the studies, including deception. Others have asked that questionable practices be rated on such dimensions as psychological discomfort or invasion of privacy. One such study revealed that college students are quite concerned about exposure to pain, are only moderately concerned about various kinds of psychological stress, and show little concern about data-gathering procedures that would appear to invade their privacy (Farr & Seaver, 1975). Another discovered that the extent to which an experimental procedure was judged unethical was influenced by the frequency with which it produced undesirable behavior (i.e., obedience to requests to harm others and commit crimes) but not by the frequency of emotional suffering that resulted (Schlenker & Forsyth, 1977). A third reported that the frequency with which college students judged experiments involving deception and stress to be unethical decreased if they were given information about the value of the research (Glaskow, Sadowski, & Davis, 1977). Of special interest is the fact that social scientists give more negative ratings than do college students to procedures that involve stress, cause physical pain, lower self-esteem, and/or produce undesirable behavior.

The evidence from these studies makes it clear that social scientists cannot be sure how the participants in their studies will feel about questionable practices to which they are exposed. Moreover, the scientists may anticipate stronger negative feelings toward some practices than will be found to occur. One group of investigators have made an innovative suggestion that would seem to surmount some of this uncertainty. They propose that a sample from the potential pool of research subjects be provided with information about a projected study and asked whether they would consent to participate. Included in the information provided would be a description of the procedures the subjects would experience and estimates of the type of behavior, desirable and undesirable, that they might display. In a study of the feasibility of this idea, these investigators found that they could predict quite well from the reactions of their sample the percent of actual research participants who had, in fact, expressed regret at having participated in a stressful experiment. The predictions held equally well for persons who had and had not been debriefed (Berscheid et al., 1973).

Aside from these direct costs to research participants, there are potential costs to society and future scientific work. For example, some research—in particular the type in which confederates enact roles in natural settings—may contribute to a social climate of suspicion, distrust, or manipulation. Other research, including that employing covert recording of intimate personal behavior, might turn society against social science and reduce future financial support of social research. It should be noted that scientists differ in how seriously they take these possibilities. For example, with respect to the possibility that questionable practices in research may contribute to a social climate of suspicion and mistrust, doubters make two points: (1) Research could add, at most, a trivial amount to the manipulation and deception that pervade a society plagued by high-pressure salespeople, dishonest repair people, and thieves; (2) participants in experiments distinguished readily between the deception in experiments and that of everyday life; from the former they draw no implications regarding the latter.

The process of balancing potential benefits against possible costs involves questions of degree as well as of kind. Is a potential contribution to scientific theory or to the solution of a social problem *important enough* to warrant high costs to the research participants? For example, granting that research in which the participant followed orders to give another person dangerous electric shocks promised to be an important contribution to knowledge, was it of enough significance to justify leading participants to commit acts that might diminish their self-respect? A parallel question may be asked about the research on cooperating interracial groups. Were societal needs for knowledge about the social management of desegregation great enough to justify involving students in research without telling them its true nature? Sometimes there is general agreement on the answer to such questions; this often happens, for example, when the research is planned as an analogue to an important social phenomenon. Usually, however, it is difficult to foresee the importance of a single investigation. When this is the case, the investigator's decision about proceeding with the research becomes more difficult.

Parallel questions may be asked about questionable practices with research participants and the harm they do. How serious is a given questionable practice? How likely is it to harm the participant? How serious might the harm be? Will it be fleeting or long range?

Answers to these questions are subject to considerable disagreement. A few examples of positions taken by some but rejected by others will illustrate. Studies involving active deception (providing misinformation) are of greater concern than those involving passive deception (withholding information). Field experiments introducing some new element into the environment (e.g., feigned heart attack) are more serious than those simply varying some ongoing activity (e.g., introducing alternative methods of charitable solicitation). Feigning an illness in a public place is a more questionable practice than feigning a minor accident. The induction of stress caused by fear for one's life (e.g., smoke seeping under a door into a locked room) is potentially more harmful than is inducing stress by false feedback of poor performance on a test. An invasion of privacy involving eavesdropping on conversations in a crowded lobby is less offensive to research participants than is covert observation of more intimate relationships. Inducing participants to perform acts that reduce their self-esteem is to be viewed less seriously when they yield to pressure to change an opinion than when they yield to pressure to mistreat another.

Some social scientists are influenced in their judgments of the seriousness of questionable practices in research by comparing them to similar practices in everyday life. For example, some experimenters point out that the stress involved in research is trivial compared to that felt in reality; this leads them to feel that inducing stress experimentally is ethically a minor matter. In the same vein, others see invasion of privacy as it occurs in research to be benign and harmless because they contrast it to more threatening invasions carried out by credit bureaus, police, and potential employers. Deception for research purposes is compared to everyday deception that has as its purpose taking advantage of others for personal gain; this makes research deception seem of little consequence.

Though there is no question about the validity of these comparisons, the inferences drawn from them are difficult to defend. They have the character of justifying a lesser evil because a greater one exists. As such they should carry little, if any, weight in the balancing of arguments for and against conducting a given investigation.

Judgments about the seriousness of questionable practices and their cost to research participants may hinge on yet another consideration, namely, whether the cost can be promptly alleviated. This argues that a deception that can be corrected immediately after an experiment is less serious than one that cannot. Similar arguments would apply to stress and to acts that lower self-esteem; they could be regarded as less-serious costs in an experiment if effective remedial actions are taken when the experiment is finished.

In balancing potential contributions against possible costs to participants, investigators must recognize a personal bias. It is reasonable, and to be expected, that they attach importance to the research they hope to carry out. If they did not, it is unlikely that they would have planned it. This means that if the research involves questionable practices, they should not trust themselves to make an objective assessment of relative benefits and costs. Rather, it is wise for them to seek consultation in this process.

Helpful consultation may be obtained from a number of sources. For example, colleagues doing similar research will constitute a valuable resource; they may well have faced a parallel decision in which they balanced factors similar to those under consideration.

However, colleagues may fall short on one score. Being in the same field as the experimenter, they may share too strongly the experimenter's values. Understanding the theoretical potential of the research, they may rate its contribution higher than would others from a different background. This suggests that it would be wise to consult, also, with persons from other disciplines, with intelligent laypeople, and with individuals like those who would be serving as research participants. Those in the last category will be especially valuable in helping the investigator assess the human costs of the experiment, particularly if they are different from the researcher in age, education, and socioeconomic class. It is informative to carry out a pilot project and discuss with the participants their feelings about the experience.

Sometimes, because of the potential for harm to the participants, there is a need for consultants with special backgrounds. For example, if physical stress were being employed, a medical advisor should be consulted. Or if mental stress were involved, it would be appropriate to call in a specialist in the area of personality or psychopathology. In general, the amount and variety of consultation should increase with the seriousness of the questionable practices being considered.

Consultation on ethical issues may be sought either from individuals or from an ethics advisory group. The former procedure is more flexible in that advisors appropriate to the issues raised by a specific experiment may be sought out. However, this approach is more time-consuming because it requires seeking out new advisors for each occasion. Time is saved by constituting a standing advisory group. This may be done by a group of experimenters with similar research interests or by an administrative unit such as an academic social science department. An advantage of the advisory group is that it will accumulate useful experience with ethical issues. On the other hand, if the range of studies about which it is consulted is too great, it may be unhelpful in some cases.

It is important to distinguish an ethics advisory group from institutional committees set up to monitor the "protection of human subjects." The function of these committees is to fulfill the ethical and moral responsibility of the university, hospital, prison, or clinic in which they operate. Typically, they give institutional clearance to the ethical aspects of an experiment. Often they have the additional responsibility of periodic review of ongoing studies to ensure that changes in research procedures have not introduced new concerns for the participants' welfare. Rarely do they have the time or expertise to advise researchers on the ethical decision they must make.

Neither the use of ethical advisors nor ethical clearance by an institutional advisory committee changes the fact that the ethical responsibility for the welfare of research participants remains with the individual investigator. Hence, the researchers may decide to proceed with the study even though the weight of advice suggests that the costs to the participants outweigh the study's potential contributions. Or conversely, the investigator may decide not to proceed despite advice that supports the project. To take any other position than this risks establishing a climate in which investigators seek to present their research plans in a manner that will secure endorsement rather than in a form conducive to securing helpful ethical analysis and advice.

In summary, a few general guidelines may be offered. These, of course, represent an oversimplification of the relevant considerations. The first consideration is whether the research problem is of sufficient importance and likely enough to produce results that will outweigh the possible cost to the research participant. When there is uncertainty, priority must be given to protecting the participant's dignity and welfare. The participants should emerge unharmed from the experience; if temporary harm is a possibility, satisfactory arrangements for its prompt alleviation should be available. When questionable practices are employed, they should be of such a nature that the participant, when informed of them, may be expected to find them reasonable and suffer no loss of confidence in the integrity of the investigator. The participant should gain some identifiable benefit from the research. The experience should be such that after its completion the participant would be willing to take part in further research of a similar nature. The conditions of the research should be such that investigators would be willing for members of their own families to take part. The investigator should have made plans to deal with any anticipated long-term aftereffects of the research.

Questionable Practices Involving Research Participants

The questionable practices encountered in social science research may be grouped into ten categories as follows:

1. Involving people in research without their knowledge or consent
2. Coercing people to participate
3. Withholding from the participant the true nature of the research
4. Deceiving the participant
5. Leading the participants to commit acts that diminish their self-respect
6. Violating the right to self-determination: research on behavior control and character change
7. Exposing the participant to physical or mental stress
8. Invading the privacy of the participant
9. Withholding benefits from participants in control groups
10. Failing to treat participants fairly and to show them consideration and respect

Involving People in Research without Their Knowledge or Consent

In some of the most significant research in the area of social relations the subjects never know that they have been participants in a research project. There are various reasons for this: Sometimes it is impossible or impractical to tell them. Sometimes the investigator decides that the information would lead the participants to display unnatural behavior and thus distort the results. But for whatever reason, the investigator involves the participants in research without their consent and hence has infringed on their right to make their own decision whether or not to participate. The investigator must always seek ways to avoid the prospect of involuntary participation. If unsuccessful, the investigator must then carefully weigh the benefits of the research against its ethical costs.

The several types of studies in which this problem arises are considered separately. The reader will note that many of these studies give rise to additional ethical issues, such as invasion of privacy.

Observational studies of group life   In a famous study often used to illustrate observational methods of data collection the investigator undertook to study "street-corner" groups of young men (Whyte, 1943). To gain access to needed information, he made friends with the group members and took part in their activities.

In another study the purpose of the investigators was to explore the manner in which a middle-class teacher related to lower-class children. The observations needed for the study were made by a person who the children thought was a student teacher.

This **participant observer** method has been used to study workers in factories, members of tribal groups, residents of small towns, and so on. Key people in such settings usually know of the research. Often, however, others who are observed do not.

Sometimes it is not possible to use the observer method because rules prohibit it or because the presence of a third party or stranger would modify the behavior under observation. An example is provided by a study of the jury system (Meltzer, 1953). The investigators wished to learn how juries functioned and whether the jury system was effective in dealing with the complexities of modern litigation. As by law no one is permitted to be present at jury deliberations, the investigators found it necessary to devise a substitute method of observation. They secured the permission of the judge and the lawyers for both the plaintiffs and the defendants to use hidden microphones to record jury deliberations in five trials.

Studies in which research is added to ongoing programs or operations   An often-cited instance of involving uninformed participants in research by adding research to ongoing operations occurred when a social scientist ran for mayor of his home town (Hartmann, 1936). Without the knowledge of the voters he distributed "emotional" campaign leaflets in some precincts and "rational" ones in other, comparable precincts. From the size of the favorable vote in the two sets of precincts he inferred the relative effectiveness of the two types of appeal.

Involving students in educational research without their knowledge is quite common. In one such experiment teachers added "motivating" comments to the papers of some students before returning them; no such comments were entered on the papers of comparable students (Page, 1958). The outcome was assessed from the students' performance on a later test. In other educational studies students who have received different types of instruction or who are in classrooms differing in ethnic composition have been compared to determine the effect of such differences on achievement, attitudes to schoolwork, and ethnic attitudes.

Field experiments In field experiments the investigator presents contrasting experiences to two or more groups of persons or to the same individuals at two different times. The outcome is often an action that can be counted or whose onset can be timed. A test of restaurant discrimination against blacks in the neighborhood of the U.N. headquarters in New York City, made 20 years ago, still provides an example (Selltiz, 1955). The experimenter sent a same-sex white pair and a same-sex black pair of diners to the same restaurants. In a substantial proportion of the restaurants the black diners received inferior service, as indicated by delays in serving, out-of-the-way seating, and other inconveniences. The study highlights the purpose of not informing the research participants. Had the restaurant personnel known that an experiment was in progress it seems unlikely that they would have shown such discrimination.

Some of the most dramatic of social science experiments have dealt with altruistic and helpful behavior in natural settings. The experimenters have set up opportunities for people to contribute or to help others. The influence of such factors as size of onlooker group, the helping behavior of a "model," and the ethnic membership of the person needing help have been examined. Some examples of helping behavior employed in field experiments are these: putting contributions into a Salvation Army kettle (Bryan & Test, 1967), helping a woman with a flat tire (Bryan & Test, 1967), helping a person with an epileptic seizure (Darley & Latané, 1968), or helping an ill person on a subway train (Piliavin, Rodin, & Piliavin, 1969).

Discussion As already noted, the questionable practice common to all these studies is that they engage persons in research without their knowledge or consent. Thus in varying degrees they limit the right of free choice and in so doing raise an ethical problem.

With few exceptions, social scientists believe that to seek consent in the types of studies described would completely change the behavior being studied and, hence, would render the research meaningless. The choice, it appears, is either to abandon the research or to carry it out despite its ethical question marks. This precipitates a value conflict between the scientists' obligations to add to knowledge and their responsibility to protect their research participants.

Although it is true that these studies generate the same ethical concern, it is possible to separate them on the basis of how much they impose on participants' time, patience, and welfare by involving them in activities in which they otherwise might not have engaged. If the extent of such imposition is minimal, the cost to the participants seems minor. If the imposition is substantial, the cost increases correspondingly; for example, experimenters who artfully disguise their confederates as injured, bloody survivors of a car wreck, seeking aid at night from rural residents, push the costs to participants to a high level.

In contrast, observational studies and the studies in which research is added to ongoing programs cause little concern in this respect; participation in the research would not alter the experiences of the participants to a significant degree. In field experiments, on the other hand, the participants' experiences are arranged by the investigator. Such experiments differ in an important way: whether the experiences are commonplace and unimportant, such as a car dallying at a green light, or are potentially more disturbing, such as an epileptic seizure on a sidewalk. In summary, the less the research procedure inconveniences the participants or involves them emotionally, the less severe the ethical question over engaging them in research without their knowledge or consent.

Apart from the fact that the studies of this type limit participants' rights to consent to activities in which they are to be involved, these experimental procedures concern social scientists because of the possibility of their cumulative impact on society. Some fear that as the research procedures become known through the mass media and through textbooks, many people will react to *real* crises by thinking that they are "just another experiment." The degree of indifference to needs for help in everyday life is already serious; might it become worse if the public became convinced that people in trouble might be playacting? It should be noted that some social scientists do not believe that there is any danger of this happening. They feel that such fears overestimate just how much people know about what goes on in social science and how much impact social research has on everyday affairs.

Concern for another kind of impact on society is reflected by the sequel to the jury-recording study cited previously. Members of Congress reacted to the jury recordings as a threat to fundamental institutions. When news of the study came out, a congressional investigation resulted. Legislation was passed establishing a fine of a thousand dollars and imprisonment for a year for whoever might attempt to record the proceedings of any jury in the United States while the jury is deliberating or voting.

Coercing People to Participate

The fact that scientists studying human behavior need people to take part in their research occasionally causes questionable practices to occur. Under some circumstances, as indicated in the preceding section, they meet this need by involving subjects in research without their knowledge or consent. Typically, however, the potential participant knows that research will take place.

Ideally, consent should be obtained only after a potential subject has been given adequate information about the research in question. What we shall examine in this section is the point that consent to participate may be free or it may be wholly or partially coerced. The latter happens in several ways: for example, an investigator may be in a position to *require* individuals to participate. Sometimes an employer or an institution may require participation of persons over whom they have authority. At other times an investigator will offer such strong incentives that the potential participant is unable to resist, such as the case when $20 is offered to a poor person. In all such cases, the ideal of complete freedom of choice is abridged.

In extreme cases, as when persons are ordered by their employer or commanding officer to report for research, coercion is clear. In less-extreme cases, however, it may be difficult to distinguish between coercion and legitimate persuasion or between coercion and a fair exchange of rewards and services.

When the freedom of individuals is restricted at their place of work or residence, such restrictions are likely to carry over into research done in these settings. Thus, employees, patients, prisoners, or soldiers may be required to participate in research projects. If a branch of the military service needs to find the sources of a morale problem, soldiers will be expected to take part in research without objecting. Or if an industry wishes to experiment with methods that may increase productivity, workers will be expected to participate. Similar expectations may hold for patients in mental hospitals with respect to research on therapeutic methods or prisoners with respect to procedures for rehabilitation.

It may be the case, however, that the potential participants are not in sympathy with the research objectives and would not take part if allowed to decide for themselves. The worker in the factory may see productivity research as a step toward greater exploitation, and the prisoner may feel that society, not he or she, needs changing. Under such circumstances, investigators face a difficult conflict between their desire, and often their obligation, to conduct potentially significant research and the questionable practice of engaging people who have been completely or partially coerced into participating.

Three variations of this conflict may be distinguished; the ethical issues they pose are somewhat different. The first arises in research projects in which some feature of the program or the organization in question is being studied with a view to increasing its effectiveness. The second occurs in research that is meaningful only if carried out with the cooperation of the particular type of person residing in an institution, for example, a study of any type of mental illness. The third is encountered in research that utilizes participants from institutional and organizational settings but has no special relationship to the program or to the people in the setting, for example, when prisoners are participants in a study of group problem solving.

Research related to organizational programs Research dealing with variations in the program of an organization provides the clearest justification for coerced participation. Under these circumstances it will often be true that the participants will feel no additional abridgment of their freedom beyond that already surrendered in the situation; that is, they will accept the research as one more aspect of their responsibilities. This is less likely to be the case when major changes in work arrangements or therapeutic regimes are introduced and studied. At such times persons included in (or perhaps those excluded from) the innovative program may object. This happened in a mental hospital when the staff decided to experiment with a treatment program that involved working with patients in groups. When a number of patients objected, they were given the alternative of being transferred to a less-attractive, locked-ward section of the hospital. However, whether or not there are objections, investigators may not shift responsibility for the ethical decision to the institution or organization. If they are unable to arrange for uncoerced consent from participants, investigators must assess for themselves the costs and benefits of proceeding with the research.

Research intended to be of value to particular types of persons Research requiring the participation of persons who might be found in a given organizational or institutional setting presents a more difficult dilemma. Research staff members working in such settings feel a professional obligation to contribute to knowledge about the kinds of problems the institution deals with and about methods that might alleviate such problems. If they are to succeed, they must have the cooperation of the patients or prisoners in their research activity. They may believe that such persons are obligated to take part in research programs that in the long run are oriented to their own welfare and to the welfare of others in their same situation. Believing this, the researchers might understandably feel warranted in employing strong incentives to obtain consent; that is, they might justify the use of social pressure or granting of special favors.

But the residents in the institution may not have this sense of obligation to the research. They may doubt its relevance to themselves and object to the time, the discomfort, and the possible curtailment of privileges. Or as noted earlier, they may believe they have no problem—that the problem resides in the institution or in society. Soldiers with a record of imprisonment or repeated violations of army regulations become candidates for resocialization research in which they are deprived of all comforts and privileges, winning them back only by exhibiting specified examples of cooperative and compliant behavior. Some enter such a program with apparent willingness; others do so only as an alternative to the threat of lengthy imprisonment and dishonorable discharge. For the latter, as with the mental patients mentioned earlier, the coercion to consent is clear, and indeed, the researcher may judge it justifiable. For those apparently willing to participate, the coercion is less evident but undoubtedly present; it is to such instances that the investigator must be especially alert.

Research utilizing persons who are especially vulnerable to requests to participate   When the problem studied has no special relationship to the program or the persons in the organization or institution, the question of free consent hinges on the incentives the investigator employs. The potential participants are approached, not because of any presumed obligation to participate, but because they have the time and are likely to consent. Owing to their circumstances, financial incentives and social approval, on which depend later favors, take on special force. For example, a prisoner may need money for cigarettes or may be building a record of good behavior for early parole. In such cases, those incentives that ordinarily would represent a poor exchange of rewards for services rendered by participants now acquire irresistible strength and, in effect, coerce consent.

Problems paralleling those just mentioned arise in the use of incentives to secure participation among disadvantaged groups in the population. Poor people will find it difficult to resist participation when money is offered. For this reason an employment service is a dependable place to recruit; persons looking for jobs can be counted on to volunteer for research paying the minimum hourly wage. Similarly, persons needing money for special purposes, such as addicts in search of money to buy drugs or alcohol, are usually more than willing to take part.

Questionable incentives may also be used to induce participation of persons who do not have special needs or organizational connections. Appeals to sympathy for the investigator may be made; the plea "If you help me I can finish my dissertation and get a job" is frequently used. Shame may be employed, as in "Women are afraid of electric shock, but most men can take it." Altruistic contributions may be stressed, for example, "You can help science learn more about the process of negotiation, and this may help head off another world war." When potential participants are inexperienced and have unquestioned respect for the social scientists who approach them, false and exaggerated claims may coerce participation and represent a misuse of interpersonal trust. It does not follow, of course, that a modest description of the potential value of proposed research is out of order. To the contrary, it is one of the elements needed for an informed decision to participate.

Discussion Complete or partial coercion to participate in research occurs either as a result of the power of institutions and organizations over individuals or as a result of the use of incentives too strong for the potential participant to reject. It is essential for the investigator to be aware of this power and to recognize the special responsibility to protect potential participants' freedom to decide. In some cases, it would be reasonable to assume that the potential participant has an obligation to assist in the research. This assumption is dangerous for two reasons: First, it may not be shared by the individuals in question, and second, it may serve as a convenient rationalization that consent is unnecessary. It will be tempting to conclude that if the organization is willing to limit freedom to consent, the investigator need not feel responsible; such a position is ethically unacceptable.

In some cases, it will seem to be to the obvious advantage of persons to participate. They have time on their hands, the research will be an interesting variation from their usual routine, or they can make good use of the money paid for participation. Although all this may be true and represents legitimate considerations, investigators must strive to provide as much freedom of choice under such circumstances as they would if none of these conditions prevailed—for example, if the potential participants were busy and in less need of money or social approval.

None of the preceding should be taken as negating the appropriateness of a modest and persuasive description of the potential value of proposed research and the use of rewards, financial and otherwise, in exchange for participation. What it implies, instead, is that such incentives should be employed with full awareness of their potential for limiting a participant's freedom in choosing to take part.

The special case of coercion to participate in research in universities and colleges: "the subject pool" A widespread practice is to require that students enrolled in a college course, such as introductory psychology, serve as research participants for a specified number of hours. Typically, each student chooses among a number of alternative experiments for which brief descriptions are available.

This requirement is a special case of the use of institutional authority to limit the freedom of consent. It will be of particular interest to readers of this chapter, for most have been exposed to it in the course of their own education. The ethical considerations involved have been debated extensively and opinions on the practice vary widely. A thorough account of this debate has been published in *Ethical Principles in the Conduct of Research with Human Participants* (APA, 1973).

An argument frequently offered for this requirement is that participation in ongoing research provides a more realistic and valuable educational experience than taking part in laboratory experiments especially arranged for training purposes. Another argument is that teachers have the right to require students to make a contribution to the advancement of the science they are studying. Current students profit from contributions of time and effort made by student research participants who have preceded them, it is argued, so it is right to expect them to make a parallel contribution to those who study social science in the future. A third argument is that if this requirement did not exist, recruitment of people to serve in research would become much more difficult and often prohibitively expensive. Some potentially valuable research would not get done. Also, the participants who would remain available as volunteers for research would be self-selected, introducing probable biases in the conclusions.

The position that prevails at most universities and colleges at the moment is that the spirit of uncoerced consent can be maintained and the recruitment of students to serve as research participants continued if the recruitment procedure preserves a substantial amount of free choice and otherwise protects the participants from undue coercion. When these precautions are combined with procedures that ensure an educational benefit to the participant, the demands of uncoerced consent appear to be satisfied. For this reason a number of university departments have developed detailed procedures to guarantee the accomplishment of educational objectives and to minimize the element of coercion. For a review of these procedures the interested reader is referred to *Ethical Principles in the Conduct of Research with Human Participants* (APA, 1973).

Withholding from the Participant the True Nature of the Research

Unlike others who are involved in studies without their knowledge or consent, some individuals may willingly participate in a research project but not be told of its true intent. Usually, their participation is explained to these subjects in terms that although true, tell only part of the story. Misleading explanations of this kind have acquired the label "cover story"; they cover up the experiment's true nature. Their function is to satisfy the participants' curiosity about what is occurring. Most often the participants are not misled about the nature of the experiences they will have or the discomforts to be encountered. The ethical problems of studies that do involve such deception are discussed in several of the sections to follow.

When subjects consent to take part in research without being told its true characteristics, they are not giving what is commonly called their *informed consent.* This term had its origins in relation to medical treatment and research and designates patients' rights to consider a type of treatment or research participation with full knowledge of the risks to their personal safety. As applied to social science research, the term has acquired connotations extending considerably beyond this original usage.

Withholding information about research in which a person consents to participate is a questionable practice for reasons previously noted: The right of free choice has been curtailed, and as a result, human dignity has been diminished. Social scientists are obliged to avoid such acts if at all possible. If they cannot, they must give careful consideration to the ethical costs of carrying out the research and the values to be served in so doing.

Studies in which the true purpose is not revealed   One example is a study of a UNESCO publicity campaign (Star & Hughes, 1950). The research in this case was planned around the fact that the campaign was to take place. Respondents were interviewed about UNESCO, some before and others after the publicity campaign. None was told of the connection between the interviews and the plan to evaluate the effectiveness of the campaign.

Social scientists studying the effects of variations in teaching methods have withheld information under similar circumstances. One such study was interested in students' racial attitudes; it compared the effects of being on cooperative interdependent classroom teams with the usual kind of intergroup contact that happens in the traditional classroom (Weigel, Wiser, & Cook, 1975). The junior and senior high school students who were the participants did not know the research was underway. When attitudes were to be assessed at the end of the school year, the investigators approached the students in their homes, posing as public opinion pollsters interested in the views of teenagers on social issues, a true but incomplete description of the purpose of the interview.

The information withheld   In the examples cited, the participants are not told of the purpose of the research; that is, they are parties to answering a research question about which they are not informed. Moreover, if their normal routine has been altered, as was true in the educational experiment, this fact also is withheld. Also, they are not told in advance of the probable uses to which the research results will be put, even though in the case of practical application to educational or social policy they may be opposed to such applications. Although they are not deliberately misled about the experiences they will have in the course of the research, even here the emphasis may be somewhat different from their expectations based on the vague description they receive. In studies other than those described still other information may be concealed; for example, when persons are selected for research because they are low achievers, have inferiority feelings, or are prejudiced, they will not be told the criterion. Or if they are to be exposed to stressful experiences such as failure or fright, this is almost certain not to be mentioned.

Discussion There are two versions of the ethical ideal that are relevant to withholding information from a research participant. One is that all information about the research should be provided. Illustrative wording for this version is found in a bill proposed to the New York State Legislature in 1971:

> ... there shall be made known to him the nature, duration, and purpose of the experiment; the method and means by which it is to be conducted; all inconveniences and hazards reasonably to be expected; and the effects upon his health or person which may possibly result from participation in the experiment.

Most social scientists consider this version of **informed consent** to be both unnecessary and impractical. They feel that some aspects of a research plan are of little interest or concern to participants and that other, more technical aspects are beyond their comprehension. Moreover, developments occur in the course of some research that could not be anticipated and, hence, could not be described to participants in advance. As a result, these social scientists favor a statement of principle that omits these undesirable features. Wording from the ethics code of one of the social science disciplines reflects this:

> Ethical practice requires the investigator to inform the participant of all features of the research that reasonably might be expected to influence willingness to participate, and to explain all other aspects of the research about which the participant inquires (APA, 1973).

The experience of researchers indicates that if they operate according to this second version of informed consent, they will find that most participants are concerned about what will happen to them in the research, how long the research will take, and any inconveniences or risks that are involved. In contrast, most participants *are unconcerned* about the nature of the research question being asked and are as likely to be willing to answer one kind of question as another. (However, participants do judge research involving pain, stress, or undesirable behavior as more ethical if they believe the research topic to be an important one. See section entitled Balancing the Costs of Objectionable Practices Against the Potential Benefits of the Research.)

Special questions arise over how the research results will be used. For example, some potential subjects would not willingly participate in research intended to increase war-making efficiency. Members of religious groups or ethnic minority groups would not wish to take part in the research if results were expected to reflect discredit on their group. A researcher finds it difficult to respond to such concerns for two reasons. First, it is not always possible to predict the applied value of the research. Second, once the results become public, the researcher has no way to control the use to which others put the findings. (This issue will be discussed at great length later in the chapter.)

One approach to informed consent would limit its applicability to research in which the participant has been put "at risk." Guidelines for the protection of human subjects disseminated by the U.S. Department of Health, Education, and Welfare of the federal government define this concept as follows:

Subject at risk means any individual who might be exposed to the possibility of harm (physical, psychological, sociological, or other) as a consequence of participation of the subject in any research development or demonstration activity which goes beyond the application of established and accepted methods necessary to meet his needs.

Risk is recognized by the guidelines to be a matter of professional judgment by the investigator and by ethics review committees at the investigator's institution. If the research does not involve risk, the investigator is not obliged to secure informed consent. This orientation highlights the origin in medical treatment and research of the informed consent concept. In social science research, by comparison, concern for the participant's dignity, self-esteem, and self-determination becomes central. Hence, the ethical ideal is to obtain informed and uncoerced consent regardless of the risk factor.

Another approach is derived from the version of informed consent (described previously) that would inform participants only of the features of the research that reasonably might be expected to influence their willingness to participate. An early example of this developed in the area of research in the then new psychoactive drugs. Any such drug has at least two effects: one is pharmacological and the other psychological, or suggestive. To control the latter, the drug researcher compares the effect of the real drug with that of a fake drug, or placebo. To tell participants which of the two they are receiving greatly reduces the value of the research. To avoid this and yet give informed consent, drug researchers developed the practice of informing individuals that they would be involved in research in which they would receive either a drug (in varying strengths) or a **placebo** but would not be told which until the research was over. The analogy in social research is to tell participants what experiences they will encounter in the experiment, whether there are inconveniences or possible harm involved, and that they *may* or *may not* be deceived. They are assured, in addition, that when the research is over, they will be given a full account of the results and have their questions answered.

None of these various approaches takes care of all the considerations that lead to withholding information from research participants. When investigators decide that information must be withheld if the research is to be meaningful, they face a value conflict between abandoning the research and proceeding with it despite the ethical question that it involves.

Deceiving the Research Participant

In the research discussed in the preceding sections, the participants have been misled by withholding information from them, either about the fact that research was in progress or about the nature of it. In the research to be discussed in this section, the investigators have felt it necessary to take the additional step of giving the participants incorrect information.

The distinction between *deceiving others passively by telling only part of the truth* versus *actively by telling an untruth* has little, if any, moral standing in our opinion. Nevertheless, social scientists take the latter more seriously because it brings an additional element into the picture, namely, a violation of participants' assumptions that they can trust what the researcher says. The ideal in the relationship between scientist and research participant is that of openness and honesty. Deliberate lying in the interest of manipulating the participant's perceptions and actions goes directly against this ideal. Yet often the choice appears to be between carrying out such deception and abandoning the research.

Deception is employed for a number of reasons. Three of the more common ones follow:

Deception to conceal the true purpose of the research A study of the effect of status differences between ethnic groups on the nature of social interaction within and across ethnic lines illustrates this type of deception (Katz, Goldston, & Benjamin, 1958). The investigators anticipated that members of a lower-status ethnic minority would be more passive and submissive in racially mixed groups than would members of a majority ethnic group. They studied this by setting four-person racially mixed groups to work on tasks requiring cooperation and discussion. Believing that a description of their hypothesis would distort the participants' behavior, they "employed" the participants to try out a group of tasks described as being under development for use as vocational aptitude tests.

A second example comes from a study of the effects of the expectations of teachers on gains in IQ of children in their classes (Rosenthal & Jacobson, 1966). Twenty percent of children in each of 18 classrooms were identified as having scored high on a test designed to predict academic "blooming" or intellectual gain. This was false; these children had been selected at random. Results showed the predicted bloomers increasing in IQ significantly more than equally able comparison children. Clearly, such a study with its sweeping implications for education would have been impossible had the teachers not been deceived.

Deception to conceal the true function of the research participants' actions Many studies have been carried out with the general aim of discovering whether subjects convince themselves in the process of giving arguments for a position they do not believe in or extolling the virtues of a product that they know is of little value. Considerable evidence is available that this happens, but there is much disagreement about why. In one of the experiments attempting to solve this puzzle, the investigators succeeded in getting a group of college students to believe that they were thinking up arguments in favor of a program they opposed, namely, to send other college students to the Soviet Union for four years in order to study the Soviet system of government and the history of communism (Elms & Janis, 1965). The researchers accomplished this by representing themselves as staff members of the U.S. State Department (or alternatively, the Soviet Embassy) who needed the arguments for a pamphlet. Their purpose in doing this was to direct the students' attention away from the effect of this activity on their own opinions.

Deceptions similar to the preceding are regularly practiced by social scientists investigating theories of cognitive consistency or *cognitive dissonance*. In order to engage research participants in actions counter to their opinions (presumably creating cognitive dissonance), investigators have devised various misleading reasons for engaging them in the production of oral or written counterattitudinal arguments, such as participation in debates in which they represent the side opposed to their own position (see, e.g., W. A. Scott, 1959).

Other deceptions to conceal the true function of the participant's actions take the form of announcing that the participant is interacting with one other person—usually a peer—when in fact the "other person" is the experimenter or a confederate of the experimenter or even a computer. The purpose of such deception is to present the research participant with a *standardized experience* and *one that can be varied in a controlled manner along a dimension being studied*. One example of this procedure is found in a study in which the investigators were interested in the reaction of one opponent to a conciliatory initiative from another—a phenomenon of importance in international negotiation (Pilisuk & Skolnick, 1968). The participant was informed that he or she was engaged in competitive-cooperative interaction (the so-called prisoners' dilemma game) with someone in another room: in fact, the responses from the latter were preprogrammed and originated with the experimenter.

Deception to conceal the experiences the research participant will have   In many studies research participants cannot be told in advance about the critical experiences they are to have. Instead they must be led to encounter this experience as a natural, unplanned development. One example comes from an experiment in which the participants were to be induced to lie to a second person. From cognitive consistency theory it was deduced that persons who received a large bribe to lie would feel less need to reduce the dissonance between their beliefs and their public "lie" than would those who lied for a trivial bribe; the latter presumably would be under more pressure to reconcile their own beliefs with the untruthful account they gave to a second person (Festinger & Carlsmith, 1959). Since telling the participants what was in store for them would have completely changed the nature of their experience in the experiment, the investigator decided to recruit persons instead for a study of "measures of performance."

Discussion With few, if any, exceptions, social scientists regard deception of research participants as a questionable practice to be avoided if at all possible. It diminishes the respect due to others and violates the expectations of mutual trust on which organized society is based. When the deceiver is a respected scientist, it may have the undesirable effect of modeling deceit as an acceptable practice. Conceivably, it may contribute to the growing climate of cynicism and mistrust bred by widespread use of deception by important public figures, as symbolized by the expression *credibility gap.*

Within this band of general agreement among social scientists, however, two positions may be identified. One is that deception is an inadmissible affront to individual autonomy and self-respect and is inconsistent with the scientific objective of discovering the truth. The other, more widely held, is that deception is occasionally a legitimate means to be used in the service of a higher value, namely, the development of a meaningful, "nontrivial" science of human behavior.

Several alternatives to the use of deception have been considered. One of these is to provide the subjects with no information about the purpose of the experiment or about what will happen to them in the course of it, promising them full information when the experiment is over. In some cases, this would seem a feasible alternative. In others, it would not because of the well-recognized tendency of participants to formulate their own hypotheses about what is happening. Such hypotheses influence their behavior and introduce unknown and untraceable error into the results.

A second alternative is to provide the participants with full information about the experiment's purpose. One study has suggested that such information would not affect the findings. In this study the investigators examined the influence of exposure to prior judgments of others on the participants' estimates of the comparative length of three curved lines (Gallo, Smith, & Mumford, 1973). The investigators reported that participants who were told that the study was concerned with discovering the extent to which people were conformers showed results similar to those of participants to whom the purpose of the study was not disclosed. (The latter were led to believe they were in a study of distance perception.) However, a second study reached opposite conclusions. Results obtained with participants who knew the purpose of the experiment (i.e., a conditioning study in which verbal approval was used to increase the frequency of use of selected pronouns) were opposite to those of participants who were given a misleading interpretation of the study's purpose. Perhaps we will learn eventually which questions can be answered without deception. Meanwhile, most social scientists would fear that disclosure of purpose would distort results and, accordingly, would hesitate to take this approach.

A third alternative is to tell the participants about the general experimental procedure (but not the hypothesis) and secure their cooperation in role-playing the behavior they would have supposedly shown had they gone through the experiment. In several cases, this alternative has been used with apparent success. For example, one experimenter asked participants to role-play a strategy meeting of leaders of a fictitious organization (Kelman, 1967). As expected, participants in these sessions formed different attitudes toward the organization depending on the type of action they role-played toward it. Another investigator asked participants to pretend to be in an experiment in which the investigator was asking them to administer dangerous electric shocks as a learning incentive to a second person (Mixon, 1972). He found that role-playing participants, if instructed in such a way as to create the impression that the experimenter was responsible for pain and potential injury to the learner, behaved much as had the participants in the original experiment. However, when the instructions indicated that the role players rather than the experimenter were to assume the responsibility, the behavior of the role-playing participants was very different from that shown by the true research subjects. On the other hand, there are numerous demonstrations that the results of role-played experiments differ from those in which the investigator has concealed his true purpose in order to involve the research subjects in direct and personal reactions to the conditions being studied (Miller, 1972).

Of course, differences in results leave unanswered the question of whether role-played or traditional experiments provide more meaningful and generalizable research results. This is still under debate. Some social scientists argue that role-played experiments can take into account the meaning attached by people to things they experience and thus provide results more applicable to everyday social phenomena. Others note that whereas role-players can say what they *should* or *might* do under real-life conditions, they are unable to predict what they *would* do. The reason for this, according to scientists who take this position, is that the role-player will not know which of the many aspects of the situation he would respond to in real situations. (For a debate on this issue see Forward, Canter, and Kirsch, 1976; and Cooper, 1976.)

It seems probable that their commitment to the development of a significant and relevant science of human behavior will lead many social scientists to continue to deceive research subjects. In some cases the research participants' rights will be curtailed in ways that they may not find troublesome, as in studies where they are given misleading information regarding the purpose of the study or the function of their own behavior within the study. In other cases, as in studies where they are misled regarding the nature of what they will be asked to do or what they will be exposed to during the research, their freedom will be abridged more extensively, and, hence, the moral cost of the experiment, if conducted, will be correspondingly greater.

Leading the Research Participants to Commit Acts That Diminish Their Self-Respect

An ethical dilemma tinged with irony confronts the social scientist studying the determinants of such topics as honesty, helping behavior, and resistance to dictatorial and authoritarian influence. These are matters that touch the highest of human ideals. Yet in their investigation social scientists use procedures calculated to induce behavior that conflicts with these ideals. To study honesty, for example, one creates opportunity for research participants to lie, cheat, and steal. To study helping behavior, one puts unsuspecting individuals in situations in which they may refuse to help when it is badly needed. To study resistance to authority one pressures participants to obey orders they regard as wrong or harmful.

The following paragraphs illustrate four of the more common types of undesirable behavior induced for research purposes.

Cheating, lying, stealing   Moral character is a topic of considerable interest to social scientists as well as to the rest of us. For example, among studies of this topic are some that have been conducted to determine whether honesty is a general characteristic or, instead, whether people are honest in some situations but not in others. Other studies have sought to discover the correlates of variations in honesty.

An example comes from a study in which college students were recruited to take part in a theft: This study was stimulated by the actual burglary of a political campaign headquarters—the now famous Watergate burglary in 1972 (West, Gunn, & Chernicky, 1975). The experimenters noted that whereas participants in the burglary explained their behavior in terms of environmental influences external to themselves, observers in the mass media tended to attribute their behavior to defects in their personal character. As these differences in the perceived causes of evildoing are predicted by a theory about the determinants of causal attribution, the experimenters felt it would be important to check the theory in a controlled situation that paralleled the real burglary. As a part of this experiment they offered inducements to college students to help with the theft of records from a business firm. The inducements included performing a patriotic service for a department of the federal government: A substantial number of the students agreed to take part (the actual burglary was never carried out).

Harming others Of equal interest has been the topic of harming others and its consequences for subsequent social interaction. Attempts have been made, for example, to discover the conditions under which one individual will obey (or defy) orders to harm another. One approach to studies of this type has been to have the experimenter "order" the research participant to administer painful and dangerous electric shocks to a second person (Milgram, 1965). The purpose of the shocks was presented as a means of punishing the person for his errors, so that he would be motivated to learn (the second person is an experimental confederate). Although emotionally upset, many research participants nevertheless showed the "blind obedience" some had thought to characterize only those persons living under ruthless political dictatorships.

Yielding to social pressure to deny one's own senses or convictions Another major topic in social relations is that of conforming to social influence. Human behavior of this sort underlies some of the best as well as some of the worst aspects of group life. The experimental study of conformity has generally led investigators to expose participants to social pressures that lead them to say things they disbelieve and to do things to which they are opposed, that is, to distrust and deny their own perceptions and feelings. In the best known of such experiments, some college students heard their peers (all confederates) give incorrect reports of the length of lines shown on a wall in front of them (Asch, 1951). Some of these students were unable to resist the cumulative influence of these reports and, in their turn, also reported seeing the lines as different from their true length. Other experimenters have exposed participants to an incorrect position announced by a group of peers on well-known factual items such as "In thousands of miles, how far is it from San Francisco to New York?" or to a deviant position on high-consensus opinion items such as "most people would be better off if they never went to school at all"— after which the participants' own answers and opinions were obtained (Krech, Crutchfield, & Ballachey, 1962). A common finding is that under certain conditions, participants take positions opposite to those they would ordinarily hold.

Failure to help when help is needed In the earlier discussion of involving people in research without their knowledge or consent, several studies of helping behavior were cited. One of these was intended to explore the hypothesis that a person is more likely to give help if he or she is alone than if one of a number of potential helpers. Researchers trained a confederate to fake a realistic and frightening epileptic seizure with the research participant out of sight but nearby (Darley & Latané, 1968).

In another study of this kind, investigators had a man with a cane (or alternatively, a liquor bottle) drop to the floor of a New York City subway train. Even though the man with the cane was almost always helped and the drunk often helped, most people left the scene with the knowledge that it was not they who had given assistance (Piliavin, Rodin, & Piliavin, 1969).

Discussion   For some social scientists, practices such as those just described are the most questionable of all those used in research with human participants. These are practices that are to some extent responsible for the fact that participants behave in ways that cause them shame, embarrassment, or regret—in some cases because they have violated their own moral standards and those of their group or community and in other cases because they have shown themselves to be less worthy and self-directed than they believed themselves to be.

However, this view of the matter is strongly challenged by other social scientists. Some argue vigorously that it is the participant, not the researcher, who is responsible for the participant's actions. It is the subject, they say, who chooses to cheat or not to cheat, to harm or not to harm another person, to yield or not to yield to social pressure. Others go further: They take the position that it is a service to people to give them an accurate perception of what they are like and, in particular, of their potential for committing an action even though they disapprove of it. According to this position, to help people maintain self-esteem based on false premises about themselves is a disservice to them, and the researcher should have no qualms about exposing an incorrect self-image if that stands in the way of further growth of the individual in question.

Two shortcomings of this position may be recognized. The first is that researchers have no right to impose their educational services on others who have not requested them. The second is that the process of recognizing and changing one's personal weaknesses is complex and sensitive. To be constructive, it must take place in a supportive or a therapeutic context rather than in a brief and threatening laboratory confrontation.

If we grant that practices threatening the research participant's self-respect are undesirable and yet appreciate the importance of the topic being studied with the aid of such practices, we may wish to ask whether degrees of undesirability may be distinguished among practices in common use. Agreeing to harm others, for example, may be judged by some to be potentially more distressing than failing to help others. However, if the harm is minor and the need for help is great, it may lead us to reverse this order.

Some researchers argue that the reactions of participants who have been led to commit acts that threaten their self-respect should determine whether such practices should be continued. A number of investigators have done follow-up studies on this point (Milgram, 1964; Ring, Wallston, & Corey, 1970). In general, these studies indicated that research participants report only minor and temporary disturbances and that they feel they have gained useful self-understanding from their experiences.

Violating the Right to Self-Determination: Research on Behavior Control and Character Change

The questionable practices described in the preceding sections are sometimes the backdrop for an aspect of social research that raises an even more serious problem: Do scientists have the right—even if they have the power—to produce significant changes in the behavior or the personalities of other people? Or in so doing, are they violating the individual's own right to self-determination in action and character?

It should be noted that this issue is independent of the nature of the behavior or character change produced in research. In the preceding section, for example, the investigator created conditions that led participants to commit undesirable acts such as cheating and harming others. However, the right to self-determination is violated just as clearly when the change produced is of a sort that onlookers might judge desirable, for example, a change in the direction of greater readiness to help others or a greater capacity to resist temptation to be dishonest.

The origin of the questionable practice of violating the research participant's right to self-determination is the social scientist's obligation to produce a science that is adequate for the task of guiding the development and modification of social behavior. Two examples, one of research involving behavior control and the other dealing with major changes in a significant attitude, are illustrative.

Low academic achievement in metropolitan public schools is a national problem of great concern. Observers disagree about its causes. Among the explanations suggested are such factors as poor motivation, inadequate teacher-pupil communication, and classes so large that remedial instruction for individuals is impractical. One group of investigators sought to improve academic achievement by a method that involved small-group cooperation, peer tutoring, and positive reinforcement (Hamblin, Hathaway, & Wodarski, 1971). The participating teachers organized their students into classroom teams. The amount of reward (credits that could be exchanged for various privileges) received by all the members of a given team depended not on their individual classroom performance but rather on the average performance of the three *lowest* achievers on their team. As a result of this new "social system," the better students on a team began to tutor the poorer ones, and the academic performance of all students, but especially that of the poorer students, showed improvement.

The second example is a study of racial attitude change (S. W. Cook, 1970). The investigator selected white female college students with extremely negative attitudes toward blacks to serve as research participants. For several hours a day, for 20 days, each participant worked cooperatively in an equal-status relationship with a black of equivalent education (an experimental confederate); a third co-worker in the cooperating work group was a white (also a confederate) who endorsed racial equality and desegregation. Several months after each participant left the experiment, her racial attitude was checked by another researcher in a different place in the city. Forty percent of the participants now showed markedly different racial attitudes, having changed in the direction of racial equality and desegregation.

In neither of these experiments did the participants know of the changes the procedures were expected to produce. Moreover, the changes would not have occurred had they depended on the free choice of the participants (i.e., the control participants did not change). They occurred only because the investigators had discovered the influences that would lead them to change or, as some would put it, the way to manipulate them.

Positions taken by social scientists on the conflict between the right to self-determination and efforts to make significant changes in research participants vary considerably. Some have placed primary emphasis on self-determination and freedom of choice and made proposals intended to preserve as much of this freedom as possible in research projects (e.g., Kelman, 1968). Others point to the everyday prevalence of behavior control by employers, educators, and government; they go on to argue that the focus should be on developing a type of control that operates for the individual's gain rather than for his or her disadvantage (e.g., Skinner in the debate between Rogers and Skinner, 1956). Still others minimize the difference between the two positions, pointing to the illusory nature of much apparent freedom of choice (e.g., Hoagland, 1963). They point out that salespersons and political figures often make us "choose" to acquire things or do things that we would be better off not having or doing. Hence, apparent freedom to choose or to act may itself be a result of control by others.

As yet, little concern has been shown regarding the implications of violating the research participant's right to self-determination. The principal reason for this is that social science has only begun to learn how to change people in ways that are fundamental to their conduct and outlook. As knowledge of the major determinants of basic (and sensitive) behaviors and traits accumulates, the value conflict will become more salient, both for scientists and for everyone. The fact that other methods of behavior control are being developed contemporaneously—including electrical brain stimulation, psychoactive drugs, and programs of scientifically tested reinforcement—will add to the concern. In the not-too-distant future it will be necessary for all researchers to clarify their own positions on this issue.

Exposing the Research Participant to Physical or Mental Stress

Human reactions to stress and behavior under stressful conditions are important topics in social relations. Examples of problems in this area include crowd behavior in emergencies, the relation of anxiety to the desire for social affiliation, and persuasibility under conditions of lowered self-esteem. The investigation of these and related questions has led social scientists to induce a wide variety of unpleasant emotional states in their research participants. These range from concern about one's economic security to a belief that one has seriously harmed another person.

That such practices create ethical questions is a matter of general agreement. Although it is true that in everyday affairs people induce stress in others (e.g., parents threaten their children; doctors threaten their patients) the assumption is that the person who is being shamed, deprived, made anxious, or punished will profit personally from this experience. Such a justification is absent from most research (although it is occasionally present in research on therapeutic methods).

Stressful experiences are usually presented to participants without forewarning. It is standard practice to "debrief" the participants at the close of the experiment about the deception that was used in producing the stress.

Some examples of experiments making use of different types of stress are as follows:

Horror   A researcher who believed he had discovered that the pupil of the eye would constrict when viewing unpleasant material and dilate when viewing material that was pleasing wished to determine whether this would provide a physiological measure of feelings and attitudes (Hess, 1965). As one check on this possibility he photographed the eyes of his research participants while they examined gruesome pictures of the remains of emaciated victims in Nazi concentration camps. Other investigators whose research required the arousal of emotional reactions have shown their participants pictures of mutilated persons or the distorted faces of persons who have drowned.

Threat to sexual identity   Among youth, experiences that raise questions about sexual identity are likely to arouse considerable emotion. This fact was used by an experimenter studying the effect of a communication from a prestigious source on attitude change. The nature of the experiment was such that it required an attitude to which the research participants had a strong emotional commitment. This requirement was met by a "self-referring attitude," that is, self-perceived masculinity or femininity (Bergin, 1962). In one part of this experiment the "director of personality assessment" of a psychiatry department of a university medical center gave the male participants test feedback indicating femininity and feedback indicating masculinity to female participants. Clear-cut emotional disturbance was observable in these individuals.

Failure   Exposing participants to preplanned failure is commonplace. Among the research topics in which it has been employed are motivation, level of aspiration, learning, problem solving, self-esteem, persistence, coping, and other aspects of personality. Research related to the continuing debate about reward and punishment as incentives for school achievement provides an example. In this study, five grading systems were used on the first midterm examination in a college course, and the results assessed in terms of performance on a second midterm examination (Goldberg, 1965). Under one of the grading policies ("strict"), the lowest 30 percent of students received an F. Under another ("lenient"), the lowest 30 percent received a D or C. After the second midterm, new grades for the first midterm were issued; these conformed to customary grading practices. Meanwhile some students had anxious moments—which was the experimenter's intent. (The results showed that the different grading policies produced no differences in performance on the second test.)

Fear   A dramatic use of this type of stress was made in a study of the effect of prior organization on group behavior (French, 1944). Organized and unorganized groups were assembled for what they believed were to be group discussions. After the discussions got under way, smoke was observed to be seeping under the door. When the group members tried to leave the room, they found that the door had been locked.

   Among the most extreme uses of fear have been those employed in studies of soldiers in emergencies simulating combat. In these studies investigators were looking for selection and training procedures that they believed would save lives in real emergencies (Berkun et al., 1962). Among the stress-producing situations they used were realistically faked ditching of aircraft in the ocean, reports of accidental radioactive fallout, fake forest fires surrounding an occupied outpost, and misdirected artillery shells exploding close by. During several of the emergencies the participants had the task of repairing a malfunctioning radio which was needed to send the message they believed would save their lives.

Emotional shock   An illustration of this type of stress comes from a study designed to test drivers' reaction to a sudden hazardous situation. The participant was driving. As the car passed a construction job, a realistic dummy fell into the path of the car too late for the driver to avoid hitting it.

Discussion   It is a questionable practice to expose research participants to physical or mental stress without their informed consent, and it is entirely unacceptable to submit them to experiences that may cause them serious or lasting harm. However, as the preceding examples indicate, the degree of stress involved in experiments varies widely. Some stressful experiences are less upsetting than others, and some are more frequently encountered than others in everyday life. The goal should always be for researchers to try to achieve their objectives with less-extreme stress experiences.

It may be possible in some instances for investigators to plan research around naturally occurring emotional stress. Everyday examples are patients awaiting injections, surgery, or their turns in a dentist's chair. Good examples of such research may be found in the work of investigators studying the effects of prior information and modeling in reducing emotional reactions to stressful events in hospitals (see, e.g., Vernon, 1973).

There will remain, however, a sizable difference of opinion among scientists regarding research in which the experimenter exposes others to physical and emotional discomfort. Some will be convinced that a scientist has no moral right to do this, whereas others will believe just as strongly that scientists must do this in order to study those matters that in everyday life cause excitement, raise concern, are motivating, lead to conflict, and in general, are most important to understand.

Invading the Privacy of the Research Participant

Research on some topics in social relations leads investigators to engage in a number of ethically ambiguous practices that we have grouped under the label of *invasion of privacy*. Included are several data-collection procedures such as participant observation, covert observation (sometimes utilizing one-way mirrors and audiotape and videotape recording), interview and questionnaire inquiries into intimate personal matters, and disguised indirect tests in which the test takers are unaware of what they are revealing.

The recent concern attached to the invasion of privacy derives not from its use by scientists but from its abuse by police, private detectives, credit bureaus, and the government. Wiretapping of telephones, secret tape recordings of conversations, "security" interviews with neighbors and acquaintances, checks on personal financial records, and the planting of intelligence agents in political organizations are types of "snooping" and spying that have become all too familiar.

In part, the objection to these procedures is that typically they are used to the disadvantage of the person whose privacy is invaded; for example, they may be used as a basis for potential criminal prosecution. Another objection, however, is to their abridgment of the "right to privacy." This is one's right not to have personal information or private affairs disclosed publicly and to determine for oneself how much of one's beliefs, actions, and personal attributes to disclose. For almost all of us, this would include privacy for intimate and affectionate relationships between adults and between parents and children. Many would also include privacy in matters of personal hygiene. For many, financial status and the nature of one's religious and political beliefs should be considered as private. For some, the right to privacy also covers things that though done in public, are not expected to be the focus of attention by others, for example, a conversation with a friend in a crowded lobby.

Studies involving some degree of invasion of privacy fall into five groups: those using techniques of participant observation, those involving covert observation and recording procedures, those asking personal questions in interviews or questionnaires, those employing disguised indirect tests, and those obtaining information from third parties.

Participant observation   Many of the more-interesting aspects of human behavior do not lend themselves to laboratory experimentation. Examples include delinquency in street gangs, family influence in voting for president, homosexual practices, the activities of "doomsday" groups, and the customs of primitive tribes. One of the ways scientists have approached the study of such matters is to become a party to the ongoing activity and, unknown to the other participants (or to no more than a few of them), to make systematic notes about what they observe. The study of street-corner groups mentioned earlier was conducted in this way (Whyte, 1943).

A researcher interested in developing a more adequate description of the different types of male homosexuality assumed the role of lookout for pairs of men who were engaged in oral sexual practices in public restrooms. A year later the same men were interviewed in their homes as part of a large social health survey without being informed that the interviewer had had any previous knowledge of the activities (Humphreys, 1970).

Other investigators interested in cognitive consistency theory studied the adjustment of members of a group to the failure of their prediction that the earth would come to an end on a certain day (Festinger, Riecken, & Schachter, 1956). To do this, they began attending the group's meetings; to avoid suspicion, they represented themselves as having had psychic experiences in the past.

The procedures used in the preceding studies may be distinguished from two similar procedures about which ethical questions are rarely raised. One is the conduct of a study in a situation where one is both a true participant and a scientist, a real patient in a hospital or a real taxi driver. The other is open prearranged observation in settings ordinarily considered private, such as observations of families carried out in their homes. In the latter, the participants rapidly grow accustomed to the observer and return to uninhibited, normal activity.

Covert structured observation   When social scientists are convinced that the act of open and obvious data collection will change the behavior being observed, they may conceal an observer or use concealed recording equipment. Sometimes this is accomplished by having the observer pose as an apparent bystander. For example, an investigator who was interested in the part played by informal private negotiation in proceedings at the United Nations took note of small international subgroups conversing in hallways and lobbies, recording the nationalities involved, who initiated the contact, and its duration (Alger, 1966). Other investigators, studying sex differences in interests, walked through crowded theater lobbies at intermission, eavesdropping to discover the topics of conversation in all-male and all-female groupings (Carlson, Cook, & Stromberg, 1936). Sometimes the concealment of the observer is quite literal, as was the case in a study designed to check on egocentricity in conversations; the observers hid under dormitory beds (Henle & Hubbell, 1938).

Often **covert structured** (or concealed) **observation** is best accomplished behind one-way mirrors. Typically the research participant is told of the observation but given a false reason for it. For example, in a study in which the social interaction of members of interracial groups was being observed, the participants were led to believe that the observation was related to the possible revision of a task on which their group was working (Katz, Goldston, & Benjamin, 1958). In another study in which the interaction of mother and child was under observation, the mother thought that only the behavior of the child was being recorded (Bishop, 1951). What is questionable about procedures such as these, of course, is that what people do in areas supposedly not under observation reveals aspects of themselves that they may have elected to keep private. This raises again the issue of what is to be considered private. More will be said about this later.

In some research the nature of the question and the setting are such that no method of collecting information other than by concealed recording seems likely to produce uninhibited and uncensored data. This was the basis for using a concealed audio recording in a study of the ability of a family to survive an extended stay in an underground fallout shelter.

The recording of concealed observations makes invasion of privacy an even more questionable practice. The fact that a tape or film exists broadens the potential audience for the behavior in question and, hence, increases the potential for embarrassment and discomfort should confidentiality not be observed. To the extent that the behavior recorded can be used against the participant, the danger in this practice is increased still further.

Asking personal questions in interviews and questionnaires Many problems in social relations are studied by asking participants to respond to questions on interviews or questionnaires in regard to their beliefs, feelings, actions, past experiences, or hopes for the future. Some of these questions deal with intimate relationships; the well-known Kinsey studies of sexual practices were one such example. Others deal with illegal practices; studies of social and cultural factors in the backgrounds of drug users are illustrative. In studies of the development of personality characteristics, researchers have asked children to describe the child-rearing practices of their parents, for example, to agree or disagree with "Dad always seems too busy to pal around with me." Researchers in other studies have asked questions about personal habits, including whether to agree or disagree with "I enjoy soaking in a bathtub" or "Sometimes I tell dirty jokes when I would rather not."

Disguised, indirect, or projective tests   Data-collection instruments of this sort are used by social scientists primarily for two reasons. The first is to measure personality traits or behavioral tendencies about which the research participants either are unaware or, if aware, do not know their position on the trait continuum and, hence, are unable to provide accurate self-description. The second is to measure some characteristic about which it is assumed that respondents are motivated to conceal the truth and give self-descriptions they know to be incorrect. In either case, the investigator is obtaining from participants information they do not know they are revealing and, in this sense, is invading the privacy of the subject's inner life. In some cases the information would be held back if the participant knew what was happening.

An example of using indirect tests to measure a characteristic about which the respondent is unable to give an adequate self-description is the use of stories told about pictures in the Thematic Apperception Test to assess strength of achievement motivation (McClelland et al., 1953). Studies of child-rearing practices have used this technique to assess the impact of different methods of child rearing on the development of this attribute.

In the literature on attitudes there are many examples of measurement of characteristics when it is feared that the respondents may inhibit or censor answers that correctly describe the characteristics. In one study, for example, groups differing in racial attitude were readily distinguished from each other by asking them to rate the plausibility or convincingness of one set of arguments for segregation and another set of arguments for desegregation (Selltiz & Cook, 1966). The participants were asked explicitly not to indicate their own agreement or disagreement with the arguments but rather to judge their effectiveness as support for whichever policy was endorsed by the argument. The indirect detection of racial attitude was possible because their attitudes led the respondents to judge as more convincing those arguments that supported the policy in which they believed; that is, those with favorable racial attitudes thought arguments for desegregation to be stronger than those with less-favorable attitudes.

Obtaining information from third parties   The information in some research can better be provided by third parties than by the research participants themselves. For example, the impact of an experimental program, such as training in human relations, on the effectiveness of a baseball manager's communication with his players, is best determined by obtaining information from the players. Similarly, the effectiveness of a program intended to prepare mentally retarded persons for work on assembly lines can best be determined by information obtained from the persons in charge. When the consent of the research participant has been obtained, such contacts with third parties present no problems. However, when the investigator fears that the act of obtaining such consent might put the participants on guard and influence their behavior (a reasonable possibility in the first example given), the investigator may decide to proceed without requesting consent. In both these illustrations, the behavior inquired about is public, and for this reason some scientists would not find the use of third-party informants questionable. However, third parties can also provide information on such matters as the religious practices of their acquaintances, their study habits, or their use of alcohol and other drugs. Getting information such as this by interviewing the respondents themselves introduces the danger that responses will be distorted in the direction of "proper" behavior. The cooperation of third parties can often be obtained by pointing this out and by promising that information supplied to the interviewer will be held in confidence. When the investigator follows this course, an invasion of privacy occurs. When, if ever, this may be justified is discussed later in the chapter.

Discussion   The examples just given suggest that privacy may be invaded in two ways: (1) by the observation of acts that an individual may prefer to keep private and (2) by the fact of being observed systematically in the absence of knowledge that this is happening. In the first case, an individual may dislike to reveal certain information, regardless of the method by which this happens. In the second, such people may object to being observed when they were not expecting to be, whether the activity involved was a casual conversation in a public place or a more-intimate relationship in their home.

Threats to privacy vary in strength on these two dimensions. With respect to the first, observation of normally public activity such as working, eating, and recreation will meet little, if any, objection, whereas observation of activity customarily occurring in private settings, such as the home, the toilet, or the bedroom, will meet a great deal. With respect to being observed systematically, several degrees of invasion of privacy may be discerned. At the least-objectionable extreme we may place observation about which participants are aware in general but about the focus of which they have been misled. More objectionable is observation about which the participant is entirely uninformed; this is true in some (but not all) participant observation. More objectionable yet is concealed observation but without audio or video recording. Most objectionable of all is concealed observation with audio or video recording. Needless to say, the two dimensions will cumulate in determining the extent to which privacy is invaded; for example, secret videotaping of extremely intimate activity will be seen as intolerable.

The preceding comments are concerned with human "cost" of invading privacy. Thus, although it may be granted that any invasion of privacy is a questionable practice in research, it is also clear that some types of invasion are more costly than others and, if undertaken, require correspondingly greater justification.

Not all the statements made about invasion of privacy in this discussion are matters of general agreement. It may be argued, for example, that activities occurring in public places should be considered open to systematic observation for research purposes just as they are to unsystematic observation by curious bystanders. This argument would open to concealed observation anything that happens in work settings, waiting rooms, restaurants, and public means of transportation. Some social scientists have extended this position to cover events that happen in private when the parties involved are engaged in government or industrial activities in which they are accountable to the public.

Another argument minimizes the seriousness of observing aspects of behavior about which the research participant has not been explicitly warned. It is enough, according to this argument, to make it known that observation is occurring; one may object to observing additional behavior as deceptive but not as an invasion of privacy.

A third argument is that participant observation does not invade privacy, although it may be judged undesirable in violating the mutual trust usually assumed in social relationships. As already noted, this argument seems more compelling when the observer is a legitimate participant, that is, a real patient, taxi driver, or production line worker. If, however, invasion of privacy is used to cover the fact of being systematically observed in the absence of knowledge that this is happening, the legitimate versus planted status of the participant observer seems of little consequence.

As noted earlier, invasion of privacy takes on many of its negative connotations from the purposes for which it is used in everyday life. In research, by contrast, data from an intimate question or from a concealed observation are rarely of interest for themselves or in relation to the specific individual to whom they refer. Rather, individual observations merge into measurement indexes or scale scores, and these, in turn, merge into group averages. This difference is not appreciated by persons unfamiliar with research, and for this reason they view procedures of the sort discussed in this section more negatively than the scientists utilizing them. Those who keep this in mind and inform concerned segments of the community in advance will reduce the danger of misunderstanding and hostile reaction. To illustrate, one pair of investigators, who explained their study by letter to both parents and children and obtained their consent in writing to participate, encountered no objection when they asked high school students the question "Have you ever engaged in sexual intercourse with someone of the opposite sex?" (Jessor & Jessor, 1975).

9. Withholding Benefits from Participants in Control Groups

Ordinarily the fact that a study has a control group composed of subjects who are not exposed to the experimental experience raises no ethical issues. But there are two exceptions. One occurs when the experimenter or others who know of the research become convinced of the value of a new program or treatment and believe that it would benefit all the research participants, including those in the control group. The other occurs when the subjects in the control group are deprived of some recognized benefit to which they had earlier had access in order to provide a more accurate assessment of the value of the new program or treatment.

Such circumstances are most likely to be encountered when the study deals with the effects of some remedial or supportive measure such as a new therapy, a promising educational innovation, a new preventive health measure, or an economic benefit. At such times, even though participants have been chosen for a control group purely by chance, investigators may feel concerned that they are being deprived of something that is important to their present or future welfare. Even if researchers do not develop such a concern, it may be expressed by others who, in some cases, may be in positions of authority.

Examples of studies in which potential benefits have been withheld from control groups An example from outside the area of social relations research will help to point up the reality of this dilemma. In the early 1970s the news media uncovered the fact that several decades earlier a government-supported experiment had been carried out to evaluate the effectiveness of a new treatment of syphilis. The reporters discovered that the health of a number of persons in the untreated **control group** had deteriorated as a result of the disease; it was clear in retrospect that had these individuals also received the new treatment they would now be in better health (Jones, 1981).

Two experiments will illustrate the parallel concern with deprived control group participants in social relations research. The first took place in the early 1960s near the beginning of the period in which social scientists began their efforts to find ways to overcome the retardation in school achievement found among children from economically and educationally disadvantaged homes. One approach was to attempt to discover compensatory methods for preparing preschool children for their first year of schoolwork. (The governmental program with this objective was called Head Start.) Basing their reasoning on the nature of the intellectual deficiencies shown by the disadvantaged children, the experimenters devised remedial educational experiences. One group of children received this training for three summers and one for two summers preceding school entrance (Klaus & Gray, 1968). Children from equally deprived homes were assigned to control groups, one such group coming from the home-town of the experimental group and another from a similar town near by. Although doubt has been raised about the effectiveness of the Head Start program in general, the experimental program in Klaus and Gray's study produced differences in average IQs between experimental and control groups that persisted at least through the fourth grade. As in the previous study, there is in this experiment a strong indication that a long-term dis-advantage to some children hinged on the chance factor of their assign-ment to the control group. Again, however, it must be remembered that the same failure to receive adequate preparation for school attendance is characteristic of many thousands of children born into disadvantaged circumstances.

The second experiment dealt with the effect of a guaranteed annual income on a person's incentive to work (Kershaw, 1972). Approximately 600 men in four-person families received government payments bringing their income up to a level between $3,000 and $4,000 per year. This con-tinued for three years. The amount received varied, always being only enough to bring them up to a specified level. Another 600 men, neighbors in the same communities, constituted a control group. Although in equal need, none received the supplemental government payments. Persons in both groups were selected randomly. (Results indicated no reduction in work incentive among those receiving payments.)

Occasionally, the concern about what the control group participants are being deprived of is sufficiently strong to cause those who have autho-rized the experiment or who are cooperating with the experimenter in car-rying it out to withdraw their support. One instance of this occurred in the course of study dealing with the phenomenon caricatured by the expression "some of my best friends are Jews." This refers to the recur-rent observation that liked or admired persons from a disliked ethnic group are categorized as "good" exceptions to the disliked groups. As a result, the experience of knowing them usually has little effect on attitude change. A group of researchers developed the hypothesis that this "com-partmentalization" and isolation of new experience contradicting old prej-udices might be prevented by encouraging the development of cross-racial friendships under conditions in which the ethnic identity of the newly made friends was repeatedly verbalized (Chein, Cook, & Harding, 1948). The experiment was conducted in a recreational center with trained group workers as leaders of experimental and control groups. In the experimen-tal groups the staff workers were to call attention to ethnic identity when-ever the children in the groups were having satisfying and enjoyable inter-changes; they were not to do this in the control groups. Midway through the research the experimenters observed that the experimental procedure was being employed in the control groups as well as in the experimental groups. In a conference about the matter, the group leaders confessed that they had become convinced that the experimental procedure was a valuable antidote to prejudice and felt morally obliged, therefore, to use it with *all* the children with whom they worked.

Discussion   What has just been said suggests that withholding potential benefits from subjects in a control group creates an ethical question in only a small proportion of the cases in which it happens. These are the instances in which control group participants are deprived of benefits that would be available normally were the research not under way. In other cases, the deprivation associated with assignment to control groups is no different from that prevailing outside the experiment and, hence, cannot be attributed to the research.

Despite this, many researchers will feel they have incurred some responsibility for control group participants in studies where it turns out that substantial benefits and advantages have accrued to members of their experimental groups. It will sometimes be possible to fulfill this sense of obligation by applying the newly tested procedures to control group participants at the close of the experiment. This is likely to be expensive and time-consuming; hence it must be anticipated when the study is being planned and budgeted.

Finally, the social scientist must remember that persons without scientific training, who may not understand the necessity for control groups in research, will not be sympathetic to experiments in which beneficial experiences are withheld from some participants. This fact should also be anticipated, and the investigator must be prepared to explain the long-range value of such experiments in the event criticism is encountered.

Failing to Treat Research Participants Fairly and to Show Them Consideration and Respect

Although social scientists obtain data from individuals or from their interactions in groups and organizations, the purpose is to establish generalizable principles of human behavior. A given research participant is only one among many persons whose thoughts and actions are studied in a single project. One consequence of this is an insidious tendency to treat the participants as research objects and forget their human sensitivities.

One extreme and, fortunately, rare indication of this tendency is to treat research participants unfairly and with a lack of consideration and respect. A minor example is to arrive late for appointments, an affront to participants who have often gone to considerable inconvenience in scheduling the time of their own appearance. A more-serious example is not to fulfill commitments to the participant. Subjects who have been promised large sums of money to take part may, instead, be paid at the going hourly rates; in such cases the experimenter "persuades" the participant that the misleading promise was necessary to the success of the research and that the research project does not, in fact, have the money for the promised larger payment. Or a promise to furnish postexperimental reports of the research may not be carried out. Sometimes such promises are "fulfilled" with reports that are incomprehensible to a reader not familiar with technical terms. A final example is the failure to provide personal benefits that participants have been led to expect, such as improved self-understanding. Sometimes the benefits that are not delivered may have been promised to groups to which the research participants belong, groups such as ethnic minorities or poverty-level neighborhoods.

Although the questionable practices just enumerated are generally thoughtless rather than ill intentioned, they cannot be excused. In this sense, they differ from the questionable practices discussed earlier in the chapter, all of which followed from the nature of research procedures to which the investigator was committed.

Discussion   A number of steps may be taken to minimize unfair and inconsiderate behavior toward research participants. The first, perhaps, is to recognize the situational context in which such behavior takes place and which facilitates its occurrence. An aspect of this context is a mutually accepted difference in status between experimenter and participant. For example, the experimenter is often a professor whereas the participant is a student. Or the difference may be that the experimenter is well educated and of comfortable economic status whereas the participant is economically disadvantaged. The experimenter is typically well established and successful whereas the participant may be mentally ill, a drug addict, or a delinquent. The experimenter often represents organizational authority when the participant is a worker or a soldier. Often without being aware of the fact, the two parties generalize this difference in status to their behavior in the research setting. For example, the experimenter may assume that the participant will display a compliant and submissive orientation and the participant, sharing this assumption, does so.

Although resolutions by the experimenter to do otherwise are appropriate, they are likely to underestimate the seductive power of the status relationship just described. Unless experimenters build a number of practices into their research routine, they are likely to find that from time to time they have again unintentionally treated the participant in ways that they regret. Among these practices are the following.

However simple the arrangements with the research participants, it is helpful to put them in writing. This is not a legalistic step; rather it is intended to remind the experimenter to be sure that participants understand the nature of their commitment, on the one hand, and the nature of the benefits they may anticipate from the experience, on the other. In the case of children or other, less-competent participants such as the mentally ill or retarded, this obligation is not fulfilled by arrangements made with legal guardians; the participants themselves are also due explanations at a level they can comprehend.

To avoid promising benefits beyond those that can be delivered, researchers will find it wise to adopt the deliberate policy of underselling. This is not to suggest that it is inappropriate for researchers to describe the potential scientific and social importance of their research as they see it or to promise interest and excitement in participating if they know this to be forthcoming. In contrast, to say that the research will produce increased self-understanding or that it will improve life circumstances for a social group to which the participant belongs is a promise hard to keep and should be avoided. If money or other rewards are promised, they must not be exaggerated, and of course, they must be honored in a literal sense. In those cases where the research calls for studying the consequences of overreward, the experimenter should go no further than to explain the research problem and invite the participants to return the overpayment. Even this should be done at a time when the participants are no longer under direct social pressure in the experimental situation.

The investigator can remind participants of their autonomy and freedom in the research situation by telling them in writing two things. One is that they are free to withdraw from the study at any time. As such withdrawal introduces bias into the research results, the experimenter should explain this problem to any participant who is considering such action. The second piece of information is the name and address of someone administratively superior to the researcher to whom the participant can report dissatisfaction with the treatment received. The participant should, of course, be encouraged to make a prior complaint to the experimenter and should be assured that relief will be forthcoming from this source.

The final step should occur in the experimenter's postexperimental contact with the participant. This is the point at which most can be done to show full consideration and respect. One objective is to do whatever possible at this time to assure that the participants have gained something from their experience. Sometimes the gain will be limited largely to the promised material reward. Often, however, interesting and useful information may be communicated about scientific theory, research methods, or social problems. In addition, and of great importance, is the opportunity to clarify the sense in which the participant has made an important contribution to scientific inquiry. Procedures for doing this will be discussed in greater detail in a later section.

Responsibilities to Research Participants after Completion of the Research

Even though the conduct of a research project has generated no ethical questions in its treatment of participants, the investigators incur certain obligations that must be fulfilled following its completion. Among these are the following: They must follow through on any commitments made to the participants when soliciting their cooperation, they must give them such additional information about the research and its results as they desire, and they must assure subjects' anonymity and keep in confidence subjects' responses.

In addition, when the research has involved one or more of the ethical questions reviewed earlier in the chapter, the investigator incurs other obligations. For example, if the methodological requirements of the study have necessitated concealment or deception, the researcher must clarify to the participant the reasons for this and restore a relationship of mutual trust and respect. This is discussed in the following subsection, Clarifying the Nature of the Research. If the research procedure has involved discomfort or stress or has diminished the participant's dignity or self-esteem, the investigator must do everything possible to alleviate such consequences. This responsibility is discussed in the subsection Removing Harmful Aftereffects. When there are circumstances that may make it difficult to protect the participant's anonymity and the confidentiality of data, the investigator must make sure that the participant understands this in advance. In the subsection Maintaining Anonymity and Confidentiality this problem is reviewed.

Clarifying the Nature of the Research

The obligation to reveal concealment or deception, that is, to "debrief," is widely accepted although its advisability and practicality may be questioned under certain conditions (see further on in this chapter). This obligation does not depend for its moral justification on a favorable outcome of the debriefing process. Nevertheless, it is reassuring to know that if done properly, misconceptions that might otherwise have persisted can be removed. This has been demonstrated in a number of studies in which the research participants were falsely told that they had unfavorable personality traits, for example, immaturity, poor social skills, low intelligence. With minor exceptions, debriefing has eliminated the negative effects of the false reports; this has been true for effects measured by physiological and behavioral methods as well as by self-description (Holmes, 1976a). Indications are that debriefing is more effective when it includes a discussion of the tendency for the negative impact of false information to perseverate than when this tendency is not discussed (Ross, Lepper, & Hubbard, 1975).

In clarifying the true nature of research that has involved concealment or deception, the investigator should strive to achieve the following:

1. Convey to the participants the investigator's sense of the potential value of the research.
2. Give the participants an appreciation of the contributions they have made to the research.

3. Provide the participants with an educational experience that includes an understanding of behavioral science research as used in the study in which they have taken part.
4. Develop in the participants an understanding of the necessity (as the investigator sees it) of employing questionable practices to obtain meaningful answers to the research question asked in the study.
5. Immunize the participants against the tendency for negative impressions of self that are developed in experiments to perseverate even after attempts have been made to correct them.
6. Convince the participant of the investigator's regrets over the need to employ questionable practices and concern over the participant's feelings about having been subjected to these practices.
7. Give the participants a perspective on their experiences that minimizes any feeling that they might have been manipulated, made fools of, shown to be gullible, or revealed character weaknesses.

To accomplish these objectives, time must be set aside for a full discussion of the participants' questions about their own behavior. Such a discussion will provide an opportunity to clarify confusion and correct misinformation and will help to minimize feelings of annoyance and resentment. It will help to detect and alleviate any harm suffered by the participants. Perhaps it will also restore respect for and trust in the investigator and protect social science against the reputation of being secretive and manipulative in character.

Though recognizing the desirability of revealing questionable practices to the participant, some investigators feel that under many circumstances the disadvantages of doing this outweigh the advantages. For example, if research participants are being drawn from a small community, such as a college or other small institution, the early participants in a study may inform later ones of the experimental deception even though they have pledged secrecy. Such actions lead to serious questions about the validity of the research and argue for the desirability of not debriefing. Even when participants who have been debriefed do not reveal what they have been told to others who are to take part in the same study, there remains the problem that potential participants in other studies hear of the deception and may become generally suspicious. If, as is likely, this leads them to guess that something unannounced is afoot in every study in which they take part, it will influence the outcome of all research in this setting in unpredictable ways.

To take another example, there are circumstances in which revealing deception may negate a positive outcome felt by the research participants. Suppose, for example, that individuals had been induced by experimental arrangements to help a team member who was having difficulty. We know that the individuals assume that they have helped at their own initiative and derive satisfaction from so doing (Blanchard & Cook, 1976). Some social scientists have suggested that debriefing participants under these conditions may reduce their self-esteem and possibly do more harm than good.

Such an analysis has led to a search for a compromise by means of which postexperimental discussions would be held with participants in some studies but not in others. One suggestion for such a compromise would be to debrief only when the experimental experience went beyond the limits of the participant's ordinary, everyday experience (Campbell, 1969c). This would make debriefing unnecessary in all field experiments and in many laboratory experiments. It would still be called for, however, in obedience studies where the research participants were persuaded to harm others, in compliance studies where they were led to deny their own perceptions, in studies where they were influenced to believe fictitious facts about important topics, and in a number of other areas. As will be evident, difficulties would arise in choosing those studies in which postexperimental discussions with participants were advisable and those in which they were not.

Still other disadvantages to dispelling deception have been pointed out. Among them is the argument that it gives publicity to the fact that deception is practiced by respected people such as scientists. Two answers may be given to this argument. One is that deception in research will be revealed in other ways, including textbooks. The other is that the deception may be discovered by the participant; it is better to avoid this danger and to reveal the deception under conditions in which it can be interpreted and justified and its consequences for the deceived person dealt with.

If debriefing is to be undertaken, it may be carried out in either of two ways. One is factual in emphasis whereas the other is feeling-oriented. The emphasis in factual debriefing is on providing information about a study's purpose and its methods, as well as the questionable practices used and why they were necessary. Appreciation for taking part is expressed, an apology may be made, and an offer to answer questions is extended. It is sometimes difficult during factual debriefings to avoid the atmosphere that the deception in the study was clever; the participants themselves often introduce this idea. Another danger is that in the debriefing the participants' attention may become fixed on the fact that they were easily fooled. Shame and embarrassment may inhibit their asking questions. Following the debriefing, resentment, self-doubts, and loss of self-esteem may surface. These feelings may be accompanied by disillusionment and loss of trust in social relationships.

The feeling-oriented debriefing covers essentially the same content as the factual. It differs primarily in achieving each objective of the debriefing through discussion. An effort is made to be sure that the research participants think about and understand the value of the research and their contribution to it, why an answer to the research question required studying natural rather than self-conscious behavior, how this necessitated deception and other questionable practices, and finally, the manner in which they themselves were deceived. The investigators' regrets about employing questionable practices and their concern for the participants' reaction to this are brought into the discussion. The investigators attempt to promote uninhibited discussion by the participants by assuming that they have negative reactions to having been deceived, subjected to stress, or led to commit acts that lowered their self-esteem. The discussion may conclude with a balancing of these negative feelings against each participant's estimate of the potential value of the research (e.g., Blanchard & Cook, 1976).

Removing Harmful Aftereffects

One of the advantages of postexperimental discussions with research participants is that they provide an opportunity for the investigator to detect and deal with negative aftereffects of the experience. Anxiety and feelings of inadequacy may develop inadvertently in the course of research that was thought by the investigator to be entirely free of such possibilities. For example, poor performance by a participant in a learning or problem-solving experiment may be interpreted by the participant as indicating a general inadequacy. Similarly, one's submissiveness or vacillation in a decision-making study may confirm one's own preexperimental apprehensions about lack of self-confidence. Or after answering questions in a personality inventory, the participant may come to the conclusion that his or her responses indicate some kind of abnormality or uncertainty about masculinity or femininity.

Unexpected reactions to research experiences may be encountered also in children. An experiment that involved recording **galvanic skin responses** from the palm of the hand will illustrate this. As it happened, the wires to the GSR electrodes used in the experiment had a red plastic exterior. Also, the pen on the moving recorder, which could be seen by the participant, wrote in red ink. An eight-year-old child participating in the study became emotionally upset and left the building. Later the experimenter discovered that the juxtaposition of the red wires and the red ink had meant to the child that blood was being withdrawn from the hand to which the electrodes were attached.

Although reactions such as these are probably rare in the type of research described, they will occur more often when research experiences are stressful. As noted in the earlier discussion of questionable practices, research participants may be exposed to experiences such as failure, fright, or embarrassment. They may be put into situations in which they cheat, lie, or steal. They may be persuaded by the experimenter to harm others by reading to them derogatory evaluations of their personalities or by administering painful punishment. Or they may be led to believe that they have been responsible unintentionally for serious injury or possible death.

Of great concern are those reactions that manifest themselves later. Accounts of such reactions are not uncommon. One such report involved a male college student who was convinced by means of a fake physiological response displayed to him on an oscilloscope that he had sexual tendencies previously unknown to him. Although he was debriefed, the experience initiated (or perhaps reinforced) a concern that two years later brought the student to a psychotherapist.

On the other hand, studies of the effect of debriefing in preventing the occurrence of longterm negative effects of stressful experiments are reassuring. However, in all such studies the type of debriefing employed went beyond a simple explanation of the deception used and attempted, in addition, to minimize possible stress reactions, for example, by assuring the participants that their behavior had been normal or had reflected positive personality characteristics or would not be expected to generalize beyond a laboratory situation. One such study employed both a questionnaire and a psychiatric interview, finding not only no evidence of trauma but also a considerable amount of satisfaction at having participated in the experiment (Milgram, 1964). Another compared a form of debriefing that concerned itself with ameliorating stress with a debriefing focused only on correcting deception; the former was found to be more effective in reducing emotional upset and in promoting a positive evaluation of the experiment (Ring, Wallston, & Corey, 1970). A third compared a stress-reduction debriefing with no debriefing, finding a clear advantage for the former (Holmes, 1976b). Of special interest is the fact that the latter study measured stress arousal reactions physiologically as well as by participant's self-description. This fact lessens somewhat a concern that research participants, rather than accurately reflecting their true emotional condition, may be giving supportive answers in a desire to respond reassuringly to a considerate investigator.

If, in considering whether or not to conduct a study, the investigators cannot be reasonably confident of their abilities to reverse potential negative effects on the participants, they should decide against proceeding with their project. When they decide to proceed, they incur the obligation to detect and remove the negative effects as soon as possible. This has several implications. In long-term or multiple-session research, it indicates the need for a system to monitor the participants' reactions during the course of the research. It implies the use in all studies of a postexperimental discussion session of a kind that facilitates discovery of emotional disturbances when they are present. Finally, in many cases, it requires procedures for long-term follow-up to detect and remove disturbances that develop after the research has come to an end.

Precautions taken in a study of the effects of exposure of adults to pornographic materials will illustrate each of the preceding procedures. As exposure was repeated periodically over a considerable period of time, the emotional condition of the participants was monitored by having them fill out mood scales each day. In addition, they were given names and addresses of psychiatrists associated with the project and urged to consult them immediately if they felt the need. After the completion of the study each participant was examined carefully for evidence of disturbance. In addition, to check for the possibility that harmful effects might develop later, all participants were reinterviewed after eight weeks.

Detecting and removing negative aftereffects in field experiments will generally be impossible; for example, the passerby who fails to help a fake heart-attack victim is not accessible to follow-up. The limitation further increases the investigator's uncertainty about costs to the research participant and requires additional assurance that the experiment under consideration promises important benefits.

A type of negative aftereffect that presents a special dilemma is that which occurs as a consequence of terminating a beneficial experimental program. An example has been described by investigators who were studying the outcomes of providing retirement home residents with a predictable and controllable adjunct to their otherwise routinized and dependent existence (Schulz & Hanusa, 1978). (The experimental program consisted of visits by undergraduates on a schedule that could be predicted and controlled by the person visited.) The study found a statistically significant improvement in health status and zest for life among those participating in the experimental program. This had the effect of arresting and reversing the typical decline in physical and psychological status characteristic of aged individuals receiving institutional care. However, to the alarm of the investigators a follow-up approximately three years after termination of the study found a greater mortality rate among the individuals who had participated in the experimental program than among those who had not. They worried that this may have been due to the contrast between the experimental program and the postexperimental return to a life of uneventful dependence following its termination. Although other evidence supported an alternative interpretation in this case, the investigators presented their ethical dilemma as one that must confront all social scientists who experiment with programs of great potential value to their research subject. It is parallel, for example, to the ethical question faced by those who conducted the guaranteed annual income experiment, discussed earlier (Kershaw, 1972). In that study income maintenance payments to poverty-stricken research participants were terminated after they had had three years to become accustomed to them.

Maintaining Anonymity and Confidentiality

The obligation to protect research participants' anonymity and keep research data in confidence is an all-inclusive one and should be fulfilled unless specific arrangements to the contrary are made with the participants themselves. Moreover, the more intimate and sensitive the responses and the less open the procedures by which they were gathered, the greater is the transgression in releasing them to others. When measures are obtained covertly and deal with private matters, the investigator incurs an especially heavy responsibility to keep them in confidence.

A questionable practice not mentioned earlier is the use of secret procedures to identify persons who assume they are providing research data anonymously. An example is the device of putting stamps in precoded precisely measured locations on return envelopes containing **"anonymous" questionnaires;** from the location of the stamp the name of the person returning the questionnaire can be determined. The purpose of these procedures is always the same, namely, to obtain frank and truthful responses which the respondent might be ashamed or afraid to give on a signed questionnaire. The name is needed to make possible comparison of these responses with background data or with opinions or actions measured in some second situation. The investigator who proceeds in this way undoubtedly will not reveal the research participant's identity to others. Nevertheless, the deviation from ethical principles is so blatant in such procedures that in our opinion, only the promise of substantial scientific or social gain could possibly justify their use.

Sometimes the problem just described can be circumvented with the cooperation of the research participants. For example, if their test or interview responses at two different times must be compared, this can be accomplished anonymously through the use of code numbers supplied by the participants themselves. Such numbers may be derived from the year, month, and day of birth of a close relative. An even simpler procedure is the use of a separate identification sheet with the assurance that a code number to be assigned by the investigator will be entered on all materials and that the investigator will personally keep confidential the lists of names and associated code numbers.

The use of code numbers for data records that are to be filed and retained for later use is desirable as a routine procedure. Among its advantages are that it symbolizes to everyone associated with the research the emphasis placed on anonymity and confidentiality. In addition it protects against deliberate efforts by others to use research data for purposes other than those intended. This may be of critical importance if access to the data is demanded by those in authority, such as institutional administrators or the courts (see further on in this chapter).

Whenever data are collected only once and no comparison with data from other sources or with follow-up data collected later is planned, it is wise for the investigator not to collect names. Questionnaires, for example, may be anonymously mailed in or deposited anonymously at some collection point.

Maintaining anonymity and confidentiality would be greatly simplified were it not for the many plausible requests and demands for access to research data by others. These include third parties such as parents and friends, institutional administrators such as school principals, professional associates such as other research investigators, and compilers of data banks.

Requests from third parties   When parents consent to the participation of their children in research, it seems entirely reasonable to them for the investigator to give them information on the things the child said and did in the course of the study. Similarly, friends who feel quite close to and concerned about a research participant will see no reason why the friend's responses cannot be shared with them. Were such disclosures to be made, they would often violate implicit assumptions by the research participant that only the investigator would learn of the subject's opinions or behavior. In some cases what was revealed might cause the participant embarrassment and discomfort. Hence, however well-intentioned the third party's request, and however harmless might appear the information requested, the investigator must not release information without the participant's explicit permission. In the case of parents, it is advisable to have a clear-cut understanding about the confidentiality of their children's research behavior before the research begins.

Requests from institutions   When research is carried out on employees, students, prisoners, soldiers, or members of any institution, administrative personnel of that institution may wish access to the data. Typically they will want the information in order to be more helpful to the research participants—perhaps to give them more effective guidance, to supplement their personal files, and so on. Occasionally, there will be other reasons, such as to increase the institution's morale or effectiveness, to locate troublemakers, or to assist in the investigation of theft or other crime. When the researchers are staff members of the institution, they may come under pressure or even under a direct order to release information. It is prudent to anticipate this and, if possible, to work out in advance arrangements for confidentiality that will be honored by administrators. When this is not possible, the investigators must either inform research participants of their inability to protect their anonymity or, if they do not do this, they must be prepared to suffer the punitive consequences of defying the institution's request.

Requests from professional associates   Sometimes one investigator will collect data from the same research participants that another has already used. A merging of data from the two studies may make it possible to answer interesting questions that neither study could answer alone. In some institutional settings this possibility may be anticipated by maintaining cumulative research files containing data on individuals who served as participants in several different studies.

This situation raises two ethical problems. The first is taking data provided by an individual for one purpose and using it for a second purpose of which the subject has no knowledge and with which he or she might not wish to cooperate. This is a questionable practice akin to that of involving persons in research without their knowledge or consent. The second is the threat to anonymity and confidentiality created by files to which a number of people have access. A suggestion for controlling the latter problem is to have a designated person charged with the responsibility for keeping the list of names and corresponding code numbers and of providing an investigator with merged sets of data identified by code number only.

Requests from data banks   The seriousness of the problem discussed in the preceding paragraphs is multiplied many times by the so-called data banks. A data bank is any collection of coded information about individuals kept in a form that makes the information easily retrievable, often by automated means. The potential of data banks for social science research is only beginning to be realized. They make it possible to reanalyze large collections of data and to analyze new data in the context of much data already stored on the same individuals. Among the major data banks are those maintained by agencies of the government. Here one may find records of employment, earnings, taxes paid, and census data on topics such as housing and age. If we wished to do a long-term follow-up of the effects of a job training program, for example, we would find in the data bank of the Social Security Administration records of the trainees' later earnings and unemployment payments.

Occasionally, social scientists are asked to contribute to data banks, sometimes to permit supplementary analysis of their data by others interested in similar questions and sometimes to supplement data already available on the same individuals (e.g., welfare recipients). The dangers in doing this are recognized and are receiving much attention both from scientists and the federal government. Many methods of coding and disguising data so that individuals may not be identified are in use, and others are being developed. No investigators who supply information to a data bank should do so without assuring themselves that a sophisticated system of this type is in operation. If it is possible to contact research participants, investigators should inform them regarding precautions taken to protect anonymity and confidentiality and seek their permission to use their data in this way.

Potential loss of anonymity and confidentiality through court order   Even more threatening to the maintenance of anonymity and confidentiality than the various requests and demands already enumerated is the fact that the confidentiality of research data is not recognized in law. This means that a court may order the release of such data for use in criminal prosecutions and, in addition, may require the social scientists to testify about individuals who have been research participants. This may happen whenever the data involve illegal behavior such as drug use, violation of sex laws, and participation in illegal demonstrations. For example, a court order was obtained by a prosecutor to have the director of an experimental drug therapy program furnish photographs of all male participants. The purpose of the order was to assist legal authorities in detecting persons responsible for an armed burglary; the prosecutor's action was based on the assumption that drug users steal to buy the drugs their habit requires.

Researchers who may face court orders to surrender data have several alternatives. One is to advise their research participants of this possibility so that they can take this into account when deciding whether to participate. Another is to render the data files anonymous in a manner already described; often this will not be feasible because the study is one that continues over time. A third is to code the data and send the name-code list outside the country for safekeeping. Refusal to produce the list can be expected to lead to punitive action by the courts, and the investigators must reconcile themselves to this possibility.

Loss of anonymity and confidentiality through reports and publications In research focused on the social life of a group or a community, problems of maintaining anonymity arise when a report is written. Even though pseudonyms for both the groups and individuals in the group are used, experience indicates that the true identity of the group or community soon becomes known. When this happens, it is often possible for group members or residents of the community to identify key individuals in the report. If detailed accounts are given of the behavior of such individuals, their mode of operating, and their relationships with others in the community, the effect can be embarrassing and, in some cases, disruptive to the life of the community and damaging to the reputation and well-being of the individuals.

Scientists differ considerably in their points of view on this matter. Some have argued that details and anecdotes damaging to individuals should not be included in reports, or if they are, that they should be adequately disguised. Some take the position, in addition, that as the report should focus on general principles, such modification or omission of details about individuals represents little, if any, loss in the value of the report. Others, however, have argued that truth must come first—in other words, that the obligation to truth is higher than the obligation to protect anonymity.

One implication of this latter position has been stated earlier. Investigators who adopt it must have a clear understanding with individuals in the research project that details of what the researchers observe and learn will be published. If the researchers do not plan to show subjects what they will write and give the subjects an opportunity to modify or withdraw it, this too should be made clear.

It must be noted, however, that not all social scientists feel that such warnings are necessary. On the contrary, some take the position that publicly accountable behavior—defined as anything that occurs in the course of one's job or in the conduct of public office—must be open to observation and study and that anonymity and confidentiality for such behavior should never be promised. A difficulty with this position is that a trusting relationship is very likely to develop in which the research participant assumes confidentiality even though this has not been promised. The investigator has an obligation to be alert to such a development and not take advantage of it.

Anonymity for valued groups   It may happen that an individual who participates in research remains anonymous but that his or her data have contributed to averages reported for a group to which the person belongs. For example, a boy may take part in a study of anti-Semitism, not knowing that he is contributing to a comparison of parochial and public schools on this variable. Or he may not know that his score on an achievement test will be used with others to derive an average achievement score for his ethnic group. When a man's attitude toward a political candidate is solicited, he may not realize that his answers will contribute to an average attitude score for the department in a factory where he works.

The question of whether research participants should have a veto over such uses of their data—that is, to be told in advance of the uses planned or, alternatively, allowed to withdraw their data after learning of these uses—precipitates a severe value conflict. On one side is the value of autonomy for individuals in determining what research purposes they will contribute to. On the other is the value that truth should not be suppressed and the faith that truth will be used to good ends rather than bad.

Whether the investigator should ever elect to violate anonymity and confidentiality   It has happened that in the course of research an investigator discovers alarming information about a research participant. For example, the participant may be planning to injure others or may be contemplating suicide. The subject may have committed an armed robbery or a rape. Or a test used in the research may show that several participants are emotionally disturbed and need immediate help.

One can do little other than present this conflict. However strongly scientists may value their commitment to anonymity and confidentiality, they may on some occasion face a situation in which what is for them a higher value must prevail.

Ethical Issues in the Utilization of Research

The preceding sections of the chapter examined the ethical issues that arise in social scientists' relations with their human research participants and the special obligations they incur when they decide to proceed with research involving questionable practices. The remaining discussion deals with other ethical issues, namely, those concerned with the utilization of social research. Certain of these issues focus on researchers' responsibility for preventing misuse of their findings, especially when the research involves disadvantaged cultural groups or is conducted in developing countries. Others deal with their responsibility for promoting the utilization of research. Although social scientists agree about the importance of these issues, they disagree on their solution. In view of this, the following discussion will present unresolved problems to which thoughtful social scientists will continue to give serious attention for the foreseeable future.

Preventing the Misuse of Research Results

Concern about the misuse of research results may arise in a number of ways. Some examples follow:

Misuse for aggression   An investigator who undertook a study of the behavioral effects of a chemical substance discovered that the material lowered the readiness of persons to protest or resist when attacked. This led to the realization that the research might be applied by military forces for war-making purposes and aroused doubts in the investigator about whether the research should be continued.

Misuse in other cultures   Another investigator was commissioned by a major religious group to study the performance of missionaries working in an underdeveloped area in the hope of determining what accounted for differences in their success in making converts. In the course of this research the researcher developed doubts that a Western religion was meaningful for the people with whom the missionaries were working. As a result, the researcher seriously considered the possibility that the study should be discontinued.

Misuse in explaining social problems   A social scientist hoping to understand the causes and possible remedies for juvenile delinquency collected data on the personal attributes and family backgrounds of research participants. The results were limited necessarily to factors in these two areas; they included such findings as the relative prevalence of fatherless homes among delinquents and their low level of ability to "postpone gratification," that is, to work for a larger but postponed reward. To the investigator's dismay, others interpreted these findings as revealing basic causes of delinquency and concluded from them that delinquency might be reduced by remedial work with individuals and families. In contrast, the researcher's own interpretation was that the basic causes were to be found in the economic and educational deprivations that led to the broken homes in which the delinquents grew up and to their ineffective personalities. However, the research did not bear on such an interpretation. This led the researcher to conclude that a misleading rather than enlightening contribution to knowledge about the origins of delinquency had been made and to decide that further research of this type should be abandoned.

Misuse in explaining group differences   Many studies have compared the achievement test scores of blacks and whites. Some social scientists argue that these studies were important and desirable. According to their view, the comparisons not only documented the regrettable inadequacies in the school achievement of black children but also spurred a search for the causes and remedies of this condition. Others, however, argue that such studies should never have been done. They reason that whites will inevitably interpret the results as indicative of inherited black inferiority although the test scores, in fact, reflect any of a number of environmental determinants of low achievement, such as low income level of parents or inferior prior schooling. Having made an interpretation of racial inferiority, the whites, according to this argument, will use this interpretation to support segregation and other discriminatory social policies.

Misuse for exploitation   Concern about the possible misuse of research sometimes focuses on its application by the organization or institution in which the research was done. One such example comes from industry. One of the well-established findings in social relations research is that when workers participate in decisions about how their jobs are to be performed, their morale usually increases. Moreover, this increase in morale is sometimes accompanied by an increase in productivity. This discovery has spawned a great interest in participative management and new leadership styles. Some social scientists interpret the application of this research as highly desirable; from it, they point out, workers gain a new sense of self-direction and personal significance. Others see this same application as misleading and harmful. They feel that employers support such research only to make workers happier and more resistant to unionization. This, in turn, makes it possible for the employers to continue their exploitation, if the higher productivity can be converted to higher profits rather than to increased wages.

Misuse in the political life of other nations   Another example comes from research on social change in developing nations. A study was planned to explore the sources of internal conflict in such nations as well as ways of preventing and coping with guerrilla activities when these threatened (I. L. Horowitz, 1967). The study was openly planned and fully described in public documents. Its financial sponsor was the U.S. Army Research and Development Office. Unknown to the project's leadership, a staff consultant in Chile misrepresented the implications of the source of financial backing for the study. When the source was publicized, the press of Chile charged that the study was a covert operation of U.S. military forces. In the resulting uproar, the study was canceled.

A parallel charge was made about the purpose of American anthropological field research in Thailand (Wolf & Jorgenson, 1970). It is evident from these two examples that when a military unit with the responsibility for combating guerilla activities sponsors research on matters potentially related to its mission, the assumption will be made that it plans to apply the research results. The individual investigator involved in the research may oppose this, be sympathetic to it, or find it a matter of indifference. However, in such cases, social scientists not participating in the study will also become concerned. To many of them, the use of data from basic research for counterinsurgency operations should be prohibited—even though some researchers are willing to go along with this objective.

Discussion Three concerns about the potential misuse of research findings emerge from these examples. One is that the results will be misinterpreted, either intentionally or unintentionally, and hence used to support the wrong policies; the potential misuse of delinquency research and of racial comparison studies are of this type. Another is that the results, although interpreted correctly, will be used for a purpose of which the investigator disapproves; the studies of the behavioral effects of a chemical and of the effectiveness of a missionary program are of this type. The third concern arises when the application is evaluated differently by different people, as the research on worker participation in industrial decision making and on coping with guerrilla activities illustrates. What is at issue in the last case is not the appropriateness of applying the research findings to bring about increased worker satisfaction and productivity or decreased guerrilla activity; rather, it is a judgment about whether such an outcome is to the long-range advantage or disadvantage of people affected by the research.

Faced with such concerns, the reactions of social scientists will vary considerably. Some will take the position that their responsibility ends with the effective conduct and proper interpretation of their research. Others will show their concern for the possible misuse of their research by anticipating probable misinterpretations and attempting to counter them in publications and public statements. Still others will, in addition, feel responsible to oppose actively any misinterpretations of their work about which they learn. A fourth group will be so concerned with the possible misuse of the findings of a given research project that they will decide against carrying it out.

It seems certain that concern for possible misuses of social research findings will take on added importance with time. The critical factor will be the success with which social science is applied to everyday affairs. As this increases, the ability to make use of social science findings will represent a powerful resource. When this happens, social scientists must confront the question of who uses their product and to what ends.

Promoting the Utilization of Research Results

In deciding whether or not to promote the utilization of their research results, social scientists confront one or more of three ethical issues. One is whether an investigator has the responsibility for promoting such utilization; this is the counterpart to the issue of his or her responsibility for preventing the misuse of results. A second has to do with the timing of the application of research findings—in particular, whether the application may be premature. The third has to do with rectifying what many regard as an undemocratic imbalance in the utilization of research knowledge— an imbalance characterized by the greater availability of social science to those with educational and financial resources than to those without.

Responsibility for encouraging research application The proposition— that research scientists are responsible for encouraging the application of their results—draws support from two directions. The first is from the public. Support of social science by society is based not so much on an interest in knowledge for its own sake as on an interest in its practical utilization. Social scientists are looked to primarily for their help in alleviating and preventing social problems and social conflict. The second direction is from social scientists themselves. Many people enter the social sciences, in part, because of their concern for human welfare. It is natural for them to ask whether their work contributes to its development. However, as noted in the discussion of preventing misuse of research results, there is widespread opposition to the idea that the scientist has any special responsibility for research utilization. According to this view, the scientist's function is the production of knowledge. This knowledge is available to all, and it is the responsibility of practical people in society to apply it.

Degree of certainty prior to research application Among investigators who feel responsible for encouraging utilization of their research there will still be differences of opinion on a second issue, that is, timing. Some will feel that the possibility of utilization should be examined in connection with every study. Others will disagree, feeling that such attempts at application are premature. They argue that a theory based on many studies is the only sound basis for applying science. According to this view, attempts to base application on the results of single studies will mislead people who do not have scientific training and is, hence, an ethically questionable practice. To some extent this difference of opinion may be minimized by considering the nature of the research. Immediate application will be justified when, for example, the researcher is studying a complex programmatic activity in a natural setting. One reason for this is that the similarity of the program studied and the setting in which it was studied to other programs is great enough to make generalization appropriate. In comparison, laboratory studies aimed at developing an aspect of a theory will suggest little by way of immediate application. The results of such studies, in combination with other research, may later provide the social scientist with a basis for developing innovative programs or new social institutions. However, not until such programs or institutions are evaluated will it be timely to foster application under field conditions.

Unequal access to research applications   The third ethical issue has to do with the potential for differential utilization of research findings by different components of society. Large industries and government agencies have the resources to be alert to scientific developments and to utilize them. Schools and public service agencies, owing to financial restrictions, have this capacity to a significantly lesser degree. Community groups and organizations with low levels of economic and educational resources are the least well equipped to make use of potentially applicable research knowledge. Social scientists have recognized this and many have attempted to correct it (e.g., Levin, 1970). As yet, however, their efforts have met with only slight success.

Summary

Ethical concerns can arise from several aspects of the research process. For example, they can be generated by the kinds of questions studied by researchers and by the methods used to obtain answers. The procedures used when subjects are chosen, the ways that they are treated, and the uses to which the data are put are all of concern. Whereas researchers have an obligation to contribute to knowledge, they have an equally binding obligation to protect the welfare of their subjects.

This chapter has reviewed ten types of questionable practices that may be encountered in social research. For each of these the concerns were raised, several examples were presented, and the issue was discussed.

Sometimes ethically questionable practices can be avoided or minimized by the use of alternative research procedures. However, they often cannot, and in this case, social scientists face a conflict between two values. The potential contributions of the proposed research must be weighed against the costs to participants who were exposed to the questionable practices. If the possible benefits are too limited to justify the costs, the research should not be done. It is suggested that investigators consult with colleagues or other types of consultants in seeking to determine the relative costs and rewards of research that involves questionable practices.

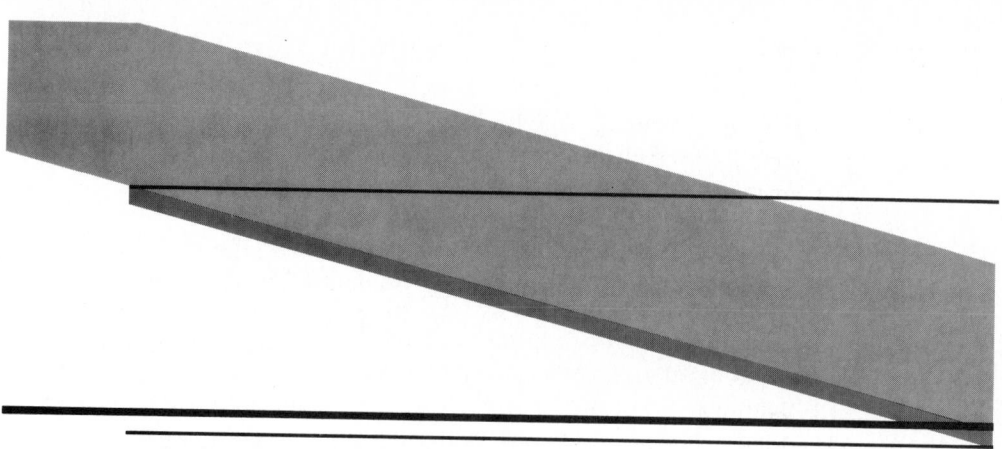

Glossary

Abstract A brief summary of the content and purpose of an article or report.

Assumption of operationalism The assumption that constructs can be measured, albeit imperfectly. It is a necessary assumption for the conduct of empirical research.

Behavior range A technique used in ecological research that involves listing the different physical settings occupied by an individual in a specified period of time, such as a typical day or week.

Behavior setting survey A technique used in ecological research that describes particular settings or environments in terms of their important characteristics, such as the predominant activities in evidence.

Census A count of all the elements of a population and a determination of the distributions of their characteristics.

Closed-ended A question in which the subject's responses are limited to given alternatives.

Cluster sampling A sampling procedure in which one randomly samples clusters or aggregations of units and then within sampled clusters one further randomly samples units.

Codebook A record of the variables one measures in empirical research, the possible values of those variables, and what those values mean in terms of the underlying constructs.

Coding The act of categorizing raw data into groups or giving the data numerical values.

Coding frame A statement of what is to be coded and how it is to be coded, to prepare data for analysis.

Cognitive dissonance A state in which the person holds two beliefs, or cognitions, which are inconsistent with each other.

Constructs The abstract concepts used in social science theories such as social status, power, and intelligence.

Construct validation Determination that a measurement taps the construct in question, that it is distinct from other constructs, and that it has the properties described by theories which employ that construct.

Content analysis A research method usually applied to mass communications, such as newspapers or television, for purposes of identifying specified characteristics of the material.

Context effects On *ratings:* influences on ratings of a given object (e.g., an attitude statement) exerted by extraneous variables such as the rater's own position or salient stimuli recalled from the past. In *questionnaires:* influences on responses to a particular question exerted by prior questions in a sequence.

Contextual variables In data analysis, the characteristics of units at higher levels of analysis that encompass the unit of analysis with which we are concerned.

Contingency table A breakdown of frequencies of values on two variables simultaneously. Such a table is useful for examining relationships between the two variables.

Continuous real time measurement A method of recording used in systematic observation in which every onset of a specified behavior is coded as well as the actual elapsed time of the behavior so as to yield measures of frequency (the total number of onsets of the behavior) and duration (the total amount of time taken up by the behavior).

Contrast error The tendency to rate objects, qualities, or persons, as more different than they really are, based upon a comparison with previous ratings.

Control group In an experiment, those subjects to whom no experimental stimulus is administered, but who resemble members of the experimental group in all respects.

Correlation Covariation of two variables in a group of people, that is, the tendency for certain values of or levels of one variable to occur with particular values of or levels of another variable.

Correlation coefficient A measure of association between two variables; it can range from 0 (no relationship) to -1.00 (perfect negative relationship) or $+1.00$ (perfect positive relationship).

Covert structured observation Observations of predetermined aspects of people's behavior made without their knowledge.

Criterion A proved, accepted, valid measure of some variable.

Datum Singular; plural is data. A piece of information ready for analysis.

Deduction   The process of making inferences from a general rule or theory to specific instances or examples. Used in generating theoretically motivated research.

Dependent variable   The presumed effect; the variable that is measured to see how it has responded to a treatment or cause.

Dimension   An inferred continuum, along which different responses can be placed at different points.

Dummy variable   A procedure for coding the values of a dichotomous variable. One arbitrarily assigns ones to individuals in one category and zeros to individuals in the other category of the variable.

Ecological fallacy   The assumption that relationships that hold at the group level also hold for specific individuals within these groups.

Elaboration   The detailed examination of an established relationship between two variables that is carried out by introducing additional variables as statistical controls.

Epistemic correlation   The relationship between a variable like dollar income and a construct like social status; the epistemic correlation must be surmised; it cannot be computed because there is no direct measure of the construct.

Experimental group   In an experiment, those research participants exposed to the stimulus condition under study.

Experimental realism   The amount of impact and meaningfulness of the independent variables for the experimental subject.

Experimental variable   A variable manipulated by the experimenter; a treatment condition to which subjects are assigned.

External validity   The generalizability of a research finding, for example, to other populations, settings, treatment arrangements, and measurement arrangements.

Field notes   The written or tape recorded notes that contain descriptions of the people, setting, actions, and dialogues for each period of participant observation.

Field study   A study for which the data are collected from persons acting out their typical roles in the everyday world, rather than as subjects in the laboratory.

Filter question   A preliminary question used to screen out respondents who do not have an opinion on a particular issue, so that they will not be asked about the content of their opinion.

Fixed-alternative   In a questionnaire or interview, a question in which the responses of the subject are limited to stated alternatives. *See* Closed-ended.

Focal individual sampling   A method of recording used in systematic observation in which during a given sampling period all individual behaviors of a particular person are scored as well as all social interactions involving this individual. Behaviors not involving this person are completely ignored.

Frequency distribution   A listing of the frequency with which different values on some variable were obtained in some batch of data.

Frequency histogram   A graphic presentation of the information contained in a frequency distribution. Values of a variable are plotted on the horizontal axis and frequencies are plotted on the vertical axis.

Free-answer   *See* Open-ended.

Galvanic skin response   A measure of the flow of electricity between two electrodes placed at different points on the skin; sometimes called the electrodermal response.

Generosity error   The tendency for raters to bend over backwards to give favorable ratings to others, out of concern that a too severe rating would harm the ratee's opportunities.

Halo effect   A rating error in which the rater lets his or her general, overall impression of another influence the rating he or she gives the other person on some specific characteristic.

Hypothesis   A tentative explanation of a relationship or a supposition that a relationship may exist. The hypothesis generates an empirical study to confirm or disconfirm the supposition.

Hypothetico-deductive method   The process of logical reasoning from premises to conclusions; used in deriving predictions from a theory.

Independent variable   The presumed cause; the variable that is manipulated or measured to see what effects it has on other variables.

Induction   The process of making inferences from some specific observations to a more general rule. Used in constructing a theory on the basis of some observed facts.

Inductive method   The process of making inferences from some specific observations to a more general rule. Used in constructing a hypothesis or theory from data.

Informed consent   The principle of research ethics that requires investigators to inform research subjects of all questionable features of the research before the subjects decide whether to participate.

Interaction effect   The combined effect of two or more independent variables on a dependent variable above and beyond the sum of the two main effects.

Intercept   When one fits a straight line to a scatterplot of data, that line has an intercept. It is the predicted value of the variable on the vertical axis when the variable on the horizontal axis equals zero.

Internal validity   The conclusiveness with which the effects of the independent variables are established in a scientific investigation, as opposed to the possibility that some confounding variables may have caused the observed results.

Interquartile range   A measure of spread of a distribution. It is the difference in scores between the twenty-fifth and seventy-fifth percentiles of the distribution.

Interval scale Any measuring device that not only is capable of placing people in their rank order on a characteristic, but also can measure the differences between them in regard to that characteristic.

Interviewer effects or interviewer bias Effects on the respondent's answers in an interview that are produced by characteristics of the interviewer (including the interviewer's attitudes or physical characteristics like sex or race).

Kurtosis A quality of the distribution of a set of data, dealing with whether or how much the data "pile up" around some central point.

Lambda A measure of association between two variables that are dichotomously coded.

Least squares regression line The straight line prediction function that is fit to a scatterplot of data in such a way that the squared residuals are minimized.

Likert-type scale A type of attitude scale that poses statements and asks the respondent to indicate how much he or she agrees or disagrees with each statement.

Main effect The effect of any one independent variable on a dependent variable.

Margin of error The variance within which results are accurate; the limits of accuracy.

Matrix A two-dimensional organization. Each dimension is composed of several positions or alternatives.

Mean The arithmetic average.

Median A measure of central tendency; the middle score of a sample, separating the upper half of the cases from the lower half.

Monotone item An item in an attitude scale that represents a position that is clearly favorable or unfavorable toward the attitude object, not a middle-of-the-road position.

Mundane realism The degree to which an experimental setting or independent variable resembles those found in everyday life.

Multistage sampling A sampling procedure that moves through a set of stages from more inclusive to less inclusive sampling units.

Multitrait-multimethod matrix A table of correlations among two or more traits measured by two or more methods, used to determine the validity of the measurements.

Naturally occurring phenomena Processes and variables measuring processes that occur in the normal course of events. For example, the relationships of sex and race with occupational attainment would reflect naturally occurring processes. Sex and race are naturally occurring variables.

Negative case analysis The systematic search for disconfirming instances in the analysis of participant observation data; used to generate and revise hypotheses.

Null hypothesis The hypothesis that one seeks to reject in statistical inference. It usually represents the inverse of one's research hypothesis.

Observer drift A problem of reliability in systematic observation research in which observers become less accurate in their observations over time.

Open-ended A type of question on an interview that does not limit the respondent's response to any preselected alternatives.

Operational definition Procedures used by a researcher to manipulate or measure a concept.

Ordinal scale A measurement that rank orders individuals on a particular characteristic, but cannot distinguish *how* different each is from the others.

Panel survey design A survey research strategy where respondents in a survey are interviewed more than once at points separated in time with the aim of studying change in respondent characteristics over time.

Partial correlation coefficient The square root of the partial r-squared.

Partial lambda A measure of the partial relationship between two dichotomously coded variables.

Partial relationship The relationship between two variables when one controls for or statistically holds constant a third variable.

Partial r-squared A measure of the partial relationship between variables measured on interval scales. More precisely, it is the proportion by which our predictions of one variable are improved when we make those predictions contingent on not only a second variable, but a third as well.

Participant observer A researcher who joins a group or organization and acts as a typical participant in order to study the behavior of the group or organization.

Pilot subjects Subjects used in a preliminary stage of a research project to help the researcher validate scales or other measures, test research procedures, or train observers or experimenters.

Placebo A substance that has no effects upon a person when ingested. Used for a control condition in a variety of studies.

Population A designated part of a universe from which a sample is drawn; also, the aggregation of people or other research subjects to which one wishes to generalize his or her research.

Pretest The administration of a measure prior to other testing in a study. One function of a pretest is to identify, or verify the identification of, differing groups on some measure.

Probability sampling The type of sampling from a population in which one can specify, for each element of the population, the relative likelihood that it will be included in the sample.

Projective methods   Those tests that provide the respondent a series of ambiguous stimuli to which to respond. The assumption is that the respondent will project his or her values, needs, and attitudes into the responses to these stimuli.

Random assignment (or randomization)   A process of assigning people or groups to experimental conditions such that each person has an equal chance of being assigned to any particular condition as is done with the flip of a coin.

Random digit dialing   A technique that assures the inclusion of unlisted telephone numbers in the sampling frame. Random sequences of digits are dialed within working exchanges.

Random error   That deviation from a true score that is the result of transitory aspects of the person, the situation, or the measuring instrument.

Randomized experiment   A research design in which subjects are randomly assigned to levels of the independent variable.

Randomized response techniques   Methods for asking questions about sensitive topics in which respondents either answer the sensitive question or give a nonsensitive response depending on a random event (such as the toss of a coin) whose outcome is not known to the interviewer.

Rapport   A state of empathy or harmony between interviewer and respondent.

Relative deprivation   The concept that one's position is not evaluated in absolute terms, but rather in relation to the position of others or in relation to unfulfilled expectations.

Reliability   The consistency in results of a test, including the tendency of a test or measurement to produce the same results when it measures twice some entity or attribute believed not to have changed in the interval between measurements.

Repeated measures design   A research design in which each group or person is repeatedly tested after exposure to more than one experimental condition.

Replication   Empirical research that attempts to reproduce the results of earlier research in a different setting or with different samples.

Residual   The difference between the value one predicts for a given individual on a variable, based on some prediction function, and that individual's actual score.

Resistance   A characteristic of a good or useful statistic. A resistant statistic is one that is minimally influenced by the presence of outliers.

Response rate   The number of completed interviews or questionnaires divided by the number of eligible respondents in the sample.

r-**squared**   A measure of association between two variables that are measured on interval scales. It tells us by what proportion our predictions are improved when we use one variable to predict a second, compared to simply predicting the mean of the second variable for all individuals.

Sampling   The selection of a sample of individuals or measurements from the total population to be studied. Sampling may involve elaborate selection procedures if the inferences from the sample are to be sound.

Sampling distribution   The distribution of the means of many different samples of different sizes. This sampling distribution is used to determine the degree of possible error in samples of different sizes.

Scale   An instrument for assigning scores to objects to yield a measure of a construct. There are two types: single rating scales (such as graphic rating scales) and multiple-item scales.

Scalogram method   A method of attitude measurement which determines if all the attitude statements can be placed on a single dimension.

Scatterplot   A plot of individual values on two variables simultaneously. The values of one variable constitute the horizontal axis; the vertical axis represents the second variable. Individual units are located in the resulting two dimensional space by their location on the two axes.

Selective perception   Hearing or seeing only what one *wants* to see or hear, rather than what was actually communicated.

Sense modalities   Ways of perceiving the environment—hearing, vision, touch, and so on.

Simple random sampling   A sampling procedure in which units are randomly sampled from the entire population.

Skewness   A quality of the distribution of a set of data dealing with whether the data are or are not symmetrically distributed around a central point.

Slope   When one fits a straight line to a scatterplot of data, that line has a slope. It tells the predicted increase or decrease in one variable as the other variable increases one unit.

Social indicators   Statistical records of such phenomena as incidence of crime or unemployment tallies that are used to chart the status and change in the quality of life.

Social desirability   A response set to answer questions about oneself in the socially approved manner.

Sociodrama   A device in which a group of people are given a series of roles to act out as if in a real-life situation. By observing how the person acts out a certain role, we may understand his or her social attitudes better.

Sociometry   The study of social interactions and social preferences among a group of people. Sociometry identifies friendship and work-relationship preferences within a group.

Specimen records   A technique used in ecological research in which observers provide a narrative running account of all the actions performed by one person over an extended period of time.

Spurious correlation An observed correlation between two variables that exists because both are caused by a common variable.

Standard deviation The square root of the variance.

Standardized In referring to interviews, those in which the questions and the choices for answers are predetermined.

Static group comparison design A research design in which groups that differ on an independent variable are compared on a dependent variable of interest. This is a pre-experimental research design, in that groups have not been randomly assigned to levels of the independent variable.

Statistical test of significance A determination of whether a difference between conditions or a relationship is so large that the possibility of its happening by chance is minimal.

Stem and leaf diagram A frequency histogram that preserves the raw data.

Stratified random sampling A sampling procedure in which the population is broken up into strata, and within each stratum units are randomly sampled.

Stratum Some subdivision of a population, based on one or more specifications.

Structural variables In data analysis, those characteristics that are formed by combining units from lower levels of analysis.

Subject variable A variable that is a property of a person; a condition or characteristic that a subject brings to a study, such as age, gender, and group affiliations.

"Subtle" item An item in a scale having no apparent content relationship to the attitude object; included because it is empirically found to be related to the attitude of interest.

Summated scales Those attitude scales on which respondents indicate their agreement or disagreement with each item; the scores for their responses are summed to obtain a total score reflecting their attitude.

Survey research The research strategy where one collects data from all or part of a population to assess the relative incidence, distribution, and interrelations of naturally occurring variables.

Theory A set of linked or conceptually related hypotheses, often in syllogistic form.

Threats to validity Alternative explanations for the occurrence of an effect.

Thurstone scale A type of attitude scale in which judges first rate the favorability of statements about an attitude object, then subjects select those statements with which they agree. The goal is to form an equal-interval scale of statements.

Time-interval sampling A method of recording observations in which each observed behavior is scored once and only once during successive intervals of a session (for example, 30 seconds) regardless of the actual number of occurrences in the interval.

Time-point sampling A method of recording observations in which recording occurs instantaneously at regularly spaced points during the session (for example, every tenth second).

Type I error A conclusion that there *is* a true difference between two populations when in fact there is *not*.

Type II error A conclusion that two populations are *not* different from each other when in fact they *are*.

Unidimensional Reflecting the presence of only one dimension, as opposed to multidimensional.

Unit of analysis The specific variable being used in data analysis; in social research, the unit of analysis might be something as specific as "the answer to Question 1" or as broad as the size of a city.

Unobtrusive measures Measurement techniques in which the subjects are unaware of being studied, either because their naturally occurring behaviors are observed without the observation being evident, or because archival records or naturally occurring traces (such as amounts of litter left in a park) are used as data.

Unstructured In referring to interviews, those in which neither the questions nor the answer categories are predetermined.

Validity The capacity of a measuring instrument to predict what it was designed to predict; stated most often in terms of the correlation between scores on the instrument and measures of performance on some criterion. The accuracy of observations.

Variable A concrete representation of an abstract construct; a means of measuring a construct. Income, for instance, is a variable used to measure the construct of social status.

Variance A measure of spread of a distribution. It is the average squared deviation of observations from the mean of the distribution.

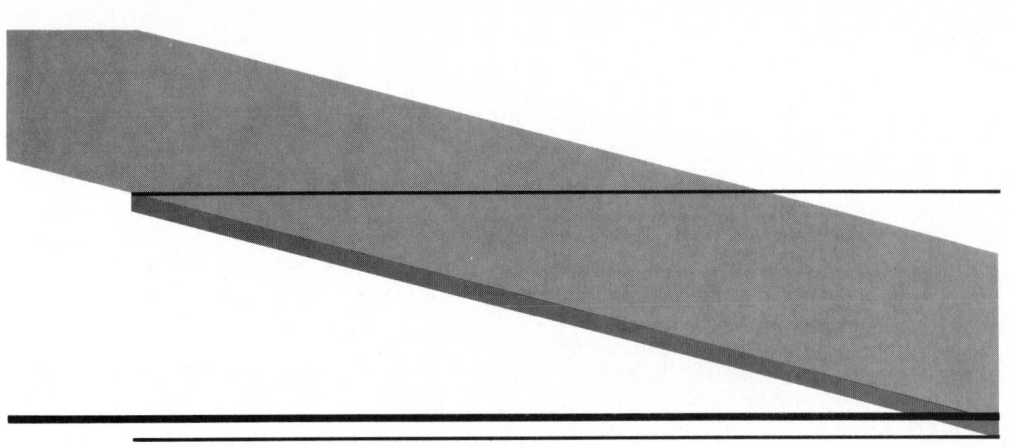

Bibliography

Abelson, R. P., & Rosenberg, M. J. Symbolic psycho-logic: A model of attitudinal cognition. *Behavioral Science*, 1958, *3*, 1–13.

Abramson, L. Y., Seligman, M. E. P., & Teasdale, J. D. Learned helplessness in humans: Critique and reformulation. *Journal of Abnormal Psychology*, 1978, *87*, 49–74.

Ackerman, N. W., & Jahoda, M. *Antisemitism and emotional disorder: A psychoanalytic interpretation.* New York: Harper, 1950.

Adler, F. Operational definitions in sociology. *American Journal of Sociology*, 1947, *52*, 438–444.

Adorno, T. W., Frenkel-Brunswik, E., Levinson, D. J., & Sanford, R. N. *The authoritarian personality.* New York: Harper, 1950.

Ager, J. W., & Dawes, R. M. Effect of judge's attitudes on judgment. *Journal of Personality and Social Psychology*, 1965, *1*(5), 533–538.

Alger, C. F. Interaction in a committee of the United Nations General Assembly. *Midwest Journal of Political Science*, 1966, *10*, 411–447.

Alker, H. R., Jr. *Mathematics and politics.* New York: Macmillan, 1965.

Alper, T. G. Achievement motivation in college women: A now-you-see-it-now-you-don't phenomenon. *American Psychologist*, 1974, *29*, 194–203.

Alper, T., & Korchin, S. J. Memory for socially relevant material. *Journal of Abnormal and Social Psychology*, 1952, *47*, 25–37.

Altmann, J. Observational study of behavior: Sampling methods. *Behaviour*, 1973, *49*, 228–267.

American Anthropological Association (AAA). *Professional ethics.* Washington, D.C.: American Anthropological Association, 1973.

American Political Science Association Committee on Professional Standards and Responsibilities (APSA). Ethical problems of academic political scientists. *P.S., Newsletter of the American Political Science Association*, 1968, *1*(3).

American Psychological Association (APA). *APA Publication Manual.* Washington, D.C.: American Psychological Association, 1974. (Change sheet 2, Guidelines for nonsexist language, published in *American Psychologist,* 1977, *32*(6), 487–494.)

American Psychological Association (APA). *Ethical principles in the conduct of research with human participants.* Washington, D.C.: American Psychological Association, 1973.

American Sociological Association (ASA). *Code of Ethics.* Washington, D.C.: American Sociological Association, 1971.

Anderson, H. H., & Anderson, G. L. *An introduction to protective techniques and other devices for understanding the dynamics of human behavior.* Englewood Cliffs, N.J.: Prentice-Hall, 1951.

Anderson, N. H. Scales and statistics: Parametric and nonparametric. *Psychological Bulletin,* 1961, *58,* 305–316.

Andrews, F. M., & Withey, S. B. *Social indicators of wellbeing.* New York: Plenum, 1976.

Argyle, M., & Cook, M. *Gaze and mutual gaze.* Cambridge, Eng.: Cambridge University Press, 1976.

Aronson, E., Stephan, C., Sikes, J., Blaney, N., & Snapp, M. *The Jigsaw Classroom.* Beverly Hills, Calif.: Sage Publications, 1978.

Asch, S. E. Effects of group pressure upon the modification and distortion of judgments. In H. Guetzkow (Ed.). *Groups, leadership and men.* Pittsburgh: Carnegie Press, 1951.

Atkinson, J. W. (Ed.). *Motives in fantasy, action, and society.* New York: Van Nostrand, 1958.

Atkinson, J. W., Heyns, R. S., & Veroff, J. The effect of experimental arousal of the affiliation motive on thematic apperception. *Journal of Abnormal and Social Psychology,* 1954, *49,* 405–410.

Atkinson, J. W., & Feather, N. T. (Eds.). *A theory of achievement motivation.* New York: Wiley, 1966.

Babbie, E. R. *Survey research methods.* Belmont, Calif.: Wadsworth, 1973.

Bagby, J. W. A cross-cultural study of perceptual predominance in binocular rivalry. *Journal of Abnormal and Social Psychology,* 1957, *54,* 331–334.

Bakeman, R. Untangling streams of behavior: Sequential analysis of observational data. In G. Sackett (Ed.). *Observing behavior: Volume II: Data collection and analysis methods.* Baltimore: University Park Press, 1978.

Balch, G. I. Multiple indicators in survey research: The concept "sense of political efficacy." *Political Methodology,* 1974, *1,* 1–43.

Bales, R. F. *Personality and interpersonal behavior.* New York: Holt, 1970.

Bales, R. F., & Cohen, S. P. *SYMLOG: A system for the multiple level observation of groups.* New York: Free Press, 1979.

Barash, D. P. Human ethology: Displacement activities in a dental office. *Psychological Reports,* 1974, *34,* 947–949.

Barber, B., Lally, J. J., Makarushka, J. L., & Sullivan, O. *Research on human subjects: Problems of social control in medical experimentation.* New York: Russell Sage Foundation, 1973.

Barker, R. G. *The stream of behavior.* New York: Appleton-Century-Crofts, 1963.

Barker, R. G. *Ecological psychology: Concepts and methods for studying the environment of human behavior.* Stanford, Calif.: Stanford University Press, 1968.

Barker, R. G., & Schoggen, P. *Qualities of community life.* San Francisco: Jossey-Bass, 1973.

Barker, R. G., & Wright, H. F. *One boy's day.* New York: Harper, 1951.

Bartlett, F. C. *Remembering.* Cambridge, Eng.: Cambridge University Press, 1932.

Bechtel, R. Hodometer research in architecture. *Milieu*, 1967, *1*, 1–9.

Bechtel, R. *Enclosing behavior.* New York: Dowden, Hutchinson & Ross, 1977.

Becker, H. S. Becoming a marihuana user. *Outsiders*, pp. 41–58. New York: Free Press, 1963.

Becker, H. S. Whose side are we on? *Journal of Social Problems*, 1967, *14*, 239–247.

Becker, H. S., & Geer, B. Participant observation and interviewing: A comparison. *Human Organization*, 1957, *16*(3), 28–32.

Becker, H. S., Geer, B., Hughes, E. C., & Strauss, A. L. *Boys in white: Student culture in medical school.* Chicago: University of Chicago Press, 1961.

Becker, L. J., & Seligman, C. Reducing air conditioning waste by signalling it is cool outside. *Personality and Social Psychology Bulletin*, 1978, *4*, 412–415.

Becker, L. J., Seligman, C., & Darley, J. M. Psychological strategies to reduce energy consumption. Center for Energy and Environmental Studies, Report 90, June 1979.

Bem, S. L., & Bem, D. J. Does sex-biased job advertising "aid and abet" sex discrimination? *Journal of Applied Social Psychology*, 1973, *3*, 6–18.

Benson, O. *Political science laboratory.* Columbus, Ohio: Charles E. Merrill, 1969.

Berelson, B. *Content analysis in communication research.* New York: Free Press, 1952.

Berelson, B., Lazarsfeld, P. F., & McPhee, W. N. *Voting: A study of opinion formation in a presidential campaign.* Chicago: University of Chicago Press, 1954.

Bergin, A. E. The effect of dissonant persuasive communications upon changes in a self-referring attitude. *Journal of Personality*, 1962, *30*, 423–438.

Berk, R. A., & Rossi, P. H. Doing good or worse: Evaluation research politically examined. In M. Guttentag & S. Saar (Eds.). *Evaluation Studies Review Annual*, Vol. 2. Beverly Hills, Calif.: Sage Publications, 1977.

Berkowitz, L., & Donnerstein, E. External validity is more than skin deep: Some answers to criticisms of laboratory experiments. *American Psychologist*, 1982, *37*, 245–257.

Berkun, M. M., Bialek, H. M., Kern, R. P., & Yagi, K. Experimental studies of psychological stress in man. *Psychological Monographs*, 1962, *76*(15, Whole No. 534).

Berscheid, E., Baron, R. S., Dermer, M., & Libman, M. Anticipating informed consent: An empirical approach. *American Psychologist*, 1973, *28*, 913–925.

Bertell, R., Jacobson, N., & Stogre, M. Environmental influence on survival of low birth weight infants in Wisconsin, 1963–1975. *International Perspectives in Public Health*, Fall 1984, *1*(2), 12–24.

Beyle, H. C.   A scale for the measurement of attitude toward candidates for elective governmental office. *American Political Science Review*, 1932, *26*, 527–544.

Birnbaum, M. H.   Controversies in psychological measurement. In B. Wegener (Ed.). *Social attitudes and psychophysical measurement*. Hillsdale, N.J.: Erlbaum, 1982.

Bishop, B. M.   Mother-child interaction and the social behavior of children. *Psychological Monographs*, 1951, *65*(11, Whole No. 328).

Bishop, G. F., Oldendick, R. W., & Tuchfarber, A. J.   Effects of filter questions in public opinion surveys. *Public Opinion Quarterly*, 1983, *47*, 528–546.

Blanchard, F. A., & Cook, S. W.   Effects of helping a less competent member of a cooperating interracial group on the development of interpersonal attraction. *Journal of Personality and Social Psychology*, 1976, *34*, 1,245–1,255.

Blau, P. M., & Duncan, O. D.   *The American occupational structure*. New York: Wiley, 1967.

Blurton-Jones, N. (Ed.).   *Ethological studies of child behavior*. London: Cambridge University Press, 1972.

Bobo, L.   Whites' opposition to busing: Symbolic racism or realistic group conflict? *Journal of Personality and Social Psychology*, 1983, *45*, 1,196–1,210.

Bogardus, E. S.   Measuring social distances. *Journal of Applied Sociology*, 1925, *9*, 299–308.

Bogardus, E. S.   *Immigration and race attitudes*. Lexington, Mass.: Heath, 1928.

Bogardus, E. S.   A social distance scale. *Sociology and Social Research*, 1933, *17*, 265–271.

Bogden, R.   *Participant observation in organizational settings*. Syracuse, N.Y.: Syracuse University Press, 1972.

Bogden, R., & Taylor, S. J.   *Introduction to qualitative research methods*. New York: Wiley, 1975.

Borgatta, E. F., & Bohrnstedt, G. W.   Some limitations on generalizability from social psychological experiments. *Sociological Methods and Research*, 1974, *3*, 111–120.

Borgida, E., & Nisbet, R. F.   The differential impact of abstract versus concrete information on decisions. *Journal of Applied Social Psychology*, 1977, *7*, 258–271.

Boruch, R. F.   On common contentions about randomized field experiments. In R. F. Boruch & H. W. Riecken (Eds.). *Experimental tests of public policy*, pp. 108–145. Boulder, Col.: Westview Press, 1975.

Boyer, E. G., Simon, A., & Karafin, G. R.   *Measures of maturation: An anthology of early childhood observational instruments*. Philadelphia: Research for Better Schools, 1973.

Bradburn, N., & Sudman, S.   *Improving interview method and questionnaire design*. San Francisco: Jossey-Bass, 1979.

Brannigan, C. R., & Humphries, D. A.   Human non-verbal behavior, a means of communication. In N. Blurton-Jones (Ed.). *Ethological studies of child behavior*. London: Cambridge University Press, 1972.

Breed, W., & Ktsanes, T.   Pluralistic ignorance in the process of opinion formation. *Public Opinion Quarterly*, 1961, *25*, 382–392.

Brenner, M. H. *Mental illness and the economy.* Cambridge, Mass.: Harvard University Press, 1973.

Brickman, P., & Stearns, A. Help that is not called help. *Personality and Social Psychology Bulletin,* 1978, *4,* 314–317.

Brickman, P., Folger, R., Goode, E., & Schul, Y. Micro and macro justice. In M. J. Lerner (Ed.). *The justice motive and social behavior.* New York: Plenum, 1981.

Brigham, J. C., & Cook, S. W. The influence of attitude on the recall of controversial material: A failure to confirm. *Journal of Experimental Social Psychology,* 1969, *5,* 240–243.

Brigham, J. C., & Cook, S. W. The influence of attitude on judgments of plausibility: A replication and extension. *Educational and Psychological Measurement,* 1970, *30*(2), 283–292.

Bromet, E. B., Parkinson, D. K., Schulberg, H. C., Dunn, L. O., & Gondek, P. C. Mental health of residents near the Three Mile Island reactor: A comparative study of selected groups. *Journal of Preventive Psychiatry,* 1982, *1,* 225–276.

Bromet, E., Schulberg, H. D., & Dunn, L. *The TMI nuclear accident and patterns of psychopathology in mothers of infant children.* Paper presented at the 90th annual convention of the American Psychological Association, Washington, D.C., August 1982.

Brown, E. M. Influence of training, method, and relationship on the halo effect. *Journal of Applied Psychology,* 1968, *52,* 195–199.

Brown, J. F. A modification of the Rosenzweig picture-frustration test to study hostile interracial attitudes. *Journal of Psychology,* 1947, *24,* 247–272.

Brown, S. R., & Ellithorp, J. D. Emotional experiences in political groups: The case of the McCarthy phenomenon. *American Political Science Review,* 1970, *64,* 349–366.

Bryan, J. H., & Test, M. A. Models and helping: Naturalistic studies in aiding behavior. *Journal of Personality and Social Psychology,* 1967, *6,* 400–407.

Burisch, M. Construction strategies for multiscale personality inventories. *Applied Psychological Measurement,* 1978, *2,* 97–111.

Burwen, L. S., & Campbell, D. T. The generality of attitudes toward authority and nonauthority figures. *Journal of Abnormal and Social Psychology,* 1957, *54,* 24–31.

Burwen, L. S., Campbell, D. T., & Kidd, J. The use of a sentence completion test in measuring attitudes toward superiors and subordinates. *Journal of Applied Psychology,* 1956, *40,* 248–250.

Bush, M., & Gordon, A. C. Client choice and bureaucratic accountability: Possibilities for responsiveness in a social welfare bureaucracy. *Journal of Social Issues,* 1978, *34*(4), 22–43.

Byrne, D., Ervin, C. R., & Lamberth, J. Continuity between the experimental study of attraction and real-life computer dating. *Journal of Personality and Social Psychology,* 1970, *16,* 157–165.

Cain, L. D., Jr. Life course and social structure. In R. E. L. Faris (Ed.). *Handbook of modern sociology,* pp. 272–309. Chicago: Rand McNally, 1964.

Cairns, R. B. (Ed.). *The analysis of social interactions: Methods, issues and illustrations.* Hillsdale, N.J.: Erlbaum, 1979.

Campbell, A., Converse, P. E., Miller, W. E., & Stokes, D. E.   *The voter decides.* Evanston, Ill.: Row, Peterson, 1954.

Campbell, A. et al.   *The American voter.* New York: Wiley, 1960.

Campbell, A. et al.   *Elections and the political order.* New York: Wiley, 1966.

Campbell, D. T.   The indirect assessment of social attitudes. *Psychological Bulletin,* 1950, *47,* 15–38.

Campbell, D. T.   The informant in quantitative research. *American Journal of Sociology,* 1955, *60,* 339–342.

Campbell, D. T.   Definitional versus multiple operationalism. *et al.,* 1969a, *2,* 14–17.

Campbell, D. T.   Prospective: Artifact and control. In R. Rosenthal & R. L. Rosnow (Eds.). *Artifact in behavioral research.* New York: Academic Press, 1969b.

Campbell, D. T.   Reforms as experiments. *American Psychologist,* 1969c, *24,* 409–429.

Campbell, D. T.   *Qualitative knowing in action research.* Kurt Lewin Award Address, Society for the Psychological Study of Social Issues, Meeting with the American Psychological Association, New Orleans, September 1, 1974.

Campbell, D. T.   Assessing the impact of planned social change. In G. M. Lyons (Ed.). *Social research and public policy.* Hanover, N.H.: Public Affairs Center, Dartmouth College, 1975.

Campbell, D. T., & Damarin, F. L.   Measuring leadership attitudes through an information test. *Journal of Social Psychology,* 1961, *55,* 159–176.

Campbell, D. T., & Erlebacher, A.   How regression artifacts in quasi-experimental evaluations can mistakenly make compensatory education look harmful. In J. Hellmuth (Ed.). *The disadvantaged child* (Vol. 3), *Compensatory education: A national debate.* New York: Brunner/Mazel, 1970.

Campbell, D. T., & Fiske, D. W.   Convergent and discriminant validation by the multitrait-multimethod matrix. *Psychological Bulletin,* 1959, *56,* 81–105.

Campbell, D. T., Miller, N., Lubetsky, J., & O'Connell, E. J.   Varieties of projection in trait attribution. *Psychological Monographs,* 1964, *78*(15, Whole No. 592).

Campbell, D. T., & Ross, H. L.   The Connecticut crackdown on speeding: Time-series data in quasi-experimental analysis. In N. E. Tufte (Ed.). *The quantitative analysis of social problems.* Reading, Mass.: Addison-Wesley, 1970.

Campbell, D. T., & Stanley, J. C.   Experimental and quasi-experimental designs for research on teaching. In N. L. Gage (Ed.). *Handbook of research on teaching.* Chicago: Rand McNally, 1963.

Campbell, D. T., & Stanley, J. C.   *Experimental and quasi-experimental designs for research.* Chicago: Rand McNally, 1966.

Cannell, C. F., Fisher, G., & Bakker, T.   Reporting of hospitalization in the health service interview. *Vital and Health Statistics,* 1965a, Ser. 2, No. 6.

Cannell, C. F., & Kahn, R. L.   Interviewing. In G. Lindzey & E. Aronson (Eds.). *Handbook of social psychology* (Vol. 2, 2nd ed.). Reading, Mass.: Addison-Wesley, 1968.

Cannell, C. F., Miller, P. V., & Oksenberg, L.   Research on interviewing techniques. In S. Leinhardt (Ed.). *Sociological methodology 1981.* San Francisco: Jossey-Bass, 1981.

Carlsmith, J. M., & Anderson, C. A.   Ambient temperature and the occurrence of collective violence: A new analysis. *Journal of Personality and Social Psychology*, 1979, *37*, 337–344.

Carlsmith, J. M., Ellsworth, P. C., & Aronson, E.   *Methods of research in social psychology.* Reading, Mass.: Addison-Wesley, 1976.

Carlson, J., Cook, S. W., & Stromberg, E. L.   Sex differences in conversation. *Journal of Applied Psychology*, 1936, *20*, 727–735.

Carter, H.   Recent American studies in attitudes toward war: A summary and evaluation. *American Sociological Review*, 1945, *10*, 343–352.

Carter, L. F.   Inadvertent sociological theory. *Social Focus*, 1971, *50*, 12–25.

Cataldo, E. F., Johnson, R. M., Kellstedt, L. A., & Milbrath, L. W.   Card sorting as a technique for survey interviewing. *Public Opinion Quarterly*, 1970, *34*, 202–215.

Cattell, R. B., & Luborsky, L. B.   T-technique demonstrated as a new clinical method for determining personality and symptom structure. *Journal of General Psychology*, 1950, *42*, 3–24.

Cattell, R. B., Maxwell, E. F., Light, B. H., & Unger, M. P.   The objective measurement of attitudes. *British Journal of Psychology*, 1949, *40*, 81–90.

Cedric X (Clark).   The white research in black society. *Journal of Social Issues*, 1973, *29*(1).

Center for Human Resource Research.   *The national longitudinal: Handbook.* Columbus, Ohio: College of Administrative Science, Ohio State University, 1977. (This handbook contains a 21-page bibliography of technical publications about the surveys and of publications reporting results of the surveys.)

Chein, I.   Narcotics use among juveniles. *Social Work*, 1956, *1*, 50–60.

Chein, I., Cook, S. W., & Harding, J.   The field of action research. *American Psychologist*, 1948, *3*, 43–50.

Cherlin, A., & Walters, P. B.   Trends in United States men's and women's sex-role attitudes: 1972 to 1978. *American Sociological Review*, 1981, *46*, 453–460.

Christie, R., & Geis, F. L.   *Studies in Machiavellianism.* New York: Academic Press, 1970.

Cicarelli, V., & Granger, R.   *The impact of Head Start: An evaluation of the effects of Head Start on children's cognitive and affective development.* A report presented to the Office of Economic Opportunity pursuant to Contract B89–4536, June 1969. Westinghouse Learning Corporation, Ohio University. (Distributed by Clearinghouse for Federal Scientific and Technical Information, U.S. Department of Commerce, National Bureau of Standards, Institute for Applied Technology. PB 184–328.)

Cicourel, A. V.   *Method and measurement in sociology.* New York: Free Press, 1964.

Clark, K. B., & Clark, M. P.   Emotional factors in racial identification and preference in Negro children. *Journal of Negro Education*, 1950, *19*, 341–350.

Clark, R. D., & Word, L. E.   Why don't bystanders help? Because of ambiguity? *Journal of Personality and Social Psychology*, 1972, *24*, 392–400.

Cochran, W. G.   *Sampling techniques* (2nd ed.). New York: Wiley, 1963.

Collier, J., Jr.   Photography in anthropology: A report on two experiments. *American Anthropologist*, 1957, *59*, 843–859.

Colombotos, J. Personal versus telephone interviews: Effect on responses. *Public Health Reports*, 1969, *84*(9), 773–782.

Cook, F. L. *Who should be helped?* Beverly Hills, Calif.: Sage Publications, 1979.

Cook, S. W. *Studies of attitude and attitude measurement* (mimeograph). AFOSR Technical Report, 1968. Boulder: Institute of Behavioral Science, University of Colorado.

Cook, S. W. Motives in a conceptual analysis of attitude-related behavior. In W. J. Arnold & D. Levine (Eds.). *Nebraska symposium on motivation, 1969.* Lincoln: University of Nebraska Press, 1970.

Cook, S. W., & Selltiz, C. A. A multi-indicator approach to attitude measurement. *Psychological Bulletin*, 1964, *62*, 36–55.

Cook, T. D. Program evaluation. In O. Lindzey & E. Aronson (Eds.). *Handbook of social psychology.* New York: Random House, 1985.

Cook, T. D., & Campbell, D. T. The design and conduct of quasi-experiments and true experiments in field settings. In M. D. Dunnett (Ed.). *Handbook of industrial and organizational psychology.* New York: Rand McNally, 1975.

Cook, T. D., & Campbell, D. T. *Quasi-Experimentation: Design and analysis issues for field settings.* Chicago: Rand McNally, 1979.

Cook, T. D., & Gruder, C. L. Metaevaluation research. *Evaluation Quarterly*, (1978), *2*, 5–51.

Coombs, C. H. *A theory of data.* New York: Wiley, 1964.

Cooper, J. Deception and role playing: On telling the good guys from the bad guys. *American Psychologist*, 1976, *31*, 605–610.

Cooper, J. B., & Pollock, D. The identification of prejudicial attitudes by the GSR. *Journal of Social Psychology*, 1959, *50*, 241–245.

Cooper, J. B., & Siegel, H. E. The galvanic skin response as a measure of emotion in prejudice. *Journal of Psychology*, 1956, *42*, 149–155.

Cooper, J. B., & Singer, D. N. The role of emotion in prejudice. *Journal of Social Psychology*, 1956, *44*, 241–247.

Cooper, W. H. Ubiquitous halo. *Psychological Bulletin*, 1981, *90*, 218–244.

Costrich, N., Feinstein, J., Kidder, L. H., Marecek, J., & Pascale, L. When stereotypes hurt: Three studies of penalties for sex-role reversals. *Journal of Experimental Psychology*, 1975, *11*, 520–530.

Cox, K. Social effects of integrated advertising. *Journal of Advertising Research*, 1971, *10*, 41–44.

Cressey, D. R. *Other people's money: A study in the social psychology of embezzlement.* New York: The Free Press, 1953.

Criswell, J. H. Racial cleavages in Negro-white groups. *Sociometry*, 1937, *1*, 87–89.

Cronbach, L., Gleser, G. C., Nanda, H., & Rajaratnam, N. *The Dependability of Behavioral Measurements: Theory of Generalizability for Scores and Profiles.* New York: Wiley, 1972.

Cronbach, L. J., & Meehl, P. E. Construct validity in psychological tests. *Psychological Bulletin*, 1955, *52*, 281–302.

Crosby, F., Bromley, S., & Saxe, L. Recent unobtrusive studies of black and white discrimination and prejudice: A literature review. *Psychological Bulletin*, 1980, *87*, 546–563.

Dabbs, J. M., Jr. *Physiological and physical activity measures of attitudes.* Paper presented at the Navy-Smithsonian Conference on Survey Alternatives, Santa Fe, New Mexico, April 1975.

Darley, J. M., & Latané, B. Bystander intervention in emergencies: Diffusion of responsibility. *Journal of Personality and Social Psychology*, 1968, *8*, 377–383.

Davidson, D., Suppes, P., & Siegel, S. *Decision making: An experimental approach.* Stanford, Calif.: Stanford University Press, 1957.

Davis, J. A. *Elementary survey analysis.* Englewood Cliffs, N.J.: Prentice-Hall, 1968.

Davis, J. A. *General social surveys, 1972–1982: Cumulative codebook.* Chicago: National Opinion Research Center, 1982.

Dawes, R. M. *Measures and indicators of attitude.* New York: Wiley, 1971.

Dawes, R. M. *Fundamentals of attitude measurement.* New York: Wiley, 1972.

Dawes, R. M. Suppose we measured height with rating scales instead of rulers. *Applied Psychological Measurement*, 1977, *1*, 267–273.

Dawes, R. M., & Moore, M. Guttman scaling orthodox and randomized responses. In F. Peterman (Ed.). *Attitude measurement.* 1979.

Dawes, R. M., Singer, D., & Lemons, F. An experimental analysis of the contrast effect and its implications for intergroup communications and the indirect assessment of attitudes. *Journal of Personality and Social Psychology*, 1972, *21*, 281–295.

Dawes, R. M., & Smith, T. L. Attitude and opinion measurement. In Lindzey, O., & Aronson, E. (Eds.). *Handbook of social psychology.* New York: Random House, 1985.

Deutsch, M., & Collins, M. E. *Interracial housing: A psychological evaluation of a social experiment.* Minneapolis: University of Minnesota Press, 1951.

Dew, M. A., Bromet, E. J., & Schulberg, H. C. Mental health effects of chronic stress in two community samples. Paper presented at the American Psychological Association Convention, August 1985, Los Angeles, California.

Diener, E., & Crandall, R. *Ethics in social and behavioral research.* Chicago: University of Chicago Press, 1978.

Diller, J. V., & Cook, S. W. *Differential recall recognition for faces of liked and disliked groups: A failure to confirm* (mimeograph). Boulder: University of Colorado, 1969.

Dillman, D. A. Increasing mail questionnaire response in large samples of the general public. *Public Opinion Quarterly*, 1972, *36*, 254–257.

Dillman, D. A. *Mail and telephone surveys.* New York: Wiley, 1978.

Dipboye, R. L., & Flanagan, M. F. Research settings in industrial and organizational psychology: Are findings in the field more generalizable than in the laboratory? *American Psychologist*, 1979, *34*, 141–150.

Dipboye, R. L., & Flanagan, M. F. Reply to Willems and Howard. *American Psychologist*, 1980, *35*, 388–390.

Donley, R. E., & Winter, D. G. Measuring the motives of public officials at a distance: An exploratory study of American Presidents. *Behavioral Science*, 1970, *15*, 227–236.

Doob, L. W. Effects of initial serial position and attitude upon recall under conditions of low motivation. *Journal of Abnormal and Social Psychology*, 1953, *48*, 199–205.

Duncan, G., & Morgan, J. N. *Five Thousand American Families—Patterns of Economic Progress: Analysis of the Panel Study of Income Dynamics, Vol. 7.* Ann Arbor, Mich.: Institute for Social Research, 1979.

Duncan, O. D. *Toward social reporting: Next steps.* New York: Russell Sage Foundation, 1969.

Durand, J. Mortality estimates from Roman tombstone inscriptions. *American Journal of Sociology,* 1960, *65,* 365–373.

Durkheim, E. *Suicide.* J. A. Spaulding & G. Simpson (Trans.). New York: Free Press, 1951.

Economic report of the President together with the annual report of the Council of Economic Advisers, transmitted to the Congress, January 1964. Washington, D.C.: U.S. Government Printing Office, 1964.

Edney, J. J. Property, possession and permanence: A field study in human territoriality. *Journal of Applied Social Psychology,* 1972, *2,* 275–282.

Edwards, A. L. *Techniques of attitude scale construction.* New York: Appleton-Century-Crofts, 1957.

Edwards, A. L., & Kilpatrick, F. P. A technique for construction of attitude scales. *Journal of Applied Psychology,* 1948, *32,* 374–384.

Eibl-Eibesfeldt, I. *Ethology: The biology of behavior.* New York: Holt, 1970.

Ekman, P., & Friesen, W. V. Nonverbal leakage and clues to deception. *Psychiatry,* 1969a, *32,* 88–106.

Ekman, P., & Friesen, W. V. The repertoire of nonverbal behavior: Categories, origins, usage and coding. *Semiotica,* 1969b, *1,* 1–20.

Ekman, P., & Friesen, W. V. *The facial action coding system (FACS).* Palo Alto, Calif.: Consulting Psychologists Press, 1978.

Elms, A. C., & Janis, I. L. Counter-norm attitudes induced by consonant vs. dissonant conditions of role-playing. *Journal of Experimental Research in Personality,* 1965, *1,* 50–60.

Epstein, C. F. *Women's place: Options and limits in professional careers.* Berkeley and Los Angeles: University of California Press, 1970.

Erdos, P. L. *Professional mail surveys.* New York: McGraw-Hill, 1970.

Erickson, B. H., & Nosanchuk, T. A. *Understanding data.* Toronto: McGraw-Hill Ryerson, 1977.

Erikson, K. T. *Everything in its path.* New York: Simon & Schuster, 1976.

Eulau, H., & Eyestone, R. Policy maps of city councils and policy outcomes: A developmental analysis. *American Political Science Review,* 1968, *62,* 124–143.

Evans, M. C., & Chein, I. *The movie story game: A projective test of interracial attitudes for use with Negro and white children.* Paper presented at the meeting of the American Psychological Association, Boston, September 1948.

Eysenck, H. J., & Crown, S. An experimental study in opinion-attitude methodology. *International Journal of Opinion and Attitude Research,* 1949, *3,* 47–86.

Farr, J. L., & Seaver, W. B. Stress and discomfort in psychological research: Subject perceptions of experimental procedures. *American Psychologist,* 1975, *30,* 770–773.

Fawl, C. L. Disturbances experienced by children in their natural habitats. In R. G. Barker (Ed.). *The stream of behavior.* New York: Appleton-Century-Crofts, 1963.

Fazio, R. H., Powell, M. C., & Herr, P. M. Toward a process model of the attitude-behavior relation: Accessing one's attitude upon mere observation of the attitude object. *Journal of Personality and Social Psychology*, 1983, *44*, 723–735.

Feather, N. T. Acceptance and rejection of arguments in relation to attitude strength, critical ability, and intolerance of inconsistency. *Journal of Abnormal and Social Psychology*, 1964, *69*(2), 127–136.

Ferguson, L. W. The influence of individual attitudes on construction of an attitude scale. *Journal of Social Psychology*, 1935, *6*, 115–117.

Ferguson, L. W. More measurement than validation. *Contemporary Psychology*, 1957, *2*, 237–238.

Festinger, L. A. *A theory of cognitive dissonance.* Stanford, Calif.: Stanford University Press, 1957.

Festinger, L., & Carlsmith, J. N. Cognitive consequences of forced compliance. *Journal of Abnormal and Social Psychology*, 1959, *58*, 203–210.

Festinger, L., Riecken, H. W., & Schachter, S. *When prophecy fails.* Minneapolis: University of Minnesota Press, 1956.

Festinger, L., Schachter, S., & Back, K. *Social pressures in informal groups: A study of human factors in housing.* New York: Harper, 1950.

Filstead, W. J. Introduction. In W. J. Filstead (Ed.). *Qualitative methodology: Firsthand involvement with the social world.* Chicago: Markham, 1970.

Fine, M. Perspectives on inequity: Voices from urban schools. In L. Bickman (Ed.). *Applied Social Psychology Annual, Vol. 4.* Beverly Hills, Calif.: Sage Publications, 1983.

Fine, M. Coping with rape: Critical perspectives on consciousness. *Imagination, Cognition and Personality*, 1984, *3*(3), 249–267.

Firebaugh, G. Scale economy or scale entropy? Country size and rate of economic growth, 1950–1977. *American Sociological Review*, 1983, *48*, 257–269.

Flanders, N. A. *Analyzing teaching behavior.* Reading, Mass.: Addison-Wesley, 1970.

Forward, J., Canter, R., & Kirsch, N. Role-enactment and deception methodologies: Alternative paradigms? *American Psychologist*, 1976, *31*, 595–604.

French, J. R. P., Jr. Organized and unorganized groups under fear and frustration. *University of Iowa Studies of Child Welfare*, 1944, *20*, 229–308.

Friedman, H. S., DiMatteo, M. R., & Mertz, T. I. Nonverbal communication on television news: Facial expressions of broadcasters during coverage of a presidential election campaign. *Personality and Social Psychology Bulletin*, 1980, *6*, 427–435.

Fromme, A. On the use of certain qualitative methods of attitude research: A study of opinions on the methods of preventing war. *Journal of Social Psychology*, 1941, *13*, 425–459.

Gallo, P. S., Smith, S., & Mumford, S. Effects of deceiving subjects upon experimental results. *Journal of Social Psychology*, 1973, *89*, 99–107.

Galtung, J. *Theory and methods of social research.* New York: Columbia University Press, 1967.

Gans, H. On the methods used in this (The West End: An Urban Village) study. In M. P. Golden (Ed.). *The research experience.* Itasca, Ill.: F. E. Peacock, 1976.

Garfinkel, H. *Studies in ethnomethodology.* Englewood Cliffs, N.J.: Prentice-Hall, 1967.

Gerbner, F., Holsti, O. R., Krippendorf, K., Paisley, W. J., & Stone, P. J. (Eds.). *The analysis of communication content: Developments in scientific theories and computer techniques.* New York: Wiley, 1969.

Getzels, J. W. *The assessment of personality and prejudice by the method of paired direct and projective questions.* Unpublished doctoral dissertation, Harvard University, 1951.

Glaser, B. G., & Strauss, A. L. *The discovery of grounded theory.* Chicago: Aldine, 1967.

Glaskow, D. R., Sadowski, C. J., & Davis, S. F. The project must count: Fostering positive attitudes toward the conduct of research. *Bulletin of the Psychonomic Society,* 1977, *10,* 471–474.

Glass, D. The ethical basis of science. *Science,* 1965, *150,* 1,254–1,261.

Glass, D. C., & Singer, J. E. *Urban stress: Experiments on noise and social stressors.* New York: Academic Press, 1972.

Glazer, E. M. *An experiment in the development of critical thinking.* New York: Bureau of Publications, Teachers College, Columbia University, 1941. (Teachers College Contributions to Education, 843)

Glenn, N. D., & Weaver, C. N. Education's effects on psychological well-being. *Public Opinion Quarterly,* 1981, *45,* 22–39.

Glock, C. Y. Survey design and analysis in sociology. In C. Y. Glock (Ed.). *Survey research in the social sciences.* New York: Russell Sage Foundation, 1967.

Goldberg, L. R. Grades as motivants. *Psychology in the Schools,* 1965, *2,* 17–24.

Goodman, L. A., & Kruskal, W. H. Measures of association for cross classifications. *Journal of the American Statistical Association,* 1954, *49,* 732–764.

Goodman, M. E. *Race awareness in young children.* Reading, Mass.: Addison-Wesley, 1952.

Gorsuch, R. L. *Factor analysis.* Philadelphia: Saunders, 1974.

Gottman, J. M. Nonsequential data analysis techniques in observational research. In G. Sackett (Ed.). *Observing behavior, Vol. II: Data collection and analysis methods.* Baltimore: University Park Press, 1978.

Graber, D. The press as opinion resource during the 1968 presidential campaign. *Public Opinion Quarterly,* 1971, *35,* 168–182.

Granneberg, R. T. The influence of individual attitude and attitude-intelligence interaction upon scale values of attitude items. (Abstract.) *American Psychologist,* 1955, *10,* 330–331.

Green, B. F. A method of scalogram analysis using summary statistics. *Psychometrika,* 1956, *21,* 79–88.

Green, R. T., & Stacey, B. G. A flexible projective technique applied to the measurement of the self-image of voters. *Journal of Projective Techniques and Personality Assessment,* 1966, *30*(1), 12–15.

Greenberg, B. C., Abdula, A. L., Simmons, W. R., & Horvitz, D. G. The unrelated question in randomized response model: Theoretical framework. *Journal of the American Statistical Association,* 1969, *64,* 520–539.

Greenwald, A. B., & Sakumura, J. S. Attitude and selective learning: Where are the phenomena of yesteryear? *Journal of Personality and Social Psychology,* 1967, *7,* 387–397.

Griffin, J. H. *Black like me.* New York: American Library (Signet), 1962.

Grings, W. W. The verbal summator technique and abnormal mental states. *Journal of Abnormal and Social Psychology,* 1942, *37,* 529–545.

Groves, R. M., & Kahn, R. L. *Surveys by telephone.* New York: Academic Press, 1979.

Guilford, J. P. *Psychometric methods* (2nd ed.). New York: McGraw-Hill, 1954.

Gurr, T. R. A causal model of civil strife: A comparative analysis using new indices. *American Political Science Review,* 1968, *62,* 1,104–1,124.

Gutek, B. A. Strategies for studying client satisfaction. *Journal of Social Issues,* 1978, *34*(4), 44–56.

Guttman, L. A basis for scaling quantitative data. *American Sociological Review,* 1944, *9,* 139–150.

Habenstein, R. W. Occupational uptake: Professionalizing. In R. W. Habenstein (Ed.). *Pathways to data: Field methods for studying ongoing social organizations.* Chicago: Aldine-Atherton, 1970.

Haire, M. Projective techniques in marketing research. *Journal of Marketing,* 1950, *14,* 649–656.

Hall, J. A. Gender effects in decoding nonverbal cues. *Psychological Bulletin,* 1978, *85,* 845–857.

Hamblin, R. L., Hathaway, C., & Wodarski, J. S. Group contingencies, peer tutoring, and accelerating academic achievement. In E. Ramp & B. Hopkins (Eds.). *A new direction for education: Behavior analysis.* Lawrence: University of Kansas, 1971.

Hammond, K. R. Measuring attitudes by error-choice: An indirect method. *Journal of Abnormal and Social Psychology,* 1948, *43,* 38–48.

Harding, J., & Hogrefe, R. Attitudes of white department store employees toward Negro co-workers. *Journal of Social Issues,* 1952, *8*(1), 18–28.

Harmon, H. H. *Modern factor analysis* (2nd ed.). Chicago: University of Chicago Press, 1967.

Hartley, E. L., & Schwartz, S. *A pictorial doll play approach for the study of children's intergroup attitudes* (mimeograph). New York: American Jewish Congress, 1948.

Hartmann, E. W. A field experiment on the comparative effectiveness of "emotional" and "rational" political leaflets in determining election results. *Journal of Abnormal and Social Psychology,* 1936, *31,* 99–114.

Hartsough, D. M., & Savitsky, J. C. Three Mile Island: Psychology and Environmental Policy at a Crossroads. *American Psychologist,* 1984, *39*(10), 1,113–1,122.

Hays, W. L. *Statistics for psychologists.* New York: Holt, 1963.

Helgerson, E. The relative significance of race, sex, and facial expression in choice of playmate by the pre-school child. *Journal of Negro Education,* 1943, *12,* 617–622.

Henle, M., & Hubbell, M. B. "Egocentricity" in adult conversation. *Journal of Social Psychology,* 1938, *9,* 227–234.

Henley, N. M. *Body politics: Power, sex, and nonverbal communication.* Englewood Cliffs, N.J.: Prentice-Hall, 1977.

Hess, E. H. Attitude and pupil size. *Scientific American,* 1965, *212,* 46–54.

Hess, E. H., & Polt, J. M. Pupil size as related to interest value of visual stimuli. *Science,* 1960, *132,* 349–350.

Higbee, K., & Wells, G. Some research trends in social psychology during the 1960s. *American Psychologist*, 1972, *27*, 963–966.

Himmelfarb, S., & Edgell, S. E. Additive constants model: A randomized response technique for eliminating evasiveness to quantitative response questions. *Psychological Bulletin*, 1980, *87*, 525–530.

Hinckley, E. D. The influence of individual opinion on construction of an attitude scale. *Journal of Social Psychology*, 1932, *3*, 283–296.

Hoagland, H. Potentialities in the control of behavior. In G. Wolstenholme (Ed.). *Man and his future*. Boston: Little, Brown, 1963.

Hochstim, J. R. A critical comparison of three strategies of collecting data from households. *Journal of the American Statistical Association*, 1967, *62*, 976–989.

Holmes, D. S. Debriefing after psychological experiments. I. Effectiveness of postdeception dehoaxing. *American Psychologist*, 1976a, *31*, 858–867.

Holmes, D. S. Debriefing after psychological experiments. II. Effectiveness of postexperimental desensitizing. *American Psychologist*, 1976b, *31*, 868–875.

Holsti, O. R. *Content analysis for the social sciences and humanities*. Reading, Mass.: Addison-Wesley, 1969.

Horner, M. W. Toward an understanding of achievement-related conflicts in women. *Journal of Social Issues*, 1972, *28*(2), 157–175.

Horowitz, E. L. The development of attitude toward the Negro. *Archives of Psychology*, 1936, No. 194.

Horowitz, E. L., & Horowitz, R. E. Development of social attitudes in children. *Sociometry*, 1938, *1*, 301–338.

Horowitz, I. L. (Ed.). *The rise and fall of Project Camelot*. Cambridge, Mass.: MIT Press, 1967.

Horowitz, R. E. Racial aspects of self-identification in nursery school children. *Journal of Psychology*, 1939, *7*, 91–99.

Horst, P. *Psychological measurement and prediction*. Belmont, Calif.: Wadsworth, 1968.

Houts, P. S. *Health-related behavioral impact of the Three Mile Island nuclear incident: Part I*. Report to the TMI Advisory Panel on Health Research Studies, Pennsylvania Department of Health. Hershey: Pennsylvania State University of Medicine, 1980a.

Houts, P. S. *Health-related behavioral impact of the Three Mile Island nuclear incident: Part II*. Report to the TMI Advisory Panel on Health Research Studies, Pennsylvania Department of Health. Hershey: Pennsylvania State University, College of Medicine, 1980b.

Hovland, C. I., & Sherif, M. Judgmental phenomena and scales of attitude measurement: Item displacement in Thurstone scales. *Journal of Abnormal and Social Psychology*, 1952, *47*, 822–832.

Hsu, E. H. An experimental study of rationalization. *Journal of Abnormal and Social Psychology*, 1949, *44*, 277–278.

Humphreys, L. *Tearoom trade: Impersonal sex in public places*. Chicago: Aldine-Atherton, 1970.

Hyman, H. H. *Survey design and analysis: Principles, cases, and procedures*. New York: Free Press, 1955.

Hyman, H. H. *Interviewing in social research*. Chicago: University of Chicago Press, 1975.

Ickes, W., & Barnes, R. Boys and girls together—and alienated: On enacting stereotyped sex roles in mixed-sex dyads. *Journal of Personality and Social Psychology*, 1978, *36*, 669–683.

Jackson, D. N., & Paunonen, S. V. Personality structure and assessment. *Annual Review of Psychology*, 1980, *31*, 503–551.

Janis, I. L. *Victims of groupthink: A psychological study of foreign policy decision and fiascos.* Boston: Houghton Mifflin, 1972.

Jennings, H. H. *Leadership and isolation* (2nd ed., 1950). New York: Longmans, 1943.

Jessor, S. L., & Jessor, R. Transition from virginity to nonvirginity among youth: A social-psychological study over time. *Developmental Psychology*, 1975, *11*, 473–484.

Johnson, J. T., & Judd, C. M. Overlooking the incongruent: Categorization biases in the identification of political statements. *Journal of Personality and Social Psychology*, 1983, *45*, 978–996.

Jones, E. E., & Sigall, H. The bogus pipeline: A new paradigm for measuring affect and attitude. *Psychological Bulletin*, 1971, *76*, 349–364.

Jones, J. H. *Bad Blood: The Tuskegee Syphilis Experiment.* New York: Free Press, 1981.

Jones, S. H., & Cook, S. W. *The influence of attitude on judgments of the effectiveness of alternative social policies* (mimeograph). Boulder: University of Colorado, 1975.

Jorgensen, D. O., & Lange, C. Graffiti content as an index of political interest. *Perceptual and Motor Skills*, 1975, *40*, 616–618.

Judd, C. M., & Kenny, D. A. *Estimating the effects of social interventions.* New York: Cambridge University Press, 1981.

Kaplan, A. *The conduct of inquiry: Methodology for behavioral science.* San Francisco: Chandler, 1964.

Kasarda, J. D. The use of census data in secondary analysis: The context of ecological discovery. In M. P. Golden (Ed.). *The research experience.* Itasca, Ill.: F. E. Peacock, 1976.

Katz, D. Social psychology and group process. In C. P. Stone (Ed.). *Annual review of psychology.* Palo Alto, Calif.: Annual Reviews, 1951.

Katz, I., Goldston, J., & Benjamin, L. Behavior and productivity in biracial work groups. *Human Relations*, 1958, *11*, 123–141.

Katz, J. *Experimentation with human beings.* New York: Russell Sage Foundation, 1972.

Kehrer, K. C. The Gary income maintenance experiment: Summary of initial findings. In Cook, T. D., Del Rosario, M. L., Hennigan, K. M., Mark, M. M., & Trochim, W. M. K. (Eds.). *Evaluation studies review annual* (Vol. 3). Beverly Hills, Calif.: Sage Publications, 1978.

Kelley, H. H., Hovland, C. I., Schwartz, M., & Abelson, R. P. The influence of judges' attitudes in three methods of attitude scaling. *Journal of Social Psychology*, 1955, *42*, 147–158.

Kelly, E. L., & Fiske, D. W. The prediction of success in the VA training program in clinical psychology. *American Psychologist*, 1950, *5*, 395–406.

Kelman, H. C. Human use of human subjects: The problem of deception in social psychological experiments. *Psychological Bulletin*, 1967, *67*, 1–11.

Kelman, H. C. *A time to speak: On human values and social research.* San Francisco: Jossey-Bass, 1968.

Kendall, P. L., & Lazarsfeld, P. F. Problems of survey analysis. In. R. K. Merton & P. F. Lazarsfeld (Eds.). *Continuities in social research.* New York: Free Press, 1950.

Kendon, A. Some relationships between body motion and speech: An analysis of an example. In A. Siegman and B. Pope (Eds.). *Studies in dyadic communication.* New York: Pergamon, 1970.

Keniston, K. *The uncommitted: Alienated youth in American society.* New York: Harcourt, 1965.

Kenny, D. A., & Berman, J. S. Statistical approaches for the correction of correlational bias. *Psychological Bulletin,* 1980, *88,* 288–295.

Kerlinger, F. N. *Foundations of behavioral research.* New York: Holt, 1964.

Kerr, M. An experimental investigation of national stereotypes. *Sociological Review,* 1943, *35,* 37–43.

Kershaw, D. N. A negative income tax experiment. *Scientific American,* 1972, *227,* 19–25.

Kidder, L. H. *Foreign visitors: A study of the changes in selves, skills, and attitudes of westerners in India.* Unpublished doctoral dissertation, Northwestern University, 1971.

Kidder, L. H. On becoming hypnotized: How skeptics become convinced: A case of attitude change? *Journal of Abnormal Psychology,* 1972, *80*(3) 317–322.

Kidder, L. H. The inadvertent creation of a neocolonial culture: A study of western sojourners in India. *International Journal of Intercultural Relations,* 1977, *1*(1), 48–60.

Kidder, L. H. Qualitative research and quasi-experimental frameworks. In M. B. Brewer & B. E. Collins (Eds.). *Knowing and validating: A tribute to Donald T. Campbell.* San Francisco: Jossey-Bass, 1981.

Kidder, L. H. Face validity from multiple perspectives. In D. Brinberg and L. H. Kidder (Eds.). *New directions for methodology of social and behavioral science: Forms of validity.* San Francisco: Jossey-Bass, 1982.

Kidder, L. H., & Campbell, D. T. The indirect testing of social attitude. In G. F. Summers (Ed.). *Attitude measurement.* Chicago: Rand McNally, 1970.

Kidder, L. H., & Cohn, E. S. Public views of crime and crime prevention. In I. H. Frieze, D. Bar-Tal, & J. S. Carroll (Eds.). *New approaches to social problems: Applications of attribution theory.* San Francisco: Jossey-Bass, 1979.

Kinsey, A. C., Pomeroy, W. B., & Martin, C. E. *Sexual behavior in the human male.* Philadelphia: Saunders, 1948.

Kish, L. *Survey sampling.* New York: Wiley, 1965.

Klaus, R. A., & Gray, S. W. The early training project for disadvantaged children: A report after five years. *Monographs of the Society for Research in Child Development,* 1968, *33*(4, Whole No. 120).

Kluegel, J. R., & Smith, E. R. Whites' beliefs about blacks' opportunity. *American Sociological Review,* 1982, *47,* 518–532.

Koslowski, M., Pratt, G. L., & Wintrob, R. N. The application of Guttman scale analysis to physicians' attitudes regarding abortion. *Journal of Applied Psychology,* 1976, *61,* 301–304.

Kraut, R. E., & Johnston, R. E. Social and emotional messages of smiling: An ethological approach. *Journal of Personality and Social Psychology,* 1979, *37,* 1,539–1,553.

Krech, D., & Crutchfield, R. S. *Theory and problems of social psychology.* New York: McGraw-Hill, 1948.

Krech, D., Crutchfield, R. S., & Ballachey, E. L. *Individual in society: A textbook in social psychology.* New York: McGraw-Hill, 1962.

Kretsinger, E. A. An experimental study of gross bodily movement as an index to audience interest. *Speech Monographs,* 1952, *19,* 244–248.

Kuethe, J. L. Prejudice and aggression: A study of specific social schemata. *Perceptual and Motor Skills,* 1964, *18*(1), 107–115.

Ladner, J. A. *Tomorrow's tomorrow: The black woman.* Garden City, N.Y.: Doubleday, 1971.

LaFrance, M. Nonverbal synchrony and rapport: Analysis by the cross-lag panel technique. *Social Psychology Quarterly,* 1979, *42,* 66–70.

LaFrance, M., & Mayo, C. Racial differences in gaze behavior during conversation: Two systematic observational studies. *Journal of Personality and Social Psychology,* 1976, *33,* 547–552.

LaFrance, M., & Mayo, C. *Moving bodies: Nonverbal communication in social relationships.* Monterey, Calif.: Brooks/Cole, 1978.

Lane, R. E. *Political ideology.* New York: Free Press, 1962.

Langbein, L. I., & Lichtman, A. J. *Ecological Inference.* Beverly Hills, Calif.: Sage Publications, 1978.

Lansing, J. B., & Heyns, R. W. Need affiliation and frequency of four types of communication. *Journal of Abnormal and Social Psychology,* 1959, *58,* 365–372.

Lanyon, R. I. Personality assessment. *Annual Review of Psychology,* 1984, *35,* 667–701.

Laswell, H. D., Leites, N., and associates, *Language of politics: Studies in quantitative semantics.* New York: G. W. Stewart, 1949.

Latané, B., & Darley, J. M. Group inhibition of bystander intervention in emergencies. *Journal of Personality and Social Psychology,* 1968, *10,* 215–221.

Laughlin, P. R., & Laughlin, R. M. Source effects in the judgment of social argot. *Journal of Social Psychology,* 1968, *78,* 249–254.

Lawler, E. E., III., & Hackman, J. R. Impact of employee participation in the development of pay incentive plans: A field experiment. *Journal of Applied Psychology,* 1969, *53,* 467–471.

Lazarsfeld, P. F. *Latent structure analysis* (mimeograph). New York: Bureau of Applied Social Research, Columbia University, 1957.

Lazarsfeld, P. F., & Rosenberg, M. *The language of social research: A reader in the methodology of social research.* New York: Free Press, 1955.

Lee, R. S. *The family of the addict: A comparison of the family experiences of male juvenile heroin addicts and controls.* Unpublished doctoral dissertation, New York University, 1957.

Lefton, M., Skipper, J. K., & McCaghy, C. H. *Approaches to deviance.* New York: Appleton-Century-Crofts, 1968.

Lemon, N. *Attitudes and their measurement.* New York: Wiley, 1973.

Letters of an Indian judge to an English gentlewoman. London: Futura Publications Ltd., 1978.

Leuthold, D. A., & Scheele, R. Patterns of bias in samples based on telephone directories. *Public Opinion Quarterly,* 1971, *35,* 249–257.

Levin, H. Psychologist to the powerless. In E. F. Korten, S. W. Cook, & J. I. Lacey (Eds.). *Psychology and the problems of society.* Washington, D.C.: American Psychological Association, 1970.

Levin, H. M. A decade of policy developments in improving education and training for low-income populations. In T. D. Cook et al. *Evaluation studies review annual*, pp. 521–570. Beverly Hills, Calif.: Sage Publications, 1978.

Levine, J. M., & Murphy, G. The learning and forgetting of controversial material. *Journal of Abnormal and Social Psychology*, 1943, *38*, 507–517.

Levine, R. V., West, L. J., & Reis, H. T. Perceptions of time and punctuality in the United States and Brazil. *Journal of Personality and Social Psychology*, 1980, *38*, 541–550.

Lewin, K., Lippitt, R., & White, R. K. Patterns of aggressive behavior in experimentally created "social climates." *Journal of Social Psychology*, 1939, *10*, 271–299.

Likert, R. A technique for the measurement of attitudes. *Archives of Psychology*, 1932, No. 140.

Little, K. B. Personal space. *Journal of Experimental Social Psychology*, 1965, *1*, 237–247.

Little, K. B. Cultural variations in social schemata. *Journal of Personality and Social Psychology*, 1968, *10*(1), 1–7.

Loevinger, J. A systematic approach to the construction and evaluation of tests of ability. *Psychological Monographs*, 1947, *61* (4, Whole No. 285).

Loevinger, J. The technic of homogenous tests compared with some aspects of "scale analysis" and factor analysis. *Psychological Bulletin*, 1948, *45*, 507–529.

Loevinger, J. Construct validity of the sentence completion test of ego development. *Applied Psychological Measurement*, 1979, *3*, 281–311.

Loevinger, J., & Wessler, R. *Measuring ego development* (Vol. 1). *Construction and use of a sentence completion test.* San Francisco: Jossey-Bass, 1970.

Loevinger, J., Wessler, R., & Redmore, C. *Measuring ego development* (Vol. 2). *Scoring manual for women and girls.* San Francisco: Jossey-Bass, 1970.

Loewenfeld, I. E. Mechanisms of reflect dilation of the pupil: Historical review and experimental analysis. *Documenta Ophthalmologica*, 1958, *12*, 185–448.

Loewenfeld, I. E. Comment on Hess' findings. *Survey of Ophthalmology*, 1966, *11*, 293–294.

Lofland, J. *Analyzing social settings: A guide to qualitative observation and analysis.* Belmont, Calif.: Wadsworth, 1971.

LoSciuto, L. A. A national inventory of television viewing behavior. In E. A. Rubenstein, G. A. Comstock, and J. P. Murray (Eds.). *Television and social behavior* (Vol. 4). Washington, D.C.: U.S. Government Printing Office, 1971.

Lynn, L. E., Jr. Policy relevant social research: What does it look like? In M. Guttentag & S. Saar (Eds.). *Evaluation studies review annual* (Vol. 2). Beverly Hills, Calif.: Sage Publications, 1977.

Maccoby, E. E., & Maccoby, N. The interview: A tool of social science. In G. Lindzey (Ed.). *Handbook of social psychology* (Vol. 1). Reading, Mass.: Addison-Wesley, 1954.

McCall, G. J., & Simmons, J. L. *Issues in participant observation: A text and reader.* Reading, Mass.: Addison-Wesley, 1969.

McCleary, R. How parole officers use records. *Social Problems*, 1977, *24*(5).

McCleary, R. *Dangerous men: The sociology of parole.* Beverly Hills, Calif.: Sage Publications, 1978.

McClelland, D. C. *Personality.* New York: Dryden, 1951.

McClelland, D. C. Toward a theory of motive acquisition. *American Psychologist*, 1965, *20*, 321–322.

McClelland, D. C., Atkinson, J. W., Clark, R. A., & Lowell, E. L. *The achievement motive.* New York: Appleton-Century-Crofts, 1953.

McCord, J. A thirty-year follow-up of treatment effects. *American Psychologist,* 1978, *33,* 284–289.

McCord, J. *Treatment that did not help.* Paper presented at the American Psychological Association Meetings, New York, September 1979.

MacCrone, I. D. *Race attitudes in South Africa.* Oxford, Eng.: Oxford University Press, 1937.

McDill, E. L., McDill, M. S., & Sprehe, J. T. *Strategies for success in compensatory education: An appraisal of evaluation research.* Baltimore: Johns Hopkins Press, 1969.

McDill, E. L., & Rigsby, L. C. *Structure and process in secondary schools.* Baltimore: Johns Hopkins Press, 1973.

McGee, M. G., & Snyder, M. Attribution and behavior: Two field studies. *Journal of Personality and Social Psychology,* 1975, *32,* 185–190.

McGovern, J. L., & Holmes, D. S. Influence of sex and dress on cooperation: An instance of "person" chauvinism. *Journal of Applied Social Psychology,* 1976, *6,* 206–220.

Maher, B. A., Watt, N., & Campbell, D. T. Comparative validity of two projective and two structured attitude tests in a prison population. *Journal of Applied Psychology,* 1960, *44,* 284–288.

Martyna, W. What does "He" mean? *Journal of Communication,* 1978, *28,* 131–138.

Masters, J. R. The relationship between number of response categories and reliability of Likert-type questionnaires. *Journal of Educational Measurement,* 1974, *11,* 49–53.

Mauldin, W. P., & Marks, E. S. Problems of response in enumerative surveys. *American Sociological Review,* 1950, *15,* 5.

Meltzer, B. A. A projected study of the jury as a working institution. *The Annals of the American Academy of Political and Social Sciences,* 1953, *287,* 97–102.

Merton, R. K., Fiske, M., & Kendall, P. L. *The focused interview.* New York: Free Press, 1956.

Meyer, N. *The seven-per-cent solution.* New York: E. P. Dutton, 1974.

Michaelis, A. *Research films in biology, anthropology, psychology, and medicine.* New York: Academic Press, 1955.

Milgram, S. Issues in the study of obedience: A reply to Baumrind. *American Psychologist,* 1964, *19,* 848–852.

Milgram, S. Some conditions of obedience and disobedience to authority. *Human Relations,* 1965, *18,* 57–76.

Milgram, S. *Obedience to authority: An experimental view.* New York: Harper & Row, 1974.

Miller, A. *Political issues and trust in government: 1964-1970.* Paper presented at the meeting of the American Political Science Association, Washington, D.C., September 1972.

Miller, D. C. *Handbook of research design and social measurement.* New York: David McKay, 1964.

Mitchell, S. K. Interobserver agreement, reliability, and generalizability of data collected in observational studies. *Psychological Bulletin,* 1979, *86,* 376–390.

Mixon, D. Instead of deception. *Journal of the Theory of Social Behaviour,* 1972, *2,* 139–177.

Monahan, L., Kuhn, D., & Shaver, P. Intrapsychic versus cultural explanations of the "fear of success" motive. *Journal of Personality and Social Psychology*, 1974, *29*, 60–64.

Moreno, J. L. *Who shall survive?* (rev. ed. 1953, Beacon House). Washington, D.C.: Nervous and Mental Disease Publishing, Series No. 58, 1934.

Morgan, J. N., & Duncan, G. I. *Five thousand American families—Patterns of economic progress.* Analysis of the Panel Study of Income Dynamics. Vols. 1–7. Ann Arbor, Mich.: Institute for Social Research, 1974–1979.

Moser, C. A., & Kalton, G. *Survey methods in social investigation* (2nd ed.). New York: Basic Books, 1972.

Muehl, D. (Ed.). *Content analysis at the Survey Research Center: A manual for coders.* Ann Arbor, Mich.: Institute for Social Research, 1961.

Mueller, C. In search of a constituency for the "New Religious Right." *Public Opinion Quarterly*, 1983, *47*, 213–229.

Murphy, G., & Likert, R. *Public opinion and the individual.* New York: Harper, 1938.

Murphy, G. L., Murphy, L. B., & Newcomb, T. M. *Experimental social psychology*, New York: Harper, 1937.

Murray, H. A. *Explorations in personality.* Oxford, Eng.: Oxford University Press, 1938.

Mussen, P. H. The reliability and validity of the Horowitz faces test. *Journal of Abnormal and Social Psychology*, 1950, *45*, 504–506.

Myers, J. L. *Fundamentals of experimental design.* Boston: Allyn & Bacon, 1966.

Myers, R. J. Errors and bias in the reporting of ages in census data. *Transactions, Actuarial Society of America*, 1940, *41*, 395–415.

Newcomb, T. M. An experiment designed to test the validity of a rating technique. *Journal of Educational Psychology*, 1931, *22*, 279–289.

New York Times encyclopedic almanac, 1970. New York: *New York Times*, 1969.

Oberdorfer, D. Political polling and electoral strategy: The 1968 election. In E. C. Dreyer & W. A. Rosenbaum (Eds.). *Public opinion and behavior: Essays and studies* (2nd ed.). New York: Duxbury, 1970.

Office of Science and Technology, Executive Office of the President. *Privacy and behavioral research.* Washington, D.C.: U.S. Government Printing Office, 1967.

Orne, M. T. Demand characteristics and the concept of quasi-controls. In R. Rosenthal & R. L. Rosnow (Eds.). *Artifact in behavioral research.* New York: Academic Press, 1969.

Osgood, C. E., Suci, C. J., & Tannenbaum, P. H. *The measurement of meaning.* Urbana: University of Illinois Press, 1957.

Oskamp, S. (Ed.). *Applied Social Psychology Annual, Vol. 5: Applications in Organizational Settings.* Beverly Hills, Calif.: Sage Publications, 1984.

Page, E. D. Teacher comments and student performance: A 74-classroom experiment in school motivation. *Journal of Educational Psychology*, 1958, *49*, 173–181.

PANE (People Against Nuclear Energy) v. *United States Nuclear Regulatory Commission*, 673 F. 2d 552 (D.C. Cir. 1982) (order vacating NRC decision); 678 F. 2d 222, 235 (D.C. Cir. Filed April 2, 1982) (amended interim order); 678 F. 2d 222, 228 (D.C. Cir. 1982) (Wilkey dissenting in part).

Parke, R. D., & Savin, D. B. *Infant characteristic and behaviors as elicitors of* *maternal and paternal responsivity.* Paper presented at the Biennial Meeting of the Society for Research in Child Development, Denver, 1975.

Parry, H. J., & Crossley, H. M. Validity of responses to survey questions. *Public Opinion Quarterly,* 1950, *14,* 61–80.

Parten, M. B. *Surveys, polls, and samples.* New York: Harper, 1950.

Parten, M. B. *Surveys, polls, and samples: Practical procedures.* New York: Cooper Square Publishers, 1966.

Patterson, S. C. Patterns of interpersonal relations in a state legislative group: The Wisconsin Assembly. *Public Opinion Quarterly,* 1959, *23,* 101–109.

Payne, S. L. *The art of asking questions.* Princeton, N.J.: Princeton University Press, 1951.

Petzel, T. P., Johnson, J. E., & McKillip, J. Response bias in drug surveys. *Journal of Consulting and Clinical Psychology,* 1973, *40,* 437–439.

Phillips, D. *Knowledge from what? Theories and methods in social research.* Chicago: Rand McNally, 1971.

Piliavin, I. M., Rodin, J., & Piliavin, J. A. Good samaritanism: An underground phenomenon? *Journal of Personality and Social Psychology,* 1969, *13,* 289–299.

Pilisuk, M., & Skolnick, P. Inducing trust: A test of the Osgood proposal. *Journal of Personality and Social Psychology,* 1968, *8,* 121–133.

Pintner, R., & Forlano, G. The influence of attitude upon scaling of attitude items. *Journal of Social Psychology,* 1937, *8,* 39–45.

Politz, A., & Simmons, W. An attempt to get the "not-at-homes" into the sample without call-backs. *Journal of the American Statistical Association,* 1949, *44,* 9–31.

Powell, M. C., & Fazio, R. H. Attitude accessibility as a function of repeated attitudinal expression. *Personality and Social Psychology Bulletin,* 1984, *10,* 139–148.

Price, R. H., & Blashfield, R. K. Explorations in the taxonomy of behavior settings: Analysis of dimensions and classifications. *American Journal of Community Psychology,* 1975, *3,* 335–351.

Proctor, C. H., & Loomis, C. P. Analysis of sociometric data. In M. Jahoda, M. Deutsch, & S. W. Cook (Eds.). *Research methods in social relations* (Vol. 2). New York: Dryden, 1951.

Proshansky, H. M. A projective method for the study of attitudes. *Journal of Abnormal and Social Psychology,* 1943, *38,* 393–395.

Quinn, R. P., Gutek, B. A., & Walsh, J. T. Telephone interviewing: A reappraisal and a field experiment. *Basic and Applied Social Psychology,* 1980.

Rajecki, D. W. Ethological elements in social psychology. In C. Hendricks (Ed.). *Perspectives on social psychology.* Hillsdale, N.J.: Erlbaum, 1977.

Rankin, R. E., & Campbell, D. T. Galvanic skin response to Negro and white experimenters. *Journal of Abnormal and Social Psychology,* 1959, *51,* 30–33.

Rathje, W. L., & Hughes, W. W. The garbage project as a nonreactive approach: Garbage in . . . garbage out? In H. W. Sinaiko & L. A. Broedling (Eds.). *Perspectives on attitude assessment: Surveys and their alternatives.* Washington, D.C.: Smithsonian Institution, 1975.

Rechtschaffen, A., & Mednick, S. A. The autokinetic word technique. *Journal of Abnormal and Social Psychology,* 1955, *51,* 346.

Rice, S. A. Contagious bias in the interview: A methodological note. *American Journal of Sociology*, 1929, *35*, 420–423.

Riley, M. W. *Sociological research* (Vol. II): *Exercises and manual.* New York: Harcourt, 1963.

Ring, K., Wallston, K., & Corey, M. Mode of debriefing as a factor affecting subjective reaction to a Milgram-type obedience experiment: An ethical inquiry. *Representative Research in Social Psychology*, 1970, *1*, 67–88.

Robinson, J. P. *How Americans use time: A social psychological analysis of everyday behavior.* New York: Praeger, 1977.

Robinson, J. P., & Shaver, P. R. *Measures of social psychological attitudes.* Ann Arbor, Mich.: Institute for Social Research, 1969.

Robinson, W. S. Ecological correlations and the behavior of individuals. *American Sociological Review*, 1950, *15*, 351–357.

Rogers, C. R., & Skinner, B. F. Some issues concerning the control of human behavior. *Science*, 1956, *124*, 1,057–1,066.

Rohde, A. R. Explorations in personality by the sentence completion method. *Journal of Applied Psychology*, 1946, *30*, 169–181.

Rorer, L. G. The great response-style myth. *Psychological Bulletin*, 1965, *63*, 129–156.

Rosenberg, M. *The logic of survey analysis.* New York: Basic Books, 1968.

Rosenhan, D. L. On being sane in insane places. *Science*, 1973, *79*, 250–258.

Rosenthal, R. *Experimenter effects in behavioral research.* New York: Appleton-Century-Crofts, 1966.

Rosenthal, R. *Experimenter effects in behavioral research.* New York: Wiley, 1976.

Rosenthal, R., & Jacobson, L. Teachers' expectancies: Determinants of pupils' I.Q. gains. *Psychological Reports*, 1966, *19*, 115–118.

Rosenthal, R., & Rosnow, R. L. (Eds.) *Artifact in behavioral research.* New York: Academic Press, 1969.

Rosenthal, R., & Rosnow, R. L. *The volunteer subject.* New York: Wiley-Interscience, 1975.

Rosnow, R. L., & Davis, D. J. Demand characteristics and the psychological experiment. *Et Cetera*, 1977, *34*(3), 301–313.

Rosnow, R. L., & Rosenthal, R. The volunteer subject revisited. *Australian Journal of Psychology*, 1976, *28* (2), 97–108.

Ross, L., Amabile, T. M., & Steinmetz, J. L. Social roles, social control, and biases in social perception processes. *Journal of Personality and Social Psychology*, 1977, *35*, 485–494.

Ross, L., Lepper, M. R., & Hubbard, M. Perseverance in self-perception and social perception: Biased attributional processes in the debriefing paradigm. *Journal of Personality and Social Psychology*, 1975, *32*, 880–892.

Rothbart, M., Evans, M., & Fulero, S. Recall for confirming events: Memory processes and the maintenance of social stereotypes. *Journal of Experimental Social Psychology*, 1979, *15*, 343–355.

Rotter, J. B. Word association and sentence completion methods. In H. H. Anderson & G. L. Anderson (Eds.). *Projective techniques.* Englewood Cliffs, N.J.: Prentice-Hall, 1951.

Rotter, J. B., & Willerman, B. The incomplete sentence test as a method of studying personality. *Journal of Consulting Psychology*, 1947, *11*, 43–48.

Rubin, Z. Measurement of romantic love. *Journal of Personality and Social Psychology*, 1970, *16*, 265–273.

Rummel, R. J. *Applied factor analysis.* Evanston, Ill.: Northwestern University Press, 1970.

Sackett, G. Measurement in observational research. In G. Sackett (Ed.). *Observing behavior: Vol. II, Data collection and analysis methods.* Baltimore: University Park Press, 1978a.

Sackett, G. *Observing behavior: Vol. I, Theory and applications in mental retardation.* Baltimore: University Park Press, 1978b.

Sackett, G. *Observing behavior: Vol. II, Data collection and analysis methods.* Baltimore: University Park Press, 1978c.

Saffir, M. A. A comparative study of scales constructed by three psychophysical methods. *Psychometrika*, 1937, *2*, 179–198.

Samph, T. Observer effects on teacher verbal classroom behavior. *Journal of Educational Psychology*, 1976, *68*, 736–741.

Scheflen, A. E. The significance of posture in communication systems. *Psychiatry*, 1964, *27*, 316–331.

Schlenker, B. R., & Forsyth, D. R. On the ethics of psychological research. *Journal of Experimental Social Psychology*, 1977, *13*, 369–396.

Schoggen, P. Ecological psychology and mental retardation. In G. Sackett (Ed.). *Observing behavior: Vol. I, Theory and applications in mental retardation.* Baltimore: University Park Press, 1978.

Schultz, D. P. The human subject in psychological research. *Psychological Bulletin*, 1969, *72*, 214–228.

Schulz, R. Effects of control and predictability on the physical and psychological well-being of the institutionalized aged. *Journal of Personality and Social Psychology*, 1976, *33*(5), 563–573.

Schulz, R., & Hanusa, B. H. Long-term effects of control and predictability-enhancing interventions: Findings and ethical issues. *Journal of Personality and Social Psychology*, 1978, *36*, 1,194–1,201.

Schuman, H., & Duncan, O. D. Questions about attitude survey questions. In H. L. Costner (Ed.). *Sociological methodology 1973–1974.* San Francisco: Jossey-Bass, 1974.

Schuman, H., & Presser, S. The open and closed question. *American Sociological Review*, 1979, *44*, 692–712.

Schuman, H., & Presser, S. *Questions and answers in attitude surveys.* New York: Academic Press, 1981.

Schwartz, B., & Barsky, S. F. The home advantage. *Social Forces*, 1977, *55*, 641–661.

Schwitzgebel, R. L. Survey of electromechanical devices for behavior modification. *Psychological Bulletin*, 1968, *70*, 444–459.

Scott, J. E., & Franklin, J. L. The changing nature of sex references in mass circulation magazines. *Public Opinion Quarterly*, 1972, *36*, 80–86.

Scott, R. *The making of blind men: A study of adult socialization.* New York: Russell Sage Foundation, 1969.

Scott, W. A. Attitude change by response reinforcement: Replication and extension. *Sociometry*, 1959, *22*, 328–335.

Scott, W. A. Attitude measurement. In G. Lindzey & E. Aronson (Eds.). *Handbook of social psychology* (Vol. 2, 2nd ed.). Reading, Mass.: Addison-Wesley, 1968.

Seligman, C., & Hutton, R. B. Evaluating energy conservation programs. *Journal of Social Issues*, 1981, *37*(2), 51–71.

Seligman, M. E. P. *Helplessness.* San Francisco: Freeman, 1975.

Selltiz, C. The use of survey methods in a citizens' campaign against discrimination. *Human Organization*, 1955, *14*, 19–25.

Selltiz, C., & Cook, S. W. Racial attitude as a determinant of judgments of plausibility. *Journal of Social Psychology*, 1966, *70*, 139–147.

Selltiz, C., Edrich, M., & Cook, S. W. Ratings of favorableness of statements about a social group as an indicator of attitude toward the group. *Journal of Personality and Social Psychology*, 1965, *2*, 408–415.

Shaw, M. E., & Wright, J. M. *Scales for the measurement of attitudes.* New York: McGraw-Hill, 1967.

Sherif, M., & Hovland, C. I. *Social judgment—Assimilation and contrast effects in communication and attitude change.* New Haven, Conn.: Yale University Press, 1961.

Sherif, M., & Sherif, C. W. *Social psychology.* New York: Harper, 1969.

Sherif, C., Sherif, M., & Nebergall, R. E. *Attitude and attitude change: The social judgment-involvement approach.* Philadelphia: Saunders, 1965.

Sherif, C. W. Bias in psychology. In J. A. Sherman & E. T. Beck (Eds.). *The prism of sex.* Madison: University of Wisconsin Press, 1979.

Shils, E. A. Social inquiry and the autonomy of the individual. In D. Lerner (Ed.). *The Human Meaning of the Social Sciences.* New York: World Publishing Co., 1959.

Shrauger, J. S., & Osberg, T. M. The relative accuracy of self-predictions and judgments by others in psychological assessment. *Psychological Bulletin*, 1981, *90*, 322–351.

Shuman, H., & Presser, S. Open and closed questions. *American Sociological Review*, 1979, *44*, 692–712.

Shweder, R. A., & D'Andrade, R. G. The systematic distortion hypothesis. In R. A. Shweder & D. W. Fiske (Eds.). *New directions for methodology of behavioral science: Fallible judgment in behavioral research.* San Francisco: Jossey-Bass, 1980.

Siegel, S. *Nonparametric statistics for the behavioral sciences.* New York: McGraw-Hill, 1956.

Simonton, D. K. Eminence, creativity, and geographic marginality: A recursive structural equation model. *Journal of Personality and Social Psychology*, 1977, *35*, 805–816.

Singer, E., Frankel, M. R., & Glassman, M. B. The effect of interviewer characteristics and expectations on response. *Public Opinion Quarterly*, 1983, *47*, 68–83.

Smith, E. R., & Kluegel, J. R. Beliefs and attitudes about women's opportunity. *Social Psychology Quarterly*, 1984, *47*, 81–95.

Smith, G. H. *Motivation research in advertising and marketing.* New York: McGraw-Hill, 1954.

Smith, W. J., Chase, J., & Lieblich, A. K. Tongue showing: A facial display of humans and other primate species. *Semiotica*, 1974, *11*, 201–246.

Snyder, M., & Swann, W. B., Jr. Hypothesis testing processes in social interaction. *Journal of Personality and Social Psychology*, 1978, *36*, 1,202–1,212.

Sobel, S. B. Throwing the baby out with the bathwater: The hazards of follow-up research. *American Psychologist,* 1978, *33,* 290–291.

Sommer, R. On the Brown adaptation of the Rosenzweig P-F assessing social attitudes. *Journal of Abnormal and Social Psychology,* 1954, *49,* 125–128.

Sommer, R. *Personal space: The behavioral basis of design.* Englewood Cliffs, N.J.: Prentice-Hall, 1969.

Spaeth, H. J. Interdimensionality and item invariance in judicial scaling. *Behavioral Science,* 1965, *10,* 290–304.

Stack, C. B. *All our kin: Strategies for survival in a black community.* New York: Harper Colophon Books, 1975.

Stanton, H. R., Back, K. W., & Litwak, E. Role-playing in survey research. *American Journal of Sociology,* 1956, *62,* 172–176.

Stanton, H. R., & Litwak, E. Toward the development of a short form test of interpersonal competence. *American Sociological Review,* 1955, *20,* 638–647.

Star, S. A., & Hughes, H. M. Report on an educational campaign: The Cincinnati Plan for the United Nations. *American Journal of Sociology,* 1950, *55,* 355–361.

Stein, M. I. The use of a sentence completion test for the diagnosis of personality. *Journal of Clinical Psychology,* 1947, *3,* 47–56.

Stephan, F. F., & McCarthy, P. J. *Sampling opinions: An analysis of survey procedure.* New York: Wiley, 1958.

Stevens, S. S. Measurement, statistics, and the schemapiric view. *Science,* 1968, *161,* 849–856.

Stouffer, S. A., Guttman, L., Suchman, E. A., Lazarsfeld, P. E., Star, S. A., & Clausen, J. A. *Measurement and prediction.* Studies in social psychology in World War II (Vol. 4). Princeton, N.J.: Princeton University Press, 1950.

Strayer, F. F., & Strayer, J. An ethological analysis of social agonism and dominance relations among preschool children. *Child Development,* 1976, *47,* 980–989.

Strunk, W., Jr., & White, E. B. *The elements of style* (3rd ed.). New York: Macmillan, 1979.

Sudman, S. *Reducing the cost of surveys.* Chicago: Aldine-Atherton, 1967.

Sudman, S. The uses of telephone directories for survey sampling. *Journal of Marketing Research,* 1973, *10,* 204–207.

Symposium on Operationism. *Psychological Review,* 1945, 241–294.

Tetlock, P. E. Identifying victims of groupthink from public statements of decision makers. *Journal of Personality and Social Psychology,* 1979, *37,* 1,314–1,324.

Thomas, W. I., & Znaniecki, F. *The Polish peasant in Europe and America: Monograph of an immigrant group.* Chicago: University of Chicago Press, 1918.

Thorndike, E. L. A constant error in psychological ratings. *Journal of Applied Psychology,* 1920, *4,* 25–29.

Thornton, G. C. Psychometric properties of self-appraisals of job performance. *Personnel Psychology,* 1980, *33,* 263–271.

Thouless, R. H. Effect of prejudice on reasoning. *British Journal of Psychology,* 1959, *50,* 289–293.

Thurstone, L. L.   The method of paired comparisons for social values. *Journal of Abnormal and Social Psychology*, 1927, *21*, 384–400.

Thurstone, L. L.   An experimental study of nationality preferences. *Journal of Genetic Psychology*, 1928, *1*, 405–425.

Thurstone, L. L.   Theory of attitude measurement. *Psychological Bulletin*, 1929, *36*, 222–241.

Thurstone, L. L.   The measurement of social attitudes. *Journal of Abnormal and Social Psychology*, 1931, *26*, 249–269.

Thurstone, L. L., & Chave, E. J.   *The measurement of attitude.* Chicago: University of Chicago Press, 1929.

Tittle, C. R., & Hill, R. J.   Attitude measurement and prediction of behavior: An evaluation of conditions and measurement techniques. *Sociometry*, 1967, *30*, 199–213.

Torgerson, W. S.   *Theory and methods of scaling.* New York: Wiley, 1958.

Triandis, H. C.   *Attitude and attitude change.* New York: Wiley, 1971.

Tuchfarber, A., & Klecka, W.   *Demographic similarities between samples collected by random digit dialing vs. complex sampling techniques.* A paper delivered at the 30th Annual Conference of the American Association for Public Opinion Research. Itasca, Ill., May 1975.

Tucker, C.   Interviewer effects in telephone surveys. *Public Opinion Quarterly*, 1983, *47*, 84–95.

Tukey, J. W.   *Exploratory data analysis.* Reading, Mass.: Addison-Wesley, 1977.

Tunnell, G. B.   Three dimensions of naturalness: An expanded definition of field research. *Psychological Bulletin*, 1977, *84*, 426–437.

U. S. Office of Federal Statistical Policy Standards.   *Social indicators, 1976.* Washington, D.C.: U.S. Government Printing Office, 1976.

Upshaw, H. S.   Own attitude as an anchor in equal-appearing intervals. *Journal of Abnormal and Social Psychology*, 1962, *64*, 85–96.

Upshaw, H. S.   The effects of variable perspectives on judgments of opinion statements for Thurstone Scales: Equal appearing intervals. *Journal of Personality and Social Psychology*, 1965, *2*, 60–69.

Upshaw, H. S.   Attitude measurement. In H. M. Blalock, Jr., & A. B. Blalock (Eds.). *Methodology in social research.* New York: McGraw-Hill, 1968.

Upshaw, H. S.   Output processes in judgment. In R. S. Wyer & T. K. Srull (Eds.). *Handbook of social cognition* (Vol. 3). Hillsdale, N.J.: Erlbaum, 1984.

Vaughan, G. M., & Thompson, R. T.   New Zealand children's attitudes toward Maoris. *Journal of Abnormal and Social Psychology*, 1961, *62*, 701–704.

Vernon, D. T. A.   The use of modeling to modify children's responses to a natural potentially stressful situation. *Journal of Applied Psychology*, 1973, *58*, 351–356.

Vidich, A. J., & Shapiro, G. A.   Comparison of participant observation and survey data. *American Sociological Review*, 1955, *20*, 28–33.

Viney, L. L.   The assessment of psychological states through content analysis of verbal communications. *Psychological Bulletin*, 1983, *94*, 542–563.

Volkova, B. D.   Some characteristics of conditional reflex formation to verbal stimuli in children. *Sechenov Psychological Journal (USSR)*, 1953, *39*, 668–674.

Walker, T. G., & Main, E. C.   Choice shifts in political decision making: Federal judges and civil liberties cases. *Journal of Applied Social Psychology*, 1973, *2*, 39–48.

Waly, P., & Cook, S. W. Attitude as a determinant of learning and memory: A failure to confirm. *Journal of Personality and Social Psychology*, 1966, *4*, 280–288.

Warner, S. L. Randomized response: A survey technique for eliminating evasive answer bias. *Journal of the American Statistical Association*, 1965, *60*, 63–69.

Warwick, D. P., & Lininger, C. A. *The sample survey: Theory and practice.* New York: McGraw-Hill, 1975.

Watson, G. B. *The measurement of fairmindedness.* Teachers College Contributions to Education, 176. New York: Teachers College, Columbia University, 1925.

Webb, E. J., Campbell, D. T., Schwartz, R. D., & Sechrest, L. *Unobtrusive measures: Non-reactive research in the social sciences.* Chicago: Rand McNally, 1966.

Webb, E. J., Campbell, D. T., Schwartz, R. D., Sechrest, L., & Grove, J. B. *Nonreactive measures in the social sciences* (2nd ed.). Boston: Houghton Mifflin, 1981.

Weick, K. E. Systematic observational methods. In G. Lindzey & E. Aronson (Eds.). *The handbook of social psychology* (Vol. 2). Reading, Mass.: Addison-Wesley, 1968.

Weigel, R. H., Wiser, P. L., & Cook, S. W. The impact of cooperative learning experiences on cross-ethnic relations and attitudes. *Journal of Social Issues*, 1975, *31*(1), 219–244.

Weiss, C. Validity of welfare mothers' interview responses. *Public Opinion Quarterly*, 1968, *32*, 622–633.

Weiss, C. H. *Evaluating action programs.* Boston: Allyn & Bacon, 1972.

Weitz, J., & Nuckols, R. C. The validity of direct and indirect questions in measuring job satisfaction. *Personnel Psychology*, 1953, *6*, 487–494.

West, S. G., Gunn, S. P., & Chernicky, P. Ubiquitous Watergate: An attributional analysis. *Journal of Personality and Social Psychology*, 1975, *32*, 55–65.

Westie, F. R., & DeFleur, M. L. Autonomic responses and their relationship to race attitudes. *Journal of Abnormal and Social Psychology*, 1959, *58*, 340–347.

White, G. D. The effects of observer presence on the activity level of families. *Journal of Applied Behavior Analysis*, 1977, *10*, 734.

Whyte, W. F. *Street corner society.* Chicago: University of Chicago Press, 1943.

Whyte, W. F. On asking indirect questions. *Human Organization*, 1957, *15*, 21–23.

Wicker, A. W. *An introduction to ecological psychology.* Monterey, Calif.: Brooks/Cole, 1979.

Willems, E. P. Planning a rationale for naturalistic research. In E. P. Willems & H. L. Raush (Eds.). *Naturalistic viewpoint in psychological research.* New York: Holt, 1969.

Williams, J., Meyerson, L., & Eron, L. Peer-rated aggression and aggressive responses elicited in an experimental situation. *Child Development*, 1967, *38*, 181–189.

Williams, W., & Evans, J. W.   The politics of evaluation: The case of Head Start. In P. H. Rossi & W. Williams (Eds.). *Evaluating social programs: Theory, practice and politics.* New York: Seminar Press, 1972.

Williamson, J., & Karp, D.   *The research craft: An introduction to social science methods.* Boston: Little-Brown, 1977.

Wolf, E. R., & Jorgenson, J. G.   Anthropology on the warpath in Thailand. *New York Review of Books*, 1970, *15*(9), 26–35.

Woodmansee, J. J.   The pupil response as a measure of social attitudes. In G. Summers (Ed.). *Attitude measurement.* Chicago: Rand McNally, 1970.

Wortman, C. B., & Rabinovitz, V. C.   Random assignment: The fairest of them all. In Sechrest, L., West, S. G., Phillips, M., Redner, R., & Yeaton, W. (Eds.). *Evaluation Studies Review Annual* (Vol. 4). Beverly Hills, Calif.: Sage Publications, 1979.

Wright, H. F.   *Recording and analyzing child behavior.* New York: Harper & Row, 1967.

Wrightsman, L. S.   Wallace supporters and adherence to "law and order." *Journal of Personality and Social Psychology*, 1969, *13*, 17–22.

Yarrow, M. R., & Waxler, C. Z.   Observing interaction: A confrontation with methodology. In R. B. Cairns (Ed.). *The analysis of social interactions: Methods, issues, and illustrations.* Hillsdale, N.J.: Erlbaum, 1979.

Zegiob, L. E., & Forehand, R.   Parent-child interactions: Observer effects and social class differences. *Behavior Therapy*, 1978, *9*, 118–123.

Zigler, E., & Child, I. L.   Socialization. In G. Lindzey & E. Aronson (Eds.). *The handbook of social psychology* (Vol. 3, 2nd ed.). Reading, Mass.: Addison-Wesley, 1969.

Zimbardo, P. G.   The human choice: Individuation, reason, and order versus deindividuation, impulse, and chaos. In W. A. Arnold & D. Levin (Eds.). *Nebraska symposium on motivation* (Vol. 17). Lincoln: University of Nebraska Press, 1969.

Zimbardo, P. G.   *The psychological power and pathology of imprisonment.* Statement prepared for the U.S. House of Representatives Committee on the Judiciary; Subcommittee No. 3: Hearings on Prison Reform, San Francisco, Calif., October 25, 1971.

Zubin, J., Eron, L. D., & Shumer, F.   *An experimental approach to projective techniques.* New York: Wiley, 1965.

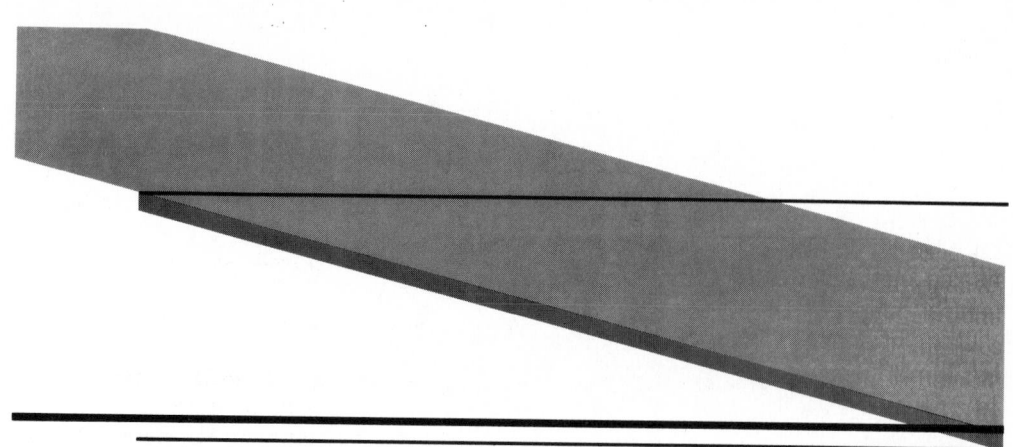

Name Index

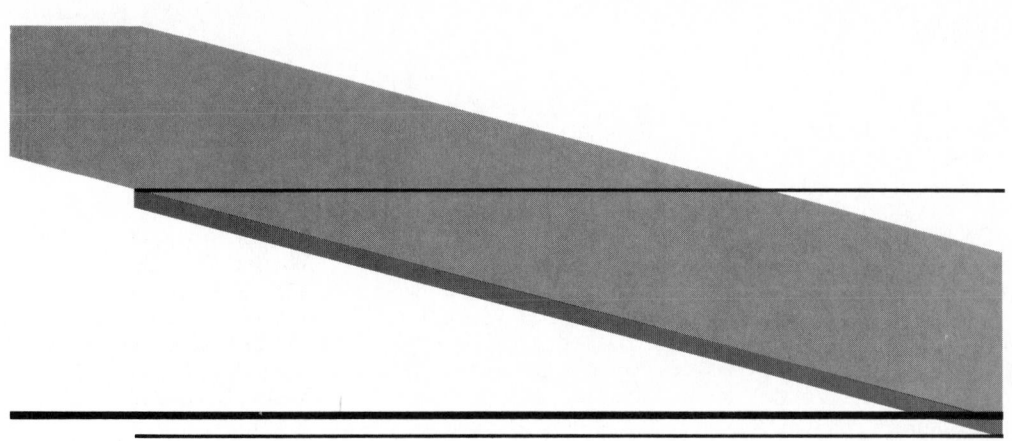

Subject Index

abstract, 445
accidental samples, compared with quota samples, 152
accidental sampling, 150
bias in, 148
acquiescent response style, 204
Adler's C_N Test, 44, 48–50, 53
analogy, used in field work, 184–186
anonymity and confidentiality, 500–505
maintaining in face of requests for information, 501–503
maintaining in questionnaires, 501
potential loss of, 503–505
for valued groups, 505
violation of, 505
applied research
compared with basic research, 396–397
environmental impact studies, 397–399
intervention, 401–402
need for, 423–426
on-site interviews and observations, 403
simulation, 400–401

applied research *(cont.)*
see also evaluation research
archival data, 299–310
construct validity of, 309
issues for users of, 309–310
potential for bias in, 309–310
reliability of, 309
statistical records, 300–303: census data, 302–303; characteristics of, 302; examples of use of, 301–302; used as social indicators, 301
survey archives, 304–305
written records, 305–309: mass communications, 306–309; public and private documents, 305–306
assumption of operationalism, 18
attitudes, questions about, for questionnaires, 238–242
authority
to support naive hypotheses, 14–15
symbols of, 14

average interim correlation, 48
average item-total correlation, 48

basic research
compared with applied research, 396–397
differences from evaluation research, 406–408
before-after two-group experimental design, 85–87
behavior, questions about, for questionnaires, 242
behavior range, 296
behavior setting survey, 296
beliefs, questions about, for questionnaires, 238–242
bias
in accidental sampling, 148
in archival data, 309–310
avoiding, 17–18: in interviewing, 222, 271–273; in questionnaire wording, 245–246, 247; rater bias, 298–299; in scientific studies, 17–18

553